Freedom's Teacher

KATHERINE MELLEN CHARRON

Freedom's
TEACHER

The Life of

Septima Clark

THE UNIVERSITY OF NORTH CAROLINA PRESS

CHAPEL HILL

This book was published with the assistance of the
Center for the Study of the American South of
the University of North Carolina at Chapel Hill.

The paper in this book meets the guidelines for permanence and durability of
the Committee on Production Guidelines for Book Longevity of the Council
on Library Resources.

The University of North Carolina Press has been a member of the Green Press
Initiative since 2003.

Library of Congress Cataloging-in-Publication Data
Charron, Katherine Mellen.
Freedom's teacher : the life of Septima Clark / Katherine Mellen Charron.
p. cm.
Includes bibliographical references and index.
ISBN 978-0-8078-3332-2 (cloth : alk. paper)
ISBN 978-0-8078-7222-2 (pbk. : alk. paper)
1. Clark, Septima Poinsette, 1898–1987. 2. African American women political activists — Southern
States — Biography. 3. African American civil rights workers — Southern States — Biography.
4. Civil rights workers — Southern States — Biography. 5. African American women teachers —
South Carolina — Biography. 6. African Americans — Education — South Carolina — History — 20th
century. 7. African Americans — Civil rights — Southern States — History — 20th century.
8. Civil rights movements — Southern States — History — 20th century. 9. Southern States — Race
relations — History — 20th century. 10. United States — Race relations — History — 20th century.
I. University of North Carolina at Chapel Hill. Center for the Study of the American South.
II. Title.
E185.97.C59C48 2009
323.4092 — dc22
[B]
2009022449

cloth 13 12 11 10 09   5 4 3 2 1
paper 15 14 13 12 11   5 4 3 2 1

In memory of Patsy Berry Nixon

Mama, this is my love letter to you.

Contents

Illustrations

Acknowledgments

Of all the lessons I have learned in twelve years of working on this project, the realization that I cannot truly express my gratitude to all who have assisted me remains one of the most profound. I received research support from the John Perry Miller Fund and a John F. Enders grant at Yale University; the Institute for Southern Studies at the University of South Carolina; and the Carrie Chapman Catt Center for Women and Politics at Iowa State University. I am grateful to all the staff in the archives and libraries that I visited, without whom my research would have been much more difficult. I extend special thanks to Elaine Hall at the King Center; Joellen ElBashir at Howard University; Robin Copp and Herb Hartsook at the University of South Carolina; and to the South Carolina Historical Society's Karen Stokes and Jane Aldrich, who drove me around to many historical sites despite her busy schedule. Given that I practically lived at the Avery Research Center for the Study of African American History and Culture in the spring of 2002, I am indebted to everyone there. Sherman Pyatt was most helpful; Deborah Wright pulled numerous collections and did a lot of copying for me; Harlan Greene helped with photo permissions; and conversations with Curtis Franks have convinced me to join his church as soon as he opens it.

I met many new friends in the course of my travels. Frank and Margaret Adams entertained me in the Garden of the Good and Sardonic in Asheville, while Bill and Lorna Chafe gave me a place to stay in Chapel Hill. In Columbia, Dan and Val Littlefield graciously opened their home to me, as did Wim Roefs. After work in the archives all day, I enjoyed sharing a beer with Bobby Donaldson, Peter Lau, and Miles Richards. In Charleston, Emily Nixon and Stan Young offered me a room of my own. Miriam DeCosta-Willis kept in touch with supportive words, and talking politics with Jonathan Wale Cain kept me on my toes. To this day, whenever I see stunning ironwork, I think fondly of Jay Rice. Lois Simms invited me to a delicious lunch one afternoon.

Joan Algar proved an indefatigable tour guide and an inspiration; she and her husband, John, have become cherished friends, as has Sophie Heltai, whose reflections on Septima Clark have meant the world to me. Cynthia Brown generously mailed her tape-recorded interviews with Clark to a stranger, and I am so delighted that I got to meet her in person. J. Herman Blake reminisced about Clark as he treated me to a scrumptious lunch in Ames, Iowa, and then insisted that I order dessert. *Every* person I interviewed passed on invaluable insight, and it is an honor to be entrusted with so many distinctive tales and tender memories. I offer special thanks to Clark's family, particularly to Elizabeth Poinsette-Fisher and Stephen Howard, who opened the family home place on Cannon Street so that Langhorne Howard could photograph the heirloom portraits of Clark's parents for this book.

A yearlong writing grant from the Spencer Foundation enabled me to complete the first draft of this project and introduced me to a magnificent cohort of fellows. I have to give a quick shout out to my fellow dancers on the rotating floor at the disco in Montreal: Andrew Ho, Lorena Llosa, Jordan Matsudaira, and Erendira Rueda. Karen Benjamin, Tina Collins, and Marc Van Overbeke, the only other historians in the bunch, read a chapter draft and offered astute suggestions, as did the members of my reading group at the Schlesinger Library 2007 Summer Seminar on Gender and Biography. I especially thank Nancy F. Cott, whom I had worked with in graduate school, and Benjamin Wise for their much-appreciated encouragement. Steve Dubb was another discerning reader, and Jane Dailey definitely made this a better book. The comments of scholars on conference panels, including Bill Chafe, Barbara Ransby, and Jacqueline Anne Rouse, enriched my efforts. In 2006–7, Amy Wood and I shared the honor of being the inaugural postdoctoral fellows at University of North Carolina's Center for the Study of the American South, where I met Harry Watson and Barb Call; they, along with Amy, shored me up at an unexpectedly difficult time. Thanks to Paul Betz at the University of North Carolina Press for all his patience. Though I met David Perry, my editor, in 1998, his benevolence through the years has only increased my affection for him. Then there's the Brazilian connection. *Obregada*, David Perry, for putting me in touch with Julio Pinto and Claudia Neto; I cannot imagine better hosts who so quickly became friends. I also express my heartfelt appreciation to Brenda Flanagan, Vera Galante, and all the wonderful Brazilian friends I made while serving as coleader of the Fifth American Studies Colloquium in Belo Horizonte in the summer of 2008, and to the Brazilian students I met when they came to North Carolina State to study our country's elections that fall.

I have been so fortunate in the students I have encountered: they have taught me much. Thanks go to all but especially to Emily Bone, Laura Hepp Bradshaw, Tess Bundy, Andrew Cantor, Rodney Cavazo, Pierre Dunbar, Zach Gillan, Tanner Hayes, Jennifer Howard, Rachel Idehen, Valerie Idehen, Adam Jackson, Robert James, Jenny Jamison, Benita Jones, Myesha Jones, Rebecca Koerselman, Amanda Lambert, Erin Liotta, Colin Madden, Carrie McMillan, Aishalyn Mock, Benjamin Rose, Rebecca Sherman, Natasha Silber, Jonathan Spellman, Michelle Talbott, Andrew Wall, and Sam Yurrow. I am particularly proud of Nikki Jones, Tom Levanthall, and Wende Nichols for their efforts in bringing the Ella Baker Tour to North Carolina State's campus in the spring of 2008.

Working with great colleagues has made a difference as well. In Ames, Iowa, fellow southerners Chris and Karen Curtis invited me to a real supper, complete with hoppin' John, sweet potatoes, collards, and sweet tea. Paul Griffiths and Pamela Riney-Kehrberg made me feel welcome in the history department, while Michael D. Bailey, Sara Gregg, Leonard Sadosky, and Matthew and Janelle Stanley helped me relax outside of work. At North Carolina State, history department head Jonathan Ocko has been a real supporter. I look forward to greeting everyone in the hallway but have appreciated conversations with David Ambaras, Matthew Booker, and Craig Thompson Friend. Occupying the office beside Blair L. M. Kelley affords plenty of opportunity to talk about everything that matters and has been a real privilege. I enjoy time spent talking history or home and garden improvement with Susanna Lee and Watson Jennison. I also value the two scholars who came to North Carolina State the same year I did. Hearing native New Yorker Thomas Ort recount his experience riding the bus to school still tickles me, and reviewing music and politics over cocktails with Brent Sirota and his wife, Alexandra, has broadened my horizons and remains a true delight.

Many teachers have influenced me along the way. Glenda Kale changed my thinking during ninth grade, a most opportune moment. Lucy Lustig taught me how to cook with consciousness and glee. Rick Chess, Peg Downes, Michael Gillum, Cynthia Ho, David Hopes, Dee James, and Merritt Moseley cultivated my love of literature at the University of North Carolina at Asheville, while Dwight and Dolly Mullen and Mark West challenged me to make sense of the world. In the Department of Afro-American Studies at the University of Wisconsin at Madison, I had the pleasure to work with Bill Van Deburg, Craig Werner, and Nellie Y. McKay, one of the most gracious scholars I have ever met. After I completed my master's thesis on Clark,

Nellie planted the first seed for this book by giving me a list of autobiographies written by black women teachers. In the final stretch, Craig read the entire manuscript and provided a much-needed fresh eye and top-notch suggestions. Stephen Kantrowitz and Pernille Ipsen are warm-hearted and brilliant Madison-based historians I am so lucky to count as friends, as is Christina Greene.

Tim Tyson's Insurgent South class made all the disparate strands of my past come together and helped me understand how I had ended up in Madison. I could say that that's when Tim inspired me to become a historian. In reality, however, it was over the course of many afternoons eating homemade pimento cheese and sweet potato biscuits in his kitchen and many nights drinking whiskey at the Harmony Bar. As a mentor, Tim introduced me to the efficacy of sports metaphors like "Throw long" and "You can't make the shot if you're not down court." As a friend, Tim sustained me body and soul. He could not have done so without assistance from the fabulous Perri Morgan and Hope and Sam.

Tim also introduced me to David Cecelski, who became first my coeditor and later a co-conspirator. On the best days, David regales me with stories of his adventures, whether as one of the finest oral historians anywhere or as a food blogger in search of a life-changing recipe. He even shares what he finds; indeed, I never knew I liked smoked bluefish so much. At the roughest moments, David saves my sanity by taking the time to listen. Always, he has encouraged me as a writer to remain sensitive to the complexities of the human heart.

Arriving at Yale in 1998, I had the good fortune to work with David Brion Davis, Paul Gilroy, and, during a semester visit, Ira Berlin. Teaching for Seth Fein and Joanne Freeman made me a better historian. I also relished conversations with Jon Butler, Matthew Jacobson, Ben Kiernan, and Stephen Pitti. Nancy Godleski ordered John Henry McCray's papers for me without even asking why. Essie Lucky-Barros and Florence Thomas had the answers that no one else in the history department did, and Victorine Shepard had a smile to share. I could have not gotten a job without the dossier office's invaluable Yvette Barnard. Nor can I imagine having a more supportive dissertation committee. Jonathan Holloway gives new meaning to the phrase "the hardest working man in show business"; serving as his teaching assistant twice provided me with a front-row seat. As a reader, Jonathan asked the right questions and gently pushed me to develop my thoughts. I always looked forward to talking to Hazel Carby, who has a rare talent for distilling the essence of the most complex ideas into elegant statements that continue to inform my thinking many moons later. Hearing her describe my work gave me confidence and made me bolder.

My gratitude to Glenda Gilmore is boundless. As an adviser, Glenda combines the wisdom of experience with tireless advocacy on behalf of her students. Everything she's done has left me better positioned in the long run. Then there is watching her in action. I know no one who is savvier or whom I would rather have as an ally. As a dear friend, Glenda has brightened my days with her humor and irreverence; in the darkest hours she has been there for me and would not let me give up. The only way I can truly repay her is to pass on to my own students the marvelous gifts she has bestowed on me. Glenda, I am a better human being for knowing you.

Many folks sweetened my days in New Haven and since. I could not have survived graduate school without Adriane Lentz-Smith. Not only is she a smart, original thinker, but she lights up any room she enters. Talking with Christian Lentz teaches me a new way of seeing the world, and sometimes I think I help him, too. Such was the case when Zora Holloway Lentz decided to make her debut in the world. Everyone thinks they have the best dissertation-writing group, but Adriane, Claire Nee Nelson, and George Trumbull IV ensured my ability to say it and mean it. Tammy Ingram's sass cannot conceal her thoughtfulness and makes me love her even more. Aaron Wong's frustrated declaration, "Fashion's not just for you, it's for everyone who has to *look* at you," made me comb my hair more than once before leaving the house. Jason Ward is a real trouper, having suffered through his first two years of graduate school as my roommate. Marisa Fuentes recently reminded me that if you love the people in your life, you have to tell them. Other friends who have helped me keep on keeping on include Heather and Dave Abernathy, Lori Brooks, Michael Cohen, Crystal Feimster, Tucker Foehl, Shannon Frystak, Eric Grant, Alison Greene, Joshua Guild, Françoise Hamlin, David Howell, Miles Johnson, Derry Kiernan, Jean Klingler, Kristin Knuteson, Michael Kwas, Rob Lalka, Wayne and Rhonda Lee, Danielle McGuire, Maureen McGuire, Leigh Raiford, Mary Lou Vitek, Anders Walker, Heather Williams, and Nathan Wolf.

Friends elsewhere have loved me all along. Holly Orr has been by my side since we shared a very Mary and Rhoda apartment on Magnolia Street. Again, Eunice Cat only chased you because you ran! I always look forward to hanging with Jenn Lindenauer and my godson, Quincy Scavron Orr. I love dining with Bob Miller more than anyone else. With my chosen family of Charles Shumolis, Theresa Steingress, and Terry Vess, I have shared abundant joy and passed through every unavoidable sorrow for the past twenty years. Among the many things they have taught me is that pee-in-your-pants laughter is essential to survival, as is a disco ball and a table to dance around. Words cannot express how grateful I am that the threads of our lives are so interwoven. Last summer, Lucy Grace arrived from Spring Hope. Though I rue the lost pairs of glasses, chewed computer cord, torn carpet, and holes dug in the backyard, I love her sweetness — especially when she's sleeping — and having her accompany me through the woods.

And then there is the family I did not choose but am so blessed to have. My aunt, Linda Burns, taught me how to do genealogical research and keeps everybody in touch. I eagerly anticipate seeing my cousin, Ron Charron, at family reunions; I appreciate the kindness of Veronica Charron and the sensitivity of my little sister Nicole Elstad and my baby brother Matthew Charron. My legal father, Gillis Mellen, amazes me with his keen intellect and his compassion. I could not be happier at how our relationship continues to grow in new and unexpected ways, and at being included in family gatherings with the inestimable Carol Mellen and Christine Cooney. I am indebted to Mark Nixon for making my mother so happy the last fifteen years of her life; I am so glad it was you, Mark. I must also give thanks to the ancestors, Hazel and Alvin Berry, Joseph Charron, Solange Hamelin, and Mary Morrison Mellen, for their nurturing and their love, so freely given.

My biological father, Ronald Edward Charron passed away as this book went to press. He turned me on to Gil Scott Heron at the impressionable age of fourteen; over the years, music helped us find the common ground. Now, this legacy endures as a song in my heart.

Last, but never least, there is my mother, Pat Nixon, a teacher and warrior in her own right. Going through her things after she passed, I found a laminated article that appeared in the Garinger High School *Rambler* in May 1984. It begins, "She is interested in what she does. She is also a little crazy. At least that is what she says." It surprised me that I sometimes tell my students the same thing. Reading further, I discovered additional unknown similarities in our approaches to teaching, which I can only credit to growing up in her house. At the end of the article, my mother told the student reporter what she wanted everyone to know: "Life's the most exciting thing in the world!" All my life, my mother's courage and invincible optimism have inspired me to live to the fullest and to find something to appreciate in each day. No one else has known me better or believed in me more.

Freedom's Teacher

Introduction

Septima Clark's Civil Rights Movement

It is night. A lone black woman walks through a cornfield in South Carolina. The stars wink above her. Crickets and cicadas grow quiet as she passes and then resume their orchestral humming, now punctuated by the sound of rustling leaves a little farther off. She moves toward an unpainted one-room building. When she gets there, she will have to rely on oil lamps for light. A group of African American adults will be waiting, eager to learn what she has come to teach them. It could be 1863 or 1916 or 1935. She could be a slave from the big house whose mistress taught her to read, a recent graduate of an American Missionary Association teacher training institute, or an instructor in a New Deal–era adult education program. Instead, it is 1964, and she is a Citizenship School teacher.[1]

There are hundreds like her conducting classes in the southern states. Each one has received a week's worth of training in a program designed by Septima Poinsette Clark. They have learned to signal their commitment to the civil rights movement by teaching their neighbors to read and write, by taking them to register to vote, and by establishing or working with any organization that will improve their communities. Their training has taught them that grassroots civil rights activism remains inseparable from grassroots education. In this process, Clark has guaranteed that each Citizenship School teacher carries forward an organizing tradition forged by countless southern black women activist educators before her.

Born in Charleston, South Carolina, in 1898, Septima Clark spent a long career teaching in public schools and devoting her spare time to civic work. She accepted her first job in a rural one-room schoolhouse in 1916. Three years later, she participated in her first organized political action when she joined the Charleston branch of the National Association for the Advancement of Colored People (NAACP) in a successful campaign to force the city to hire black teachers in its segregated public schools. Her experience at the end of World War I convinced the young Clark that activism worked, and allowed her to establish a pattern that influenced her choices for the rest of her life: advocating both on behalf of black children and to expand professional options for black women. During the interwar years, Clark learned to function within a broader network of black women. Her involvement in the all-black Palmetto State Teachers' Association and local women's clubs fed her vision of the politically possible. At the same time, teaching adult literacy classes equipped her with concrete skills on which she came to rely in formulating the Citizenship School pedagogy.

As it did for so many others, World War II marked a watershed for Clark. Her involvement with the South Carolina NAACP's wartime campaign to equalize teacher salaries meant directly challenging her employer, the white state.[2] Convinced that the momentum of local postwar activism could be harnessed to federal opportunities to dismantle Jim Crow, Clark took a stand for integration in 1950, an unpopular choice with most white Charlestonians and many of her black colleagues. In 1956, when the Charleston City School Board fired Clark for refusing to conceal her membership in the NAACP, it inadvertently freed her to devote her full attention to issues that had long been on her mind. Four decades of teaching and civic organizing shaped how she perceived the fundamental problems confronting the southern black community, including the need for better schools, better health care, better job opportunities and wages, and increased voter participation — particularly among black women — in local, state, and federal affairs. The challenge this former public school teacher accepted was to find a means to solve them.

Clark articulated her citizenship pedagogy in the mid-1950s while working for the Highlander Folk School, an interracial adult education center in Tennessee. Highlander sponsored the first Citizenship School classes until state repression forced it to transfer the program to the Southern Christian Leadership Conference (SCLC) in 1961. Clark migrated from Highlander to SCLC and helped make citizenship education a cornerstone of SCLC's mobilization strategy. According to former U.N. ambassador Andrew Young, who worked with SCLC, the Citizenship Schools "really became a foundation for Martin Luther King's non-violent movement," with graduates playing "a very strong role" in most of SCLC's campaigns. From 1961 to 1970, Clark and her coworkers prepared a network of Citizenship School teachers, "people with Ph.D. minds who never had the chance to get an education," to train others to become community activists. Those teachers collectively taught more than twenty-five thousand people.[3]

Inside the city churches, country homes, beauty parlors, and tents that served as classrooms, black adults studied so that they would pass the literacy tests that southern states administered to prospective African American registrants. Typical comments when they succeeded included "First time I have felt like a human being" and "So proud to get my registration certificate, I almost ran a stoplight."[4] Beyond practicing reading and writing, however, students learned of citizenship responsibilities that ranged from establishing local voting leagues to paying taxes and lobbying for improved municipal services. They came to understand citizenship not only as an individual legal right they possessed but as a tool that might be deployed on behalf of the wider community. African Americans who passed through the Citizenship Schools acquired the knowledge and the confidence to act.

The Citizenship Schools represent the pinnacle of Clark's activist career and easily merit a book-length study.[5] Yet to evaluate Clark's place in the African American freedom struggle by focusing solely on the Citizenship Schools is to obscure both their historical significance and hers. The program Clark fashioned stemmed directly from her forty years of practice as an activist educator: teaching citizenship by helping people to help themselves and then to participate in bettering their communities. Thus, the roots of the Citizenship Schools lay in the historical experiences of African American women teachers and in a frequently misunderstood tradition of black schooling in the segregated South.

Our perception of the black freedom struggle changes when we place the worldview and deeds of black women activist educators such as Septima Clark at the center. Education was never a politically neutral issue in the Jim Crow South. Clark's career demonstrates how segregated schools functioned as sites of citizenship struggles and how a predominantly female teaching force propagated a communal vision of citizenship that emerged alongside freedom itself.[6] No longer does the black church stand alone as the primary institutional base for the civil rights movement; the schoolhouse — often the *very* same building — becomes an equally important site.[7] More broadly, Clark's life provides a framework for measuring the transformations of southern black women's educational and social justice activism in relation to national, state, and judicial politics from the Progressive Era through the Cold War civil rights movement and beyond.

The rural segregated educational world that Clark entered in 1916 demanded that black teachers improvise pedagogically in the classroom. To generate community support for schools, these teachers had to meet community expectations. In other words, they had to learn how to become community organizers who balanced flexibility and specificity.[8] Over the course of her career, Clark also taught in urban elementary schools, which afforded her the opportunity to increase her civic commitments. Southern cities provided hubs where black teachers' activism meshed with the organizational culture of black clubwomen. Together, they created national networks of support that extended back into remote rural communities and educated both children and adults. Innumerable black women across the South shared Clark's outlook: do what is doable, and do what is needed.

Examining "education for citizenship" as a daily practice helps to create a more precise picture of teachers' historical role in the freedom struggle. Since Emancipation, African American educators had battled on the front lines.[9] As the World War II civil rights movement climbed into high gear, however, black teachers grew more wary in their public support.[10] Understanding this shift requires making explicit the gendered methods by which black educators negotiated the lines between the school — state-run education in the hands of white supremacists — and learning in the community. The black men who acted as administrative school liaisons had a political mission distinct from that of the black women teachers at the grassroots, who served as liaisons between the schoolhouse and the neighborhood. Different proximities to white oversight informed these men's and women's decisions to act politically at specific historical moments as well as how they measured progress.

Another way to bring teachers' roles in the long arc of the freedom struggle into sharper focus is to decentralize *Brown v. Board of Education*. Paying attention to earlier court battles involving education sheds light on teacher activism and its transformation in the wake of the white state's response. Significantly, southern white supremacists who sought to outmaneuver Supreme Court decisions requiring the equalization of black and white education gained valuable experience in the decade preceding *Brown* and relied on that experience to stymie desegregation after 1954.[11] Beginning in the early 1940s, increased white surveillance of black education — itself a response to black teachers' demands for equal salaries, black students' fight for access to higher education, and black activists' battle for the ballot — replaced decades of white neglect. Worse, state legislatures began taking punitive measures. Black educators continued to support the NAACP secretly, but the majority refused to imperil their livelihoods by directly challenging the status quo. Instead, they continued laboring in the trenches, teaching their students. In addition, some black educators disagreed with the NAACP's shift from the goal of equalization to integration in the latter part of the 1940s. Septima Clark was not one of them. Because her colleagues declined to step forward en masse, she had to craft a technique for passing their organizational know-how to others who would.

Clark chose to continue to express her commitment to education and social justice at Highlander. The school based its philosophy on cooperative problem solving, and its goal of fostering leadership among ordinary citizens discarded the Progressive Era belief that the right to lead belonged to their social betters.[12] Highlander affected Clark's thinking about who could serve as a leader in the Cold War civil rights struggle, even as it allowed her to use the expertise she had previously acquired. For the first Citizenship School, which began on Johns Island, South Carolina, in 1957, she devised an adult education program grounded in her conviction that lasting social change had to simultaneously emerge from and radicalize everyday experience.[13]

Disappointments certainly taught Clark much. "Don't ever think that everything went right," she cautioned. "It didn't. Many times there were failures. But we had to mull over those failures and work until we could get them ironed out." Characterizing the Citizenship Schools as "an experiment I was trying," Clark confessed that she had not been certain that her ideas would work. Her confirmation came "when people went down to register and vote and they were able to register and vote."[14]

Registering to vote had long represented a primary goal of the black freedom struggle, but it had never been the only one. Black southerners did not define citizenship so narrowly. In the early 1950s, African Americans' failure to make their influence felt in Charleston through voting convinced Clark that before people could stand up, they needed to build their confidence. Her program mobilized the masses not because they had less to lose materially but because of what individuals gained personally from literacy and the empowered sense of self that accompanied it. Linking practical literacy with political and economic literacy, Clark's citizenship education decreased local people's fear of white reprisals and made them willing to accept the responsibilities of leading citizens. Equally instructive is how Clark defined the program's accomplishments. "As I saw people work in their communities, and decide to attempt some of the things we recommended, then succeed in doing things like being able to get checks signed at banks and getting recognized among their own people and in their churches, then I knew that the experiment had worked out."[15]

Extending across the South under SCLC's auspices, the Citizenship Schools became all-black sites of movement mobilization. They thrived for several reasons. First, Clark devised an adult education program that was truly radical yet appeared nonthreatening because it looked like what black women teachers had been doing in the Jim Crow South for decades. Few moderate whites would have argued that teaching semiliterate black adults to read and write amounted to anything less than a worthy activity. Even so, such educational camouflage lasted only until graduates put what they had learned into practice. Second, by answering concerns that people considered necessary to improve their daily lives, Clark's pedagogy drew on a defining feature of the southern African American educational tradition: the reciprocal expectation and obligation between teacher and community. Every Citizenship School teacher came from the community in which she taught and began class by asking her neighbors what they wanted to learn. As a result, the schools became the conduit through which local people defined the movement in their town in terms of how they applied that knowledge.[16] Third, classes provided a space in which adult African Americans could begin to dismantle their internalized sense of white supremacy, the feeling that "white was right."[17] Segregation dictated such racial separatism as a necessary training strategy, but it remained temporary. Like its founder and the organization for which she worked, the program ultimately sought integration into the political system. Graduates expressed this goal by joining existing political parties or establishing independent groups and by raising their voices at municipal meetings. Finally, Citizenship Schools gave teachers and students a specific goal around which to organize, and each new registered voter testified to the possibility of achieving this aim. That, in turn, spurred alumni to do more.

Women outnumbered men as both teachers and students in the Citizenship Schools. Clark's program attracted women in part because she accentuated everyday experience in the political preparation process. In teacher training sessions, grassroots women discovered how to address the political, economic, social, and maternal issues that they identified as important. After they returned home, Citizenship School teachers relied on a curriculum intended for adaptation to local circumstances. Steering their own ships fostered black women's confidence in the value of their ideas and abilities, which manifested itself in practice as they worked alongside others. The common assumption that education equaled women's work also informed this gendered division of labor and leadership within the movement. It seemed as natural for black women to lead in the schoolhouse as it did for African American preachers to stand in the pulpit. Clark's citizenship education produced a cadre of local women leaders who created an environment in which change was possible.[18]

This was Septima Clark's civil rights movement: direct action meant registering to vote, but also combining education, protest, and advocacy to force the state to become more responsive to the black community. Her approach incorporated the young people of the Student Nonviolent Coordinating Committee, but they were not its focus. Building an educational foundation required slow, methodical work and yielded unpredictable results. Black youth invigorated the freedom struggle but often rejected the patience Clark's educational process required. Similarly, citizenship education relied on assistance from white allies, and the program even trained poor whites in interracial sessions before the end of the 1960s, but Clark's strategy first and foremost targeted the needs of black adults. Clark's civil rights movement was not captured in newspaper photographs or broadcast on television, though many of the anonymous faces in the crowds belonged to those who had passed through citizenship education classes. Most important, her movement was sustained, to various degrees in different communities, by grassroots Citizenship School teachers, a corps of go-to women who used their skills to mobilize their neighbors, reconcile conflicts, and answer community welfare needs.

Examining the activism of women who became Citizenship School teachers in the 1950s and 1960s thus modifies existing narratives of the women's movement. As Septima Clark asserted, "Many people think the women's liberation movement came out of the civil rights movement, but the women's movement started quite a number of years before the civil rights movement."[19] She referred both to the evolutions within a tradition of southern black women's activism and to women's importance in realizing civil rights goals. Putting Clark's program at the center enables us to retell the story of both the civil rights and the women's movements from the perspectives of southern black women.

The black community had long judged its women's ability to balance their responsibilities as workers and mothers with civic organizing as a source of strength, not a liability.[20] Even so, Clark's citizenship education enabled grassroots women to connect their personal problems to political action in a distinct milieu.[21] Training sessions and teaching offered women the chance to think about community development from their perspective, while the civil rights movement provided them with the vehicle for action. The imperative of banding together as a community to end legal segregation helps explain why these black women did not identify disrespect from male colleagues as the first problem that needed tackling, though that hardly meant that women did not notice the problem. Instead, they addressed issues at the intersection of their personal concerns — as mothers, sisters, daughters, and wives — and the community's welfare and survival.[22] At its core, women's freedom struggle, in all its manifestations, aimed to ensure a better future for children.

Taking a longer view of southern black women's ongoing activism at the local level, particularly in conjunction with President Lyndon Johnson's War on Poverty, also facilitates a reevaluation of our received wisdom regarding the civil rights movement's decline. From the mid- to late 1960s, a new generation of civic activists, trained by black women, took up the work in their communities. Southern black women translated practical literacy into political and economic literacy in the voting booth and the Head Start class, at the courthouse and at the school board meeting, and by running for office. Their tenacity in the face of shrinking resources, both from civil rights supporters and the state, heightens our awareness of the impact of national and international developments on southern movements. Federal legislation represented concrete victory, but federal economic intervention proved critical for the viability of the programs into which many Citizenship School alumni channeled their energies. Government oversight, however, introduced new standards of accountability and opened new avenues of attack for the movement's political foes. Government assistance also spawned new struggles for local control of federal dollars, prompting competition between not only black and white southerners but also among black organizations.

Too often, the civil rights and women's movements we collectively remember are mirages, shimmering across the decades reflecting partial historical truths and contemporary nostalgic desires. Too often, the civil rights story begins in 1954 and ends in 1968, and white women seem to have taken the central initiative in launching the women's liberation movement. Representations of these intertwined movements are equally mediated, gendered, classed, and raced in ways that eclipse our view of black women in them. The problem began in and with the movements themselves. For example, sexism within the civil rights movement was nowhere as problematic as it was within SCLC, an organization led by ministers who replicated the church's gender hierarchy in their political work, which had serious repercussions. Both the media at the time and the publicity generated by SCLC overwhelmingly highlighted men's roles as leaders. These, in turn, defined the earliest narratives and obscured women's contributions.[23] That trend persists. "The tragedy, I think," maintained Victoria Gray Adams, who served as the Mississippi state supervisor of Citizenship Schools, "is that in all the media so-called celebrations, they never talk about the real core of what happened back there."[24] This book joins many others in attempting to correct that oversight.

⌒✾⌒

A biographer embarks on a long excursion. Fortunately, for this one, Septima Clark left behind two autobiographies that provide excellent insight into her thinking at two discrete historical moments. Yet by its nature, the genre conceals as much as it reveals. Writing the self signifies at best an act of selective remembering. Autobiographers must review their life stories and arrange them into a cohesive narrative that demonstrates both their representative ordinariness and what makes them exceptional. The question of audience is of utmost importance, particularly for African American autobiographers, who have historically confronted the reality that documenting one's life could put it at risk.[25] In this sense, the provenance of an autobiography from its genesis to its publication must be considered when evaluating an author's constructed self.

Clark began work on her first autobiography a little more than a year after Tennessee state authorities had raided Highlander and arrested her. The fate of the school remained uncertain, with court decisions pending regarding the revocation of its charter. In *Echo in My Soul*, published in 1962, Clark joined her life story with a vigorous defense of Highlander. She also meticulously cataloged the injustices of Jim Crow in South Carolina to argue more broadly for the legitimacy of the civil rights movement. As a result of the timing—and most likely due to the fact that a white male southern liberal served as her coauthor—she remained guarded in her critique of activist coworkers and chose to reveal only certain details of her private life.

By the time Clark recorded her recollections in a series of oral history interviews in 1979, published as *Ready from Within* seven years later, she could speak more freely. Her editor for this project was a white antiracist woman and educator from the West Coast. The dynamics between the two women of course shaped the topics discussed. Clark adopted a narrative posture that differed considerably from the one she had fashioned in the early 1960s. Most notably, the theoretical insights she gained from the women's movement of the 1970s infused Clark's later framing of her life. For example, she pointed to the center of American political, economic, and social hierarchies when she proclaimed, "This country was built up from women keeping their mouths shut."[26] A biographer must acknowledge that *how* Septima Clark told the story of her life at different moments and to different people — that is, her language and her rhetoric — constituted as much a part of her ongoing resistance to oppression as the dramatic events of the past she described. A historian must question the meaning of the differences between two versions of the same story and then compare them to the historical record.

Readers of biography usually anticipate that the subject will walk across every page. This biography operates on a different assumption, namely that events influenced Clark from afar just as Clark's influence extended far from her physical person. Federal, state, and local realities shaped Clark's activism. *Freedom's Teacher* is both an individual biography and a biography of the freedom struggle that combines the political, educational, and social in a way that renders more discernable the world — with all its possibilities and limitations — that made Clark and that she helped to remake.

In a 2002 oral history interview, one-hundred-year-old former teacher Ruby Cornwell confirmed the importance of identifying the particulars of southern black women's educational philosophy and practice. When queried about the difference between her teaching of black adults in lay-by schools in the 1920s and the teaching done by community women in the Citizenship Schools of the 1950s and 1960s, Cornwell emphatically declared, "It's the same thing!"[27] The goal of helping people to help themselves was certainly the same, as was the method: gaining people's trust, listening to what they considered the greatest obstacles of everyday life, and then devising a pedagogy to meet their needs. What differed between the 1920s and the civil rights era were the opportunities to connect learning directly to political action in a social and economic justice movement that had unprecedented if imperfect federal support.

Clark's activism also differed at various stages in her life. Her civil rights movement appears distinctive in part because of the generational perspectives she brought to it.[28] Personal failure mattered too. If growing up in Charleston provided the foundation that set a young Septima Poinsette on a path of service, disappointment in marriage depleted her self-confidence, forced her to wrestle with depression, and robbed her of a secure position among the leading women of her hometown. Septima Clark did not regain her self-assurance until she moved to Columbia, the state capital, where entrance into civic organizing circles remained more open to those who expressed interest. Few Columbians knew the details of her personal tragedy, and she could more easily assume the identity of "Mrs. Clark."

Yet in 1925 she had become a mother. Perhaps the greatest silence in both of Clark's autobiographies and in her many interviews concerns her relationship with her son. On the one hand, Clark's financial insecurity during the interwar years obliged her to pursue employment outside of the classroom and in the summers, but she also derived great satisfaction from participating in professional and civic groups. Together, these factors influenced her decision to send her son to live with his paternal grandparents. The legacy of slavery meant that members of the black community considered it neither unusual nor an abdication of parental responsibility for mothers to rely on kin for help with child rearing. Children, in general, did not occupy the central position in families that they do today. On the other hand, it is a quintessentially Charlestonian trait not to discuss painful aspects of one's life, even among intimate associates, let alone with strangers. Additionally, Clark might have consciously chosen to omit certain personal details as she constructed the public persona of "civil rights veteran" in narratives that became stock tales.

For Clark, familial relationships both reflected her private priorities and became a casualty of her public activist choices. From the early 1950s forward, Clark's activism distressed family members — chiefly her mother and the sister with whom she shared a home in Charleston. The incessant travel her movement work demanded removed her from day-to-day family routines, and the danger associated with it meant that her silence preserved their safety. Nevertheless, Clark regularly scheduled time to see family despite her unrelenting obligations. During the movement's heyday, family visits constituted an opportunity for her to relax.[29] Moreover, throughout her life, Clark reconnected with her siblings, including an older half-sister, in the North at least once a year. She also made sure that her oldest granddaughter, whom she helped to rear, spent some vacation time with these relatives annually. After assuming care for two of her six grandchildren, Clark recognized how things had come full circle. The youngest, David, "was born with a damaged brain. This little handicapped boy stayed with me until he was twelve, so I say that my son's grandmother kept him and I had his little boy."[30]

Contemplating Clark's silences and reading between the lines of what she did say clarifies her radicalism. We can more readily ascertain, for example, how her financial struggles as a widowed mother probably influenced her decision to support the NAACP's teacher salary equalization campaign, which she later described as her first "radical" act. Those who would judge Clark's educationally based political vision as conservative, both then and now, fail to appreciate that overthrowing Jim Crow was a radical goal and that empowering black grassroots southerners represented a radical means of accomplishing it. Nor should we forget that Clark was taking a militant stand while the movement's young people were still learning to walk. From the outset, age and generational organizing approaches separated Clark from younger radical activists.[31] Clark freely shared the wisdom she had gleaned from experience, serving as a mentor to younger members of the movement. What created the most distance between Clark and this cohort, however, was their repudiation of nonviolence. The crux of the matter lay in the differing means judged critical to achieve the same ends.

Septima Clark joined early and stayed for the duration. As she changed, she brought change to familiar places and charted new territory by making those places familiar to others. She helped grassroots black women realize that the civil rights movement was their movement, and she offered testimony from her life to assist them as they made their way.[32] She appeared grandmotherly during the movement's zenith, which led the Federal Bureau of Investigation to dismiss her as "an old lady," insignificant and nonthreatening.[33] She did not often lose her temper, but when she did, folks remembered. She could be stubborn and single-minded with colleagues yet gentle and nurturing to students young and old. She definitely had opinions about how things ought to get done, and she spent a long life training those who would try.

"It's not that you have just grown old," Clark asserted in her eighth decade, "it is how you have grown old."[34] Septima Clark, much like her movement sister, Ella Baker, viewed change as an ongoing process. She believed in the necessity of adapting to meet new problems as they arose. She grasped the frailty of the human condition and the challenge of not losing hope. Her citizenship education program allowed many others to undertake a journey similar to the one she traveled and propelled an organizing tradition of southern black women forward into our own time. Clark's life reminds us that despite the constancy of struggle, the privilege of longevity occasionally brings attendant lessons in patience, endurance, and clarity. Today, in a world where millions of citizens struggle to have a voice in the decisions that shape their daily lives, Septima Clark has much to teach us.

CHAPTER ONE

Home Lessons

Mondays were the hardest. After getting her children off to school, Victoria Poinsette had to organize the giant piles of laundry she would wash and iron during the week. She loathed the work because it confirmed the gap between her idea of what her station in life should be and its reality. Despite the fact that her husband, Peter, worked steadily, their combined incomes barely covered expenses. The ruined smoothness of her hands betrayed the hours spent toiling over steaming tubs, scrubbing and wringing garments. But washing white people's clothes was infinitely preferable to cleaning their houses or serving them tea. That she absolutely refused to do. A black woman in a southern city had few employment options. Taking in laundry meant that Victoria Poinsette controlled her time and could balance such onerous labor with the responsibilities of her household, which eventually included seven children crowded into a house with four rooms and a kitchen. For this, the family owed five dollars a week in rent; and every Monday, the white landlord came to collect. Victoria Poinsette knew that if she did not have the money, she would suffer the indignity of listening to his threats or suggestions about how to get it. "Put that boy to work," the man once barked after seeing her son on his way to a violin lesson. Chances are he never really saw the young black girl sitting on the porch steps watching and listening. She, however, never forgot how he habitually insulted her mother.[1]

Septima Poinsette Clark used this memory from her childhood to explain her decision to become a teacher. With her salary, she planned to buy a house and thus spare her mother such humiliation. Her recollection underscores how public power arrangements in the Jim Crow South—which granted white men ultimate authority, limited black men and black women's job opportunities, and rendered little black girls invisible — ordered the daily lives of African Americans. Yet it also hints at the private values of ordinary southern black families, and the possibilities afforded by urban living. The Poinsettes routinely sent one of their children to violin lessons, despite the fact that the family pinched pennies to pay rent. The money Victoria Poinsette earned also contributed to tuition for her children at private schools. If rent day made stark the limitations family members confronted, the rest of the week testified to their steadfast will to thrive.

Born in Charleston, South Carolina, on May 3, 1898, Septima Earthaline Poinsette entered a world that had been shaped as African Americans gained and lost political power after the Civil War. Freedom for most black Carolinians, including her slave-born father, had arrived only three decades earlier, and the Low Country, with its majority black population, had served as the epicenter of black militancy and political activism. Beginning in 1867, African American voters elected black congressmen, state legislators, and city councilmen who refashioned public policy and, with the aid of their constituents, changed the civic landscape. During Reconstruction, black politicians wielded power within the state's Republican Party and attempted to establish an interracial democracy protected by law. They wrote a new state constitution in 1868 that, among other things, guaranteed universal male suffrage, expanded women's legal contract and property rights, and created a state-supported free public school system with compulsory attendance. An 1867 sit-in to protest mistreatment on Charleston streetcars, combined with problems encountered by black legislators while traveling, soon led to laws barring racial discrimination in public transportation and accommodation.[2] African American community activists complemented such work by founding a plethora of institutions — militias, churches, schools, newspapers, mutual aid societies, and memorial celebrations — to defend their freedom, promote their autonomy, train future leaders, and bequeath a legacy of black pride to subsequent generations. Young Septima Poinsette could not walk the streets of her hometown without passing innumerable reminders of such recent history. The efforts of this Reconstruction generation endured every Sunday she sat in church and every weekday she attended school.

Nevertheless, Poinsette spent her girlhood traversing a terrain scarred by white supremacy's hatefulness. Nearly every action by the Republican legislature had called forth strong opposition from the members of the state's Democratic white planter class, who abhorred the extension of citizenship to African Americans and who balked at assuming the tax burdens for measures that benefited their former slaves. White elites, united by a passionate conviction that black political power was illegitimate and committed to regaining control of the state's black agricultural labor force, led the counter-revolution that ultimately depended on violence for its success. Twenty-two years before Septima Poinsette's birth, white Democrats seized control of the state government and moved swiftly to circumscribe black political rights.[3] They did not succeed completely until 1895, when, overriding the objections of six black delegates, members of the state constitutional convention formally disfranchised thousands of poor Carolinians, both black and white. Reestablishing a racial caste system based on the social subordination of African Americans proved difficult, and the effort continued into Septima Poinsette's adolescence. She was fourteen years old when Charleston passed a law segregating seating on streetcars.[4]

Charleston, nestled on a peninsula between the Cooper and Ashley Rivers, has always had a long memory and self-conscious pride. "What city in America has more history of significance than Charleston?" Septima Clark once asked.[5] Few white Charlestonians, however, wanted to recall 1865–76. Those interested in colonial history could begin by noting that white settlers established Charles Towne as a British colony in 1670 and might observe that the immigrant society of the colonial Low Country was led by a generation of sons who sought to replicate their fathers' success as sugar planters in the Caribbean. They could point with pride to the grand eighteenth- and nineteenth-century residences that lined White Point Gardens, more commonly known as the Battery, as evidence of the fortunes amassed by the rice planters who became the city's founding fathers. Others might concede their forefathers' reluctance to embrace the American Revolution. Still others could dismiss the fact that Charleston's economic fortunes had peaked by the mid-1830s and brag that, in terms of culture and refinement, it continued to rank above every other southern city. Then too, their city served as the antebellum seat of state political power, and its influence changed the course of the nation's history. Charleston's sons led the South out of the Union in 1860.[6]

Rendered invisible but nonetheless central to all of these narratives, black Charlestonians would relate a different story. They might start by mentioning that the African presence in the area dated back to 1526, meaning that Africans preceded white settlers by 144 years. They could remark that their city's port surpassed all others in colonial America as a point of disembarkation for African slaves. Some of these slaves gambled for freedom by joining the British in the American Revolution; forty thousand more arrived in

Charleston between 1804 and 1808, when the legal prohibition on the slave trade written into the U.S. Constitution took effect. Those uncomfortable with the stigma of slavery might prioritize the achievements of the city's antebellum free black community, and consider the parallels between the three-tiered Caribbean slave societies—in which free blacks and people of mixed race served as a buffer class between white planters and slaves—and Charleston. Others could comment with pride that their ancestors, free black and slave artisans and craftsmen, built many of Charleston's luxurious mansions and elegant churches or fashioned the gorgeous wrought iron gates adorning them. They might affirm that the distinct piazzas that stretch the entire length of one side of most houses, providing breezy relief in the hottest months, were a West Indian–inspired design. They would certainly add that former slaves continued to live in the alleyways behind the majestic residences south of Broad Street, the most fashionable address for the city's white bluebloods. Indeed, well into the twentieth century, Charleston's residential patterns reflected white reliance on African American labor and the necessity of keeping it close.[7]

African American and white southerners have long used memory and place to locate themselves in history, though segregation forced them to map a racially inseparable past by attaching different meanings to the same geography. Among the spoils of victory in post-Reconstruction political battles, white southerners claimed the right to control the public memory of their region and to interpret it for the rest of the nation. They recast the story of 1861–76 as a tragedy, replete with social chaos and political corruption. Both the absence of African Americans in narratives of the Lost Cause and the centrality of their presence in stories of Reconstruction legitimated power relations in the white South of Septima Poinsette's youth. Moreover, throughout her adult life, white supremacists invoked the horrors of "Radical misrule" during Reconstruction to combat the slightest hint of black political activism. Such "memory-work" did not belong to white political leaders alone. Linking the individual wrongs they experienced at the hands of Union troops to the collective malaise of postwar "Yankee imperialism," a divided and diverse white South attempted to reconstitute itself as a community—specifically a racially superior Us vis-à-vis a black inferior Them.[8] White southerners used memory as both a cultural and political tool.

The same held true for southern African Americans. The white people who rewrote the region's history to erase or distort black contributions could never silence the stories black people told each other to explain what had happened. From individual testimonies of slave life and Emancipation to bearing witness to Jim Crow injustices, black southerners fashioned their collective narrative of southern history. Significantly, theirs was not a counter-memory per se but *the* memory on which they drew to join their personal experiences to broader social and political movements. Still, the task remained daunting. In theory, Jim Crow meant that race trumped everything else in terms of defining community because it legally and ideologically erased differences among black individuals.[9] In reality, differences of gender, class, and geography shaped the ways that black men and women in the urban and rural South recalled the past, attached meaning to it, and then passed their stories on to the generations that toppled segregation.

In Septima Poinsette's Charleston, African American memories recalled not merely events but circles of relationships, both with white Charlestonians and within the black community.[10] First came the matter of literal genealogy: more than a few African Americans were related to aristocratic white families in the Low Country, and such connections were well-known, if whispered. One native black Charlestonian recalled that as a boy, he asked his mother to identify someone he passed on the street: "Child, let me tell you; let me tell you about their mama, grandmother, who's their real daddy," she answered. Genealogical information did more than identify who was who. It provided a blueprint of who had access to power and how much. "Charleston is a city of 'come here' and 'been here.' If you've been here four or five generations, that gives you access to whites, and that's how you work politics and certain people," he concluded.[11]

Second, black Charlestonians made distinctions based on interracial familial relations and their ancestors' status as free or slave. Caste—the lightness or darkness of one's skin—mattered, too. For example, in 1790, members of the city's free black community, similar to their counterparts in the North, with whom they maintained contact, established the Brown Fellowship Society, a benevolent organization that admitted only light-skinned persons. Darker-skinned free blacks responded by creating other, equally restrictive groups such as the Humane Brotherhood. Free black men and women, who comprised 17.7 percent of the city's population in 1861, perceived themselves as a people in the middle.[12] Maintaining relationships with aristocratic white Charlestonians meant distinguishing themselves from the slaves in their midst. In nineteenth-century Charleston, members of the free black community accumulated property, ran successful businesses, and founded schools, churches, and literary and debating societies. If, after Emancipation, free black men and women looked back with pride on the cultural and institutional legacies of their community, they also looked forward in fear. Afraid of losing their privilege and everything else, they closed their circle tighter and policed its boundaries more carefully. And they used memories of difference, rather than similarity, to do so. Thus, the social divisions within Charleston's black community hampered the forging of collective strategies of resistance premised on shared memories of inequality because not all black Charlestonians were unequal to the same degree. "I really feel that if we didn't have so much 'black' this and 'brown' that, 'mulatto,' and so forth, we could have done more in Charleston," black Charlestonian Mamie Garvin Fields claimed; "our organizations often suffered from it."[13]

Southern women played an especially important role in institutionalizing the region's memory. As a generation of white women's efforts to memorialize the Lost Cause demonstrated, women's exclusion from formal participation in politics did not hamper their ability to shape the white South's mythic historical representations, which most accepted as unquestioned fact. The silent white granite Confederate soldiers who stood guard over town squares in the remotest southern hamlets provided constant reminders of white men's right to rule and their willingness to die for that right. The authority to reinscribe and by extension naturalize white supremacy in the civic arena carried high stakes. Such deliberate misremembering helped ease the general anxiety about maintaining political and social hierarchies based on race and gender and affected local allocations of material resources and social services.[14] Segregation relegated black women to challenging white women's version of the past within the confines of the black community. Black women did so by using racial uplift organizations to foster a sense of cultural pride. Unable to commemorate the bravery of preceding generations, both slave and free, with public markers, they kept the story alive in the black community's oral traditions and Emancipation celebrations. Perhaps more influential in terms of practical numbers and potential effect were the thousands of ordinary women who taught school. Throughout the twentieth century, black teachers, including those who instructed young Septima Poinsette, self-consciously occupied a position at the center of the memory-work of African American communities.

Septima Poinsette came of age in a community proud of its traditions and fearful of losing its hard-won accomplishments. Lessons for negotiating the contradictory emotional gap between that pride and fear began at home. At the same time, family history, more than any other factor, determined an individual's status in caste-conscious black Charleston. Parents, playmates, deportment, church and club memberships, connections to prominent white Charlestonians, and even the choice of a funeral home reflected people's stations. Simply put, local African Americans came in with a place, passed it onto their children, and took it out with them.[15]

Slavery's vicious pruning disfigured Septima Earthaline Poinsette's family tree. Socially, her father's enslavement neutralized her mother's boast of being a "free issue" and barred their daughter from black Charleston's most exclusive circles presided over by descendants of the antebellum free elite. Lineage served as the elite's first line of defense, and Poinsette could not trace hers back more than one generation on either side. The Poinsettes' situation was not unique, but earning social respect demanded attitude and required differentiating the family from others. Throughout her life, Victoria Poinsette maintained, "We were very particular, we didn't socialize with two-for-fives," a local term for commoners.[16] Marrying a former slave had not automatically lowered her station. Exactly which white family had owned her husband made a difference. Another subtle distinction involved whether he had worked in the big house or the fields. Indeed, in Charleston, the full meaning of Peter Poinsette's freedom could not be defined apart from what constituted an appropriate slave past. This expectation, in turn, profoundly shaped the personal stories of slavery he fashioned for his heirs.

Narrating the events of her childhood, Septima Poinsette Clark confronted such burdens of memory and place as she constructed a reputable account of family origins and her coming of age. Problematic silences echoed throughout the stories her parents passed down, reinforced by their notion that certain things were not discussed with children.[17] Assigning meaning to the memories her parents did share entailed an act of historical imagination on Clark's part, set against the backdrop of her own experiences. To describe her upbringing, Clark had to show the ways her self had been molded by her parents' hopes and frustrations, by the social and cultural traditions of her native city, and by the fact that she was born black and female in the Jim Crow South. That the Poinsettes responded to the hardening of segregation by attempting to shield the family reputation from Charleston's worst abuses placed their grown daughter in dialogue with both the possibilities and the limitations of the past.[18] As a woman who challenged white supremacy, Septima Clark had to reconsider Peter and Victoria Poinsette's lives to make sense of her own.

⸏᚜⸖᚛⸏

This much is certain: prior to the Civil War, a slave woman who lived on the White House plantation, near Georgetown, South Carolina, gave birth to a son and named him Peter. Peter spent his childhood at White House, perhaps an ironic name, given that the only white people in the immediate vicinity were the master and his family and the overseer. The young boy took his place among approximately one hundred black slaves, the majority of whom cultivated rice in the marshy tidal swamps formed by the confluence of the Pee Dee and Black Rivers.[19] He saw them leave at sunrise, dressed in drab gray, headed toward the rice fields. There, they labored barefoot, "knee deep in stagnant muck, surrounded by buzzing insects, under a scorching sun," stopping for a dinner that might consist of soft-boiled brown beans and corn pone. Field hands in Peter's community possessed the complex specialized knowledge required for rice production. They toiled under a black driver named Daniel for as long as it took to complete each day's assigned task, which varied depending on the growing cycle. All were designed to last until sunset.[20]

After work, the adults in Peter's world retired to the slave village. Here, among two clustered rows of "small, whitewashed wooden houses," each free-standing with "a little yard or garden and generally with two or three trees about it," Peter's kin used the precious time they controlled to grow sweet potatoes, beans, and Indian corn to enhance their diet. The land offered additional supplements. Nearby rivers and streams bequeathed trout, perch, bream, and in springtime spawning herring and shad, a true if bony delicacy. Succulent blackberries abounded. White House slaves also raised pigs and chickens to sell and saved the money or spent it on such luxuries as molasses. On Sunday mornings, some members of Peter's community gathered, "well dressed and well behaved," to hear sermons by white ministers. On Sunday evenings, a group reconvened in the village to worship, this time led by one of their own, who, "with great fervor and great gesticulation, thumping on the table with his clinched fists," preached of a Christ who would "make us free."[21]

Peter's first master, Joel Roberts Poinsett, had led a cosmopolitan and distinguished life. According to one admiring biographer, "He rode with the Cossacks and alongside South American revolutionaries," "served five Presidents and almost single-handedly organized a militia," and "was a scholar, a botanist, history buff, [and] linguist" who spoke six languages. This white South Carolina son, born in 1779 to a prominent Charleston physician of Huguenot descent and a well-connected English mother, received his education at Timothy Dwight's elite academy in Connecticut and later in Great Britain. In 1816, Poinsett won the first of his two terms in the state legislature before succeeding Charles Pinckney in the U.S. House of Representatives in 1821. President John Quincy Adams subsequently appointed Poinsett as the first U.S. ambassador to Mexico. After four years, the Mexican government demanded that the diplomat, who had earned a reputation as a baneful interloper, be recalled.[22]

Joel Poinsett arrived home just as the contentious debate over federal tariffs accelerated. Vice President John C. Calhoun, like Poinsett a South Carolinian, spearheaded the states' rights movement that peaked with the nullification crisis of 1832–33. Poinsett, however, sided with an old friend, President Andrew Jackson, and assumed leadership of the state's Unionist Party and the militia organized to defend its cause. The aging grandee withdrew from politics after the controversy but returned in 1837 when President Martin Van Buren appointed him secretary of war. Poinsett improved internal military operations, but his tenure also represented a culminating moment in the years following the 1830 passage of the Indian Removal Act. Hence, he supervised attempts to quash Indian guerrilla resistance during the Second Seminole War in Florida as well as the forced migration of more than forty thousand Native Americans west of the Mississippi River.[23]

Poinsett became a substantial slaveholder in 1833, when, at the age of fifty-four, he married Mary Izard Pringle, a widow one year his junior, and took up residence at her plantation, White House. He brought his love of botany to his new home and planted a lavish garden featuring both native and exotic species. A lane garlanded on each side by pink and white rosebushes greeted visitors, who then proceeded along an avenue of live oaks stretching beside the Pee Dee and passed the vegetable and flower gardens before arriving at the house. In the blooming months, brown-spotted wood thrushes, bright-winged bluebirds, and trilling robins darted among cape jessamine, magnolia, Japanese honeysuckle, azalea, gardenia, and roses so brilliant that Poinsett once bragged they "put all Pedee & black river to blush." Gray mockingbirds danced minuets between dogwood and peach blossom, mossy oak and pine. In the mornings, Mary Poinsett delighted in feeding rice grains to showy cardinals and prosaic sparrows on the piazza. And however they spent the days, evenings found the couple safely nestled inside a house furnished in "good old-fashioned aristocratic taste and comfort."[24] Thus, they passed their twilight years, comfortably sustained by the wealth that the labor of several generations of African Americans had created.

Despite the fact that he owned a hundred slaves, the Unionist Poinsett is remembered as an abolitionist. An 1850 visitor to White House provided a more accurate assessment, noting that Poinsett "earnestly desires that his native land should free itself from this moral obliquity" but that as a pragmatist, he recognized "the difficulties attending any change so great, that he leaves the question to be solved for the future."[25] That future proved indefinite. Joel Poinsett died shortly before Christmas in 1851 and left all of his property, including his slaves, to his wife. When Mary Poinsett died in 1857, her only son, John Julius Izard Pringle, who lived with his wife and children on the Greenfield plantation six miles up the Black River, became the new master of White House and owner of all its slaves, including Peter.[26]

Years later, sitting by a potbellied stove in his home, Peter Poinsette reminisced about his days as a slave. Septima Clark admitted that the exact details of his early years had always confused her, but she selected a specific few stories to retell as she reconstructed his narrative and related it to her own life.[27] She incorporated slavery's disruption of family ties by commenting, "I never heard him speak of a father at all." Moreover, the possibility that her grandmother had been raped lingered beside the blunt truth of southern interracial familial relations. Following Peter's birth, Clark noted, his mother delivered four more children: a black daughter; two brown sons, Samuel and Henry; and a blue-eyed white son named Thomas.[28]

Peter Poinsette also shared his attitude toward plantation discipline. As a young boy working in the big house, Peter probably spent considerable time in the kitchen, for he described for his daughter how the cook would sometimes leave the key to the smokehouse where the other slaves could find it and procure some meat for themselves. When caught, they got whipped. Peter believed they deserved it. "It sort of amused him, I guess," Clark stated frankly, "as a boy to see a man wincing and receiving a whipping . . . and actually not knowing what it really meant." Clark also added details that underscored African American traditions of resistance. If the young slave Peter accepted the world as it was and his place in it, "there were always some people" in his community "who were against this thing," she asserted. Referring to the instigator of an alleged 1822 slave conspiracy in Charleston, Clark speculated that Denmark Vesey "would not have been a friend" of her father's "because he didn't have that kind of feeling."[29]

Nevertheless, Clark drew a valuable lesson from Peter Poinsette's past and connected it to her own time. Many African Americans, she recognized, grew up unaware "that it was wrong for them to have to stand back until every white person was served." She included herself in this group. "That's what I had to do—to stay back. . . . I didn't feel angry about it, and they didn't either."[30] Having changed, Clark understood that awakening to the idea of freedom was a gradual process. Peter Poinsette's life story reminded her to be patient when she encountered people who hesitated to join in her civil rights organizing.

Another tale Clark repeated reflected her central concern with education. When he grew a little older, Peter was assigned to accompany two of the master's children to school. "They rode on horseback, while he carried their books," she envisioned. When the group reached the schoolhouse, the slave boy carried the young masters' books into the classroom and then waited outside, despite the weather, until the day's lessons concluded. Joel Poinsett had no white children. His wife's only son, who inherited White House in 1857, however, had four. They were Pringles.[31]

Clark refashioned her father's personal history to express a yearning that never quite abated. "I like to think," she proposed, "that although the little boy who years later would be my father did not have the opportunity to learn what was in those books he was carrying for the other little boy, he then got the desire to discover some day for himself the exciting and stimulating things in them." In her version, slavery taught young Peter the importance of education, and he emerged from its crucible more determined that his children obtain it. The only time Clark mentioned being disciplined by her father was when she did not want to go to school. Still, Poinsette did not pursue an education after he became free and learned to write his name only during World War I.[32] That neither his educated wife nor children taught him to read earlier speaks volumes about family politics and perhaps his own pride.

Peter Poinsette's family also heard stories of how he served his master's side in the Civil War. All of the Pringle boys enlisted in Company K of the Fourth South Carolina Calvary. Commanded by Colonel Benjamin H. Rutledge, the regiment included members of the Charleston Light Dragoons, an elite militia dating back to the eighteenth century. The Pringles soon gained admittance to the Drags, who were "distinguished from the other companies by their superior uniforms, equipments, and horses."[33] In all likelihood, Peter, who had once escorted the boys to school, now accompanied them to war as a manservant.

Beginning in late 1862, the Pringles' regiment saw action near Pocotaligo and around Port Royal Ferry near Beaufort before being ordered to Charleston in August 1863. Septima Clark recalled that her father "went down on that Battery" and carried water to Rebel soldiers and wood to stoke the cannons aimed at "Yankee ships in the harbor that came to free the slaves."[34] Thus, he aided the defense of the city during the 587-day federal bombardment that began that August. Other family members assigned Peter the equally dramatic role of "taking messages down to the Confederate Army people in Beaufort" on horseback.[35] A teenage slave boy certainly would have attracted less attention on the road to Union-occupied Beaufort than any white man, though the horse would have been a beacon to beleaguered troops on both sides. But other questions emerge from this portrait. How could Peter's master be certain that the critical message would reach its destination and not be delivered to the wrong person, perhaps intentionally? How did he know his slave courier would return? How long did it take him to weigh these risks before entrusting Peter with this responsibility?

Peter Poinsette's fidelity to the Confederates was rewarded sixty years later. On March 17, 1924, he appeared before the Charleston County Pension Board and swore that he had been a servant under "Captain B. H. Rutledge," had "served the state of South Carolina for more than six months," and had "remained faithful to the Confederacy during the said war." Rutledge's son testified to the validity of Poinsette's claim and left his signature beside the former slave's mark. With freedom, Clark's father had chosen the name Peter Porcher (pronounced Por-shay) Poinsette, most likely to commemorate Joel Roberts Poinsett Pringle and Percival R. Porcher, both of whom died in battle. Retaining the name "Poinsett" rather than "Pringle" allowed him to claim a link to a famous diplomat and botanist, which would have carried clout in the Low Country. Though Peter Poinsette never completely severed his connection to the prominent white people who had been willing to die to keep him enslaved, he might have played to their expectations of a loyal, illiterate servant by signing his pension application with an "X." For the remaining three years of his life, he received eight dollars annually in recognition of his wartime service.[36]

The Confederate defeat had brought an uneasy freedom for Peter and his White House kin. "He claimed that lots of people cried because they didn't know that they were going to be able to have any food," Clark recounted. Nor could they be sure of securing shelter, clothing, and work in the world beyond the only home they had known. Some stayed and negotiated labor contracts with their former master.[37] Peter Poinsette and his three brothers were among those who sought a future in Charleston. A single familial generation later, Septima Poinsette could see clearly what a difference that choice made. Growing up, she remembered some of her father's cousins who still lived on plantations in the countryside visiting on the weekends. "They'd sit down in our yard and be telling tales of their life on that plantation," she observed. "We felt they were so silly, you know, not to hate the people who had them living like that."[38] Such comments echo the antebellum cleavage between house and field slaves, which Clark transposed onto the dissimilarity between urban and rural life.

Postwar Charleston had hardly been a welcoming place, however. The city lay in ruins, so devastated that General William T. Sherman, whose troops reached the Palmetto State in early 1865, instructed that it was "hardly worth the time it would take to starve it out." Those who had the means had fled, leaving a mostly destitute population to scramble for food and shelter amid the rubble. Even so, Charleston became an important early staging ground for both black pride and Union victory. African American and white Union troops took control of the city in mid-February. Six weeks later, after welcoming Major Martin R. Delany, the highest-ranking black officer in the Union army, four thousand African Americans paraded through the city's streets, celebrating their freedom. Schoolchildren carried placards that read, "We know no masters but ourselves," and a hearse surrounded by "mourners" dressed in black announced, "Slavery is dead." Other prominent national figures made their way to Charleston as well. Northern abolitionists Henry Ward Beecher and William Lloyd Garrison joined Delany, local war hero Robert Smalls, a former slave; and the son of Denmark Vesey in an April 14 ceremony to restore the U.S. flag above Fort Sumter. Later the same evening, John Wilkes Booth shot President Abraham Lincoln in Washington, D.C.[39]

Thousands of rural migrants pursuing opportunity, the Poinsette brothers among them, gave the city a majority black population, a change in composition that had important political and social repercussions during Reconstruction, particularly when African Americans gained the right to vote. At the same time, the depressed local economy, which never regained its antebellum strength, could not absorb the excess labor. As an illiterate former slave, Peter Poinsette competed in an overcrowded labor market dominated by unskilled workers. After the passage of the Black Codes in October 1865, he had to find work or risk being arrested for vagrancy and then involuntarily returned to a plantation to work off his fine. Migrants' hopes that the federal government would offer jobs and protection were quickly dashed as both the occupying U.S. troops and the Freedmen's Bureau showed more concern for stemming the massive influx by restoring the members of the agrarian labor force to the plantations from which they had fled. Established members of Charleston's black community, middle-class artisans and craftsmen, and especially the antebellum free elite did not exactly welcome these strangers from the country, though their mutual aid organizations sought to augment the bureau's social welfare work.[40]

Tense race relations made Charleston a dangerous place. Gone was the culture of deference that had characterized prewar black-white interactions as freedpeople gave public expression to their new status. Returning white Charlestonians flinched at the sight of their former domestics dressed in finery and carrying parasols. They complained of being jostled off sidewalks by impudent African Americans and of being publicly taunted with songs such as "Hang Jeff Davis on the sour apple tree." Black and white Charlestonians regularly engaged in battles on the Battery, a scenic promenade that had been off-limits to African Americans in the antebellum era, and freedmen and -women did not hesitate to physically confront abusive white civilian authorities. Nor did they suffer gladly white Union troops when it became clear that these former liberators shared the racism of southern white people.[41]

Civilian African Americans' willingness to embrace self-defense to resist the reimposition of white control bolstered membership in black militia companies. When one white newspaper editor complained in 1868 that African Americans intended "to overawe the white man, to keep him down by force," the Reverend Richard Harvey Cain, an African Methodist Episcopal minister and later a U.S. congressman, defended African Americans' intent to abide by the law. Still, he warned that they stood "prepared to stand by their liberties . . . and see that the liberties of their children are guarded with sleepless vigilance. Let their foes beware!"[42] At the heart of such matters lay the question of full citizenship rights. Black Carolinians, like black people across the South, did not wait for others to give meaning to their freedom. Cain's rhetoric of "liberty" suggests that African Americans likened the Civil War to a second American Revolution and now insisted that the nation live up to its founding ideals. They well understood that the Second Amendment's right to bear arms went hand in hand with protecting freedom.[43]

South Carolina's black political leaders amassed real political power during Reconstruction. Black legislators chaired key committees, controlled patronage in their home counties, and most importantly, "gained the ability to reward friends and punish enemies."[44] Still, statewide political cohesion proved nearly impossible to come by, and divisions within Republican ranks aided the white supremacist counterrevolution as it gained strength. Internal distinctions among African Americans persisted, and white allies vacillated. With black loyalty to the party assured, white Republicans acted to attract white support, often voting against their black counterparts on key matters. GOP factions competing to control local political machines also undermined party unity. Meanwhile, white Democrats' efforts to wrest out-right control of the state government differed in South Carolina's upper and lower regions, but blood spilled everywhere. The turning point occurred in 1876. White and black Democrats in and around Charleston, however, shed more blood at the hands of Republicans throughout that venomous fall.[45]

In stark contrast to such black militancy and reading the past through her present, Septima Clark claimed that her father emerged from slavery "non-violent." Such a description provided one way for her to resolve the contra-diction between her life as a civil rights warrior and his as a former defender of the Confederacy who discussed the "fightings" of the Reconstruction years but avowed that he had not participated in postbellum politics. Reminders of that bloody recent past lingered throughout her childhood. "On election day particularly," Clark noted, "we stayed in the house because election time in Charleston was a pretty hard time."[46]

Peter Poinsette nonetheless made political choices. His impecunious circumstances probably led him to rely on the contacts with leading white Carolinians that he had forged while defending the Confederacy. Even so, his Confederate service and personal loyalties or his periods of unemploy-ment might have endangered him. The mobility that accompanied freedom may have influenced his decision to take a job with the Clyde Line Steam-ship Company, which sailed between New York and the Caribbean. By Janu-ary 1880, he had married and become a father to a daughter named Alice. Following his wife's death, Poinsette found someone to care for Alice and resumed his work on the Clyde Line. In Jacksonville, Florida, he met and married Victoria Warren Anderson sometime between 1890 and 1892.[47]

Anderson had been born in 1870 in Charleston. Family lore held that one of her parents was part Native American.[48] She lived on Marsh Street, near the Cooper River, with her two sisters, Masaline and Martha, at least until she reached the age of ten. Their mother, Rebecca, a widow who could not read or write and took in laundry, sent all three of her youngest daughters to school.[49] Following Rebecca's death sometime after 1880, the remaining family members gambled on a better future in Haiti. The young Anderson sisters moved in with their older half-brothers who worked in a cigar factory in the independent black nation. Living in a household with several mem-bers earning decent wages allowed the girls to complete their education. Septima Clark believed that being able to read and write helped to make Victoria Poinsette "the proud soul she was all her life." The experience, how-ever, also sharpened Victoria's personal biases, including her caste-conscious disdain for dark-skinned black people. Haiti so profoundly shaped Victoria's personality that Clark described her mother as a "real West Indian" despite the fact she resided there for less than eight years. By the age of eighteen, Victoria Anderson had resettled in Jacksonville.[50]

Clark did not embellish the story of her parents' meeting, marriage, and subsequent relationship. Peter Poinsette was not a complete stranger to the Anderson family because Victoria's older half-sister, a dressmaker named Eliza, had married Peter's brother, Samuel, who worked as a carpenter in Charleston. Clark believed that her mother's decision to marry had grown out of a painful rejection. Victoria apparently had been dating bricklayer Fletcher Robinson when her younger sister, Martha, announced that he had asked her to marry him. "I think that triggered [Victoria] to feel as if 'I want to marry,'" Clark suggested, "so she married the first person that came along." After the ceremony, the couple celebrated with a pig roast in the backyard. The early years of the marriage were good, and Victoria Poinsette, reputedly a "great dancer," enjoyed accompanying her husband to parties. Only after the couple moved back to Charleston and started a family did she realize the full consequences of her choice.[51]

The Poinsettes settled at 105 Wentworth Street, where Victoria gave birth to their second daughter in 1898. They named the baby after her half-sister, Septima Anderson Peace, who lived in Haiti. A son followed a year later.[52] With three young children to support, Peter Poinsette worked as a waiter for W. G. Barron, whose establishment on State Street catered functions for Charleston's white aristocracy, including the exclusive St. Cecilia Society's annual ball. In 1902, he joined with John "Brownie" Richardson to open the Richardson and Poinsett Lunchroom at the same location. It was not unusual for black men to work so near Broad Street, but it was extraordinary for black men to own a business there. Had elites in the white community not sanctioned the effort, Poinsette and Richardson could never have obtained a lease. "People knew my father," Septima Clark confirmed, "because he catered parties, because he had that little restaurant . . . and because he was a former slave of Joel Poinsette [sic]."[53] But the business soon failed, and Peter Poinsette subsequently moved between jobs as a waiter and a custodian.

When Septima Poinsette was six, her family moved to 26 Henrietta Street, the street where she spent the rest of her childhood and much of her adult life as well. Two more daughters and three more sons, the youngest born in 1914, completed the family. The Poinsettes' neighbors worked as longshoremen and ship joiners, carpenters, masons, electricians, dressmakers, shoemakers,

Peter Porcher Poinsette, n.d. Photograph by Langhorne Howard.
Courtesy of Elizabeth Poinsette-Fisher and Steven Howard.

Victoria Warren Anderson Poinsette, n.d. Photograph by Langhorne Howard. Courtesy of Elizabeth Poinsette-Fisher and Steven Howard.

chauffeurs, cooks, and domestics. Because the segregated housing patterns that prevailed in New South cities such as Atlanta never took root in Charleston, an Old South city that stubbornly clung to its veneer of antebellum gentility, the family always lived in a racially mixed neighborhood. Henrietta Street's residents included not only African Americans but also native white Carolinian, Irish, Italian, and German families, though the children rarely played together.[54] Alvin Anderson, who grew up in the neighborhood during the 1930s and 1940s, reflected on the difference that living among white people made. "You're always going to meet some decent white person, on your street or around the corner," he explained; "they may not even speak to you, but you know Mrs. So-and-So is a nice lady."[55] From his perspective, the interracial awareness spawned by these simple encounters, along with the more intimate ties between white and black families, alleviated some racial tension.

More troubling for Victoria Poinsette were Henrietta Street's few interracial couples — specifically, white men who fathered children with black women but were barred by law from marrying them. She apparently did not consider the possibility that genuine ties of affection existed for these couples and saw such women as nothing more than "kept" women who lived in sin and birthed children out of wedlock. She did not allow her children to play with the offspring of such mixed relationships. She also detested neighbors who "comb[ed] their hair" or "use[d] a dishcloth" to bathe half naked on their porches. Preserving the family's reputation mandated vigilance. Poinsette drove away the bootleggers who occasionally sat on her porch by pouring water underneath her doorsill.[56]

For most of her married life, Victoria Poinsette struggled mightily with the frustration that accompanied managing her desire for a middle-class lifestyle on a working-class budget. She compensated with her attitude. "She walked like she was Queen Elizabeth" and "was always well dressed," a family friend recalled. With members of her intimate circle, "Mama Vickie," as she was affectionately known, could be warm and generous, but "most people would be afraid of her" because "she didn't talk and grin and all that stuff with people."[57] She also blamed her husband for not providing for the family. As a girl, Septima often heard her mother lamenting the fact that "the clothes that I put over my head [when I was younger], I'll never put over again." She missed her former finery, at times refusing to go to church because of her wardrobe's shortcomings. The nadir came when her nine-month-old baby died. With no funds to pay for the infant's burial, Victoria sought help from Eliza Poinsett. "My mother had to get four dollars from this sister of hers to pay for the digging of this grave," Clark remembered, "and she cried bitterly; she hated that sister after that."[58] Pride and shame sprouted through the cracks in Victoria Poinsette's armor of invulnerability. Septima Clark alternatively characterized her mother as "haughty," "high strung," and "emotional," but Victoria's heart held deep sorrows, too.

Clark described her father as much more "even-tempered." Where Victoria Poinsette refused to talk to those she considered beneath her, her husband would speak to anyone and often went out of his way to help strangers. "I can never forget," Septima Clark asserted, "nor do I wish to—those little incidents when my unlearned, humble, serving father expressed in his simple way his love for people, all people. I can see him now," she continued, "running up to some woman, white or black, it made no difference, struggling along with arms filled with packages. . . . 'Here Missus,' he would say, 'now let me take that! It's too heavy for you; it will break you down.'"[59] On the evenings his wife attended meetings of the United Tents of America, a women's organization for which she served as treasurer, or various other clubs to which she belonged, Peter Poinsette instructed his children on the necessity of trying to find something noble in everyone. "He wanted you not to exalt yourself, but to look at the culture of others and see whether or not you could strengthen their weaknesses and try to investigate how you could improve yourselves toward them," Clark commented. She took his lessons to heart and "never looked down on anybody," Alvin Anderson confirmed. "I never heard her say, 'I'm not going to have anything to do with this person' or 'I don't care about them.' Never heard that."[60]

Still, his wife's general unhappiness bothered Peter Poinsette. Most of the time he responded by trying to put the small inconveniences into a larger perspective. "Vickie, a hundred years from today you'll never know the difference, and none of these things will make any sense," he gently chided. When it came to the children, however, he deferred to her judgment. "Whatever your Ma says," he told them if they complained about something she had done.[61] He never took sides or talked against her, and since he spent most of his time at work, Victoria Poinsette ruled the roost.

Family members always joked that Mama Vickie had "fire in her hands," meaning she did not hesitate to punish her children physically. She fully expected them to obey the Bible's Fifth Commandment, to honor their parents. Her word was law, and the children dared not talk back to her. Once, when young Septima attempted to correct her mother in the presence of an aunt, Victoria slapped the girl hard enough to knock out one of her teeth. Later that night, Victoria tried to force her daughter to include "God bless

Mama" in her nightly prayers, but Septima stubbornly refused and earned another whipping. "I learned from that it was best not to antagonize her," Clark recalled. Another time, as the family walked down King Street, the heart of Charleston's shopping district, Septima spied some candy that a little white girl had dropped on the ground. When she started to pick it up, her mother spanked her, right there on the street. "I was very cautious of things she did not like," Clark later noted, confessing that she was also angered by her mother's strictness.[62]

The rules and routines in the Poinsette household reflected the family's fiscal difficulties as well as the larger problems of being African American in a segregated society. Having the right manners and morals rendered other limitations less acute. Victoria Poinsette insisted that her daughters act like ladies in public, which meant that they did not leave the house without wearing gloves, that they kept the reasons for their outings to themselves, that they did not eat while walking down the street, and that they did not holler hellos to acquaintances. Ladies rarely went to stores, because stores sold beer and liquor. Ladies addressed people, including family members, by their proper titles; always, Victoria Poinsette referred to her husband as "Mr. Poinsette" or "your father." As the lady of the house, she did not venture into the street to examine the wares of the vendors who hawked vegetables, fish, charcoal, and kindling; instead, she waited for them to come to her porch steps. For safety reasons, girls never went to the door after six o'clock in the evening, when Peter Poinsette "closed all the blinds" in the house. And girls never played or walked home from school with boys. Victoria Poinsette "had a feeling that men were out there waiting," and she told her daughters, "You'll be attractive to men. Men are here to ask and women to refuse until the proper time. And if you accept favors from men, men are going to mark you and then you will be no good."[63]

Poinsette kept her children busy with chores. "She had a schedule for every child and every day of the week," Clark observed. Each older child bore responsibility for caring for a younger sibling. Septima had to ensure that her youngest sister, Lorene, had breakfast and clean clothes to wear to school. Whenever a piece of Lorene's clothing needed mending, Septima attended to it or risked a whipping. With no plumbing in the house, the children took turns hauling buckets of water from the fountain in Marion Square, located across Meeting Street at the western end of their block. Victoria Poinsette would not allow her offspring to accept money when elderly neighbors solicited their help, admonishing her children, "You must learn to share your services." She expected older children, however, to contribute to the family purse. From the age of ten, Septima arrived home from school on Mondays, Tuesdays, and Wednesdays and found loads of clothes set aside for her to wash. On Thursdays and Fridays, she pressed the garments with a heavy flat iron. The work lasted until suppertime at six o'clock; an hour of study followed, and bedtime was around eight.[64]

Victoria Poinsette also strictly oversaw what little free time her children had. Every potential playmate had to provide satisfactory answers to questions such as "Who are you? What's your mother's name? Where do you live?" or was promptly sent home. The Poinsette children usually played with their cousins or acquaintances from church on Friday afternoons. According to Clark, her parents' status prevented her from attending "any of the parties that were given by the upper-class people in Charleston, the middle-class people who had money and whose mothers didn't have to work."[65] Yet if certain social snubs could not be avoided, others could be passed along. Victoria Poinsette expected her children to walk and act like they were "somebodies" and sanctioned their social rejection of those beneath them to signal the family's pride.

Victoria Poinsette marshaled that pride to stand up to white men and white authority as well. Septima once watched as her mother confronted one of their Irish neighbors, Michael Barry, for refusing to let black children skate on the sidewalk he had had paved in front of his house. On another occasion, Clark recalled, when the family's dog scratched a white child, whose mother then called the police, Victoria Poinsette refused to let the officer into her house to investigate, saying, "Don't you put your feet across the sill of my door."[66] On still another occasion, she accused a policeman of trespassing as he pursued a suspect into her backyard. It did not matter that the alleged criminal was also in the backyard, having found refuge behind the family goat and under the house: "What are you doing in my yard?," Poinsette snapped. Finding the officer's answer insufficient, she asserted, "I'm a little piece of leather, but I'm well put together, so don't you come in here." Thus, Victoria Poinsette's silence when insulted by the white landlord seemed the exception rather than the rule — and made sense given the necessity of keeping a roof over the family's head. Indeed, as Clark also divulged, "My mother did many things like this. I appreciate them because I really feel that it helped me to be able to stand in front of the Klansmen and White Citizens' Councils, of large groups that were hostile. I never felt afraid and I think it was because my mother showed so much courage back in those early days. I felt that if she could do it way back then, then I could."[67]

For Septima Poinsette, growing up in an urban community augmented family lessons in self-respect and pride. Charleston offered numerous examples of African American prosperity and good citizenship, including an all-black fire company, six African American doctors, one black dentist, and the McClennan-Banks Hospital and Training School, which educated black nurses. Members of the city's black community had acquired an estimated one million dollars worth of personal property by 1904, and the black-owned Charleston Land and Improvement Company, which held "hundreds of acres of land and one of the finest resorts for picnics" in the state, leased its property for white people to use.[68] Residents could peruse not one but two local black newspapers, the *Charleston Messenger* and the *Southern Reporter.*[69] Charleston's Labor Day parade featured members of the African American bricklayers' and carpenters' unions, painters, barbers, and bakers strutting in step with the strains of an all-black band. White organizers relegated the African American participants to the rear of the parade, but many observers felt that they had saved the best for last. In Charleston, although black women could not sit on benches in the city's parks, they could put their babies in carriages every bit as fine as those of white women and then stroll around the parks, alongside black women pushing white babies.[70]

Less formal memory-work occurred on the city's streets as well. Mamie Garvin Fields, who was born in 1888, described regularly encountering "Aunt Jane," who sold groundnut cakes and other tasty treats near the College of Charleston. "If you would stay, she would tell you stories about her home 'cross the sea,' and she would tell about our old folks right here in South Carolina." Then too, black professionals in the city used their manners and dress to combat the external limitations imposed by the law and white attitudes. Dr. William Johnson regularly rode through Charleston's streets atop "the most sumptuous maroon surrey you ever saw, gold fringe and gold trim on the wheels," Fields remarked, adding that a smile and a wave from Johnson "uplifted your spirit whenever you saw him."[71] For young Septima Poinsette, who walked everywhere, the streets of her hometown offered important lessons in black history and achievement.

Weekends allowed the Poinsette family some leisure time. Saturday was shopping day. A better cook than his wife, Peter Poinsette usually bought the groceries, rounding out meals with okra, corn, tomatoes, and string beans from the family garden. Accompanying their parents on shopping trips, the Poinsette children probably stopped to listen to the young black musicians in the Jenkins Orphanage Band, which regularly performed for donations on King Street.[72] On Saturday afternoons, fish vendors made their way down Henrietta Street advertising their wares by singing, "Shimpee—Roe, Roe,

Roe, Roe" or "Shark steak don't need no gravy," meaning its own juices made the gravy in the pan. Every Saturday, the Poinsettes treated themselves to three pecks of shrimp or three strings of fish for a quarter. The children cleaned them the same day in preparation for a "big Sunday breakfast" of fish and grits with tomato sauce. Because they believed in honoring the Sabbath, the Poinsettes also roasted the meat and cooked the rice for Sunday dinner a day ahead and then kept the food warm in the woodstove. Honoring the Sabbath, however, made Sundays boring. Playing was forbidden, unless one enjoyed playing the organ in the parlor. On the plus side, from the children's perspective, Victoria Poinsette did not whip her children on Sundays. Someone caught sneaking a morsel of ham prior to dinner would remain unpunished until Monday.[73]

As their reverence for the Sabbath suggests, religious training ranked high on the Poinsettes' priority list, though the family members worshipped at different churches. When he was not working on Sunday mornings, Peter Poinsette and his son, Peter T., attended Centenary United Methodist Church, where he had married his first wife. The girls usually went with their mother. Victoria Poinsette joined Old Bethel United Methodist and attended Sunday evening services closer to home at Emanuel African Methodist Episcopal. After gobbling up breakfast, the children headed off to morning Sunday school at Zion Presbyterian and to afternoon religious classes at Old Bethel. Members of both Centenary and Old Bethel had eschewed affiliating with the Methodist Episcopal Church, South, opting instead to align with northern white Methodists. Thus, the Poinsettes joined a denomination that had an integrated membership at the national level and whose mostly white governing body disavowed black inferiority and racial oppression. Not until the 1890s had the United Methodists begun a slow capitulation to the principle of segregation. Septima Poinsette eventually chose Old Bethel as her spiritual home.[74]

If Septima Poinsette had considered the history of the churches she attended while growing up, she would have had much to ponder. Knowing what had happened inside those buildings amounted to a comprehensive study of days past. In the spring and summer of 1865, for example, Zion Presbyterian had hosted daily debates and nightly mass meetings, with the overflow crowds spilling onto Calhoun Street. Inside, Low Country black leaders deliberated tactics and strategies as they sought to articulate the collective aspirations of freedmen and -women. The rallying culminated on November 25 as forty-six delegates from across the state assembled at Zion for the Colored People's Convention. Over the next several days, they adopted a variety of resolutions, including one that denounced slavery and one that demanded "even-handed Justice." Both "Big Zion" and Emanuel African Methodist Episcopal held numerous such political gatherings during the early years of freedom.[75]

Churches of all denominations helped to institutionalize African Americans' nascent social, political, and economic autonomy. Because black clergymen served as intermediaries between the masses in their congregations and white authorities, black voters frequently elected ministers to state and national office. Church members established mutual aid societies and relief organizations as well, thereby creating an important social welfare infrastructure. God's house also became the schoolhouse. Black ministers, working alone or with northern sympathizers and the Freedmen's Bureau, founded schools and often taught classes.[76]

Septima Poinsette's generation smarted most from the pain of what African Americans lost when the white supremacists won. During Reconstruction, black legislators had engineered state funding for a host of public initiatives that mirrored those emanating from black congregations at the local level. Facing the certain disfranchisement of his people, black state representative Thomas Ezekiel Miller of Beaufort County attempted to set both the record and the public's memory straight at the 1895 constitutional convention. "We were eight years in power," Miller pronounced. "We had built school houses, established charitable institutions, built and maintained the penitentiary system, provided for the education of the deaf and dumb, rebuilt the jails and court houses, rebuilt the bridges and re-established the ferries. In short, we had reconstructed the state and placed it on the road to prosperity." All this had been accomplished, Miller noted, while increasing South Carolina's debt by just $2.5 million from its 1868 level. After 1895, a more miserly state, led by white elites averse to paying taxes, turned its back on such duties, starving schools and social welfare services for both black and white Carolinians.[77] Black churches stepped into the breach, continuing to offer services that extended well beyond spiritual guidance.

Participation in the church provided a social foundation for black Charlestonians and introduced younger members to the finer points of fund-raising and public speaking, thereby bolstering their self-confidence. It was normal to hear announcements every week pertaining to church-sponsored community activities and to participate in the bake sales or raffles that financed those endeavors. "Guest rallies" gave young people a chance to entertain various congregations by singing or reciting poetry and Bible verses. "That was building character," one Charlestonian observed, "service without being taught service. It was expected."[78] As a teenager, Septima Poinsette chaired her youth group, taught Sunday school, and helped to raise four thousand dollars to purchase a new organ for Old Bethel.[79] These experiences endowed her with a service-oriented ideological framework, which, as a teacher, she would adapt to educational organizing to rally community support for cash-poor black schools.

A commitment to obtain an education by any means necessary flowed like an undercurrent through Septima Poinsette's world. Immediately after the Civil War, a plethora of schooling options had existed for freed people in the Low Country. Some attended classes conducted by black veterans who had learned to read while serving in the Union army. Others looked to the church, where Sunday school curricula reached far beyond Bible study and evening classes for adults became routine. Many more former slaves crowded into the public schools that began opening a mere three weeks after Union troops captured Charleston. By early March 1865, the city's new school superintendent, abolitionist James Redpath, had enrolled one thousand black and two hundred white students at the Morris Street School. More than half of their teachers were African American, most of them native Charlestonians. Along with northern whites and Union army officers, they taught more than four thousand students in five schools by July. Aid from northern philanthropic groups and missionary societies facilitated the expansion of schools by providing funds to buy land, construct buildings, and pay teachers' salaries.[80] In Charleston, no group achieved greater success than the American Missionary Association (AMA).

Founded in 1846 by abolitionists disgusted with churches' tepid stances on slavery, the AMA sought to transfer the venerated traditions of New England to the South and its institutions, with the long-term goal of establishing schools to train southern black teachers. The AMA's chief emissary in Charleston was the Reverend Francis L. Cardozo, a native of the city and an organizer in local Republican postbellum politics. In October 1865, he formally organized the Saxton School and hired ten southern African American and ten northern white teachers. Cardozo recognized that Saxton's curriculum would have to focus on basic material until it produced enough students for advanced teacher training. Yet only three years later, the AMA purchased a lot on Bull Street and, after the Freedmen's Bureau completed construction of a school building, renamed Saxton the Avery Normal Institute. By 1868, most northern relief societies had begun to scale back their southern educational commitments. The Freedmen's Bureau got out of the education business altogether in 1870, when the state, in accordance with its 1868 con-

Old Bethel United Methodist Church, located on Calhoun Street in Charleston, n.d. Courtesy of the Avery Research Center for African American History and Culture, College of Charleston.

stitutional mandate, assumed responsibility for providing a system of free public schools.[81] The AMA's relationship with Avery lasted until 1947.

Ex-slaves valued education as a consequence of being denied it while in bondage. Freedmen and -women well understood that their future economic and political security depended on securing basic literacy skills and pursued them with equal fervor in both the city and the country. How else could one be certain of the terms of the annual labor contracts he or she signed? How else might one retain the privilege of owning property by identifying the letter in the mailbox as a tax bill? How else would one recognize the name of the man for whom he wanted to vote? Most of all, former slaves wanted black control of black schools. Though they welcomed the assistance of the Union army, the federal government, and northern white missionaries, circumstances demanded a clean break from white oversight and manipulation. Equally important, many African Americans adopted an "each one, teach one" philosophy: those who acquired some education promptly passed it on.[82]

By the time Septima Poinsette reached school age, however, Jim Crow's ascent had turned the tide. Under the control of the white state, the school as an institution proved essential to the maintenance of white supremacy, and public schooling assigned people particular social destinies. Rather than recalling the difficulties inherent in the preservation of the racial order, school curricula made it appear unchangeable. The predominantly female teaching force played a tremendous role in expanding or curtailing imagined possibilities of citizenship. In segregated classrooms, white teachers instilled in generations of white students the ideological and practical meaning of their racial privilege, which cut across class differences to further promote unity within the white community. Yet, on the other side of the color line, black teachers battled with equal fervor to provide black students with the skills and cultural capital to succeed in a world controlled by white people.[83]

Despite their differences in so many areas, Peter and Victoria Poinsette agreed on the importance of educating their children. In 1904, Septima began attending Shaw Memorial School, a public institution. Built in 1866 by black soldiers stationed in the city, its name honored Robert Gould Shaw, commander of the Fifty-fourth Massachusetts U.S. Colored Troops, who died at the Civil War's Battle of Fort Wagner. If the name of Septima Poinsette's first school conjured a reminder of the hope of that historical moment, the less than ideal conditions there testified to the cruel reality of segregated education. Charleston had a white teacher training institute, and to ensure that its graduates found jobs, city fathers employed only white teachers in the public schools. At Shaw, according to Clark, a hundred black first-graders sat on bleachers in what was called the ABC gallery, and their white teachers spent most of the day escorting students to the bathroom, which was outdoors. "We didn't learn too much," she commented. Fearful of the health risks—particularly lice—generated by such close contact with the masses and aware that the instruction was substandard, Victoria Poinsette withdrew Septima from Shaw after one year and sent her to one of the many private schools independently operated by local black women.[84]

Victoria Poinsette's carefully calculated choice acknowledged the shortcomings of white teachers who expressed their gratitude for their jobs by reinforcing white ideas of black inferiority. As Clark asserted, these white women "didn't like for black children to speak to them in the streets; I guess they didn't want other people to know they were teaching blacks. They were embarrassed to be teaching black children and they would have you whipped." For the young African American student excited to greet his or her teacher, being snubbed generated negative associations with education itself. Clark, "a timid child," found such incidents disheartening and translated them into a dislike of school: "I soon hated the school and I thought little of" the teachers.[85] Her three years at the independent private school gave her a much more positive view of education. Even the most socially distant black teacher remained more sensitive to her pupils' feelings.

At a time when the family "zealously hoarded coupons" to exchange as birthday and holiday gifts, Victoria Poinsette scraped together a dollar tuition each month so that Septima could attend a private school on Logan Street. The new environment did more than improve the girl's chances for educational success. The school's operators, a Mrs. Nuckles and her niece, "didn't take just anybody who had the money for tuition," Clark later observed. Nuckles "chose her pupils from the Negroes who boasted of being free issues," those who "constituted a sort of upper caste." Poinsette's enrollment testified to her mother's standing in the community and secured her a place in at least one exclusive social circle. Moreover, Nuckles's nonacademic lessons of culture and manners dovetailed perfectly with Victoria Poinsette's home teachings. Nuckles "required that we act in a manner befitting our superior position," Clark noted. The failure to perform academically had immediate consequences as well. Students who made mistakes during spelling lessons could expect to be summoned to the front of the room and have the correct letters whipped into their open palms.[86]

Nuckles also taught by example. Septima Poinsette, for one, "delighted to see her in those skirts with the many gores and high-necked shirtwaists with the boned necks." On Sundays in particular, "this woman was a fashion plate indeed." Nuckles strengthened both black cultural pride and her pupils' sense of community outside of the classroom by inviting them to hear her sing at various local churches. Her glamour and her commitment to excellence impressed Poinsette, who acknowledged, "I suspect that my admiration for her influenced in some way at least my early ambition to be a teacher." Equally significant, private instruction by Charleston's black women circumvented the inadequacies of large classes and short academic terms that plagued white-controlled black public schools.[87] Moreover, these teachers were free to offer lessons in black history and achievement.

Such seditious pedagogy was not limited to the classroom but spilled over into Charleston's public thoroughfares. Mamie Fields remembered how Anna Izzard, the teacher at the private school she attended, led older students on walking tours around the city, using her storytelling skills and their questions to instruct them. Izzard and her class ignored the custom that rendered the Battery off-limits to African Americans except on the Yankee July 4 holiday, and students' inquiries about the cannons there provided an opportunity to discuss the Civil War and to point out Fort Sumter in Charleston Harbor. Similarly, students asked about the mansions lining Battery Park: "Who were those people? How did they get the money to build such great houses?" In this way, recalled Fields, "we found out about the Revolutionary War, the Civil War, how people made money during slavery." Such lessons in the ways of white folks were balanced by black history. "She taught us how strong our ancestors back in slavery were and what fine people they were." Izzard's creative pedagogical approach not only challenged the city's de facto segregation but also subverted white people's memorialization of public space. Black teachers thus composed narratives that located African American actors at the core of a civic landscape whose monuments to white supremacy intended to erase the presence of nonwhites.[88]

Perhaps because of financial hardship, Septima Poinsette returned to public school after fourth grade and finished eighth grade at the newly built Charleston Colored Industrial School, later renamed Burke High School. For decades, Burke was the county's lone public institution offering black children anything beyond an elementary education.[89] Only one of all Poinsette's white teachers in these years, Miss Seabrook, made a positive impression on the girl. Instead of teaching by rote memorization, Seabrook used maps and socioeconomic data to teach world geography. Her methods spurred Septima to continue further study outside of the classroom. Graduating from eighth grade would have qualified Septima to teach, but Victoria Poinsette insisted that her daughter "must get some more education. You'll go to Avery next year."[90]

At Avery, Septima found an academic "paradise." Every student in the three-story brick building had a seat at a desk. Her astronomy course provided intellectual stimulation, which she valued as much as the practical instruction she gained in sewing and cooking classes, and she appreciated the dedication of the integrated faculty. Passing a portrait of Francis Cardozo in the hall made her feel proud. During her four years at Avery, Poinsette sang in the glee club, played for the girls' basketball team, and served as the assistant editor of the school yearbook and as vice president of her senior class. She also joined the King's Daughters, a group established to aid the less fortunate, particularly the community's elderly and infirm.[91] Avery's pedagogical philosophy reflected its sponsor's sense of Christian missionary duty and reinforced the lessons of community service that Poinsette had first learned at home and at church.

Yet for some of its darker-skinned pupils, the school proved less than a social paradise, earning notoriety for perpetuating the caste line within black Charleston. Despite her apparent success on the campus, Poinsette encountered exclusion. If her friends ignored the class and caste distinctions that divided Charleston's African American community, their families did not. "I was considered beneath a lot of the students there since my mother was a washerwoman and my father had been a slave," she noted, "and so I couldn't go to any of the parties that were given by the parents of my classmates."[92] At the same time, attending Avery raised her standing above all of those who went to public schools. To pay Avery's $1.50 monthly tuition, fourteen-year-old Septima took a live-in job cleaning house and babysitting for a black neighbor, Ella Sanders, who feared staying alone when her husband was away for his job as a railroad porter.[93]

As a teacher training institute, Avery's pedagogical approach reflected broader educational trends popular at the turn of the twentieth century, particularly the philosophies of Johann Heinrich Pestalozzi, John Dewey, and Harvard child psychologist William James. The importance of "'object lessons,' or learning from experience" stressed by Pestalozzi's disciples, who "discouraged rote learning and physical punishment," fit well with Dewey's emphasis on "learning by doing." Required textbooks included Emerson E. White's *The Art of Teaching*, which pedagogically linked Pestalozzi's theories to James's, and Reuben Post Halleck's *Psychology and Psychic Culture*, which James endorsed.[94] Poinsette's theoretical training emphasized the close relationship between the curriculum and students' life experiences.

During her time at the school, however, Avery found itself caught up in national debates about the role of black education in the South. A bitter ideological battle pitted northern philanthropists and white southerners who believed in universal schooling against the white supremacists who controlled southern politics. Reformers reasoned that an economically prosperous and modern society could be secured only by educating the labor force to develop efficient work habits and to become responsible citizens. Northern businessmen who presided over philanthropic foundations—and their contributors—took a special interest in how educating the South's black agricultural workers might best facilitate the region's economic modernization, thereby strengthening its ties to industry, while teaching African Americans to accept a subordinate place in the southern social order. Members of this faction advocated industrial education similar to that promulgated by the Hampton Institute in Virginia and, more famously, Booker T. Washington's Tuskegee Institute in Alabama. White supremacists, conversely, having only recently wrested political power from black southerners, perceived education as a Pandora's box, arguing that "any large-scale expansion of black education, even industrial education, would set in motion a revolution in race relations that would undermine the South's existing political and economic arrangements."[95] In theory, the white supremacists were right. In practice, it would take African American educators and their students four decades to finish the "revolutionary" task.

Responding to the spirit of the times, the AMA added an industrial department to Avery in 1900. Parents and alumni, proud of the school's educational excellence and its role in the development of a black professional class, resisted efforts to scale back the school's emphasis on classical education. As the AMA moved toward developing industrial normal schools to serve rural southern constituencies, Avery supporters insisted that it continue as a college preparatory and normal school in its existing urban location or be upgraded to a college. Benjamin F. Cox, who in 1914 became Avery's first black principal since Cardozo in 1868, mediated the growing rift between the school's benefactors and his local constituency. Aware that AMA leaders hoped for biracial cooperation in southern black education, Cox conscientiously solicited the support of prominent local white Charlestonians, including two of the city's mayors and some influential ministers. Nevertheless, during Septima Poinsette's junior year, the financially burdened AMA considered closing her school. Cox mimicked the methods of his AMA-sponsored alma mater, Fisk University, as he devised additional ways to assuage Avery's economic difficulties. "Every time the trustees came from the North, we had to sing the spirituals," Clark remembered. "I didn't know the history of the spirituals and I disliked them greatly, so I'd stand to the back and just move my mouth and wouldn't sing."[96]

A new form of segregation arrived at Avery the same year as Cox and his wife, Jeanette, did. White northern women had taught at the school since its founding and had earned the respect of parents and students. Unlike their southern counterparts, these women used their position to challenge segregation by accompanying their pupils to performances at the local theater and sitting with them in the second-floor balcony reserved for black patrons. White teachers also visited their students' homes. Such defiance of local custom, along with the fact that Avery's white and black faculty shared the teachers' dormitory, "provoked considerable talk in Charleston," Clark averred, and city officials responded by prohibiting interracial living arrangements. Two of the most beloved white teachers, Mattie M. Marsh and Elsie B. Tuttle, "had been there thirty years," Clark reflected, "and they were as reluctant to leave as we were to have them go." They remained until her graduation, but after their departure, Avery joined McClennan-Banks as the only two institutions in the city where all-black faculty instructed black students.[97]

Reflecting other Progressive Era trends, training at Avery reserved a special role for black women as moral agents in the community. In the late nineteenth century, African American educator Anna Julia Cooper had intervened in larger debates regarding woman's proper place by asserting that "the position of woman in society determines the vital elements of its regeneration. . . . Woman's work and woman's influence are needed as never before," she argued, "needed to bring a heart power into this money getting, dollar-worshipping civilization; needed to bring a moral force into the utilitarian motives and interests of the time."[98] Cooper's observations distilled the thinking of a whole generation of black women, shaped by the discrimination they confronted as African Americans and women and by their activism within churches, schools, and social welfare organizations. These women believed that maintaining noble womanhood was part of their duty to resist white supremacy; Septima Poinsette and other teachers had to conform to these precepts. "You had to be very cautious, to a certain extent, in how you lived your life," another black educator from Charleston affirmed, "certain places they just didn't expect teachers to be seen."[99]

Teaching was respectable work. Not only would it provide Poinsette with a relatively decent income, a portion of which she could send home, but it was one of the few occupations available to southern black women who wanted to do something other than serve white people. In the early 1920s, just over 35,000 black women in South Carolina worked in domestic service, whereas only 3,457 black women taught school. Victoria Poinsette vowed that none of her children would ever nurse a white baby, and her husband refused to allow his daughters to work as domestics or at hotels because he "feared the temptations and possible dangers sometimes associated with that sort of work."[100] Temptation meant receiving gifts from the white man of the house or the white boss in exchange for sexual favors. The dangers included physical and verbal abuse as well as rape, which routinely went unpunished.

Septima Poinsette earned her licentiate of instruction, which equaled two years of college training, from Avery in the spring of 1916. She was now qualified to teach in South Carolina — if she could find a job. Marsh and Tuttle had other ideas. "Septima is college material," they informed Cox, who then urged Victoria and Peter Poinsette to consider sending their daughter to Fisk to continue her studies. Septima's parents welcomed the idea, particularly because a college graduate would be a first in the family. Paying Fisk's tuition of nineteen dollars a month however, seemed beyond what their daughter could imagine. "I knew what a struggle we were having to get along even at that time and how hard it was to get the $1.50 a month for the Avery tuition," she reasoned. "So I argued against their trying to send me to Fisk. Had the situation been different I would have loved to go."[101] Instead, she enlisted the aid of the Reverend Edward B. Burroughs, a black Methodist minister who had connections to the white school trustees on Johns Island and had heard of an opening at a two-room school. Forgoing Fisk and accepting this teaching position marked a turning point in Septima's life, both because of the possibilities it foreclosed and because of those it opened.

The fact that Charleston offered no jobs to its black public school teachers meant that Avery prepared the majority of its graduates to teach in rural county systems. "It is in the country that our teachers must find their work," the school's white principal observed in 1909. But, he noted, "the jungles of Africa can hardly present more dangers than the [malaria and yellow] fever abounding the coast regions of the South." Into these backwoods of "ignorance and superstition," Avery alumni trod to teach "habits of thrift and cleanliness" along with the fundamentals of reading, writing, and arithmetic.[102] Yet these sentiments, penned for a northern white benefactor, speak only partially to how Septima Poinsette and other freshly minted teachers envisioned both their mission and their constituency. The school's emphasis on racial uplift dated back to its Reconstruction-era origins and paralleled the local black community's firm belief in fostering self-improvement through intellectual and cultural enrichment. Avery tried to prepare its teachers to bridge the gap between the opportunities afforded by urban living and the realities of rural life. Additional chasms awaited crossing.

Septima Poinsette knew nothing about Johns Island, the everyday texture of the Sea Island people's lives, or their history. She did not know that while the Civil War still raged, Robert Smalls had joined three other African Americans in a delegation from the Sea Islands that attempted to gain seating at the 1864 Republican National Convention. Nor was she aware that by the summer of 1865, an estimated thirty thousand freedmen and -women, many of them recent migrants, resided on Edisto, James, Wadmalaw, and Johns Islands and that they waged a fierce battle to prevent white planters from reclaiming land that the settlers believed was rightfully theirs. She probably could not have imagined island residents preparing a petition reminding President Andrew Johnson of the government's obligation to them. She was not acquainted with the fact that by early 1866, officials at the Freedmen's Bureau had validated a mere 450 land claims filed by freed people. Instead, what Poinsette would have seen was the aftermath of Reconstruction: that most rural residents had turned to tenant farming and sharecropping because they figured that such arrangements would best preserve their self-sufficiency, and how much time had proven them wrong.[103]

Postwar Sea Islanders' failures had far-reaching consequences. Rural freedmen and -women had tried to tie their future to landownership because they perceived how it strengthened their community's economic autonomy. They had recognized that their children's and grandchildren's daily independence and self-protection also depended on the earth. Fifty years in the future, those who had gained pieces of land provided room and board for young teachers in their midst, including Septima Poinsette. By the time she arrived on Johns Island in 1916, only a tiny flame of the radically democratic political activism of that earlier generation still flickered. Yet forty years after Poinsette's initial sojourn to Johns Island, it would be the independent landowners who hosted and mentored the civil rights activists who came to help finish the revolution begun in Reconstruction.[104] And it would be Septima Clark's adult literacy program that mobilized their neighbors.

❧

"I stood on a platform built by my mother and father," Septima Poinsette Clark claimed. As a civil rights veteran, Clark looked back on her childhood and credited her father's gentleness and patience as laying the foundation for her approach to working with people. "You don't exalt yourself," Peter

Poinsette had counseled his children. By contrast, her mother's anger and courage provided Clark with the motivation to act in dangerous situations. Clark conceded that she felt closer to her father than to her mother and that she wanted to be more like him. She admitted sharing Mama Vickie's "emotional" nature but maintained that "it takes much more to arouse me than it did my mother." Victoria Poinsette's inability to "see changes in people," her belief that "if I can do a thing, you can do it," bothered her second daughter. Nor did Clark care for the way her mother scolded her father for his inability to imagine a different world. "You can't see what's happening," she often told Peter Poinsette; "You're just no good."[105] However, Clark appreciated the fact that in a society that attempted to silence black women, her mother "talked back and let people know that she wasn't going to stand for any foolishness." And she came to value her mother's strictness and home teachings, because "it helped us to be real women."[106] As the white South fixed Jim Crow as the law of the land, Septima Poinsette learned to balance her father's emphasis on the importance of flexibility with her mother's insistence on standing firm. Like a tree with multiple branches and deep roots, she knew how to bend with the wind and hold steady in the storm.

Septima Poinsette bridged the generation between slavery and freedom, and the broader sensibilities of Charleston's black community supplemented the planks in the platform that Peter and Victoria Poinsette built. Their daughter's participation in the church and her schooling reinforced their lessons of service and nurtured her self-confidence. Moreover, black Charleston's institutions and its educators preserved memories that contested Jim Crow's logic of black inferiority. Even so, black Charlestonians feared the indignities and the material losses white supremacy imposed on all black people, which reinforced their penchant to preserve distinctions among themselves and rendered the community's internal divisions difficult to surmount. Growing up in Charleston, Septima Poinsette could not entirely escape the stigma of her father's former enslavement and the fact that her mother worked as a washerwoman.

Narrating her coming of age in a time and place where "nobody ever thought about voting," Clark had to show how her radicalism emerged not despite her family and society's history but because of it, which meant leaving room for the unresolved contradictions in her parents' and her native city's past.[107] How else could she explain Peter Porcher Poinsette's loyalty to the Confederacy? Or rationalize Victoria Poinsette's adherence to aristocratic Charleston's social exclusivity, even when the distressing social rejections she experienced stemmed from such practices? More broadly, what new meanings might we, Clark's "listeners," derive from her narrative? One final meditation seems appropriate here.

When the botany-loving Joel Poinsett returned from serving as the nation's first ambassador to Mexico, he brought a special cutting back and grew it in the gardens at White House. In Mexico, the plant was known as the Flower of the Holy Night because it bloomed during the Christmas season. In the United States, it became known as the "poinsettia" to honor the man—diplomat, scholar, remover of Native Americans, Unionist, slaveholder—who introduced it to this country.[108] With its flaming red and rich dark green leaves, the poinsettia calls to mind the festive Christmas season. Yet the plant's symbolic meaning changes when viewed through the lens of Septima Poinsette Clark's life. Born the daughter of a slave from the Poinsett plantation, she grew up to become a fighter in the southern struggle for her people's freedom. First cultivated deep in the antebellum slave South, the poinsettia—like the woman whose name recalls it—reminds us that the pain of the past and the promise of the future are rooted in the same soil.

CHAPTER TWO

Taking Up the Work

The afternoon sun battled storm clouds to reach the Ashley River that Saturday, September 9, 1916. As the clock neared half past two, Septima Poinsette,
her mother, and Ella Sanders, her neighbor and patron, made their way to
the public wharf at the end of Tradd Street. The two older women had come
to see the eighteen-year-old Septima embark on her new life as a teacher. For
Victoria Poinsette, pride in her second child's accomplishments mixed with
relief that she had escaped the dreariness and the dangers of domestic service. Her daughter was leaving home for the first time, having accepted a job
on isolated Johns Island because her native city refused to employ African
American teachers in its segregated public schools. Reaching Johns Island
by gasoline launch would take about eight hours. It required navigating narrow intracoastal waterways and creeks, sometimes waiting for the tide to
rise enough to cover the long, wide mud flats that separated deeper channels
of water from shore. Growing up, Septima had heard stories of the island,
its abundance of fish and game, mild climate, and fertile soil, but not much
about its people. Conversation did not flow easily as the three women stood
on the dock waiting for the small boat that would carry the young teacher
away. Their silence acknowledged that it might be a long time before they
reunited. Gazing across the brackish water, Septima Poinsette contemplated
the separation from loved ones but resolved to make the most of every opportunity the adventure afforded.[1]

The days ahead would test her mettle more than she knew. She would
exchange the comfort of familial Henrietta Street for the privation of rural
living among strangers. A dilapidated schoolhouse overflowing with chil-

dren of all ages would replace Avery's exclusive academic environment. She would endure physical hardships and would never again take some things for granted—a well-heated classroom, nutritious meals, access to doctors. Conversely, she would learn to fashion creative solutions to the tasks at hand. She would find the depth of her commitment strengthened by these trials. She would discover that she had the wherewithal to survive.

Teaching and living on Johns Island from 1916 to 1918 marked a point of departure for Septima Poinsette, prompting her to start thinking about "getting things done."[2] Confronting for the first time the brutality of rural poverty, she saw up close how severely the agricultural economy constrained the lives of her students, their families, and everyone dependent on and enmeshed within it. Such an intimate view challenged her preconceptions of poor people. It is not so much that she would have turned away from a life of service. Her parents had taught her the duty of giving back to the community, and church involvement and training at Avery had reinforced this lesson. But spending time on Johns Island caused Poinsette to consider new methods of answering the call to serve. Her inexperience meant that she had to discover her own ways of "getting things done" with few resources apart from the people themselves. Johns Island changed the way Septima Poinsette saw the world.

Of course, Miss Poinsette knew that the educational world she entered that day was rife with inequality, but the idea that white Carolinians fared better than their African American neighbors says both too much and too little. As the rest of the nation embraced Progressive Era educational reforms, the Palmetto State lagged far behind, adamantly resisting attempts to standardize its public school system. South Carolina had no state school tax in 1916, no statewide compulsory attendance law, and no minimum school term. In 1915–16, annual per-pupil expenditures ranged from a high of $48.59 for white children in Sumter County to a low of $0.95 for black children in Colleton County. The disparity ultimately hurt everyone. South Carolina's average expenditure for pupils of both races totaled $13.45, a mere 32 percent of the national average. Seven out of ten South Carolina students never started the fifth grade, and only 5 percent entered high school.[3]

Into this academic wilderness Septima Poinsette journeyed, joining almost nine thousand other teachers, 80 percent of them women and the majority stationed in rural schools. Though they confronted similar problems—too many pupils crowded into classrooms on some days and too few during harvest season—Poinsette's white colleagues could at least take comfort in what relief the currency of their whiteness bought them. They could expect to be treated with courtesy by the district trustees who employed them and set their salaries. They could depend on those trustees to provide minimum supplies, including textbooks and firewood to heat the schoolhouse. They could anticipate greeting, on average, thirty-five students in their classrooms. They could plan to deposit their paychecks in the bank for five and a half months of the year. If they were among the lucky few, working in one of seven counties, they might benefit from the innovative suggestions of a county teaching supervisor. And if all else failed, they could look forward to leaving the profession when they married.[4]

African American teachers operated with a different set of assumptions. They could look forward to meeting indifferent district trustees who felt little obligation to address them with proper titles and who provided only the most rudimentary school supplies, if any. The majority could expect to report to work in old, weather-beaten shacks or churches, and to welcome at least sixty-nine students, usually many more, into their classrooms. They could anticipate receiving one-third the salary of their white counterparts at best, and had to stretch it further since they only taught for an average three and a half months each year. Most could count on being left entirely to their own devices, with no outside supervision or guidance. And unless they married economically independent men, they could assume that they would spend the rest of their lives laboring under these miserable conditions. Taking up the work required a missionary's faith of purpose and a true believer's zeal.[5]

Yet to be black and a teacher in the Jim Crow South was to be a "precious symbol" of a people's dreams from days gone by and of hope for the future. Teaching afforded high esteem in a community that remembered the high cost of education barely a generation earlier. "Once I was whipped simply because it was thought I had opened a book," a former slave recalled in 1922.[6] The idea of the power of the book rippled relentlessly across the twentieth century. For those whose dreams of acquiring a bit of learning had been vanquished, educating their children signaled resistance to a sharecropping and tenant-farming present that too often resembled the slave past. A child who could read, write, and figure numbers had a better chance to survive, to prosper, and, given the inclination and the chance, to escape. For every parent who had been told to keep his child in the fields or else, education marked a small triumph against a deadening systematic oppression.

More broadly, disfranchised African Americans in South Carolina and across the region viewed education as a primary battlefield in the struggle to undermine white supremacy and to reestablish themselves as citizens.

They faced a formidable enemy in a white state equally determined to use education to maintain the racial and economic status quo. "The objections to negro education arise chiefly from the feeling that it unfits the negro for the place he must fill in the state" as a manual or agricultural laborer, one white South Carolina educational official reported in 1911, "and that the so-called educated negro too often becomes a loafer or a political agitator." At his inauguration the same year, Governor Coleman Blease declared, "I am opposed to white people's taxes being used to educate Negroes."[7]

Keeping black backs bent and black hands busy ranked high among South Carolina's priorities. Still, Governor Blease's vitriol represented only the most visible expression of the state's determination to control black labor and black lives. Year after year, South Carolina demonstrated its disregard through miserly spending on facilities, equipment, and teacher salaries for black schools.[8] This situation was never a matter of benign neglect. Rather, it represented a deliberate attempt to tack down the horizons of African American aspiration and opportunity. Separate and unequal education targeted children, whose value the white state measured only by the economic potential of their labor. It was an insidious evil, sustaining itself throughout the twentieth century. But the denial of equal educational opportunity did not look evil at all. On the contrary, it appeared as normal as the noonday sun.

How did southern African American educators confront ordinary evil when neither flight nor fright was an option and progress was a necessary mandate? From the earliest days, they relied on two considerable resources, one external, the other internal, and both entangled in geographic, social, economic, and political realities. First, they depended on northern philanthropy to construct and maintain schools and to extend teacher training. By the end of the first decade of the twentieth century, however, the philanthropic landscape had changed, and its long-term goals had begun to evolve in a new direction.[9] The support of black rural communities provided a second crucial resource. Yet conditions varied widely from place to place, and the promise of education remained tethered to local circumstances. Communities where some farmers had achieved a degree of economic independence or that had benefited from the organizing of an industrious teacher responded more readily than those who had neither. "Don't need no education to work in the fields," was a sentiment sometimes voiced by black tenant or sharecropping parents, especially within earshot of the white landlords on whom their livelihoods depended.[10]

The eighteen-year-old Septima Poinsette had enlisted in a small but growing army of black teachers, shock troops who carried the fight to south-ern rural communities. In these hinterlands, they forged an activist educa-tional culture that had long-term political consequences. Their activism was created in the absence of white state supervision, shaped by improvisational pedagogical strategies, and underscored by a commitment to local people. Success depended not on confrontation but on driving a wedge, gaining ground an inch at a time and holding it. Victories remained uneven. Many rural teachers lacked sufficient training and had only acquired a bit more education than the students they endeavored to teach.[11] But the strivings of the best and the most competent instructors mattered. Understanding how they evaluated their labors and responsibilities, how they measured progress, is critical to appreciating the lifework of thousands of southern black women. To judge their world solely through the eyes of educational leaders—whether allies or foes—is to obscure the magnitude of their ac-complishments.

This world of black teachers in the rural Jim Crow South contains the roots of Septima Poinsette Clark's vision of citizenship education. Sprouts appeared over the next few decades, fertilized by her wider experiences in the world. After nearly a lifetime of cultivation, they reached maturity— ironically, when she lost her job as a teacher in 1956. But Johns Island in 1916 is where it all began.

⌐⊱⊰⌐

Septima Poinsette Clark spent nearly forty years teaching in both rural and urban areas in South Carolina, a state that ran its schools the way it played its politics, favoring home rule at the county level over establishing state-wide standards. Deference to local control shaped the public school system from its inception and made sense in a state still recovering from the social upheaval and financial devastation of the Civil War. In 1868, both white and black Carolinians fretted over the prospect of integrated classrooms. African American delegates to that year's state constitutional convention remained most concerned about the potential negative impact of white prejudice on black education and about guaranteeing employment for future black teachers. The delegates conceded that the black majority preferred separate schools in practice but refused to write segregation into the new constitution. At the same time, because they benefited from a political system based on local control, they left it intact. The 1870 School Act reserved administra-tive power for counties, which guaranteed African American supervision of schools in black-majority districts where black men held office.[12]

Merely creating a system of public schools had constituted an ambitious task. Though white hostility to bankrolling universal free education stemmed from the fact that the state's Reconstruction government had constructed the modus operandi, deeper reasons lay in antebellum society. Strident arguments against growing a strong central government reflected a historic aversion to state interference. White Carolinians believed that authority properly belonged to an independent yeomanry, male heads of households. Objections that public schools cost too much meshed with the low-tax realities of the former plantation economy. Reconstruction added insult to injury. First, it officially excluded antebellum elites, former leading Confederates, from the decision-making process. Then it placed an unprecedented tax burden on this already battered ruling class, with the money to be used to build the first state-supported public services, which they had never envisioned, had little use for, and therefore viewed as illegitimate. After white Democrats regained power in 1876, the specter of educated and enfranchised African Americans posing a perennial threat to the preservation of white supremacy galvanized resistance to publicly supported schools.[13]

The debates involving education and politics came to a head at the 1895 state constitutional convention. By that time, Governor "Pitchfork" Ben Tillman had effected a revolution within a revolution in South Carolina political affairs, pitting the interests of the state's agricultural producers against those aristocrats who had presided over the reconstruction of white supremacy in 1876–77. Tillman, a member of the elite, manipulated antebellum ideas of the inherent nobility of white yeomen to reconstruct a polity whose ordering principle was the rule of white men. Though he did little to help farmers retain their declining independence, Tillman won the right to rule by organizing this group of white men against the white men they believed sought to subjugate them. Moreover, he fathomed the practical political lessons of 1876. Power must remain in the hands of local lieutenants, leaders and supporters who could be counted on to defend, with force if necessary, this branch of the Democratic Party's interests. As a result, the 1895 state constitution deliberately strengthened the power of county governments.[14]

Governor Tillman chaired the committee on suffrage at the constitutional convention, where the primary discussion revolved around how best to disfranchise African Americans without robbing too many poor white men of the right to vote. Most delegates agreed that an educational restriction in the form of a literacy test was necessary, but some worried that educated black men would retain the vote while a large number of illiterate white men would not. Formally restricting black access to public schools was not an option because doing so would garner resistance from black Carolinians, generate pressure from groups outside of the South, and risk federal aid to white agricultural colleges. Shoring up white schools provided an alternative; to that end, delegates agreed to raise the school property tax from two to three mils, or three-tenths of one cent. "It is foolish to say any other race can get control of this State if we are educated," proponents reasoned, and education "can be gotten only by taxation." Tillman also knew that his supporters could not prosper without at least rudimentary schooling. Nevertheless, African American delegate R. B. Anderson's resolution to require compulsory attendance for all students age seven to twelve, which would also have served as a way to undermine compulsory child labor, went down to defeat.[15]

Tillmanites accomplished their goal of restricting suffrage. The literacy test stayed, augmented by a poll tax, property restrictions, and an "understanding" clause that persisted through 1898. White men who could not read or write could still vote if they paid taxes on three hundred dollars worth of property; failing landownership, would-be voters had to demonstrate that they "understood" a section of the state constitution. South Carolina purged all voting rolls, requiring universal reregistration in 1896. The electorate narrowed to fifty thousand white men and fifty-five hundred black men, with the poor of both races effectively prevented from voting.[16]

Black education remained secure only as long as African Americans retained a vestige of political power in state government. Without the vote, black Carolinians had no voice in electing the men who ran the system, from the governor down to the county superintendents. That these elected officials appointed members to county boards of education closed the circle of exclusion. Equitable spending soon emerged as a most critical issue. South Carolina law stipulated that counties distributed school monies according to enrollment. With black voters neutralized, white educational leaders in black-majority counties faced little opposition as they channeled all property tax revenue into white schools.[17]

By 1916, when Septima Poinsette began teaching, the precarious political unity among white men fostered in 1895 had again collapsed. The up-country cotton mill boom of the 1890s remade the state's economic, political, and social landscape. In its wake, two distinct groups of white people disputed the meaning of citizenship and the role of the state: urban middle-class men and women, who advocated using the power of the state to address social ills and promote reform, and mill operatives, who eyed these self-proclaimed leaders with suspicion and fought state intrusion into private life.[18]

Mill people found their champion in Coleman Livingston Blease, a Tillman protégé, a racist demagogue, and the ultimate anti-Progressive. Stirring new anxieties about whiteness and manhood into the political cauldron, "Coley" brought South Carolina's simmering class tensions to a boil.[19] Offering little in terms of concrete policy, Blease rewarded his constituents by rhetorically prioritizing their concerns above those of town reformers, especially in the realm of education. Education itself was not undesirable. "I am in favor of building up a free school system so that every white child in South Carolina may be given a good common school education," Blease conceded in his inaugural address. The state should spend money for better facilities, higher salaries for teachers, and history books, "especially histories, by Southern authors for Southern children." But when state-sponsored schooling interfered in the relationship between parents and children, Blease drew the line. "In my opinion, compulsory education in the hands of the State means disrupting the home, for it dethrones the authority of the parents and places the paid agents of the State in control of the children, and destroys family government," he declared.[20] The governor's listeners understood what he did not say: compulsory attendance laws would cripple mill families who relied on the money their children earned. The incremental pace of educational progress in South Carolina crystallizes only against this political backdrop.

These up-country battles influenced Septima Poinsette's professional world from afar. Most relevant for teachers such as Poinsette was the lack of economic opportunity in rural areas and the inherent problems compulsory schooling legislation posed for sharecropping and tenant children. Agriculture still dominated South Carolina's economy, and farm families could not survive unless all members worked. When it came to the question of education, white farm interests joined millhands in opposing compulsory schooling. African American farmers could not vote, but a number of them sided with their white neighbors. As one rural black educator observed, "If the school board held a meeting on a proposal for six months of schooling, Negro parents would fill the hall to protest." They did so under the threat of eviction from white landlords. Some black parents believed that book learning might either ruin their children for farmwork or endanger them by making them "uppity," but others made great sacrifices so that at least one of their children could obtain an education.[21] The dearth of economic options left all black tenants and sharecroppers few alternatives.

The politics of education in South Carolina guaranteed that the state's forty-five counties operated with considerable sovereignty. Each delineated its own school districts, raised and dispensed the majority of its educational funds, and hired its own teachers.[22] Reformers found curbing the power of county school officials a nearly impossible task. Just as county delegates to the General Assembly acted as local political bosses, passing laws to raise revenue and then channeling funds back to their home counties, county superintendents, elected for two-year terms, functioned as what the first state supervisor of rural schools, W. K. Tate, called "educational engineers" who controlled all money raised at the county level. Frustrated reformers complained continually that too much power was vested in the county superintendents, and that they prevented the state superintendent of education from making needed changes. Worse, the county-level officeholders were often chosen based on political connections rather than expertise.[23]

Educational home rule bred deeper problems in South Carolina's schools. Because the county served as the basic source for all revenue, differences in population and resources created huge statewide disparities in the quality of public education. Voters in counties with greater concentrations of wealth and higher tax bases, by-products of industrialization and the growth of an urban middle class, usually were willing to pay more for good schools. Sparsely populated rural counties with lower enrollments had to make less money go further. The smaller the number of districts in each county, the better educational services provided, but conditions varied widely even among districts in the same county. Counties with the fewest resources, highest enrollments, and most districts faced the greatest difficulties.[24]

Johns Island was in Charleston County, which had the state's second-largest education budget and a relatively low number of districts, nineteen. It should have been a premier place for Septima Poinsette to work. Charleston's teachers of both races received the highest salaries in the state. For African Americans teachers, this meant pocketing nearly three times as much as their colleagues elsewhere. Black per-pupil expenditures crested at a state high of $7.31 in 1916–17 in Charleston, which earned it first place in the annual rankings.[25] Yet the county's numbers were so high because only white teachers taught in the city's black public schools, where trustees provided books, furniture, fuel, and any other necessary supplies. Black teachers, compelled to teach in the country, fared much worse, as Miss Poinsette soon discovered.

Local control denied state officials any role in hiring employees, including ensuring their competency. Urban schools remained most likely to attract the best instructors, but urban teachers comprised only a small minority of the state's teaching corps.[26] According to state educational official

William H. Hand, because each county certified its teachers, the state had forty-five different methods for evaluating candidates' fitness. In response, Hand urged the creation of a state board of examiners to evaluate teacher competency. Moreover, Hand pointed out, hiring practices hindered state-wide efforts to weed out the worst elements of the labor force. Normally, prospective white employees wrote to their county boards to request jobs, stating the extent of their training and experience and offering references. Poinsette, like most African American teachers, had to procure recommendations from local white neighbors or from black leaders in good standing with white officials. Either way, Hand argued, few county boards had the resources to investigate fully each application and too often relied on fundamentally flawed criteria.[27]

The state's agricultural economy guaranteed that the majority of its children, black and white, who lived in rural districts fared worst. Just five years before Poinsette began teaching, State Supervisor of Rural Schools Tate admitted, "As a field of special effort, the rural schools of South Carolina is a virgin one." Tate could take satisfaction in the fact that the state's counties had recently completed organizing rural school districts for whites, but supervising those 1,866 districts remained a daunting task. In addition to establishing statewide teacher certification and a system of classification for students, Tate recommended consolidation, streamlining taxation at the local and county levels, and better supervision in white country schools. Supervision for African American rural schools, Tate confessed, had even further to go: "It has been my observation that the negro schools of South Carolina are for the most part without supervision of any kind. Frequently, the [white] county superintendent does not know where they are located."[28]

When Septima Poinsette began her teaching career, South Carolina spent nearly $3.5 million annually educating white students and just over $400,000 for black pupils, even though the state had almost eighteen thousand more African American children enrolled. Furthermore, black schoolhouses and grounds accounted for more than half of the state's public schools but were valued at a mere 9 percent of all school property. "No one can get a real picture of such a situation without actually seeing it," J. H. Brannon, the first state agent for Negro schools, testified in 1918, at the end of his inaugural year on the job. Summarizing what he had seen, Brannon wrote, "We usually find a shabbily constructed, unceiled and poorly equipped building, often a church, in which we find the teacher endeavoring to teach fifty to a hundred children, with a session of from three to four months." It came as no surprise, then, that black students lagged behind white students. "The real wonder," Brannon continued, "is that they learn as much as they do." He recommended that physical facilities be improved through such "modern" amenities as "blackboards, heaters and enough desks to seat the children."[29]

Septima Poinsette had already been teaching at Promise Land School, one of the eleven schools for black children on Johns Island, for two years by the time Brannon filed his first report. Brannon had not visited one Sea Island school, but his description fit Promise Land. Poinsette met her class in a log cabin with one long room divided in half by a chimney. Mud filled the cracks in the walls, while a creosote varnish covered the outside, preserving the wood but giving the building the appearance of having been painted with black tar. The windows had no glass; shutters kept the wind at bay but darkened the room considerably. The chimney smoked; the fireplace provided too much warmth for those who sat closest to it, none for the students farthest away. Homemade benches without back support offered pupils little comfort. District trustees William Andell, W. H. Hanahan, and F. Bartow Wilson shared responsibility for supplying the school's equipment—a water bucket and dipper, one table, one chair, and an ax with which the teacher or older students could chop firewood. There were blackboards but no chalk or erasers. There were a few dog-eared textbooks; none of them matched.[30]

Theoretically, school terms on Johns Island ran for eight months. Septima Clark later confirmed that she "stayed on the island most of the time from September to Christmas and then from Christmas to June." In reality, however, attendance hinged on the time of year and weather. Older children began appearing at the school regularly after the last cotton had been picked, usually just before Thanksgiving. They stopped going in the early spring, when the agricultural clock signaled that it was time to begin preparing the fields. Rainy days were the most crowded, at least until the sun came out and a plantation overseer arrived to call tenant children back to work. At harvest time, only the youngest children came to school, since parents signed contracts obligating older children to labor in the fields.[31]

Within South Carolina, systemic change in African American education always rested on courting white favor and downplaying black initiative. Black Carolinians, however, did not sit by idly. In the 1920–21 term, when the General Assembly appropriated $15,000 for their rural schools, black patrons raised $28,038 in private subscriptions. But the black community had to be careful that their white neighbors did not suspect that black schools were gaining even a slight advantage. Reformers attempting to ameliorate the grossest inequities used the utmost caution when they described how white taxpayers' money was spent. As the state agent for colored schools reassured his white readers, "Under no circumstances was a district given more than the Trustees allotted, or more than the negroes subscribed, or more than one dollar per pupil." He also insisted that the legislature's beneficence "has done more to convince our negro population of the liberal and sympathetic attitude of our Lawmakers, as well as the white folks at large."[32]

Regional resistance compromised federal assistance. The Smith-Lever Act of 1914, for example, provided funds to land-grant colleges for extension services conducted by agricultural and home demonstration agents. The measure presented a potential problem in states with both white and black institutions as it might have ceded the latter a slight degree of financial autonomy. Southern pressure in Congress preserved local white control by guaranteeing that state legislatures retained the right to decide whether black or white institutions would manage both the work and the money. In 1918, as another bill that aimed to secure state cooperation in federal educational initiatives worked its way through Congress, South Carolina's state superintendent of education, John Eldred Swearingen, alerted his U.S. senators to key provisions he found objectionable. Conceding that "equality of public school opportunity" across the nation "can never be secured without Federal legislation," the superintendent warned against the vague language that accompanied proposed standards of federal oversight. He asserted that a provision that would allow the federal government to regulate how states prepared teachers would make the U.S. secretary of education "the absolute dictator of teacher-training standards in America." Swearingen believed that "State Legislators and the State educational authorities ought not to be penalized for exercising their own discretion."[33]

Outside intervention in the form of northern white philanthropy had long served as the most substantial financial resource for southern black education. J. H. Brannon would not have had a job as the Palmetto State's agent for African American schools had not the General Education Board, founded in 1902 "to standardize southern black education," paid his salary and expenses. Then, too, the "modern" schoolhouses Brannon advocated would not have been built without the aid of the Rosenwald Fund, established in 1917 by Julius Rosenwald to erect schools for black children in the South. Nor would county training schools, as black high schools were called, have existed without contributions from the Slater Fund, established in 1881 to promote industrial education. These training schools, which ran for seven to nine months and served pupils in grades eight through twelve, greatly expanded the educational opportunities available to African Americans and trained significant numbers of teachers.[34]

Similarly, fewer African American teachers would have traveled to the Tuskegee Institute in Alabama, the Hampton Institute in Virginia, or to the black state college in Orangeburg for summer school sessions to enhance their credentials had the General Educational Board not helped to defray their expenses. Fewer still would have received pedagogical help inside their destitute rural classrooms without the Anna T. Jeanes Fund, founded in 1907, which provided African American supervising teachers. By 1917, South Carolina had fourteen Jeanes teachers and only six white rural county supervising teachers, since the state had to pay for those positions.[35] Certainly there was an ironic potential inherent in philanthropic assistance: at times black schools surpassed white schools in accessing specific kinds of educational opportunity.

Such broad support, however, reflected a seismic shift in the philanthropic terrain. In the first decade of the twentieth century, foundations concerned with southern black education discarded the religious, missionary approach of earlier sponsors as a new generation of Progressive leaders assumed command of the most influential organizations. More secular in orientation, these men viewed themselves as a moderating force in the often virulent world of biracial southern education. They had learned from earlier mistakes, and by 1911 they had changed tactics. Where the business of establishing and overseeing African American schools had previously proceeded with little input from local whites or the state, philanthropists now reasoned that they should play a central role. Philanthropic generosity began to arrive with qualifications that aimed to cajole intransigent white states into assuming more fiscal responsibility for black education. At the same time, philanthropists demonstrated their sensitivity to white southerners' concerns. Policy changes, for example, included curriculum adjustments to enhance vocational training, which both northern and southern white businessmen believed more suitable for black children's future role in the labor force. Most importantly, all monies were routed through white hands.[36]

These developments meant that philanthropic planners consulted less and less with southern black educational leaders. African Americans occasionally found allies in white southern Progressives, who reasoned that although black people would always be subordinate in the social order, the reform of society as a whole could not proceed without including them in the effort. Yet as support for private schools diminished in favor of public education, whatever voice black leaders had earned — as representatives of parents, teachers, and students — had to be retuned to local styles of accommodation.[37] It was much easier to pen paeans to distant benefactors who visited a few times a year than to charm the foxes guarding the henhouse of white supremacy next door.

In practice, the new realities accentuated the difference in the ways black male and female educators fought back. Accountability mattered most. The black men who became educational leaders, at either the state or county level, functioned as liaisons to the white state. Theirs was the work of securing financial resources to institutionalize improvements in facilities and teacher training. Teachers at the grassroots, the majority of whom were women, served as liaisons to the black community. Relying on personal and communal resources, they worked to nurture local interest and participation in education. Leaders had to negotiate prevailing political winds. Teachers rolled up their sleeves and did what needed doing. Equally significant, these contrasting roles fostered distinct visions of achievement and evaluations of success. Where white animosity required delicate dissembling to secure even modest advancement, the proverbial glass most often looked half empty. From the classroom, where community appreciation balanced crushing workloads, that glass could easily appear half full.

Along with black home demonstration agents, whose numbers slowly grew after the passage of the 1914 Smith-Lever Act and the 1917 Smith-Hughes Act, Jeanes teachers functioned as intermediaries among the white state, black educational leaders, black teachers, and rural communities.[38] Technically, these women worked under the county superintendents who selected them, but the superintendents' unfamiliarity with black schools gave Jeanes teachers wide latitude, and they often functioned as de facto African American county superintendents. In addition to consulting with district trustees about hiring teachers and observing rural classroom instruction, Jeanes teachers devoted considerable time to showing women and their daughters how to organize homemakers' clubs, to sew, and to can fruits and vegetables.[39] No county superintendent, white or black, would have had a reach that extended so far into the domestic realm.

Young and inexperienced, Septima Poinsette certainly could have used the help of a Jeanes teacher, but Charleston County had not yet secured such services when she was hired, and no other philanthropic support had yet reached Johns Island. Poinsette likely did not question her ability to do the job because her training at Avery ranked among the best in the state and guaranteed her competency as an instructor. She probably felt excited by the challenge. But had she known exactly what she was getting into, she might not have gone.

�''⋇''⋅

From Charleston on a clear day, Septima Poinsette could glimpse a few of the tree-covered Sea Islands that cluster off the coast from South Carolina to Georgia. Though most inhabitants remained isolated geographically and culturally, the islands had long been commercially integrated with city. By 1910, daily steamboat service connected more prosperous islanders to the mainland. White planters journeyed to Charleston to conduct their most important business: marketing their crops, purchasing supplies, banking, and visiting the children they often sent to school in the city. That year, planters shipped approximately twelve thousand bags — worth between one and two million dollars — of long-staple cotton out of Charleston Harbor. With the handsome profits, planters bought such amenities for their homes as phonographs and telephones. Some also began to diversify their crops, experimenting with growing short-staple cotton and produce. Land still remained relatively cheap, and prior to the arrival of the boll weevil, the future looked bright. "There is perhaps no place in the world," the *Charleston News and Courier* boasted, "where a man who intends to plant could do so with such great hopes of excellent success."[40]

For African Americans, who comprised the majority of Sea Island residents, life was much more precarious and would remain so until after World War II. Those who owned land had more self-sufficiency and fared better than their neighbors. Indeed, black farm owners on Edisto Island produced three-fifths of the long-staple cotton shipped to market in 1910 and ginned it themselves. Elsewhere, African Americans struggled for a small degree of autonomy. Their resistance to working for whites forced the *News and Courier* to confess that "the labor situation is not good," though it blamed "ease of living." Planters paid their field hands fifty cents a day, and "it is an old saying that a negro with fifty cents is not looking for a job," the newspaper asserted, implying that shiftless, lazy black people would rather go hunting and fishing or steal seed cotton than obtain honest work year-round. Influential white Sea Islanders promoted the establishment of a rural police force to prevent theft and to arrest the visibly unemployed for vagrancy. "The truth is that negroes on the islands are the most prosperous in the state, if not in the South," the *News and Courier* declared.[41] Nothing could have been further from the truth.

Conditions on Johns Island were more typical. Thirty-two miles long and ten miles wide, Johns Island's arable acres produced their share of cotton, but were better suited to growing vegetables, especially corn, sweet potatoes, cabbage, lima beans, okra, and peas. Sweet fruit ripened on the branches of apple, fig, peach, and plum trees. Crab and shrimp proliferated all summer; fall and winter brought oysters and mullet. Few of the people who labored on white-owned plantations, however, enjoyed this bounty. Even many small independent black farmers sent the vegetables they grew to market in Charleston as a matter of economic survival. Others supplemented their meager incomes by catching and selling fish. As a result, the basic diet of black Johns Islanders consisted of rice, grits, fatback and a few vegetables. "For dinner we eat peas and some corn grits, little sweet potato and drink some water," one resident recalled. Or they made ash cake — cornmeal wrapped in hot ashes, baked in chimneys, cut, and served cold. They roasted corn for coffee and grits for tea.[42] The living on Johns Island was anything but easy.

Saying her good-byes to her mother and Ella Sanders, Septima Poinsette boarded the gasoline launch for a destination that, in her own words, could have been "for all I knew about it, on the other side of the Atlantic." Her adventure began sooner than she anticipated when the small watercraft's engine died, leaving its passengers stranded. The new teacher spent her first night in the middle of a river. Jerry Blake arrived in his diminutive boat the next morning to convey her the remaining distance. When they landed at Mullet Hall, Blake's wife, Queen, who had been waiting a little too long, had a few choice words for her husband. As soon as he could get a word in edgewise, Blake introduced Poinsette as the new teacher and added that he had promised to carry her ten miles further down the road. Queen Blake composed herself — a teacher, after all, was an important guest — and offered to feed Poinsette breakfast first.[43]

Miss Poinsette got her initial look at the island later that Sunday morning, when she and Queen Blake climbed into her hostess's gig, a two-person, horse-drawn carriage, and headed south to the Humbert Wood community. Poinsette would have traveled roads lined with oaks, their supine limbs raising gnarled hands, gloved with luminous skeins of Spanish moss. She would have felt where their tangled roots made the road bumpy. She would have seen open fields, grassy and bare, empty to the untrained eye unless her hostess pointed out where small clusters of trees memorialized slave burial grounds. Poinsette would have passed plantations where the grandchildren of those slaves still labored between rows of cotton. She would have viewed homes with wide-gapped walls made from too-green lumber, without plumbing or screens to keep out flies and mosquitoes. Salt air, marsh mud, crushed oyster shells, crickets' loud singing, fecund soil, and pine needles— these sensory details would have been both familiar and strange to a city girl arriving in the country.

Along the way, Queen Blake introduced Miss Poinsette to churchgoers they passed and let them know where she would be staying. Timmy Bishop's place was one of the best in the neighborhood. A farmer who owned his land, Bishop also dabbled in storekeeping, undertaking, and preaching. Nevertheless, the rustic features of the house Bishop had built himself shocked Poinsette's urban sensibilities. A lantern hung on a nail illuminated her attic room. Here she sponge bathed quickly, in the absence of heat. After the family had gone to bed on Saturdays, she tiptoed downstairs for a longer bath in front of the big fireplace. Come winter, the wind yowled through cracks in the walls and floors. Water was scarce, and Poinsette worried that it came from impure surface wells, but no alternative existed. Rural culinary arts also surprised her. Mrs. Bishop stocked her kitchen with large cans instead of pots and used them to cook the family staples of fatback and grits. A frying pan came in handy for the fresh fish occasionally served for breakfast or supper. To Poinsette, the best Johns Island offered fell short. The Bishop place could never match the comfort of Henrietta Street. Its "crude" conditions unsettled the eighteen-year-old teacher, already nervous about living with strangers. These circumstances shocked even the indomitable Victoria Poinsette the one time she visited.[44]

Physical trials often accompanied residence in bucolic communities. Nearly seventy years later, Septima Clark admitted that living on Johns Island "was quite a struggle for me." Like her students, she walked to school. After winter set in, the daily trek combined with the lack of adequate heat in the classroom made her feet "so cold they were swollen and red." She soon suffered from what island people called chilblains (frostbite). Well-meaning neighbors advised her to roast white potato and put her heel in it, which she did, but the treatment "only made things worse." Since there were no doctors on Johns Island, Poinsette had to bide her time until she could seek medical attention in the city. By then, her condition had become critical. "I thought I was going to lose my toes there for a while," she confessed.[45]

Humbert Wood was a poor community even by local standards, and few residents had even a rudimentary education. Miss Poinsette now lived among field hands, the majority working on white-owned plantations, and they influenced how she perceived the larger contours of her new world. She thought her neighbors "led listless, indifferent lives" and "cared little, in fact, about improving themselves." Most could not read or write, and they gossiped too much for her taste. A Christian woman, she viewed skeptically their notions of the supernatural. She questioned people's fears of "'conjur' men and women," their belief in evil eyes and spells, and the tales of dying men "cough[ing] up small animals" as their souls descended into hell. Living with a part-time undertaker might have exposed her to the burial practices she found outright scandalous. Johns Islanders relied on homemade coffins pieced together from the extra boards folk used to build their "rough shanties." When a coffin proved too short, Clark remembered, "the corpse was taken out — this I have known of, for a fact — and the legs broken to permit it to be squeezed into its inadequate resting place." The lack of organizations for self-improvement combined with too many wagging tongues and superstitious minds caused her initially to characterize Johns Island people as "primitive."[46]

More than anything else, the lack of health care and health education appalled the new teacher. Unsanitary living and poor diet bred disease and death. Hookworm and pellagra flourished. Children whose legs had been lashed by dew-laden brambles on the walk to school arrived at the schoolhouse with running sores on their legs. Had there been a doctor on Johns Island, residents probably could not have afforded his services. No one, including those who owned small farms, had much cash. In times of illness, they ministered to one another and relied on folk remedies. "Lison molasses" and lemon juice brought down a fever; "jimsey weed" and a few drops of turpentine helped rid children of worms; spiderwebs healed minor cuts and abrasions.[47]

The island's high infant mortality rates especially horrified Septima Poinsette. Young unwed mothers, whom she later carefully distinguished as "not so much immoral" as "unmoral," lacked basic child-care knowledge. Given that most "residents were desperately poor anyway," she reasoned, "it was but natural that there were large numbers of these half-clothed, ill-fed, and improperly cared-for illegitimate children."[48] Mothers working in the fields often had no one to watch their babies and consequently left them unattended, putting a "sugar tit," a mixture of lard and sugar tied in cloth, in the baby's mouth. In no time, swarms of mosquitoes and flies would cover the infant. Many children died before they turned two. "The people were

The original Promise Land School on Johns Island, 1954–55.
Septima Poinsette began her teaching career at this school in 1916.
Courtesy of the Avery Research Center for African American
History and Culture, College of Charleston.

virtual slaves," Clark recalled. "They had no choice but to work in the fields for white people. That's one of the reasons we had so many babies to die."[49] Little in her previous experience had driven home so intensely the necessity of saving black women and black children's lives, and she never forgot this lesson.

Similarly, nothing in Poinsette's training at Avery could have fully prepared her for the abysmal conditions she encountered during her first days as a teacher. Trustees Andell, Hanahan, and Wilson designated Poinsette as the principal of the dilapidated schoolhouse and hired one of her former Avery classmates to assist her. Together, the women endeavored to instruct 132 students in all grade levels. Miss Poinsette had charge of the students whose ages qualified them for fifth through eighth grades. Some of them were as old as their teacher. "Grade" was a term used loosely in any case. "It wasn't any use to do graded reading when they had not had any basic words at all," she later remarked. By February, the other teacher at Promise Land had thrown in the towel. Septima Poinsette believed life on Johns Island "too rigorous" for her colleague, a Charlestonian who hailed from a more solidly economic middle-class background. "Perhaps had I been reared as she had, I would have been forced to give up too," she surmised.[50]

For all her efforts, Septima Poinsette earned thirty-five dollars a month.

She paid eight dollars board to the Bishops. She gave twenty dollars to her family and spent two more to purchase fresh meat to send to them. That left her five dollars to buy school supplies or to keep for herself. Meanwhile, a white teacher in a nearby school who held a comparable teaching certificate taught only three children. She did not have to chop the wood that heated her classroom stove. She had textbooks. And she got paid eighty-five dollars a month—"the rankest discrimination," Clark called it almost forty years afterward.[51] But when she began teaching, she had no means of redress and precious little time to brood. On Johns Island, as elsewhere, more important work needed to be done.

⤳✳⤵

From afar and in theory, white concern for black education remained hostile; up close and in practice, it manifested itself as indifference. As long as these circumstances prevailed, black teachers in rural southern schools operated with a considerable degree of autonomy. Recalling her early years teaching in Texas, Dorothy Robinson confirmed that she was a "free agent . . . as long as I did not ask for anything that would entail the expenditure of money." Robinson recognized that the "extreme flexibility" with which she worked signaled that her small rural school was a "nonentity" in the eyes of whites, and acknowledged that the combination of state negligence and her zeal to help students "resulted in severe personal frustration."[52] State apathy bred disappointment, but teachers who daily encountered eager faces in their classrooms had no choice but to channel their energies toward more constructive ends.

At times, white hostility had to be negotiated. Asking for help usually guaranteed a visit from a white trustee. Charlestonian Mamie Garvin Fields, whom Septima Clark later came to know, taught on Johns Island from 1909 to 1913. When enrollment shot above one hundred at her one-teacher Miller Hill School, Fields requested an assistant. Trustee F. Bartow Wilson arrived unannounced one afternoon to investigate. Students sounded the alarm by screaming with fright when he rode up on horseback with "a dozen dogs a-yipping and a-snapping," carrying his gun. Smoking a pipe and leaving mud from his boots all over the floor, Wilson inspected Fields's classroom and declared, "I diddin know th' was s' minny damn niggers up here on this hill." All the while he cradled his gun in his arm. If Fields had more than she could handle, he advised, she should "shut it *daln*." "Right there in the middle of all the children wanting to learn, he said that," Fields later fumed.[53]

More often, African American teachers capitalized on the absence of state supervision. As a student in Florida, Madge Scott sang "Lift Every Voice and Sing," the African American national anthem, every day before class, and her teachers secretly added black history to the curriculum. They "knew that the supervisor or superintendent only came around every five or six months and when they came everything had to be exactly so," she recalled. "Any information we were learning about black people would be set aside and all teachers made sure we were working on the official curriculum." Scott characterized her teachers' actions as "subversive" because she perceived that instilling race pride in students significantly countered the devaluation of black life.[54]

Ethel Grimball, who attended elementary school on Johns Island during the 1940s, also praised her teacher, Johns Island native Isadora Richardson, for her curriculum additions. "She taught us about Harriet Tubman, she taught us about Frederick Douglass, the poets. She was the best history teacher we ever had. She was the one who taught us about black history." Grimball saw white people at her school only after her grandfather had constructed a little building on school property, which Richardson used to start a hot lunch program: "They didn't come in our classroom. They came to see what our little building for the lunch room was all about."[55]

Grimball's 1940s school differed little from Promise Land when Septima Poinsette began her teaching career — "a one-room, two-windows, one door black creosote school." According to Grimball, "There was no electricity, no heating system — you had one pot-bellied stove in the middle of the floor — no indoor bathroom." "The condition in that school we attended I will never forget as long as I live," she continued, "but we had a very, *very* good teacher." Richardson's practical and pedagogical efforts bore fruit. When Grimball began attending Burke High School in Charleston, her algebra teacher expressed surprise at the extent of her preparation. Richardson provided an education that "surpassed any city schools or whatever they had. She prepared us for the city school, for high school. She really did."[56] With determined teachers and students who wanted to learn, rural schools could achieve excellence against all odds.

Conditions in black country schools necessitated a different kind of teaching. The lack of funding, facilities, and equipment demanded that teachers hone their improvisational skills and combine them with creative genius. In the absence of textbooks, Miss Poinsette encouraged her children to tell stories of their everyday lives, which she then incorporated into reading and spelling lessons. When she secured a few books from the county, she had students compose a story based on the illustrations, an exercise that gave her an important insight. She could not just "say 'Get a book and open it.'" Instead, she had to ask, "Look at this picture. Does it look like people are living here?" Smoke rising from a house with a chimney, for example, would signal the affirmative. "This is the way you build up your story," she counseled, "*Your* creative ability is the thing that you need to pull out of these children *their* creative ability, make their eyes see what is in that picture."[57] Other teachers, including Richardson, made their own reading and math workbooks, tailored to students' needs, while first-time educators frequently relied on the examples of those who had taught them. "By remembering their improvisations, substitutions, and ingenuity," Dorothy Robinson provided herself "with a sort of built-in ability to cope with the complete lack of aids, materials, equipment, and supervision that even then were considered basic." Educators also extended their improvisational skills if and when they received professional teaching guides. Such guides made basic assumptions regarding available facilities and equipment; without adaptation, their suggestions proved useless.[58] At every turn, success mandated creativity.

Johns Island presented Miss Poinsette with an additional challenge: most of her students spoke Gullah, and she had to adapt her reading lessons accordingly: "When I taught reading, I put down 'de' for 'the' because that's the way they said 'the.'" Then she made it a point to tell her pupils the difference between what they would see printed in the book and the sounds they actually used.[59] Without such adaptations, the linguistic barrier not only might have posed a serious problem to Poinsette's teaching but also could have prevented the community from accepting her. A product of the islands' geographical isolation dating back to the seventeenth century, Gullah preserved the language and culture fashioned by Sea Islanders' enslaved African ancestors. Like slaves elsewhere, those on the Sea Islands "learned new words—in English, Spanish, Portuguese or French—but they spoke these words with a West African pronunciation, and poured their new vocabulary into the mold of West African grammatical and idiomatic forms."[60] Over time, Gullah had worked its way across the water and into the speech patterns of both white and black Charlestonians. Gullah-speaking whites inadvertently testified to the influence of the black women who raised Charleston's white children and left their telltale mark on the tongues of their young charges.[61] As a girl, Septima Poinsette had heard Gullah spoken by fish vendors peddling their wares on Henrietta Street. As a young teacher, she identified her familiarity with the dialect as one of her biggest advantages: "I could communicate with" the students because "I myself spoke very much like them."[62] Islanders tended to regard strangers warily. Poinsette's language skills helped her earn their trust, an essential prerequisite for any rural teacher's larger mission.

Facing an enormous task with scant funds, African American teachers depended on the resources of the communities in which they taught and to whom they were most accountable. As one teacher confirmed, "Our duties did not end in the schoolroom but flowed out to meet the demands of community life in which we were involved and expected to participate from habit, experience and duty." Educators at the grassroots knew that improving educational opportunity for African Americans meant instilling the desire to learn in both children and adults and that a "good teacher meets her learners where they are."[63] Where there was community interest and support, it had to be deployed to its fullest potential. Where there was lack of motivation, ambition had to be fostered.

Women who lived in the communities where they taught had experiences quite distinct from their colleagues who commuted. For many, including Poinsette, life in rural communities challenged educated, middle-class preconceptions of poverty and ignorance. "The people were simple," one teacher explained, "and by simple I do not by any means infer they were foolish. Whatever pertained to the community, you got the good with the bad without any affectation. There was no show of whitewashing." Mamie Fields observed that teachers had to know how students lived, if they had adequate provisions at home or if they had to work to help make ends meet, to understand classroom performance. "You didn't necessarily know these things if you were reared in the city or a better-off family," she noted.[64] Familiarity enriched teachers' views of community needs, desires, and potential and gave them a fuller sense of the raw material with which they were working. Rural communities likewise took pride in "our teacher" and often celebrated her arrival as a communal event. Ella Cotton remembered that the rural Alabama church that doubled as her school was "packed" the first time she visited on Christmas Eve. She left that night, her arms loaded with gifts, hoping "I could as worthily measure up to them as a teacher."[65]

After new teachers settled in and started the school year, they began the work of getting to know the community. Most had learned of the necessity of forging these relationships during their training. Fields's instructors had "encouraged" her "to get to know the community, adults as well as children, and try to help the community as a whole." Clark recalled that soon after arriving on Johns Island, she began "to get interested in the children and their parents." In a world where educational improvement hinged not on state resources but on local constituencies, teachers judged instructors who missed "the pulse of the people" as "inept."[66]

Establishing relationships allowed rural educators to hone the rudimentary skills at the heart of their activism. First, they understood visiting as an essential organizing tool, fully aware that the success of future projects would emanate from this foundation. Frederick Celestine Jenkins-Andrews, who taught on a neighboring Sea Island, believed that teachers had a duty to inspire students "to *be somebody*, to *do something* so the world might be a better place because they lived in it." To do so meant "you must know the child, know what he knows, even what he feels. Here is the necessity to live with the children, play with them on the playground, visit them in their homes." Rural teachers willingly sacrificed afternoon, evening, and weekend hours. Poinsette, for example, taught women to sew two days a week after school. On other afternoons, as she walked backed to the Bishops' house, she stopped "to help" her neighbors "drop seed in their garden." On Saturdays, she did more visiting. Johns Islanders soon recognized their new teacher, whom they called "Miss Seppie" because they had trouble pronouncing "Septima."[67] As strangers became neighbors, Poinsette's commitment deepened.

More broadly, such visiting dissolved the boundaries between the school and the home. Teachers regularly crossed those lines as part of their prosaic duties and their moral mission. The first task was to make people — many of whom either harbored unpleasant memories of the classroom or failed to appreciate how a little education might benefit their children — feel at ease. Doing so took time.

The larger goal of arousing interest in learning meant discovering the values and inconsistencies of the people, which required an educational organizer to pay attention and to listen. A good teacher, Estelle Hicks, who worked in Alabama, claimed, "should strive to be an ever-learning student of human nature, and allow for human differences, remembering at all times that no two things in the world are exactly alike." And, she emphasized, educators "should refrain from sitting on the gossip bench." Talking with parents provided important lessons for teachers. Sitting on the porch with a rural family as "the day slowly poured out its last rays of light and softened into the evening dusk," Ella Cotton found herself "amazed at the sum and quality of the principles underlying the foundations of that family in which both the father and mother were illiterate."[68] Life experience bequeathed valuable insight. In a very real sense, these teachers became students.

After trust had been established, local people confided in their teachers.

People rendered invisible in the white South's historical drama stepped from the shadows to claim center stage. "Many ex-slaves were still living," Cotton noted. "Occasionally they would plumb the depths of their still-sore hearts and memories for some searing experiences they'd gone through." Two aged brothers told Cotton how their masters had forced them to torture, beat, and sometimes kill errant slaves. Another woman, whom Cotton described as having "as much real dignity as I've seen in one person," confessed that she had killed all but one of her fifteen children to save them from slavery.[69] Others told of the violence of disfranchisement. Meeting people in East Texas in the 1930s, Dorothy Robinson remarked "there was still fresh in the minds of the black population an incident in which respectable black men and women had been beaten away from the polls with ax handles." "Equally fresh in their memory," Robinson continued, "were the horrors of a race riot in Slocum that had erupted a few years previously." Related in "hushed tones," such stories revealed "a weird mixture of deep-seated bitterness, smoldering anger, and helpless surrender."[70] The transmission of painful memories, reaching back several generations, cemented the bonds between teacher and community. If education was the road, shared stories delineated where a community aspired to travel—beyond "helpless surrender"—as surely as they marked where it had been.

Communities expressed their approval of teachers in a variety of ways, sending them gifts of food or inviting them to supper. On a practical level, sharing cooking responsibilities relieved the burdens placed on boarding families who were not much better off than their neighbors. Local people also invited teachers to parties. On Johns Island, Miss Seppie enjoyed the festivities at the end of harvest when parents and neighbors treated her to "fruits and candies and whatnot" and entertained her with "fiddlers and dancing late into the night." Another favorite event was islanders' annual celebration while making molasses. As the sugarcane syrup "bubbled and boiled" in its big iron pot, "the men and women and children assembled there sang old hymns and ballads and spirituals, told and listened to old tales." Around midnight, when the molasses was done, Poinsette joined her neighbors in savoring fresh gra-nut cakes, candy made from roasted peanuts coated with leftover drippings after the syrup had been poured out of the pot. "Delicious!," she exclaimed.[71] If participating in community festivities and learning about local culture eased the loneliness some rural teachers felt, it also meant identifying parents who could become allies in accomplishing the educational tasks at hand.

Parental approval climaxed at school programs. Perhaps none surpassed

the annual end-of-year program, described by one teacher as the "gala social event of the year." Everyone dressed in their finest and craned for a
better view as children displayed their acting, reciting, singing, or dancing
talents. Parents of those who performed well "had the added pleasure of publicly proving that they had produced superior progeny." Aside from parental pride, school performances also stimulated interest in education itself.
"Every parent loves to see his child in a show," Fields commented. "If the
child does well, the parent thinks the school is doing well—which would
influence school attendance." Small victories counted, especially when they
motivated improved scholarship. Having her students win a spelling bee
"made us heroes and heroines in the eyes of our parents and the community," Cotton avowed, "and the memory of the little event was kept alive to
stimulate lagging scholars."[72]

Without state support or organizational outlets, teachers in country
schools played a primary role in fostering educational and civic awareness.
Fields's students offered all kinds of excuses for not attending school every
day, "but the biggest reason," she maintained, "was that the parents weren't
trained to send their children to school regularly. The teacher could have a
lot to do with that." After rural parents became interested, they were more
likely to be involved in their child's school than were urban parents. Ethel
Grimball believed "the parents in the rural area were more supportive of
their children in school than parents in the urban areas." That assistance had
noteworthy consequences. On Johns Island, "parents supported the teacher
whenever there was any difficulty with the pupil," Clark later observed, and
the teacher's authority "was not questioned." Discipline was less difficult as
a result.[73]

Many teachers, including Poinsette, organized parent-teacher associations (PTAs) in their communities. Johns Island "parents, for persons illiterate and entirely unused to modern ways," she discovered, "did remarkably
well and were most cooperative." That they attended meetings surprised the
first-time teacher. Robinson described her PTA as a "vital social force" that
garnered "the support of parents and non-parents alike." Among one of its
first tasks was Campus Improvement Day, which soon became a community
event that drew children, parents, and grandparents to the school. As the
elders stood by, smiling, "the children scampered about with a new-found
sense of self importance." So precious was the organization's work in the eyes
of Robinson's community that the treasurer "kept the PTA funds tied up in
a handkerchief, often secreted in her bosom." Similarly, a Jeanes teacher
characterized the PTA at one of the schools she supervised as "a live wire. If

we had PTA's in all communities like this," she continued, "we could do more effective work."[74]

Yet another board in the bridge between home and school, rural PTAs facilitated the parental education that activist teachers at the grassroots identified as crucial. Rural PTAs were more homogenous in membership and more likely to involve broader segments of the community than their urban counterparts. By the same token, women who taught in the one- and two-teacher schools that predominated in the country took more active roles in PTAs than their urban colleagues. They were, after all, the only teachers. "Probably the most distinguishing characteristic of the rural associations," one commentator reflected, "is the fact that it is truly a community organization."[75] As such, rural PTAs provided a forum for pondering and then articulating communal goals. Campus Improvement Days not only increased black students' sense of self-worth but functioned as social gatherings in which a community could signal its resistance to separate and unequal education and express an independent pride. Most significantly, by establishing PTAs, rural teachers such as Poinsette fostered the development of lay leaders in the community who would remain in place even after the teachers moved on. Such modest beginnings remained essential to the long-term goal of teaching citizenship by helping people to help themselves.

Indeed, local people gave generously of their hard-earned nickels and dimes to finance new schools or to purchase paint, nails, and lumber to improve old ones. At the schoolhouse, men, women and children labored for their own benefit. They devoted time and muscle to clearing tree stumps, making desks, and planting flowers. Describing their efforts in South Carolina, a white state official remarked, "The colored patrons in every instance have subscribed liberally and have been glad to work on the buildings." "In one community," another white Carolinian reported, "the colored children picked cotton one day and gave the money earned for the erection of a new building." Parents occasionally even mustered funds to supplement teachers' salaries so that school terms could be lengthened.[76]

In exchange, rural communities expected that teachers would aid in the business of daily life: writing letters, filling out mail order forms, and figuring crop prices and wages. While fulfilling these duties, Poinsette began to see how her early evaluation of Johns Islanders as a people who "led listless, indifferent, lives" was erroneous. Sometime after her arrival, Poinsette learned that a group of men on Johns Island had joined together to form a black fraternal organization. They called themselves the Odd Fellows, kept the rituals of the club shrouded in secrecy, and through membership enhanced their standing in the community.[77] Members had to make speeches and do some bookkeeping, meaning that involvement required people to know how to read and write. Johns Island's Odd Fellows logically turned to their community's teachers.

In the beginning, several of the men approached Miss Poinsette and the other teacher and asked for help in preparing a speech. The teachers responded by writing a speech and reading it to the men, who then memorized it. "One thing about people who can't read," Poinsette discerned, is that "they have good memories." Before long, the men wanted to read and write their own speeches, so they began going to meet with the teachers regularly in the evenings. To Poinsette, the men's desire to improve themselves provided the key to the success of these informal adult education efforts. They learned faster because they applied themselves to a specific and personally relevant goal. The Odd Fellows also started thinking about how to improve their community and voiced their concerns to others. As word of the tutoring spread, younger girls and boys sought out the teachers in the evenings to learn to read and to write. This "pastime," Clark later affirmed, "gave us a lot of joy." It also ignited her interest in adult literacy, "the work that would command in later years so much of my time and zeal."[78]

Adult education was a common extracurricular duty for southern rural teachers of both races. The problem of illiteracy was especially acute, however, among African Americans. In South Carolina, the 1920 census listed 181,422 black men and women as illiterate. In Charleston County, where Poinsette taught, 26.6 percent of the African American adult population could not read, compared to only 1.5 percent of native-born whites. J. B. Felton, the second state agent for African American schools, praised the "unselfish service" of black teachers and the "missionary spirit" with which they approached "the removal of illiteracy." He recognized that the task could not "be accomplished without the sacrificial labor of hundreds of negro teachers."[79] Septima Poinsette was one of many.

⟶❊⟵

African American teachers in the rural South served a disfranchised constituency and understood well the long-term political implications of their job. Still, theirs was not an educational culture that advocated a direct attack on white supremacy. The approach favored by these teachers at the grassroots is more readily apparent in a father's advice to his daughter as she began her teaching career: "Listen and Look. Don't be a crusader. Find a point of entry where you can fight segregation." Forged within the heart of the Jim Crow

South, this educational world reflected the political and social constraints of that time and place. Change came slowly. In 1934, Felton confessed that black teachers "are really making bricks without straw."[80] These masons and their bricks left a legacy to the freedom struggle akin to landownership: a greater possibility for self-sufficiency and an independence of the mind. But teachers could never furnish the economic independence necessary to sustain these gains. As a result, the abject conditions of Johns Island's schools changed little over the two decades that separated Septima Poinsette's time there and that of Isadora Richardson. Generation after generation of rural African Americans faced the same problems. Structural change in southern segregated public schools, as in southern politics and society, would require at least the threat of federal intervention.

Black women teachers' lives and work nevertheless bear witness to an intervention against the state-sponsored denial of equal educational opportunity. And everywhere they looked, a "point of entry" to fight Jim Crow's worst abuses could be found. Since the end of the nineteenth century, for example, suffrage had been shackled to the ability to interpret the written word. In an era when the right to vote lay beyond the realm of political possibility for most rural black southerners, literacy had more personal and concrete significance. It meant they could exchange correspondence with sons, daughters, brothers, sisters, cousins, and others who had joined the northward exodus known as the Great Migration. They could peruse mail order catalogs and exercise a choice as a consumer by spending their money that way rather than at the white man's store. They did not have to rely on the white man's figures when it came time to settle debts. They could pay their property taxes without the aid of white people, who might use the opportunity to swindle African Americans out of their land. They could keep up with the news and find solace after a long day's work by reading the Bible. Literacy and the feelings of self-sufficiency it generated meant that African Americans could hold their heads a little higher.[81]

Poverty and ignorance, deprivation and indifference might have been the first things noticed by black rural teachers, especially those with urban backgrounds. The longer they worked in their communities, however, the more their vision evolved. The economic and social realities of rural black life mandated that teachers adopt practical approaches to solving the problems at hand. They attuned teachers to the necessity of doing what was doable. More importantly, teaching in rural schools fostered an indigenous activism and homegrown criteria for success. Where white officials complained that "because of the absolute incompetency and unfitness of negro teachers," the state wasted its money investing in improvement for rural schools, Cotton asserted, "No teacher can be termed a 'failure' who has taught her pupils to read—and well." Similarly, Jenkins-Andrews reminded her Edisto Island colleagues how Jesus Christ recruited twelve disciples, gave them three years of training, and sent them out "to redeem humanity and transform society." Thus, she concluded, "the teacher in the small school may well not despise the day of small things."[82]

Finding a "point of entry," driving a wedge into the walls of segregation, demanded specific activist approaches. A teacher had to have personal determination. After four months on Johns Island, Miss Seppie "felt I was beginning to accomplish something, even though I was still but a child and I was facing a discouraging and almost impossible task. But I was not discouraged, despite the sea of faces that confronted me every day I walked into our crude and uncomfortable classroom."[83] Like her colleagues across the South, Poinsette attempted to connect rural education to rural life by improvising, drawing upon her own creativity to make up for the lack of materials.

Outside of the schoolhouse, black rural teachers pursued their larger goal of teaching citizenship. As Clark later claimed, "I felt I was in a position as the school teacher in the community to help them in some small way at least toward achieving a better life." Doing so required teachers to tap the community's primary resource, its people. Visiting and listening came first. Only then could teachers motivate children and adults to want to learn and help them devise strategies for applying that learning. From their perspective, "the Negro teacher, the Negro children, the Negro homes, all are involved and inseparable in the eternal circle that goes round and round in an increasing and diminishing strength."[84] Progress ebbed and flowed, but the reciprocal obligations that bound rural teachers, students, and parents stimulated communal participation in education even as they promoted rural civic awareness and individual self-improvement.

The experience of rural teaching simultaneously schooled women such as Poinsette in how to become more effective community organizers and provided them with a particular orientation toward short- and long-term goals. "The philosophy that sustains a teacher," Dorothy Robinson theorized, "is based on the knowledge that all does not end with each day's effort." Teachers who organized PTAs or taught adults in the evenings encouraged the proliferation of lay community leaders. Teachers who established mother-daughter sewing or canning classes knew that they promoted the strengthening of family bonds. In impoverished communities, ensuring that people had food to eat and skills they could use also amounted the work of survival.

Poinsette would have agreed with a teacher who asserted, "Never did I feel that we weren't doing anything, because whatever we were doing, it was better than the day before."[85]

Taking up the work of teaching in the rural Jim Crow South conditioned Septima Poinsette's later approach to political activism. "If they did not set me on my course," she remarked, Johns Islanders "surely did confirm me in a course."[86] Visiting with her neighbors, Miss Seppie learned to listen more keenly, learned to be sensitive to community expectation, and learned that even a little substantive change demanded that a teacher "meet her learners where they are." She gained a more astute understanding of how people responded to oppression and limited opportunity and perhaps why they sometimes did not respond. These lessons did not immediately undo all of her urban sensibilities. Her journey had just begun. But Septima Poinsette Clark would carry this knowledge with her for the next forty years before she would return to Johns Island and use it to help launch an educational program that would remake the South's political landscape.

CHAPTER THREE

Singing the Blues in the New Reconstruction

Home beckoned Septima Poinsette. Summers brought a return to the familial embrace of Henrietta Street, a chance to rekindle acquaintances with friends, and to participate once again in services at Old Bethel United Methodist Church. Nonetheless, the season itself rarely allowed a break from hard work. The family still struggled to make ends meet, and younger siblings' tuition at Avery still had to be paid. Poinsette spent the summer of 1918 serving three meals a day in a boardinghouse. Though that meant long hours, from six o'clock in the morning until nine o'clock at night, sometimes seven days in a row, she considered the nine dollars she collected each week "big money."[1]

Before fall arrived, a new opportunity presented itself. When Avery principal Benjamin Cox decided to expand the fifth- and sixth-grade classes, he visited Henrietta Street to offer Poinsette a job. She accepted, reasoning that she "would have a chance to learn about teaching in an urban community."[2] The occasion also provided her first lesson in political action as well. Toward the end of 1918, Poinsette joined a community-wide effort to get black teachers hired in the city's black public schools. To do so required challenging the city's all-white Board of School Commissioners and then its General Assembly delegation. The local chapter of the National Association for the Advancement of Colored People (NAACP) initiated the campaign, and the twenty-year-old Poinsette added her name to its membership rolls.

Black Charlestonians' willingness to confront the white state reflected the renewed militancy that characterized the national black freedom struggle during and after World War I. African Americans interpreted the era as one of a "New Reconstruction," and by that they meant finding a way back into politics.[3] For Poinsette and her neighbors, Reconstruction survived in the memories of those who had lived through it and in the institutions they had built. More important, some nineteenth-century black activists remained in the city. The man at the forefront of the teacher campaign, Thomas Ezekiel Miller, had served as a Reconstruction-era congressman and state legislator. His presence dramatized the direct ideological and strategic ties between the two postwar eras. Dividing them were the plethora of segregation statutes that legally designated African Americans as second-class citizens; a federal government that barely even bothered to feign interest in the welfare of black people; and an entrenched group of white southern Democrats — including some who had presided over the end of the first Reconstruction — that effectively controlled Congress.

Both within and outside of the South, migration and mobilization in the great war for freedom accentuated the shortcomings of American democracy for black citizens. Trumpeting the age-old belief that anyone willing to sacrifice his life in service of the nation merited full citizenship, black leaders called on the community and its veterans to demand payment. Looking back to an earlier postwar era, W. E. B. Du Bois asked, "Fifty-eight years ago Frederick Douglass and his fellows appealed to your fathers and grandfathers. . . . They responded and won their freedom on the field of battle. *Are Free Men Less Brave Than Slaves?* Men of color, brothers and fathers, we appeal to you!" A few anonymous black Charlestonians responded to the nation's hypocrisy in an equally militant fashion during a May 1919 race riot. More broadly, the rhetoric of black manhood that complemented the goal of full citizenship in this era suggests that electoral politics had not lost its masculine associations for African Americans. Ironically, southern black women rather than black men obtained suffrage during the New Reconstruction, though white supremacists largely prevented these women from voting.[4]

As a teacher employed at the prestigious Avery Institute and as a soldier in the local battle for racial justice, Septima Poinsette seemed to be moving in all the right directions. Her inclusion among the city's black professional class would help to improve her family's economic fortunes, and she still dreamed of buying her mother a house. Participation in the NAACP should have led to invitations to join like-minded black women in the work of racial uplift as a member of local and state women's clubs. Instead of auguring a new activist life course, however, Poinsette's first organized political action dissipated into nearly a decade of private anguish. She fell in love for the first time, married, and became a mother, and then a widow.

Septima Poinsette Clark's major misstep was to marry a stranger and a sailor; respectable black Charleston judged neither very highly. In fact, the traumatic events of her short marriage meant that Clark's personal experience during the New Reconstruction proved most akin to the kinds of trials and tribulations that the era's black women blues singers described. As a properly reared Charlestonian and a teacher, Clark would have been horrified to be publicly associated with blueswomen, who celebrated an independent sexuality that contested black clubwomen's chaste politics of respectability. As a young woman, she upheld the codes of silence embraced by black women as a defense against stereotypes of their sexual licentiousness. Yet many years later, Clark would rely on a similar kind of blues testifying, choosing to share details of her private sufferings as she worked to empower grassroots women in the civil rights movement.[5]

⥈⁂⥆

Poinsette reported to work on her first day at Avery with a new perspective. Despite her familiarity with her alma mater, the two years she had spent on Johns Island had heightened her awareness of the advantages afforded by working in an institution with modern facilities and a tradition of organized extracurricular activity. Where the Promise Land School amounted to little more than a dilapidated shack, Avery's solid brick building had heat and glass windows, a library full of the classics, desks for all its students, and ample supplies for its teachers. Faculty spent afternoons and evenings supporting students who performed in plays, gave choral concerts, and scored points for the basketball team. According to one Avery graduate, its "teachers took on a greater role than just instructors. They were counselors, part parents, friends of a sort, truly amazing."[6]

Poinsette had traded the autonomy of little supervision to work for a black principal at a black-controlled institution. Unlike the white county school district trustees, who often did not know the location of the black schools they supposedly supervised, Cox cut a conspicuous figure at Avery. Students viewed him as a "father figure for sure" and understood that "he wanted them to be tops in behavior as well as in subject matter," alumna Lois Averetta Simms remembered. Cox at times injected dramatic humor into his lectures, playing the clown to "show us how we looked chewing gum," which he disliked.[7] A good principal knew how to balance the necessity of developing a good rapport with students and maintaining discipline. At Avery, Poinsette discovered what it was like to work with a concerned supervisor who provided strong leadership.

Poinsette soon realized, however, that Avery's better facilities and higher academic standards did not automatically translate into an easier job. The difference in the socioeconomic backgrounds between students at Avery and those on Johns Island "meant I would have a different sort of reckoning with my pupils' parents," she ascertained. On Johns Island, parents and students alike respected a teacher's authority. By contrast, Avery parents "were positive that their children were all 'A' students and that their conduct was exemplary." If a teacher recounted something less than stellar about their little Johnny's behavior or their little Susie's progress, they refused to believe it. "Visits to [parents] by the teacher to report on the work of their children accomplished little," Poinsette noticed. "Consequently, some of the problems of discipline" proved difficult to solve; "sometimes I was more on my own — and on my mettle — than I had been during the two years on the island."[8] Though Septima Poinsette Clark later characterized the experience as "good training for me," she neglected to mention the particular difficulties she encountered in challenging members of Charleston's African American elite. Most of these people did not consider her family to be of any social consequence. Why would they value her word or estimation of their children over their own entrenched sense of superiority?

Poinsette's lack of social status and her youth might also have contributed to what would become her first professional setback. In her one year teaching stint at Avery, Poinsette failed to establish herself as an equal among a group of colleagues. "I didn't have many friends," she later conceded. Perhaps Poinsette preferred running her own show in a rural schoolhouse to navigating the fault lines of internal faculty rivalries at an urban facility. Yet working in the city also allowed Poinsette the opportunity to expand her educational activism, leading her to describe "teaching at Avery [as] one of the most important and formative experiences of my life. It was then that I first became actively concerned in an organized effort to improve the lot of my fellow Negroes."[9]

In a sense, Poinsette had returned to a new Charleston in the summer of 1918. Ongoing advances in civic and social welfare services — sewer lines, paved streets, garbage collection — signaled the arrival of Progressive Era sensibilities in the Low Country, and World War I had contributed to the strongest economic upsurge the city had experienced in more than twenty years. White Charlestonians benefited most from these improvements, but migrants crowding the streets looking for wartime work and housing strained all city services.[10] The biggest difference, however, was that Charleston's race-conscious black men and women had established an NAACP branch in 1917 to redress the injustices that plagued the black community and to negotiate concrete solutions.

Charlestonian Edwin "Teddy" Harleston took the lead. Born in 1882 to one of the city's elite African American families, Harleston attended Avery before enrolling at Atlanta University, where he befriended his sociology and political economy professor, W. E. B. Du Bois. After graduation, Harleston chose to pursue a career as an artist. He studied at Boston's School of the Museum of Fine Art, specializing in portrait painting. At his father's insistence that he take a more active role in the family's funeral business, Teddy Harleston moved on to the Renouard School for Embalmers in New York City. While there, he likely renewed his acquaintance with Du Bois. On February 23, 1917, after Harleston had returned home, he gathered twenty-nine people and established South Carolina's first NAACP branch, with himself as president.[11]

Avery graduates predominated among the charter members, demonstrating the extent to which independent black educational institutions provided an important foundation for civil rights organizing in the Jim Crow South. Other early members hailed from the urban black professional class. Harleston even belonged to the small minority of black Charlestonians who voted. Harleston logically began organizing the chapter by recruiting the people he encountered every day: family members, business associates, and friends from Avery. Still, black Charlestonians' exclusive social practices meant that the NAACP's leaders would have to learn how to reach beyond their closed circles to attract new members and score concrete victories on the wider community's behalf. Provoking interracial confrontation represented a novel strategy, as did reaching across the historical fissures that divided black activists from each other.[12]

Septima Poinsette knew who the Harlestons were. She could see the funeral parlor that Edwin G. "Captain" Harleston had built in 1913, an imposing three-story structure located on Calhoun Street, from her home. But she did not socialize with members of the family. According to Edwina Harleston Whitlock, Teddy Harleston's niece, whom he adopted, "The Harlestons were light, and we didn't associate with people who were much darker than we were."[13] The fact that Poinsette did not learn of the NAACP's work from friends in her hometown accentuates her social distance from the people who formed the branch.

Instead, she first heard of the NAACP while teaching on Johns Island. African American residents in rural areas expected their teachers to participate in community meetings, and Poinsette attended one Presbyterian convention that included speakers from outside of South Carolina. "They told about the NAACP and what it was doing," she commented, "they were trying to get groups organized." The practice of blending spiritual and political work inside the church that had taken root during Reconstruction fifty years earlier still held, fortified in the Progressive Era by black women's role in expanding the church's racial uplift and social service work.[14] Involving themselves in community affairs, southern black women teachers such as Poinsette labored to make the public schoolhouse an equally important institutional site in the black freedom struggle.

One week after the Charleston NAACP chapter's founding, Du Bois arrived in the city to rally the new troops. The situation in Charleston's public schools provided an immediate motivation. "Of all the cities in the South," Du Bois wrote in the *Crisis* two months later, "Charleston is guilty of the meanest act toward colored folks. It keeps in their schools white teachers who do not want to be there; teachers who despise the work and who work mainly for the money it brings them." He then issued a call to action. "Colored Charleston should register and vote and get rid of this abomination . . . then, if need be, strike and let every colored child stay home until teachers were installed who believed them human beings."[15]

Mamie Garvin Fields served on the committee that gave the distinguished visitor a tour of the city. "In the car, Dr. Du Bois got restless," she remembered, as they passed city landmarks that did not allow African Americans access. "All you are showing me is what the white people did," Du Bois complained; "I want to see what the colored people of Charleston have built." Du Bois chided his hosts for not striving to do more locally. "Oh, Du Bois was hard on us," Fields recalled, "but it woke us up."[16]

Two months later, the NAACP chapter got busy. America's entry into World War I in April 1917 opened new employment prospects at the Charleston Navy Yard, including jobs for women sewing sailor's uniforms. The navy sought six hundred women to fill these positions but told African Americans they need not apply. In May, Teddy Harleston delivered a petition to officials protesting black women's exclusion. When they failed to respond, the national NAACP took the issue to Capitol Hill, securing the support of representatives and senators from Minnesota, who then prodded the Navy Department to address the situation. Secretary of the navy Josephus Daniels, former editor of the *Raleigh News and Observer* who had fanned the flames of the North Carolina white supremacy campaigns that culminated in the

1898 Wilmington racial massacre, maintained that hiring decisions belonged in the hands of local authorities. The Minnesota delegation refused to back down, eventually forcing the navy to amend its position and enabling 250 black women to secure jobs as seamstresses. By the end of the year, membership in Charleston's NAACP chapter had swelled to more than 200.[17]

The discrimination against African American women at the Charleston Navy Yard was part of the larger problem of how to manage the war effort in Jim Crow's backyard. As southern states scrambled for a share of the federal dollars that flowed from the arrival of army training camps, leaders confronted the thorny question of what to do with the black soldiers who would certainly be sent to the region. White officials and white residents feared that interracial contact at the facilities would lead to violence and bloodshed, especially if northern black troops—who had not been schooled in the proper deference that defined southern race relations—were stationed in the South.[18] As in the first Reconstruction, federal money also carried with it the risk of federal intervention in southern affairs, exactly the type of interference that white southerners wanted to avoid and that organizations such as the NAACP hoped to exploit. Racial justice could not be obtained without it.

The branch's second major campaign focused on two shocking white-on-black crimes that occurred in the city: the murder of a black man by a white streetcar conductor, and a white man's attempted rape of a ten-year-old black girl. When authorities neglected to do anything about either incident, Harleston and company interviewed witnesses and pressured city prosecutors to take action. In the end, an all-white jury returned a not-guilty verdict in the homicide. A grand jury's refusal to indict in the rape case underscored the limits of justice available for black women and girls in a society that had accepted white men's sexual violence against black women as a master's prerogative during slavery and had subsequently propagated myths of black women's sexual immorality. Recognizing sexual violence against black women would have been tantamount to overturning an entire social order based on the racial subordination of both black men and black women as well as all women's subordination to all men.[19]

The first Charleston NAACP fight that attracted Septima Poinsette's attention involved another child, "a black boy who had been accused of theft." A white woman believed that the youngster had stolen her watch while delivering ice and had him arrested. After she found the watch in the pocket of an apron that had been sent to the laundry, she notified authorities, who then released the boy. "When that happened," Clark remembered, "Edwin Harleston got a group of people together and asked her to make restitution to this boy and pay for the time he had spent in jail and make a public statement." Harleston reasoned that "when this fellow went to school, if she didn't make a statement, children would be teasing him about being arrested and call him a 'jailbird.'"[20] By including the potential ramifications the boy faced at school, Clark retold the story of the NAACP's action from a teacher's perspective. Her budding activist consciousness remained tied to the problems black students confronted, and not only the academic ones. Indeed, by 1918, white leaders engaged in increasingly hostile attempts to control the extracurricular activities of Charleston's African American youth, particularly boys.

The problem hinged on the broader criminalization of black bodies that began after Reconstruction and the specific ways white southern Progressives recast Jim Crow's social controls as social reforms. Few white southerners questioned the prevailing wisdom that African Americans, as a group, "were by nature more prone to criminality." Those who lived in urban areas became especially wary of rising crime rates that actually resulted more from the economic and social dislocations spawned by industrialization than from an amplified presence of black "criminals." In Charleston, white police remained more likely to round up poor black men, rather than white men, charge the black men for vagrancy, and save the city a little revenue by sending them to the chain gang. Moreover, if the city's policemen represented the most visible enforcers of Jim Crow — both written laws and unwritten custom — the local press abetted this work. Routine articles that highlighted the disproportionate number of black arrests led readers to conclude that crime often had a black face.[21]

African American boys had to be especially careful. In the "perilous world" of the segregated South, native Carolinian and educator Benjamin Mays wrote, "if a black boy wanted to live a halfway normal life and die a natural death he had to learn early the art of how to get along with white folks." By 1916, getting along with Charleston's white folks meant no skating down King Street, the city's major business thoroughfare; no loitering; and no throwing stones. Police reports for that year reveal a large disparity in the number of black and white youth who came into contact with the criminal justice system. Officers arrested 167 African American boys — 23 of them age ten or younger — but only 37 white boys. The majority of the black youth who ran afoul of the law were between eleven and fourteen years old.[22] Actions that might earn white children stern warnings could mean arrest for black children.

Since her days as a teenager, Septima Poinsette had been concerned with finding constructive activities for the youngsters on Henrietta Street. "I loved children so much in the early days," she later wrote, "that I would gather them and take them to a parade or for some recreation or to Sunday School on Sunday mornings. The people in the neighborhood called me 'Little Ma' . . . for I was considered a little mother to all these children." Poinsette's creative pastimes spoke to the lack of recreational facilities for African American youth. Barred from public parks and playgrounds, those who did not find their way to the black Y or the black-owned union halls that doubled as recreation centers had no alternative but to play in the streets.[23] The arrest of 167 black boys in a single year proved that informal recreation programs, like Poinsette's, were no match for the tactics of an expanding police state that lurked underneath white Charleston's veneer of racial paternalism.

Perhaps such unsatisfactory responses to the problem of juvenile delinquency inspired Poinsette's decision to get involved with the local NAACP's campaign to have black teachers hired in the city's black public schools. Local African American educators knew that intervention in the classroom would go a long way toward molding black children into responsible adults. The NAACP's argument that "there must be reciprocity in love, affection, and sympathy between teacher and pupil" resonated with Poinsette's experiences with Charleston's white teachers. She knew firsthand that "without the aforesaid reciprocity," there could "be no hope planted in the breast of the pupil by the teacher to elevate him and make him a strong man or woman." Another motivation included the potential benefits for teachers, such as the right to choose whether to work in the county's rural schoolhouses. From a teacher's point of view, the campaign represented a chance both to advocate on behalf of black children and to expand personal and professional options. Poinsette understood that she was entering a political fight, and she characterized her participation as "my first experience with any sort of political action."[24]

The 1918–19 Charleston teacher campaign represented the final battle to secure black teachers for black children in the segregated schools of the urban South. This movement by southern African American educational activists had begun in the aftermath of Reconstruction; by the 1890s, these efforts had succeeded in all but two cities in the region. New Orleans acquiesced completely in 1916, leaving Charleston alone in its obdurate refusal to change.[25] The upheaval generated by World War I, however, changed the city's black activists.

The contest began in earnest in the fall of 1918, though the great influenza epidemic that hit Charleston that September slowed its start. Authorities closed schools, theaters, and churches and halted public gatherings until the danger passed. The quarantine bought NAACP organizers time; after it ended, they held sixteen mass meetings to generate community support. Poinsette attended several of them.[26]

By November, debates concerning the wisdom of as well as the appropriate strategy for pursuing the teacher campaign emerged in the local black press. A writer to the editor of the *Charleston Messenger* took issue with the paper's portrayal of those who favored the change to an all-black teaching force as "agitators." "No one is fighting white people and these 'agitators' are sufficiently intelligent to know that it would amount to nothing if they did. They realize that they must appeal to the innate justice of the authorities to see that we are properly treated," he argued. "Can you show me one man of prominence in the city who was educated in the public schools?" He also suggested that by fostering race pride, black teachers schooling black students would also bolster future sales of black newspapers.[27]

Edwin Harleston's brother-in-law, the Reverend Daniel Jenkins, founder of the Jenkins Orphanage, published the *Messenger*. As the head of an institution that received nominal support from white city fathers, Jenkins had to exercise caution and not publicly appear to endorse challenges to their authority. The *Messenger*'s editor responded to this letter by questioning whether black educators were prepared to shoulder the responsibility of managing black schools — an argument that closely resembled the one advanced by white people — and suggesting that leaders had undertaken the effort without garnering enough community support. "We are simply calling for the full co-operation of the colored people of this city," he penned, "and before asking for anything they should unite, especially the parents of the children." Given that Charleston's socially exclusive elite dominated the local NAACP's executive committee, persuading leaders to be more inclusive could increase the chances for success. The editor also provided a view of the extent of teachers' support for the effort by commenting, "The teachers must not go ahead of the parents."[28]

On the last day of November, the NAACP formally presented its request to the city school board, demanding relief from the "abnormal" conditions that prevailed in Charleston's public schools. The fifty-five years that had passed since the end of slavery had afforded more than enough time to train a competent black teaching corps, the petitioners asserted. Reminding the school board that African Americans had been "faithful, obedient toilers . . . in the service of our city, county, State and nation," they asked why black Charlestonians were deprived of "this natural, pfilial, God-given right to teach our children in the public schools?"[29] In essence, these crusaders argued that the logic of segregation dictated that white teachers did not belong in black schools. This approach placed the NAACP in the awkward position of making a case for upholding a segregationist principle in education even as it protested racial discrimination in every other aspect of Low Country life. Yet such tactical conservatism also aligned with the broader goal of dismantling Jim Crow. Black educational autonomy ultimately guaranteed the persistence of demands for full inclusion in the nation's economic and political life.

The Board of School Commissioners met with the NAACP's committee on January 9, 1919. Two days later, the white men ruled that since a bond to expand public school facilities was pending voter approval, "the board at present is not in a position to change the personnel of the teaching staff in the colored schools." It was a classic delay tactic. The board members said that they hoped to consider the petition favorably in the future but estimated that if the bond issue passed, the expansion would take three years. Three years was too long for Charleston's black leaders, who saw their campaign as part of the national upsurge in activism generated by World War I and had deliberately picked this moment. The NAACP's committee responded by upping the ante. Since the school board had admitted its powerlessness to make the change, African American leaders concluded that their only recourse was to take the fight to the state legislature.[30]

Clark remembered that such a bold riposte "enraged some of the white citizens of Charleston and they shouted for all to hear that mulattoes . . . were the only ones who wanted Negro teachers for their children. The cooks and the laundresses, they declared, didn't want their children taught by Negro teachers." White school board members gambled that exploiting class divisions within the black community would impede the campaign. If Charleston was the only place in the South that inverted segregation's logic by having white instructors teach black children, defending a principle mattered more. Local white authorities expected their word to be taken as law and remained invested in exercising complete control over black public schools and the learning that occurred inside of them.[31]

The school board's assertion that only well-to-do African Americans wanted black teachers prompted NAACP organizers to launch a massive drive to collect signatures from black parents whose children attended the public schools. Septima Poinsette volunteered. So did many others. Mamie Fields enlisted in the army canvassing door to door, a force so big that she "wonder[ed] who was left at home just to sign." It was natural for the teachers and activist-minded women who ordinarily assumed responsibility for parental visitation to lead in the community outreach. Working at Avery, Poinsette risked little, though she later claimed that Cox objected to his faculty's participation in the effort and that some of her colleagues refused to associate themselves with the controversy. "The older teachers at Avery didn't want to be involved," she commented, "but I didn't have many friends and I didn't care."[32] Moreover, well schooled in the notion that black teachers taught by example, Poinsette recruited some of her sixth-graders to help, thereby initiating them into political action as well.

Not everyone signed the NAACP's petition cards. Some residents, Clark recalled, "had the feeling that they didn't know. Of course, when you don't understand things, you are against it. And there were some who had the feeling [that black teachers] wouldn't be worthwhile."[33] Those who worked for whites might have feared losing their jobs, and those who worked for themselves but had white clients might have anticipated boycotts if word spread that they had aligned themselves with a group of troublemakers. Organizers had also told canvassers to warn people against signing a competing petition that favored retaining white teachers. Septima Poinsette recognized how explaining the issues at stake helped to raise her neighbors' educational and political consciousness. Residents who added their signatures to the NAACP's appeal could feel satisfied that they had participated in the black community's largest organized political effort since Reconstruction. Stripped of the right to vote, the black Charlestonians who signed raised their collective voice to declare, "We dissent!" Canvassers ultimately collected 4,551 signatures from households representing 22,755 individuals, or two-thirds of the city's black population.[34] The NAACP's representatives had solid evidence to refute the school board's arguments that black parents preferred white teachers.

Thomas E. Miller probably relished the opportunity to lead the delegation to Columbia to present the petition to the General Assembly, for it signaled his reentry into the game of state politics after a forced retirement. Born free in 1849 in Ferrebeeville, Miller had attended Charleston's antebellum private schools and then pursued his education at Lincoln University in Pennsylvania, graduating in 1872. Taking advantage of a brief opportunity for black Carolinians, he went home to study law at the University of South Carolina and under the tutelage of a state supreme court justice. He was admitted to the South Carolina bar in 1875, one year after voters from the black majority stronghold of Beaufort elected him to the state House. Miller still held a seat in the state legislature in 1895 and served as a delegate to the convention that rewrote the state constitution that disfranchised black Carolinians. Yet he also persuaded his colleagues to establish a separate land-grant college for African Americans. On March 3, 1896, state legislators created the Colored, Normal, Industrial, Agricultural, and Mechanical College of South Carolina, known more simply as South Carolina State, in Orangeburg. Three days later, Miller nominated three of the six white men chosen to serve on the college's board of trustees; one day after that, he resigned his seat in the legislature. The trustees then named Miller the school's first president.[35]

Miller had negotiated the best deal possible. In exchange for his removal from legislative politics, he had gained the top job at the only state-funded black higher educational facility in South Carolina. Unlike the lack of supervision that prevailed in black elementary and secondary schools, however, South Carolina State's white board of trustees assumed a much greater role in decision making and overseeing operations at the college. Such arrangements required Miller to astutely engage the politics of education, particularly by muting his objections to his lack of control of the school. He even kept his mouth shut when the legislature elected the rabidly racist Coleman Blease to the trustee board in 1906. When Blease won the governorship four years later, Miller could no longer hold his tongue. Thus, one of Governor Blease's first orders of business in 1911 was to demand Miller's resignation "on the grounds of pernicious activity in politics." To clarify his actions, the deposed college president sent a copy of his letter of resignation to the state's major newspapers. "I am guilty of having begged voters not to vote for you," Miller told Blease. "I counted the cost before I opposed you," he continued, "hence, I am prepared for the blow of your official act."[36] Unemployed but ever proud, Thomas Miller resettled in Charleston.

Miller returned to the state legislature in January 1919 as the chair of the NAACP delegation. A large crowd gathered at the train station to see the men off and to signal its approval of the updated petition they carried. Though much of the original wording remained, the latest version included the assertion, "We are not a committee of a few educated negroes . . . we are the chosen representatives of the petitioners, namely of more than ten thousand adult men and women." On Saturday, January 18, Harleston led several hundred of those petitioners on a march through the streets of Columbia. Three days later, Miller got down to business, relying on the practical experience he had gained during his tenure in the General Assembly. Knowing that the Charleston County delegation sided with the school board, Miller exploited the historical animosity between upstate and Low Country politicians by persuading Senator J. H. Wharton of Laurens County and Representative

R. A. Meares of Fairfield County to introduce legislation in their respective chambers. Miller also soon reiterated to the press that he had a petition with the signatures of ten thousand black Charlestonians.[37] Thomas Miller knew the value of a good bluff.

The proposed measure and the NAACP's petition went beyond asking for the removal of white teachers from Charleston's black public schools. It requested that the legislature amend Section 1780 of the state Civil Code of 1912 to read, "It shall be unlawful for a person of the white race to teach in the free public schools of South Carolina provided and set aside for the children of the negro race." In other words, the bill would formalize what had merely been a widespread custom of segregation. The NAACP conceded that the provision generated controversy because "colored people did not want to put themselves as on record as willing to increase discriminatory statutes on the law books of South Carolina." Before the bill could be formally presented, it had to pass through the House Committee on Education, and its opponents had to have a chance to speak. With a hearing scheduled for January 30, the NAACP delegation went back to Charleston and secured an affidavit of the validity of the signatures by African American heads of families who endorsed having black teachers teach their children.[38] Thomas Miller also retrieved a very large suitcase.

Charleston County senator A. R. Young spoke for school board members and superintendent Andrew Butler Rhett at the committee hearing. Young began by praising the city's white teachers and insisting that "it was an outrage to dismiss these 'white ladies' on a petition of Negroes." While every white lawmaker had to concede this point, it soon became apparent that a majority favored the change. Young then explained the pending bond issue. Still losing ground, he returned to the school board's original objection, that the effort represented the wishes only of highbrows in the black community. At that moment, Thomas Miller dramatically lifted the suitcase at his side, causing it to fall open. According to Mamie Garvin Fields, "More papers scattered across the room than the people could pick up," and "every sheet they did pick up was black with the names of black people who signed."[39]

The presentation of the petition cards settled the debate, and the House voted in favor of the measure. A day later, Meares informed Young that Miller and the NAACP remained willing to delay action on the bill if the school commissioners would reconsider, thereby rendering legislative action unnecessary. This outcome would also enable black Carolinians to avoid going on record in support of a Jim Crow law. On February 3, Superintendent Rhett sent Teddy Harleston a copy of a resolution passed by the school board that said "on or before the scholastic year commencing Sept. 1st 1920 . . . Negro teachers will be employed to teach the Negro pupils" in the city. Meares received two silver candlesticks from black Charlestonians for his efforts on their behalf. In the fall of 1919, the city hired seventeen black teachers. A year later, when the resolution took effect, fifty-five black teachers, all but one of them women, three black principals, and two black vice principals began work in Charleston's public schools.[40]

The NAACP's victory mattered in concrete ways. It meant that African American youth in Charleston could begin learning things that black children elsewhere in the state already knew. "The Negroes in the South Carolina Legislature during the Reconstruction and post-Reconstruction years were the men held up to us in high school history classes as being great men," Greenwood County's Benjamin Mays recalled, "and not the Negro-hating Benjamin Ryan Tillman and his kind, who strove so long and hard to deprive the black man of his vote." Like Mays, Charleston's black pupils might now come to feel that they "had identity." Victory also gave the national NAACP a chance to highlight one of its few triumphs south of the Mason-Dixon Line. Du Bois asked Harleston to give an impromptu account of the campaign at the organization's 1919 national convention. Equally significant, black Charleston's conquest sent a message to white city leaders. As the editor of the *Messenger* observed, the initial accusation that the desired change did not represent the views of the majority of black Charlestonians had backfired because it represented "a tacit admission of the principle of the right of colored people to participate in matters of public concern."[41] To Septima Poinsette, the outcome meant that activism worked.

Poinsette's involvement in a fight steered strategically by Miller exposes the deeper roots of southern black political insurgency during the New Reconstruction. Like their predecessors after the Civil War, black Charlestonians in the second decade of the twentieth century battled for black educational autonomy. But just as the struggle had subsequently shifted to more secular terrain, so too did the organized opposition. Achieving cohesion in this campaign allowed the NAACP to serve as the institutional vehicle for transmitting nineteenth-century memories of black political activism — as well as adaptations of earlier tactics — to a cohort of World War I– era insurgents. Those who attended the mass meetings where Miller spoke, including Poinsette, and volunteered in the petition drive accepted the activist torch he passed on. Their deeds subsequently influenced others. Future teacher Ruby Middleton Forsythe, then a student at Avery, remembered the excitement generated by the community-wide canvass and the feeling of winning.

"That made a lasting impression on me," she remarked. "It convinced me that things can change when black people organize."[42] Forsythe carried this knowledge with her when she began community organizing as a teacher in a Mount Pleasant school two years later.

Yet the Charleston NAACP's victory also set a dangerous local precedent. Having lost, the white school board redoubled its efforts to control black education. First it had to align itself with the principles of segregated education that existed elsewhere. In May 1919, Rhett recommended that the Board of School Commissioners formally adopt a salary schedule that differentiated between white and black teachers. The state's NAACP did not challenge this reactionary measure until twenty-four years and another world war had intervened. Next, the school board decided that only single black women could teach in the city schools; those already married would have to continue working in the rural county system. And after black teachers and administrators were hired in 1920, the board appointed the former white principal at Shaw Elementary as the first supervisor of Negro schools. Rhett defended incurring the extra expense of the new position by observing the action demonstrated to black principals, teachers, and students that "the white people still have an interest in the schools and an authority over the schools, which they are prepared to exercise."[43] Rhett's tenure as superintendent would last until 1946.

White Charlestonians also took a greater interest in black teachers, watching for signs of additional dissident activism that might come from belonging to the NAACP. The local NAACP thus resorted to surreptitious means of collecting dues from African American educators in the 1920s. Mary Alice LaSaine, the Jeanes supervisor for Charleston County's black schools, would wait outside the courthouse, where teachers who worked in rural areas came to cash their paychecks. When the women left, according to Clark, LaSaine "was standing right there holding a nearly closed parasol upside down." Teachers "slipped our dollar membership dues into that parasol as we walked past her. We didn't want anybody to see us putting it in because we knew the trouble it would cause."[44] Despite the new systematic white surveillance, however, black educators had taken one giant step forward.

❧

In the short run, the Charleston branch of the NAACP emerged stronger and more determined to follow up on its success. World War I had ended, and with black soldiers beginning to return home, opportunities to advocate for racial justice seemed numerous. On May 15, 1919, Thomas Miller stood be-

hind another podium at the Victory Club to address a ~~~
by the forty-five African American soldiers who belong~
War Veterans Association.[45] Five days earlier, the Red S~
in Charleston.

It was the bloodiest single season anyone could reme~
the end of the Civil War. Isolated race riots in which whit~
attacked entire black communities had exploded in Ar~
the turn of the century, but 1919 differed in both scope ~~~ ~~~~~. Between
April and October, approximately 250 black men, women, and children died
in twenty-five urban race riots and a racial pogrom in Elaine, Arkansas. By
December, white mobs had lynched 78 black people, 18 more than the previous year. Ten of these victims wore military uniforms; 11 of them were
burned alive at the stake. The tide of this bloody wave surged north, south,
east, and west, wherever African Americans and whites were competing for
housing, jobs, and educational and recreational facilities.[46]

Charleston's trouble began about 8:30 on Saturday evening, May 10, when
Isaac Doctor, a black man, got into an argument with Jacob Cohen and George
Holloday, two white bluejackets, at a pool hall on Beaufain Street. The dispute spread outside to the street, and when it turned physical, the two sailors
fatally shot Doctor. The situation escalated, and an estimated two thousand
navy men fanned out across the peninsula to "get the negroes." Some white
sailors armed themselves with cue sticks and balls procured from pool halls.
Others raided shooting galleries, grabbing rifles, pistols, and ammunition.
One hour later, Roper Hospital, which served African Americans, admitted
its first riot victim for treatment. Over the next several hours, the number of
patients increased so rapidly that hospital officials could not keep an accurate
count. The outnumbered and overwhelmed police force soon realized that it
could not restore order and contacted officials at the naval training camp to
send provost guards as backup. By midnight, a detachment of marines had
begun patrolling the city, but more than three more hours passed before the
situation was under control.[47]

The riot started early enough that plenty of people found themselves
caught in the melee. White patrons dining at a popular restaurant on King
Street watched in horror as members of the mob pulled a black man from a
streetcar and then beat and shot him. Responding to shouts of "The sailors
are coming," black cobbler James Frayer closed his shop, took refuge behind
the counter, and refused to open the door. A random shot fired by a sailor outside hit his apprentice in the lower back. Making his way home from work,
Peter Poinsette encountered two white men who demanded his money, but

him pass when he said he had none. At home, sewing a dress for her [...]er, Septima Poinsette heard "a mass of screaming and hollering" that sounded like it was coming from Marion Square. The riot had reached the western end of her block. "We stood on our porch," she remembered, "and when we hear them bursting down the street screaming and hollering, we run back in the house. We couldn't help it none. . . . I know I was afraid."[48]

Her neighbor, Ed Mitchell, was not as lucky. He was attacked at the corner of Henrietta and Meeting Streets and had to be treated for wounds to his head, abdomen, right arm, and both hands. At a dance Septima Poinsette had considered attending, members of the mob "beat most of the people who were up there — Blacks — and some of them had to run and hide in alleys until they could get back home." Elsewhere, a black man had his kneecap shot off, at least two others sustained gunshot wounds in the hip and thigh, and many more suffered wounds from flying bottles and bricks. The mob also shot a thirteen-year-old black boy in the back, paralyzing him from the waist down, while a young black girl was hit by a stray bullet. Before dawn, two black men lay dead, at least twenty-seven people — seventeen of them African Americans — were wounded, and authorities had made fifty arrests.[49] No one went to church that Sunday.

Charlestonians recoiled. For his part, Mayor Tristram Hyde promised a full investigation and the imposition of martial law if any more violence erupted. He also declared his intent to ask W. G. Fridie, the African American owner of a barber shop on King Street that catered to whites and had been destroyed, to submit a bill for damages to the city. "This might set a precedent," Hyde conceded, "but the negroes of Charleston must be protected." Hyde's statement embodied the racial paternalism that had long characterized local interracial relations by essentially reasserting white men's right to oversee public safety. White Charlestonians wondered "whether or not the outbreak was the culmination of a series of incidents or hard feelings between enlisted men and negroes" or if it "was a spontaneous outburst."[50] In other words, did outsiders bear the primary responsibility for the trouble? If so, white residents could consider the riot an aberration and breathe a little easier. But something unexpected and infinitely more frightening to white Charlestonians had made this violence radically different from earlier incidents: a few black Charlestonians had fought back.

When the first police officer responded to gunshots in the Beaufain Street area, witnesses pointed to the house from which a group of black men had launched attacks on bluejackets roaming the streets. None of the African Americans resisted arrest. When a mob of white men rushed into a pool hall in search of makeshift weapons, its owner saw a group of black men grabbing whatever remained and following the mob out the door. A mere two hours into the riot, reports began filtering in that African American snipers had positioned themselves on several of the streets leading to the Navy Yard, aiming at cars whose passengers wore service hats. Taxi drivers refused to return sailors to the training camp. Streetcar conductors brave enough to pass through the area instructed riders to remove their hats and sit on the floor. Marines apprehended a black man waving a large gun in the streets and a black chauffeur carrying a concealed .32-caliber revolver. Rumors of targeted attacks by black Charlestonians persisted in the aftermath of the riot. According to one account, African Americans riding in a "mysterious gray automobile" had fired shots into the Roper Hospital lobby; other observers claimed that bullets had hit the police station, and police later confirmed that shots had been fired at marines standing outside of the building.[51] Amid the chaos, nobody knew for certain whether the race war that white people had feared since slavery days had finally begun.

Authorities captured Cohen and Holloday, who confessed to firing two shots each at Doctor. Nevertheless, the jury at the coroner's inquest blamed the killing on "enlisted men," without naming anyone. Additional information also came to light at the inquest. Early reports had contended that Doctor had jostled his way past the two bluejackets and then responded to their remonstrations by hurling epithets and assaulting them with a weapon. Police chief Joseph A. Black, who had loaded Doctor's body into the coroner's wagon, testified, "I examined the negro and could find no trace of any weapon, nor was there any signs that a scuffle had taken place." Cohen and Holloday gave arresting officers a different story: "An army officer with two gold bars told us that if, when we told a negro to halt and he didn't do it, we were to shoot him." They asserted that Doctor "was throwing rocks."[52]

Septima Poinsette heard yet another version: "Some soldiers went down on Beaufain Street and they claimed they bought some whiskey from a black man, and the whiskey proved to be water. He was cheating them." The secrecy surrounding Prohibition violations in Charleston kept local newspapers from mentioning the possibility that alcohol might have been a factor in the dispute. The city had long ignored state liquor laws, and "blind tigers" had flourished there for more than two decades. Bemoaning his inability to rein in wet Charleston with state legislation, Governor Richard I. Manning remained determined to enforce federal Prohibition. Mayor Hyde played along so well during the war that Manning ordered state constables in the city relieved of duty except on the waterfront and in rural areas.[53] Charleston officials would not jeopardize the governor's newfound trust by revealing that illegal alcohol traffic in the heart of the city might have sparked the riot. A group of rowdy sailors offered a better explanation.

Charleston's African American leaders understood the hidden factors contributing to the racial tensions that had flared into violence—most notably, the difference in living conditions and life opportunity that white supremacy rendered normal. NAACP leaders and a committee of African American ministers asked city officials for better "housing, lighting, sanitary, and educational conditions" and suggested that the police force hire African Americans, a proposal that generated no results for thirty-one years. The men also recommended establishing a biracial committee with reform-minded white Charlestonians to develop a concrete program. Though it took white residents a little longer to recognize that they might benefit from such a committee, community leaders formed the Charleston Interracial Committee in 1921. Teddy Harleston served on it for the remainder of the decade.[54]

In the meantime, black women had stepped from the wings to assume a starring political role in the New Reconstruction. Less than a month after the passage of the Nineteenth Amendment in August 1920, South Carolina's women began presenting themselves at registrars' offices. In a single day, 168 black Charlestonian women registered. In Columbia, black women surprised registrars on the first day, forcing the franchise's gatekeepers to improvise by making them wait until all white women had been registered. Undeterred, the black women returned the next day, only to discover that a new prerequisite—proof of having paid three hundred dollars in property taxes—had been adopted overnight. Elsewhere in the state, a group of black women filed suit when a registrar turned them away. Newspapers described the black vote as "negligible" on Election Day but noted that "it was larger than ever before due to the women taking part."[55]

Like their white counterparts, black suffragists had argued for formal political inclusion based on their moral superiority as mothers and as wives who attended to the welfare of the entire community. If black men premised their postwar claims to full citizenship on wartime service, black women relied on their community service as antilynching crusaders, teachers introducing civic organizing to rural areas, and racial diplomats procuring state funding for social welfare benefits. In the wake of the legal and extralegal maneuvering that denied them their constitutional right to vote, southern black women did not turn away from politics in the 1920s. Rather, they redoubled their efforts to influence white male politicians and to persuade their wives to assume more active roles promoting racial justice.[56]

Septima Poinsette neither involved herself with Charleston's interracial group nor joined other black activists attempting to capitalize on postwar possibilities. By 1920, her life had changed dramatically. And it would take her nearly the whole decade to recover to the point where she could effectively reengage with the African American freedom struggle.

⌒◦❧◦⌒

Septima Poinsette's first sweet taste of romance followed close on the heels of her first sweet taste of victory in the NAACP teacher campaign. The end of World War I brought a daily influx of servicemen into Charleston Harbor, and black community leaders asked teachers to host the returning heroes at the segregated United Service Organization. One evening in late January, a particular sailor caught Poinsette's eye. Nerie (pronounced Nee-rye) David Clark hailed from Hickory, North Carolina, and had served as a navy wardroom cook during the war. When Poinsette learned that his ship would be docked in the port through the weekend, she did what all interested but respectable young women of her community did: she invited him to church. To her surprise, Clark showed up at Old Bethel on Sunday morning with four other sailors in tow. "That Sunday I was the talk of the church and the community; I had been accompanied not by one sailor but by five!" she mused. Poinsette then invited them all back to Henrietta Street, where they sat on the porch talking. She knew better than to ask them inside for a bite to eat. But even entertaining five sailors on the family's stoop, in plain sight of all the neighbors, was not the sort of thing respectable women — especially teachers — did. "Charleston wasn't especially fond of sailors; in those days they had the reputation of being rough fellows," she later conceded.[57]

The gossip that followed should have been Septima Poinsette's first red flag. Charlestonians had always distinguished between natives and newcomers, and this attitude extended to servicemen. Victoria Poinsette gave her daughter quite a tongue lashing after they left. For the first time in her life, Septima did not care: she had "been impressed, even excited by Nerie Clark."[58]

The brouhaha might have died down except that Clark appeared in Charleston again in May, after the race riot. He came from Norfolk, Virginia, on a three-day pass, spending the first day traveling to the Low Country and the last back to Virginia. Unfortunately, the one day Poinsette and her suitor did have together coincided with Avery's commencement exercises, and she had little time to talk to him. Clark showed up alone at the evening graduation ceremonies and waited for Miss Poinsette to finish her duties.[59]

Chances are Poinsette's colleagues and her students' parents clucked their teeth, shook their heads, and kept their distance.

Poinsette again invited Clark back to her house to sit and talk on the porch. She learned that he had been born on December 15, 1889, that he had a twin brother and a younger set of twin siblings, and that he had completed the sixth grade. She admired his self-declared penchant for the good life, including a fondness for fashionable clothes. When she accompanied him to the train station, he turned and kissed her passionately. "We were both misty-eyed," she recalled, as the train pulled away, but the mist cleared quickly when she saw blue dye from his uniform staining "the tucks of my starched white crepe de chine shirtwaist." She realized what awaited her at home: "a lecture on going out unchaperoned in a taxi with 'one of those wild sailors.'"[60]

Romance had escaped Poinsette during her high school years. "I guess . . . when you just work and go to school and come home and be with your parents," she came to understand, "that's the most dangerous situation. You need to have wider experience." No man had yet captured her fancy as much as Nerie Clark. He must have been a real sweet talker, and the fact that he was a stranger might have increased his allure. It made her parents nervous, however. "Somebody must have put some voodoo on you, 'cause you never bothered about boys," Victoria Poinsette warned her daughter. The elder Poinsette needed only one look at Clark to know that he was not a suitable man for her daughter. "He was of a darker-brown complexion than were members of our family," Septima Clark recalled, but she might as well have said that Nerie Clark was too black. "He was extremely dark, and Mama Vickie did not like dark people," a family friend agreed.[61] Mama Vickie may also have feared that her daughter was repeating her mistakes by falling for a darker, less educated man. But her child was a grown woman, and Victoria Poinsette could only hope and pray that Nerie Clark would never tread on her stoop again.

In the fall of 1919, Septima Poinsette took a job in a three-teacher rural school in McClellanville, a sleepy fishing village forty-one miles from Charleston. She later claimed that a salary increase had attracted her, but other, equally compelling, factors pushed her away from Charleston. Poinsette's support for the NAACP teacher campaign had been unpopular with some of her Avery colleagues. Teaching there probably also opened old wounds from her student days—the feeling of exclusion that reaffirmed her status as a perennial outsider. Moreover, Poinsette had spent two years living by her own pluck on Johns Island. Going home meant readjusting to Victoria

Poinsette's strict routines and hawkish oversight. Her mother's disapproval of Nerie Clark might have proven the last straw.

Poinsette was assigned to teach fourth-, fifth-, and sixth-graders. The school's principal moonlighted as a minister on the weekends, leaving early on Friday and returning late Monday night, so she soon taught his sixth- and seventh-graders during his absences as well. Nerie Clark's recent attentions had affected Poinsette's confidence when interacting with men. She was young, she was beautiful, and she befriended this principal, enjoying long walks with him after school. By spring he was smitten; a marriage proposal followed. Poinsette hesitated: "I feared I couldn't be a minister's wife — as I supposed ministers' wives should be and had observed some of them to be. So I refused him."[62]

The decision reveals much about Poinsette's personal insecurities, concern for privacy, and determination to become her own woman. Black ministers occupied the brightest spotlight in the community, and the church expected their wives to share it. In addition to household duties, preachers' wives had to perform as gracious hostesses at church functions and to act as helpmates in ministering to the community's needs. "I didn't know . . . just how I could live and please all the people," the young teacher admitted, "because I didn't feel as if I wanted to do all those things." Poinsette not only turned down the man but rejected the lifestyle that accompanied being a first lady in the black church. "My behavior would be on display," she recognized, "and I was afraid that I would fail." Her refusal of the minister also reflected her desire to escape Victoria Poinsette's dominating influence. "My mother was so strict and had all those strict religious ideas, and I felt that I'd be jumping into another frying pan" by marrying this man, Septima explained.[63] And her heart still belonged to Nerie Clark, even though she had not seen him in a year.

He found her in McClellanville that May. He had been to Henrietta Street to get her parents' permission to marry her, but Victoria Poinsette had "adamantly refused." Someone else must have told him where to find her. He rode up with the mailman, and when he asked, she said yes. He went back to Charleston to get the license and the ring. Since no one had a telephone, he told the family the news in person. There was no celebration. The Reverend Graham Howard, "an old preacher who had been a slave," married the couple on May 14, 1920, in the home where she boarded, and they enjoyed their wedding supper aboard a launch "powered by an engine that also turned a cotton gin and a corn mill." He shipped out to the Netherlands the next day. She finished the school year in McClellanville.[64]

There comes a time in life when daughters are moved to say "no" to their mamas. "Since I had never fallen in love before, I had a feeling that this was my chance. This was my life, so I went ahead with it," Septima Clark later asserted. For the young bride, love and marriage marked a new phase of womanhood. Professionally, she had already made the transition from girlhood. Marriage meant the start of a more personal journey, one bound up with her awakening sexuality and yielding its own intimate lessons in self-knowledge. Poinsette had been raised to believe that marriage sanctioned the pleasurable fulfillment of sexual desire between a man and a woman, but she had also been raised by a mother who had sacrificed much so that her daughters might achieve more in their lives than she had. Victoria Poinsette viewed the union as an impudent expression of ingratitude as well as an outright rejection of all her teachings. A smoldering anger settled between mother and daughter. Peter Poinsette felt differently about his new son-in-law, but "he dared not speak out" because his wife "would have jumped down his throat if he had."[65] It required hardheaded resolve to rebel against her mother's wishes. The private joys of being in love provided quite a shield.

Septima Poinsette's choice of a stranger and her elopement defied her community's expectations as well. Charleston had long been an endogamous city. As one native son observed, people "marry within groups" and "stay within [their] own kind of people." Unlike her brother, Peter, who romanced and married a girl from a prominent local family, Septima wed somebody she hardly knew and "all my people were against that," she divulged. More-over, Charlestonians had their own sensibilities about how to put on a proper wedding. "Everybody wanted to do something for you, but mind, they might be hurt if they were not asked to do what they wanted to do for you," Mamie Garvin Fields remarked. "One thing the bride had to do was to make sure all the various people of the community who loved the family were happy taking part in the wedding."[66] By her community's standards, Septima Clark had failed to make a wise choice and had failed at her bridal duties. Such decisions did not help her establish herself as a respectable woman in her hometown. More significant, and perhaps unconsidered by a young woman who had rejected a proposal that would have propelled her further into pub-lic prominence, her choices had broader implications for any aspirations to do activist work in Charleston.

Black Charleston's married leading ladies saw continuity between their private domestic duties and their public roles. Those who had entered com-panionate marriages and developed good home lives also strengthened the platform from which they engaged in racial uplift, translating their roles as

Septima Clark (right), with her brother, Peter T. Poinsette, and his future wife, Lucille Mears, mid-1920s. Courtesy of the Avery Research Center for African American History and Culture, College of Charleston.

daughters, sisters, wives, and mothers to benefit the community. Embracing a decidedly Victorian morality to combat the negative stereotypes of black women's sexual profligacy, they presented a refined and chaste public demeanor that privileged female duty and civic responsibility while obscuring their private sexuality as wives. Of course, marriage itself did not serve as a prerequisite for activism. Many single professional women stood in the civil rights vanguard of this era because educated black women had a special obligation to answer the call to civic service. And marrying a less educated man did not automatically mean abandoning such responsibilities. Speaking before a women's Bible class, one Charlestonian man noted, "If an educated man marries an illiterate woman, his children will have lost much; but if an educated woman shall marry an illiterate man, she could still give her children her own standards." Civic activism strengthened those standards, he continued: "Unless a woman is a useful factor in the world, she is limited in usefulness in the home."[67] Nevertheless, the choice of a husband—his standing in the local community—signaled how far a woman might rise socially and by extension in the circle of female civic leaders.

Jeannette Cox, wife of Avery's principal, epitomized the ideal wife who complemented her husband's work. In addition to mentoring women students, she served as the first delegate of the Charleston City Federation of Colored Women's Clubs at the 1916 annual meeting of the state federation of black clubwomen. That fall, because she "greatly missed my Albany, Ga. club," Cox organized the exclusive Phyllis Wheatley Literary and Social Club, with membership limited to twenty women, though they could be married or single. Most of them were Averyites. A recent migrant to the city whose social eminence reflected her husband's high-profile position, Cox hoped the Phyllis Wheatley members would surmount "prescribed social lines" and envisioned the club as "a sort of social crucible in which we might begin a mixture of the perfect social compound."[68] Including young, unmarried women meant teaching them by example the art of performing the social responsibilities of a dutiful wife.

Cox observed that when the group was founded in 1916, "all of Charleston's ills were laid to the lack of unity among its social groups. And it must also be remembered that that mighty leveler—Negro teachers in the city schools—was still the substance of things hoped for."[69] From Cox's perspective, at least, the NAACP's teacher campaign promised to bring unity among the women already engaged in civic affairs. Septima Poinsette might have even been asked to join had she formed friendships with her colleagues at Avery.

Septima Clark, however, would not have been considered. In addition to their local civic improvement efforts, the women in the Phyllis Wheatley prided themselves on serving as cultured hostesses for important visitors to their fair city. For example, in 1928–29, they hosted ladies attending the African American Palmetto Medical Association's annual meeting in Charleston. According to Cox, such endeavors, were "no small undertaking," requiring the club members "to select good working committees, to prepare a home attractively, to choose suitable refreshments, to serve them appetizingly, to buy economically, to keep accurate accounts, to send invitations to all who should be invited, to forget none, to prepare ourselves, to report to the home punctually." Ultimately, "no matter how worn or weary we may be," the hostesses had "to smile and continue smiling to the bitter end in order that our guests may catch the spirit of cheer and depart with joy and appreciation for the courtesy."[70] In Charleston, no sailor's wife—even one who was a teacher—could hope for an invitation to such receptions for black professionals. Moreover, without her own home, she could not anticipate hosting similarly distinguished gatherings of prominent citizens.

The Phyllis Wheatley ladies also imagined themselves as ambassadors to the white community. When the club sponsored a concert by Marian Anderson, Cox remarked, "many white friends attended and were very enthusiastic in their commendation." In this way, the women shored up the work of their husbands who had business dealings with white Charlestonians. Again, a sailor's wife had little value for the critical task of cultivating white goodwill, on which the success of racial uplift initiatives often depended.[71] Septima Clark's marital choice prohibited her entry into important statewide networks of black leaders.

Nerie Clark returned to his bride two months after their marriage, and the newlyweds lived in a rooming house until the fall, when he shipped out to the Pacific and she traveled to Jacksonville, Florida, to visit family. As the wife of an enlisted sailor, Clark could rely on his salary and forgo teaching. She saw her husband again in Florida and then met him in Charleston in the spring of 1921, when she gave birth to a daughter. To make amends with the baby's grandmother, they named the infant Victoria Irma. Twenty-three days later, the baby died. A midwife had attended the home delivery and "hadn't noticed that the baby didn't have a rectum and that the stools were coming through the vagina, until it got very sick and had a fever," Clark admitted sixty years later. By the time the family got the infant to the hospital for an operation, it was too late.[72] Grief-stricken, Septima Clark buried her daughter without her husband because he had already gone back to sea.

Septima Clark sank into a numbing depression and found it difficult to envision any kind of future. Her mind turned to dangerous meditations. "I felt that I was being punished for having disobeyed my mother," she recalled; "I thought what I had done was against the will of God, according to the religious laws that I learned, and I felt very strongly about that." In a fog of self-doubt and self-loathing, Clark walked alone to the end of a pier near the Battery and contemplated suicide, but Victoria Poinsette sent one of her sons out on his bike to find his sister and bring her home. Though it would have only taken a few words to absolve her daughter's sense of having sinned against God by marrying Nerie Clark, Victoria Poinsette held her tongue. "She never forgave me," Septima Clark maintained. "She was strict like that." Victoria Poinsette also never tried to make peace with her son-in-law. "I know he was afraid of my mother," Clark observed. Nerie Clark never returned to Henrietta Street.[73]

Septima Clark could not remain there long either. As the wife of an enlisted man, she was entitled to a federal stipend, but when it failed to arrive, she "knew nothing about the procedures to follow in inquiring about it." Short on cash, too proud to ask her parents for help, and needing a change, she took a job as a live-in caretaker for an elderly white woman who planned to summer in the mountains of Hendersonville, North Carolina. The woman constantly criticized Clark's performance. The situation worsened when her son and daughter-in-law arrived with their new infant son and asked Clark to take charge of changing its diapers. "I couldn't," she realized. "It made me think too much of my own child. I just sat and cried."[74] Only prayer and the end of her tenure in September brought relief. Still unable to face possible censure at home, Clark went to live with her in-laws in Hickory, North Carolina.

Hickory differed from Charleston in just about every way. The sloping hillsides surrounding Hickory provided a dramatic contrast to Charleston's flat marshes and salty expanse. Ample snowfall and colder weather required sturdier clothing and complicated outdoor laundry chores. Fewer black people lived in western North Carolina—only 1,043 African Americans called Hickory home, whereas Charleston's black population topped 32,300. The few black entrepreneurs clustered their businesses along Twelfth and Thirteenth Streets. S. A. Brown, the town's sole black undertaker, ran a barbershop and a grocery from the same location as his funeral parlor. African American travelers refilled their tanks at the one black-owned gas station and found overnight refuge solely at the Carlton Hotel. Hickory's black residents could avail themselves of the services of one dentist, one blacksmith, one shoemaker, one taxi company, and three eating houses but no restaurants. Their children went to one school, and churchgoers attended eight African American houses of worship.[75]

George W. and Matilda Clark, Nerie's parents, had achieved more financial stability than Peter and Victoria Poinsette. They had enough land to keep a cow and grow a garden full of fresh vegetables, and Matilda Clark did not work. They belonged to Mount Pisgah African Methodist Episcopal Church rather than a United Methodist congregation. Though they were "key people in the community," the Clarks did not subscribe to the same limited social mores as Charlestonians, and Septima Clark believed that they held "a more advanced idea of what being a Christian really means than the more strict code under which I had been reared." She joined their church "for the privilege of being acknowledged and really being accepted by my in-laws." However, Matilda Clark ran her household much in the same way that Victoria Poinsette ruled hers, dictating to its members her expectations and their obligations. Seeking to make a life for herself in North Carolina, Septima Clark accepted a job instructing fourteen students in a tiny Mars Hill school, near Boone, in the fall of 1922. It was the smallest class she ever taught during her forty-year career.[76]

After earning his honorable discharge from the navy the next May, Nerie Clark joined his wife in Hickory, but he had trouble finding a job that suited him. He was, after all, a black man who had traveled the world and who aspired to the good life. He decided to return to the country club in Dayton, Ohio, where he had worked as a waiter prior to the war. Although Septima Clark had never resided in such a large city, the move presented her with her first chance to make a home for herself and her husband. She seems to have welcomed that opportunity and did not teach in Dayton. She attended a Baptist church across the street from her house as well as a few Methodist ones, apparently without her husband. She learned about the city's most famous African American son, poet Paul Laurence Dunbar. She befriended a neighbor, a woman living in a common-law arrangement, and soon earned a new respect for the bonds of love that could flourish in this less traditional type of relationship, though she rejected it for herself. Living in Dayton, she recalled, "made me see that there are people in the world who have different ideas . . . and I started looking for the differences."[77] By 1924, she also looked forward to welcoming another child into the world.

This birth, on February 12, 1925, occurred in a hospital. Clark named her healthy son Nerie, after his father. Just when it seemed within reach, however, happiness once again eluded Septima Clark. "While I was still in the hospital," she noted, "I learned that my husband had been divorced from one woman and was virtually living with another right there in Dayton." The shame of having married a divorced man might have been bearable; no one else, particularly in Charleston, would ever have to know. But the emotional shock of her husband's betrayal caused Septima Clark to fall physically ill. A high fever kept her from nursing the baby and from attending to household matters. The neighbor she had befriended lent a hand with the laundry until Clark could recover physically. When she finally mustered the courage to confront her husband, he asked her to leave. By June, she had taken her infant son back to her in-laws' house in Hickory. That fall, she was teaching again, this time in the nearby small village of Hildebran.[78]

In December, Septima Clark was called back to Dayton as her husband lay dying of kidney failure. After sitting disconsolately by his bedside in the hospital all day, she spent sleepless nights at his home weighing the pros and cons of becoming a foreign missionary. She had never been so alone. Offering her life in Christian service, spreading the Gospel among strangers in a faraway place, might have seemed the best way to amend for the error of her ways, the original sin of disobedience from which her current sorrow sprang. But she also feared being separated from her infant son. How could she protect him from an adverse reaction to the climate of the Far East, where she imagined going? If she left Nerie Jr. behind, how could she be sure his needs would be met? More practically, perhaps, Septima Clark realized that she had no idea of how to get the information she needed to make a sound decision. Again, paralyzing self-doubt troubled her mind. Nerie Clark Sr. passed away ten months to the day after the birth of his son, three days before his thirty-sixth birthday. His twin brother, Eli, and an undertaker from S. A. Brown's funeral parlor arrived to help his twenty-seven-year-old widow pack and escort his body back to North Carolina.[79]

The funeral dictated that Septima Clark play the role of dignified grieving widow. She tried to collect "all the sweet notes he had written me, so the minister could make the family feel good." She did not make a fuss when a spray of roses sent by her husband's girlfriend arrived or when one of her brothers-in-law threw it into the trash. Sitting in Matilda Clark's living room, she watched her son, "just learning to walk," swing from the casket handles "as if it were a toy."[80] And Septima Clark decided she never wanted to marry again.

Clark could discuss the emotional trauma of the past few months with no one, especially her proper Charleston family. "The classic difference among Charlestonians," explained a family friend, "is that you don't air your con-

Nerie David Clark Jr. and his paternal grandmother, Matilda Clark,
1926 or 1927. Courtesy of the Avery Research Center for African
American History and Culture, College of Charleston.

cerns, you don't tell people stuff."[81] If she listened to the radio, however, Clark would have heard plenty of other women testifying to the heartache of being left, two-timed, and disrespected by a man. Blueswomen including Ma Rainey, Bessie Smith, Alberta Hunter, and Ethel Waters often sang of the "rage of women against male infidelity and desertion" that Septima Clark had come to know too well. In a 1928 rendition of "Used to Be Your Sweet Mama," Bessie Smith lamented,

Yes I'm mad and have a right to be
After what my Daddy did to me.
I lavished all my love on him
But I swear I'll never love again.
All you women understand what it is to be
In love with a two-time man.
The next time he calls me sweet Mama in his loving way
This is what I'm going to say:
I used to be your sweet Mama, sweet Papa,
But now I'm just as sour as can be.

Yet blueswomen simultaneously celebrated the subsequent independence they gained to control their lives. Later in the song, Smith declares, "I ain't gonna let no man worry me sick / Or turn this hair of mine gray." "Used to Be Your Sweet Mama" begins as a lament but ends as an affirmation, with Smith acknowledging both tremendous pain and a determination to overcome it that ultimately sustains a new sense of self.[82] Septima Clark would do the same.

In time, Clark developed more concrete explanations of her decision not to remarry that reflected more about the woman she became than about the widow she was in the late 1920s. First, she disliked the way Nerie had treated her both privately and publicly: "I had a husband," Clark once disclosed, "who used to say to people all the time that 'She doesn't know. You know women don't know too much of anything.'" Victoria Poinsette's daughter knew better. Whatever expectations of a companionate marriage Clark imagined as a young bride, her husband's dismissal of women's opinions signaled his upholding both a sexual and an intellectual inequality within their marriage. She also worried about how a new man would treat Nerie Jr.: "I never felt as if another man would take the other man's child, and I didn't want him shunted aside by anybody. And there was so much of that, and I just felt so badly." Over the years, she came to feel that "I never could take a lot of foolishness off a man." Clark continued, "I heard someone saying that they went home and their lights were out—[the husband] didn't pay the light bill; their water was gone—they didn't pay the water bill. And I just wouldn't put up with that, because I'd been doing it so long for myself."[83]

Dating taught her a few more lessons about men's "foolishness." Once, during the 1930s, she and a "friend" took a stroll down the streets of Columbia. Nerie Jr. ambled along behind them, "scraping his shoes on the sidewalk like children do." "Just go ahead and scrape them up," the man told her son; "Your mama got plenty of money." Teaching might have provided Septima Clark with a steadier income than her would-be paramour, but she was also a widowed mother struggling to make ends meet in the middle of the Depression. "I got real mad at that man," she remembered, "and I never talked to him anymore." Another time, a "very good friend" whom she accompanied to a dance instructed her not to dance with anyone else. "Didn't want anybody putting his arm around his girl, he said. Men are so funny," Clark reflected. But she knew right then and there that this man was not for her. More important, Clark valued the freedom to make her own life decisions without needing to obtain a man's opinion or approval. During the heyday of the civil rights movement, when Clark resided far away from South Carolina and when fund-raising demanded constant travel, she realized, "I don't think I would have been able [to do] very much. I'm very sure a man wouldn't put up with it."[84]

After her husband's death in 1925, Septima Clark stayed in Hickory and continued teaching in Hildebran long enough to start feeling like more of an outsider in western North Carolina than she did in the Low Country. Her accent told most of her neighbors that she hailed from somewhere else. Attending the African Methodist Episcopal church, Clark surveyed the congregation and saw "hardly a soul that I knew, and not one of whom I could call my people." The region's topography also frightened her. "As I walked up one hill and down another and could not see a house," Clark recalled, "my heart would literally throb." In a region more sparsely populated by African Americans, she lacked the familiar feeling of safety in numbers. One afternoon, as she rode home from school with her brother-in-law, Martin Clark, their car collided with one driven by a white woman. As the drivers exchanged "angry words," Septima Clark began to worry that her brother-in-law "might be lynched." And though she appreciated her in-laws' kindness and hospitality, Clark grew weary of living in another woman's household and obeying her rules.[85]

A different kind of loneliness set in. Her anger with Victoria Poinsette paled by comparison, and after two years, Septima Clark felt positively homesick. Her father's passing away in 1927 only reinforced for her the importance of being close to family. Time had also rendered the explosive circumstances of her marriage less acute, and her husband's death freed her from having to mediate his encounters with her mother. No matter what hard feelings might still linger on Henrietta Street, Clark decided to return to her "beloved Charleston."[86] In a very real sense, she went home a new woman.

❧❧❧

Septima Poinsette Clark had stepped into a larger activist stream coursing through black America in the World War I era. Because it represented a challenge to the white men who ran Charleston's schools and the white men who represented Charleston in the General Assembly, the local NAACP's teacher campaign constituted her first organized "political" action, as she recognized. Education and politics remained inseparable in the Jim Crow South, providing the rationale for the national NAACP's strong encouragement of its southern chapters to "organize the citizens to secure better schools and longer terms, and . . . guard against a lowering of school standards" during the New Reconstruction. Doing so provided a way for disenfranchised black southerners to educate themselves and each other, practically and politically, about the benefits and responsibilities of citizenship. Perhaps the more far-sighted among the organization's leaders recognized the inherent irony of their situation: how strengthening black institutions in response to discrimination and injustice might eventually foster the end of segregation itself.[87]

As with the first Reconstruction, racial violence and federal indifference gutted the promise of the short-lived New Reconstruction. Effectively barred from exercising their new constitutional right to vote, black teachers and clubwomen led efforts to develop broader educational initiatives to bolster the community's well-being. Teaching among the rural poor on Johns Island, Septima Poinsette had already witnessed the pressing need for broader access to health care, economic self-sufficiency, and adult literacy training for African Americans. As a mother whose infant daughter had died, she understood the importance of disseminating pertinent medical information to women, who bore the responsibility for their children's health and safety. Septima Clark would soon join other black clubwomen and teachers working in the state capital to expand social welfare services, a process that often entailed training would-be clients in the fundamentals of citizenship as well. But first, in the wake of a failed marriage, she had to reinvent herself.

It is easy to understand a young woman's willful blindness as she fell in love for the first time. Now, a widow and a mother at twenty-nine, Clark had to negotiate the unforeseen consequences of listening to her heart instead of to the counsel of others. Adopting the attitudes and values of black Charleston's elite, particularly with regard to status, Victoria Poinsette had attempted to place her children on an upwardly mobile social path. Wedding Nerie Clark, Septima Poinsette had not only rebelled against her mother but had also rejected her community's standards for making a good match and the politics of respectability embraced by Charleston's civic-minded black women.

The isolation born of her marriage ultimately reinforced Clark's sense of belonging to a larger community. Yet her marriage was more than a tragic detour along her path to becoming an activist. Instead, the internal oppression that defined her most intimate relationship with a man yielded a more firm conviction in the value of her opinions and the importance of voicing them in public.[88] Painful private silences helped Septima Clark learn to speak.

CHAPTER FOUR

Political Training Grounds

Septima Clark noticed several improvements at the Promise Land School on Johns Island when she returned to teach there in the fall of 1927. Someone had begun mowing the grass around the school yard, and new outdoor privies stood nearby. Creosote-painted wood covered once gaping holes on the outside of the school building, which helped a newer stove more evenly heat the inside. The district trustees had even started supplying firewood. Better yet, the county had retained teaching and health supervisors to visit the island schools. On the downside, too many children still crowded into the classroom, and Clark and another teacher still struggled to classify students of all ages with different amounts of learning into some semblance of grade groups. But anyone unfamiliar with conditions at Promise Land ten years earlier might have missed the significance of such small enhancements, whereas Clark recognized that "in the mid-twenties on Johns Island they represented a distinct advancement."[1]

Living on Johns Island, however, presented unanticipated difficulties for a widowed mother with a young child. The house where they boarded was drafty, and ever-present swarms of mosquitoes reminded Clark of the vulnerability of Nerie Jr.'s health. "We hadn't been on the island long," she noted, "before he went down with a siege of whooping cough and the measles." Clark confronted a difficult decision. She wanted her son "to grow up under my own care and guidance," but she had to protect him. Sending Nerie to live on Henrietta Street would have meant seeing him more often, but Victoria Poinsette had already taken in one grandson after her daughter

Ruby's death. Clark's in-laws in Hickory had more room and more economic stability, so Nerie went to live with them. Septima Clark described being separated from her son as "a real heartache."[2] She saw him in the summertime, except for the weeks she worked or attended summer training sessions.

In 1929, Clark enrolled in a program for African American teachers in Columbia, the state capital. Cornell A. (C. A.) Johnson, principal of Booker T. Washington School, the best black public school in South Carolina, serving students in grades one through eleven, taught her class. Clark's work impressed him so much that he asked if she would be interested in relocating to Columbia. This was no small offer. According to one Booker T. Washington faculty member, not just anyone taught in the capital city. "You could have been the smartest person at your school . . . but that alone did not get you a job in Columbia, South Carolina. Sometimes it took that and a lot of pull. And of course they were always trying to find the best person they could."[3] Clark's commitment to the people of Johns Island gave her pause, but the prestige of teaching in Columbia and a higher salary boded well for her future. Greater financial security could even mean reuniting with her son. She applied for a job and began teaching the third grade at Booker T. that fall. Years later, Clark recognized the momentousness of this decision. "I have often wondered what my life would have been like had I elected to stay on Johns Island," she reflected. "It might have run a smoother course, I suspect. But I suspect also that I wouldn't have been able to accomplish as many of the things I have always wanted to do, or come so close to the goals I set myself in my early years."[4]

Septima Poinsette Clark was thirty-one years old when she relocated to Columbia. Aside from the personal and professional benefits, the move enabled her to become part of a larger network of black Carolinians involved in a multifaceted challenge to Jim Crow. Clark asserted that her Columbia years "strengthened my determination to make my own life count in the fight to aid the underprivileged" and "gave me excellent training in procedures that could be used effectively in the struggle."[5] The Depression contributed to a decline in membership in state chapters of the National Association for the Advancement of Colored People (NAACP) and its political inertia. Yet this also guaranteed that at least some of Clark's procedural training occurred in alternative organizations, most notably the Palmetto State Teachers' Association and the South Carolina Federation of Colored Women's Clubs. Teaching adult literacy classes for educational reformer Wil Lou Gray, moreover, provided Clark with valuable pedagogical experience and practical insights. For Septima Clark, Columbia during the interwar years proved the right time and place to rejoin the African American freedom struggle.

A superficial glance at black Carolinians' actions during the 1930s might seem to indicate that they failed to mount a large-scale frontal attack on racial injustice and instead settled for "token protests," characterized by humble supplications to white officials.[6] Such a view obscures the full range of southern African Americans' political actions and how much was at stake. Taking a more optimistic approach, we might characterize this as a time when many of the people who played decisive roles during the 1950s and 1960s began sowing seeds that later bore fruit. Clark located herself among this generation of activists. Other larger structural changes that prepared the ground for the civil rights revolution included African American migration out of the South, New Deal intervention and material relief, and the historic shift of the northern black electorate to the Democratic Party in 1936 and the consequent intraparty realignments.[7]

Closer attention to the pressure black southern activists brought to bear on the segregated system demonstrates how they forced a powerful but imperfect white supremacy to adjust.[8] The leaders of Clark's educational world pursued long-term goals that sought to make southern black schools equal rather than subordinate to white educational institutions. Doing so required particular strategies at the state level, but help also came from beyond South Carolina's borders. By the early 1930s, regional and national educational bodies — those that oversaw accreditation and adult education, for example — had begun to include African Americans on their agenda. This trend emanated from Washington as well in the form of an unprecedented degree of federal attention to black education, which broadened conversations about teaching citizenship.

Citizenship itself assumed new resonance in the 1930s as a consequence of the crushing weight of the Depression, fears of the rising influence of the Communist Party, and emerging domestic and international fascist threats. Education for young and old alike certainly offered one method for inoculating citizens against these dangers and reinscribing faith in the American democratic ideal. Yet the paradox of circumscribing pedagogy to fit within a Jim Crow context could not be ignored and ultimately necessitated the articulation of both local and national forms of citizenship participation. Equally relevant, an economic crisis that undermined the traditional links between individual self-sufficiency and a citizen's status forced educational theorists to reexamine the relationship between individual and community well-being. These theorists then advised educators to strengthen both. Southern black teachers who did so tapped into an indigenous black political tradition that had long conceptualized citizenship as grounded in communal autonomy.[9]

Clark's interwar activism expressed itself in woman-centered professional and civic organizations whose collective impact proved potent fertilizer for some of the most important germinations of the period. Together, teachers and clubwomen continued to fortify a social service infrastructure in response to both the opportunities occasioned by Franklin Delano Roosevelt's New Deal and the limitations imposed by white state indifference and/or hostility. Clark gained access to this network of women for the first time in the 1930s, and they significantly shaped her vision of leadership. In distinctly nonelectoral milieus, she also acquired political lessons that sharpened her understanding of how educational outreach informed successful community organizing. More broadly, black women's strategies for securing citizenship served as a critical foundation for the next phase of the freedom struggle, inaugurated by World War II. Illuminating the interdependence of their organizational culture and their educational practices allows us to see the world as Septima Clark and her colleagues saw it.

꒰ঌ⋆৲꒱

Septima Clark picked a propitious moment to move. King Cotton had been seriously ailing since the end of World War I, as falling demand resulted in overproduction and plummeting prices. Land values and wages followed accordingly. Cotton pickers who earned ninety-five cents per hundred pounds in 1924 collected only fifty-two cents for the same amount in 1930. In a state whose economy depended on agriculture, bad news for the farmers meant bad news for everyone else, including the bankers who provided loans and the merchants who provided annual supplies on credit. Nearly half of the state's banks closed in the 1920s.[10]

As the state capital, a commercial hub, and an educational center, Columbia weathered the decade's economic downturns relatively well. In addition to state government, the city's industrial economy revolved around textiles, railroads, lumber, and publishing. In the first two years of the Great Depression, each industry experienced setbacks, but they occurred in waves rather than simultaneously, thereby preventing massive unemployment. Yet if the city offered better options than starving to death on a farm, the Depression's storm hit with full force during the last year of Herbert Hoover's presidency. By 1932, Clark's third year of teaching in Columbia, city and University of

South Carolina employees were paid in scrip rather than money, and more than twelve thousand local residents and an influx of drifters crowded the streets looking for work. Local relief remained overburdened, and federal assistance had yet to arrive.[11]

Racial prejudice, political disfranchisement, legal discrimination, and limited access to employment guaranteed that most African Americans in Columbia, where they comprised nearly 40 percent of the population in 1930, were worse off than their white counterparts. The majority worked as manual laborers and as domestics. Only 2.3 percent of white Columbians could not read, but 22.2 percent of the black adult population was illiterate.[12] Nevertheless, the city was one of the state's two urban centers where significant opportunity existed for African Americans.

By the late 1920s, a small professional class of black men and women had carved a comfortable niche for itself in the state capital. Septima Clark first settled among the working class on Blossom Street, near the University of South Carolina and a mere two-block walk from Booker T. Washington. She boarded with the Hoover family, which owned a grocery next door. After a few years, she relocated to the northeast Waverly neighborhood. African Americans who lived there were materially better off than most blacks and more than a few whites, which influenced their attitude toward others. According to one black Columbian, "Waverly was considered by the Waverly people as being superior."[13] For Clark, however, a Waverly address signaled her new sense of belonging in the world of black professionals. Many residents worked nearby at Benedict College and Allen University, two private schools affiliated with the Baptist and African Methodist Episcopal Churches, respectively, or at Good Samaritan or Waverly Sanatorium, two small hospitals that treated African Americans. Septima Clark's neighbors included professors, schoolteachers, ministers, doctors, bankers, and insurance salesmen.

Ten blocks due west of Waverly lay the heart of the city's black business district, known to black residents in the early days as Little Harlem and during World War II as Congo Square. Little Harlem reflected the community's vitality. More than a few black Columbians visited Richard S. Roberts's photography studio at 1119 Washington Street to sit for portraits. Those who wanted to publicize community events could stop in at the offices of the African American weekly newspaper, the *Palmetto Leader*, which occupied the same lot. Across the street, they might have grabbed lunch at the Baltimore Café. Those who had paychecks to deposit or who needed loans only ventured a few doors down to the black-owned Victory Savings Bank. Members of the Knights of Pythias met around the corner from Roberts's studio. Women who volunteered at the Phillis Wheatley YWCA or patrons seeking a book from the branch library established there in 1930 walked one block south and took a right. Everything else black Columbians needed could be found at the offices of physicians and dentists, funeral homes, bakeries, barbershops, and beauty parlors clustered within a five block radius.[14]

Many activists who played a critical role in the interwar freedom struggle passed through this area daily. The residential and professional proximity of community leaders afforded them the chance to speak often and informally about significant developments, to arrange meetings, or to invite each other to supper. It also guaranteed that people encountered one another outside of the churches or schools that formed the foundation of their communal alliances. Annual medical, educational, and religious conferences made the capital city a nexus where black Carolinians exchanged news. Following a 1930 visit, *Pittsburgh Courier* journalist George S. Schuyler affirmed the unique opportunities that such a lively community offered local residents: "Here also one finds what is all too rare in the South and the North, a considerable circle of Negroes who can read and think and are vitally interested in the play of ideals and the consideration of social, economic, educational, and political questions."[15] In this, Columbia did not differ greatly from Charleston.

In terms of who could participate in those discussions, Clark soon realized that Columbia seemed refreshingly democratic in comparison to tradition-bound Charleston, where inclusion or exclusion from certain social and activist circles depended on familial and marital status. In Columbia, "no one knew or cared that my father had been born a slave or that my mother had done laundry to help provide a living for her family," Clark observed. Nor did they know anything about the details of her marriage. "In Columbia, everyone mixed, and the schoolteacher was considered rather high up on the social ladder," she recalled; "the doctor's wife and the schoolteacher and the woman working as a domestic sat down together at the bridge table." Such social integration across class lines would have been impossible in Charleston. "When the Negro doctors in Columbia had their meetings," she continued, "they would invite not only their wives and their more elite friends to social functions but also all of their patients. They left out no one."[16] Clark welcomed the feeling of inclusion and consequently found the confidence to participate in a broad range of organizations.

Black Carolinians in the state capital took a keen interest in politics and like their counterparts across the nation warily eyed the 1932 presidential election. A northern Democrat with national ambitions, Franklin Delano Roosevelt had always abided by the unspoken agreement to leave the white South to handle its own affairs. The candidate said nothing about African Americans during the campaign as he courted the backing of white southerners. He also let local white supporters offer their own interpretations of what his election might mean. At one Camden, South Carolina, rally for FDR, a group of "Red Shirt marchers and Red Shirt orators" likened 1932 to 1876. African Americans worried that a Roosevelt victory would strengthen the hand of southern Democrats in the nation's capital and compared his election to Woodrow Wilson's 1912 ascendancy. Though alienated by Herbert Hoover's attempt to appeal to white southerners by refashioning the GOP as a party for white men, 77 percent of African American voters across the nation cast their ballot for the incumbent in 1932.[17]

White southern Democrats rejoiced when Roosevelt prevailed. Ordinarily staunch supporters of a minimal federal presence in state affairs, they responded favorably to the flurry of legislation the new president presented to Congress in his first hundred days despite the fact that it strengthened the federal government's power to stimulate economic recovery. How the New Deal would play out in a region whose economic health depended on a poorly paid, racially segregated, and nonunion labor force remained to be seen, but seniority in Congress and control of key legislative committees meant that southern politicos panicked little. They wielded their influence to keep the power to distribute agricultural relief in white hands, benefiting planters at the expense of their black tenants and sharecroppers. African Americans in urban areas encountered discrimination securing jobs on federal works projects as well. Corrie Wingard of Columbia described what happened to her brother. When the "woman what went to his house saw he had nice bedroom and livin' room suits," she "told him he didn't need no work 'cause he had nice furniture. I reckon she allowed they could eat that."[18]

Southern congressional veto power over all proposed legislation reined in the president throughout the first phase of the New Deal, which lasted until 1935. Had Roosevelt been inclined to extend relief to African Americans on near-equal terms or to champion racial justice issues, he could not have acted. As he informed the NAACP's executive secretary, Walter White, in the mid-1930s, in reference to proposed anti-lynching legislation: "I did not choose the tools with which I must work. Had I been permitted to choose them I would have selected quite different ones. But I've got to get legislation passed by Congress to save America." FDR knew that if he spent political capital endorsing the antilynching bill, conservative southerners "will block every bill I ask Congress to pass to keep America from collapsing." Ongoing discrimination in federal work projects and public housing programs, as well as the climbing number of unemployed African Americans on the relief rolls, prompted some black critics to dub FDR's social and economic vision the Raw Deal.[19]

Even so, Roosevelt's administration went further than any of its predecessors in acknowledging issues that concerned black America. In his effort to find solutions to the national emergency, FDR cast a wide net. Those who went to Washington, D.C., included a group of liberal white southerners linked by the shared recognition of the South as a critical battleground for the New Deal and sensitive to the centrality of race as a determining factor in shaping its success or failure. Black advisers also accrued increasing numbers of positions in the federal bureaucracy, bringing their expertise on the social and economic problems of African Americans to bear within the governmental departments where they worked.[20] Yet because it nurtured a new mind-set among ordinary Americans of both races, the New Deal amounted to more than a collection of experimental programs and a symbolic politics of inclusion. It changed the way the average southerner, including Septima Clark, thought about government and citizenship and how they responded as political actors.

Clark had landed a plum job at Booker T. Washington. The *Palmetto Leader* credited Principal C. A. Johnson with making the school "one of the best in the southeast," with a "substantial and modern plant." However, a 1931 survey of the black public schools in Richland County's District 1 exposed the real inequalities that plagued this educational oasis. That year, Columbia spent just over one million dollars educating white students and just under one hundred thousand on its black pupils. Overcrowded classrooms in all but one of the elementary schools made teaching more difficult and posed serious health risks. Booker T. Washington had no electric lights, "fairly sanitary" toilets in the basement, and one microscope for 170 biology students. Black teachers earned significantly less than their white counterparts, even those with fewer credentials.[21]

According to Johnson's daughter, Maude J. Robinson, the school "had wonderful teachers," and they made up for the less than ideal physical conditions. In an era when the State Board of Education approved history textbooks that championed the Lost Cause, Columbia's African American teachers labored to convey a more accurate portrait of the state's past. Celia Dial Saxon, the history and civics teacher at Booker T. Washington, had briefly attended the University of South Carolina during Reconstruction and taught in the system for more than fifty years until the day of her death in 1935. Robinson recalled that Saxon "gave us wonderful instruction, including African American history. We were not deprived there of learning about our history and our background."[22] Black faculty also endeavored to make students feel they had a stake in learning. "The teachers made you do. You were capable so you went ahead and did it," another Booker T. Washington alumna affirmed.[23] Posting the names of honor roll students on the walls reinforced their sense of accomplishment. Administrators took the time to walk the halls and to speak with students, inquiring about their day and their needs.

Clark would have easily recognized that her colleagues in this urban public school district embraced the same educational culture as rural teachers in the segregated South. As on Johns Island, urban educators prioritized the establishment of relationships with parents. Fannie Phelps Adams, a teacher who spent much of her career at Booker T. Washington, confirmed, "You had to know the parents, and the only way you could know them was to visit. We were expected to visit the homes of the children so that you would know the family conditions and know from whence the children had come." As Clark already knew, the bridge teachers built between the home and the school earned parental trust. Trust fostered parental support, and support in turn facilitated teachers' success in the classroom. "Parents respected us," Adams continued. "You had better opportunity to do with children what needed to be done." Such connections also improved fund-raising, which was necessary for athletics and other school programs. In addition, according to Adams, "every teacher was expected to sponsor an activity club of some sort."[24]

The biggest difference between urban and rural public schools was the level of administrative supervision, as Clark immediately noticed: "From the beginning, teaching in Columbia opened my eyes. In the first years there, at any rate, I'm sure I learned more than I taught." Johnson held two types of weekly faculty meetings. During "building" meetings, "he would discuss the routine things that necessarily were done for the advancement of the school." At "professional" meetings, "the teachers would work on problems of teaching," mainly pedagogical planning and methodology. Many of Clark's colleagues "grumbled" about staying after school two days a week, sometimes for three hours, after a long day's work, but she felt that the meetings were beneficial and "really prepared me for the teacher's examination I had to take later on."[25]

At the end of Clark's first year in Columbia, the school board appointed Johnson as the city's first supervisor of Negro schools. The *Palmetto Leader* predicted that Johnson "will do for the city schools what he has done for 'Booker T.,'" accomplishments that included earning a class "A" rating from the State Board of Education. The promotion reflected Johnson's skill as an ambassador to white school officials even as it introduced him to a new level of responsibility by making him directly accountable to white superintendent Abram Cline Flora. Because he ran a tight ship, Johnson had tremendous leeway to make his own decisions. "C. A. Johnson saw to it that his schools did what they were supposed to do," Adams remembered. As long as the work was getting done, white supervision did not pose a threat. "I don't think they cared," she concluded, but "we had conferences and everything that were overseen by the very top structure."[26]

Clark's new colleagues had impressive credentials, and Columbia's African American educators took advantage of opportunities for professional development. All of the black elementary teachers in Richland County District 1, including Clark, held first-grade certificates, which required two years of normal or college training; all of the city's black high school teachers had college degrees or "at least four years of training after high school."[27] Since entering the profession, Clark had looked for ways to strengthen her credentials by attending summer school sessions. Working in the state capital led her to consider options outside of the South. Johnson had earned his master's degree at Columbia University in New York, thereby establishing precedents — from the idea itself to concrete recommendations for course work — for the many members of his faculty who followed. The summer after her first year at Booker T., Clark headed to Columbia University, where she studied curriculum building and adult education.[28]

Living near Benedict College allowed Clark to act on her desire for enhanced professional training during the school year as well. Along these lines, she asserted, "the biggest thing I did in Columbia was to go to school and get my bachelor's degree." Clark took classes at Benedict in the mornings or evenings, depending on her teaching schedule. Overcrowding in the city's elementary schools helped her realize this goal. "Segregation caused us to have double sessions," she recalled, "so I taught from twelve o'clock in the day till five in the afternoon. In the mornings I could take two or three classes . . . and at night I could take two or three more."[29]

Personal trials delayed Clark's graduation from Benedict until 1942, however. In the mid-1930s, she transferred to Saxon Elementary School, moved out of the Waverly neighborhood, and began boarding with Jennie M. Willis closer to downtown. In 1936, she took a job at Howard Elementary School, followed Willis back to Waverly, and sent for Nerie Jr., now eleven and a half,

Nerie David Clark Jr., early 1930s. Courtesy of the
Avery Research Center for African American
History and Culture, College of Charleston.

and enrolled him in seventh grade. She imagined that she and her son would be together until he graduated from high school and went on to college to undertake "training for one of the professions."[30] She wanted her son to be more like her than his father.

Boarding with a boy on the verge of adolescence presented difficulties that Clark had not anticipated. First, Nerie had an insatiable appetite. The "dainty salads and dry cereals" that Willis served "were simply not for him." Willis had two growing children of her own to feed as well as several other boarders, also teachers, and Clark remained sensitive to the hardship her landlady faced. "I remember how embarrassed I was at Nerie's eating," she recalled, even though she tried to dull his hunger with between-meal snacks. Another problem soon surfaced. Nerie did not exactly step lightly, and his shoes "made marks on [Willis's] polished floors and she was fearful of her furniture." When Willis gave Nerie "a special chair to sit in which would stand his heavy pounding," Clark decided it was time to relocate. "I moved three times that year," she observed. "I'll never forget how I tried so hard at each of our boarding places to supplement his meals by buying him pickled pigs' feet, ham, bologna, onions, cheese and crackers, and bread with which I fixed sandwiches before or after regular meals."[31]

Clark also had trouble keeping her son outfitted. By the time he turned twelve, Nerie wore a size sixteen suit. He criticized the clothes his mother bought him at department stores, informing her that the "sleeves are too short and the pants won't hold the crease." In such moments, long-buried memories returned, and Clark "would think how much he was like his father."[32] It must have been difficult for her to live suspended between the heartache of separation and feelings of maternal inadequacy. Still, these had to be balanced with practicality and the necessity of making decisions that would best benefit her son. At the end of the school year, Nerie Jr. returned to Hickory to live with his grandparents. Clark returned to teaching at Saxon and moved in with Susie Lane Bailey, a friend of her younger sister, Lorene Poinsette.[33]

Freed of the daily responsibilities of motherhood, Clark resumed her pursuit of professional betterment. Her efforts dovetailed with those of her colleagues throughout the South in the 1930s. A mere 15.6 percent of black teachers in the thirteen southern states held bachelor's degrees in 1930; a decade later, 35.1 percent of them had obtained such qualifications. In rural areas, where the majority of black women taught in one-teacher schools, teacher preparation improved even more dramatically: the number of teachers who had six years or more of training beyond elementary school more

Lorene Poinsette, late 1920s–early 1930s.
Courtesy of the Avery Research Center for
African American History and Culture,
College of Charleston.

than doubled between 1930 and 1935.[34] Whether they traveled out of state
or enrolled in local summer training sessions, southern black teachers took
the initiative because they linked their professional development to the possibility of raising their salaries and because the leaders of their educational
world argued that improving schooling for black southerners — on which the
progress of the race rested — depended on well-trained teachers.

Significantly, those leaders who sought to advance professional opportunity for African American teachers without offending southern white sensibilities routinely emphasized teachers' shortcomings more than they touted
their successes. Indeed, most characterizations of black teachers stereotyped
them as unprepared or underqualified. A predominantly male cohort propagated this message far and wide, perhaps nowhere with more urgency or
impact than in the segregated teachers' associations they oversaw. Every
teacher at Clark's new school, for example, belonged to the Palmetto State
Teachers' Association (PSTA), which likely influenced her decision to join
the group.[35]

Retaining black control of black education formed the core of the PSTA's mission. The state's leading black educators—Thomas Ezekiel Miller and his successor as president of South Carolina State, Robert Shaw Wilkinson, among them—established the organization in 1900 in response to a move by white officials to curtail black oversight of summer teacher training sessions. The PSTA grew slowly at first, hampered by the incremental expansion of state-funded public schools for African Americans. Representatives from a few counties usually met in correlation with South Carolina State's summer programs until 1918, when members wrote the group's first formal constitution and began organizing and recruiting at the county level. Given the racial militancy of the post–World War I years, perhaps it was no coincidence the PSTA's membership and convention attendance quintupled in 1919.[36]

As the 1920s began, PSTA officials fortified the program that would define their leadership and their activism for the next thirty years. Their primary objective was to make South Carolina's separate education equal—particularly in terms of school funding and facilities, teacher preparation and pay, and term length—without sacrificing black educators' right to manage black schools. The PSTA first sought to gain recognition as the voice of the state's black educators. The association's executive committee began collecting data on African American schools with the hope of being "in a position to furnish the County Superintendents and State Department of Education any information desired."[37] PSTA leaders recognized that white indifference to poor conditions in black schools, coupled with white anxiety if those schools showed too much improvement, mandated that the organization develop institutional mechanisms for measuring progress.

The PSTA's male leaders fully understood the political stakes of their advocacy, though they would never have publicly described themselves as political activists. Instead, they always tailored their public statements for a white audience. In a 1931 report, for example, C. A. Johnson, serving not only as supervisor of Negro schools but also as PSTA president, wrote, "Negro leaders and white people interested in Negro education frequently come to see our schools. They seem to be especially interested in our vocational program which we regard as a mere beginning of what we hope to do." The astute Johnson knew that the South's best white people had long championed the spread of industrial schools and vocational training for African Americans. He then added humility to his remarks, acknowledging that "those of us who are in the work are not unaware of our weaknesses and shortcomings."[38]

Johnson concluded by providing a detailed outline of the steps needed to make Columbia's black schools academically equal to its white schools in terms of classroom instruction, curriculum, and testing.

C. A. Johnson undoubtedly believed in the importance of vocational education. As Fannie Phelps Adams remembered, at Booker T. Washington, "we had not only the academic courses, which proved outstanding, we also had the trades." Offerings included Latin, literature, and geometry as well as vocational, domestic, and manual arts. As Booker T.'s principal, Johnson had helped secure college scholarships for his students, but he also knew that some students were not academically inclined and that black teachers—not white school boards or well-meaning white allies—were best positioned to evaluate pupils' strengths and weaknesses and steer students onto academic or vocational tracks accordingly. Protecting that autonomy mattered most. Moreover, Johnson understood that a strong vocational program would enhance job opportunities for African Americans. His endorsement of comprehensive vocational education assuaged whites and paved the way for better funding.[39] More important, vocational training would put money in black people's pockets and food on their tables. As one of Columbia's leading black activists, Modjeska Simkins, commented, "You couldn't think about improving a person's mind when he had an empty belly."[40]

PSTA leaders pursued curricular improvements and strengthening faculty credentials as part of their larger goal of gaining accreditation for African American schools. Within a separate and unequal system, accreditation conferred a legitimacy that everyone could recognize as progress.[41] Most enlightened white people held that black schools could not possibly meet the standards expected of white ones, since the white state's purposeful lack of funding guaranteed that black school buildings and equipment would remain inferior. Still, African American educational leaders argued against establishing a double standard. "We ask that we be rated by the same standards used in rating the white schools," Johnson informed the South Carolina high school inspector in the late 1920s, before regional accreditation of black high schools by the Southern Association of Colleges and Secondary Schools began in 1931. The Southern Association ceded the point. Black educational leaders reasoned that a different accreditation scale increased the stigma of inferiority in black schools because it legitimated lower funding and sanctioned substandard training for black teachers. If the uniform standards initially slowed the increase in the number of qualifying black institutions, accreditation on equal terms meant more equal schools in the future.

In 1933, Booker T. Washington became the only black public high school in South Carolina to earn regional accreditation, an honor it shared with three private schools.[42]

By the time Septima Clark joined the PSTA in the early 1930s, its leaders oversaw one of the state's most influential African American professional groups. Membership had increased by a factor of seven during the 1920s, and it would double again over the next decade. In thirty-eight counties, 100 percent of teachers joined. Primary, elementary, high school, vocational, and college instructors added their names to the organization's roster because they appreciated its accomplishments on their behalf. By 1937, the extra training promoted by the association had paid off: 75 percent of the state's black teaching corps qualified for first-grade certificates and consequently earned higher salaries—though still far less than white teachers received.[43]

For thousands of black Carolinian teachers, including Clark, membership in the PSTA offered an introduction to the battle to equalize educational opportunity. "Those teachers who failed to participate" in the association, the *Palmetto Leader* commented, were "relegating themselves to the rear with double quick time." Particularly important were the county chapters' legal and legislative committees, which acted as watchdogs "to study proposed school legislation and conduct conferences on them; to plan a program of action; to facilitate their passage if we indorse them or to insure their deport if we do not . . . to propose legislation and work for [its] passage."[44] The few teachers who served on such committees attended to the business of politics and educated members on pertinent developments at a time when the Depression's devastating financial woes rendered the state's NAACP branches virtually defunct and when internal battles about whether to commit to a legalistic civil rights strategy or one that stressed economic justice hampered the national NAACP's efficacy.[45]

The PSTA both kept one eye on progress within the state and raised rank-and-file teacher awareness of national developments. In 1934, secretary of the interior Harold L. Ickes called the National Conference on Fundamental Problems in the Education of Negroes, which featured First Lady Eleanor Roosevelt as a speaker. In its official organ, the *Teachers' Bulletin*, the PSTA informed members of resolutions made at the Washington, D.C., conference that pertained to "ultimate educational objectives and ideals," including "equal economic opportunity, and political and social justice for all."[46] No PSTA official would have jeopardized his standing with the state's white educational establishment, many of whom participated in the association's annual conferences, by uttering the words "political" and "justice" in the same sentence. Instead, the PSTA let a federal voice do so. Teachers who read the bulletin got the message.

Becoming a member of the PSTA allowed Septima Clark to stay abreast of current trends in conceptualizing and teaching citizenship in the segregated South. Aware of the limitations black southerners confronted, the Committee on Citizenship at the National Conference made several recommendations. It urged "the shifting of emphases upon objectives in education according to the community needs and the application of this principle to the problems of citizenship training." This reaffirmed in theory what African American teachers at the grassroots already knew from practice: teaching citizenship began with local communities' desires. "Citizenship education must embrace citizenship in all its ramifications," the committee advised, clarifying that voting and officeholding alone did not define "good citizenship."[47] In other words, black educators bore responsibility for *expanding* definitions of citizenship for a population disfranchised in the present and most likely the foreseeable future.

To do so, these national experts suggested that southern black teachers create "school activities which will bring the child into immediate relationship and knowledge of governmental functions," especially by providing practical instruction in the duties of various state and local officials as well as tax collecting and public spending. They also recommended that the "Negro child, as a member of a minority group, should have special training in how to judge worthy leadership."[48] Simply put, southern black teachers should demystify political processes for their students — and by extension their parents — and provide them with the critical thinking skills to evaluate government officials. The committee left unstated what such citizenship training could mean, particularly if black southerners ever gained the right to vote. In fact, a six-year-old black child in South Carolina who started the first grade in 1934 would not have been old enough to vote in 1948, when a federal court decision finally opened the state's Democratic primary to African Americans.

In 1935, the PSTA adopted "Training for Character and Citizenship" as the theme for its annual convention and invited Ambrose Calivar, the first African American specialist to join the U.S. Office of Education and director of the 1934 conference, to give the keynote speech. Attending the sessions for elementary school teachers, Clark heard discussions that "emphasized the function of the school in relation to the child" and the school's role in determining "the most pertinent needs of the community and how these needs can be met."[49] The parts played by teachers, the school, and the home in fostering "good citizenship" took on new meaning amid the appeal of more radical solutions to the economic and social problems unleashed by the Depression. These might be led by fascists in nearby Atlanta or by antifascist liberals and communists united under the umbrella of the Popular Front. Either way, the presence of such groups explains the PSTA's assertion that "influences from without are at work in our country, trying to poison the minds of many people against our government" as well as the PSTA's emphasis on teachers' duty to inculcate respect for the law.[50] Regardless of how they actually viewed the latent impact of more radical groups, PSTA leaders publicly appeared to respect Jim Crow's local boundaries. At the same time, they demonstrated their loyalty to a national government they hoped would intervene more definitively.

Power within the PSTA had always been concentrated in the hands of a few, mostly men, who filled prestigious administrative positions in South Carolina's black public schools and private colleges. Through hard work, association leaders had earned a reputation among white educational officials as being "earnest and enthusiastic men, who are able to get their people to see the advantages of co-operating with the public school authorities toward the uplift of the race."[51] The majority of the PSTA's rank-and-file members, however, were women, who comprised 80 percent of the state's black teaching force by 1932 and who mostly worked in rural schools. Black women's commitment to their students and their communities did not waiver during the leanest years of the national emergency. "Teachers have been called upon to work without immediate pay," one white South Carolina official observed, and "have gladly done this in practically every case and hardly any teacher has refused to continue work on this account."[52]

Membership in the PSTA inspired Septima Clark. She appreciated hearing "excellent speakers" at the association's annual meetings, but "perhaps more important than the addresses we heard . . . was the mere coming together of this large and potentially influential group." Participation in the PSTA allowed her and other members to witness the power of collective self-respect, which sustained them in their labors. More practically, it gave black women teachers new ideas for tackling old problems by providing a forum for venting frustrations to sympathetic listeners and then culling advice from the wisdom of shared experience. From each other and from the educational organizers among them, black women teachers learned how to implement practical strategies for change, whether in the classroom, the community, or the state legislature. Attending PSTA conventions, Clark realized, "we teachers had a visible demonstration of our importance, of what we *already* were; it didn't take much imagination to visualize what we might be in the life of our state."[53]

A broader perspective informed her sense of the impact these women might make. Surveying her PSTA colleagues, Clark saw many women who, like herself, devoted their spare time to civic organizing. Indeed, more important to Clark "than the teacher-training programs and even the teaching itself, as far as my own development was concerned . . . were the opportunities I had in Columbia to participate in civic activities."[54] Southern black women educators hardly limited their activism to the school or the PSTA. Rather, they integrated it into the expansive organizational culture forged by clubwomen engaged in social welfare work. Septima Clark's vision of political possibility in the interwar years took into account the potential power of both teachers and clubwomen.

⋖⁕⋗

Marion Birnie Wilkinson, a native of Charleston married to the president of South Carolina State, and Booker T. Washington history teacher Celia Saxon were among the women who founded the South Carolina Federation of Colored Women (SCFCW) in a Columbia church in 1909 and affiliated with the National Association of Colored Women soon thereafter. According to the SCFCW constitution, the group sought to "promote [the] education of colored women and to hold an educational convention annually"; "to work for the social, moral, economic, and religious welfare of women and children"; and "to secure and enforce civil and political rights for our group." Over the next few decades, women in a growing number of local clubs built an extensive network that reached into every city, town, and hamlet across South Carolina. The SCFCW divided the state into districts, each of which had a president who worked closely with department directors to implement programs at the local level. By 1929, departments included suffrage, temperance, health, home economics, and rural education.[55]

Simultaneous participation in several organizations reinforced these women's activist alliances and made the SCFCW one of the state's preeminent uplift vehicles. In addition to overseeing the construction of the first YWCA building on any black college campus, Wilkinson belonged to the state Interracial Commission and the executive committee of the Red Cross. Similarly, Columbia's black YWCA owed its existence to the vision and leadership of Saxon, who also served as treasurer of the PSTA for many years. Clubwoman Belle E. Vincent, president of the SCFCW's Orangeburg District in

1931, figured prominently in the Columbia YWCA and in the city's NAACP chapter.[56] Moreover, clubwomen specifically targeted teachers in their recruiting efforts. Clark commented that at the start of every school year "the Federated Women of Columbia held a big teachers' party at which the new teachers were welcomed."[57] She, for one, jumped at the chance to become involved with a Columbia chapter of the SCFCW, particularly since participation had been denied to her in Charleston.

South Carolina's black clubwomen took singular pride in establishing the Fairwold Home for Delinquent Girls, just ten miles down the road from Columbia, in the post–World War I era. "I vividly recall the tramp, tramp, tramp thro the wooded areas of Cayce, South Carolina, hunting the present spot" of the home, clubwoman Etta B. Rowe reminisced. The work among young girls at Fairwold, renamed the Wilkinson Home for Underprivileged Orphans in 1931, especially appealed to Septima Clark. "The good that this institution has done over the years," she remarked in 1962, "is inestimable in my opinion."[58] The sense that they needed to give back what had been given to them represented the cornerstone of clubwomen's philosophy, and they considered their civic organizing educational work. As former teacher and Charlestonian clubwoman Mamie Garvin Fields observed, "The point was to have the next generation come up knowing how to organize themselves and take their rightful place in the community." Just like teachers who worked in underfunded and dilapidated schools, women of the SCFCW had to improvise useful strategies for answering community needs in the face of constant financial restraints. They also set modest practical goals. Amid the Depression, SCFCW leaders planned to have a poultry plant built and to purchase a "good milk cow" to help the Wilkinson Home become more self-sufficient.[59]

A shared commitment to helping younger black women compelled Columbia's teachers and clubwomen to unite in fund-raising efforts. At Thanksgiving, they held a turkey raffle; at Christmas, they sponsored a dance where everyone wore white. According to Clark, "This white dance was always held before the teachers left for the holidays," and "teachers were always at the head of any list of persons invited to such functions" because "they were considered the best economic group." In the spring, Federated Women staged dramatic productions to raise money, and "many of the teachers either acted in the plays or helped with the producing, staging, or ticket selling." In fact, a presentation of *Lady Windermere's Fan* put on by the women of Columbia's Sunlight Club and featuring "a special cast of local teachers" kicked off the PSTA's 1931 annual convention. Clark later credited these productions as beneficial to her organizational training because they incorporated role-playing and taught her how to deal with programs and audiences.[60]

Black women activists who aimed to improve health conditions for black Carolinians also turned to the state's teaching force and clubwomen to reach local communities. In 1931, Modjeska Simkins became a field worker for the South Carolina Tuberculosis Association, charged with the duty of raising health awareness through education. She approached teachers first, addressing them at state and county meetings and parent-teacher association gatherings. Next, Simkins organized a two-day institute in the summer teacher training sessions at South Carolina State. With funds from the Federal Emergency Relief Act, 20 unemployed teachers joined her in 1933; in that year alone, they visited 203 schools, reaching 1,266 teachers and 54,383 students. Simkins's success depended on tapping into preexisting networks.[61] Teachers who attended county PSTA meetings and summer sessions or who, as Septima Clark had on Johns Island in the 1910s, organized local parent-teacher groups buttressed that statewide infrastructure. As community liaisons and community leaders, teachers also played a pivotal role in getting the message to parents.

Evolving medical knowledge and the education programs of the South Carolina Department of Health certainly underlay the fact that "the incidence of parasitic, epidemic, and contagious diseases diminished notably" during the interwar years. Still, Jim Crow health care afforded white Carolinians greater treatment options at the state's public health facilities. Although more black Carolinians suffered from tuberculosis, the state sanitarium had more beds for white patients, and many African Americans died with their names on its waiting list. Black women conducted educational spadework in communities to promote health awareness and better health in general. In this case, progress meant prevention. Among black Carolinians, African American teachers and clubwomen helped contribute to a 53 percent decline in the tuberculosis death rate between the wars.[62]

Involvement in the SCFCW provided Clark with concrete methods for adapting the educational values she had gleaned as a rural teacher to urban civic activism, and vice versa. The degree to which being a clubwoman raised Clark's consciousness might best be reflected in the fact that although she lived and worked in an urban environment, she enrolled in a rural sociology course at Atlanta University in the summer of 1937. "Everybody" in her professional world at the time "was talking curriculum," Clark later explained. She shrewdly perceived that because the majority of black southerners lived in rural areas, urban teachers needed to assist in developing rural curricula.[63]

At the same time, the organizational practice of club work had underscored for Clark the imperative to create stronger social welfare programs and services that answered the needs of rural people.

After she arrived at Atlanta University, another course, Interpersonal Relationships of Human Beings, and its instructor, W. E. B. Du Bois, attracted Clark's attention. She could not pass up the chance to study with a man she recognized as "one of the greatest black intellectuals in the country." A young and socially unimportant Septima Poinsette would hardly have imagined meeting and talking with Du Bois when he had visited with the leaders of Charleston's NAACP chapter twenty years earlier. That a more mature and civically engaged Clark could sign up for his course provides better insight into just how much self-confidence she had accumulated since moving to Columbia.[64]

Riding in the back of a streetcar on the way to Du Bois's seminar one afternoon, Clark watched as a young black mother climbed aboard holding a baby in her arms and a two-year-old by the hand. "I'm Momma's little man," the toddler announced as he sat down in the front seat, "and I can sit up here." Clark remembered, "His mother was so nervous that she shook" as she admonished her son to move to the back. When Clark told her class what had happened, Du Bois responded, "There will come a time when this will be changed," particularly when black people registered and voted. Clark's classmates grew annoyed at her. "What she bring that up for? You know she just wants to start something," they gossiped. Clark interpreted their response as indicative of the different material conditions and their resultant mindsets that defined rural and urban living. Some of these students "hadn't been too long from the plantation, and some of them were still living on contract farms," she observed. "They thought I was a terribly controversial person, just stirring up trouble by talking."[65]

Clark drew a different lesson from Du Bois's pedagogy and her civic engagement. Teaching and club work had schooled her in a woman-centered approach to community leadership. "*Real leadership*," Etta B. Rowe asserted, "does not mean standing at the head of an organization—real leadership is that technique . . . that induces others to work and perform in a like manner."[66] Clark saw black women as bearing responsibility for helping their students and neighbors comprehend that they had to do something to bring change. Identifying problems in everyday life, analyzing them in a group, and then discussing possible solutions represented an important first step.

Hearing Mary McLeod Bethune—a native South Carolinian; founder and president of Bethune-Cookman College in Daytona, Florida; president of the

National Council of Negro Women; member of FDR's informal Black Cabinet; and personal friend of the First Lady — also stirred Clark. As head of the Division of Negro Affairs in the National Youth Administration, Bethune traveled more than forty thousand miles up and down the East Coast in 1937, lecturing audiences on how best to meet the problems confronting black students. Not surprisingly, Bethune exhorted African American educators simultaneously to embrace multiple strategies. To address local needs, they should direct group advocacy at state educational policymakers, but they should also familiarize themselves with the opportunities that accompanied New Deal relief. The flip side of becoming federal clients included recognizing federal shortcomings, such as Washington's failure to force southern states to distribute federal emergency grants equitably, and the right to pressure the federal government to do more. Bethune also advocated southern African Americans' reentry into formal politics, telling her listeners on one occasion, "You must as rapidly as possible qualify for and exercise the right of the ballot so that your voice is really heard."[67] Bethune's prominence reinforced Clark's sense of what was possible. Referring to her proximity to the nation's leaders, Clark recalled that Bethune "said, 'I'm a fly in that bowl of milk, but I'm certainly there.' And that gave me a real great feeling that a black woman that was that type could be sitting in Roosevelt's . . . [Black] cabinet."[68]

Clark soon decided that she, too, needed to make her presence felt by engaging with white people. African American clubwomen in the segregated South routinely cultivated relationships with white state officials and strategically joined forces with white women, even as they increasingly demanded that those allies recognize interracial work as a cooperative effort among equals. A women's health issue drew Clark to one interracial group headed by a white doctor. According to her, unmarried women who went to the hospital to give birth were routinely sterilized after delivering their third child. The doctor called together "blacks and whites" in discussions "at Benedict College, and he talked about what was happening in Columbia."[69] Clark had not attended interracial meetings prior to her arrival in Columbia, and she did not formally join any interracial groups while there. But she did begin working with a white woman for the first time.

～✿～

Teaching on Johns Island, Septima Clark had attempted to meet the adult community's desire to learn. Living in Columbia, amid constant refrains of professional betterment and a flurry of civic service, raised her awareness of the necessity of participating in a more systematic program of adult education. Perusing her March 1935 copy of the *Teachers' Bulletin*, for example, Clark would have read a recommendation from PSTA president H. H. Butler that "every teacher and every County unit will throw their full strength behind the efforts of Miss Wil Lou Gray in her campaign for stamping out adult illiteracy among our group." On March 25, Clark began teaching three men and eleven women in Gray's Richland County Adult School program.[70]

A white Progressive Era educational reformer, Wil Lou Gray helped to pioneer the field of adult education in South Carolina and then became its leading voice for most of the twentieth century. Born in Laurens County in 1883 to an upper-class family, Gray graduated from the state's Columbia College and began her teaching career in a rural one-room school. The frustration of that experience convinced her to pursue graduate study, first at Vanderbilt University and later at Columbia University, where she obtained a master's degree in political economy. Returning to South Carolina, Gray accepted a position as supervisor of rural schools in Laurens County, probably the best job available for an educated white woman aspiring to a professional career. In 1915, the General Assembly made its first appropriation for adult education, and Gray responded by inaugurating night classes for her Laurens County constituents. Appointed the state supervisor of adult education four years later, she headed the nation's first state-supported adult education program. By the 1930s, Gray oversaw schools for adults in every South Carolina county and had institutionalized the Opportunity School, a segregated summer program for both black and white Carolinians that she had originally created for white textile workers in 1921.[71]

Gray's Adult Schools had first flourished among women in South Carolina's mill villages, where students learned the three Rs in conjunction with "broader socialization in utilitarian values and religious piety." Such pedagogy reflected Gray's familiarity with Denmark's "folk school" movement, which blended religious beliefs and secular nationalism and aimed for cultural revival through cooperative living and problem solving. Many southern educational reformers, black and white, of Gray's generation saw the Danish folk schools as a useful model for addressing illiteracy and poverty.[72]

The Depression lent special urgency to the task. "The problem of adult elementary education in South Carolina," Gray declared in 1938, "is not only an educational one, but social and economic." If modern amenities had transformed daily life by instilling in people "a desire for better living," those who lacked the education to fulfill that desire became "liabilities to the State." Dependency ran counter to the ideal of a virtuous citizenry, while ignorance bred disease and crime. Gray advised her recruiting teachers to target people "who have good minds, are willing to work, and wish to be somebody." Classroom instruction focused on problems that students confronted in their daily lives, including the relationship between work habits and wages, health education and domestic science, and becoming "better informed" citizens. As one student affirmed, "You learn how to live not just exist."[73]

In many respects, the educational philosophy and organizing sensibility that defined Gray's career resembled the uplift efforts of Clark and other black teachers and clubwomen. As part of her early teacher training, Gray had been encouraged to get to know the adults whose children she taught by visiting their homes and participating in community activities. She taught recruiters for her Adult Schools to do likewise. In just two months during 1935, black and white organizers knocked on 117,940 doors and reported that 82 percent of the men and women with whom they talked indicated that they "would like to study." As a county supervisor, Gray had promoted professional development among her teachers by encouraging them to participate in county, state, and national teacher associations, aware that more members meant more lobbying power with state officials. Clark had realized this by attending the PSTA's annual conventions. And as a reformer interested in adult education, Gray frequently joined hands with white clubwomen.[74] Integrating African Americans into adult education programs, however, forced southern white women such as Gray to build relationships with black women and strengthened interracial endeavors.

Politicking with white men required a different approach. To expand her Adult Schools, Gray continually worked to persuade the reluctant South Carolina legislature that the state should spend money advancing the general welfare of its citizens. Some legislators viewed Gray as a nuisance: said one, "She was worse than chewing gum in your hair in her persistence for support for her work."[75] But Gray proved a savvy practitioner of both politics and public relations, particularly as she incorporated black Carolinians into her activities. Stepping carefully across the color line, Gray cited 1930 census figures that revealed that 26.9 percent of black Carolinians could not read and write, five times the rate for their white neighbors. She then appealed to white Carolinian pride by asserting that the entire state's "progress" was "seriously retarded because of this burden of illiteracy and ignorance." Still, the white community had benefited from nearly a decade of advancement before classes for African Americans began, and even then philanthropic contributions were needed. Black adults responded enthusiastically to the opportunity. In 1928, they had comprised 24 percent of Gray's total enrollment; by 1930, they accounted for more than two-thirds.[76]

Septima Clark understood from her own experience that neither the practice of nor the interest in adult education was new. As one race leader explained, "There has been adult education for Negroes in this country for three hundred years. Negro education began with adult education. . . . [W]e have always had it." By the time FDR took office, the broader purposes of educating adults had matured, both philosophically and pedagogically. Turning away from their earlier emphasis on Americanization classes for foreign immigrants, national leaders in the field instead looked to advances in sociology as they developed a methodology to equip people to improve their daily lives.[77] The most significant difference in the 1930s was federal sponsorship of adult education via the New Deal; in the southern context, national government involvement sparked new debates about teaching citizenship.

Both African American and white proponents of adult education attempted to avoid the ire of southern white people by defining citizenship in a variety of nonpolitical guises. Black sociologist Ira De A. Reid identified reviving American culture as a goal of educating the nation's citizens, noting that "when we say 'culture' we only mean the most perfect adaptation that an individual makes to his environment in order that he might live most successfully and happily." On the surface, such careful articulations appeared nonthreatening because the apparent end was to help black individuals achieve the greatest amount of personal satisfaction possible within segregation. Beneath the surface, however, no consensus existed about what exactly constituted living "most successfully and happily." Adult education to foster economic self-sufficiency, for example, implicitly challenged black southerners' economic dependence on white employers.[78]

Adult education designed to boost "the morale of both children and parents" and by extension "the entire community" appeared equally nonpolitical, but education for citizenship in this context accentuated citizen obligations with regard to community improvement.[79] It also complemented the political traditions and the political practices of black teachers and clubwomen. Given the high level of unemployment, instructing people to make wise use of their leisure time represented another preoccupation for adult educators in the New Deal era. As Clark recognized, teaching classes became an important expression of community service, while attending classes served as one of the most constructive ways men and women could spend their time. The adult education classroom functioned as a communal space in which students could see more clearly how their neighbors shared particular problems. Students also could begin to learn more about how to help themselves and about local and federal sources of assistance.

African American participation in Richland County's Adult Schools far exceeded white participation. Clark and eleven other black instructors taught 252 students, while five white teachers held classes for 89 white pupils. Whether because of economic circumstances or for practical and social reasons, sessions attracted more women than men — 181 black and 50 white women enrolled compared to 71 black and 39 white men. Classes for African Americans also had higher average attendance, perhaps because white Carolinians averaged slightly more initial schooling and thus fewer of them lacked literacy. Teaching these classes supplemented black teachers' salaries as well. Clark taught three evenings a week for nine weeks at Booker T. Washington and earned thirty-three dollars a month.[80]

In her classroom, Clark promoted economic and social citizenship and introduced her students to the basics of political citizenship. Her fourteen students ranged in age from seventeen to sixty-five, and the majority worked at a fourth-grade level. Two could not read or write at all; Clark taught them to sign their names, "fill out money orders," and read street signs, "simple directions," and the "name of occupation[s]." To the end of teaching them to use their "leisure time more profitably," she stimulated their "desire to read to gain information" in magazines, newspapers, and the Bible. Clark even highlighted several practical achievements that would help her students in their interactions with white people. Training in language skills meant "helpers in domestic work can converse better in answering [the] telephone," while lessons in arithmetic contributed to "problem solving." More important, with regard to improving "community ideals and attitudes," "health standards" had been "built up from Social Science," instruction and "worthy citizens" had been "developed from understanding the laws through language discussions." When asked what might be done to improve the work, Clark took a cue from C. A. Johnson. "Have group meetings for adult teachers twice a month to improve methods of presentation of the work," she suggested.[81]

Gray had a "big influence" on Clark. Practically, she gained a better understanding of the difficulties of adult education, which included "having enough patience" to work with people who could not read and write. Tutoring adults on Johns Island, she had pretty much relied on an improvisational curriculum. "If they wanted to make a speech, or if they wanted to read the

Bible, or if they wanted to read a newspaper," Clark recalled, "we worked with that." Gray's program introduced Clark to "much better" methods.[82]

Specifically, Gray relied on two distinct pedagogical techniques to teach adult learners. First, instructors gave pupils pieces of cardboard on which to trace their names until they learned how to write. "Night after night, night after night, they traced over their names," Clark observed. "In two weeks they could write their names without tracing." Second, to teach reading, Gray had compiled a booklet full of information on South Carolina, such as "population figures" or "the amount of acreage devoted to the different crops." Gray's reader reflected the era's central concern with developing curricula relevant to everyday life, but it had a more practical purpose as well. Teachers used it in lieu of traditional elementary primers that Gray recognized embarrassed grown men and women. "Even though they couldn't read and write," Clark commented, "she felt that she could do better than to teach them about Henry Penny and Chicken Little and Baby Ray." Gray's primer included pictures of the statehouse in Columbia, which Clark encouraged her adult students—like her elementary children on Johns Island—to use to "make stories." In all likelihood, she relied on the same pictures to help develop "worthy citizens" who understood "the laws through language discussions."[83]

Indeed, the citizenship component of Gray's pedagogy, tailored to inculcate respect for political and institutional authority, fed African American visions of political inclusion. Aware that offering people relief from monotonous routines held tremendous inspirational power, Gray had established an annual pilgrimage to the state capital as part of her citizenship training. Bringing students to the institutional center of state politics would demystify state government. Ideally, a firsthand glimpse of the people who attended to its business would enable adult learners to imagine themselves as engaged citizens in their own communities. Of course, some people might have found the experience intimidating. A good number of South Carolina's rural residents had never traveled to such a big city. The poverty that threatened to suffocate their lives meant that a pair of shoes was a pretty luxury, let alone a new dress or a suit. Reflecting on the trip, Adult School students admitted to having trouble sleeping the night before, described how it felt to see so many people in one place, and promised to remember the day for the rest of their lives.[84] The annual pilgrimage began as a white-only event, but by the mid-1930s, African Americans participated as well.

In April 1935, four thousand black pilgrims, dressed in their Sunday best, congregated in Columbia and spent a day doing many of the same things as their white counterparts who had visited a week earlier. After being welcomed personally by the state superintendent of education, James H. Hope, and Gray, the group toured the graves of white state fathers, including some who had enslaved their ancestors and disfranchised them. But just as whites students had, African Americans entered the State House to sign the register. Many black visitors undoubtedly read this demonstration of literacy as another step on the long road to full citizenship. Literacy requirements, after all, were among the first obstacles that had to be surmounted to register to vote. The visitors also attended a pageant, "Vanguards of Our Race," that offered them the opportunity to ruminate on the lessons of black history and black achievement. Clark devoted six extra teaching nights to prepare her students to participate in the pageant, yet another way of boosting the sense of community in her classroom and then extending it to benefit the community at large. Finally, black Carolinians gathered to hear guest speaker Dr. Channing H. Tobias, a black representative of the national YMCA. Seeing such a large group of black southerners assembled for a secular educational purpose impressed Tobias, who later remarked that he knew of "no record of a similar occasion anywhere."[85] The pilgrimage combined lessons in government with cultural pride that celebrated community achievement. Hearing nationally known speakers; learning about African American poets, musicians, and scientists; and signing the State House register meant returning pilgrims had interesting stories to tell their family and friends.

Septima Clark remembered Gray as racially progressive for the era: "I think when she came over to the place where we were . . . she had just as much of a good feeling about the blacks as she did about the whites, but they were segregated." When Gray invited Mary McLeod Bethune to speak in Columbia in 1938, a few of the city's black residents joined their white neighbors in the audience at the Washington Street Methodist Church.[86] Equally significant, Gray's concern for the plight of black Carolinians and her commitment to adult education led her to interracial meetings at which participants gave voice to the more radical implications of the work.

Attending the First Annual Conference on Adult Education and the Negro at Virginia's Hampton Institute in 1938, Gray heard Luther P. Jackson, a black professor at Virginia State College, address the matter most explicitly. "I want to narrow 'Adult Education for Civic Participation' to 'Adult Education for Governmental Participation,'" Jackson began. He proposed that teachers working with African Americans "include some features that would fit them to the need of some contacts with . . . government officers." Jackson offered three methods to help grown students gain a fuller understanding of their right to be heard as citizens. First, "the adult teacher could tell her adult students to vote, even in the Southland." Second, people "should petition the government for redress of their grievances." Finally, they should "use . . . letters and telegrams" to "bring about pressure on the government." Jackson concluded by insisting that teachers should teach by example by paying their poll taxes and registering to vote.[87]

Though Jackson went furthest out on the limb with his analysis, others lent their support. A panel discussing the "major objectives" of adult education for African Americans insisted that "literacy today requires more than reading and writing," including "the elementary understanding of political issues and parties in local and state contests." By contrast, Morse Cartwright, director of the American Adult Education Association, stressed the interdependence of the individual, family, community, state, and nation but observed that the goal of nurturing an enlightened body politic "involves no social action." The representative from the U.S. Commission on Education reminded everyone of the New Deal's boundaries when he commented that "the government feels it ought to give states a chance to work out their problems."[88]

Adult educators thus developed plans of action within the parameters of segregation. For example, the Committee on State Government and State Aid in Negro Education, on which Gray served, recommended that states lacking adult education programs begin by establishing such programs "with Negro directors for Negro clients and white directors for white clients." Gray and other white committee members placed a premium on progress, whatever the means, while their African American colleagues understood the importance of retaining black control of black education in all its manifestations. At a plenary session, Bethune echoed this sentiment, affirming that "Negroes will have to interpret Negroes and their needs."[89] At root, black educational leaders defended such autonomy with the expectation that black teachers replicate the emphasis on self-determination as they instructed students.

Wil Lou Gray was a realist, unwilling to jeopardize her political power. Yet her modest acts of racial goodwill, coupled with her support for an interventionist state, increasingly placed her at odds with South Carolina's political leaders. Gray approved of Governor Olin D. Johnston's prolabor stance and his educational reform legislation, but she believed that FDR's New Deal had an equally important impact. "We made little progress in the state until Roosevelt came to office," she later wrote, "and gave us a new social philosophy which embraced not just the top level of our society but made an effort to raise all levels. I can't see how anyone can call that socialism."[90] By the mid-1930s, however, white southern politicians were sounding alarms.

Southern conservatives, convinced that the role of government should not go beyond preserving "conditions of fair play and equal opportunity," began to view the New Deal as a dangerous exercise in "social and economic planning." As the 1936 election loomed, the Democratic Party seemed to have become completely beholden to northern urban constituencies, including labor and African Americans. Black activism at the local level contributed to the heightened sensitivity of southern lawmakers in Congress, thereby increasing their aversion to Roosevelt's programmatic reforms. In 1935, for example, Modjeska Simkins and Robert Mance had responded to a proposed antilynching bill in Congress by founding the State Negro Citizens Committee, which sent telegrams of support to the White House and every member of South Carolina's congressional delegation. This willingness to speak out, coupled with decisions by others to quit their farms and seek federal relief work, confirmed the erosion of the black dependency on which the entire system rested. Southern politicians also took notice of the black community's affinity for Roosevelt, which amplified white disdain for the president. According to Peter Epps, an African American agricultural laborer, black Carolinians "talked more politics since [Mr.] Roosevelt been in than ever [before]."[91]

African Americans in South Carolina went beyond talking. In 1936, a record number of the state's black residents registered to vote in the general election. By September, approximately seven hundred had added their names to the voting rolls in Richland County alone — seven times as many black people as who had participated in the 1932 general election there. To show their appreciation to Roosevelt, the majority registered as Democrats.[92] In addition to paying poll taxes, receiving a registration certificate required reading and interpreting a section of the state constitution to the satisfaction of the white registrar, which also meant possessing basic literacy skills. Who knows how many of the new black voters on South Carolina's rolls had first signed their names in the State House register as pilgrim students of Wil Lou Gray's a year earlier?

⟶⟨❉⟩⟵

At the intersections within southern black women's activist educational culture, Septima Clark learned more about how to organize people and teach them to be citizens. Black southern educational associations of the 1930s urged teachers to participate in the crusade to equalize black schools by strengthening their credentials and by building a statewide educational network with enough muscle to lobby state legislatures. Local and national black leaders attempted to harness nascent federal support, both by advising teachers to capitalize on the educational prospects stemming from the New Deal and by pushing conversations about citizenship beyond ambiguity.

Civic organizing reinforced such approaches and further refined activists' sensibilities about how to get things done. "Women in public life must learn to listen to everybody's opinion," Albertha Johnston Murray, an elementary school teacher, PSTA member, clubwoman, and contemporary of Clark's, advised. "They must never be prejudiced or dogmatic, they must keep an open mind, and when they have listened and know what they think themselves, they must have the courage to stand by that."[93] Becoming a clubwoman imbued Clark with a particular vision of leadership that emphasized collective responsibility and cultivating participation by as many like-minded women as possible. Better living conditions, better schools, better health care, and respect for black womanhood could materialize only with cooperative and concerted effort.

Working with Gray provided Clark with a specific set of tools with which to build a new society. Teaching reading to black adults helped Clark to realize that her students could not exercise citizenship—and would never feel like citizens—without literacy; moreover, she learned, literacy itself represented merely an initial first step. More broadly, adult education efforts of the interwar years must be contextualized within the far-reaching changes spawned by the New Deal's impact on the South. The controversy over how simultaneously to promote and contain black southerners' citizenship aspirations could not be neatly reconciled with the goal of helping "people to think for themselves." Adult education leaders advanced a pedagogy rooted in Progressive Era conceptions of the relationship between citizens and the state but rewrote Booker T. Washington's vision of schooling to acquire basic literacy and vocational skills. By 1938, at least some African American leaders had begun to argue that students had to comprehend that "vocational education must be accompanied with political competence."[94] Moreover, adult education proponents continually preached that learning constituted an ongoing process. Teacher training stressed fashioning models that could be modified in the future.

Septima Clark was not a leader in the PSTA, the SCFCW, or Gray's Adult School program during the 1930s. Better, she was a rank-and-file member and participant. Clark's activism during the interwar years reflected a practical response to specific problems that black children and black adults—

particularly women—confronted. Her experience allows us to more fully understand a political training received by thousands of black women educators and civic activists in the segregated South and the organizing tradition that they fashioned from it. The core belief of that tradition stressed the interdependence of education and an expansive vision of social uplift; by the 1930s, this idea included citizens' right to pressure local, state, and federal officials to access resources and opportunity.[95] Professional development, club work, and formal training as an adult educator led Clark to think differently about the interconnectedness of political, economic, social, and educational problems. She soon translated this understanding into what she described as her first "radical" act.

CHAPTER FIVE

The Battle Transformed

By the late 1930s, Septima Clark had reached a point where she had always wanted to be, professionally and socially. As she observed, "My days and nights in Columbia were very busy ones. Not only was I teaching a full schedule and attending teacher training courses and going to civic club meetings of one sort and another, but I was also going to bridge parties and taking part in other social activities. I was being accepted."[1] That might have been enough for most people, but not for Clark. She knew how much further there was to go. And the activist journey she had begun on rural Johns Island in 1916 changed dramatically during her last six years in the state capital. Before she left Columbia in 1947, Clark would have a blueprint for how to harness southern black women's activist educational and organizational practices to South Carolina's nascent civil rights movement.

World War II transformed the African American freedom struggle. Foremost, it exposed the hypocrisy of a nation that claimed to fight fascism abroad yet preserved segregation in both its military and society. Black leaders used this paradox to increase their pressure on the federal government to end its discriminatory practices. In June 1941, for example, A. Philip Randolph's all-black March on Washington Movement garnered Executive Order 8802 from President Franklin Delano Roosevelt. The order prohibited racial discrimination in defense industry firms that held federal government contracts and created the Fair Employment Practices Committee to monitor compliance. The social and economic dislocations spawned by the U.S. entry into the conflict six months later amplified black civil rights militancy. Black migration intensified throughout the war years as people moved north and west and from rural to urban areas in the South in search of better opportunities. Migrants signaled their disgust with ongoing competition for jobs, housing, and services by joining established civil rights organizations and keeping abreast of the struggle for racial justice. Membership in the National Association for the Advancement of Colored People (NAACP) increased ninefold during the war, while circulation of black newspapers rose 40 percent. In 1942, the *Pittsburgh Courier* launched its Double V campaign calling for victory against fascism abroad and racism at home, thereby fostering solidarity in the attack on government and civic policies that sanctioned racial inequality. In short, World War II emboldened rank-and-file black activists everywhere. Before the fighting ended, the Congress of Racial Equality began testing nonviolent direct action tactics to end segregation in the North; students at Howard University conducted "sit-downs" on two occasions to desegregate restaurants in the nation's capital; and southern African Americans, with the Supreme Court's 1944 decision in *Smith v. Allwright*, won the right to vote in Democratic primaries.[2] That victory sent a clear signal that it was time to renew widespread voter registration campaigns, which is precisely what black Carolinians did.

Septima Clark concentrated her activist energies in a revitalized battle to make separate education equal—specifically, in the NAACP's campaign to equalize salaries for black and white teachers. A favorable 1940 U.S. Supreme Court ruling had set a precedent for the adoption of new, more confrontational tactics. In South Carolina, however, Palmetto State Teachers' Association (PSTA) leaders refused to cooperate, much to the dismay of some of their members.[3] Teacher activism of the early 1940s—not the lack of it—split the PSTA into two factions: the Young Turks, who supported a direct assault on educational inequalities by going to court, and those determined to scuttle protest to preserve the peace.

Though hardly a "young" Turk, when confronted with the option of following the PSTA or the NAACP, Septima Clark chose the NAACP. She characterized her participation in the teacher salary campaign as her first "radical" act, "the first time I had worked *against* people directing a system for which I was working." Many of Clark's colleagues opposed taking court action because rumor had it that they would be forced to take a more rigid examination for teacher certification to equalize their salaries. Even before a plaintiff had been chosen and a suit had been filed, state senator W. Brantley Harvey Sr. assured his friends in the General Assembly, "We intend to get around the matter of equalizing teacher salaries on the basis of our plan to re-certify Negro teachers."[4] After several years of delay, the South Carolina

NAACP filed two salary equalization suits, one in Charleston in 1944 and the other in Columbia in 1945. The association won both, and white lawmakers kept their pledge.

Clark's decision to cast her lot with the NAACP demonstrated her willingness to take a stand and earned her the respect of her more timid coworkers. Clark "was well known by the educational professional set," one Columbia educator remembered. "She was an excellent teacher and she was well thought of." Clark's active role in the salary crusade also facilitated her transition from rank-and-file NAACP member in Columbia to NAACP leader in postwar Charleston. Indeed, in one recounting of her life, she claimed, "I want to start my story with the end of World War II because that is when the civil rights movement really got going for me personally and for people all over the South."[5] Participation in the salary equalization battle transformed Septima Clark.

The national NAACP's educational litigation campaign took shape during Clark's earliest years in Columbia, in the beginning of the 1930s, and had several interrelated goals. First, by forcing the state to equalize expenditures on black and white schools, the association hoped to bankrupt segregation. Second, aware of the likelihood of appeal by local authorities, NAACP leaders wanted to win higher court decisions as a way to establish legal precedents and to focus national attention on the wretched conditions that prevailed in separate and unequal southern schools. Third, officials envisioned these legal challenges as part of a broader process of community mobilization. National leaders reasoned that involvement in individual suits would invigorate the freedom struggle in local black communities. Lawyers for the NAACP pursued three types of educational cases between 1933 and 1950: desegregating graduate and professional schools, equalizing teacher salaries, and equalizing educational facilities. They expected that the higher education cases would be the easiest to win. Teacher salary equalization proved a trickier proposition because pay scales differed from district to district, so suits had to be filed one district at a time. Potential reprisals against black teachers, the segment of the community most likely to have joined the NAACP, increased the risks. Equalizing physical facilities in black elementary and secondary schools represented the most difficult cases, requiring ongoing support from entire communities through protracted court fights.[6] Under the able guidance of Charles Hamilton Houston, a Howard University law professor who became the organization's chief legal strategist, and his protégé, Thurgood

Marshall, who joined the staff in 1936, the NAACP decided to begin the fight in the Upper South, where white opposition might be weakest.

Between 1936 and 1940, African American teachers in Maryland and Virginia went to court demanding equal pay for equal work. In June 1940, federal judge John J. Parker reversed the decision of a lower court that had dismissed a salary equalization suit brought by Melvin Alston, a teacher and president of the Norfolk Teachers' Association. In October, the Supreme Court refused to review *Alston v. City School Board of City of Norfolk*, thereby letting Parker's decision stand and demonstrating the Court's intention to enforce the equality provisions of *Plessy v. Ferguson*. Segregation would henceforth become much more of a burden to state budgets. African American teachers in four additional southern states then filed suit.[7] White school officials realized they had two choices. They could begin paying the same salaries to black and white teachers with comparable experience and training, or they could invent new salary schedules that appeared race-neutral on the surface.

On the eve of the 1940s, the disparity between white and black schools in South Carolina had lessened somewhat. Average term lengths for black elementary and high school students ran 141 days, versus 175 for white students. Black teachers taught an average of 40 pupils per class, just 11 more than white teachers, a significant improvement from Septima Poinsette's days at the head of a classroom with more than 130 black students on Johns Island while her white colleague nearby taught 3 white children. Moreover, 79 percent of all black teachers held first-grade teaching certificates. Nevertheless, 803 of South Carolina's African American educators still labored in rural one-room schools as the 1940s began, whereas only 240 white teachers did so, and the total property value for white schools was 6.4 times higher than that for black schools.[8]

Beneath the surface of segregation, such disparities reflected the reality that school consolidation had proceeded at an uneven pace, particularly in rural areas, which led the state supervisor of rural schools to recommend abolishing the district system altogether. Centralizing all school operations at the county level would yield less dramatic discrepancies between urban and rural schools. Yet consolidation also required expending more funds on pupil transportation. By the 1940–41 school year, South Carolina provided more than a million dollars to operate 1,703 buses for white students but allotted less than six thousand dollars on 8 buses for African Americans. Overall, the state spent 4 times more per white pupil than per black student, and white teachers earned 2.4 times as much as black teachers.[9] African American activist educators had a solid case should they choose to go to court.

The Columbia NAACP branch "quickly commanded" Clark's "attention and support," and she "joined with enthusiasm" in the early 1930s. As a rank-and-file member of the organization, Clark "walked the streets recruiting memberships" for her chapter, but she was not privy to the executive committee's decision-making processes. Belonging to the largest branch in South Carolina, however, kept Clark informed about the association's progress in attacking educational inequalities elsewhere. Ironically, perhaps, the lack of coordination among the other seven functioning chapters within the state prompted the 1939 formation of the South Carolina State Conference of Branches of the NAACP. Geography dictated Columbia as the logical choice for its headquarters. In June 1941, members of the State Conference elected the Reverend James M. Hinton, pastor of Columbia's Second Calvary Baptist Church and a salesman with the Pilgrim Life Insurance Company, as president and Modjeska Simkins as secretary.[10]

By 1941, the State Conference also had an unofficial organ in John McCray's newspaper, the *Lighthouse and Informer*. McCray had grown up in the all-black town of Lincolnville, South Carolina, and had attended Clark's alma mater, the Avery Normal Institute. After graduating as class valedictorian in 1931, McCray headed to Alabama's Talladega College. He resettled in Charleston five years later and took a job with the North Carolina Mutual Life Insurance Company. He also briefly assumed the presidency of its NAACP chapter. In 1938, McCray began publishing the *Charleston Lighthouse*, which merged with the *People's Informer* of Sumter in 1940. At the urging of black activists in the state capital, McCray relocated to Columbia at the end of 1941. Osceola McKaine joined him as associate editor of the *Lighthouse and Informer* soon thereafter. The World War I veteran had spent twenty years as a nightclub owner in Ghent, Belgium, but in December 1940 had returned to his native Sumter, where he enjoyed semicelebrity status as a result of his cosmopolitan experience.[11] Teacher salary equalization would become their first editorial crusade.

Meanwhile, black Carolinians had been watching the courts. In November 1940, a month to the day after the Supreme Court refused to review *Alston*, L. Raymond Bailey, assistant secretary for the Columbia NAACP branch, wrote to Thurgood Marshall to request information on how to initiate teacher pay equalization cases in the Palmetto State. Bailey admitted he acted surreptitiously and asked that Marshall keep the matter confidential "because of the small size of our group and the type of people with whom we must deal." Marshall replied by explaining the general process established through trial and error in the previous decade. First, a committee "composed of equal numbers of teachers and citizens" should form with the understanding that "the names of the citizens are made public but the names of the teachers are not made public for obvious reasons." Next, the group should select a treasurer and begin fund-raising to pay for expenses associated with bringing suit and "to guarantee one year's salary to the teachers who might be discharged as a result of the case." After a plaintiff had been found and local counsel had been secured, the national NAACP would provide legal services free of charge.[12]

White Carolinians also began formulating a response to *Alston*. More progressive leaders sought genuine reform, though they took pains not to allude directly to the prospect of salary equalization. Concluding that salaries had remained static for the past five years despite rising costs of living, members of the Columbia City School Board recommended immediate relief for teachers, adding "We believe that this fund should be equally distributed among all teachers." White legislators, by contrast, merely wanted to appear willing to comply with the new law of the land. In its January 1941 session, the General Assembly voted to increase salaries for all teachers by a flat ten dollars. When the bill reached his office, however, Governor Burnet R. Maybank Sr. confronted a dilemma. As one white informer to the national NAACP explained, Maybank had already announced his candidacy for the U.S. Senate seat vacated by the appointment of James F. Byrnes to the Supreme Court. Yet Maybank's political foes had worded the bill to make no distinction between African American and white teachers despite the fact that the issue had been "thoroughly debated on the floor of both houses." The aspiring senator knew he could "not afford to deny" white teachers a raise, but he did "not want to sign for the increase of the Negro teachers salary." Instead, Maybank let the bill gather dust on his desk and began meeting with members of the State Board of Education to discuss methods for "re-classifying the teachers so as to eliminate or deprive Negro teachers the benefits of [the] legislation."[13]

Outright defiance also emerged. In May, South Carolina state senator Olin Sawyer, a physician and farmer from Georgetown, proclaimed, "If the supreme court does say we must pay the Negroes, how are they going to make us do it? Are they going to send the army to South Carolina to make us do it? We're running this government."[14] In 1941 America sent its army abroad instead. It would be sixteen years before President Dwight D. Eisenhower, in just such a show of federal power, dispatched the National Guard to Little Rock, Arkansas, to protect the black students attempting to integrate Central High School.

Running for the U.S. Senate as the country prepared for war, Maybank dared not go as far as Sawyer. In August, the governor signed the bill raising teachers' salaries according to a "merit system" devised by a provisional committee that he had appointed. After the initial raises had been granted, white teachers still earned 2.2 times more than African Americans. White men who taught high school saw the biggest increase in their salaries, followed by black men who taught elementary school. Black women elementary school teachers like Clark, who comprised the majority of the state's black teaching force, received the least. The governor's temporary committee also advised that a two-year study of "the entire program of teacher education and certification should be undertaken," ostensibly so that teachers' salaries might better reflect their qualifications and training in the future.[15]

The PSTA leadership had been charting a course as well. In 1941, the organization set aside money for a Teachers' Defense Fund but otherwise did nothing to organize a court challenge. Despite pleas from two NAACP spokesmen that "Negro teachers will not accept any compromise and nothing less than equalization of salaries," the PSTA endorsed a gradual plan to begin in the 1941–42 school year and to be completed two years later. It then sent representatives to negotiate with state officials. Prior to signing the bill to raise teachers' salaries, Maybank publicly announced that "various agreements" had eased his mind. Though he did not mention specifics, observers presumed that the governor "referred to some understandings with Negro educators to the effect [that] the Negroes would not press court actions at once to force immediate salary equality."[16]

The threat of immediate litigation clearly gave members of the PSTA's upper echelons leverage in their conversations with state officials. As association president John P. Burgess informed a white ally in 1941, "Many of us believe that equalization of salaries in one year might be asking too much, but we certainly believe that a beginning should be made this year." In exchange for delaying court action, they hoped to secure a legitimate role in designing the state's new certification plan and maybe even representation on the Board of Examiners to ensure more equitable evaluations of African American teachers. From their perspective, embracing a gradual approach bought both parties time to work toward an amicable compromise, whereas forcing the state's hand would lead only to swift retribution. If push came to shove, PSTA leaders also knew that white allies who wanted to preserve their positions and influence would have no choice but to side publicly with the defenders of educational inequality, which more progressive white people conceded thwarted educational advancement for all Carolinians. Moreover, the PSTA men sensed the strong support for the governor among white educational officials, particularly those who had been calling for South Carolina to "modernize" its teacher certification process, because his new proposals dovetailed with their agenda.[17]

Nevertheless, South Carolina's more militant black teachers and activists questioned the association's chosen course. In addition to helping revitalize the Sumter NAACP branch, Osceola McKaine offered his opinion on the salary equalization issue in the *Lighthouse and Informer*, cautioning against an overreliance on legislation and judicial rulings to generate change in the court of public opinion. Grassroots organization, conversely, was imperative. "In South Carolina, the NAACP has exactly 1,140 members," McKaine wrote, "and there are more than 5,000 Negro teachers in this state." Excoriating teachers for their failure to support an organization willing to fight on their behalf, he found "this lack of gratitude . . . so shameful as to be scandalous" and urged both teachers and the PSTA to contribute financially to the NAACP. In October 1941, PSTA officials responded by hiring McKaine "to canvas the state by county and collect data on black teachers' salaries," with the understanding that he would pay his own expenses. McKaine did more than collect data during his travels: he organized support for a court challenge.[18]

Septima Clark and others who backed the NAACP would have to learn key talking points to persuade their colleagues to join the struggle. The first question that must have been on the tip of every teacher's tongue was whether suing in court or actively supporting the cause would lead to dismissal. "No," an NAACP circular assured them; "South Carolina law requires that well-founded accusations of misconduct or inefficiency be proved before a teacher can be discharged." Though private correspondence with Thurgood Marshall suggested otherwise, the brochure reminded teachers that they had little reason to worry because the NAACP had never lost a salary suit. With regard to the practical specifics of equalization, the publication called attention to the fact that the state had announced "an anticipated SURPLUS of between $8,000,000 and $9,000,000" for the 1943 fiscal year. Additional factors indicated that the time was ripe to seize the initiative. World War II had already begun to cause an acute teacher shortage: by the 1942–43 school term, 23 percent of white and nearly 16 percent of African American schools lacked adequate faculty, as men and women secured more lucrative teaching positions elsewhere and left the profession altogether for higher-paying defense industry jobs or to enlist in the armed services. In the absence of a state tenure law, the shortage should have provided an extra layer of protection against dismissal for teachers willing to inaugurate court challenges. Still, if a teacher wondered why the PSTA was not leading the fight, the pamphlet answered that "the Executive Committee of the Association has persistently refused or purposely neglected to carry out the demands of its members."[19]

Pushed to defend its actions, a powerful bloc within the PSTA Executive Committee adopted an obstructionist posture. As one official observed, "We know what the teachers want us to do, but we are not going to do it."[20] PSTA leaders had been pursuing equalization on their own terms for twenty years and resented the NAACP's interference. More broadly, the PSTA would not have been naive enough to predict, as the NAACP circular did, perhaps disingenuously, that even the least trained black teacher would have her salary increased to match a similarly situated white teacher. The PSTA men knew that the least trained would be the most vulnerable, whereas the NAACP implied that equalizing the salary of the best and the brightest would yield positive benefits for all.

The activists pushed forward. Early the next year, J. Andrew Simmons, a Charlestonian and the principal of Booker T. Washington in Columbia, volunteered to help find a plaintiff. Black teachers and noneducators alike held Simmons in high esteem. "He was a top man," Fannie Phelps Adams, who taught at Booker T., declared. Septima Clark, who had known the principal in her hometown, concurred: "I did all I could to support Mr. Simmons."[21] As part of his master's degree work in 1935, Simmons had researched the pay disparities between the state's white and black teachers. He persuaded his cousin, Malissa T. Smith, a graduate of Avery who taught at Burke Normal and Industrial School in Charleston, to become the first plaintiff. J. Arthur Brown, a former Simmons student and NAACP member, helped galvanize support in the Low Country. With a willing plaintiff and grassroots backing, the State Conference of the NAACP played its first major card. In March 1943, James Hinton released a statement announcing that black Carolinians intended to sue before the end of the current school term to equalize black teachers' salaries.[22]

A showdown between PSTA members who supported the NAACP and those who did not could no longer be avoided. It occurred during an April 9 meeting of the PSTA House of Delegates. Perhaps in an attempt to delay while appearing to compromise, the PSTA's executive committee had already voted to set aside another twelve hundred dollars in 1943 for a teachers' defense fund. But when the executive secretary referred to the matter, some delegates protested that they had not been informed of it. A "lengthy discussion" over the purpose of the fund followed and resulted in a motion that the monies be used for "fighting for equalization of salaries for teachers and transportation facilities and other facilities for Negro children to start this year." The motion carried by an "almost unanimous vote." The Young Turks seemed to have triumphed, at least until salary equalization reemerged as the first item on the agenda at the evening session. At this point, "twelve very influential members" made it clear that they did not favor suing the state to equalize teachers' salaries. J. L. Dixon, who endorsed legal action, brought matters to a head when he moved that the entire twelve hundred dollars be turned over to the NAACP. The opposition stalled until another delegate moved that the motion "be tabled indefinitely," which it was by a vote of thirty-nine to thirty-one. Thus, a faction led by twelve men had prevailed over nearly half the members of the House of Delegates, who represented the interests of teachers in their home counties.[23]

NAACP leaders could afford to be more militant because none of them relied on the white state for their paycheck. Too often, however, NAACP activists, particularly McCray and McKaine, oversimplified their critique and downplayed the very real hazards of PSTA members' involvement. Given historical precedent, the expectation that teachers would assume a position on the front lines of the struggle fed NAACP organizers' frustration, but caustic editorials hardly facilitated teachers' conversion. When activist teachers in Columbia, including Clark, failed to persuade 75 percent of their colleagues to sign an equal pay petition, McCray publicly rebuked all of them. "More and more (though it is a sinister feeling)," he wrote, "I am reaching the conclusion that Negro teachers, as spineless and unworthy as those in Columbia have proven themselves, should be left to slave and starve and receive the wages of a serf." For her part, Simkins—every bit as militant as McCray and McKaine, and perhaps more so—distinguished between teachers and their leaders in the PSTA. In a 1943 article, "Negro Teachers Called to Arms," Simkins addressed her audience, "hundreds of whom are my personal friends and former co-workers," and declared, "Swear vengeance against your 'misleaders.'"[24]

Beyond what she read in the newspaper and the gossip she heard on the street, at school, and at NAACP meetings, Septima Clark was not privy to any of this internal wrangling. Yet she was all too familiar with the frustration of trying to make ends meet on a pitifully small salary. Clark finished her bachelor's degree at Benedict College in 1942 and wanted to pursue a master's degree. The state's plan to revise its teacher certification procedure and to adjust salaries accordingly might have influenced her ambition, but Clark could not obtain a master's in South Carolina. In the aftermath of *Alston*, a few southern legislatures had increased their funding for scholarships that would enable black teachers to earn advanced degrees out of state.[25] Palmetto State legislators did not. Septima Clark could not afford to stop teaching, and school-year obligations left only summers available for study. Financial constraints, however, forced Clark to use this free time to supplement her income.

In the summers of 1942 and 1943, she went to work at Camp Green Shadows in Harrison, Maine, a private vacation spot used by a vice president of the John C. Winston publishing company. Clark's job consisted of duties Victoria Poinsette would have never deigned to perform: cleaning white people's homes and serving them dinner. The experience introduced her to the strange ways of the wealthy. The lady of the house "had different colored dust cloths for the different colored rooms," Clark noted, "and she would go around behind me to see that I used the blue in the blue room, the yellow in the yellow room." For dinner, the hostess would "buy a whole side of beef, and we'd serve it all that night." Clark was amazed. "I thought, 'How *in the world* could you spend that much money?'" Referring to her own childhood, she continued, "It was hard for me to see that when we would buy ten cents worth of beef and make it go around our family." At night, Clark read to her boss, whom she described as not having "the patience" for the task. The next day she watched incredulously as the woman paraded her newfound knowledge before her guests: "She was sitting down there telling those people that thing just like she had read it herself!"[26]

Still, Clark considered herself lucky to have secured the job. She appreciated the plethora of books available to read in her spare time. Seeing this rich woman worry about her pristine furniture and white carpets, Clark told herself, "I never will have money like this. When I get a house I want one that I can use soap and water to clean." Most important, however, "It was good pay for me, ten dollars a week, forty dollars a month. And then the guests who came gave me good tips. I thought I was real wealthy then." Elsewhere, Clark explained, my "salary was so little, and I had a child to support, too. My husband was dead, I wanted to buy a house for my parents, and so I went up there and worked for the summer. *And it cleared my money that I made in the winter.*"[27]

World War II provided Clark with other opportunities to earn a little extra income. She resumed her teaching of African American adult students for Wil Lou Gray in 1941. "A large group of inductees had come to Fort Jackson who were unable even able to sign their names to get their payroll

Septima Clark (far left) with friends at Camp Green Shadows, Harrison, Maine, summer 1942. Courtesy of the Avery Research Center for African American History and Culture, College of Charleston.

checks and the Army wanted to do something about it," Clark observed. "So they asked Miss Gray to work out a plan, and she asked me to help her instruct the soldiers who would be in the classes she was arranging." In segregated classes, Clark's students learned to write their names in two weeks. "And from then on they were able at least to sign the payroll, which was a great achievement for them." The men also learned how to write their company numbers, their occupations, "such as baker, electrician, truck driver and whatnot," and how to "read the names of the buses going out to the fort." Working with these black soldiers, men willing to give their lives for their country in a segregated army, Clark saw up close how much their state had failed them. In 1940, though 35 percent of South Carolina's population lacked fifth-grade educations and 81 percent lacked high school diplomas, these native black sons lacked even the basic literacy skills to attend to the most mundane tasks.[28] The gap between the rhetoric of fighting a war for democracy abroad and the segregated reality at home could not have been clearer or more infuriating.

Personal matters underscored Clark's sensitivity to the nation's hypocrisy. Nerie Jr. finished high school in 1941 and enrolled at North Carolina Agricultural and Technical College in Greensboro. Then he was drafted into the army. "That was the hardest thing in my life," Clark recalled; "I said, 'If he just had a father alive, then we could share this.'" After seeing her son off, she volunteered at the bus station in Columbia, where she had plenty of opportunity to talk with other anxious mothers watching their sons leave for war. Keeping occupied was Clark's way of dealing with difficult personal transitions. "I could usually work under stress," she confirmed. "I did a whole [master's] thesis while he was in that army." When the war ended, she went to meet her son and did not recognize him in the crowd. "You mean you don't know me?," Nerie exclaimed as he approached. "I didn't," Clark confessed; "He had grown so much."[29]

Throughout his adolescence, Clark had spent more time apart from her son than in his company, which testified further to the limited options for self-supporting black mothers trying to survive in an economy that ranked the value of their labor lowest and paid them the least. Financially, Clark had no choice but to rely on kin to help raise her son, yet this also resulted in tremendous personal costs. She missed the daily events of his growing up; each time she visited she had to try to recover the lost days as best she could, and she cried each time she left. Other aspects of their relationship reflected the distance. "He never said 'Mama,'" Clark once commented, "He said 'Septima.' This is something I dislike."[30] Life in Hickory, however, pro-

Septima Clark (standing, far right) and her son, Nerie David Clark Jr.
(seated, far right), at a Clark family reunion, Hickory, North Carolina,
n.d. Courtesy of the Avery Research Center for African American
History and Culture, College of Charleston.

vided Nerie with extensive contact with his uncles, and Clark understood
that young black men needed male role models. Moreover, her son's daily
presence in her life would have forced Clark to readjust her personal goals,
leaving her less time for professional development and civic organizing.
Knowing that her son was in good hands allowed her to pursue a life somewhat independent of him. Even so, the personal financial difficulties that
had prevented Clark from raising Nerie herself surely influenced her belief
in the justness of salary equalization.

෴

By 1943, turmoil had expanded beyond South Carolina's African American
educational community to white school boards. Caught between the pressure generated by black activists and their reliance on the General Assembly for state aid to subsidize teachers' salaries, local school officials faced the
unwelcome prospect of reducing the salaries of white teachers if the state
legislature failed to act. Charleston's City Board of School Commissioners

received Malissa Smith's petition to equalize her salary on June 24, 1943, and immediately contacted attorney H. L. Erckmann, who assured the board of its legal right to refuse employment to any teacher who disrupted school operations. Erckmann took this opportunity to advise the board "to abolish present salary schedules" and reclassify all teachers and principals "with due regard to character, ability, experience and fitness, and to contract with and pay them accordingly, without regard to race or color." He left it to the board to determine the practicality of implementing his suggestions but added, "If something is not done, the taxpayers through their representatives may decide to take matters into their own hands *and refuse to pay for more than a Grammar School Education.*"[31] While the idea of eliminating funding for secondary education seemed slightly hysterical, it eerily foreshadowed Governor James Byrnes's threat to close all of South Carolina's public schools rather than desegregate them nine years later.

Harold Boulware, a black lawyer in Columbia and the national NAACP's legal point man in the Palmetto State, had initially anticipated taking Smith's case to court in February 1943, but figuring out South Carolina's labyrinthine process of teacher hiring and remuneration proved time-consuming. By August, Boulware had yet to file Smith's suit, and the delay embarrassed James Hinton, who had promised imminent action five months earlier. McKaine soon apprised Marshall that the situation in South Carolina had become "critical" and that the campaign had reached a "standstill."[32]

Summer ended and Smith returned to Burke when the next school year began. On Monday, September 27, she called in sick and failed to report to work for the rest of the week. School officials soon learned that she had gone to Columbia on Wednesday and had gotten married on Thursday. By this time, marriage no longer automatically brought dismissal. As a consequence of the teaching shortage, the board had reserved the right to hire married women on a case-by-case basis. After board members decided that "the services of Malissa Smith [would] be dispensed with," Erckmann confirmed that they had the legal grounds to fire her for failing to obtain the "proper permission" for her absence.[33] Because marriage increased women's job vulnerability, NAACP organizers next looked for a male plaintiff. They approached Eugene C. Hunt but learned that the draft board had recently classified Hunt as 1-A. Filing suit might lead the board to draft Hunt sooner. Hunt directed the NAACP to one of his Burke colleagues, Viola Louise Duvall, who agreed to become the next plaintiff. NAACP lawyers filed *Duvall v. J. F. Seignous et al.* in federal district court on November 10, 1943. Federal judge J. Waties Waring would preside over the case.[34]

The news that Waring would hear the case gave Thurgood Marshall and Harold R. Boulware cause for concern. Descended from a long line of Charleston aristocrats, Waring had served as a political campaign manager for the notoriously white supremacist U.S. senator Ellison "Cotton Ed" Smith and had close ties to Maybank, now serving as South Carolina's junior U.S. senator. Indeed, Smith and Maybank had engineered Waring's appointment to the federal bench. Erckmann initially tried to have the case dismissed on the grounds that the school board had acted in good faith when it passed its August 1943 resolution to pay teachers on the basis of their "character, ability, experience and fitness . . . without regard to race or color." He also contended that the "federal government cannot interfere with the operations of schools financed by state funds unless there is prima facie evidence of racial discrimination." Under the Due Protection Clause of the Fourteenth Amendment, the plaintiff's counsel rejoined, "the mere fact that you say you are going to do something is no grounds to dismiss the suit."[35] Judge Waring concurred.

Spectators packed the courtroom the next morning; regardless of what happened, both black and white Charlestonians expected the trial to provide "a good conversation piece for posterity." Waring entered, took his seat, and turned his back to the plaintiff's table to face the defendants. How long, Waring asked, had it been since federal Judge John J. Parker had ruled in black teachers' favor in *Alston*? As the school board's lawyers shuffled through their records, Marshall attempted to answer. Waring stopped him short: "I didn't ask you, Mr. Marshall." When defense attorneys finally replied, Waring fired off another question. How long had it been since a similar suit had been heard by a state court in Maryland? Marshall again attempted to answer, but Waring again cut him off: "Not you, Mr. Marshall." A wave of murmurs broke through the crowd. "See there," a black woman's voice echoed above the low din, "they won't even let her lawyer talk." Judge Waring waited patiently for the defense's response and followed up with a few more questions before swiveling around in his chair to face the plaintiffs. "Mr. Marshall, I don't want you to think I was being rude in not permitting you to answer those questions," Waring apologized. "I know you know the answers. You were the attorney of record in most of them. What I was trying to determine is how long it has been that the School Board has known it must pay equal salaries to its teachers. This is a simple case and there isn't need to take up the court's time." Waring asked Marshall whether he would like an order to equalize salaries immediately or if he wished to give the Charleston City School Board time to comply. An astonished Marshall said he wanted to consult with defense attorneys. "Very well," the judge agreed. After setting a deadline for the attorneys to get back to him, Waring announced, "Court's adjourned."[36] The entire trial had lasted fifteen minutes.

Supporters of the NAACP celebrated. On February 15, newspapers reported James Hinton's announcement that "lawyers were preparing similar suits for Columbia and for 'an upstate city.'" White Carolinians panicked. The next day's *Charleston News and Courier* carried an editorial, "The Submissive South," that recommended privatizing public schools as an end run around the federal court ruling.[37] State representative M. V. Horne soon submitted a bill that "would declare *every school* in South Carolina to be a separate unit, and provides for each unit the office of a 'trustee-manager' whose duty it would be to administer the affairs of the school," including setting salaries. Such decentralization would have undermined all of South Carolina's progress toward consolidation, but opponents sought to thwart court decisions that would bind the entire state.[38] Though the bill did not pass, it demonstrated how far legislators imagined going ten years before *Brown v. Board of Education*.

The General Assembly did, however, succeed in attaching a provision to the 1944 Deficiency Appropriations Act that established a grievance procedure for any teacher who contemplated court action. An aggrieved teacher first had to appear before her county board of education and could only register complaints on her own behalf, a blatant attempt to prevent the filing of class-action suits like the *Duvall* case. The General Assembly thereby empowered county boards of education to act as civil courts but did not force them to follow civil court rules.[39] If a county board decided against the teacher, she had thirty days to appeal to the State Board of Education; it, in turn, had thirty days to procure a transcript from a county board and schedule a hearing. Two months afforded white authorities plenty of time to make their displeasure known in any local black community. Moreover, the bill provided that the State Board of Education, "upon its own initiative, in the accomplishment of justice in the matter, shall have *the right to require all teachers in said district from which the appeal came to be examined and recertified*."[40] Thus, not only would one brave soul face potential repercussions, so would every single one of her colleagues, those she knew and those she had never met. While the language of the law appeared racially unbiased, it hardly seemed plausible that South Carolina would enforce this castigatory measure against its white teachers. Only after seeking relief through these channels could a teacher take her complaint to a state court of common pleas and ultimately the state supreme court.

State senator Edgar Brown of Barnwell, one of the two most influential men in the General Assembly, defended the statute, asserting that it was "not in any sense a scheme to evade federal court decisions." Rather, Brown declared, it "will develop clearly whether or not any discrimination is being practiced in connection with salaries or anything else upon white and colored teachers." The NAACP disparaged the bill's provision that "the findings of fact by the state board of education shall be final and conclusive to all parties" as "just so much wasted verbiage."[41] Federal law trumped state law, and African American teachers still had the right to federal protection. Yet the white state's maneuvering significantly muddled the issue and burdened the NAACP with the task of reeducating its members.

Septima Clark "enthusiastically" lent her talents to this chore as she helped rally support for the Columbia salary equalization suit. Drawing on her experience in 1919, when the Charleston NAACP had forced the city to hire black teachers, Clark proposed the idea of canvassing door to door to apprise the black community of the pertinent issues in the campaign. In the intervening years, she had learned that "a good teacher meets her learners where they are."[42] She valued listening to parental concerns but also knew that generating such grassroots support might embolden teachers. In short, Clark recognized that the everyday practices of black women activist educators, properly channeled, could play a fundamental role in the emerging civil rights movement.

Not all of Columbia's black teachers shared Clark's enthusiasm for challenging their inequitable pay in court. "We had several meetings," Clark recalled, "and the discussions at times were lively." C. A. Johnson, the former principal at Booker T. Washington and supervisor of African American schools for the past thirteen years, "felt that we were foolish in bringing the issue into the courts." Still, he did not attempt to dissuade supporters. "I had attended a meeting, held in one of the churches," Clark observed, "and Mr. Johnson felt that this was one session we should not have attended. But though he knew I had been to the meeting, he never questioned me about it." A white reporter also covered that meeting and published its proceedings in the newspaper. "This frightened some of the teachers," Clark added, "but others were completely unafraid. One teacher even was anxious for the reporter to get her name; she said she was proud to be a part of this movement."[43]

As in Charleston, J. Andrew Simmons helped locate a plaintiff in Columbia. Albert N. Thompson had taught at Booker Washington Heights Elementary School for two years when he submitted his petition to the Richland County School Board on June 7, 1944. The document neglected to request a hearing before the board, in accordance with South Carolina's new law. If Thompson wanted to pursue his complaint, defense attorney Frank A. Graham concluded, the "Board will be glad to fix a time and place for the hearing." Marshall advised Hinton to skip the grievance procedure altogether and carry the battle directly to the federal district court. Doing so took seven months.[44]

In the interim, black Carolinian activists launched another direct assault on white supremacy. On April 3, 1944, the Supreme Court handed down its ruling in *Smith v. Allwright*, outlawing the all-white Democratic primary on the basis that it violated African Americans' right to vote as guaranteed by the Fifteenth Amendment. It was the most momentous voting rights decision since Reconstruction. Eleven days later, South Carolina governor Olin D. Johnston convened an emergency session of the state legislature and told members that the Supreme Court's action had rendered it "absolutely necessary that we repeal *all* laws pertaining to primaries in order to maintain white supremacy." Nothing less than "the preservation of morals and decency in government is involved," the governor maintained before reminding his audience of history's horrible lessons. "Where you now sit, there sat a majority of Negroes," he spat. "They left a stench in the nostrils of the people of South Carolina that will exist for generations to come." The General Assembly then repealed almost two hundred statutes that referred specifically to primary elections. In effect, this "South Carolina Plan" asserted that the Democratic Party was a private organization. As such, its internal decisions—including the right to exclude African Americans from membership and thereby prevent them from voting in primary elections—remained legally immune from federal judicial authority.[45]

McCray and McKaine responded by establishing the Progressive Democratic Party (PDP). Speaking at the group's inaugural gathering, held at Columbia's Masonic Temple on May 24, McKaine also invoked the lessons of the past—specifically, those of African American participation in government. "Our main purpose for being here today is to help history to repeat itself," he pronounced. Hinton followed McKaine at the podium and placed events in a more contemporary context. "We are living under a greater dictatorship than Hitler has ever given, and we don't like it," the NAACP's state president proclaimed. The fact that his son was fighting in the South Pacific crystallized the issue. "He is good enough to die," Hinton shouted, "but he is not good enough to vote in this hellish South Carolina. Black boys are dying on battlefields, and these South Carolina demagogues meet in extra session to further disfranchise what we are fighting for."[46]

The PDP ultimately sought to add African Americans to the state's voting rolls. By the time delegates assembled, however, organizers had decided to challenge the seating of South Carolina's all-white delegation at the 1944 Democratic National Convention in Chicago in hopes of bringing federal pressure to bear on their obstinate state. They would be confronting a wartime president pursuing an unprecedented fourth term with the assertion that he should reward his southern black supporters by confirming their right to full participation in party affairs, both locally and nationally. Indeed, the two competing delegations from South Carolina starkly confirmed the growing tensions within the Democratic Party caused by the impossibility of appeasing both its black constituency and its southern white supremacists. National leaders understood that party unity could best be preserved if the PDP failed. Accordingly, at preconvention meetings with the group's leaders in Washington, D.C., Democratic officials argued that the PDP had not followed the national party's rules by organizing at the precinct, ward, and county levels and predicted that the credentials committee would dismiss the PDP's challenge on a technicality. Twenty PDP delegates nevertheless headed to Chicago by train on July 13. Four days later, PDP leaders presented their case to a special subcommittee. Maybank spoke for South Carolina's all-white delegation, which, as expected, won the right to be seated. In a conciliatory gesture, national Democratic Party officials assured the PDP that an integrated South Carolina delegation would be seated in 1948.[47]

The Palmetto State's black activists were far from finished. The PDP returned home to launch a massive voter registration drive and linked it to a bid by McKaine to win election to the U.S. Senate, the first time since Reconstruction that a black man in South Carolina had run for such high office. McKaine's opponent was none other than Governor Johnston. When official figures showed that Johnston had defeated McKaine 94,556 votes to 3,214, the PDP cried foul. It then submitted affidavits to the Justice Department and asked that it bring criminal charges against election officials. Next, the PDP challenged Johnston's seating in the Senate and implored the other members to investigate. Neither the Senate nor the Justice Department responded.[48] The lack of federal support hardly boded well for black activists engaged in the simultaneous battle to equalize teachers' salaries.

Septima Clark's pursuit of professional excellence removed her from the front lines of the PDP's political battles. By scrimping and saving, she enrolled at Hampton Institute in the summer of 1944 to begin earning her master's degree. When she returned to Columbia for the 1944–45 school year, she took a more active role in the salary equalization campaign. The PDP's summertime challenges had raised the stakes for participating teachers, and her activity provided Clark with entry into the circle of NAACP and PDP leaders. This, in turn, heightened her strategic importance. "I was able to get some affidavits from both white and black teachers," Clark revealed, that demonstrated "the discrepancies" in their salaries. Some of the white teachers "let us have copies of their checks." By spring, however, the Columbia salary equalization suit had run into difficulty, mostly because of the lackluster performance of the new local counsel, Shadrack Morgan, a black lawyer from Orangeburg who had replaced Harold R. Boulware when he entered the armed forces. According to Clark, "When Mr. Marshall came down to Columbia, he discovered that this attorney hadn't done the work he had been assigned." As a result, the national NAACP lawyer "spent practically the entire night working on the case, getting affidavits and doing other chores that should have been done before his arrival."[49]

J. Waties Waring heard arguments in *Thompson v. Gibbes et al.* on May 9, 1945. Again, curious observers packed the standing-room-only courtroom. Witnesses for the Board of School Commissioners in Richland County's District 1 testified that existing salary inequities resulted from factors that had nothing to do with racial discrimination. Training, experience, and ability mattered, as did choices made by African American teachers. "In every case," board chair J. Heyward Gibbes explained, "the starting [annual] salary offer is $900. White teachers refuse it and we have to go higher. Negro teachers accept it and consequently get lower salaries." Edward R. Dudley, a NAACP attorney from New York, asked whether Gibbes believed "that a Negro teacher of equal qualifications and experience should get the same salary as a white teacher." "Yes, of course," Gibbes said, "unless . . . the teacher agrees to work for less." He also asserted that the board had been working to decrease salary differentials since 1941. "On the basis of qualification, a discrepancy in white and Negro teachers' salaries that has 200 years of social, educational, and political background for a basis is being eliminated," Gibbes maintained; "Nothing but a more or less violent action can change it overnight."[50]

Abram C. Flora, superintendent of Columbia schools, provided specific examples of instances where a few black teachers earned more than their white counterparts. When cross-examined by Dudley, however, Flora admitted that a black auto mechanics teacher had been paid an annual salary of $1,500, while a white teacher of the same subject collected $2,200. Flora attributed the discrepancy to "specialized work and the need." Dudley persisted, forcing Flora to divulge that a local white high school principal earned $437 a month and his two assistant principals $288, while Booker T.'s Simmons had no comparable help and earned a mere $260. When pushed to account for this disparity, Flora chalked it up to "length of service," and "service to the institution." But Simmons had a master's degree from Columbia University and more than twenty years of experience, including sixteen as principal. At this point, Judge Waring asked the superintendent, "You think that school should have a better principal?" "It probably should," Flora responded, though he had earlier described Simmons as "a competent person."[51]

The relatively progressive Flora found himself in a difficult position. On the one hand, he defended the school board's existing unequal system and its efforts toward improvement, remarking, "I think in the main we have gone a long way." On the other hand, Flora rhetorically nodded toward African American educational leaders when he added, "We have had wonderful cooperation." He also impressed Waring as a fair man, a "clean cut, decent, able, fine kind of chap, perfectly frank." Clark viewed Flora sympathetically as well: "I have always believed that the white superintendent of schools thought that we were right in demanding equalization of salaries."[52] Unlike Charleston's hearing, Columbia's lasted all day.

Sixteen days later, Waring handed down his decision for the plaintiffs, distinguishing between the good intentions of upstate white school officials and those in the Low Country. During the *Thompson* hearing, Waring had recognized a genuine attempt on the part of the school board to remedy its racially discriminatory salary schedules. "The old cliché that Rome was not built in a day, is applicable to this situation," Waring wrote. Those who sought "over night" remedies had to be "persons motivated either by idealistic abstractions or by a spirit of political revenge and self-seeking aggrandizement."[53] Waring was neither a militant nor a race traitor, but he believed that the court should facilitate equalization in accordance with federal law. He ordered the Richland County Board to set a new salary schedule by April 1946 and then make it retroactive to the 1945–46 school term.

Between the time the *Thompson* case was filed and when it was heard in court, the South Carolina state legislature had taken further precautions, notably in the first session that followed black Carolinians' overt political defiance in the summer of 1944. The State Board of Education had submitted two new salary schedules for the legislature's consideration, one for all beginning teachers and one for current teachers who chose not to apply for recertification. The General Assembly "decided that such was legally unsound and provided only one state aid salary schedule, which in effect made recertification mandatory for all teachers receiving state aid." Senator Edgar Brown again defended the legislature's action: "If you don't accept a recertification plan now, $3,250,000 will be gouged out of the taxpayers by federal court orders making pay for whites and Negroes equal."[54] Practically overnight, the General Assembly had passed a law that required the state's entire teaching force to become recertified.

The statute generated considerable anxiety among teachers. They soon learned that new certificates would be divided into five classes, all of which were linked to the amount of training they had received. Only teachers who held master's degrees could obtain a Class 1 certificate; those who had only bachelor's degrees and who had previously been entitled to first-class certificates now faced the psychological hurdle of receiving a Class 3 certificate. White teachers' enrollment in summer school programs jumped 375 percent in 1945; among African Americans, enrollment increased a modest 18 percent because a larger proportion of black teachers had always sought additional summer training. Moreover, each class of certificate had a corresponding grade that ranged from A to D. Teachers' salaries would depend on the grade of certificate they held, but the sole basis for determining that grade would be their score on the National Teacher's Examination (NTE). Practical considerations meant that not all teachers could immediately take the NTE, but salaries soon would reflect their performance on the exam. As Charleston superintendent A. B. Rhett noted, "The teachers, at least the white ones, are very much divided on the subject" of the NTE. A few favored taking the examination, while others were "violently opposed."[55]

The same held true for African American teachers, most of whom viewed the imposition of the NTE as the white state's retaliation against them for the salary equalization suits. According to Septima Clark, "Some of the Negro teachers gave up their positions at once," and "others declared they would not take the examination." The state NAACP advised black teachers to follow the latter strategy. During impassioned discussions at one mass meeting, Clark told those assembled, "If you say that you are not going to take that examination, I will be with you. But if some of you say tonight that you are on the fence on this proposition, then I know you will be the first ones there to take it." By this time, Clark was well on her way to earning a master's and had confidence in her ability to perform well on the NTE. She had decided to

Septima Clark (back row, far left) with the faculty of Columbia's Howard Elementary School, 1945. Courtesy of the Avery Research Center for African American History and Culture, College of Charleston.

ignore the NAACP's request. As she told her colleagues that night, "I will let you know right now that I am going. I am not afraid to take that examination."[56]

Lois Averetta Simms, then a young teacher in Charleston, participated in a similar meeting at that city's Central Baptist Church. Most of the assembled crowd opposed the test and wanted to present a united front to school authorities. Beyond the injustice, personal pride was at stake. All teachers would have to provide their NTE scores to the school office. Knowing teachers' NTE scores also meant knowing their salary brackets. Ill feelings could hardly be avoided, Simms observed, because "office folk talk, you see? And there are teachers who are in with the office folk, so they know who made the A's, they know who made the B's, and B wasn't supposed to be worthwhile." Fannie Phelps Adams explained the practical consequences of failing to score high enough on the NTE to earn a Grade B certificate in districts that required it as a minimum: "We lost a *very* good teacher. He was hired but had not taken the teacher's exam. So when he took it, he made a C. And he was one of the best teachers that we could have had, but unfortunately, he had to leave because he didn't make a B." "That score," she asserted, "does not determine your real abilities."[57]

White legislators had passed a statute that explicitly abolished racial discrimination in teacher salaries at the same time that they introduced "objective" factors that determined how much teachers got paid. As NAACP attorney Edward Dudley informed James Hinton, "Although this system may not be altogether desirable, nevertheless it is not discriminatory, and the Negro teacher has just as much chance to arrive in the higher salary brackets as the white teacher." Or did she? Figures released by the State Department of Education the next year revealed that 95 percent of white teachers had scored high enough on the NTE to have their salaries fall within the Grades A and B pay range. Only 43 percent of black teachers did so, and 57 percent of African Americans still received lower pay because their NTE scores placed them in the Grade C and Grade D salary brackets.[58] Comparable training, years of service, and competency did not guarantee a comparable salary at all.

Fannie Phelps Adams clarified one possible reason for the disparity. Most black teachers, she reasoned, had not been taught how to maximize their performance on standardized tests. "When you come to questions, if you don't know it right off, I know now, move on to something else, and you have some extra time to come back" at the end. "But I didn't learn" to take tests that way; "I learned that you stay there, you have got to get that answer, so you slow down, and as a result you miss out and you don't make a good score."[59]

Ellison D. Smith, son of Cotton Ed Smith and director of the state board's Division of Teacher Education and Certification, offered additional insight in 1946. Praising white teachers for availing themselves of opportunities for enhanced training and the "valuable" service provided by the Extension Division of the University of South Carolina, Smith remarked that "extension services for Negroes, however, are still very inadequate." The PSTA attempted to fill the gap by instituting a series of workshops and seminars designed to help black teachers navigate recertification, but it could do little to help them earn advanced degrees. Commenting on the increase of graduate study available for white teachers, including "the advent of the Ed. M. Degree," Smith admitted that "graduate work for Negroes is still woefully lacking." South Carolina might have changed how it paid all its teachers, but it had yet to equalize the funding and the resources it provided for their professional training. Thus, when Dudley counseled that "it is incumbent upon the teachers themselves to make a diligent effort to achieve as high a mark as possible" on the NTE, he failed to account for the ongoing structural inequalities that prevented them from doing so.[60]

Teachers and their representatives in the PSTA's House of Delegates apparently had taken the criticisms of the state's more militant activists into account, however. Speaking before a group of educators in Barnwell County, John McCray once declared, "The great mistake our teachers have made, and are making, is that of having a pussyfooting, yowsah boss type of state organization." Black teachers "ought to put into office only men and women of the lay teaching profession," he urged. "You commit suicide when you elect a college president, a principal, or supervisor, to executive offices in your organization. . . . These people are sitting in a hot seat and they are not going to do anything considered a departure from the prescribed fashion in South Carolina." B. W. Gallman, PSTA president from 1944 to 1946, was neither a principal nor an administrator. His successor, James T. McCain, Osceola McKaine's cousin, assumed the presidency of the PSTA in 1946. McCain, the principal of Palmetto High School in Mullins, was also the former president of the Sumter NAACP branch.[61]

Both McCain and Gallman had favored taking action on salary equalization. In its wake, these Young Turks took their turn at the organization's helm and generally steered it in support of the NAACP's activist agenda. In 1945, the PSTA endorsed the NAACP's plan to launch a suit to equalize graduate and professional training at the state's African American college and appointed a committee to work with the NAACP. It also lent its support to another ongoing campaign. As early as 1944, Osceola McKaine had begun organizing black activist parents in Darlington County to sue the local school board to provide equal transportation on school buses for their children. By 1946, the Reverend Joseph A. Delaine, who also worked as a teacher and whom McKaine had persuaded to establish a NAACP branch in Manning, had taken up the cause in Clarendon County. In 1947, the PSTA donated a thousand dollars to help Delaine's fight and for John Wrighten's suit seeking admission to the University of South Carolina Law School. Three years later, and at great personal cost, black activists in Clarendon County filed suit in *Briggs v. Elliott*.[62]

Moreover, the PSTA heeded black activists' call to participate in politics. At its April 1946 annual convention, the association went on record "urging every teacher employed in the schools and colleges of S.C. to qualify for full citizenship by obtaining their registration certificates and voting upon every possible occasion." Such a public declaration meant significantly more within the contentious atmosphere that prevailed in South Carolina between 1944 and when first voting rights case reached the courts in 1947. Indeed, PSTA leaders and activist teachers who backed the NAACP paid a high price. Prior to her trial, Viola Duvall confided to McCray that she had received hate mail from white supremacists and that she could hardly withstand "the pressure of being cut-off by her fellow teachers." Whether or not he judged his superintendent's comments in court as a bad omen, J. Andrew Simmons resigned as principal of Booker T. Washington and relocated to New York shortly after the end of the salary fight. "I have always felt," Septima Clark surmised, "that Mr. Simmons wouldn't have lost his job had he stayed on in Columbia." In July 1946, when plaintiff Albert Thompson failed to appear to answer a complaint about his "moral behavior," the school board terminated his contract. As Clark later observed, "Many folk were willing to make great sacrifices in order to obtain, or attempt to obtain, fair dealing for members of their race."[63]

After the war, people who were not educators became increasingly willing to assume the risks of civil rights protests. Black veterans returned ready to fight for first-class citizenship. Equally important, grassroots activists enlisted in the home front battles begun by the NAACP. In April 1945, a committee of African American community leaders from Johns Island appeared before the Charleston County School Board to protest their "totally inadequate" school facilities. The men requested that a high school be built, that elementary schools be consolidated, and that transportation for black students be provided. Three months later, the county board approved a recommendation by the white school trustees of Johns Island District 21 to pay Esau Jenkins seventy-five dollars a month to transport island students to Burke High School in Charleston. Though Johns Island had no NAACP chapter, such local initiative reflected the extent of the state NAACP's influence. Ten years after the state chapter's founding, the number of local NAACP branches in South Carolina had grown to ninety-one; by 1950, the Palmetto State had twenty-two NAACP youth councils and two college chapters.[64] National NAACP strategists had been right to assume that their litigation campaigns for educational equality and political rights would mobilize black communities across the South.

Yet the national NAACP could not have foreseen exactly how its success in both the equal salary and voting rights campaigns would affect one core group of members: teachers. White lawmakers in South Carolina paid little attention to precisely which African Americans were becoming activists: arousing the white state's ire placed all black educators squarely in the political crosshairs.[65] The new, supposedly race-neutral certification requirements signaled increased white surveillance from the mid-1940s forward. Because it politicized certification procedures, the NAACP's victory altered the role black teachers would play in the civil rights struggle in the Palmetto State.

After 1945, the majority of African American teachers chose not to risk their livelihoods by publicly supporting the NAACP. At the same time, many continued secretly to donate money to the organization because they believed in its work. No group was more familiar with the injustices of dedicating their lives to their profession every bit as much as white women but receiving lower salaries. African American teachers had the most intimate knowledge of the depravity of separate and unequal education because they labored in dilapidated classrooms and without the requisite equipment every day. Black women greatly resented the indignities that segregation imposed on their lives outside of school as well. Septima Clark traveled frequently by bus between Charleston and Columbia. Too often, however, the bus often stopped in places that had no restroom facilities for African Americans. Clark also recalled standing outside to wait for the bus even when it was rainy and cold: "You paid the same fare, but there was no place for you."[66]

Teachers considering taking a stand with the NAACP had to consider the fact that they would be endorsing the equally explosive goal of voting and ponder the consequences of losing their jobs. Deciding to avoid open identification with the cause carried its own burden: "It was terrible," one teacher confessed; "You couldn't be who you really wanted to be." Septima Clark, by contrast, believed that her individual courage strengthened her entire educational community. "I felt that in reality I was working for the accomplishment of something that ultimately would be good for everyone." Such a perspective provided her with an "easy conscience."[67]

More broadly, black teachers who did not openly participate in the nascent civil rights movement in South Carolina still made an important choice by staying in the classroom. Carolyn Carter, a 1959 graduate of Booker T. Washington High School, recalled, "I don't think there was a teacher there who just thought about a salary, or how far they could go." Rather, "they made us feel like we were the most important people in the world, and they taught us pride and tradition." Carter's history teacher made a profound impression. "When you go out there in the world," she told students, "whatever you do, remember you have us on your back. So therefore you don't do anything that's wrong or that would embarrass us." Carter got the message: "We were all going to accomplish something," she concluded, "We were all going to bring our people to a different level."[68]

In 1946, Septima Clark received "the greatly coveted master of arts degree" from the Hampton Institute. "I would never again attempt to earn a master's in three summers," she later admitted; "It is too strenuous — literally all work and no play." "One of my projects," Clark remembered, "was an experiment conducted with thirty-six Columbia sixth graders." She needed a tape recorder "because the project involved pupils who had speech de-

Septima Clark (front row, fourth from left) at the time she received
her master's degree from Hampton Institute in Virginia, summer 1946.
Courtesy of the Avery Research Center for African American
History and Culture, College of Charleston.

fects and I wanted to them to hear themselves reading as they sounded to other persons." Unable to purchase a tape recorder with her paltry salary, she counted herself "fortunate in having a principal who was able to obtain through the [all-white] school board the supplies I needed." But she had to spend $185 of her own money to have the report typed.[69] Beyond the everyday financial hardships black teachers endured, Clark's recollections underscore how little money they had to fund their professional aspirations. There was absolutely no room in a budget for unanticipated expense. Earning a master's degree reflected meticulous financial planning as much as an educational achievement. Moreover, if the salary equalization triumph primarily benefited the black professional class, Septima Clark's extracurricular employment, in both the summer and the school year, provides a reminder of how precarious that class status had been for teachers who were self-supporting women with multiple financial obligations.

Septima Clark embraced the NAACP's salary equalization campaign for the same reason she had joined the 1919 Charleston fight: because it offered her the chance to expand her options, both personally and professionally. Activists' efforts "paid off," Clark claimed, "not only in the satisfaction of having made the good fight, but also in actual cash." By her own estimate, Clark's salary tripled. When she started teaching in Columbia, she made sixty-five dollars a month; by the time she left, she earned nearly four hundred dollars.[70] Clark was one of only 250 black women in the state who scored high enough on the NTE to place her in the Grade A salary bracket.

In 1947, Victoria Poinsette suffered a stroke, and Septima Clark decided to move back to Charleston. At forty-nine, she returned to the Low Country having gained considerable experience in civic and political affairs. Her induction into the Alpha Kappa Alpha Sorority in May 1945 guaranteed her a better position among black women civic organizers in her hometown.[71] Participating in the teacher salary equalization campaign and earning a master's degree fortified Clark's confidence in both her own skill and the work of the NAACP. While the battle sharpened her sense of how southern black women's activist educational culture might prove adaptable to the transformations within the ongoing freedom struggle, dissent within teachers' ranks also alerted her to obstacles that would have to be overcome. At the end of World War II, Septima Clark did not know which way the freedom train was heading, but she knew that she would be on board. She was about to find out just how lonely that ride could be.

CHAPTER SIX

Crossing Broad

Charleston had always been a mercurial mixture of hidebound traditions and fleeting moods, subject to sudden agues like the fever that seized the fire-eaters of 1860. World War II, nearly as revolutionary as the Civil War in its own way, altered Charleston forever. Septima Clark moved back to a city caught between African Americans' pursuit of wartime civil rights promises and white people's determination to safeguard power. This struggle became the central drama of the postwar years. Taking cues from shifting national and international trends, an interracial cast of characters performed their scenes in courtrooms, classrooms, churches, and community centers. Behind them a dissonant chorus mixed strains of gospel, blues, jazz, and "Dixie."

Clark joined her like-minded activist neighbors in the continuing quest for educational equality and political inclusion. Most significantly, she appeared for the first time on the stage of Charleston interracial politics. Though mutual self-interest brought black and white Charlestonians together, negotiations had long proceeded according to white-defined rules. Discussions focused primarily on improving public health, housing, employment, education, and recreational facilities. Easing racial tensions that occasionally threatened to erupt served as an equally important mandate. All talk of electoral politics remained taboo, and unsanctioned publicity was anathema. Considered uncouth in this city of genteel manners, public dissent challenged the facade of white benevolence. It could even be dangerous when it challenged white control.[1]

Disfranchisement had ensured black dependency on white interracialists. These self-defined well-intentioned friends of the black community at best sought to guarantee fair treatment under "separate but equal." But if they began to suspect that African Americans were making too much progress, they worked to undermine it. Relying on the goodwill of white people was therefore a tricky business. Charleston's black community had an equally long history of raising funds to meet its educational and social welfare needs and took great pride in the autonomy and strength of its institutions. Too often, however, the presence or absence of white financing underwrote a project's success or doomed it to failure.[2]

If white Charleston had had its way, this model of interracial relations, forged in the Progressive Era, would have endured. The members of the white community were quite surprised, therefore, when one of the city's blueblood sons, federal judge J. Waties Waring, ruled in 1947 that South Carolina must "rejoin the union" and allow its black citizens to register and to vote in the Democratic primary.[3] Ironically, as black Carolinians rejoined the Union as voters, some of their white neighbors desperately sought a way out, an effort that culminated in the 1948 Dixiecrat presidential campaign of South Carolina governor Strom Thurmond. New political fissures divided old interracial allies.

In 1950, Septima Clark befriended Waring and his second wife, Elizabeth. Since the teacher salary equalization campaigns Waties Waring's conversion from well-connected upholder of the South's racial order to what white Carolinians saw as a race traitor had been under way. Between 1947 and 1951, the judge's decisions on behalf of African American plaintiffs placed him at the vanguard of the educational and political aspects of the national civil rights fight. Elizabeth Waring positioned herself similarly when she gave an incendiary speech at the black branch of the Charleston YWCA in early 1950. The couple's iconoclastic stand won approbation from the black community and white people's enmity. This white loathing endangered black activists: as Clark recalled, "My courage was to be severely tested."[4] With the exception of Clark, Ruby Cornwell, and a few others, black Charleston's public support for the Warings proved short-lived.

Clark valued her friendship with the Warings, though she did not always agree with them. The couple's counsel helped to crystallize Clark's vision that the civil rights movement needed to aim for complete integration. Years later, she assured them, "The old bridge that took me safely across to the doorway of freedom and democracy can't ever be forgotten," crediting them with being among "the persons who helped me to walk across that bridge."[5] Crossing that bridge, however, also required crossing Broad Street, angering the south-of-Broad Street bastion of white influence and power in Charleston. Clark's radicalism in the early 1950s expressed itself most in the interracial circles of social welfare advocates in which she moved. The Warings had no access to this world.

Clark certainly understood the pride and fear that limited traditional black leaders' action, but her status as both an insider and an outsider in her hometown gave her a different point of view. The greatest obstacle Charleston's leading African Americans faced in the postwar years involved their inability to effectively marshal the power of the ballot. At the same time, they confronted new internal contests for the right to dictate tactics and strategies, with some of these challenges issued by Septima Clark.[6] Clark played a major role in attempts to rid community agencies of segregation. Doing so necessitated confronting both dominant white Charlestonians and the black women who had their own reasons for resisting the integration of their organizations. Clark did not become disillusioned with local interracialist dynamics, in part because they allowed her to forge relationships with the small minority of Charleston women who shared her perspective. Rather, she grew impatient with leading black and white women who equivocated. What she perceived as the myopia of other black spokespersons added to her frustration. Her colleagues' failures, along with their reluctance to join her, would lead Septima Clark to chart a more independent course.

World War II permanently changed Charleston. In 1941, 80 percent of South Carolina's federal defense appropriation had landed in and around the city, breathing new life into its moribund port and military installations. Rural migrants arrived to take advantage of the wartime opportunities. By 1943, the number of employees at the Navy Yard had more than quadrupled, and a year later, the metropolitan population had swelled from a prewar level of 99,000 to 157,000. Defense production surpassed tourism as the city's leading industry, affording Low Country laborers a per-capita income nearly three times the state average. Flush times meant brisk business for restaurants and hotels, retail merchants and cab drivers, and prostitutes who catered to nearby military personnel, as well as contractors and construction workers eager to answer the demand for housing. And if average residents took comfort in the fact that their wallets were a little fatter, public officials and business leaders salivated at the thought of capitalizing on the economic boom. In the immediate postwar years, selling Charleston, with its resuscitated port, abundance of raw materials, available cheap labor, and mild climate, was relatively easy.[7]

Everywhere, Septima Clark saw evidence of this transformation. At the revived port, modern warehouses yawned alongside narrow rail lines and bustling docks, annually swallowing and disgorging five million tons of commercial cargo—processed timber, chrome ore, plastic, petroleum, rubber, textiles, food, fertilizers and chemicals. New neighborhoods, the first suburbs fringing the old peninsular city to the north and west, housed wartime migrants who stayed to call Charleston home. New power transmission towers stalked the landscape like awkward misshapen metallic herons, carrying 60 percent more electricity to residents' abodes and workplaces. New bridges welcomed commuters. Closer to downtown, shoppers, bankers, lawyers, and laborers crowded the streets. Their footsteps and voices merged with a cacophonous urban symphony of church bells, automobile horns, and the booming mufflers of the sixty-six city buses. Clark caught one of those buses every morning at the corner of Calhoun and Meeting Streets and rode it a mile and a half to Henry P. Archer Elementary School. On any given day, the increased number of passengers—mostly white men going to work at the Navy Yard—made it all the more likely that she would have to give up her seat in the colored section to white patrons.[8]

Arriving at Archer, however, reminded Clark how little had changed with regard to the endemic problems in Charleston's segregated schools. By 1946, nearly 4,000 African American children attended the city's three black public elementary schools—Archer, Buist, and Simonton—none of which had been built to accommodate more than 1,000 students. Conditions at Simonton were the worst; there 1,810 students crowded into a school built for 760. As city school superintendent George Rogers noted, school officials had no option but to use the fourth floor, "which according to the South Carolina building code should not be used at all."[9] Increased enrollment also mandated double and triple sessions and elevated teacher-pupil ratios. Older students hardly fared better: Charleston had only one unaccredited black high school, Burke, which was overcrowded and lacked a cafeteria, adequate toilet facilities, and heating. No African American school in Charleston provided hot lunches. Moreover, the city school board still spent only three-fifths as much money on educating black students as on white pupils. Though school officials privately acknowledged the urgency of building a new elementary school for black children, they feared white opposition to the expenditure of funds for black schools more.[10]

Septima Clark's students and their parents benefited least from the postwar expansion and diversification of the local economy, which continued to

*Septima Clark (standing, far right) with members of the Alpha Kappa
Alpha Sorority, ca. 1948. Courtesy of the Avery Research Center for African
American History and Culture, College of Charleston.*

relegate them to domestic labor and unskilled positions. Inadequate recreational facilities offered few options for those with leisure time. Most African Americans resided in the city's upper wards, squeezed by the housing shortage into deficient dwellings, with the worst slums concentrated on the east side, beginning just four blocks north of Clark's Henrietta Street. Such overcrowding continued to generate serious health problems in a community where death rates were 62 percent higher among the black population than the white population, and where two of the four county hospitals refused to treat African Americans.[11] In every facet of community life, the majority of black people in Charleston remained at the bottom.

Once resettled in her native city, Clark vigorously resumed her participation in civic affairs. As in Columbia, her civic activism meshed naturally with her teaching. She became involved with the work of the local Tuberculosis Association, which an independent committee recognized as the "most important voluntary health agency in Charleston County." As county chair of the segregated Division 2, she organized parent-teacher groups to compile a list of parents to whom Christmas Seal stamps could be sent with requests for donations. Family networks facilitated these efforts, as she had only to call on her brother, Peter Poinsette, who headed the city's black parent-teacher association. Clark also chaired a committee on public health that sought to educate community members as well as immunize African American children and treat venereal disease among adults.[12] These activities signified a mere beginning.

Over the next few years, Clark served as president of the Marion Birnie Wilkinson Club of the city Federation of Colored Women's Clubs and second vice president of the state organization. She acted as Basileus, or president, of the Gamma Xi Omega chapter of the Alpha Kappa Alpha sorority and accepted the vice presidency of the newly formed chapter of the National Council of Negro Women. When she became involved in the African American YWCA branch on Coming Street, its board elected her chair. She also held various positions on the board of the local National Association for the Advancement of Colored People (NAACP). Clark spent her after-school hours attending meetings—sometimes more than one a day—and she did not drive. Clark accepted such a rigorous schedule as part of her normal routine. She took naps and developed the habit of working in the wee morning hours, when all was "quiet and peaceful."[13]

With the exception of the NAACP, Clark's civic activism continued to express itself in woman-centered organizations, and she became well known among the cadre of black women busy in both communal and interracial social welfare work. Clark greeted sorority sisters Ruby Cornwell and M. Alice LaSaine, Charleston's Jeanes supervisor, at NAACP meetings. There she also encountered Mamie Garvin Fields, a former teacher and ardent clubwoman, and Irma Clement, wife of outspoken local leader Arthur Clement Jr. Helen Stiles and Mamie Rodolph, fellow members of her federated club, joined Clark at the YWCA events, along with Clement; Susan Dart Butler, the driving force behind the opening of the city's first African American public library; and another sorority sister and teacher, Jessica Brown. Clark attended gatherings of the local chapter of the National Council of Negro Women with all of these women as well as Rose Huggins, executive director of the black YWCA on Coming Street; Susie Simmons, whom Clark knew from the Tuberculosis Association; Julia DeCosta; and Maude Veal.[14]

Clark's extensive participation in black women's organizations confirmed her status as a Charleston insider just as her profession guaranteed her membership in the black middle class. But organizational contacts alone rarely fostered close personal friendships in the caste-conscious city. Even at the age of fifty, Clark remained excluded from the closed circle of black aristocracy as a consequence of her parents' status, her ill-fated choice of a husband, and the darkness of her skin. "I wasn't considered too well by that group," she claimed, "because they were very fair-skinned people with straight hair."

The home at 17 Henrietta Street that Septima Clark purchased in 1948, n.d.
Courtesy of the Avery Research Center for African American
History and Culture, College of Charleston.

The civic leaders who traveled in Charleston's most select African American social circles and who had long memories did not extend social invitations to her. "They would not come to my house. I wasn't good enough. Neither could I go to their house."[15]

Exclusion from one small part of the community did not diminish Clark's social life, which revolved around her family. Clark finally realized her girlhood dream of buying her mother a house in 1948, when she purchased the one that she; her sister, Lorene; and Victoria Poinsette shared on Henrietta Street. Her brother, Peter, and his family lived several blocks away. All visited together after church on Sundays and frequently met each other at big cultural events, hearing Roland Hayes, Marian Anderson, and Paul Robeson when they came to town. Each sibling still had a role to play in the family. With the assistance of a hired nurse, "Seppie," as her family called Clark, shouldered the burden of nursing Mama Vickie back to health after her stroke, and she recovered enough to once again chop wood. All the women of Henrietta Street counted on Peter to handle legal matters, while Seppie depended on Lorene to drive. The two sisters went everywhere together and stayed very close despite their very different personalities. Clark also took pleasure in socializing with her sorority sisters, although she did not share their penchant for high-society life and rarely wore fancy clothes or jewelry. "Why waste my money on that?" Clark reasoned; "I get what I need." She had a gown if she needed a gown, and she even had a fur cape, but her overall style was more down-to-earth.[16]

Charleston's black women rarely waited for white women to take the lead in social welfare projects but recognized the benefits that white support could bestow. At times, such backing was critical to the survival of the institutions to which so much time and energy had been devoted. For example, in 1907, feeling that their auxiliary efforts at the black YMCA "assist[ed] the men to save the boys" but that "the girls were being neglected," a group of ten black women had decided to launch a program for young women. They chose not to affiliate with the national YWCA because its board had ruled that it would recognize only one association in any geographical area and Charleston's white women had founded an association three years earlier. The black Y women continued to operate as an auxiliary of the local black YMCA and thus retained their autonomy. In February 1911, after years of fundraising, they purchased a lot with several buildings at 106 Coming Street and immediately established a kindergarten, a primary school, a girls' athletic club, and sewing classes.

By the time of World War I, the Coming Street Y was near default on its mortgage and its black women faced a difficult choice. The national YWCA's War Work Council intervened, promising to fund programs if Coming Street switched its affiliation, a process that entailed relinquishing its charter and deeding its property to the white YWCA. On one hand, the change meant surrendering the group's hard-won independence; on the other, it meant freedom from mortgage debt. The black Y women debated their options, considering both the short- and long-term consequences. World War I had created an influx of working women who sorely needed Coming Street's services, and the possibility of obtaining future appropriations from the national Y augured well for the survival and expansion of its work. The leaders reluctantly agreed but signed over their property with the stipulation that it forever remain the African American YWCA.[17]

To coordinate projects and allocate funds in a city that had both a "central," or white, Y, located on Society Street, and an African American branch, black women began attending interracial meetings. Doing so brought them into contact with the white women who saw themselves as moral guardians in the civic arena and acted accordingly. In public, white women cultivated the modesty of proper white southern ladies. Behind the scenes, they marshaled the influence of their social position, their networks, their access to powerful men—husbands, sons, neighbors, fellow church members—and the ballot to secure social legislation that would bolster human welfare and check industrial abuses. A racially paternalistic sense of Christian duty had first led white Y women across the color line, but after World War II, Charleston's all-white central Y board increasingly disagreed with the national organization's positions, particularly when it took a stand against segregation at its 1946 national convention.[18]

A lifetime of activism and influence in building local social services made Charleston's civic-minded white women resistant to changes in interracial relations. Such transformations struck at the heart of their identity as women and as political actors. Paradoxically, their empowered sense of self had taken shape in the 1910s as they fought for the right to vote, the same right that African Americans so forcefully pursued after World War II. White interracialist women missed the irony in their fear of extending suffrage to their black neighbors, perceiving only how the extension of the ballot threatened to rend the social welfare fabric they had so diligently woven. Their ideology had reached maturity in the World War I years and reflected the shining promise of the Progressive Era in spite of the dark cloud of institutionalized white supremacy. Many of these white women took satisfaction in their status as "experts," interpreting black life for state officials and their less progressive neighbors. Segregation gave their accomplishments meaning.

White female interracialists, like their male counterparts, felt at a loss when black people began to demand political rights. Most of these women would have concurred with Charlestonian Harriet Simons when she argued that improved race relations came when "many of the negro leaders" realized "how difficult it sometimes is, even with the best will in the world, to get things accomplished."[19] The only realistic timeline for improvement had to acknowledge that meaningful change came slowly but surely, not swiftly. But change could occur promptly at some times, which underscored the reality that what white women wanted to preserve most was their control. Such was the case in 1947, when Septima Clark brought a problem at the Coming Street Y to the attention of the Society Street Y women.

Certain neighborhood boys, bored and perhaps jealous that they lacked a program of their own, had begun harassing the Coming Street Y girls and playing pranks on its director, Rose Huggins, whom Clark described as "shy" and "sometimes even fearful." As a teacher, Clark understood mischievous boys. If a no-nonsense mien commanded their attention, a policeman stationed at the door during Y functions would certainly deflate their bravado and send them off whimpering. But where would they go? Years in the classroom had also taught Clark the necessity of finding creative ways to channel the excess energy that led to such shenanigans. The Y women discussed the problem and decided to send Clark and two white ministers' wives to talk with Mayor Edward Wehman Jr. to see what could be done.

Clark, then teaching the early session at Archer, took the morning off to attend the meeting. When the women arrived, Wehman promptly seated Clark's companions and then sat down with his back to her. The white women bristled, though Clark remained calm. "We had come down there for a purpose and I resolved to let nothing keep me from doing my part to see the purpose accomplished," she remembered. When her turn to speak came, she quietly but firmly asked if the city would provide a policeman for Coming Street events. "But Mr. Mayor," Clark continued, "that is only the short-range solution." She then requested the mayor's help in developing a recreational program to keep the boys occupied and out of trouble. Wehman phoned the chief of police and after a brief conversation informed the ladies that on days when the Y had events scheduled, they had only to call the station before the men left for their beats.[20]

That problem solved, the women took their leave, but as soon as they got outside, Clark's white friends told her how much the mayor's bad manners had embarrassed them. She appreciated the sentiment but asserted that success mattered more. She also instructed them in the broader implications of her racial diplomacy: "Regardless of the way he treated me, I think that he must now feel that hereafter he can sit with his face toward a Negro woman." Nearly thirty years of teaching in the segregated South had fine-tuned Clark's pragmatism, just as her decision to check her anger reflected the awareness possessed by any southern black woman engaged in the politics of social welfare. Clark later conceded that the episode affirmed for her the "virtue and efficacy of having patience" and "not permitting myself the costly luxury of losing my temper."[21] Both the women of Society Street and those of Coming Street could take satisfaction in how easily they had accomplished their goals. Things might have proceeded like this indefinitely, with white women running interference for black women and apologizing for white male officials, had political dramas not begun unfolding near and far.

The events of July 12, 1947, stuck most in the minds of Carolinians watching the courts. That day, Judge Waring handed down two decisions in separate cases of alleged racial discrimination. The first involved equal educational access. Edisto Island native, Avery graduate, and World War II veteran John Wrighten had applied to the all-white University of South Carolina Law School, which refused him admission. Wrighten sued on the grounds that in 1938 the Supreme Court had ruled in *Gaines v. Canada* that states must make their separate law schools equal or admit African Americans to white institutions. Waring offered state officials three options. They could establish a law school at South Carolina State, admit Wrighten to the University of South Carolina, or close the existing program and provide no state-funded legal education for white or black students. South Carolina chose the first solution, and during its next session, the General Assembly released two hundred thousand dollars for a building and thirty thousand dollars for a library at South Carolina State.[22]

The second case proved much more contentious. On August 12, 1946, George Elmore, secretary of the Richland County Progressive Democratic Party (PDP), had gone to his polling place in Columbia's Ward 9 to vote in the Democratic primary. When party officials turned him away, he filed suit. In the resulting case, *Elmore v. Rice*, Waties Waring finally voiced unequivocally his dissent from South Carolina's racial order. His opinion decried Olin Johnston's 1944 special legislative session — in which the General Assembly had essentially remade the Democratic Party into a whites-only private club to evade the Supreme Court's ruling in *Smith v. Allwright* — as "pure sophistry." Waring dismissed the change on the grounds that private clubs did not elect public officials and that the Democratic primary was tantamount to election in South Carolina. Before concluding, the judge quoted President Harry S. Truman: "We can no longer afford the luxury of a leisurely attack upon prejudice and discrimination. There is much that state and local governments can do in providing positive safe-guards for civil rights."[23] Ruling for the plaintiff, Waring cast his lot with the Union.

Southern lawmakers had initially felt they had a friend in Truman, who hailed from a border state and who had appointed several southerners to key positions in his administration. In 1947, conservative and liberal Democrats alike fell in line behind the president's tough new stance toward the Soviet Union and his foreign policy strategy of "containment" to check Soviet aggression. Most southerners also supported Executive Order 9835, in which

Truman directed that all government employees be investigated to root out communist or "subversive" elements and instituted a loyalty oath for all those who remained.[24] The Cold War had officially begun.

Nevertheless, white supremacist Democrats underestimated Truman's fealty. When a postwar wave of racial violence engulfed the nation in 1946, as it had in the Red Summer of 1919, Truman was genuinely repulsed. Much of the violence was directed against black veterans such as Isaac Woodard, who was brutally beaten by a white bus driver in Batesburg, South Carolina, and blinded for life. Truman responded by establishing the President's Committee on Civil Rights to investigate abuses and make policy suggestions. In February 1948, he appeared before Congress to outline a ten-point legislative program based on the committee's report, *To Secure These Rights*. The president's proposals included creating a civil rights division in the Justice Department and signaled his support for federal protection of the right to vote, banning discrimination in interstate transportation, and eliminating Jim Crow in the armed services. Though he stopped short of publicly sanctioning his committee's condemnation of segregation, Truman promised to circumvent congressional opposition through executive fiat whenever possible.[25]

Feeling the talons of the federal eagle poised to sink into their necks, white southerners crafted a defense that blended an acknowledgment of the South's "race problem" with familiar warnings against the dangers of federal interference in local affairs. Many residents of the region shared South Carolina governor Strom Thurmond's conviction that economic investment, not federal intervention, would resolve the racial quagmire. Thurmond joined his regional comrades at a meeting in Wakulla Springs, Florida, to debate an appropriate response to Truman's civil rights message. All participants agreed that the South must reassert its power in the national Democratic Party, but they disagreed about how far to go. Mississippi's delegates, along with half of Alabama's, walked out of the Democratic National Convention that summer. The rebels then formed the States' Rights Democratic Party, more commonly tagged the Dixiecrats, and launched an insurgent bid for the presidency with Thurmond as their candidate.[26]

Ordinary white Carolinians joined the chorus of dissent. "I would rather see every school and church in the State of South Carolina burned to the ground," one of them announced to J. Howard McGrath, chair of the Democratic National Committee, "than to force by law the white children to attend the same churches and schools with negroes." For good measure, he added,

"Truman is a carbuncle on the rump of degenerate political demagogery."[27] In South Carolina, 1948 was late, not early.

Meanwhile, Palmetto State Democrats formulated a two-pronged strategy to skirt *Elmore v. Rice* on the grounds that Waring's decision applied solely to Richland County. First, they reaffirmed that only white people could belong to the Democratic Party. African Americans would be allowed to vote in the primary if they presented their general registration certificates, an extra step not required of members of the white electorate. Second, the Democrats instituted an oath for all would-be voters. Registrants had to avow their support for "social and educational separation of the races" and profess their allegiance to "the principles of States' Rights."[28] The more sly among them probably reasoned that the federal government could not possibly object to such a "loyalty" oath given that Truman had already required one of all government employees. Officials in Beaufort County also rationalized that membership in the PDP conflicted with the rules of the regular Democratic Party and removed the names of several African Americans from the rolls. One of those purged, David Brown, agreed to serve as plaintiff when the NAACP brought suit against county Democratic chair William P. Baskin in early July 1948.

Peeved that he had to return to court almost a year to the day after the *Elmore* ruling, Judge Waring made himself clear in *Brown v. Baskin*: "I'm going to say to the people of South Carolina that the time has come when racial discrimination in political affairs has got to stop." He abolished the oath, extended the registration deadline to July 31, and ordered state Democratic Party leaders to enroll all qualified electors regardless of "race, color, creed, or condition." He also threatened officials who obstructed African American enrollment, as well as any Election Day troublemakers, with contempt of court and imprisonment. Even so, the next day's *Charleston News and Courier* ran a front-page article, "How to Stop the Club Enrolling." Later that afternoon, as he accepted the Dixiecrat presidential nomination in Birmingham, Thurmond thundered, "There's not enough troops in the Army to force the southern people to break down segregation and admit the Negro into our theaters, into our swimming pools, into schools, and into our homes."[29] So far African Americans had only been admitted to the voting booth.

Black Carolinians had just two weeks to register. In Septima Clark's hometown, 4,360 African Americans added their names to the books in just three days, and on August 10, an estimated 30,000 black people braved the high summer heat across the state to cast their ballots in the Democratic primary. Poll watchers in Charleston County reported a "steady" stream of black voters throughout the day. Waties and Elizabeth Waring passed the afternoon driving to polling places in the city's predominantly black Wards 9–12. Septima Clark remembered the day as "quiet"—a pleasant change. "Election day used to be a terrible thing around Charleston. Guns were always out. There would always be some death. Judge Waring stopped that."[30] The ballot gave black Carolinians more powerful ammunition in the struggle for civil rights. The stakes had changed, and across the spectrum, from militant to accommodating African Americans and from segregationist to moderate white people, everyone took up a new position.

White Charlestonians soon had confirmation that African American enfranchisement would lead to the more horrible specter of "social equality." By late 1949, some of Charleston's leading black citizens had begun socializing with the Warings. In the aftermath of *Elmore v. Rice*, the judge had become a pariah among white residents in his hometown, who claimed that the couple forged these interracial friendships to legitimate the civil rights résumé they had been building since 1947. As white Charlestonians stopped making social calls at the Warings' home south of Broad Street, the subdued and reflective judge and his more outgoing, strong-willed wife reached out to well-educated, economically successful, and accomplished members of the black community.[31]

Ruby Pendergrass Cornwell fit that profile. Born in 1902, in Foreston, South Carolina, the young Ruby grew up in the Low Country. With her father assigned to preach in a rural area, she was raised by relatives in Charleston and attended Avery Institute for one year before transferring to Mary McLeod Bethune's Daytona Educational and Industrial Institute in Florida. After graduating from Talladega College, Pendergrass studied vocal performance in Harlem. She returned to Charleston in 1925 to teach at Avery, counting two of Clark's younger siblings, Lorene and Wilfred Poinsette, among her students. Pendergrass moved easily in Charleston's elite social circles. The women of the Phyllis Wheatley Literary and Social Club asked her to join them, as did the women of the Entre Nous Bridge Club. Her teaching career ended in 1930, when she married Charleston dentist A. T. "Connie" Cornwell.[32]

Ruby Cornwell first met the Warings in the spring of 1949 but did not really get to know them until she attended a New Year's Eve party at Harry and Corinne Guenveur's home at the end of that year. Those black Charlestonians not dependent on white goodwill for their economic well-being had the least to fear as they forged a relationship with the controversial white couple. Septima Clark would not have been invited to this fete, but not because she worked for the state. According to Cornwell, her family "did not rate socially" or "club-wise" in that part of the black community.[33] As the assembled guests lifted their glasses to toast the birth of the New Year, few probably imagined how turbulent 1950 would become. J. Waties Waring had by now become a household name in South Carolina. Sixteen days later, Elizabeth Waring grabbed her chance to join him in the spotlight.

✧✧✧

Rose Huggins, executive director of the Coming Street Y, heard Elizabeth Waring give a speech and suggested that the black Y women invite her to address their 1950 annual meeting. The women, including Septima Clark, who was serving as chair of the Y's Committee on Management, agreed and began planning the event. When the announcement appeared in the *Charleston News and Courier*, white women at the Society Street Y immediately objected. Judge Waring had sent seismic tremors rippling through the state's political community with his controversial primary ruling, and for this reason alone the choice might have been deemed inappropriate. But he had sent even greater shock waves through Charleston's social community in 1945 when he divorced Annie Gammell Waring, his wife of three decades, to marry a twice-divorced Yankee woman. The fact that Elizabeth and her ex-husband had been bridge partners with Waties and Annie Waring set tongues wagging. The fact that the judge had asked Annie to go to Florida to terminate their marriage since South Carolina law forbade divorce was seen as at best scandalous, at worst unethical. The fact that the judge continued to live in Annie's family home while she moved into a carriage house around the corner — where she had a clear view of Waties and the new Mrs. Waring carrying on — was perceived as downright dishonorable and barbaric.[34]

Elizabeth Waring's pernicious influence, aristocratic white Charlestonians liked to believe, led her husband to snub his family and his few remaining friends. They also thought that she pushed him further in his support for racial justice.[35] In style and philosophical mind-set, Elizabeth Waring played the perfect foil for traditional white Charleston. Together, she and her new husband had the social stature and personal networks to focus national attention on their publicity-shy city. Even if all the Y women of Society Street did not travel in the south-of-Broad social world that hated Elizabeth Waring, they certainly followed its lead and were repulsed by the idea of her speaking to any group affiliated with their YWCA.

Society Street Y women called a meeting on January 12 to persuade the Coming Street Y women to rescind their invitation. Septima Clark listened to their objections and offered an alternative argument. Black women, she reasoned, would know little or nothing of the gossip surrounding the Warings' social life. When Clark refused to rescind the invitation to the judge's wife, Society Street representatives responded that her stance threatened the possibility of having an African American woman appointed to the central white board. "All of this work we have been doing to get this representation will be lost," one woman contended. "This is a hot potato whichever way you take it," Clark realized. She knew that either choice would create anger, but she could not think of a reasonable excuse for canceling the speech. She stood her ground but decided to inform Elizabeth Waring of the new developments.[36]

Clark visited the Warings for the first time that evening, aware that she and Huggins were on a delicate mission when they knocked on the front door of 61 Meeting Street. Though familiar with Judge Waring's court rulings, Clark had never met him or his wife. After explaining the situation to Elizabeth Waring, Clark made two requests: "If the white people ask you not to speak, will you please speak? And if the Negroes ask you not to speak, please let me know."[37] Clark and Huggins would not have failed to apprehend the significant connections their hostess had at her disposal when an indignant Waring immediately phoned the Y's national headquarters to express her outrage at the white women's actions. By the time Clark returned to Henrietta Street that night, a telegram from New York asking for confirmation of Waring's complaint awaited her. Over the next few days, local gossips had a field day, and Septima Clark began receiving threatening phone calls at home.

Approximately 150 Charlestonians turned out to hear what Elizabeth Waring had to say four nights later. The few white people who attended took pains to avoid the featured guest. Expecting trouble from the Klan, Judge Waring had advised organizers to position men around the room and next to the light switches. Clark sat on the dais as Waring delivered what she called her "shock treatment" speech, written "deliberately to break down the stone wall of silence on the subject" of civil rights, "which the velvet glove method had never penetrated."[38] Most contemporary observers and subsequent commentators have focused on her description of white southerners as a "sick, confused, and decadent people," a statement picked up by the national press. But she also uttered words that reflected her bravery and defiance as much as they revealed the shortsightedness of her social privilege.

Following her introductory remarks, Elizabeth Waring took the suggested topic, "achievement," to heart and spoke as someone whose vantage point allowed her to see civil rights change as part of national and international trends. She urged black Charlestonians to harness it to combat white intransigence. Waring pronounced herself most encouraged, however, by "the strength and courage, the purpose and self-respect and dignity" of "the man and woman on the street—particularly the Negro women." By this time, walking the streets of Charleston had become something of a challenge for the judge's wife. White Charlestonians no longer looked her in the eye. Worse, they pretended not to see her. Those who acknowledged her presence did so by stopping dead in the middle of the sidewalk, locking arms, and, with whispers of "hold your ground," forcing Waring to step into the street. Waring parlayed her travails into a gift that had bequeathed a special insight: "There is a new look," she claimed, "in the eyes of the Negro women I pass on the streets."[39] One wonders which black women she meant. Did Waring refer to those she passed as they were on their way to clean the houses of her neighbors, the one she employed in her own home? Or is it more likely that she thought of the educated and the civic-minded black women she had come to know?

Equally palpable to Waring was "the rising tide of inspiration and self-assurance of the plain everyday person who has no desire or opportunity perhaps for public importance, but is spreading his influence all around." That influence, both Elizabeth Waring and her husband believed, would be felt most effectively in the wise use of the ballot. Black Charlestonians agreed but still groped for a method to ensure such use. Waring warned her audience against listening to the advice of "those timid ones" who preached gradualism, which the Warings judged far more dangerous than white supremacist hostility. "You must take the final push now or never," she concluded; "More power to you and I am proud to be a part of your movement."[40]

How must it have felt, listening to the white wife of a federal judge saying such things? It was just 1950 after all. *Briggs v. Elliott*, the Clarendon County school case, would not be argued in Judge Waring's court for another year; the Supreme Court's decision in *Brown v. Board* loomed four years in the future; the Montgomery Bus Boycott, five; the March on Washington, thirteen. Waring's listeners undoubtedly understood that this white woman had crossed the line separating herself from her white neighbors and could never go back. Some in the audience, like Clark, probably recognized the Warings as powerful allies with important national connections and were both thrilled and amazed. Others feared for their lives. Victoria Poinsette "became so frightened" that someone would shoot through the window "that she lost the use of her legs" and had to be carried out of the meeting hall.[41]

The varying white responses to the Coming Street Y affair indicated how Elizabeth Waring's confrontational style in challenging the racial status quo fed anxieties about women's behavior in a society whose men retained their power by controlling both women and African Americans. The most extreme response, from a writer in New York, succinctly linked white men's racial superiority to their sexual privilege when he "expressed hope that" Waring "would be '*raped* by a diseased *nigger.*'" On the other end of the spectrum, the southern press trivialized Waring's searing social critique by dismissing her as "just the girl who didn't get invited to the party" who retaliated by saying "something catty about the hostess." South Carolina's political leaders took a position somewhere in between, according Elizabeth Waring the status of a "professional" though "uninformed agitator." Undeterred, Waring continued her public crusade and upped the ante by appearing on national television's *Meet the Press* and endorsing interracial marriage, the greatest taboo of all. Before the end of summer, the South Carolina General Assembly had passed a resolution to buy the Warings a one-way ticket out of the state. A statewide petition effort eventually garnered more than twenty thousand signatures from people who supported the judge's impeachment.[42]

Flaming crosses also answered Elizabeth Waring's fiery words. A small wooden one burned in front of the couple's home on March 11, while they vacationed in New York. City police dismissed the incident as the work of pranksters. On May 27, another cross blazed in front of the all-white Murray Vocational School, beside two crude signs reading, "Nigger, don't try to go to white school" and "Waring, nigger-lover, get out of town." Again, police declined to investigate. A Klan motorcade paraded through the city for the first time in nearly thirty years that same month. Though law enforcement and white officials issued denials, Judge Waring estimated that the Klan had eight hundred members in Charleston County alone. Perhaps encouraged by the lack of an official response, unknown assailants hurled several large bricks at the Warings' home on the night of October 9, smashing their living room window and damaging the front door. After this, the U.S. Marshal's Office assigned guards to protect the judge day and night.[43]

Genuinely concerned for their safety, the Warings exploited these events in hopes of prompting federal action in the South. Waties Waring described the stoning of his home as "an attack upon the Union which I represent" and as "evidence of the stubborn, savage sentiment of this community in fighting the American creed." Elizabeth Waring believed that it was "wholesome to have the volcano erupt for all to realize the truth." Moreover, the couple began expressing their willingness to become civil rights martyrs. "Perhaps," the judge told a sympathetic interviewer, "there could be nothing better than that the white supremacists should kill me." Denying that he had a death wish, the seventy-year-old Waring maintained, "It is time some whites die to wake up America."[44] The couple vowed that they would not be intimidated or driven out of town but would stay in the South to fight for freedom and democracy.

In their attempt to "wake up America," however, the Warings may have played both ends against the middle. Segregation complicated the task of acquiring accurate information about the levels of white intimidation the black community encountered as well as responses to it. Then, too, white ignorance often worked to black Charleston's advantage when charting a navigable course in any given situation. Elizabeth Waring believed that black friends could provide the couple with valuable ammunition. "There are so many things you can do for us, so many things that we can't find out that you can," she later instructed Clark; "You get on that end and bring us the information we need." At other times, Waring seemed to piece together her own story. Eight days after she spoke at the Coming Street Y, NAACP executive secretary Walter White offered John McCray a scoop for the *Lighthouse and Informer* if he would verify what White had heard from "a reliable source"—presumably his personal friend, Elizabeth Waring. White's source informed him that Society Street Y women had prepared another press release repudiating Waring's speech for the black women of Coming Street to sign. They had refused, according to White's informant, "despite veiled threats and other pressure." Before closing his letter, White cautioned McCray against contacting anyone but "Septimus B. Clark," for he had also been alerted to the fact that "two employees" of the Coming Street Y "are paid extra by some of the white people to report all that goes on" in their branch. "One of them is said to be a young woman by the name of Huggins," White offered, admitting that he had no idea if "these reports are accurate."[45]

Clark had declined to sign the press release and denied to McCray that she had been pressured to do so. Her answers to the reporter's questions demonstrated a typically Charlestonian strategy to keep the issue quietly within the Y. She even refused to give him the NAACP branch secretary's name. Relating the story to Elizabeth Waring, Clark concluded, "I admire Mr. McCray very much but I dislike his idea of injecting his personal opinion or unofficial rumors into newspaper articles. The YWCA issue was too big to be tampered without thoroughness in thinking through."[46] As a fair-minded, respectable civic activist concerned about her reputation, Clark was less interested in a titillating story than in an accurate representation of the facts. It bothered her that neither the white nor the black press appeared to share her view. And on this important tactical question, she diverged from Elizabeth Waring, who had tried to give White the Y story.

The civil rights movement that Elizabeth Waring envisioned began with her husband's judicial rulings. She reserved a messianic role for the judge because he had "rolled away the stone from the grave and brought life to our Negro people as people and as human beings." Even so, she understood that African Americans had to walk through that open door, had to take the lead while she and the judge played supportive roles. Thus, she denounced black Charlestonians who capitulated to segregation as harshly as she condemned white supremacists. In "this battle for Negro Rights we cannot weaken our stand and make exceptions"; those who would not toe the line "will have to be spanked," she informed Ruby Cornwell. Women, especially wives of prominent men engaged in the civil rights struggle, had a special mandate: as hostesses, it was their duty to hasten social integration by presiding over interracial gatherings in their homes.[47] Waring divided the world into those who were for and against her and her husband. Given her defiance and its social consequences, Waring reasoned that black Charlestonians had no choice but to side with her and the judge; former friends became "traitors" with alarming alacrity. Despite her patronizing and uneven temper, Elizabeth Waring's honesty and courage attracted Clark and Cornwell, women who dared to confront the system and were prepared to make unpopular choices to do so.[48]

Septima Clark sipped tea at 61 Meeting Street less than a month after the Y affair and soon joined the Warings for luncheons and evening meals as well. She was there when a journalist and photographer from *Collier's* magazine visited. The resulting article, "Lonesomest Man in Town," appeared in late April and pictured Clark seated between Susan Dart Butler and Ruby Cornwell. Associating with whites initially left Clark uneasy and self-conscious: "Having been reared in an environment away from all white people it has been hard to feel comfortable just sitting and talking together," she later explained to Elizabeth Waring. True to the Broad Street aristocracy, the Warings entertained in the most elegant style. Fine china, linen napkins, and finger bowls adorned even their luncheon table, while caterers and a cook prepared the meals and a butler served. The refined atmosphere made Clark "conscious of my appearance"; she "wanted to have something extraordinary to wear to your house with a fresh hair-do every time." Clark surmounted her discomfort because the experience held great educational potential. "I really felt I could get a better insight into the political way of doing things and learn more of Charleston and South Carolina politics simply by going to the Waring home and listening to the talk there than I could in any other way," she remarked. Still, because many black Charlestonians objected, Clark recalled, "I had to make a decision to go regardless of what happened."[49]

From the beginning, the Warings mentored Clark in a number of ways. In addition to offering insight into national and international politics, they provided her with valuable advice regarding strategic voting closer to home. African Americans had no good choice in the 1950 U.S. Senate race between Olin D. Johnston, the incumbent Democrat, and Strom Thurmond, the former Dixiecrat presidential candidate. During one interracial campaign rally in Charleston, black attendees hissed in protest when Johnston accused Thurmond of appointing a "nigger physician" to the state medical board. In response, the senator demanded that someone "make those niggers keep quiet!" Yet Clark intervened in a political debate among summer school faculty and, as she wrote to Elizabeth Waring, took "the opportunity of telling the group all the information you gave me about Johnston's seniority and the wisdom [in] back of defeating Thurmond."[50]

Moreover, Elizabeth Waring's friendship helped Clark "to crash the caste system here." Being included on Waring's guest list made Clark feel that people she could not otherwise engage now paid attention when she spoke her mind about racial justice. "I don't know whether they ever learned to like me too well, but they listened to me. They listened to the things I had to say around that table," she asserted. Clark occasionally relished the ways in which Waring made Charleston's black socialites uncomfortable. "There were times when I felt that you were playing pranks on the Bourgeois group," she confessed, because "they had to listen to you tell them about me (a slave and a washerwoman's offspring)."[51] Social exclusion from Charleston's most elite circles, albeit for very different reasons, provided common ground for Clark and Waring.

Septima Clark's sensitivity to her status as both insider and outsider also prompted her to invite Elizabeth Waring to tea on Henrietta Street. Clark admitted that the invitation was a test: "Being a proud Charlestonian myself," she wanted to see if the refined Waring "could sip tea in a common, humble, ordinary house." When the judge's wife accepted, Clark felt better. Victoria Poinsette, who disliked white people intensely and would never have deigned even to serve them a glass of water, was livid and stayed in her room the entire time. The sight of the federal guards who accompanied the Warings everywhere created quite a stir among the neighbors, many of whom shared Clark's pride if not her nerve. "As long as Septima Clark have them white people coming to her house, we're gonna always have trouble," Henrietta Street residents worried.[52]

Clark's escalating activism certainly complicated her familial relationships. Lorene Poinsette, a teacher, belonged to her sister's federated women's club and worked with the YWCA but declined to get involved with more explicitly political work that might invoke the wrath of white Charlestonians. Peter Poinsette, a postal carrier, acted more cautiously as well, even though his job as a federal employee granted him protection against economic reprisals. Clark later reflected, "They weren't fighters. They didn't feel like they could fight for freedom or for justice; they just didn't have that kind of feeling."[53] She accepted her family members' different perspectives and knew not to ask them to do certain things, but she still took the steps she deemed necessary to bring about change.

Victoria Poinsette increasingly feared that her daughter's actions made the entire family a target. The Sunday after the attack on the Warings' home, she and Lorene were especially nervous when Peter's daughters came for their usual visit. "She didn't want us to get out of the car," Elizabeth Poinsette-Fisher remembered. Rushing them off, she told the girls, "We don't want you over here. We don't know what's going to happen. We don't know if she's being watched."[54] If Mama Vickie no longer had the strength to prevent her daughter from continuing on a dangerous course, she had sense enough to know how easy it would be to find out that Peter Poinsette was Septima Clark's brother. Family looked out for family in the Poinsette clan. Loyalty to the Warings meant violating the family trust.

Soon thereafter, Victoria Poinsette fell ill again and slipped into a coma. On the evening of February 3, 1951, she passed away in her sleep. Sixty cars formed the funeral procession from Old Bethel to the cemetery, even though the family had hired only four. Friends and acquaintances, including members the Society Street Y board, visited Henrietta Street to offer their condolences. The visitors could not have failed to notice the photographs of the Warings that Clark had "very prominently placed" on her living room table.[55]

Clark remained calm despite the storm raging around her. According to her niece, she took the view that "whatever's going to happen is going to happen." Aunt Seppie used to say, "If this is the way I'm supposed to die, then this is the way I'm supposed to die." Death was not an abstract impossibility. One afternoon while visiting 61 Meeting Street, Clark encountered a white garbage man who muttered, "Damn niggers coming into this house. I'm going to kill them all and kill myself too and we'll all be in hell together." Elizabeth Waring disavowed fear when Clark told her about the threats, arguing, "That would be one of the best things that could happen for publicity."[56]

A belief in total integration propelled by forceful action increasingly united Clark and the Warings, but Clark did not always concur with the judge's wife. For one, she disapproved of Elizabeth Waring's condemnation of all white southerners, commenting, "I didn't like the idea of her calling them decadent." Clark admired at least some of the white women she had met at interracial Y meetings, especially those who had accompanied her to visit the mayor and Virginia Prouty, Society Street's director for young adults. When Caroline Moore, whom Clark described as a "daughter of the Confederacy," assumed the presidency of the Y's executive board, she created a stir by threatening to call off a regional conference if black women insisted on eating with white women during the proceedings. Prouty objected and promised to resign, which led Clark to suggest that Society Street and Coming Street women who shared Prouty's concern should support her by doing the same. Rank-and-file Society Street women also rebelled against their officers by proposing that all Y women meet over supper. "Sad to say only five of the Negro women attended," Clark relayed to the Warings. Everyone else "acted just like the whites," providing what she considered "frivolous excuses for not attending."[57]

Clark's alliance with the infamous couple also had professional consequences. At school, she encountered opposition from her principal, Wilmot Frasier, who warned her of the dangers of supping with the Warings. Some of her colleagues confronted her at a faculty meeting, complaining that Clark's actions legitimated segregationists' claims that "the real reason blacks wanted integration was to socialize with whites." Clark heard them out and then asked if she might respond. She calmly turned to each of her detractors and drew them in with simple questions that hardly required a second thought to answer. Did anyone tell Frasier who he should marry? Did anyone tell the teacher with a new car what kind she should buy? Did anyone tell the particularly fashion-conscious woman what kind of clothes she should select and from what stores? "Of course not," they responded. Looking each in the eye, Clark asserted her right to choose her friends.[58]

Septima Clark and Elizabeth Waring shared radical integrationist goals but acted according to their individual social locations. If, as the wealthy white wife of a federal judge, Waring relied on the power of publicity, Clark, a teacher and ardent civic activist, identified her classroom and the organizations in which she participated as pragmatic starting points. At school, Clark's seventh-grade students made a "Champions of Democracy" poster with the Warings' picture, which offered a chance to connect a civics lesson to current events. These lessons did not end when the bell rang. Wanting her students to have "first-hand information of our government," she traveled with them to Columbia to watch a session of the state legislature.[59]

In the interracial arena, Septima Clark more directly voiced her belief in integration. When asked to serve as chair of the segregated division of the Community Chest, she accepted because it gave her the "chance to let the Board of Directors know that I do not believe in a Division II." Similarly, only white women served on the YWCA executive board. Clark appeared before its members and argued that segregated boards inhibited the work of the entire organization by preventing African Americans from knowing what white people were doing and vice versa. When she finished, the women present voted unanimously to elect her as first black woman on the executive board. Bringing around members of the Tuberculosis Association amounted to a greater challenge. Eleanor Halsey, the white chair, and others were "greatly disturbed" when, in the summer of 1952, as Clark and a small group argued for the dissolution of the African American auxiliary and the creation of a single biracial board. When the issue came to a vote, as Clark informed the Warings, the black members in attendance "voted to keep the auxiliary much to our dismay."[60]

The majority had its own logic. As they had at Coming Street in the World War I years, many black women remained reluctant to forfeit control over activities in their community. Within their segregated auxiliaries, they established the priorities, devised creative fund-raising techniques, and maintained decision-making control. Many of these women probably still perceived themselves acting as shields for those who could not defend themselves. By advocating integration, Clark risked undermining black organizational structures and the resources they marshaled. Combining black and white tuberculosis prevention and treatment services, for example, might mean that black people ceded control over what had previously been their smaller yet guaranteed share of funding if they could not command power in the integrated organization. Clark's agenda placed her at cross-purposes with that of some other women in her community whose value systems she shared and with whom she had worked intimately for several years.[61]

However, association with the Warings allowed her to grow closer to

Septima Clark, early 1950s. Courtesy of the Avery Research Center for African American History and Culture, College of Charleston.

Maude Veal, another black woman who rejected accommodation. In 1951, Veal, a schoolteacher and the wife of the Reverend Frank Veal, pastor of Emanuel African Methodist Episcopal Church, broke the color line of the local chapter of the League of Women Voters (LWV). Veal submitted her membership application to the LWV by mail, with no reference to her race. When officers notified her of her acceptance, they offered Veal a ride to a meeting that same night. Veal declined and phoned league president Harriet Simons, reminding her that the two women had met at a fund-raiser for the all-black Cannon Street Hospital. Simons took the hint and hurriedly ended the call.[62]

Simons and another woman soon visited Veal at home, assuring her that although the LWV looked favorably on her application, the potential controversy could hurt the organization because it depended on contributions from the business community. In other words, these white women argued that it was not they but their husbands who were prejudiced. The women suggested that Veal set up a segregated group. Instead, she alerted the national office, which had gone on record against the formation of segregated auxiliaries. The next time Veal heard from Simons, the LWV president informed her that the application had been accepted unanimously but asked that she not talk to the press. League officers publicly continued to explain Veal's participation to the white community as "training" for her to lead a black auxiliary.[63]

Like some of the Society Street Y women, rank-and-file LWV members staged a mutiny against their leaders by inviting more black women to attend their discussions. League officers again asked Veal to form an all-black group, and again she refused. The LWV leaders then approached Clark, who also declined. But when they appealed to Mamie Fields, she consented. Her decision reflected a lifetime of participation in an interracial culture that explicitly avoided discussing politics and made sense in a political climate in which keeping white eyes shut and white ears deaf to black strategizing had concrete advantages. Moreover, after the black auxiliary began meeting in the evenings at Dart Hall, at least one of its members seized an opportunity to continue the integration of the white league. After paying her two-dollar membership dues, Mabel Greene called Simons to let her know that she had a scheduling conflict and would be attending the white women's morning sessions instead. According to Clark, Simons responded, "Oh! but you have such a fine group of Negro women to associate with." "True enough," Greene conceded, "but I have no time at night so I'll be into the morning meeting."[64]

Harriet Simons had a slightly different recollection of the Charleston LWV's integration. At a 1954 regional meeting of state presidents in Atlanta, she told the group that "after two months of deliberation," the league had "invited a dozen or so outstanding Negro women to join," neglecting to mention the segregated auxiliary. Nor did she tell her fellow southern LWV state presidents that Charleston's white women had excluded black women from a banquet honoring U.S. senator Burnet R. Maybank Sr. just six months earlier. Despite these omissions, Simons asserted that black women encumbered the organization's work. "It will never be easy," she maintained, "as no one of the women has contributed a great deal because their political education is so far behind." The finest compliment she could muster for the black league women was that "when interested they work awfully hard."[65] Simons's skewed and paternalistic account provides an early example of how southern white people came to believe that others, not themselves, had supported segregation.

Black women did not need to depend on the LWV to educate themselves about politics. In 1947, the city's clubwomen had invited PDP leader John McCray to speak at a district meeting "so that the women might know more about what is being done to gain the right to vote." Afterward, the City Federation instructed each club to begin studying registration and voting. Like other club presidents, Clark bore responsibility to "keep before her members the importance of the ballot, and to have every member registered." Contributing to broader registration efforts, clubwomen also distributed informational bulletins in black beauty shops, barbershops, and restaurants. After Judge Waring opened the primary to black voters in *Brown v. Baskin*, Marion Birnie Wilkinson, president of the South Carolina Federation of Colored Women, urged the women of the Low Country to follow the example of those upstate. "We are really politicians up this way," she wrote to Fields, "and are getting ready to arouse our citizens to participation in the coming municipal elections." She suggested asking sorority women and those in civic organizations "to join hands" so that black voters would recognize their "full responsibility and at least maintain a balance of power which means so much to us."[66]

Experience taught Septima Clark that registration was one thing, participation another, and wise use of the ballot still another. After black Charlestonians gained the franchise, only a handful translated its promise into nuts-and-bolts activism in the city's Democratic Party. Just two months following Elizabeth Waring's speech at the Coming Street Y, Clark crossed Broad again, along with five other African Americans, to attend a Democratic club meeting in Ward 1, the oldest and most aristocratic preserve on the peninsula. Though they admitted Clark's group, white club members brought in a prepared slate of candidates and adopted it within five minutes. "If we had any one to offer we could not have done it with such a small number attending," Clark realized. Nor was she satisfied with the slate. As the 1950 primary approached, she voiced her unease with the candidates' lack of political sophistication. "It is disheartening to think that the men who want to represent us know so little about vital problems. I listened to seventeen of them and not one could truthfully say that he understood the 'Taft-Hartley Act' and could discuss it or intelligently vote against it as well as other legislation."[67] Clark took her right to vote seriously and educated herself on the issues. Translating that into a community-wide awakening was the next step.

Failure in Charleston's 1951 mayoral race drove the point home. When the first Democratic primary eliminated white supremacist Nathan W. Cabell, incumbent mayor William Morrison squared off against state senator Oliver T. Wallace. White supporters found Morrison affable enough despite his known penchant for the bottle but conceded that he was "lazy." Detractors honored him with song: "Wild whiskey Bill . . . never worked and never will." African Americans eyed Morrison warily. True, he had appointed the city's first black policemen after a three-year campaign spearheaded by the Interracial Committee, but his administration had also tried to shut down the city's only all-black fire company. Members of the black community also remembered how Morrison had bent with the political winds to align himself with the Dixiecrats. Black voters did not know that in 1949 Morrison had secretly explored ways to dilute their voting strength via a redistricting plan.[68] A year later, Charleston adopted an at-large system for electing the city's aldermen.

The city's black leaders, the Warings, and their allies favored Wallace. One of the last remaining New Deal liberals in South Carolina, Wallace supported labor, opposed the Dixiecrats, and had sponsored legislation in the state senate to raise teacher salaries. Black teachers, including Clark, expressed their appreciation by canvassing on behalf of his campaign. McCray argued that Wallace "has given Charleston county Negroes about the finest consideration they have ever received from any man in public office," efforts that included publicly soliciting their vote. The Morrison machine, by contrast, attempted to court black voters only surreptitiously. Black leaders had good reason to hope that their ballots would swing the election because they had helped Wallace outpoll Morrison by 142 votes in the first primary. Before the second primary, however, several prominent black Charlestonians threw their weight behind Morrison. Elizabeth Waring labeled these folk and their ilk "segregation profiteers" and informed Ruby Cornwell — apparently without the slightest sense of historical irony — that "a more powerful weapon than words will have to be used to whip them into line."[69]

The campaign turned nasty in the days just prior to the election. The candidates hurled personal insults at each other, and rival groups engaged in fistfights at a rally in Marion Square. Wallace had challenged Morrison to make an appearance, and five thousand people turned out to witness the showdown. According to Clark, who only had to walk to the end of her block and cross Meeting Street to join the crowd, Morrison tried to leave after speaking, but Wallace called him back to the podium and "shook his finger in his face three different times." Morrison "did not deny the statements made about him being drunk most of the time and using the public funds to buy his cars and the gasoline to run them." African Americans in the audience "jumped up and screamed out, 'Yes Morrison is yellow. He's yellow all the way down his spine.'"[70]

Amid this wrangling, both candidates and much of white Charleston waited anxiously to see whether the black community would vote as a bloc. African Americans constituted almost half of the voting-age population in the city's upper wards, where 60 percent of residents had registered to vote. Black leaders knew that the election offered the best chance to date to demonstrate the power of the black vote. If they delivered the margin of victory to Wallace, they would gain unprecedented political leverage and force future candidates to accord them some respect. Clark attended three Wallace rallies and was optimistic, informing the Warings that "the Negroes have spoken out frankly condemning the men and women who are supporting Mr. Morrison."[71]

In an unusual reversal, voter turnout for the second election exceeded the first by nearly twelve hundred. As expected, Wallace carried the upper six wards of the city, including the African American strongholds in Wards 9–12. In Ward 12, however, he beat Morrison by a mere ten votes, which demonstrated the Morrison machine's effectiveness in making up lost ground there. The mayor also picked up Wards 1 and 2, below Broad Street, which had gone to Cabell in the first primary, and won reelection. Though just one day earlier the *Charleston News and Courier* had ranked the black vote as the second-most-important factor in the election, the paper gloated, "If any substantial 'bloc' of Negro votes was formed by leaders of that race on behalf of Mr. Wallace, it was totally ineffective." Clark attributed Morrison's victory to the fact that he "gave away more money" in Wards 11 and 12 and thus received more votes the second time around. She initially hoped that reform would emerge out of the campaign's bitterness, yet a few weeks later, she confided to the Warings that "the reports of the behavior of Negroes in the last election are appalling. Many of us are embarrassed greatly. They sold fine opportunities to establish worthwhile principles for chicken dinners, cokes, beer, and whiskey."[72]

Disgusted, Elizabeth Waring wrote to Ruby Cornwell and declared dramatically that the election had led her and the judge "to this grave decision that our work in Charleston is done. *It is* finished. . . . From now on you Negro people will have to work your problems out for yourselves." Aside from her irritation at the lack of unified support for Wallace, Waring had begun to feel that some African Americans had taken her and the judge "too much for granted and mistrusted and not respected our friendship." She resolved to retain "courageous characters," including Clark, in her intimate circle, but otherwise vowed to receive former friends with only the "impersonal warmth of the humanitarian." For those who contacted the couple on behalf of organizations, Waring promised to play the role of the "bountiful white lady the Uncle Toms and Aunt Jemimas think a real white lady is." In this, she sounded remarkably like the white interracialists who wanted to work with black leaders only if African Americans did what they told them to do. Henceforth, Waring continued, African Americans would have to be "tested carefully first and watched by all of you for their record in action" to gain more personal access.[73] Less than six months later, the couple abandoned Charleston for New York, moving away for good.

Keeping in mind the failures of black organization in the mayoral race of 1951, Septima Clark supported the efforts of J. Arthur Brown, Herbert Fielding, and the Reverend Frank Veal a year later when they offered themselves as candidates for the state House of Representatives. The men spoke three times before women's groups, each time asking Clark "to make an appeal for funds in their behalf" and to recruit workers. She obtained donations from clubwomen, her sorority sisters, and a group of teachers enrolled in summer school. The teachers also agreed to take voters to the polls, to help educate them in the practical operation of voting machines, and to conduct a telephone canvass to remind friends to vote on Election Day. A community-wide voter registration effort had added nearly thirteen thousand African Americans to the books, but Brown, Fielding and Veal still polled last among a field of twenty-two candidates. Brown thought that black voters had been confused by having to elect a slate of ten candidates; those who marked only the names of the three black men had their ballots discarded. Fielding agreed.[74]

Deeply engaged with the campaign and active on committees that discussed tactical strategies, Septima Clark understood the lesson. Voter confusion remained a problem. The political failures of 1951 and 1952 taught Clark that more than increased voter turnout was necessary. A new kind of voter education had to be devised. African Americans also had to surmount all the white ruses deployed to discount black votes. As Clark already knew, white officials used similarly deceptive tactics to stymie the fight for equal education.

⋯⋙⋘⋯

By 1950, the Palmetto State was well practiced in performing scripts based on circumventing Supreme Court rulings pertaining to educational equalization. Each time, the players reprised familiar roles: black litigants braving wrathful reprisals; white jurists deeming their complaints invalid; black lawyers strategically pursuing an elusive Fourteenth Amendment; white justices of the high court cautiously deploying their power to shatter or uphold precedent; southern white politicians ardently defending tradition and its illusions of purity. As they had in the 1944 and 1945 teacher salary equalization cases and the voting rights fights of 1947 and 1948, the actors reassembled in 1950 for the beginning of a very long denouement.

Two decisions by the Supreme Court in June of that year brought up the curtain. *Sweatt v. Painter*, in which the Court ordered the University of Texas Law School to admit its first black student on the grounds that the state's black law school was inadequate, established definitively that unless higher education facilities were truly equal, the Court considered separation of the races unconstitutional. The second case involved the treatment of black students within the all-white institutions that had admitted them. In *McLaurin v. Oklahoma Board of Regents*, the Court struck down restrictions that had relegated sixty-eight-year-old graduate student George McLaurin to sitting in the classroom in a roped off section marked "Reserved for Colored" and to eating alone in the lunchroom at a different hour from white students. The state could not force interactions between students in an integrated institution, the justices conceded, but it also could not sponsor such outright harassment of any individual or group within that institution.[75] Though both cases applied specifically to higher education and neither repudiated the "separate but equal" doctrine of *Plessy*, southern politicians did not miss the handwriting on the wall. South Carolina's James Byrnes was positioned better than most to read it since he had sat on the high bench for one year during the Roosevelt administration.

The seventy-year-old Byrnes had formally retired from politics in 1947, when he tendered his resignation as secretary of state in protest of Harry Truman's civil rights policies. On January 14, 1950, Byrnes threw his hat into the gubernatorial ring, claiming that his concern for political developments had forced him out of retirement. White Carolinians trusted this elder statesman—whose political résumé included a dozen years in Congress and a decade in the Senate as well as service in two presidential administrations—and viewed him as the most able to preserve states' rights and segregation. This knowledge made Byrnes's job easier. According to one seasoned observer of state politics, he ran as "a Southern gentleman, not feeling the necessity of carrying on a person-to-person candidacy as others might." He received 72 percent of the vote.[76]

In his January 1951 inaugural address, Byrnes lost no time driving home the main point of his legislative agenda. He recommended instituting a 3 percent state sales tax—the first in South Carolina's history—with proceeds used to repay the seventy-five million dollars in bonds he sought to finance a massive school equalization program. Byrnes targeted not the state's graduate schools but its elementary and secondary public schools. "When I determined to re-enter the field of politics," he later confided privately to *Charleston News and Courier* editor Thomas R. Waring Jr., "I anticipated that segregation in the public schools would become an issue." Publicly, however, the new governor spun his proposal as a "duty" shared by all Carolinians. "We should do it because it is right. For me that is sufficient reason," he solemnly preached.[77]

Byrnes's stance gave other state politicians a chance to demonstrate their concern with the need to enhance South Carolina's image. Linking high illiteracy rates with low per capita income, the speaker pro tempore of the South Carolina House, Ernest "Fritz" Hollings, announced, "We have got to educate our youth regardless of court decisions."[78] Such comments made transparent the ways in which education and the "race problem" dovetailed to complicate efforts to attract outside industry. Searching for the middle ground between regional loyalty and salvation via economic investment obliged Palmetto politicians to rally white voters to support the new sales tax, ostensibly to help themselves first.

In reality, Byrnes and his cohorts meant to launch the most expensive educational campaign in the state's history for one reason and one reason only: they wanted to make the state's black and white schools equal to keep them separate. Jimmy Byrnes acted the part of maverick two months later, when, without conferring with any other southern governor, he told a meeting of the white state teachers' association that he would close the schools before integrating them.[79] By this time, Byrnes read a far more ominous threat in another case pending in a Charleston court.

When NAACP lawyers initially filed suit in the name of Harry Briggs on behalf of black parents in Clarendon County, they sought only equal school facilities and bus transportation for black students. At a November 1950 pretrial conference, however, Waties Waring had surprised Thurgood Marshall and defense attorney Robert Figg by suggesting that the NAACP throw out the original complaint and file a new one attacking the South Carolina statutes that mandated segregated schools. Thus, Waring asked the NAACP lawyers to do nothing less than seek a ruling that would condemn separate education—regardless of how equal—as unconstitutional. Marshall knew that the prospects of winning the first battle in a Deep South state were less than favorable. More troubling, suits contesting the constitutionality of state laws required hearings before a three-judge district court panel, though they could be appealed directly to the Supreme Court. If Marshall could count on a sympathetic response from Waring, he had to gamble that at least one of the other two judges would concur, which was highly unlikely. Nevertheless, the NAACP lawyer amended the suit as requested.[80]

Septima Clark's classroom obligations prevented her from going to the courtroom on the morning of May 28, 1951. Ruby Cornwell stood at the front of a line of more than five hundred people, most of them black, that stretched around the courthouse. Walking the one block from his home to work that day, Judge Waring took heart at the sight of African Americans who had traveled long distances to catch "a little whiff of freedom." Those less schooled in the intricacies of legal arguments could not have helped but been disheartened when Figg opened the proceedings by conceding the plaintiff's main point: Clarendon County schools were unequal "in respect to buildings, equipment, facilities, curricula, and other aspects of schools." Figg then asked the court to give the state time to equalize its schools. To prove that South Carolina intended to do so, he had only to cite the seventy-five-million-dollar school program already passed by the General Assembly and the three-week-old State Educational Finance Commission that would oversee construction. The hearing before the three-judge panel lasted two days. Judge John J. Parker wrote the majority opinion in *Briggs v. Elliott*, which found that in *Sweatt* the Supreme Court had intentionally left *Plessy* intact and that the inherent constitutional right to equality differed considerably in the arenas of higher and common public school education. In a vigorous twenty-one-page dissent, Judge Waring delivered his final opinion in a significant civil rights case and concluded it by declaring, "Segregation is *per se* inequality."[81]

Even before the *Briggs* decision had been handed down, South Carolina and Byrnes responded to the threat it posed by adopting a more aggressive stance. In early 1951, the governor created a committee, chaired by state senator L. Marion Gressette, whose main purpose was to chart South Carolina's course of action and response to federal court rulings.[82] Monitoring *Briggs* and the four other cases with which it had been consolidated under the name *Brown v. Board of Education of Topeka, Kansas*, as they made their way to the Supreme Court, Byrnes next persuaded the General Assembly to approve a referendum to be presented to voters in the 1952 general election. Come November, voters could choose whether to authorize the legislature to repeal yet another article of the state constitution, the one that granted lawmakers the power to operate the state's public schools. Voting yes would signal support for closing schools in the event that the Supreme Court declared segregation unconstitutional.[83] These white leaders believed that the Supreme Court would hand down a decision no sooner than October 14, 1952. South Carolina's "School Amendment" sent an unmistakable warning to Washington and positioned Byrnes at the forefront of southern obstruction. It also empowered voters to play the role of jurist.

Septima Clark followed the debate with keen interest. In the days leading up to the election, she made her way down to the Francis Marion Hotel to hear William D. Workman Jr., a Columbia newspaperman, discuss the School Amendment. As usual, Clark informed the Warings, the next day's press coverage of the event failed to accurately represent what happened in the meeting. "The Negroes used their chances to let the whites know how they feel about this one sided separate but equal affair," she wrote. Workman argued that white children would suffer should they have to sit in the classroom next to educationally inferior black children. He also "showed his true color" by swearing that he would "scratch up enough money to send his children to private elementary schools" if the Supreme Court ordered integration. For many Carolinians, that solution was neither popular nor practical, and according to Clark, white members of the audience "hooted his idea."[84] Less than two weeks later, voters across the state nevertheless passed the School Amendment by a two-to-one margin.

Clark did not lose hope because she had confirmation that at least some white people dissented from the overwhelming majority. Attending an interracial YWCA meeting in Columbia four months later, she found "a large number of white women" voicing their opposition to political events unfolding in their state. "They spoke bitterly of the people who voted to change the public school status and chided women all over the state for not having worked hard enough against that proposal of our governor," she recounted to the Warings.[85]

Black Charlestonians, meanwhile, seized the opportunity to make South

Carolina live up to Byrnes's "separate but equal" pledge. In January 1952, representatives of the NAACP, the parent-teacher association, and the city's federated women's clubs appeared before the city and county school boards. Despite the mandate to equalize, local officials had decided to spend nearly forty thousand dollars more of the funds from the State Educational Finance Commission for improvements to white schools. Noting that black students outnumbered white students in the system and that black schools still lagged far behind, these black citizens asked the all-white board to reconsider. According to spokesman Arthur Clement Jr., group members believed that "integration is inevitable" but remained willing to work within the bounds of segregation for the present. Lest their petition be too easily dismissed, he asserted that African Americans had become more sophisticated in their analysis and better organized in the past ten years. "We seek only equal opportunities," Clement assured the board, but "when we observe a disadvantage, an inequality, we know now how to be vocal under the laws of our State and our nation."[86] Lacking a federal mandate, black activists signaled their intent to soldier on. But the Gressette Committee, charged with helping devise new laws whose constitutionality would have to be tested by black litigants, would indefinitely delay justice.

⟨⟩

Despite all of the setbacks, Charleston's power dynamics had altered irrevocably between the end of World War II and the early 1950s. African Americans could and did vote. Organizations that had been strictly segregated, such as the YWCA and the LWV, experimented with integration. Charlestonians had seen one of their own, J. Waties Waring, turn against all that he was supposed to represent and embrace an interracial future. Many people, from Jimmy Byrnes to Arthur Clement Jr., believed school desegregation unavoidable despite the fact that its inevitability meant different things to African American and white Carolinians. Postwar racial violence had also erupted in South Carolina, most famously in Woodard's 1946 beating and the 1947 lynching of Willie Earle; less famously in a white police lieutenant's fatal shooting of Moses Winn in Summerville after Winn agreed to testify about police brutality before a federal grand jury. Yet comparing her state to others where white-on-black physical brutality lasted well into the 1960s, civil rights leader Modjeska Simkins explained how South Carolina differed: "The power structure has a velvet-covered nailed fist." But the Palmetto State later avoided "wholesale night riding and all that mess" because "the power structure knew that we would move out toward the federal courts."[87]

To Septima Clark, it seemed as if even poor black people were finally going to have their day in court. In 1953, Clark served on the housing committee of the state conference of the NAACP and traveled to Columbia to plan the annual convention. "For the first time in the history of the conference," she notified the Warings, "we are planning a session to inform the low income ignorant groups of the 'Legal Procedures' common to everyday living that can be used." Organizers hoped "to awaken these people to the fact that they must have an understanding before signing any contract."[88] As she had done for years, Clark concentrated on developing a practical educational component that would effect change in everyday life, but she still searched for a model that could yield results. At the same time, her dissatisfaction with local civil rights leaders pushed her to equally important realizations.

Clark perceived lack of unity as a serious handicap. The elections of the early 1950s had accentuated the divisions within Charleston's black leadership ranks. "The members on the [NAACP] executive board are so greatly divided in their thinking," she reported to the Warings after the 1951 mayoral race, adding that she thought such divisions would undermine the organization's effectiveness. "We say so much and do too little," she opined in early 1952 as efforts to get a new school built for black children went nowhere. That summer, she attributed the NAACP's difficulties in recruiting new members to the fact that "the heart of the apple is rotten."[89] Clark thought that in every area of the struggle, Charleston's black leaders had proved themselves shortsighted. Though she praised the NAACP's stance in the school equalization fight, she worried about unnecessary vagueness: "I do want them to be specific and say to the school board exactly what they want in no uncertain terms with sound facts to back them up." Most of all, Clark had come to believe in the power of voter education. Referring to disappointing election results, she lamented, "Few of us have been trained to think profoundly or to weigh matters on all sides."[90]

To be fair, Clark was not always so pessimistic. "I never feel discouraged," she maintained on another occasion; "I know that each step is a stepping stone in the right direction." She saw the greater degree of parental involvement in the school equalization fight as a positive development, noting, "I am so happy to see the parents of the masses have at last been aroused." She also took heart from increased teacher participation in getting out the vote. Charleston's teachers canvassed for candidates and drove voters to the polls. "Even my principal is urging the parents to register, vote and watch the coming election," Clark gleefully informed her distant friends in 1952.[91]

Yet Clark's impatience with Charleston's slowness and vacillation soon prompted her to seek new arenas of action. On July 16, 1953, she wrote to the Warings and mentioned that she was working at the YWCA because its new executive director had "gone to a conference" in Monteagle, Tennessee. Clark believed it a meeting of the Southern Regional Council.[92] In actuality, Anna DeWees Kelly had gone to the Highlander Folk School. Most white southerners, if they had heard of the interracial social activist training center, considered Highlander radical. Some suspected that it might be socialist; others whispered that it might be communist. The information Kelley brought back appealed to Clark, who had earned her radical credentials in Charleston. Crossing Broad Street, Septima Clark had stepped over a line. And there would be no turning back.

CHAPTER SEVEN

Bridging Past and Future

From a distance, they appear silhouettes of reclining curvaceous women, most lovely at dusk, gathering shawls woven of the palest pink, burnt orange, and soft violet light around their shoulders and hips. Such unblushing topography defines the Appalachian Mountains that straddle the North Carolina–Tennessee state line. Septima Clark viewed this landscape as she traversed the winding roads of southeastern Tennessee's Grundy County in June 1954 to attend a workshop on school integration at the Highlander Folk School (HFS). It was a hopeful moment for a veteran activist. The Supreme Court's ruling in *Brown* striking down "separate but equal" in public schools had come barely a month earlier, bringing with it a focus on fashioning concrete strategies for integration in communities across the South. Over the next few years, Clark recruited a number of kindred spirits to make the same journey to the school in Monteagle.

Seasoned African American activists learned much at Highlander. A residential adult education center that conducted weeklong workshops, HFS strove to make the American democratic ideal a reality by equipping students to improve conditions where they lived. In this sense, its philosophy did not differ completely from that which infused Clark's activist educational world. Like black clubwomen, HFS defined leadership not as standing at the head of an organization but as assuming the responsibility to get others involved. Yet the HFS concept of leadership emphasized ordinary people — not necessarily self-conscious community leaders — taking part in the decision-making process and devising plans on their own terms and according to their own needs. Students did not gather at HFS to spin theories. Rather, they relied on their collective knowledge to decide what action could best answer the specific problems in their home communities. Identifying and cultivating potential leaders served as the school's primary goal and the standard by which it measured its success.[1]

Highlander's egalitarian commitment to social and political activism appealed to Clark, who had spent the past seven years deeply engaged in Charleston's civil rights campaigns. The school's approach underscored things Clark already knew, such as the importance of hammering out a tangible plan of action. At the same time, she learned new methods that significantly altered her activist vision. HFS training taught Clark to more effectively mentor others. Recruiting for Highlander expanded Clark's vision of latent constituencies and disabused her of the notion that poor people needed to be led by their social betters. Most significantly, HFS pushed Clark to translate adult education theory into political and community action.

Indeed, what African American activists like Clark brought to Highlander was just as important, if not more so, than what they gained from it. Director Myles Horton's focus on facilitating local people's efforts to gain a voice in the decisions that affected daily life provided a foundation on which Clark built. To Highlander, Clark carried a teacher's and a clubwoman's sensibility about how to organize southern black communities — that is, insider knowledge. After her first visit, Clark became the main conduit linking HFS to the Low Country. The school's subsequent accomplishments there stemmed from her position in a network of activists as well as her ability to recognize and nurture potential supporters.

Clark's involvement with HFS marked a major turning point in her long activist career. Under its aegis, she helped to develop the Citizenship Schools as a part of a pilot program to increase voter registration on Johns Island. Experience teaching adult literacy classes and familiarity with the shortcomings of past voter registration campaigns led Clark to conclude that the HFS project should first answer people's desire for more self-sufficiency in their daily lives. Doing so, in turn, would enhance their self-confidence to the point where they could shoulder the burdens of civil rights work in their communities. The Citizenship Schools became the most successful program in Highlander's history. That might not have been the case had not Clark insisted on the fundamental importance of teaching the three Rs in conjunction with voter registration. She, not Horton, recognized practical literacy as a key to political liberation for the black grassroots.[2]

The year 1954 signaled a beginning for Septima Clark even as it marked a culmination of some of her most important life goals. Yet the southern political terrain that she labored to transform yielded very little during that decade. As the way grew increasingly perilous, Clark's unfaltering support for integration further strained her relationships with some of her activist colleagues. Clark's refusal to conceal her opinions for the sake of political expediency ultimately cost her nearly everything, including her job. By 1954, most Charlestonians thought she had already gone too far out on a limb. Even before it snapped, she had little choice but to look elsewhere in her pursuit of a useful course of action. Before the end of the decade, however, she would have early confirmation that her efforts had not been in vain.

⋍⋎⋇⋎⋋

The educational sensibilities that spawned the founding of the social activist training center in Tennessee would have been familiar to Septima Clark. Dr. Lilian Wycoff Johnson, a native of Memphis, purchased the large parcel of land that became the school's first home. Born in 1864 to a wealthy banking family, Johnson had earned a doctorate from Cornell University in 1902 and had been active in both the woman suffrage movement and the Women's Christian Temperance Union. In 1915, she built a comfortable residence on her property, located between Monteagle and Tracy City, the county seat in a coal mining region whose rich black veins had been depleted. The desperate plight of her neighbors did not escape Johnson, who soon decided that her new home could serve as a community and educational center. She also occasionally entertained at least one African American guest, Gertrude Kennerly, the teacher at the area's only school for black children. When Clark met Kennerly in the 1950s, the elderly educator confirmed that on her return from cashing her paycheck in Tracy City, she would often hitch her buggy and visit with Johnson. By any standard, Lilian Johnson was a modern woman. By Grundy County standards, she defied all manner of conventions. Family members later characterized her as "quite a gal," with good intentions but questionable ideas.[3] Unfortunately, her endeavors never took off quite the way Johnson had hoped. As the 1930s began, she made it known that she was eager to retire but wanted to keep her community center operating. She soon received a visit from a precocious young man.

Myles Horton was a native of Tennessee who could trace his Scotch-Irish ancestors in the New World back to the eighteenth century and count soldiers who fought for the Union during the Civil War among them. Born in 1905, Horton initially became interested in adult education during his junior year of college while overseeing a vacation Bible school program in the indigent mountain community of Ozone. Memorizing Bible verses and reading Bible stories, perhaps valuable preparation for the hereafter, hardly seemed a useful education for children whose parents wrestled poverty and seemed to have few options in the here and now. Horton decided to ask the adults to gather at the church in the evenings to talk about their troubles. He was surprised to learn that the people regarded his lack of expertise as inconsequential: "That was probably the biggest discovery I ever made. You don't have to know the answers. You raise the questions, sharpen the questions, get people to discussing them."[4] At the end of the summer, Horton's mountain friends asked him to stay, but the twenty-two-year-old doubted his ability to be an effective teacher unless he got more education. Toward that end, the Reverend Abram Nightingale, an early mentor, encouraged Horton to attend Union Theological Seminary in New York.

Going north exposed the Tennessean to the teaching and ideas of some of the most radical and progressive thinkers of the day. Discussions of the moral bankruptcy of capitalism could hardly be avoided in the fall of 1929. At Union, Horton soon came under the influence of one of capitalism's most vocal critics, Reinhold Niebuhr. A Christian socialist, Niebuhr rejected the naïveté of social gospel proponents, who believed that progress was inevitable and pursued social reform rather than fundamental social change. Along with Socialist Party leader Norman Thomas, who also inspired Horton, Niebuhr formed the Fellowship of Socialist Christians to advocate a movement of labor and progressive Christianity that would hasten the transformation of society. Horton was hooked, supplementing his studies by familiarizing himself firsthand with industrial trade unionism.[5]

Reading John Dewey confirmed for Horton that education should address community needs, be based on its practical experience, and help alleviate the disparities created by modern industrial life. Everywhere he went, Horton sought counsel on how to forge vital links between an educational center and the community it served. While studying at the University of Chicago in 1930, he befriended settlement house pioneer Jane Addams, who recognized that in essence, Horton wanted to start a rural settlement house. Finally, Horton's quest led him to Denmark in the summer of 1931 to see its folk schools. Within a few, the twenty-six-year-old found an inspiring level of participation. As one folk school director told him, the schools worked to evoke "a picture of reality not as we have met it in our surroundings, but as we ourselves would have formed it if we could — a picture of what reality *ought* to be."[6]

Myles Horton arrived home in the late spring of 1932 to begin fund-raising and scouting locations for his school. At the Blue Ridge Assembly in North

Carolina, he caught up with Don West, a native of Georgia who shared his commitment to remaking society. Horton learned that West had already found a Tennessee site for an adult school but could use financial support. The two men agreed to join forces and made several visits to Johnson. According to Horton, their idea of using adult education to remake the social and economic order initially shocked Johnson, whose "approach to education and social service was structured and well-planned from top to bottom." She agreed to lease her land and its buildings to the young visionaries for one year. At the end of that time, depending on their progress, she would either resume control of the property or extend the lease.[7]

Horton and West officially opened the Highlander Folk School in November 1932. West departed six months later, displeased with his partner's tendency to dominate decision making. After securing a charter from the State of Tennessee in 1934, Horton and the HFS staff searched for the right program to match the school's two complementary goals: educating "rural and industrial leaders for a new social order" and preserving and enriching "the indigenous cultural values of the mountains." They first focused on the emerging southern labor movement. Staff members became involved with coal mining, woodcutting, and textile strikes in the region and organized workshops to educate union leaders. In the process, HFS earned a prolabor reputation that caught the attention of allies and foes alike. Meanwhile, Myles Horton personally caught the attention of Arkansas native Zilphia Mae Johnson, who married him two months after her arrival in 1935. Zilphia Horton's musical talent and love of folk music proved especially valuable in fostering solidarity among Highlander students over the years.[8]

In theory and in limited practice, HFS had welcomed black southerners from the time it opened its doors. Charles Johnson, a sociologist at Fisk University, visited the school during its first year. In 1934, J. Herman Daves, a black professor in Knoxville, joined the faculty as a part-time instructor. Yet not until ten years later did forty black and white members of the United Auto Workers Union attend the first integrated workshop. Several African Americans served on Highlander's board of directors by the end of the 1940s. In 1953, the board voted to make race relations HFS's primary focus, and the school began a series of workshops on integration.[9]

Staff members had refined Highlander's educational technique and philosophy by the time Septima Clark first visited. Recent failures in extension efforts to develop rural leadership had demonstrated that the school could not enter a community with a preset program and expect it to thrive. Instead, a sense of crisis or at the very least a problem that needed a resolution had to emanate from within the community itself. Northern and international visitors often participated in HFS workshops, but the majority of students represented a cross-section of southerners—some highly educated, a few wealthy, but most ordinary people—interested in changing their native region. HFS concentrated on transforming individuals, not established organizations, and a person's degree of education or economic status mattered less than his or her capacity for leadership. "There can never be enough full time professional workers to release the energies and stimulate the ideas needed to make democracy a reality," Myles Horton preached. "We must have leadership rooted in the community. By teaching people to train others we are spreading leadership and in so doing are reaching out in a manner that would otherwise be impossible."[10]

Clark had heard of Horton's adult education school, but she learned more of its work from a colleague in her women's organizational network. Anna DeWees Kelly, executive director of Charleston's Coming Street YWCA, had met George Mitchell, chair of the Southern Regional Council and an HFS board member, while attending an interracial conference on education in Washington, D.C. When Kelly asked Mitchell if he knew of a place in the South where black and white people could gather to discuss relevant contemporary issues, he told her about Highlander. She enrolled in a workshop on school desegregation in the summer of 1953, catching a ride with a health worker from Columbia. Kelly later described her first impression of HFS. As the women sat in their car, marveling at the beauty of the sunset and not quite sure if they were in the right place, "the first person that came out of the building to greet us was white, was straggly, shoulder length hair, no make up and no shoes." Kelly was taken aback. Black women educators and civic activists would not have been caught dead in public dressed so informally. "My first thought was 'communist,'" Kelly recalled. The subsequent workshop changed her opinion. "Participants were given opportunities and encouraged to express their feelings and ideas, to lead the discussion groups, to role play, and to practice parliamentary procedure in an atmosphere of acceptance." According to Clark, Kelly returned home exuding enthusiasm for HFS's integrated workshops, which "eliminated stereotypes" and "broke down traditional barriers" in a manner that affirmed the nation's democratic principles.[11] Eager to recruit others to travel to Monteagle, Kelly persuaded Clark to go the next summer.

Septima Clark was fifty-six years old when she enrolled in Highlander's June 27–July 5 workshop on integration. Though she had shared elegant luncheons, teas, and suppers with the Warings and their white friends, Clark had never really lived informally among white people. "I was surprised to know that white women would sleep in the same room that I slept in," she commented, "and it was really strange, very much so, to be eating at the same table with them, because we didn't do that" in Charleston. Interracial living fostered the development of personal bonds rather quickly. Discussions continued outside of workshop sessions in shared rooms, during shared meals, and over shared chores, such as washing the dishes. In the course of such activities, Clark was amazed to learn of class prejudices dividing the white community. "I found out that whites were against whites. The low income whites were considered dirt under the feet of wealthy whites, just like the blacks were." As Myles Horton averred, "There is something about the experience of living and working together and being closely associated without outside distractions for a period of days or weeks which heightens the educational process." Clark confirmed that such close interracial contact "was so new, so different and living and learning together there meant much to me."[12]

Clark worked on two brochures during her stay. The first, *A Guide to Community Action for Public School Integration*, suggested involving members of parent-teacher associations, YWCAs, United Church Women, the League of Women Voters, and, of course, the National Association for the Advancement of Colored People (NAACP) — to all of which Clark belonged — and "outlined steps that had been tried in various communities." Highlander staff presumed that any action on school integration would require the involvement of teachers, an assumption that likely increased their interest in working with Clark. Clark's extensive civic participation meant that she easily recognized the importance of uniting various organizations to garner broader support as well as the difficulty of that task. The second pamphlet, *What Is a Workshop?*, described how to incorporate the HFS approach into local organizing. It recommended a "flexible program," with the general topic well defined but subject "to change according to the interests of the group and/or the resources of the people available." Any southern black teacher or clubwoman would have appreciated the emphasis on flexibility and tapping community resources. Less familiar would have been the idea of grassroots participation in formulating a program rather than merely in presenting a plan developed by outside organizations and state agencies. By her own account, training at the school allowed Clark to hone her organizational skills to reach people more effectively. "Highlander helped me to consider numbers when thinking of memberships, to interview for concrete data, and to survey for reliable facts," she wrote in a follow-up questionnaire. She also claimed that her experiences there made her "more vociferous on the Integration angle."[13]

What one did after leaving Highlander mattered more than what occurred while there. If sessions opened with the question "What do you want to do?," they closed with the challenge "What are you going to do?" Clark began by broadening her search for civil rights supporters in Charleston. She contacted Marie Hodges, an African American officer in the Tobacco Workers' Union, and George German, the black president of the International Association of Longshoremen, and convinced them to attend another workshop that summer. The working classes, Clark told J. Waties and Elizabeth Waring, "constitute approximately two-thirds of our school patrons and can force the issue [of school integration] if they know how." Clark attempted to recruit members of the Charleston NAACP executive committee and women from the YWCA to make the trek to Tennessee as well. Reporting her progress to Horton, she declared, "They like ideas, listen attentively, but to me that's not enough. I want action."[14]

Clark also brought Highlander to the Low Country. Later that summer, she invited Myles and Zilphia Horton to participate in a one-day workshop that she had organized under the auspices of the county parent-teacher association and that stressed "home and family life, health, religion and music." Clark's dedication validated Horton's belief that "a person who has been to a session at Highlander is several times more effective than a person with whom a Highlander staff member has worked in his own community."[15]

Esau Jenkins, a native of Johns Island and a member of the Charleston NAACP's executive committee, agreed to accompany Septima Clark back to HFS in August 1954. Born in 1910, Jenkins had completed the fourth grade before leaving school to farm cotton on four and a half acres owned by his father. He married Janie Bell at sixteen, and the two began raising a family that eventually included thirteen children. Esau Jenkins had a mind for business. When he began growing vegetables instead of cotton, he noticed that most of the merchants buying his produce in town were Greek. To curry their favor, Jenkins studied their language. After a year or two, whenever he came round, word went out among them that "the colored Greek is in town." His truck farming business thrived until World War II, when Jenkins realized that the rise of mechanization would leave him unable to compete with increased levels of production. He decided to buy a bus and to use it to transport Johns Island students to Burke High School in Charleston. Next, he developed routes for islanders who worked in the city.[16]

Racial violence prompted Jenkins to begin organizing in his community.

In September 1938, two black men riding in a truck accidentally ran over a white man's dog. The dog's owner got in his car, chased the vehicle down, then shot and killed the passenger. On another occasion in the early 1940s, two dogs, one belonging to a white couple and the other to a black man named Sammy Grant, got in a fight. When the white woman confronted Grant, he allegedly replied, "Whoever said I put my dog on your dog tell a damn lie." No one ever knew what she told her husband. The next day, however, he shot Grant at point-blank range with a twelve-gauge shotgun. Grant survived, but when authorities did nothing, Jenkins and a group of men formed the Progressive Club to secure legal aid for victims of racial violence and their families. Community protection ranked high on the club's agenda, as did gaining independence from white people.[17] Indeed, Jenkins understood economic self-sufficiency as essential to solving his community's more entrenched problems. "That was Esau's whole thing," his younger colleague Bill Saunders asserted; "folk could sell stuff, because you have to have a way to make money." The right of Johns Island children to go to school motivated Jenkins as well. He once overheard a white planter tell a black woman that his beans and cabbage needed picking and that he intended to fetch her children from class. "That hurt me," Jenkins remembered, "because I felt those children's education was being hampered."[18] By 1954, he served as president of the Johns Island parent-teacher association; superintendent of Sunday schools at his church, Wesley United Methodist; and president of the Citizens Club, a group of two hundred islanders who worked on school and community issues.

Jenkins arrived at Highlander having already started a rolling voter registration school. As his bus lumbered toward Charleston one morning, a woman passenger struck up a conversation with him. Alice Wine had not finished third grade, but she wanted to learn about voter registration laws. Knowing Jenkins's reputation as a "race man," she promised him she would vote if he would help her learn how to register. Jenkins agreed, but the request gave him another idea. He typed copies of the state laws pertaining to registration and voting and began passing them out to other passengers on his bus. Driving between Johns Island and Charleston, Jenkins explained portions of the laws. As he waited to pick up passengers on the peninsula, he reviewed sections of the state constitution with those who could not read and discussed their meaning. Aside from the in-town stops, which mandated caution, the autonomous space of the bus afforded Jenkins and his passengers an ideal opportunity to engage in rudimentary voter education unbeknownst to white people.[19]

During his first HFS workshop, Jenkins raised pertinent questions about how to get his neighbors involved in his projects. Beyond the franchise, he wanted to awaken in them an understanding of their rights to better schools and community welfare services. When discussions turned to what participants hoped to do back home, Jenkins said he planned to run for the local school board. "Not that there is any hope of getting elected," he added, but because "I want to prove that a Negro can run for office and not get killed."[20]

Septima Clark had known Esau Jenkins since her early days teaching on the island, although he had never been a student in her classes. In the late 1940s, she had begun working with him, both in the Charleston NAACP and in conjunction with a vacation Bible school program for migrant farm families on the island, an effort in which Clark enlisted the help of her brother, Peter Poinsette, and his daughters. "The living conditions were terrible," Elizabeth Poinsette-Fisher remembered; "You didn't want to go over there because they had one spigot in the middle of the place. All around there it would be nasty, muddy, and wet." If family members looked askance at Clark's more explicit political organizing, they could hardly absolve themselves of the Christian duty to help the less fortunate. "Aunt Seppie would say, 'Peter, we don't have somebody for next week. Do you think you can come over?' He'd say, 'Well, you know I have to work.'" Clark did not let her brother off the hook so easily. "Well, how about Thursday?" she countered. "When you're off, you can get a group together. Maybe Esau can get somebody else for Wednesday."[21]

Women and children's health issues on the island also commanded Clark's attention. As Basileus, or president, of her Alpha Kappa Alpha chapter, Gamma Xi Omega, Clark led a 1954 fund-raising drive to provide diphtheria immunizations for local African American children. She included those on Johns Island, because sixty-eight had died from the disease the previous year. The health program that she subsequently helped to establish reflected her organizational sensibility. "It's a nice way to edge in and do something which demands protection and respect," she observed. Most Johns Island women had no way to get to the immunization clinic in Charleston, and Clark found a way to address the county health center's oversight. "We furnished the transportation, did the follow-up, helped with the registration," she remarked, "and in that way we were able to get the mothers to come out." Still, the task had not been easy. "For a long time I couldn't get the sorority women to help at all," Clark recalled, "and we had to depend upon girls we were training to be debs. In the minds of these women, the islands

Esau Jenkins's bus, 1956. Courtesy of the Avery Research Center for African American History and Culture, College of Charleston.

Children at immunization clinic on Johns Island, 1956. Courtesy of the Avery Research Center for African American History and Culture, College of Charleston.

were taboo." Equally troubling was the lack of response among the women of Johns Island themselves. In the wake of the diphtheria deaths, not one resident had complained about the lack of a clinic or asked to have one established on the island. Like Jenkins, Clark wondered aloud at the August HFS workshop "How are you going to get them to think for themselves?"[22]

By the time Clark and Jenkins returned to the Low Country, great plans were under way for a testimonial dinner in honor of Judge Waring, whose dissent in *Briggs v. Elliott* three years earlier—that "segregation *per se* is inequality"—had finally been validated by the Supreme Court. Three hundred people, including Zilphia Horton, whom Jenkins had invited, spent the evening of November 6, 1954, listening to a host of speakers praise Waring. Horton stayed as a guest at Jenkins's home through the weekend. She used the opportunity to evaluate Jenkins and his community as a pilot site for the rural leadership training course HFS had been developing for two years with the aid of a grant from the Schwartzhaupt Foundation.[23]

A few weeks later, Myles Horton traveled on a reconnaissance mission to Charleston with HFS associate director Henry Shipherd and an Antioch College student. Septima Clark arranged for them to meet first with the Charleston County black teachers' association, where discussion revolved around the relationship between integration and political action. When talk turned to the difficulties of getting black Charlestonians registered, one teacher volunteered that there was "a widespread rumor that people would have to read in order to vote" and that her students had told her that "their parents did not go to the polls because they were afraid they would be embarrassed if they could not read." The next night, the Highlander emissaries met with ten black ward leaders. While Horton praised Jenkins's "leading role" in a conversation that linked problems in the city and on Johns Island, one of his colleagues discerned that factions divided Charleston's leadership.[24]

Anxious to "cash in on the good will" created by his wife's visit, Myles Horton and his associates concluded their trip by going to a meeting of the Johns Island Citizens Club. The possibility Johns Island offered excited Horton, who believed an effective program there would benefit Charleston and other nearby islands. He characterized most of the sixty to seventy people in attendance "as potential leaders" and noted that "practically all" of them "owned their own small farms." Landownership provided a buffer against white economic reprisals, while living close together allowed members to gather "informally to discuss their plans" between meetings. The main plan was to get Esau Jenkins elected to the school board. Jenkins spearheaded the effort, securing pledges from those already registered to vote to influence two more to make the attempt and spreading trips to the courthouse over many months to avoid alarming white people. A Jenkins victory, Horton theorized, would boost local leadership "because school teachers on the Island are afraid [for] their jobs and can't be expected to do much until Negro trustees are elected."[25]

At this meeting, Septima Clark and Anna Kelly watched as Horton failed to generate a Highlander-style discussion. Johns Islanders remained suspicious of outsiders, and most residents were accustomed to listening when a white man spoke. They had certainly never met one as genuinely interested in their opinions as Horton, who harbored no illusions about how his white skin limited his effectiveness. "I know that as a white person, I'm not fully accepted among Negroes," he commented; "I recognize that I must work primarily through" community workers "like Septima, who can get their confidence." At first, the people of Johns Island chose not to engage with him; even if they had, Horton did not understand Gullah. Only gradually did he earn their trust and their praise. By contrast, Johns Islanders responded warmly to Clark because she had "learned their ways," "tuned her ears to [their] language," and "didn't put herself above them."[26] Clark's familiarity with the people proved essential to furthering HFS's plans.

In February 1955, Horton arranged for Clark to conduct research for the school on Johns Island. She would visit potential leaders, interview them, and send the results to Horton so that he could codify the information and use it for a rural leadership training manual. Horton assured Clark that his staff members "feel as I do that nobody could do a better job than you'll be able to do." Fact-finding missions led Clark to the black county agricultural agent, the tax assessor's office, the County Council, the Board of Registration, the Community Planning Board, and the superintendent of education. On the island, she approached the task of community organizing in the same way that rural teachers always had, spending untold hours listening to concerns that worried local residents. Clark strengthened her bond with Johns Island women by bringing clothes for their children and by lingering in their homes after meetings to assist with cooking or child care. From them, she learned that younger people, particularly women who had gone to college, "were beginning to want a room of their own" and better-quality homes. She recommended that they establish a community housing committee to "assemble information regarding loans."[27]

From the beginning, Clark prioritized increasing women's participation. Beyond describing what happened at meetings on Johns Island, her reports included details of women's contributions. Because women did not assume roles as speakers, Clark made sure to comment on the table decorations they prepared and the food they served. In conversations with HFS strategists, she named women who might be interested in joining the effort. After one meeting attracted more than 250 participants, almost half of them women, Clark observed that not a single question had been asked. "I think the next thing to do is to get those tongues loosened up," she wrote.[28]

When Horton asked Clark to join the Highlander staff in the summer of 1955, dividing her time between the Low Country and Monteagle, she consented. After years of spending summer vacations working for white people or improving her teaching credentials, Clark finally had the chance to devote her free time to a project about which she felt passionate and that allowed her to draw on her expertise. "This is a thing I have longed to do throughout the ages," she excitedly reported to the Warings, "and now the opportunity has come."[29]

Yet in spite of her enthusiasm for the Johns Island project, Clark could not have failed to apprehend that her connection to Horton and his school was increasingly fraught with danger. As an institution dedicated to promoting the peaceful integration of southern schools, HFS became a target for the region's staunch segregationists, who capitalized on the anticommunist hysteria that gripped the nation. In the spring of 1954, Mississippi senator James O. Eastland had opened an investigative inquiry in New Orleans. He wove Highlander into the web of communist conspiracy based on its labor affiliations in the 1930s and 1940s and testimony at the 1953 McCarthy hearings. Horton took the stand in his school's defense and ended up being dragged out of the chamber following his attempt to read a statement on civil rights by President Dwight D. Eisenhower. Horton told Clark what had happened in New Orleans shortly after he asked her to become HFS's liaison on Johns Island: "Septima, I don't want you ask me to speak to any group or connect my name with the work I've asked you to do because for about two years hence the mention of my name may hurt the work," he cautioned.[30]

Privately, Clark remained equally disturbed over her remuneration. She and Horton had initially agreed that HFS would pay her fifty dollars a month. By May 1955, Clark had made three trips to Johns Island and sent Horton three reports but still awaited her first payment. "There are a lot of things I like about Myles and his family," she complained to the Warings, "but I like honesty, truth, and justice too." At the end of the month, Horton visited the Low Country, and Clark told him of her concern about the school's reputation. "I had no fear," she wrote to her friends; "I asked him frankly about the investigation and the report and his name being attached to the Johns Island Project and he unburdened himself." That she could speak so bluntly to a southern white man indicated the strength of Clark's sense of self-assurance just as her willingness to give Horton a chance to explain underscored her affinity for his school. Gradually, she learned the details of HFS's operative and administrative procedures. For his part, Horton later admitted, "The first year was a year of dialogue between us."[31]

It also took time for Clark and Horton to convince Jenkins of the necessity of spreading leadership throughout a community. Jenkins lost the school board election by a slim margin but received 192 votes from the island's 200 registered African Americans. Common sense provided a simple remedy. Johns Island's population was nearly 68 percent black; all that was needed was to get more black people on the voting rolls. Jenkins single-mindedly dedicated himself to that goal but interpreted expanding leadership to mean securing volunteers to interest neighbors in voting and to provide transportation on registration days. When it came to developing leaders, according to Horton, Jenkins "always came back to the idea of a large meeting where a leader would speak."[32]

Clark respected Jenkins and did not want him to think her a meddler. However, she also felt that he assumed a "preacher" role at community meetings, and on more than one occasion, she had seen Jenkins talk so long that people walked out. She and Horton worked patiently with him. For example, during a strategy session in March 1955, the conversation turned to a house-to-house survey of island schoolchildren. Jenkins said that his daughter, a schoolteacher, could probably obtain the information. Clark proposed having a few of her former students help and emphasized that increased involvement would heighten the chances for success. On another occasion, Horton drew a map of Johns Island and asked Jenkins who could be contacted in different neighborhoods. "There are no leaders there," Jenkins responded. "There's a leader anywhere in relation to the people in their community, a neighborhood leader," Horton advised; "You go back and find your leaders and send them up here to a Highlander workshop."[33] By April 1955, Jenkins had adapted his thinking. "My ideas of community leadership have changed in many ways," he wrote to Horton. "I found that giving others something to do and help making better citizens in a community is very important. My old way of doing things was slow." Years later, Clark noted, "You have to give Myles the credit for being [able] to change the hearts of people so that they would know themselves. Because I think Esau wanted to teach them how [to] do things, but Myles wanted to teach others how to change themselves."[34]

Septima Clark combined her HFS research on the islands with recruiting workshop participants. In June 1955, she visited Johns Island ten times, interviewed fourteen men, five of whom said they would go to Monteagle in July, and paid a Sunday morning visit to nearby Wadmalaw Island.[35] There, she caught up with Sonny Jenkins (no relation to Esau) outside of his church. Jenkins was deep in conversation with a group of his neighbors, trying to decide what action to take regarding a black woman who recently had been accidentally killed by a white marine speeding down the highway. Jenkins invited Clark inside to give a speech for the NAACP after the service. What she said provides a better view of how she used a specific request to broaden her audience's understanding of potential resources—whether local, state, federal, or international—to address the community's problems.

Clark began her talk by establishing her familiarity with life on the islands, describing the conditions in the schools on Johns Island when she first taught there in 1916. She credited the NAACP's equalization efforts for bringing improvement and then linked those efforts to the right to vote. Next, she shifted gears, announcing that she wanted to find someone to attend a Highlander workshop on the United Nations, "where people from all over the United States and many countries from across the sea will gather to share experiences of building recognition of human rights." Clark imbued her secular recruiting with spiritual ideals: "The whole idea of the worth and dignity of man and the right of each individual to the good life comes from our Christian gospel, from the demands of the prophets for justice for all and from the teaching of Jesus that all men are brothers and all are equally loved by God." She then challenged her listeners to imagine a different world. "It is a great thing for people to adopt these rights as a goal, so different from the way of life they have long followed. Can you adopt these rights as your goal?" A few cries of "Amen" answered her from the pews. "Then show to the people around you that you have a registration certificate, that you will come out to the polls and vote when an election is on your island, that you have a membership card from the NAACP and that you will send a man to represent you at the United Nations workshop at Highlander Folk School in Monteagle Tennessee!" she declared.[36]

Fostering unity among different factions on the islands represented another key aspect of Clark's recruiting and organizing. George Bellinger owned a store on Johns Island and ran several buses in competition with Esau Jenkins. Early on, Jenkins informed his Highlander friends that Bellinger "was against political action" and would take no part in meetings. Clark respectfully asked Jenkins if he thought it "would be alright" for her to approach Bellinger. Greeting Bellinger, Clark commented that perhaps he could use a vacation since the time to lay by crops had arrived and then invited him to attend an HFS workshop. "Jenkins is mixed up with that," Bellinger countered; "Are you rejecting him?" Clark assured him that she was not but said that he could accompany her on a week when Jenkins would not be at Highlander. Bellinger then grew a little bolder and asked Clark about her husband. When she told him that Nerie Clark had been dead for thirty years, Bellinger responded, "Is that so? I could drop you a little vegetable off some time." She gracefully deflected the offer, whereupon Bellinger began to lament the fact that his tomatoes were rotting on the vines. Clark seized the opportunity: "Maybe we can think about a cannery. That's one thing you could think about and get other farmers to help you with. . . . We can get the Home Demonstration agent to come out to the island and tell a group how it can be done." By offering Bellinger a distinct project of his own, she found a way to ease the competition between him and Jenkins and to extend leadership in the community. Horton noted that Bellinger left HFS assuring staffers "that he would cooperate with Jenkins and others in the registration and housing program."[37]

For some Johns Islanders, the chance to participate in a Highlander workshop seemed an answer to long-held prayers. Elijah "Buddy" Freeman, one of Septima Clark's former students, explained that he was "kinda worried" about traveling to Tennessee "but hope to the Lord that I live to enjoy it and bring back a good message." Freeman used his decision to interact with white people at Highlander to address those who protested that they did not want their children to mix with whites: "I am not afraid of white people. And I look them in the eyes and tell them just what I have to tell them." Freeman got no response when he asked his listeners, who "would like to have integration?," so he continued, "I asked the question and I am glad to answer it." Remarking that "if war [were to] break out," the government would "carry all" to battle, he argued that integrated schools and playgrounds would promote better interracial understanding. More important, "Our children will have the privilege and a chance to receive the same thing in wages the white man receives."[38] Though perhaps a minority voice on Johns Island, Freeman understood the benefits of integration in educational, social, political, and economic terms.

Septima Clark also convinced her first cousin, Bernice Robinson, to go to Highlander's United Nations workshop. The ninth child of a brick mason and a seamstress, born in 1914, Robinson grew up in a home that stressed many of the same values esteemed in the Poinsette household. Family pride was balanced by an ethos of caring and a stress on achieving economic independence within a segregated society. Robinson joined an older sister in New York in 1929, where she completed high school. She dreamed of continuing her studies at the Boston Conservatory of Music, but the sister became ill and was unable to work, forcing Bernice to return to Charleston. She married, had a daughter, divorced, and went back to New York in 1936, securing work in the garment industry during the day and going to cosmetology school in the evenings. By 1939, Robinson had opened a beauty shop with a friend in Harlem. Despite brisk business, she could not earn enough money to quit her factory job and support her daughter, who now lived with Robinson during the school year. She opted to take the civil service exam and briefly relocated to Philadelphia in 1941. Not finding the City of Brotherly Love to her liking, she moved back to Harlem and worked a number of civil service jobs during World War II.

Robinson enjoyed living in the North, where she could go to the movies and sit anywhere she liked; where she could catch the hottest acts at the Apollo Theater as well as Carnegie Hall; and where she befriended the Armenian, German, and Jewish women who labored beside her in the garment factories. She believed that these experiences "prepared me for working in an integrated society." Relying on the city's international milieu, Robinson and another African American friend even found a way to bypass discrimination at a restaurant that refused to serve black people. "We got the wraparound turbans and we put that on our head," she gleefully reminisced. "We go into this restaurant looking elegant, big earrings and a lot of jewelry. . . . Boy, we got the royal treatment! We kind of made believe we couldn't understand exactly what was being said. They treated us like some African dignitaries. . . . All you had to do was speak some gibberish, and they would declare you were a foreigner." Robinson also registered and voted for the first time and earned extra money working as a paid staffer on an assemblyman's reelection campaign. She had no plans to return to live in the segregated South. In August 1947, however, she went back to Charleston to visit and discovered that both her parents were ill and not properly cared for, and she "just couldn't walk off again and leave like that." She never went back to live in New York. But the "first thing" she did was join the Charleston NAACP, where she got to know her cousin.[39]

The United Nations workshop spread over two sessions during the first two weeks of July 1955. Bernice Robinson attended both, joined by Septima Clark's niece, Alice Poinsette, and Esau Jenkins for the second. HFS staff had organized the workshop under the title "The United Nations and You" to connect local struggles to the nation's Cold War posturing as leader of the Free World. Organizers hoped that participants would realize how they could use the international body's interest in human rights to pressure the federal government, which would then compel the South to respect the Supreme Court's decisions and end segregation. Moreover, the United Nations language of human rights offered a broader vocabulary for challenging discrimination than the legal and political framework of civil rights. Nevertheless, when staff asked participants how support for the United Nations could be encouraged back home, Jenkins replied, "I don't want to do a thing for the United Nations."[40] Although Jenkins was primarily concerned with getting his neighbors registered to vote so that he might gain a seat on the school board, his response underscored the reality that in its concern for incorporating the big picture into a local community, HFS staffers occasionally lost sight of the urgency of conditions on the ground.

Instead of reflecting on the United Nations, Jenkins described how Alice Wine had memorized the state constitution and received her registration certificate but still could not read very well. She and others had no way to increase their community involvement beyond voting. According to Robinson, Jenkins announced, "I need a school. I need somebody to help me, tell me *how* I can get a school going to teach my people." With that, "he turned the whole workshop around," and "that's all we talked about for the last couple of days." The United Nations workshop prompted Robinson to question some things for the first time: "I was confronted with the fact that we had all this illiteracy on the island. While I knew it was there, it just never disturbed me because I accepted it as a way of life." She also realized a shortcoming in the Charleston NAACP's voter registration campaigns: "We could just deal [only] with people who *could* read."[41]

Rosa Parks participated in the workshop's second week as well. Long active in Montgomery, Alabama, she had caused quite a stir in 1948 when she had taken the NAACP's youth chapter to see the Freedom Train exhibit, sponsored by the federal government and heralded as a lesson in democracy. Curators had stipulated that segregation would not be permitted on the Freedom Train, even as it traveled below the Mason-Dixon Line. Before it pulled out of Montgomery, Parks had begun receiving threatening phone calls. Virginia Durr, a white southern liberal who had been active in the region's racially progressive campaigns since the New Deal, encouraged Parks to visit HFS in 1955 because, Durr believed, the experience would help buoy her friend's work with NAACP youth. Durr even secured funding and accompanied Parks to Atlanta to board the bus to Tennessee.[42]

Septima Clark remembered Rosa Parks as timid and painfully shy. She "wouldn't talk for two or three days in that workshop, wouldn't say a word." Parks also kept her distance from white participants until Alice Poinsette took it upon herself to make Parks feel at ease by going to her room and talking with her one evening. At the next morning's session, Clark gently suggested that Parks tell her story: "I said, 'Rosa, tell these people what a hard time you had getting their Freedom Train into Montgomery.' And she didn't want to tell it. But she finally told, and after she spoke about it, she didn't want anybody to know because she was really afraid that white people in Montgomery would hear about it." A United Nations representative at the workshop promised Parks assistance should whites retaliate. Back home, Parks said she planned to continue her work with the NAACP but, according to Clark, predicted that nothing would happen in Montgomery because the black community "wouldn't stick together."[43]

Myles Horton was visiting Septima Clark in Charleston four months later when they heard the news that Parks had been arrested for refusing to give up her seat in the white section of a segregated city bus. He immediately went to Alabama. Clark read the event as a sign of HFS's efficacy. "Had you seen Rosa Parks (the Montgomery sparkplug) when she came to Highlander," she wrote to the Warings in 1956, "you would understand just how much *guts* she got while being there."[44]

Not all workshops generated such amazing, if unpredictable, results. Clark directed a session attended by middle-class African Americans from Nashville and Chattanooga in August 1955. "I wasn't able to accomplish anything with them," she later observed. "I don't know whether they were afraid to teach others or if they had some highfalutin idea that poor people were so far beneath them that they wouldn't fool with them. . . . We got them to see what conditions they were living under," she concluded, "but we couldn't get them to do any of the work in their community to help others change."[45] Clark knew how much class prejudice within the black community hampered the work. The difficulty she encountered in Charleston as things heated up in the latter part of 1955 and throughout 1956 led to more personally painful realizations.

⌁⌖⌁

The African American children at Septima Clark's school, Archer Elementary, had offered some spirited responses to *Brown*. "They'll be plenty of fighting now," one boy predicted, while another chimed, "The first one to call me a nigger, I'll bop him in the nose." Many complained, "I don't want to go to school with them." The forward-looking expected to enter white high schools but dared their future classmates "to say anything to me." One third-grader advised his teacher "that he was leaving the next day because he lived near a white school." White students had their own reactions as well. As Clark's principal left one afternoon, he overheard a group of white boys snarl, "That's the nigger who is going to be over us."[46] Maybe they repeated what they had heard at home. What their parents said and did was infinitely more frightening.

In the months and years that followed the Supreme Court's 1954 decision and its implementation decree issued a year later, white people across the South went on the offensive to protect their segregated way of life. Robert Patterson organized the first chapter of the all-white Citizens' Council (CC) on July 11, 1954, in the Mississippi Delta. White South Carolinians established their inaugural branch in Elloree the same month that Highlander hosted its United Nations workshop in August 1955. Less than six months later, South Carolina counted a total of fifty-six CC chapters and significant backing from the state's political leaders. U.S. representative L. Mendel Rivers, from Charleston's First District, identified himself as a member. U.S. senators Strom Thurmond and Olin D. Johnston thought it best not to join but publicly affirmed their support for the organization.[47]

Solidifying public opinion behind the preservation of segregation and organizing local resistance to federal intrusion formed the backbone of the CC's agenda. It drew members from the upper and middle classes, respectable civic leaders and businessmen who literally had considerable investments in preserving white economic and political power. Participation by their wives ensured the success of the covered dish suppers and Low Country oyster roasts that served as a pretext for more serious business and validated assertions that the "Council movement is truly a people's movement . . . organized from the bottom to the top, rather than the top to the bottom." The editor of the *Charleston News and Courier*, Thomas R. Waring Jr., described CC members as "among the best people" in South Carolina, "the citizens who belong to the civic clubs and the churches . . . and do the other housekeeping chores of a community." Joe Brown, president of the Charleston NAACP branch, dubbed them "the tuxedo gang of the Ku Klux Klan." Unlike the Klan, CC leaders publicly disavowed violence, preferring to rely instead on economic intimidation and legislative action.[48]

Staying within the law was hardly difficult for the men who wrote it, and white Carolinian legislators had been preparing specifically for the *Brown* decision for a good three years before it was handed down on May 17, 1954. In his speeches before CC chapters and the state chamber of commerce, Rotary and Lions Clubs, parent-teacher associations, Sunday schools, and even the Girl Scouts, state senator Marion Gressette, chair of the school committee that bore his name, liked to brag that South Carolina had been the "first of 17 states to organize."[49] In 1956, he proclaimed that every recommendation his committee had made to the General Assembly to keep the state's schools segregated had been adopted. The legislature had invested broad power to oversee schools in the hands of local district trustees; repealed the compulsory attendance law; suspended all state funding if any child transferred into a school as a result of a court order; and provided appropriations only for schools, colleges, and recreational facilities that remained segregated. Perceptive lawmakers recognized that they needed to adopt the military strategy of "defense in depth." As the Gressette Committee's secretary, Wayne W. Freeman, remarked, "We knew that we would probably have to abandon our first lines, and fall back on the deeper ones."[50] Their battle was both legal and social.

The Klan relied on different tactics. "Since those nine buzzards on the Supreme Court have abolished the Mason-Dixon line," one anonymous hooded member told an interviewer, "we had to establish the Smith & Wesson line." Questioned further, he explained exactly what he meant: "It is a popular brand of firearms in the Klan now. We're arming as fast as we can." Klan rallies in South Carolina drew new recruits with alarming alacrity. On a single evening, 123 members joined in Conway; 800 people joined in Camden on another occasion. State highway patrolmen directed traffic to and from the gatherings. The mayor of Camden changed his mind about allowing a local Methodist church to sponsor an interracial youth conference when he received threatening phone calls and the Klan burned a cross in his front yard. Soon thereafter, the Camden Klan flogged a fifty-two-year-old white music teacher for "voicing pro-integration sentiments." Reflecting on the incident, the beaten man's pastor succinctly stated, "Fear covers South Carolina like the frost."[51]

Amid the terror and the violence, black activists signaled their willingness to fight back by defying the Klan's intimidation efforts. At one rally, a robed speaker called for seventy-year-old community leader L. A. Blackman, who had attended a Highlander workshop, to be "run out of town," whereupon Blackman stood up in the back of a friend's truck and declared, "I'm here in Elloree, I've been here for seventeen years, and I have no idea of leaving." His brazenness stumped the hooded men, who mustered no response that night. More than a few black Carolinians endorsed John McCray's approach for ridding the state of the Klan: "Everyone knows what to do about a mad dog running loose, or a rattlesnake," McCray editorialized in the *Lighthouse and Informer*; "the solution is to cancel on sight anybody crazy and wicked enough to cover themselves and maraud at night for evil intent." African Americans should defend themselves with "violence equal in strength to that of the Klan," McCray suggested. The Reverend Joseph Delaine, a leader in the Clarendon County school suit whose church was bombed and house repeatedly shot up, responded to Klan terrorism by returning fire one night. When authorities swore out a warrant for his arrest, Delaine left South Carolina for good.[52]

Black veterans had returned from World War II with extensive weapons training. At a discussion in Septima Clark's home in 1955, one man observed, "In the last Civil War, we didn't know anything about ammunition and guns," and a woman declared, "If anyone shoot at me one time and don't get me, they dead." The conversation then turned to the Klan's efforts to intimidate a Miami NAACP leader for organizing a campaign to get streets paved and garbage collected in a black neighborhood. "Because Negroes are mad as hell down there, just as mad as the white boy, nothing happened," another participant reflected. "Negroes were out there with their guns and their knives when the Ku Klux Klan came through, and they knew it, and they move on through and nothing happened because they didn't dare get out." The community got its paved streets and its garbage collection, and the men and women at Clark's house agreed that "they got it because they protected that one man and they protected themselves." For many black southerners, self-defense would remain a legitimate tactic well after Martin Luther King Jr. became the national spokesman for nonviolent resistance.[53]

By the mid-1950s, Cold War idioms of democracy and freedom meant that civil rights advocates could expose the brutal reality of American race relations to embarrass the nation on the international stage. Yet white supremacists invoked the Cold War's anticommunist rhetoric with equal fervor to combat civil rights gains and to attack civil rights organizations. Portraying the NAACP as a communist front, southern state legislatures passed laws requiring the association to hand over its membership lists and financial statements to white officials or be shut down. Clark, assigned to work with auditors on the Charleston branch's financial books and serving as the chair of the education committee in 1956, had important documents in her possession. "I would have burned the records before I would have let [state officials] have them," she later asserted. Nevertheless, southern NAACP membership rolls plummeted by almost half, dropping from 128,716 in 1955 to 79,677 two years later.[54]

Black Carolinians and their white allies felt besieged by the middle of the decade as they confronted a campaign of intimidation designed by the state's "best people." In Charleston, as elsewhere, those who had signed petitions requesting that their children attend white schools began changing their minds. "Joe Brown is taking quite a beating now," Clark informed the

Warings in late 1955. "Many petitioners are saying unkind things about him when they withdraw their names." Economically independent black farmers and small businessmen active in the NAACP found their access to supplies and credit canceled overnight. Banks began to require African American loan applicants to sign statements swearing that they neither were nor planned to become NAACP members. Beyond unemployment and economic ruin, there was plain meanness. One of the fifty-seven African American parents in Orangeburg who signed a petition for school integration was a mother whose son needed a special milk formula because he was a hemophiliac. CC members intervened to cut off her service.[55]

Black Orangeburg responded by mounting an economic defense. By October 1955, students at South Carolina State organized a community-wide boycott of twenty-two businesses whose owners or employees had ties to the CC. Local whites claimed that the boycott had no impact, but Clark heard from Modjeska Simkins that "the young people are doing a wonderful job in Orangeburg. They are not attending theatres [or] patronizing any white stores and refuse to drink Coca Cola."[56] Newly elected governor George Timmerman Jr., who had pronounced during the campaign, "Nowhere in my Bible does forcing little children in their formative years to mix with other races seem to me to be an application of the Golden Rule" and accused the NAACP of "following the Communist line," opened an investigation into faculty and student affiliation with the civil rights organization. The college's white trustees pressured the administration to expel student leaders. According to Clark, the school's president "called in the Junior NAACP president and told him if he calls a meeting on that campus he will send him home. No spine in the backbone of the professionals," she concluded with disgust. The students' bravery, however, encouraged her: "The younger generation will ride over this hump," she forecast in 1955.[57]

Clark understood that to capitalize on the promise of *Brown*, African Americans had to claim their legal rights in an atmosphere where most people weighed the costs of acting for change and paused. "I am sorry to say," she told the Warings, "that numbers of our people say it every day that they prefer segregation." By contrast, she wanted her community to realize that not all white people harbored ill will toward them: "That's the one big thing that I've been trying to carry around. I want them to know that there are some allies, that there are some people that they can trust and talk with."[58] In the mid-1950s, Clark tethered her hope to the possibility of building an interracial grassroots movement that matched the campaign conducted by white supremacists in strength and resolve. The main issue was how to get black and white colleagues in numerous organizations to take an equally passionate public stance.

To that end, Clark concentrated her efforts among teachers, YWCA women, and NAACP leaders. Appointed chair of the Legal and Legislative Committee of the Charleston County Teachers' Association in 1955, she applied herself to the "enormous task" of getting "these intimidated teachers" acquainted with "present school policies." Clark's committee targeted teaching contracts, tenure, retirement, and reducing teaching hours and loads as pertinent issues. As chair, she put the skills she had acquired at HFS to work by devising a factual questionnaire to collect data to present to local school authorities. Clark sent out six hundred letters of inquiry and received a mere ten responses. Even "the women on the committee who rave about injustices have not sent in anything," she lamented to the Warings. "Our teachers and other leaders have been conditioned so long that they are afraid to ask for and about anything." Local educators seemed less timid when dealing with white people outside of South Carolina. In 1956, Clark derived great satisfaction in organizing, with Highlander's assistance, an interracial federal credit union for teachers in Charleston.[59]

She grew particularly incensed, however, when white Y women purchased train seats in a segregated coach for her and another black woman traveling to a national conference in New York and then dismissed the action as an administrative oversight. After the trip, Clark registered her complaint as part of her report on the business of the convention. "Of course I'm the bad fellow now," she told the Warings, "but I could not report on business and leave that kind of business out of the picture." The result, she admitted, was "not a word of action taken" by either white or black Y women. "That makes me know that our people need quite an educational program. They will let you down flat and the women in that assembly were all college trained women." That many of the black women who held executive positions in the Coming Street YWCA also worked as teachers only heightened Clark's aggravation with her colleagues' reticence.[60]

Within the Charleston NAACP, Clark worried about "the general attitude of what we call our intelligent people." She bemoaned "the complete apathy of the people in general" with regard to the Mississippi murder of fourteen-year-old Emmett Till for allegedly whistling at a white woman. Foot-dragging tried her patience, and refrains of "Go cautiously" infuriated her. She grew especially annoyed at the lack of respect her ideas received from the men of the NAACP executive committee. During one meeting, Clark mentioned an article about Thurgood Marshall that had "greatly disturbed" her. "The men . . . hooted me off and really took it as a joke, saying 'Can't you see they are trying to divide the Negroes.'" At another regional session, she suggested that all churches cancel services to hold a Sunday morning rally, with the proceeds to go to boycott activists in Alabama. "Who heard me?" she raged, "No one! That was too much to ask."[61]

Yet Clark felt elated that the Charleston NAACP expanded when other southern branches were shrinking. Bernice Robinson estimated that membership increased "from about 300 to way over 1,000" after Joe Brown assumed the presidency in 1955. Robinson, who recruited members among her beauty shop clientele, was more sympathetic than Clark to the predicament of educators. "Many of them were teachers," she affirmed. "They would have the cards come to me, to my house, so that their mailman would not even see . . . any literature or anything coming to them from the NAACP because they had to be very careful." Clark had begun to pin her hopes on a different constituency. "The men from the countryside are now taking a part," she wrote to the Warings in October, while "those who have climbed the social ladder are still at the top sitting on the last round doing absolutely nothing." If Clark took comfort in rural residents' lack of fear, she still considered their paucity of experience a hurdle. "I do feel that a period of interpretation should be the next step," she asserted. "Conditioned apathetic individuals will need lots of educational discussions before they are aware of inequalities or inadequacies affecting the race."[62] By 1956, Clark preached to every major professional and civic organization in which she worked about the necessity of an educational foundation for the success of civil rights campaigns.

People who take a stand for their beliefs, despite the unpopularity of those beliefs and despite the risks, have to be stubborn. Clark's colleagues interpreted her obstinacy, particularly on the integration issue, as an unwelcome imposition. On one occasion in Columbia, Clark asked a teacher if she planned to attend a school board meeting where proposals to integrate faculty in the public schools would be discussed. "I'm not going," the woman snapped, "I leave that to you. You like to mix with white people." When Clark transferred to Rhett Elementary School in 1955, a few teachers caustically remarked, "Now she comes over here to rule." "I will speak," Clark answered in her own defense. She did not view herself as pushy. "I never try to force my ideas on anyone," she claimed; "I speak my beliefs and leave it up to the individual to decide whether I'm right or wrong." Clark described her activist approach as "militant but calm." She did not often lose her temper in public, and in the course of her fifty-seven years, she had learned to trust herself: "Each time I pass through a new crisis," she maintained, when "the sun is barely peeping through those angry storm clouds . . . I patiently wait to strike a blow when my inner self whispers, 'Now is the time.'"[63]

Clark's zeal carried additional liabilities, however. Her unrelenting activist schedule left little time for relaxation and taxed her health. "I feel worn out at nights," she confessed to the Warings. When she sprained her ankle, she allowed herself two days' rest and then "carried this bandaged foot to school and meetings," noting, "I can't be set aside." She also had little time for her personal life. "My son came to see me [at] Christmas," she wrote in January 1955, "and brought a wife. The same old story. Young people marrying for all love to hold hands and kiss with no signs of furniture or a house. The wife has not finished school. Anyhow, I wish them luck and will have to offer whatever help I can give."[64] Despite her slight disapproval of the newlyweds' lack of practicality, she refused to burden her son the way Victoria Poinsette's censure had burdened her. Still, she had not met her new daughter-in-law prior to the marriage or attended the wedding. The personal fulfillment Clark gained from her movement work was always balanced by a personal price she paid for investing so much of her time in it.

Septima Clark also defended herself to her family members. "Not any of them agree with me," she confided to the Warings. "In most cases they feel I'm right but too outspoken and too hasty. Nevertheless, I'm not interfered with and do not let any of them hinder me in the stand I take." Clark's activism caused her sister, Lorene Poinsette, with whom she shared a home, much grief. Poinsette's nerves could not withstand the pressure. "I just feel so sick," she told Clark; "I just feel like a bowl of jelly." According to Elizabeth Waring, Clark admitted, "My family are fighting me." "She told me that she was alone with no following, no friends . . . that people were calling her a '*Radical*'" and "were afraid of her."[65]

Waring's dramatic tendencies and Clark's stoicism aside, the local situation had reached a crisis point by the spring of 1956. Newspaper articles had linked her to Highlander as they blasted the school and excoriated Horton as a "champion of integration." People began to suspect that Clark was a communist. After the cc added the United Council of Church Women to its list of "subversive" groups, the city school superintendent called Clark to ask if she belonged to the group. Clark had merely attended one of their meetings with a white colleague from the ywca. "I'm a member of the Methodist Church," she replied, explaining that it provided financial support to affiliated religious organizations; "I suppose [that] makes all Methodist women members of the United Council of Church Women," she cleverly rejoined.[66] Even so, teachers had good reason to be more cautious.

On March 17, Governor Timmerman signed into law a bill that that barred city, county, and state employees from belonging to the NAACP. Local school boards, with the blessing of the State Board of Education, added a page to their annual job applications on which teachers had to list their organizational affiliations. The stress became too much for some to bear. Clark remembered that the new law especially affected Alice LaSaine, Charleston County's longtime Jeanes teacher and ardent NAACP supporter. "She knew she was going to lose her job because she was a member and she did not want to give it up. She just got terribly ill in her mind. She became senile soon and she died not too long after that," in 1957.[67]

A very few teachers chose to face the consequences. After the school board forced them to resign when they refused to answer the questionnaire, eighteen teachers filed suit in Elloree.[68] Others, including Clark, opted to complete the questionnaire but refused to deny their NAACP affiliations. Meeting in executive session on May 9, the Charleston school board voted not to renew the contracts of Clark and four other teachers. Clark received a letter apprising her of the decision a month later. Though the school board gave no reason for its action, she knew: "I had been completely outspoken in my talks and participation, though I was mindful of the fact that as a teacher in the public schools I would be vulnerable to criticism." Clark's brother scolded her. "Why didn't you resign?," Peter Poinsette asked; "You knew since January that they were getting after you." Clark believed that she would be in a better position to fight back if the board dismissed her than if she resigned.[69]

After receiving the letter, Septima Clark called Joe Brown, who contacted state NAACP president James Hinton and the executive secretary of the Columbia-based Palmetto Voters Association, in which Clark had also been active. The men met at Clark's home and discussed strategies — including filing a lawsuit — to pressure the school board. Clark believed she had a solid case on her hands. She had earned the highest marks and compliments on every annual teaching evaluation since her return to the Charleston system in 1947. By the fall, however, nothing had come of her case, though ousted colleague Henry Hutchinson had joined the fight. Clark and Hutchinson met again with Hinton, who assured them that their suit would be filed as soon as the Elloree case was heard. They also sought help from the Palmetto Education Association (formerly the Palmetto State Teachers' Association) but were informed that the association had chosen to prioritize the "Elloree case because we had action by the school board that we felt could be attacked." When Clark contacted the National Education Association, a representative replied that it would act only if the Palmetto Education Association filed the request.[70]

Having exhausted her official avenues of recourse, Clark took matters into her own hands. Knowing that if black teachers stood united, they could not all be fired, Clark sent out 726 letters to her associates asking them to protest the state's anti-NAACP legislation and the school board's actions. Twenty-six answered her, eleven agreed to meet with the school superintendent, and on the appointed day, five showed up. "I considered that one of the failures of my life," Clark claimed, "because I think I tried to push them into something that they weren't ready for." It was a bitter lesson, reinforced by Clark's craving for "action" and the reality that her associates remained too fearful to relinquish their anonymity. Yet this particular failure taught Clark an invaluable truth: "You always have to get the people with you. You can't just force them into things. When I went into Mississippi and Alabama I stayed behind the scene and tried to get the people in the town to push forward. Then I would come forth with ideas. But I wouldn't do it at first because I knew it was detrimental."[71]

Despite her unemployment, Clark still received minimal financial support from her family, and she owned the Henrietta Street house. The first job offer she received came from John F. Potts Sr., former Palmetto State Teachers' Association president and principal of Voorhees Institute in Denmark, South Carolina. When Clark informed Potts that she intended to remain vocal about issues that mattered to her, he responded that his institution frowned on such outspokenness. She declined the job. Believing that the relative freedom in the North and the substantial increase in pay would prove irresistible, the Warings urged Clark to relocate to New York and obtain a teaching job there. Clark tried to imagine residing in the city but "had never liked the idea of living in an apartment entered through a long hall where dozens of families lived and yet more than likely one never knew another and seemed never to be concerned one with the other." For a woman who had spent her life in rural and urban southern black communities, moving north would have required adopting a different method of community organizing. "I really don't want to leave the South unless I am forced to do so," Clark told her friends; "I want to stay here and fight this thing out. Like the slaves, I feel that 'trouble won't last always.'"[72]

When Myles Horton invited Septima Clark to come to work for Highlander full time, she had to weigh the decision. Along with the shocking news of Zilphia Horton's death from drinking typewriter cleaning fluid, recent personnel changes, and the school's informal administrative practices

Left to right: Clark's sister-in-law, Lucille Poinsette; Ruby Cornwell;
Septima Clark; and Mrs. E. B. Burroughs at Alpha Kappa Alpha's
testimonial dinner for Clark, December 3, 1956. The other members of her
sorority refused to be photographed with her. Courtesy of the Avery Research
Center for African American History and Culture, College of Charleston.

gave her pause. In April 1956, the HFS board had convened an emergency
meeting in Atlanta to address the potential resignations of Myles Horton,
Henry Shipherd, and his wife, Betty, who served as the school's executive
secretary. The central issue was the school's financial situation. Both parties
stressed that no improprieties had occurred, but the Shipherds felt that the
school's finances should be managed more transparently and that regulatory
oversight should be increased. Horton disagreed, arguing that the foundations that provided grants to HFS "were satisfied." He also asserted that he
and the Shipherds supported different means of achieving the school's goals.
Where he wanted to stay in the background and educate local people to
become community organizers, Henry Shipherd preferred "going to meetings, giving advice, helping people out, et. cetera." The resulting tensions
had yielded an "intolerable" situation, with Horton issuing an ultimatum
that either he or the Shipherds had to go. The board directed that an audit
be undertaken, after which Highlander would settle any remaining fiscal
obligations to the Shipherds and accept their resignations. The board also
amended the school's charter and by-laws to clarify its administrative practices.[73]

Septima Clark enjoyed working with the Shipherds, whom she praised for their "wonderful ideas of strict routine and accurate records." She perceived that "at times" Horton "tries to be democratic but there are other times when he is not." Clark also hesitated to accept the offer to come to Highlander because Grundy County, Tennessee, had a very small black population. Clark would have no church to attend regularly, and conducting daily business would become more problematic. The local bank, for example, would serve black customers only if a white person vouched for them, while more hostile white residents held that "Negroes are not allowed on the mountain." Clark did not really want to leave Charleston, but her local support had entirely eroded. Even her sorority sisters would decline to have their picture taken with her when they gave her a testimonial dinner later that year. Their rejection hurt Clark very deeply.[74]

On the positive side, the remaining staff at Highlander promised to stand behind Clark, and she expected to travel back and forth frequently between Monteagle and the Low Country. Horton thought it important that neither white nor black Charlestonians conclude that Clark had been run out of town for taking a public, pro-integration stance. Clark agreed. She also wanted to stay as active as possible in her civic organizations and did not want to abandon the work she had begun for HFS on the Sea Islands. She accepted Horton's offer, still shaken by losing her job and without complete certainty that she had made the right decision: "For three solid months, I couldn't sleep. Night after night I stayed up listening" to tapes from workshop sessions. "One morning . . . I felt a kind of free feeling in my mind, and I said, 'Now I must have been right.' I was able to fall asleep and to sleep after that. I decided that I had worried about that thing long enough."[75] Publicly, Clark rarely admitted to being afraid; privately, she spent many hours searching her soul for confirmation that she had been right to take such an uncompromising stand.

Clark's new position as director of workshops included planning and administering all summer residential programs, but she did not lead the sessions herself. According to Guy Carawan, who joined the HFS staff to provide its musical component after Zilphia Horton's death, Clark "helped get all the communication out to everybody, kept track of who was coming, made sure how much food was being prepared." In other words, she supervised all the mundane details that ensured a successful workshop experience. During the winter, she traveled to raise funds. In 1958, when her title changed to director of education, Clark began managing all of HFS's educational fieldwork. Thus, in addition to organizing residential workshops in Monteagle, she attended to all the details of Highlander's extension work. Finally, Clark prepared financial reports on all of HFS's educational activities.[76]

⌒⋇⋇⌒

By the time Septima Clark moved to Monteagle, plans to establish a voter education program to answer Esau Jenkins's appeal for help mobilizing his neighbors had been in the works for almost two years. At least twenty people from the Sea Islands had participated in Highlander workshops since Clark's first visit in 1954, and they provided the initial leadership and enthusiasm. White Carolinians, meanwhile, had responded to Jenkins's political ambitions. In the wake of the earliest voter registration successes on Johns Island, the Charleston County delegation to the state legislature voted to appoint rather than elect school board trustees.[77]

Clark claimed that a pedagogical idea came to her while she was on an airplane, returning from a National Education Association meeting with Myles Horton. "And when I went back to Highlander, that night, I started, sitting down and writing out 'Education for Citizenship.'" Clark had been moving in educational circles that specifically addressed matters of "citizenship education" for twenty years. Yet what had in the 1930s been a strategy for fighting fascism became in the 1950s a way to win the Cold War, endorsed by no less than Dwight D. Eisenhower. Beginning in the fall of 1951, for example, Charleston's city school board launched its Citizenship Education Project in two white high schools. Local newspapers praised the endeavor. One ran an article accompanied by a large photograph showing a student beside a blackboard listing the things "A good citizen should do," including "be informed," "be actively interested in his government," and "VOTE." In 1953, the school board expanded the project to Charleston's African American high school. Clark read this action as mere tokenism, especially as ardent segregationists increasingly invoked the same language of education and citizenship to preserve white supremacy. As she later informed a Highlander supporter, "You can't teach citizenship training [in black schools]. They are afraid the Negroes will learn too fast."[78]

Clark had never focused her activist energies exclusively on voter registration. Indeed, she did not really do so until after Judge Waring's decisions in the late-1940s primary cases. As an activist educator and clubwoman, she had devoted much of her attention to school and health issues affecting the black community while remaining equally concerned with mentoring young black women and garnering respect for black womanhood. As an organizer of several HFS-sponsored workshops in 1955 and 1956, she had incorporated affordable housing and consumer cooperatives into her agenda. Clark had a broad definition of "citizenship education," augmented by her involvement with Highlander but firmly rooted in southern black women's activist organizational culture.

Designing the Citizenship School program, Clark rightly suspected that literacy training would add African Americans to the voting rolls, but Horton doubted that doing so constituted the most effective approach. According to Clark, Horton thought a staff member could go into a community, explain the laws to people, prepare them specifically for the voter registration test, and then lead them to the registrar's office. Both organizers knew that only 10 percent of Johns Islanders were completely illiterate, but that did not mean that the rest read sufficiently. Clark's experiences led her to a different conclusion. "I just thought that you couldn't get people to register and vote until you teach them to read and write," she reasoned. So she argued with Horton over her preferred methodology. "Myles and I just had to shout it out," she recalled. "Myles would ask me about methods, and I would say, 'Don't ask me about methods. Let me tell you how I'm going to do this thing.'" Uniting practical, political, and economic literacy, Clark intended to guarantee that newly enfranchised African Americans made informed decisions and remained active citizens after leaving the voting booth. If Horton judged her technique outdated, he conceded the value of Clark's personal investment in the project and concluded that "her sense of the need to keep the program practical would more than make up for any weaknesses in method."[79] Thus, the curriculum's emphasis on basic literacy resulted from Clark's adamant insistence.

Clark, Horton, and Jenkins spent the fall of 1956 preparing to open the first Citizenship School. First, they needed a place to hold classes. Jenkins approached the principal of the island's four-year-old Haut Gap High School to ask if they could use a classroom. Fearful that the white superintendent would learn of the classes, the principal said no. Jenkins next sought space at a local Methodist center. Fearful that his wife might lose her teaching job in the public schools, the presiding preacher said no. Jenkins then learned that the old Mount Zion Elementary School was coming up for sale for one thousand dollars. He arranged to borrow money from an acquaintance in Charleston to buy the building. Before the deal was settled, however, a white man purchased the building; then he offered it to Jenkins for fifteen hundred dollars. With no other alternative, Jenkins obtained a loan from Highlander and bought the facility. The Progressive Club opened a cooperative store in the building's large front room. Members could save money shopping there,

The original Progressive Club on Johns Island, late 1950s.
Courtesy of the Wisconsin Historical Society, Image # 41223.

and preliminary profits would go to repay the building loan. Equally important, as Clark noted, the store provided a way "to fool white people" and to
avoid arousing suspicion about the school that would run in the two rooms
in the back.[80] Segregation provided cover.

With the classroom secured, organizers turned their attention to selecting
a teacher, immediately deciding against professional educators. Highlander
staff believed that aside from their timidity, professionally trained teachers
might prove too curriculum-oriented — or worse, too middle-class — in outlook and therefore unable to resist the temptation to usurp decision-making
roles. Though Clark would have seemed the logical choice, she traveled too
frequently as the school's fund-raiser to do the day-to-day teaching. HFS planners sought someone equally sympathetic to the Johns Island students, some
of whom lived in poverty, hewing the land for plantation owners; others of
whom worked as maids and cooks in the city homes of white people; and still
others of whom eked out a living by combining seasonal work in Charleston
with farming. "A lot of these people were doing all right economically," Pro-

gressive Club member Bill Saunders asserted, "but they were not fulfilled because somebody had to tell them what they were getting in a letter and a lot of the time, those folk were lying to them."[81] Johns Islanders needed a teacher they could trust.

Clark, Horton, and Jenkins settled on Bernice Robinson. She protested, reminding them that she had not even attended college. Clark reasoned that a college degree mattered little, given that Robinson would be teaching the most basic subject matter. Moreover, Robinson was familiar with the island people through her NAACP work, she understood Gullah reasonably well, and she had been trained at Highlander. As a beautician who ran her own shop in Charleston, she also remained less vulnerable to white economic reprisals.

Significantly, Clark's observation, "we felt that she had the most important quality; the ability to listen to people," reflected the sensibility accrued during her own earliest days teaching on Johns Island. Elsewhere, Clark noted that even Myles Horton had difficulty with this essential skill. Dedicated as he was, "It was hard for him to hear them say, 'Now this happened the night that that cow had its calf on such-and-such a moon.' . . . He wanted them to come right to the point and they wouldn't do it."[82] Robinson claimed that working in the beauty industry had endowed her with "a good ear." "When you're a beautician, you're everything. You preach to them. You listen to their problems. . . . They're going to tell you all of their life stories."[83] Black beauticians and their customers occupied a female-centered space wherein the value of listening was appreciated. The intimacy of the shop provided a safe forum in which women could unburden themselves and catch up on neighborhood gossip, and the workers there gained an enhanced sensitivity to the nuanced meanings of the stories people told to explain their lives.

HFS organizers decided that classes would run two hours a night, two nights a week, for two months during the agricultural off-season. Robinson bore responsibility for recruiting her own students. Attracting adult pupils required the same skills that had been at the heart of black women's educational culture for most of the twentieth century. Yet in the beginning, Clark did not try to impose her methods on Robinson. Instead, she helped her cousin more indirectly. "We used to ride a lot together and just by talking about the way things were happening in Charleston and on the various islands . . . she picked them up." This explains why a nervous Robinson entered class on the first night armed with elementary school reading primers borrowed from two of her sisters-in-law who were teachers, and why she never used those materials.[84]

Ten women and four men gathered in the inaugural Citizenship School class on January 7, 1957. Robinson tried to make her adult students feel at ease by diffusing the traditional classroom hierarchy. "I said to them, 'I'm really not going to be your teacher. We're going to work together and teach each other.'" In the tradition of a Highlander workshop, Robinson began by asking her students what they wanted to learn. Most wanted to read the newspaper, to read their Bible, to read letters from their children far away, and to learn how to fill out a catalog order and a money order form. "I started off with things that were familiar to them," she recalled. "I'd have them tell me stories of about what they did in the fields and what they had in their homes," which she then copied down and used for reading lessons.[85] The reemergence of the improvisational pedagogical methods that Clark had first used on Johns Island in 1916 might have been a coincidence, or it might have reflected Robinson's skills as a listener.

The men, Robinson soon discovered, had a particular interest in arithmetic. To begin teaching simple math, she relied on newspaper circulars that advertised weekly specials at the supermarket. If "two pounds of beans" cost forty-nine cents, she queried, and "if you wanted four pounds, how much would it be?" Similarly, she challenged her students to figure how much gasoline they would use to drive from the island to the city or how to combine measurements to estimate the amount of material they would need to build a fence. Again, though Robinson had never taught before, her description of her practical pedagogy echoed verbatim a sensibility embraced by African American teachers in the rural Jim Crow South: "I used all that *trying* to meet them where they were." Yet Robinson never lost sight of how far she hoped her students would progress. "I tacked up the [United Nations] Declaration of Human Rights on the wall and told them that I wanted each of them to be able to read and understand the entire thing before the end of school."[86]

Eight of Robinson's students could read "very poorly," while three could not read or write at all. Drawing on her previous experience teaching for Wil Lou Gray, Clark suggested that Robinson give all the students pieces of cardboard with their names written on them so that they could trace the letters until they learned how to write. After students grew comfortable with each other, Robinson had those who had basic literacy skills read aloud portions of the state constitution pertaining to registering and voting. She incorporated troublesome words into vocabulary lessons, reviewed their meaning, and worked on pronunciation. Robinson learned something new about how individual determination inspired educational progress. Anna Vastine was sixty-five years old and could neither read nor write when she began class. At the end of two Citizenship School sessions totaling five months of biweekly instruction, Robinson called Vastine to the front of the classroom to identify her first and last name on the board: "I will never forget the emotion I felt when she got up, took the ruler out of my hand . . . and said, 'There's my name, A-n-n-a, Anna. There's my last name . . . V-a-s-t-i-n-e.' Goose pimples came out all over me."[87]

Additional classroom instruction reflected Clark's tenure teaching adult literacy classes for Gray. Like Gray, Clark compiled a special reading booklet for students. Clark's first reader contained a history of Highlander; sections of the state's election laws and the state constitution; a copy of a registration certificate; information on the Democratic and Republican Parties; a section on "Taxes You Must Pay in South Carolina"; a description of social security and how to claim benefits; a list of health clinics in Charleston County; instructions on how to address elected officials; and blank mail order and money order forms. Because Clark understood that acquiring citizenship meant acquiring the information that citizens needed to know, materials in the booklet stressed the importance of law and procedure, making it not altogether different than Gray's primer. To ensure that community officials heard them, citizens had to speak the language. But whereas Gray's citizenship education uncritically celebrated South Carolina and sought to inculcate respect for existing political and institutional authority, Clark's curriculum connected learning directly to social change through political action. As she pointed out, "We need to think about taxes, social welfare programs, labor management relations, schools and old age pensions. These affect our daily lives and are definitely tied to the vote."[88]

Though adults composed Robinson's primary constituency, Citizenship School training from the outset included young people. Thirteen teenaged girls joined their parents in the first class. An excellent seamstress, Robinson added sewing and crocheting lessons to keep the girls occupied and quiet. Even so, "they would snicker when an adult would stumble over the word," she stated. Figuring that turnabout was fair play, Robinson assigned them stories to read and summarize for the class. "They'd stumble over some words. Then I'd say, 'Let's laugh at them too, they can't pronounce that word.'" Next, she gave the girls information on public speaking and told each of them to make a speech. "And they'd get up and start talking and put their hand over their mouth. And so I said, 'Can you imagine getting up in front of an audience and giving a talk and you putting your hand over your mouth?' . . . I did that just to criticize them so they would see that they should not be criticizing their elders."[89] Still, the premise behind training

Two girls in a Citizenship School sewing class, Sea Islands, ca. 1958–59.
Courtesy of the Wisconsin Historical Society, Image # 41222.

these young black women in public speaking dovetailed with training their parents to register to vote: it anticipated a future of community participation.

Bernice Robinson also discovered what a lifetime of teaching had taught Septima Clark—that is, that the reciprocal expectations and obligations, forged at the grassroots between teacher and community, fostered learning. "I have never before in my life seen such anxious people," Robinson wrote to Highlander after the first few weeks of class. "They really want to learn and are so proud of the little gains they have made so far. When I get to the club each night, half of them are already there and have their homework ready for me to see."[90]

Thrilled by initial reports, Horton indicated that he wanted to visit the Citizenship School class. Robinson panicked and called Clark, who was away fund-raising. "Don't worry about it," Clark counseled her cousin, "because Myles don't know nothing about teaching anybody either." She meant that although Horton asked searing questions that got people thinking about

*Esau Jenkins (left) and Myles Horton (right) in the Progressive Club store,
1958–59. Courtesy of the Wisconsin Historical Society, Image # 41217.*

how they could change themselves and then affect positive change in their
communities, he had no practical experience teaching adult literacy classes.
Robinson's ability, with the assistance of Jenkins, to keep students "busy as
bees" working on diverse tasks impressed Horton. He also noticed that thirty
or forty more people, young and old, stood in the cooperative store and listened intently to what was going on in the classroom.[91]

At the end of the first session in February, eight of the fourteen students
registered to vote. HFS decided to continue the program in December 1957
and to extend it by one month. Jenkins helped spread the word. Now, when
Jenkins approached his neighbors about learning how to register and vote,
he incorporated their more personal desires for self-fulfillment and self-
sufficiency, asking, "Do you *want* to read the letter that's coming from your
daughter in New York? Do you *want* to be able to fill out a money order?
Do you *want* to be able to pay your own taxes?" Citizenship School alumni
shared the responsibility for generating interest in the next class. Enrollment on Johns Island increased to thirty-seven. News traveled rapidly along
the grapevine. By the time classes began in 1958, three additional schools

had opened, one in North Charleston and one each on neighboring Wadmalaw and Edisto Islands.[92]

Expansion forced Horton and Clark to formalize their pedagogical procedures. The two agreed that all classes would be taught by African Americans. Well-meaning whites, Horton conceded, would have trouble breaking the habit of "dominating" discussions, and black adult students needed to begin dismantling their internalized white supremacy. Clark, too, had undergone that process: "I had to change, too, because I used to feel that whatever was white was right." Next, Horton and Clark decided that Citizenship School teachers should be well respected and come from the communities in which they taught. As for qualifications, Clark confirmed that they looked for "those who could read well aloud and write legibly." Prospective teachers were required to attend a five-day training workshop at Highlander and to return for a weekend follow-up session. Back home, Citizenship School teachers had to conduct a little research. They had to know the location and hours of the voter registration office; the names of local elected officials; when elections were held; what health services were available in the community; and where the nearest social security office was. Given such responsibilities, "dedication to the cause" represented an important credential, underwritten by the "patience" to work with adult learners. Teachers could expect to receive fifty dollars a month for travel and material expenses.[93]

Family and community networks often pulled people into local civil rights struggles. Esau Jenkins's daughter, Ethel Grimball, became the Citizenship School teacher on Wadmalaw Island. Grimball had been refused a job teaching in the public schools because of her father's activism. She had also been to an HFS workshop and had observed Robinson teaching on Johns Island. A Presbyterian church agreed to donate class space. Grimball recruited her students, again mostly women, from among members of the Wadmalaw Island Improvement Committee, the civic organization that her father had helped to establish. She enlisted the aid of Willie Smith, "the main person" who rallied "the people together so that when you have the meeting they will be there," and Anderson Mack, who enrolled in her first class. Though some of the students could read a little before they attended Grimball's class, Mack had never learned the alphabet and could not write his name. When the sessions ended three months later, "he could kind of scribble 'Anderson,'" Grimball remarked. Another student wanted to learn how to sew "because she had so many children, and she figured she could help herself." Grimball had someone come in to teach sewing and crocheting, while she focused on

*Alleen Brewer (right) with Edisto Island Citizenship School students,
ca. 1958–59. Courtesy of the Wisconsin Historical Society, Image #41220.*

teaching reading and writing. She included budget lessons to help her students save money. At the end of the class, all of Grimball's students added their names to the voting rolls.[94]

Alleen Brewer, a social worker, led the Citizenship School class on Edisto Island, which was also held in a Presbyterian church. The wife of a minister, Brewer had moved to Johns Island in 1929 and earned a reputation as a woman who "would help with anything that needed doing." As one resident observed, she "was one of the persons that we call the 'grandmoms of the islands,' instrumental in so many little things that you don't hear much about." Her proven dedication facilitated her Citizenship School recruiting efforts. Facing thirty-eight students on the first night, Brewer organized them into groups so that they might help each other. Edisto islanders advanced quickly. According to Clark, at the end of the first month, seven of the nine students Brewer accompanied to Charleston registered to vote. Like Robinson and Grimball, Brewer integrated sewing lessons into her curriculum and had her pupils make book bags for their materials. Visiting class one evening, Clark noticed that Edisto students enjoyed lingering afterward to socialize, and she overheard a man say, "Now we don't have to wait for Sunday to fellowship together." She thus realized that the program's ability to strengthen community relations contributed to its popularity. Brewer kept a sewing circle going for women after the session ended to retain the new ties that had been forged.[95]

Robinson taught the class in North Charleston at the invitation of her friend, Mary Davis, a beautician and an NAACP activist who had been to HFS. Davis lived in Charleston Heights, an area that lacked paved streets and where inattentive landlords had let their property deteriorate, which hurt Davis's economic investment. Clark claimed that Davis wanted to get her neighbors registered to vote and hoped the Citizenship School would help them "ask for better streets and to be heard when they asked." In the course of her teaching, Robinson had developed a chart that illustrated the rankings of government officials, from those in local public service, employment, and school positions all the way up to the governor. A dozen women, most of whom worked as domestics, convened in Davis's shop, where they not only prepared for the registration test but also learned how to navigate that chain of command to "get some things done for the improvement of their community."[96] After this class ended, Bernice Robinson became the supervisor for all of the Low Country Citizenship Schools.

As Septima Clark traveled to increase interest in the programs, she encountered a range of attitudes that reaffirmed her sense of strategic possibilities. On Wadmalaw Island, after screening a Highlander-made movie featuring Esau Jenkins, Clark fielded questions from the two hundred people in the audience and observed, "It gave them a real thrill to listen to Esau in the movie. It is a real pride that they feel has come to one of the islanders." Less-promising comments underscored the fact that the first step on the road to citizenship did not usually lead straight to the voting booth. Visiting Hilton Head, Clark heard a woman assert, "There is no use in voting, all the people in Columbia are white anyhow. They don't care about you." Knowing that the woman's attitude helped keep unresponsive political leaders in power, Clark conceded, "We can't touch that now, but we can work along with them." The solution was to "get a good program going."[97]

The increased numbers of African Americans on the voting rolls certainly represented one measure of the program's early triumphs. Citizenship School graduates pledged to influence those who could read and write to add their names to the voting rolls. In 1958 alone, more than 600 black people on Johns Island registered to vote. A total of 106 students, ranging in age from fifteen to seventy-six, enrolled in four classes during the 1958–59 term; 86 of them obtained registration certificates before the end of the session. By March

1960, black registration on Johns Island had risen 300 percent since the first class started. That same year, Edisto counted 200 black voters, an addition of 160 since 1958. Of the 111 students participating in Citizenship School classes on Edisto during the 1960–61 session, 105 registered to vote.[98]

Yet it would be a mistake to gauge the impact of the earliest Citizenship Schools solely by the numbers. Far more important and far more difficult to quantify are the reasons that people decided to enroll in the classes and the personal transformations they consequently experienced. John Wigfall had completed the first grade and could only spell his name. After enrolling in a Johns Island Citizenship School class, he learned to write and do simple arithmetic, and then he became an enthusiastic supporter of the Citizens Club. Eloise Reed had acquired basic literacy skills because she had attended school through the fourth grade, when she dropped out at the age of eighteen to get married. "I learned what I was already learn and forgot by worriation," she commented; "I learned lots of words in my book what I was almost forget, I could go back and pronounce those words." After completing her Citizenship School class, she kept her Bible near her bed to read "as much as she [could] anytime she [could]."[99]

Some of those who attended the Citizenship Schools had already obtained their voter registration certificates. Solomon Brown, born on Edisto Island in 1884, first registered to vote in 1905 and had voted continuously since that time. Perhaps drawn to Brewer's class for the social opportunity it afforded, Brown stated that he and his classmates "learned much of what Democracy means that we did not know before" and "were inspired to help others toward first class citizenship." Brown went on to serve as the first president of the Edisto Island Improvement Committee. Arthur Jenkins (no relation to Esau), the first president of the Wadmalaw Improvement Committee, and Willie Smith had become registered voters based on the amount of property they owned and taxes they paid. Both men enrolled in Grimball's classes. Jenkins's math skills improved; Smith learned long division and enhanced his penmanship.[100]

Legacies of citizenship rooted in personal and family history stretching back to the days of Reconstruction also motivated Sea Islanders. Alice Wine, who was born in 1906, said she "knew about voting in my mother's time." Her parents told stories of how they "used to go down to Judge Beckett and they vote and they take food with them and they be there all day long. To make things better for the rest what's coming now." Wine knew of no other black people who voted until Esau Jenkins began to organize his neighbors, but the memory of her parents' voting inspired Wine to action when an opportunity "to show she was a citizen" presented itself. After graduating from her class, she secured social security benefits originally denied her and became a clerk in the Progressive Club's cooperative store.[101]

As Clark had predicted, participation in the Citizenship Schools profoundly affected daily life. Those who learned to read, write, and figure felt more self-sufficient and less vulnerable. More important, they had the means to preserve their independence. Johns Island resident Bill Saunders cited many occasions when white people "would say they were paying property taxes" for illiterate black landowners and then not do it, causing African Americans to "end up losing their property." With the advent of citizenship education, "folk were learning that they can go and pay their own taxes and they would know when they had the receipt for their property taxes." Similarly, Bernice Robinson recalled that insurance salesmen had taken advantage of island people. "They were paying the man every week and the man just scribbled in the book. Come to find out the insurance had lapsed. They didn't have any. They were cheated in so many different ways by not being able to read and write." After finishing his Citizenship School training, Anderson Mack declared "that if a man gave him a piece of paper and said that it said something, he could see for himself rather than taking the man's word."[102]

Graduates gained marketable skills that could lead to a greater economic autonomy as well. Laura Johnson, a mother of ten and a student on Wadmalaw, wrote that before she joined Grimball's class, "I washing and wonent to lom how to read and figer & sow." After finishing class, Johnson continued, "I can make my children close and also I read and figer much better." She added that she had influenced two more people to register. Likewise, when asked by Horton why her neighbors wanted to read and write, one woman replied, "To do they own business." Completing classes encouraged some Citizenship School alumni to continue their education. Grimball noted that Mack "went on to night school." Her other students experienced additional gains: "When our people went to the courthouse, they got better treatment; health care came as a result of all that; better educational condition came as a result of all that. I can just keep naming it because after the literacy school, after people started registering and voting, you got a change in attitudes." In Clark's evaluation, "One thing spreading out starts others. It's like the pebble thrown in the mill pond."[103]

As hoped, the Sea Island Citizenship Schools also spurred the founding of local community clubs and invigorated those already in existence. Between 1957 and 1960, residents on Johns, Wadmalaw, and Edisto Islands got into the habit of attending monthly meetings, where they also learned about parliamentary procedure. Paying modest monthly dues allowed members to signal their sense of self-sufficiency and pride. Discussing current events, often news of racial violence from other areas of the South, strengthened their commitment to the local struggle. Blending the secular and the sacred, islanders propagated a political vision based on the notion that "the Lord helps those who help themselves." Their grassroots organizations, which combined collective strategizing with routine continuity, became a vehicle for spreading leadership throughout the community.[104]

From Septima Clark's perspective, one of the most important developments was women's assuming a greater role in community affairs. Initially, "women didn't speak on the islands," she remarked; "they fanned the flies and waited until the men said things." When women began saying, "Esau, we need so and so," Clark read such actions as "a new statement." From that point on, she asserted, "we were able to get more women who were willing to speak up." By mid-1959, the Voters Association of Edisto Island had elected three women to its program committee and three more to its youth activities committee.[105] If women's participation testified to a widening planning circle, Clark derived special satisfaction from strengthening their confidence in their leadership abilities because she knew that such improvements fortified communal work.

Sophisticated political organizing also emerged in the wake of the Citizenship Schools. "Everybody who needed to vote, we made sure they got out and vote," Bill Saunders confirmed. "We knew the registration certificate number, we took it down, and we could count how many people voted and if that didn't come off the machine, we knew that somebody tampered" with it. On Wadmalaw Island, an African American woman joined a precinct executive committee. After it supported the winning white candidate, he secured legislation "to send school buses down side roads, to have mail delivered to individual boxes, and to establish three day care centers."[106] Such seemingly small changes proved to those who benefited that their votes mattered.

If Clark appreciated how Citizenship School training encouraged pupils to enlist their voices along with their votes, she soon had solid evidence that the personal self-confidence students acquired decreased their fear of the white power structure. In the spring of 1959, the *Charleston News and Courier* printed a series of articles and editorials describing the true nature of what was happening on the Sea Islands but linked such efforts to the "communist-influenced" HFS and ominous international developments. The paper's editor, Thomas R. Waring Jr., observed, "On every hand, we hear warnings about the possibility that communists may take over the dark-skinned people of the world. Red China already is communist. Africa is in turmoil. So is the Middle East. White civilization, which brought order and prosperity to undeveloped lands, is in peril." He concluded by warning his readers of the danger of communist-sponsored race mixing. Citing Johns Island's most visible leader out of context, Waring announced, "As Esau Jenkins said of integration, 'It's a Revolution.'" Clark dismissed Waring's propaganda to focus on a more relevant underlying truth. "I'm sure the program will not be hurt because the editorial [has] failed to intimidate any of our students," she informed Horton.[107]

By the early 1960s, Jenkins decided that he wanted his own workshop facility on Johns Island. Jenkins reasoned that he could attract black activists from across the South who might not want to travel as far as the Tennessee mountains. After conferring with Horton, Jenkins secured the money to construct a building with a meeting hall that could accommodate five hundred people, a housing unit that could sleep sixteen, and a kitchen. The new Progressive Club retained space for the cooperative store as well. According to Clark, the Marshall Field Foundation provided money to rent a chartered bus to "bring the people from as far as eastern Texas and northern Virginia," and "we had workshops there one whole summer with those people." College students from as far away as Santa Cruz, California, later spent time at the facility, learning about the freedom struggle from Jenkins and his neighbors.[108]

Over time, Citizenship School teachers and alumni helped transform the Low Country's political landscape. In 1967, black registered voters comprised 38 percent of those on Charleston County's books. Not all of them were Sea Islanders, but island residents no longer had to make special trips to the city on the two days of the month when the books were open. Thanks to their own efforts, they could register any day of the week and in numerous public locations closer to home. That same year, black votes ensured the election of St. Julian Devine as a Charleston alderman, the first African American to hold public office in the city since Reconstruction.[109]

᯽

Septima Clark had seen her share of dark days and trying times. As the white South raised the stakes of civil rights activism, she raised her commitment and paid dearly for her choices. Yet Clark's vision of political possibility remained firmly rooted in a spirit of service that became a source of her strength. When Esau Jenkins asked for a school to teach his people to read and write, Clark heard him and obliged. As a result, where many African Americans regarded the forces of white repression as insurmountable, Clark saw a grassroots civil rights movement beginning to take shape in the South Carolina Low Country. By 1959, she recognized that it had assumed a momentum of its own.

Going to Highlander in 1954 changed Clark. Most notably, she gained a new perspective on the importance of developing indigenous community leadership. Helping people navigate the obstacles of Jim Crow failed to address deeper social inequalities. Persuading people to accept leadership responsibilities so that their communities might demand a voice in the allocation of county, state, and federal resources amounted to a more radically democratic enterprise.

From his mountain plateau, Myles Horton had spent two decades developing his pedagogy among impoverished white Appalachian farmers and white southern laborers, men and women who could vote but who lacked social and economic power. Social, economic, and political equality for African Americans seemed like a distant, radical dream when Septima Clark began teaching on Johns Island in 1916. Nevertheless, she lived long enough to see changes in the law render that dream achievable and spent many years as an activist educator helping to make it a reality. At HFS, Clark encountered a familiar philosophy of adult education premised on helping people to help themselves. The difference was that most of those Horton targeted had acquired enough of an education to be able to read and write, whereas many disfranchised black southerners had not. For Clark's people, overcoming adult illiteracy proved the definitive factor to begin building black political power on the Sea Islands.

Additional Citizenship School pedagogy grew directly out of Clark's lifelong experiences. Citizenship School teachers recruited students by visiting homes, community meetings, local churches, and beauty parlors, where they asked questions and listened to the issues residents considered most worrisome. The teachers then persuaded people to enroll in the classes by linking the ability to read, write, and vote to the expansive social and economic agenda long pursued by black women civic organizers. If registering to vote had become doable, plenty remained that needed doing. Inside the classroom, like earlier generations of black women before them, teachers endeavored to meet students where they were by improvising. Classes incorporated the same general approach and definitely aimed for the same goal, but location and student desire dictated day-to-day content. Addressing practical concerns, Citizenship School teachers tapped into the mutual reciprocity between teacher and student that had long defined southern black education.

The men and women who became the first Citizenship School students in South Carolina wanted to exercise a right that had been guaranteed to them for nearly a decade. But they thirsted more for the ability to act on their own behalf, a feeling of self-reliance and independence, privileges they had never enjoyed because they lacked formal education. They learned more rapidly because these more personal aspirations motivated them. Some even carried living memories of a time when black people had voted. Clark's program for citizenship education provided a bridge between that remote past and a hopeful future. The distance from the schoolroom to the courthouse remained considerable and the path arduous, but students traveled down the road toward personal empowerment along the way. They also learned how to use the vote to improve their community. Citizenship School graduates crossed over: they went from silently accepting things as they were to raising their voices to influence how things should be.

The degree to which individuals applied what they learned on a daily basis can never be fully measured, or underestimated. But perhaps Johns Island resident Benjamin Bligen put it best when he summed up the situation: "More light is shining. Can see more. Likewise, you can do more and think more, 'cause I believe more light is shining now than was ever shining in the past."[110] Soon, due to Septima Clark's efforts, that light would be shining across the South.

CHAPTER EIGHT

A Fight for Respect

In 1956, Ella Baker invited Septima Clark to attend a Sunday afternoon meeting at a church in Chattanooga that featured Coretta Scott King as the speaker. Clark, who had never met King, agreed to go and to stand in a receiving line with honored guest afterward. Just before the event, however, she unexpectedly greeted the wife of the church's minister in Monteagle. "She made that trek, twelve miles up the mountain that Saturday night, to see if I had something that I could wear to stand in line with Mrs. King," Clark recalled. The minister's wife had previously been to Highlander and had noticed Clark's casual wardrobe. "I had to produce a dress," she continued, "I had to show her that I had a black dress and it had some kind of net or something on the front." The episode irritated Clark. Seeing King, she remarked, "I didn't think that she looked so wonderful that I had to be so dressed up to meet her. . . . I hope the lady was satisfied after she had come to see what I had." A Charlestonian, Clark knew well the ways of the black aristocracy and understood that they sometimes had to be endured. "That's how people are about material things," she granted.[1] As a teacher and clubwoman, she was well versed in negotiating both class expectations and class tensions within the black community. Such realities always existed alongside everything else involved in working with people.

Clark's reputation among southern black women activists had most likely motivated organizers in Chattanooga to include her. Yet working for Highlander raised her profile in both the African American and white civil rights communities and expanded her activist network. Traveling on behalf of the school, she was introduced to A. Philip Randolph, president of the Brotherhood of Sleeping Car Porters and long a nationally prominent black leader. On another occasion, Clark applauded a speech on the First Amendment delivered by Anne Braden, a white ally from Louisville, Kentucky, to the Women's International League for Peace and Freedom. All the while, overseeing workshops at HFS brought Clark into contact with progressive thinkers and activists from the wider world, including former First Lady Eleanor Roosevelt and visitors from Europe and Africa. On one occasion, Clark traveled to Atlanta with a female member of the Nigerian royal family who had stopped at Highlander as part of a State Department tour. There, she first met Martin Luther King Jr. As she testified about her affiliation with HFS, "I really feel that the training, contacts, and shared experiences that I received have been more than beneficial to me."[2]

The professional fund-raising work she undertook for HFS in the North and West required Clark to fashion a movement persona for broader public consumption. For Highlander, she became an "authentic" voice of the struggle southern African Americans had long waged against the injustice of Jim Crow. Clark developed stock stories from her own life narrative — perhaps none more repeated than the conditions in Johns Island schools when she had started her teaching career in 1916 — and then linked them to changes that had come about as a result of HFS's work on the island four decades later. Her familiarity with Johns Islanders allowed her to interpret the texture of their daily lives as they labored to attain the practical literacy to qualify to vote and the political literacy to use the vote effectively. Clark was an articulate and soft-spoken black woman who had interacted with wealthy white people. To audiences of mostly white donors, she used her speech and her manner to represent the southern civil rights movement as dignified, respectable, and just. Moreover, leaving the South strengthened her faith in the likelihood of the movement's victory within it.

In the latter part of the 1950s, the school in Tennessee became an important meeting site for southern black civil rights activists, thereby affording Clark a better view of developments across the region. As early as 1958, she recognized that "even Mississippi's pot is beginning to boil." At the same time, she relied on both new and well-established contacts, particularly among black women, to find local leaders and to recruit workshop participants. When Clark met Ruby Hurley, a field secretary for the National Association for the Advancement of Colored People (NAACP), she urged Hurley to send "civic minded workers" from "Mississippi, Texas, Georgia, Louisiana, and Florida" to Highlander.[5] Despite her rising stature, Septima Clark, like Ella Baker, remained most interested in the potential of grassroots people. Shared perspectives on how best to organize the movement guaranteed that the paths of these two activists would continue to cross. Shared tribulations as black women working for men who disregarded their opinions provided additional common ground.

Indeed, serving on the Highlander staff did not come without liabilities. As the Shipherds' departure in 1956 had demonstrated, Myles Horton clung to his sense of ownership over the school's programs and direction and was willing to defend it at all costs. Clark tried to influence HFS's operations, with mixed results. An older woman with forty years of teaching and organizing behind her, Clark wanted Horton to respect her ideas. Both had strong personalities, but Clark often had to fight to be heard. By 1959, for example, she worried that Highlander's "integrated" workshops were too frequently all-black and wrote a memo to the school's trustees that pointed out the need for white recruiters to do more to attract white participants. A meticulous record keeper, Clark observed that of the 101 people who had enrolled in three residential workshops the previous summer, only 13 had been white; she concluded, "Yes, I'm *deeply concerned*."[4]

The school's perceived success on the integration front, however, made white supremacists even more determined to shut it down. Another major dispute erupted between Clark and Horton when state officials raided HFS in 1959 and Clark went to jail for the first time in her sixty-one years. The ensuing legal battles sunk Highlander and forced it to convey the Citizenship School program to the Southern Christian Leadership Conference (SCLC) in 1961. Clark stepped into the lifeboat of SCLC in what proved a difficult transition. Her health suffered. Tempers flared, and the relationship between Clark and Horton reached its nadir. Most of all, Clark's lack of a voice in the decision-making process that affected her personal and professional life angered her. The transfer shed light on the gap between HFS's democratic conception of leadership and the occasional reality of its operating practices. The resulting wounds took time to heal.

Keeping her eye on both promising developments in local communities and the long-term objective buoyed Clark's spirits. More important, her role as an agent in generating change continued to escalate. Clark's position in key networks enabled her to connect those who would with those who could. Given her familiarity with the internal politics of organizational life, she knew not to let personality conflicts and personal antagonisms eclipse larger goals. Nevertheless, Clark's loyalty to Highlander and especially to

Horton faced additional tests between 1959 and 1961. As she told the Warings, "Faith I must have and will keep to lean heavily on."[5] Along with faith, she would need courage.

✺

The attacks on Highlander hardly abated in the wake of Senator James O. Eastland's 1954 hearing, particularly because the school's integrated workshops kept it on the radar of leading white supremacists. In late 1957, segregationist governor Marvin Griffin used state tax funds to establish the Georgia Commission on Education. Determined to prove that HFS was a hotbed of communism, the commission hired a photographer to infiltrate the school's twenty-fifth anniversary celebration on Labor Day weekend. Martin Luther King Jr. attended that session and was photographed sitting near Abner Berry, an African American man who registered as a freelance writer but actually worked as a correspondent for the Communist Party's *Daily Worker*. A month later, the Georgia Commission released a four-page newspaper, *Highlander Folk School: Communist Training Center, Monteagle, Tenn.*, that featured a picture of King, Berry, Horton, and Aubrey Williams with the caption "'Four horsemen' of racial agitation." Additional photographs showed African Americans and whites eating, swimming, and dancing with each other and huddled together, allegedly discussing integration. Griffin offered an editorial statement that put the images in perspective: "It has been our purpose, as rapidly as possible, to identify the leaders and participants of this Communist training school and disseminate this information to the general public. Only through information and knowledge can we combat this alien menace to Constitutional government." The commission printed 250,000 copies of the pamphlet for distribution; the Citizens' Council and the Klan reprinted an estimated 1,000,000 more by the end of the year. By the mid-1960s, billboards reproducing the photo with the words "Martin Luther King at Communist Training School" appeared across the region.[6]

On February 12, 1959, the Tennessee General Assembly began an investigation of HFS. A special legislative committee held its first private hearing in Tracy City nine days later. Two witnesses testified that the school "was operated out of Moscow," though they admitted that they had never set foot on the property. Horton defended HFS during six hours on the witness stand at a March 4 public hearing in Nashville. The committee filed its report two days later, concluding that Highlander was not a school in the traditional sense of the word. While HFS's integrated workshops stood at the heart of the matter, the special committee made its decision on the basis of more technical considerations, the most serious of which involved a 1957 land transfer from HFS to Horton. The committee members recommended that Albert F. Sloan, the attorney general for Tennessee's Eighteenth Judicial Circuit, inaugurate a suit to revoke Highlander's charter.[7]

HFS had very few local supporters, but that small band responded immediately. Fourteen professors at the University of the South in Sewanee released a statement to the press protesting the charges of communist subversion and praising the school's commitment to democracy. They took an unpopular stand. *Charleston News and Courier* editor Thomas R. Waring Jr., a proud Sewanee alumnus, rebuked the "failure by educated, responsible citizens anywhere to recognize, identify, and oppose forces that would destroy the Republic in the stolen name of 'democracy.'" He also reminded his readers of the danger closer to home by calling attention to the HFS-sponsored educational activities on the Sea Islands, naming Esau Jenkins, Bernice Robinson, and Septima Clark as the school's "chief workers with colored people."[8] A tempest was brewing; the gale hit with full force four months later.

Friday, July 31, 1959, was a balmy evening in Monteagle. With Myles Horton in Europe, Septima Clark had presided over a weeklong workshop on community leadership. Several people she knew well were present, including Edisto Island Citizenship School teacher Alleen Brewer; Edisto Island Voters Association members Mamie Bligen, Celia Campbell, and Solomon Brown; and I. De Quincy Newman of the South Carolina NAACP. Thirteen youth had also come from Montgomery, Alabama. On this last night of the workshop, Clark screened George Mitchell's documentary, *The Face of the South*, in the dining room. Bernice Robinson decided to skip the film because she had seen it numerous times. Instead, she joined a few others on the lawn to cool off. Esau Jenkins sat talking with a group of men nearby. Robinson noticed distant headlights filtering through the trees and then disappearing but at first did not think too much of the activity. Soon, however, she thought she saw movement in the darkness and more headlights. She got up and walked toward the kitchen door on side of the main building. As she did so, a plainclothes police officer appeared and began herding the group up the lawn. It was about 8:40 P.M.[9]

Clark's six-year-old granddaughter, Yvonne, remembered waiting in the common room for the movie to end so that she could go on stage and perform a dance for the audience. After her mother's death in 1958, Yvonne had moved to Henrietta Street to live with her grandmother. Clark's residing in

Tennessee meant that Yvonne stayed with her great-aunt Lorene during the school year, but she had also been to Highlander many times. During one visit, when her grandmother had taken her for an ice cream cone at a Monteagle drugstore, Yvonne had "sat up on that seat and turned around," enjoying the treat until the store's owners had asked them to leave because "they didn't want no black girl sitting up there eating no ice cream cone." When Yvonne Clark heard a knock on the door that July night, she opened it.[10]

Seated near the projector, Septima Clark noticed a man with a camera in the hallway. She walked over to the door to investigate. Stepping out of the room, she saw another man, who she later learned was Sloan, approaching. The district attorney presented a warrant to search the premises for alcohol, a clear violation of the law in dry Grundy County. He had brought along twenty policemen and state troopers, most of them not in uniform, as well as some photographers from the *Chattanooga Free Press*. "Well go right ahead," Clark responded incredulously, "You won't even find cooking sherry in our kitchen." After a short interval, an officer returned and informed Clark that she was under arrest, not because anything had been found but because Sloan said so. She delayed long enough to advise someone to look out for her granddaughter until she got back.[11]

As the man roughly led Clark away, Brent Barksdale, a young Quaker, asked about her legal rights. Authorities grabbed him. Perry MacKay Sturges, a young teacher from New York, and musician Guy Carawan followed behind, asking officials why Clark was being arrested. "Lock those guys up, too," was the only answer they received. Another white man soon stuck his head into the room full of anxious movie watchers and demanded that someone stop the film. "But you have Septima Clark arrested," an anonymous voice answered from the dark, "and she's the only one who knows how to work the projector." The man found the cord and yanked it from the wall. The group endured another hour and a half in the darkness. They sang hymns and "We Shall Overcome," improvising "We are not afraid" in an extra verse for the first time, until another white man turned on the light and began taking names. Dr. Solomon S. Seay of the Montgomery Improvement Association volunteered his, as did a few others.[12]

When Robinson reached the back of the school, she saw that the police had Clark by the arm outside. The same image stuck in Bill Saunders's mind more than forty years later: "I don't know how come they didn't break [her arm], because it just went up in back of her head. They did something awful to her." Clark stayed cool and said nothing. "What are they doing with my Grandmommie?" Yvonne Clark screamed as she ran crying out of the house. Robinson grabbed the child and tried to calm her down. Authorities put Clark and the three young men in police cars and ordered the drivers to roll up the windows. There, they waited for what seemed an eternity. Just as Clark had predicted, the search of Highlander's main buildings yielded nothing—though the wallet, bankbook, and twenty-six dollars in cash taken from her were never returned. Authorities spread out, eventually gaining access to Horton's home on the periphery of the campus, where they found some open bottles of rum and gin and a wooden cask with clear liquid in it. Bingo! It mattered little that Horton's residence was not considered school property and therefore was not covered under the search warrant. As Sloan and his posse later discovered, the wooden barrel contained no moonshine either, just a little bit of water that had been added to keep it from cracking.[13]

Clark estimated that she did not leave Highlander until after midnight. To shake any workshop participants who might try to follow, the police went around several mountains and changed cars once on the way to the county jail at Altamont. Clark was unsure whether she would live "to see the daylight or not. I didn't feel too good riding with them, because I do know that these young mountain boys had beaten others to death, and I had a feeling that that might happen to me." Carawan sat beside her, demanding to know his rights. Clark knew that a dark mountain road was no place to argue with southern authority in 1959. There would be no witnesses. She admonished him, "This isn't the place to talk."[14]

Authorities charged Clark with illegal possession and sale of whiskey. Sloan stood nearby as she was fingerprinted, mockingly asking if she had gotten "a good taste of that liquor." Everybody who knew Septima Clark knew she was a teetotaler. Clark offered to take a blood test, but the men ignored her. They also refused to let her make a phone call before leading her to a cell. "They put me in this room and there were men above me," she recalled, "whenever they used the toilet, all that stuff would come down right through my room." Carawan, Sturges, and Barksdale were charged with "public drunkenness, interfering with officers, and resisting arrest." From his cell, Carawan heard Clark softly singing "Michael, Row the Boat Ashore," a song she had heard Harry Belafonte discuss at an HFS workshop. Vera McCampbell, whose involvement with the school stretched back to the days of Lilian Johnson, arrived shortly before 2:30 A.M. and posted Clark's $500 bail. Sloan refused to let her pay the $250 each for Clark's companions, however, claiming that he wanted to keep them overnight to give them a chance "to sober up."[15]

Clark's three-hour preliminary hearing occurred on August 6, 1959. The only witness called by Nashville defense attorney Cecil Branstetter, she denied that she had ever had liquor in her possession and reiterated that Horton's home was not HFS property. At one point, Sloan shook his finger in her face and warned her against perjuring herself. "I have never before seen a witness so abused as the Attorney-General has abused our witness — perhaps because she is colored," Branstetter told the press the next day. Carawan, Barksdale, and Sturges were arraigned six days later. A grand jury indicted all four, but in 1960, the state dismissed the case against Clark and dropped the charges against the three men.[16]

The next hearing involving Highlander occurred in mid-September. Sloan sought to suspend operations at HFS on the basis that the school illegally sold alcohol to its residential students. The district attorney also argued that the "loud and boisterous gatherings" on its grounds as well as the "immoral, lewd, and unchaste practices" among students rendered Highlander a public nuisance. State witnesses provided titillating testimony, swearing that they had seen nude interracial couples having sex in cabins and on the front lawn. Branstetter called their credibility into question and even established that one man had been jailed more than two dozen times for public drunkenness. Horton testified: "I am personally responsible for having instituted a policy at the Highlander Folk School of having beer available for people who were there for conferences." He explained that "against the advice of a number of my colleagues and friends," he had established a rotating fund where thirsty students "could put some money in a box if they wanted to." HFS then used the donations to restock the icebox with beer and soda. "Mrs. Clark was against this kind of thing," he added, "and some of her other teachers are, and the last few years, there has been very little of that." Clark later confirmed that she had argued with Horton about the policy: "I felt as if we didn't need to have the beer, because I saw quite a few of the union men that beer made almost crazy. They didn't act like themselves . . . and I didn't want to be wrestling with people with beer." Circuit Court judge Chester C. Chattin ruled that the state had failed to prove that HFS was a den of moral iniquity but concluded that the distribution of alcohol without a license violated state law. He ordered a temporary padlock placed on the school's main building. The court allowed the school to use its other facilities until November 3, the date of the final hearing on shuttering Highlander.[17]

Despite the brave countenance Septima Clark adopted in public, the experience traumatized her. Yvonne Clark recalled that the only time she ever saw her grandmother smoke a cigarette was the morning she returned from jail. Septima Clark's picture appeared on the front page of newspapers, attached to articles noting that she had been charged with possessing whiskey. The *Charleston News and Courier*'s coverage prompted the former president of the city's NAACP chapter, Arthur Clement Jr., who had relocated to North Carolina, to write a letter of protest. "I have personally known Mrs. Clark for over thirty years and she is of the highest character, with an unusually high sense of values," he proclaimed. Clement accused the paper's editor, Thomas Waring Jr., of delighting in Clark's misfortune: "Your intimations in your local publications emphasize '61-year-old woman' and 'held for grand jury action on illegal whiskey charge.' Bear in mind that Mrs. Clark has no way to fight back at this veritable character assassination technique." Waring replied that his information on Clark had come across the Associated Press wire and that she was as well positioned as any other citizen to defend herself.[18]

Letters of support arrived daily at Highlander, some from rather high-profile people. "The hope of the future rests upon dedicated lawyers like Cecil Branstetter, leaders of fortitude like Myles Horton; and women of integrity, honesty, and courage like Septima P. Clark," Martin Luther King Jr. wrote from Atlanta in a statement intended for publication. Other supporters offered more personal words. "Of course your own fine character and your long life of integrity and purity and nobility is the finest answer to such low charges," Virginia Durr assured Clark. Albertha Johnson Murray, a black Charlestonian schoolteacher and clubwoman, counseled, "Remember your friends and acquaintances and well-wishers believe in you and know you are a strong educational, spiritual, and cultured leader of the race." "Always remember that you are playing a role in which future historians will pick up their pens and list you among the great women of the 20th Century," Charleston NAACP branch president Joe Brown advised.[19]

Clark remained more worried about how the episode could damage her reputation in the present. She knew what some members of the black professional class would think: jail and alcohol separated "respectable Negroes" from "shiftless" lower-class folk. If Clark shared this perception, she likely did so because of her Christian training, and she had not let the idea interfere with her civil rights organizing. For example, when Esau Jenkins had suggested that local bootleggers should not be invited to community meetings, Clark had responded, "We have to work with everybody on this island."[20] And Clark's commitment to the movement often led her to castigate the black elite for its apparent apathy. Yet even Elizabeth Waring proved less than sympathetic to her friend's latest predicament, writing to Ruby Cornwell, "Poor Septima. I feared disaster for her when I warned her a long time ago . . . of the dangers of going to Highlander—Lack of integrity and management and as the Judge says no good common sense to have liquor in a dry state when they are on the spot being smeared."[21]

Clark soldiered valiantly on in the battle for public opinion. She soon hit the road, armed with papers and tape recordings of the hearings that had resulted in the temporary padlocking of HFS, to raise financial and public support for the ensuing court battle. Before a small group in Connecticut, Clark told of Sloan's disrespect while she was on the witness stand and maintained that "she later shook his hand" and harbored no ill will toward him. "I knew he was all stirred up inside. I could see the veins sticking out in his neck, and I thought to myself, that man won't even be able to digest his dinner tonight. Me, I went home and ate hearty as you please."[22] For nonsouthern white audiences, Clark marshaled a deliberate down-home practical style, complete with humor and forbearance, to clarify the degree to which both she and Highlander had been misrepresented in the press. That nonthreatening persona made her a great fund-raiser for the school.

She had to work harder, however, to convince black southerners of her integrity. As she informed Horton from the field, people she had never before met had "to learn to believe in me and not the adverse publicity they read or hear about me." The controversy generated by the school's alleged communist ties demanded that Clark evince a calm, reasonable mien to demonstrate her respectability for black audiences as well. As Atlanta University's John Hope II remarked during a discussion at HFS, "Septima goes into a church service and talks to them, and they say well now she looks like a normal person, if she says that there's nothing phony about this maybe we better look further."[23]

Albert Sloan finally showed all of his cards at the November hearing when he amended his original complaint against HFS to argue that its racially integrated workshops violated the state's segregation laws. *Brown*, he reasoned, did not pertain to private schools. Nevertheless, the jury considered only two main questions. First, did Horton operate Highlander for his personal gain? And second, did HFS engage in the purchase and sale of beer and other sundry commodities? The prosecution vigorously argued that Horton had resided on tax-free property for twenty-five years and then helped himself to more than thirty thousand dollars worth of land in 1957, when the HFS board had transferred the home in which he lived and seventy acres to him in recognition of the fact that he had essentially spent his entire career working without a salary. No money exchanged hands, but Horton could neither document his unsalaried years nor definitively prove that the property transfer reimbursed him for back pay. Given that Horton had basically conceded selling beer at HFS, Judge Chattin instructed the jurors to determine only whether he ran the school for personal gain. They deliberated for forty-five minutes before returning a guilty verdict.[24]

On February 16, 1960, Chattin revoked the school's charter. State law prohibited corporations from conveying property to their officers. The judge also held that Highlander's unlicensed sale of beer violated its charter and concurred with Sloan that Tennessee's segregation laws "as applied to private schools are constitutional and valid." HFS appealed, and its programs continued running. When the U.S. Supreme Court declined to hear the case on October 9, 1961, the battle ended. The Highlander Folk School ceased to exist. Expecting as much, Horton had already obtained a charter for the Highlander Research and Education Center and had moved his operations to Knoxville. As he had maintained from the beginning, "Highlander is an idea. You can't kill it and you can't close it in."[25]

⋖⟶✺⟵⋗

Amid the tumult surrounding her arrest and trial, Septima Clark continued to answer requests for help with voter education and registration from black communities in Alabama, Georgia, and Tennessee. In truth, the Citizenship Schools had expanded so much that they had become unwieldy for Highlander to manage. "We weren't interested in administering a running program," Horton averred, "we were just interested in developing it. . . . We wanted to get out of it and let other people run it."[26] The school could no longer afford to finance new projects, which meant that organizations would have to operate programs at their own expense. HFS could, however, train community representatives at minimal cost, and it had the Sea Island Citizenship Schools to offer as a working model.

During 1960–61, HFS hosted six teacher training workshops to familiarize local activists with the process of establishing Citizenship Schools. First-time teachers learned how to recruit students, to make lesson plans, to keep records, and to work in conjunction with area supervisors. Typical questions included how to handle disruptions and know-it-all students as well as how to judge educational levels among individuals and then divide the class accordingly. Discussions centered on self-motivation as a catalyst for influencing others and "stressed the importance of the teacher to see to it that her class attend community affairs, especially civic and political affairs." By late 1961, Highlander claimed that fifteen hundred adults studied in Citizenship

Schools in forty southern communities.[27] In between the training sessions, Septima Clark and Bernice Robinson carried their expertise into the field to assist in the organization and operation of the nascent extension programs.

Travel carried its own dangers, surprises, and inconveniences. In Montgomery, Alabama, Clark was staying overnight with Virginia Durr when a group of men arrived at five o'clock in the morning and announced that her husband's law office had been burglarized. Believing them to be members of the Klan, Durr refused to open the door and said she would have someone check into it the next day. That Clark spent the rest of the night calmly reading surprised her friend. Clark later admitted that driving around town with Durr, who would occasionally stop to powder her nose and then run a red light, scared her more than the Klan.[28] Clark faced a different situation when her contact was someone she had never met in person. In Bradenton, Florida, she arranged to spend the night with a Quaker woman with whom she had exchanged letters and talked on the phone and who apparently did not realize that Clark was African American. When the woman answered the door, all she could muster was "Ohhh." Inside, the woman asked Clark to pray with her. "I tried to say some words to make her know that I didn't feel bitter toward her," Clark recalled, then "she pulled her curtains down, we sat down and enjoyed supper in the kitchen." Because her hostess could not offer her a seat at the dining room table, Clark was not really surprised when she had to find alternative overnight accommodations with a black family. Yet in Tallahassee, the situation reversed itself. "There it was the Negro boycott leaders who took me for white and made a reservation at the leading hotel," Clark commented. She kept a balanced perspective on such mishaps and "was amused at both of them." As a roving organizer, Clark encountered the most difficulty in rural areas where she was a stranger. "Black people in small southern towns didn't trust black people coming in from the city," she observed. "I found out when I went into small communities that the illiterate blacks . . . were ashamed to let me know they were illiterate."[29]

Local leaders who prepared the groundwork before Clark arrived facilitated progress. In southeastern Georgia, Hosea Williams, a World War II veteran who had attended Morris Brown College in Atlanta on the GI Bill and secured a job as a chemist with the Department of Agriculture in Savannah, formed the Chatham County Crusade for Voters in 1960 and soon "molded it into a disciplined political machine."[30] Word of South Carolina Sea Island activities had reached Savannah, and Williams appealed to Highlander for help in getting a program running in his community. Clark visited Savannah that fall. She realized at once the difference her outsider status made. "I must lean heavily on" community leaders familiar with Highlander's work "for support, for trust and for faith in doing a program," she wrote to Horton. Williams and his wife, Juanita, attended a workshop at HFS in early 1961. "I must admit that I learned a lot about teaching adults," he subsequently informed Clark; "I want you to know that my wife was over-inspired. She has not stopped talking about the things we have been doing wrong yet."[31]

By late spring, Williams and local activists from thirteen other counties had established the Southeastern Georgia Crusade for Voters (SGCV) and had sent more people to Highlander. Clark and Robinson praised the political sophistication of those who participated in an April workshop: "They were alert, knew a great deal about the political set-up in their city and counties, and asked many intelligent questions about the national machinery." By June, twenty-four Citizenship School teachers taught 660 adults in southeastern Georgia.[32] The SGCV's initiative and progress so impressed Highlander officials that they secured a grant from the Schwartzhaupt Foundation to finance the Georgia programs. When the SGCV affiliated with SCLC in September, Williams claimed that the "adult citizenship schools played a very important part in registering 13,000 new voters in the First District."[33]

Clark succeeded elsewhere because she had the wherewithal to prioritize practical, everyday concerns as a way to gain entry into the community. Detailing her activities in Huntsville, Alabama, in 1960, Clark noted that Horton had given her a single name, a Miss Harris who ran a local orphanage. Clark found Harris, brought two of her daughters back to HFS for a workshop, and then returned to Huntsville with them for a few weeks. "Miss Harris was busy getting her place together," she remarked, "and I contributed $15 on a Frigidaire that she needed, which spelled a lot." Harris then introduced her new friend to the Reverend H. P. Snodgrass, minister of the First Baptist Church. Clark and Snodgrass spent two weeks just walking around, talking to people in the community. "Finally I got him to invite ten other persons . . . to have a luncheon with us," she stated. In this, Clark was relying on a strategy that she had first adopted while working with the Coming Street YWCA in Charleston — getting ten women to assist a project and asking each of them to contact ten more. At the Huntsville gathering, Clark recruited the Reverend M. C. Barrett, a Methodist minister, to go to HFS, and he subsequently volunteered to teach a class. Nevertheless, when Clark visited Barrett's church, she could not persuade members of his congregation to become involved. "He had too many middle-class black teachers who worked at a college in Huntsville," she surmised; there "was no way in the world that I could get them to do anything whatsoever. They were too scared."[34] Clark found her teachers elsewhere. From October 1960 through February 1961, 114 adults attended seven classes in Huntsville and two nearby communities, New Market and Farley. Just as generations of black parents had done when funding for public schools failed to meet their children's needs, these adult students voted to contribute two dollars a month to keep their Citizenship School running. They also organized the Madison County Voters League.[35]

In southwestern Tennessee's rural Fayette County, Clark entered a community under attack. Spurred by the desire to add their names to the jury pool after an all-white jury convicted a black man of murdering a white man, a few African Americans in this cotton farming area began registering to vote in 1959. When local whites refused to let them cast ballots in that year's Democratic primary, group members filed and won the first suit under the 1957 Civil Rights Act, which empowered the U.S. Justice Department to bring civil suits on behalf of individuals and groups who had been denied the right to vote. A group led by John McFerren, a World War II veteran and owner of a gas station, then formed the Fayette County Civic and Welfare League to organize a voter registration drive for the 1960 elections. With African Americans comprising 78 percent of the county's population, white reprisals began almost immediately. White doctors in country clinics refused to see black patients, while members of the Citizens' Council circulated registration lists and white merchants refused to sell black farmers goods. National companies initially acquiesced to local white supremacist pressure as well. By June 1960, Gulf Oil had removed McFerren's tanks, forcing him to install his own. Still, he could find no major oil company to fill them until regional and national civil rights organizations intervened on his behalf. The Southern Conference Educational Fund sent telegrams to the heads of Esso, Texaco, and Gulf Oil, all of whom denied discriminating against black customers. The NAACP provided additional leverage when it issued a call for its members to boycott the gasoline providers. Oil companies restored service to McFerren by August.[36]

Viola McFerren, a beautician, initially looked askance at her husband's activism. "I was more than afraid, I was downright scared," she remembered. The couple lived on his family's farm and received a series of threatening phone calls. One night, the situation became so bad that John McFerren "loaded up all his weapons and went out." He told his wife "not to come outside for anything" and did not return "until after daybreak." Another night, a white man phoned and said that a group of white men had offered to pay him to kill John McFerren and that he had been beaten for refusing. White intimidation proved most effective face to face. "White men would drive by at a snail's pace with the reddest faces and crudest expressions," Viola McFerren recounted. "They would throw rocks at the house and in the house. I would be standing there with my babies."[37] A mother's duty to protect her children made Viola McFerren a reluctant joiner.

Despite white terror, twelve hundred African Americans voted in Fayette County on November 8, 1960, swinging the county from the Democratic to the Republican Party for the first time since Reconstruction. Following the election and that year's harvest, white landowners began evicting black sharecropping and tenant farming families. The dispossessed now eyed winter's approach with no houses, no money, and no jobs. Sheppard Towles, an independent black farmer, donated a corner of his property for those who had nowhere else to go. Local movement leaders secured fourteen war surplus tents, and on December 14, 1960, twenty adults and fifty-six children moved into this tent city. Two weeks later, night riders fired shots into the tents, and residents set up a rotating guard to protect themselves. McFerren appealed to the Justice Department and the Farmer's Home Administration, to little immediate avail.[38] With no end to the crisis in sight, organizers also considered how to enable people more broadly to exercise their newly acquired and very costly citizenship.

The Fayette County League sent three men and nine women between the ages of twenty and seventy to HFS for a Citizenship School training workshop in April 1961. Having seen their first ballot just five months earlier, the group knew little of the local political structure. Clark complimented their eagerness to learn but asserted that they would need additional training before they could qualify as on-site teachers. All but one, she observed, had only elementary-level skills. When attempting to role-play in a skit on "Selling the Idea of the School," Fayette County residents "relied wholly on the instructors for every word." Clark characterized their presentation as poor, with "no creative ability or spontaneous conversation." As a result, she and Robinson concluded "that one of us needs to live in Fayette County for a year." Such a solution hardly seemed practical, given the rapidly growing interest in the program and subsequent appeals for both women's assistance. Yet Clark's preference for "doing the ground work there or elsewhere" may well have indicated the increasing difficulties she faced in living at Highlander. In the interim, she recommended that HFS train students from nearby Lane College to teach the first classes.[39]

A letter that Clark received from three Fayette County women might have strengthened her faith in their potential. Fannie Puckett, Mary Dowdy, and Mattie M. Shaw expressed their new consciousness as American citizens by opening the letter, "We the people of West Tennessee . . ." They continued, "Being at High Landar School have impress us to go back to Fayette County and stress the need for adult Citizenship School." The women concluded by underscoring the combined effect of their ordeal at home and their experience at HFS: "We as Freedom Fighter with all of the oppsitation we have meat . . . will fight until the Battle is faught and the victory is won."[40]

That these black women felt most comfortable expressing themselves to another black woman accentuated the importance of Clark's presence at HFS. It meant that grassroots African American women had someone in whom they could confide. Such had not always been the case in either mixed-sex or mixed-race gatherings. On Johns Island, Clark had seen women hang back and let men do all the talking. By 1958, however, she had reported, "Women on the Islands are speaking out. They were always in the background. Not now. They had to learn to speak in their homes first." But they had to raise their voices outside of the black community, too. Clark informed one HFS supporter that residential workshops were beneficial because when grassroots people "first get into an interracial situation they are very timid. The women are worse than the men. They stick together and are very glad to get home again." Clark had long discerned that black women needed to shift from racial to interracial thinking as much as their white counterparts did.[41] Regardless of the differences in personal histories and class backgrounds, she also understood the specific oppressions that accompanied being black and female in the Jim Crow South. An empathetic listener, Clark could identify veiled truths in seemingly innocuous comments and provide a model for those just beginning to walk the activist path.

Equally relevant, Puckett, Dowdy, and Shaw renewed their pledge to the struggle and redefined themselves in the space created by that commitment. These formerly disfranchised women declared themselves "Freedom Fighters." Septima Clark knew that a resolute belief that one could make a difference represented a good beginning, but it had to be followed up with the hard work of acquiring the necessary training. From there, expressions of citizenship became reality in the practice of canvassing communities, teaching classes, and sustaining programs geared toward communal improvement. Within a year, the nine women who attended the April HFS workshop were conducting Citizenship School classes in Fayette County. Eight of them taught together in four schools, while Dowdy led her own class.[42]

Clark also worked with the black women who led an effort to provide relief for the inhabitants of the tent city. In response to recruiting by Clark and Robinson, a group of fifty-two beauticians from Tennessee and Alabama convened at HFS in January 1961 for a "New Leadership Responsibilities" workshop. Eva Bowman, a former state inspector and examiner for the Tennessee Cosmetology Board who lived in Nashville, made a presentation in which she urged her colleagues to view "civic service as a responsibility of the Beautician." Less than a week after returning home, Bowman reported that the beauticians had voted to organize a health center for the homeless in Fayette County and had formed a board of directors. Bowman's familiarity with beauticians across the state significantly strengthened the endeavor.[43]

A month later, the beauticians returned to Highlander to hammer out a specific plan of action. The women agreed to set up boxes marked "For Fayette County" in their shops and brainstormed ideas for tapping into their statewide professional network. To reach their goal of raising fifteen hundred dollars, they planned to ask colleagues in the State Beauticians' Association to donate the amount charged "for one hair do" to the cause. Then they identified two women in Chattanooga who might help secure donations of medical office equipment. Clark traveled to Fayette County in late March to attend their next meeting at John McFerren's store. She went not as an HFS representative but out of personal interest. After the beauticians visited the tent city, Clark facilitated discussions of the proposed health center by asking specific questions, such as how the women planned to obtain the land and how much it would cost.[44]

A number of factors slowed the beauticians' progress. Announcements occasionally failed to communicate important details, including where donors should send money. In all probability, this resulted from the confusion that arose within the ranks of the Fayette County Civic and Welfare League. In early 1961, dissension split the founders into two groups, who then went to court to divide the money, food, clothing, and supplies that had already arrived.[45] Some of the beauticians imagined waiting until the health facility was built before beginning service to the tent city. Others proposed immediately establishing a health center in a tent. Recognizing the urgency of the situation, Clark wrote to Bowman, "Eva, again, let me beg you to get on with the original idea of a tent so the people can be helped now. Then as they vote they can push the county to give them a health center."[46] Clark's wise advice stemmed from her understanding of the necessity of meeting both short- and long-term goals.

Towles donated an acre of land for what would become the Fayette County Health and Recreation Center, providing space for health care, adult education, a kindergarten, and relaxation. At the same time, independent groups from cities across the nation that had been collecting donations for relief joined together to establish Operation Freedom, with the goal of raising $250,000 for Tennessee's beleaguered grassroots activists. Construction on the center began in November 1962, with the work performed by college students during school breaks.[47] White repression hardly lessened, but neither did African American determination. In 1963, ongoing voter registration drives were accompanied by the county's first sit-ins, and two local African American leaders announced their intention to run for county offices, the first black men to do so since Reconstruction. The same year, after nearly two years of living with no electricity or running water, residents of the tent city began moving into newly constructed homes on which they received low-interest mortgages.[48]

The original crisis in southwest Tennessee in 1960 and 1961 brought representatives of many civil rights organizations to the area and garnered financial support from labor unions and individual donors. Yet by 1963, Operation Freedom had moved across the Tennessee state line into the Mississippi Delta and had begun to channel funds to activists there. National civil rights headlines also turned the public's attention away from Tennessee. As a result, when a second crisis erupted in Fayette County, brought on by a Citizens' Council "that has learned how to avoid publicity and thus be more effective," no one was watching. Trying to restore the nation's focus on the area, a 1963 Fayette County newsletter proclaimed, "these Negroes now look around and find themselves essentially alone."[49] Outside supporters could remain ignorant of indigenous efforts — especially the fact that black beauticians had helped answer crucial needs in tent city — as much as the national spotlight, or attempts to reclaim it, could obscure them. Rural Fayette County served as but one of many sites where black women looked beyond voter registration to community welfare as they formulated responses to the local crises that resulted from civil rights battles, and where Clark herself played a guiding role.

Clark's urban organizing often proceeded more smoothly but presented different challenges. Clark traveled to Alabama in early 1961 to meet with representatives of the Montgomery Improvement Association (MIA), which had been formed at the beginning of the 1955 bus boycott. On January 22, she attended a meeting led by the Reverend Ralph Abernathy, the MIA president and an SCLC stalwart, and Dr. Solomon S. Seay, who had been at Highlander the night of the raid and who served as the MIA's executive secretary. The men appointed a group of women to consider how an adult education program could benefit the MIA's agenda. Clark spoke alone with Abernathy and Seay the next morning and reported that "they asked me to meet with the women, explain our program, answer their questions, and move them into wanting to become leaders so as to take up the training and set up the classes."[50] These black men knew that women's involvement was crucial to sustaining the church and could easily see how women's efforts could be vital in civil rights campaigns. Nevertheless, Abernathy probably did not imagine women leading in the same way that he did — for example, walking at the front of the line at mass marches.[51] Given black women's long history as schoolteachers, however, he and Seay likely considered the Citizenship Schools one area where women, as teachers and supervisors, might lead effectively.

The women who assumed the responsibility of the Citizenship School classes in Montgomery had different expectations. Clark participated in another mass meeting while there, after which MIA leaders convened a smaller session to request volunteers to chair the committees that would develop the educational program. Three women and one man stepped forward. Abernathy and Seay outlined what would be expected of committee chairs. Clark noted that the group reached consensus only "after one woman had made it clear that this would be her program and there would be no dictation."[52] She expected a degree of autonomy and would brook no orders from above.

The MIA held regular mass meetings and published a newsletter, thereby providing black activists in Montgomery with established forums for recruiting Citizenship School students. At the end of her visit, Clark recommended that the MIA devote a portion of its mass meetings to this purpose. She suggested that the group distribute a questionnaire asking what types of classes appealed to people, because some members might need citizenship training while others might want more general courses of study. Lest their enthusiasm outdistance their practicality, Clark reminded organizers that they should stay to help those who might need assistance filling out the survey. Finally, she urged the MIA to send at least eight potential teachers to the next training workshop at Highlander. Four women committed that night to making the trip in February; by April, they were instructing 235 people in five distinct classes. Three more women and one man attended a teacher training workshop in Tennessee in April; two months later, local enrollment had climbed to 435.[53]

Black Montgomery's organizational infrastructure helped produce such quick results. Clark observed that during their teacher training workshop, MIA participants "presented a skit on 'Recruiting Students and the need for more Schools' which was superbly done with on the spot conversation, handbills, and announcements." The presentation also supplied a useful model for the others present.[54] Black women's demand that male leaders not dictate how the program was run, when coupled with black men's general lack of interest, meant that the Citizenship Schools became another site in which women could exercise their leadership skills within the MIA. Moreover, they brought previous experience in both education and civic organizing to the task. Montgomery's first corps of teachers included clubwoman Irene West, who became an area supervisor; Juanita Abernathy, wife of the MIA president and a former schoolteacher; Bertha Howard, a retired schoolteacher; and Bertha Williams, a retired principal. Despite the lack of funding and materials, the first classes started on February 27. According to the March MIA newsletter, the teachers "only had some people who wanted to learn to read, write, and work some arithmetic. Also, they had plenty of faith." Finally, the curriculum of the Montgomery Citizenship Schools reflected the broader concerns of previous generations of black women activist educators. In addition to citizenship fundamentals, teachers offered instruction in "Home Arts" as well as general and health education.[55]

⋰⋰⋰

Throughout these months, Highlander battled for its existence. The stress of not knowing what would happen affected everyone differently. Septima Clark was sixty-two years old, and she had already suffered a heart attack, in 1957 while at Highlander. Nevertheless, her schedule remained as unrelenting as ever. At the end of January 1961, her body sent another warning that she could not ignore. She had returned to Charleston to address a problem in an immunization campaign, the white nurses who refused to roll up the sleeves of black children and would not "rub their arms." Clark decided to talk to a white doctor and made her way to his office above the library. "I had lots on my mind," she admitted. "When I got to the top of the steps, I sat down and couldn't go any further." A librarian took her to Roper Hospital, where a physician informed her that she had had a mild heart attack.[56] Clark had no choice but to take a short leave of absence from HFS to rest. The forced break must have been frustrating, considering the building momentum of the southern movement and the fact that Clark kept busy to keep her mind off her troubles.

Horton coped with the stress of the time by thinking through the most effective way to train teachers so that the Citizenship Schools could expand. Clark and Robinson added their two cents. Robinson too had been hospitalized, but she informed Horton that "training someone else is quite a job and not one that can be done in one workshop or done properly with only one Director in charge." When Clark directed, Robinson claimed, "I can see points that need to be stressed or explained more fully and she is grateful for my alertness. Likewise, this happens when I am directing." Aside from their desire to continue personally overseeing all teacher training, both women worried about the gendered division of labor within some existing Citizenship Schools. Describing a follow-up workshop for activists from southeastern Georgia, Robinson noted that while the teachers had mastered the methods, "the supervisors are not as alert," lacking "sufficient knowledge" of their local government to assist the teachers. "I realize that these men have been selected as supervisors because they were capable of finding places to hold classes and had influence in the community to recruit students," she added. Robinson recommended that future supervisors be selected by a workshop leader, most likely her or Clark, since they were "in a better position to determine who is better qualified." Should teacher training duties fall to someone else, Clark and Robinson conjectured that a leader from Johns Island would be most eligible because islanders had the longest involvement with the program; however, the two women stated, "As yet we do not have one person on Johns Island who could take this training course and relate it to others."[57]

By contrast, Horton thought that the women should limit their activities to preparing others to train potential teachers in local communities. Clark and Robinson resisted because the change would have moved them one step further away from a process that they understood well and on which they believed local success depended. "Septima and Bernice were not ready to go there," Candie Carawan, who first visited Highlander in 1960, remembered. "They had their valid reasons, but they really had to be pushed and pushed by Myles to take that next step which would enable the program to multiply."[58]

Part of Clark's rationale stemmed from her experience in local communities. She tried to enlighten Horton: the Sea Island project had succeeded because "I was literally a Charlestonian . . . and knew the people on the islands and in the city. . . . Therefore I could go to them with one potential leader and do a program." Everywhere else, she had discovered, earning people's trust required spending more time with grassroots leaders so that they would not "get the old feeling" of being exploited by an outsider. Specific problems also arose in various locations. "In Huntsville," Clark continued, "the city people . . . will not listen to a country leader. A leader must be gotten who is rooted in the lives of the city people and one rooted in the lives of the county people." Such annoying details had to be incorporated into the timeline for developing local Citizenship Schools. "To me this says that you expand the

Citizenship idea in a new place in the way the needs and problems are considered by the potential leaders in that particular situation," Clark reasoned. "The pattern is the same and yet different."[59]

The local situation also dictated what kind of programs would best assist local efforts. As Clark reported, leaders in Savannah "would like to do a literacy class first and leadership training with their board members later on." Horton and Clark held divergent perspectives on the distinction between the two types of preparation. "Myles wants to know if these schools are different," Clark observed; "To be technical they are. Both are working for first class citizenship but the prerequisite for states where literacy tests are given is to be literate." Activists in West Tennessee, for example, needed both literacy skills and "knowledge of the basic procedure to work as a leader to help others become leaders." Approaches and materials varied, but where Horton still separated formal literacy instruction from leadership training, Clark believed that the underlying philosophies were the same. "To my thinking, the 'Citizenship School' idea is being used in both schools," she asserted, cautioning against semantic obfuscation and divisive internal staff gossip. "I'm saying all of this," she concluded, "because I could tell by the look in Myles' eyes and the working of his facial muscles, along with the whispering campaign, that there was great dissatisfaction."[60]

When Clark and Horton had failed to reach a meeting of the minds by the spring of 1961, she wrote again. As Clark saw it, the earliest Citizenship Schools had benefited from the relative economic security of Sea Islanders, their geographical proximity, and HFS's singular focus. Programs in Alabama and Georgia, by comparison, were "reaching people more benighted than the Islanders" and had "multiplied like a multiplying onion." Average class sizes were considerably larger, and the distances supervisors had to travel to assist teachers were much greater. "The growth has been so rapid that it is frustrating to all concerned," she conceded. "I am writing all this because it is hard to communicate this thing to you. Some where along the line communication has broken down and every time I feel elated over the progress it flares up as an inflammatory substance."[61]

Threatened with being shut down, Highlander had to find a more stable organization to administer the program, further straining Horton and Clark's working relationship. HFS, not Clark, shaped the narrative of the Citizenship Schools' origins that was sold to the outside world. Attempts to describe their success highlighted Horton's role as the educational expert and devalued the nature of Clark's contribution. Around this time, HFS staff prepared a memo to send to Ralph Tyler of the U.S. Justice Department in which Horton offered his services in planning the department's voter registration campaign across the South. The message to Tyler acknowledged Clark's role in developing the Citizenship Schools but did so only by objectifying her as "the precise instrument for carrying out the experiment." Describing her limitations, it became most insulting. Clark failed to "grasp the overview," the memo maintained. Only with "the benefit of Myles Horton's constant and informal guidance" did she thrive "in organizing, training teachers, and providing supervision for the classes." Moreover, "Mrs. Clark apparently could not grasp principles or conceptualize a systematic methodology. She is not aware even that she lacks this capacity." A defiant Clark later added a rebuttal in the margin: "I was not supposed to be professional. The idea and dream was in Myles Horton['s] mind."[62] What rendered the original criticism most incredible was the fact that it referred to a woman with a master's degree in education and forty years of organizing in black communities behind her. How likely was it, then, that she could not "conceptualize a systematic methodology"?

Belying the criticisms lodged in the memo, Septima Clark had taken on new prominence in national and international adult educational circles. In 1958, for example, she participated in a Chicago conference sponsored by the Study of Liberal Education for Adults that sought to assist southern black colleges in developing community adult education programs. The only woman among sixteen college presidents and their envoys, Clark quickly perceived that "those men kept talking about a program that could not reach the rank and file." Her presentation, based on the Sea Island Citizenship Schools, turned the tide. According to Clark, one man excitedly told her, "I never could find out how to reach the people who are way down in the educational scale" and wanted "more training in line with [their] economic status and for greater recognition in [their] community." Additional validation of Clark's expertise came in 1959 when she was elected chair of the Rural Adult Education Section of the Adult Education Association. Nor had there been any problem with Clark's representing Highlander in discussions with individuals and international development groups interested in adult education. While traveling on behalf of the school the same year, Clark attended a luncheon in Philadelphia with a British group that was "planning citizenship schools in Northern Rhodesia." Over the next few years, Clark and Horton received similar requests from people working in Kenya and Mexico.[63]

Contrasting perceptions of the most effective way to propagate the Citizenship School program lay at the root of Horton's misrepresentations of Clark's competence. The Justice Department memo ended by stating, "An effort was made last winter to have Mrs. Clark make a record of her procedures and techniques. This she attempted with little success." Again, Clark responded in the margin: "The procedures and techniques in each community were different. There was no general academic pattern." Horton apparently had not listened to Clark when she had stressed that the "pattern is the same and yet different." Her comments emphasized what southern black activists had begun to discover through experience: different tactics proved most efficacious in different localities. Elsewhere, Clark claimed that Horton had not done his homework. She and other HFS staffers had collected copies of various state election laws so that they would know exactly what each state required of its registrants. "Myles hadn't read them," she stated; "He was just making a guess of what you could do."[64] Thus, where Horton saw one overarching struggle that could be waged similarly in diverse locations, Clark saw a plethora of civil rights movements with multiple overarching goals.

Clark also had trouble getting some of her other HFS coworkers to listen. Informing Perry MacKay Sturges that he would not be able to run a workshop alone as planned, Clark declared, "Twice before I tried to tell you this but we do not seem to communicate too clearly with each other." Sturges, who had been arrested with Clark on the night of the raid, worked as a teacher at the Collegiate School, a private K–12 school for boys in New York. Despite or perhaps because of his credentials, Clark judged him too impatient for the "tedious" task of training grassroots people. But she had another reason for insisting that she lead the workshop with him: "There is a great mistrust among Negroes of the white man attempting now to do something for them and more so of northerners." Clark had "found that white people who considered themselves liberals and thought they were doing Negroes a great favor to drink tea with them and discuss trivial issues aren't needed in that role anymore." In a black-led movement that increasingly relied on direct action, "one must be invited in to help with the current struggle," she observed; "You can't force them." Her advice attempted to bridge both racial and generational gaps, and she anticipated Sturges's displeasure at receiving her letter: "Knowing you as well as I do, I think you may feel that Septima is working against me but for the good of the school I'm forced to let you know my position."[65] Clark's blunt, no-nonsense manner likely irritated many people. From her standpoint, however, duty required her to do everything possible to ensure the workshops' success. Presiding over interracial gatherings inevitably meant some degree of discomfort.

That discomfort infused some of Septima Clark's most enduring personal relationships with white friends. Elizabeth Waring, for example, criticized

Highlander Reports

25th ANNUAL REPORT   Oct. 1, '56 - Sept. 30, '57

Mrs. Septima Clark, Director of Education, Highlander

PUBLISHED BY HIGHLANDER FOLK SCHOOL • MONTEAGLE, TENNESSEE

Septima Poinsette Clark, ca. 1956–57.
Courtesy of the Wisconsin Historical Society, Image # 41216.

Clark's educational approach as too akin to the gradualism preached by white southern moderates. Defending herself, Clark knew that she had to be gentle but firm, reminding Waring "how uncomfortable Negroes have felt with white people, especially in the interracial meetings before 1954," when "neither would be intellectually honest with the other." Friendship with Waring had helped Clark overcome her hesitancy: "When I sat in that little rocker in your bedroom and you told me of your plans to leave Charleston, you were laundering socks as you spoke, then I felt very close to you and my tongue became loosened." Such intimate interactions had emboldened Clark in her hometown. "A new creature had welled up within and I saw the future full of hazards but [had] no idea of turning back." Through the citizenship schools, she sought to replicate this process for others. "It's that kind of education that I'm talking about," Clark explained, "not books as such but the education that makes a man a man." More important, she wanted Waring to understand how teaching black adults to read and write prepared them to become active in the movement. Literacy was necessary not only to register and vote but also "to question power structures about housing rights, to know their strength and how to gather strength when presenting petitions." In another letter to Waring, Clark reiterated what she saw as a prominent challenge at Highlander: African Americans who "felt that everything said before the group had to be good feelings in race relations," an attitude that greatly hindered the work.[66]

As HFS's primary black staffer, Septima Clark had the job of translating evolving African American perceptions to white supporters of the movement both at the school and beyond. On one hand, her experience crossing the color line to work with whites in civic groups and civil rights organizations in South Carolina made her especially well suited to playing the role of interpreter, as did her tenure at HFS. Even so, when the school rewarded her for achievements on its behalf that depended on her interpretive skills, it occasionally neglected to inform her. Clark had been "really surprised" when she returned from netting three thousand dollars in one day of a fund-raising trip to find that she had been named the director of education. She read the announcement in a HFS newsletter.[67] On the other hand, Clark's frankness, a necessary prerequisite, could provoke responses that ranged from uneasiness to anger, from embarrassment to guilt, from anxiety to suspicion. Moreover, exposing opinions that African Americans usually expressed only privately among themselves could earn criticism, which probably made Clark more sensitive to slights. Having accepted — perhaps by default — the responsibility of representing the black perspective, she assumed that white allies would listen. That expectation extended to her views on the best way to spread the Citizenship School program.

On one point, at least, Horton and Clark agreed. In the heady months that followed the student sit-ins on February 1, 1960, the two recognized that the fight had taken a new turn. In Clark's estimation, the protests had "spread like a prairie fire" from Greensboro, North Carolina, to more than one hundred cities across the South. Clark and Horton initially had alternate visions of Highlander's role in assisting student activists. As a committed adult educator, Horton believed that HFS should work with grown people who were "already working on issues in their communities" and "shouldering adult responsibilities." In addition, the school's charter specifically defined its work as among adults. In 1953, HFS had begun hosting weekend integration conferences for college students, but the fact that it did not devote an entire week to young people indicated the difference it accorded their influence and participation. Clark's faith in youth, by comparison, had ripened in the aftermath of the 1955 student-led boycott at South Carolina State in Orangeburg, and she remained more open to student potential. Following the 1957 college workshop, Clark told the Warings, "It made me feel so good to see [the students] thinking ahead." Horton waited until the sit-ins began before reconsidering his position. According to Candie Carawan, "By 1960, Myles began to shift his opinion because then he felt like, 'Well, these students are getting involved in the community and they are taking on major responsibilities, and so now this is a constituency we could work with.'"[68]

Toward the end of March, Septima Clark contacted Ella Baker, who was then working for SCLC. On April 1–3, 1960, two weeks before the formation of the Student Nonviolent Coordinating Committee (SNCC), forty-seven African Americans and thirty-five white students, representing twenty colleges in nineteen states and three foreign countries, came to Monteagle. According to Guy Carawan, the people who gathered at Highlander "had been picked by Ella and Septima—either picked or through asking on the grapevine 'Who's really making things happen in your town?'"[69] A synopsis of the meeting confirmed, "To our knowledge this was the first occasion when a fairly wide cross-section of student leadership came together for a . . . discussion of the movement's philosophy and goals." It also vindicated Clark's belief in the promise of student activists; the school announced that henceforth, they "would participate as adults in Highlander workshops." At the same time, HFS staff learned of student apprehension when it came to embracing a few of Highlander's proven techniques: "Some were uncertain about the wisdom of seeking to work directly with community agencies, or with adults, Negro or white, in planning future strategy."[70]

The fact that the sit-ins were "Negro inspired" and "Negro led" introduced new considerations that students debated that weekend. "The question now appeared to be whether Negro and white people should from now on move in two separate groups, working presumably for the same end, but separately (which seemed a contradiction in principle)," the conference report noted, "or whether the time had come for the white liberal to retreat from the front lines and wait for direction in a completely Negro led movement."[71] The issue of white involvement in a black-led student movement thus predated SNCC's founding conference, which was held at Shaw University in North Carolina on April 16–18, 1960.

Two days before Baker gathered with student activists at Shaw, she wrote to Clark of her "deep and abiding interest in the work you have done and are doing." Baker recalled the first time she heard about the Sea Island Citizenship Schools, several years earlier: "Little did I dream, at that time, that we would have an occasion to work together here in our beloved Southland. . . . I have long since been committed to the idea of 'teaming-up' with you." She concluded by promising to attend a workshop at HFS in May and to send Clark news from the student conference. Clark had already invited Baker to serve on an educational committee at Highlander because she needed Baker's "help in planning bigger and more vitalizing workshops for the entire South."[72] Clark also probably wanted an ally. Another black woman with extensive organizing experience and contacts could help Clark persuade those at HFS who failed to listen to her or deemed her suggestions impractical.

Ella Baker likely had become interested in Septima Clark's work when Baker joined SCLC in January 1958 to organize its first major campaign, the Crusade for Citizenship. Founded in 1957 and headed by Martin Luther King Jr., SCLC linked a network of church-based southern black leaders under one umbrella and dedicated itself to using nonviolence to securing justice in public accommodations and at the voting booth. Having captured national attention with the May 1957 Prayer Pilgrimage for Freedom in Washington, D.C., which Clark attended, SCLC next sought to mobilize the grassroots. King outlined his vision of the crusade at an executive board meeting that October, and organizers eventually designated February 12, Abraham Lincoln's birthday, as the official launch date in nearly two dozen southern cities. This goal was ambitious, since SCLC lacked an experienced organizer to co-

Myles Horton (left) and Ella Baker (center, without glasses)
at a Highlander workshop, 1960–61 term. Courtesy of
the Wisconsin Historical Society, Image # 41218.

ordinate the campaign. Meeting in New York, Bayard Rustin and Stanley Levinson, who along with Baker had been instrumental in SCLC's founding, suggested that King hire Baker as the crusade's director. King initially protested, arguing that the men of SCLC might insist that a minister hold the position, but he had very few options, and time was running out. He agreed that Baker could serve as "acting director" but stipulated that SCLC would not pay her salary.[73]

Baker reached Atlanta and found that the ministers of SCLC had not thought to provide her an office, let alone a phone or support staff. "I had to function out of a telephone booth and my pocketbook," she remembered. She plunged in, working alongside SCLC's executive director, the Reverend John Tilly, to make the February 12 kickoff a big public success. Then the real work, organizing local people to oversee the voter registration drives in their communities, began. Expecting its affiliates and other community groups to conduct the local campaigns, SCLC offered them limited resources and facilitators trained to lead voting clinics. Still, over the next two years, the organization failed to realize its goal of doubling the number of African Americans on southern registration books. White resistance slowed progress and increased personal risk, as did the difficulty of passing literacy tests to the satisfaction of the white registrars.[74]

Another reason for the disappointing results was that the clergymen who led SCLC repeatedly disregarded Baker's advice. In an October 1959 memo, for example, Baker proposed that SCLC incorporate some form of literacy training into the crusade. "It was not my idea that S.C.L.C. should conduct [voter registration] classes," she wrote, "but that we could interest such groups as the Women's Baptist Convention, the National Council of Negro Women, and the national college sororities in such projects." Baker understood the long-term value of a literacy program: "More people would be equipped with basic tools (reading and writing), and would then be ready for effective social action." She was also familiar with the distinct roles adopted by men and women within the church and the community. Like Clark, Baker envisioned a solution that would bolster women's involvement and yield the desired results. Not only would it provide "respectable" cover for essentially radical work, "the literacy project could well serve as the basis for calling a Southwide meeting of women, as we proposed before," she concluded.[75]

Baker's preoccupation with getting women involved in local civil rights movements was hardly the only point of divergence between her and the men of SCLC. A fundamental conception of leadership divided them. Clark remembered that Baker "didn't see why a brochure should have sixteen pictures of Dr. King" but no images of his followers, and she resented the lack of recognition given to women's movement work. Baker's philosophy proved more akin to Clark's: "I have always thought what is needed is the development of people who are interested not in being leaders as much as in developing leadership in others," Baker later affirmed. At this point, SCLC's idea of education for leadership training translated into teaching others the philosophy and tactics of nonviolence, not providing people at the grassroots with the tools to empower themselves.[76] Repeatedly frustrated in her attempts to influence SCLC's leaders and preferring a movement strategy that emphasized training local leaders and spreading responsibility throughout a community, Baker resigned from SCLC shortly after she helped found SNCC.

Conceding that the Crusade for Citizenship had flopped, King asked Horton and the HFS staff to design a program for SCLC at the end of 1960. Plagued by financial and legal problems, Horton suggested that SCLC simply take over operation of the Citizenship Schools, which had increased both community mobilization and voter registration. James Wood, King's administrative assistant and SCLC's director of public relations, met with Horton over the second weekend in November to begin discussing arrangements.

The men agreed that Clark should continue working with the program full time and therefore considered the possibility of including her as part of the transfer. Horton knew Clark's sense of ownership and investment in the Citizenship Schools, but he might not have been sorry to see her leave Highlander. It appears that no one had consulted Clark, and the minutes of the meeting referred to her as if she were a piece of equipment: "Mrs. Clark, or her equivalent, will be available to SCLC on a full-time basis."[77]

Indeed, in the spring of 1961, acting on the assumption that Clark would leave HFS, Horton offered Andrew Young a full-time staff position directing Highlander's leadership training program. The twenty-eight-year-old from New Orleans had been living in New York and working as the associate director of the National Council of Churches' Department of Youth. His selection made sense. HFS's ability to change with the times meant cultivating college student leaders in the aftermath of the sit-ins. Young accepted because he wanted to return to the South to contribute to the movement. His inexperience showed in his description of his role to a white supporter: "Someone needs to be more directly involved in the Southern struggles who is somewhat secure in an integrated society and is able to appreciate the Negro's possible contributions." The masses' enthusiasm needed "a little theological perspective. What they hunger for most," Young continued, "is some form of ideology that can hold them together as a movement and cut down on some of the friction which seems to exist." He finished by observing, "Somehow, the 'classes' and the masses must be brought together in this struggle. My job is to find out how."[78] The sixty-three-year-old Clark was certainly in a position to enlighten him.

Financial problems complicated the transition. HFS and SCLC received a joint $26,500 grant from the Marshall Field Foundation to continue the Citizenship Schools for one year. In April 1961, when the Tennessee Supreme Court ruled that HFS would have to surrender its charter, the foundation's lawyers anticipated that the school would soon lose its tax-exempt status and pointed out that Field could administer money only to tax-exempt organizations that provided facilities for training. SCLC had neither tax-exempt status nor a location. At Horton's suggestion, Young and another member of the National Council of Churches approached Wesley Hotchkiss of the American Missionary Association's Division of the United Church Board of Homeland Ministries to ask it to sponsor the program. Hotchkiss responded enthusiastically to the chance for his organization to participate in the modern freedom struggle in a role not altogether different from the one it had assumed a hundred years earlier. The United Church Board of Homeland

Ministries also owned a Reconstruction-era school facility in Dorchester, Georgia, about forty miles from Savannah, that could be used for weeklong teacher training workshops. By June, Hotchkiss had agreed to pay Young's salary through the United Church of Christ and to administer the Field Foundation grant to SCLC. Young would join Clark at SCLC, technically as her boss.[79]

Septima Clark and Bernice Robinson sat on the Citizenship School Program Committee formed by Myles Horton to negotiate the transfer. Yet both women spent most of that spring away from Highlander, assisting in the establishment of Citizenship Schools and tending to their health, and consequently missed meetings. On June 5, Horton sent Clark a telegram informing her that she need not return to HFS because the committee's plans had changed. One week later, he notified her that the committee had decided to operate the HFS and the SCLC Citizenship Schools separately. "This will leave you free to devote full time to developing SCLC's program," Horton told her, while "Bernice will work full time developing the Citizenship classes not financed by the Field Foundation."[80] Without consulting Clark and Robinson, the committee had concluded that Clark would work for SCLC—meaning that she would have to move to Atlanta—while Robinson would remain with HFS.

The women immediately registered their outrage. "We have decided that we will work together while training, regardless of who pays who," they announced to Horton. They reiterated their argument that the job was too much for one person and declared that their services could not be separated. "Septima 'phoned Wood today," they continued, "She told Wood that we refused to be swapped around like horses. . . . We don't think anyone can plan *for* us, but *with* us." Clark and Robinson were unwilling to surrender the responsibility for planning their future to these men. The uncertainty surrounding both HFS and the program's continued existence had already led them to consider joining the Peace Corps. Certain that they could use their aptitude to benefit newly independent countries in Africa, both women took the eight-hour examination at the federal building in Chattanooga on May 29, 1961. At an HFS staff meeting three days later, Clark and Robinson said they would take three months to consider their options and agreed to remain at HFS for that period to train their replacements. Thus, by the time Horton notified Clark and Robinson of the changes, he already knew that they might no longer be involved with the Citizenship Schools at all.[81]

Horton chastised Clark for contacting Wood on her own. "I am sorry that you felt it necessary to take the planning out of my hands," he wrote on June

Bernice Robinson (standing, left) and Septima Clark (standing, right)
at a Citizenship School teacher training workshop, ca. 1961.
Courtesy of the Wisconsin Historical Society, Image # 41508.

21, "despite the fact that I can understand why Negroes sometimes become
impatient with those of us who are unable to move as fast as they think we
should." With Robinson, Horton adopted a more conciliatory tone. He confessed to being "shocked" by the women's insistence on working together
despite the plans he had arranged. However, he noted, "As I think you know,
we would like to build the non-SCLC part of the Citizenship Training Program around you, and arrange the finances so that the program can continue
regardless of what might happen to Highlander this fall."[82]

Clark responded with considerable ire. Since October, she began her letter
to Horton, "you have made pronouncements to me and to the contributors
about my salary." But SCLC had made no commitment, either verbally or in
writing, to pay her. Clark's concerns reflected personal financial responsibilities that included health care for herself and her sister as well as a home
improvement loan that she had taken without being able to list her employer
on the application. "You see, Myles," she maintained, "I've been a working
woman for years and [am] accustomed to taking care of myself. I'm not a
clinging vine. Even at age 63 I can plan for myself." She mentioned that she
had received a letter from the Peace Corps asking if she would be available
by mid-July and reasserted her competency by adding that "two countries
in West Africa need college trained women at once." Only then did Clark
reveal her true feelings: "I think you did not want to tell me that you did
not want me anymore but I'd rather you say it to me than have others treat
me so inhuman." Horton seemed ambivalent about her continued relation-

ship with HFS, and Clark wrote, "I've never seen that side of you. I don't intend to be bitter but to fight for a principle." In case Horton missed her real point, Clark wrote again four days later. "Our work with the grassroots is a great part of me. There is nothing I enjoy more than working with these people," she emphasized. "The remaining workable years of my life will be promoting citizenship programs somewhere somehow. I'll work wherever I'm needed and wanted."[83]

In the meantime, Horton wrote to the Field Foundation's Maxwell Hahn to apprise him of the situation. Worried that Clark might contact Hahn, an action that could either complicate matters further or reflect badly on Horton, Highlander's director went on the offensive. Acknowledging that the delays had "been very disconcerting to Septima," he cited her failure to trust him — and, by extension, Hahn — as the source of the problem: "Septima sometimes assumes that she is a victim of white prejudice and chicanery, even though everything possible is being done by all of us." When Clark learned of Horton's comments, she became angry: "There was friction due to inefficient staffers," she later scribbled on a copy of the letter. More troubling, Horton's remarks reflected the assumption that one white man should understand and value another's reasoning. His tone presupposed a communication between equals. Horton not only again attempted to speak for Clark but also intimated that if she spoke for herself, her comments should be taken with a grain of salt. Two months later, another HFS staffer prepared a memo for the chair of the school's executive council, stressing how "unfortunate" it was "that Mrs. Clark should at this time of tension accuse Mr. Horton of bad faith and persecution when he made such effort to provide for her security at a time when his own and that of the school are in the greatest jeopardy."[84] In reality, Clark did not want to impede the transfer; she merely wanted more consideration and respect.

Septima Clark soon had the chance to have her say. In the fall of 1960, HFS staffer Alice Cobb had begun negotiating with Scott Bartlett, an editor in chief at E. P. Dutton, about publishing Clark's autobiography. Clark remained too busy to iron out the details personally, but Cobb reported that she desired "the help of an understanding Negro scholar of her choice, who is deeply concerned with the integration movement, and would be able to help her in interpreting some of the experiences which a professional writer from your staff might not understand fully." Though Cobb denied HFS's interest in the book's potential publicity, she wrote that "since some of Mrs. Clark's more widely celebrated experiences have been related to her association here," the school wanted to guarantee that "whatever is said from the Highlander back ground be written from a clear and accurate understanding" of its history.[85] Given the tensions between Clark and Horton, Cobb's efforts represented another attempt to control the public portrayal of the school.

Working on an autobiography in 1960–61 was an overt political gesture on Clark's part. It offered her the chance to salvage her reputation in the aftermath of her arrest, and it provided a platform for establishing the validity of the southern civil rights movement before a national audience. At the same time, Clark confronted a paradox faced by countless African American autobiographers before her: documenting her life could put her in jeopardy. At the very least, writing the book would require her to expose herself to the scrutiny of a potentially hostile white audience. Clark recognized that her personal story remained inseparable from the larger narrative of the black community's struggle against white supremacy. Yet as a black woman speaking, she encountered the problem posed by her proximity to power in a society vested in white male authority. Her account would challenge her audience's implicit assumptions regarding the justness of their nation at the height of the Cold War. Clark had to tread carefully — for example, in critiquing the federal government and the Kennedy administration, which had begun to show halting support for the civil rights movement, in the aftermath of the Cuban Missile Crisis. Moreover, by speaking in her own defense, she would also be speaking for her movement allies, including Horton, who had come under attack.

Echo in My Soul represented a test of her loyalty, and Clark passed with flying colors. Dutton ignored her request for a sympathetic African American coauthor. Instead, it chose LeGette Blythe, a native North Carolinian and white southern liberal who had worked for years at the *Charlotte Observer*. Thematically, Clark highlighted her vision of democracy throughout and insisted that she was not afraid despite the numerous attempts to intimidate her. "Freedom has always been lost by a people who allowed their rights to be gradually whittled away," she testified. Persecution came with the territory. "I feel that before a person goes into work of this kind he must search his soul and decide once and for all that this is the price he may have to pay for the freedom he is trying to establish for all." She also issued a direct response to Tennessee's attempt to close HFS by asserting that the "threat to silence . . . the voice of Highlander is a threat to the very existence of every organization in this nation and to the basic freedom of thought and expression in every American."[86]

Clark knew too much was at stake to air private squabbles in public, and she devoted the last half of her personal narrative to a stoic defense of the school and its work. Still, the tension between her and Horton smoldered between the lines, as when Clark pronounced that the "key figure in the Highlander story is a woman." She was referring, of course, to Lilian Johnson. If this strategy made HFS seem less a communist threat in 1961, it also deemphasized Horton's substantial role in founding the school. Perhaps that is why in one late-1962 letter to Clark, Horton added a postscript informing her that he had borrowed a copy of *Echo in My Soul* from Bernice Robinson. Congratulating Clark for "doing such a wonderful job," Horton promised, "We are anxious to promote the sale of it in any way we can."[87]

⌒⊶⋇⊷⌒

Septima Clark had believed Highlander the most useful vehicle for addressing issues that had long been on her mind. Yet spreading the Citizenship School program to new locales introduced new challenges. Clark always viewed the evolving struggle through an educational lens and devised strategies to overcome persistent obstacles. Ironically, one of the greatest of those hurdles involved making her voice heard and garnering respect for her lived experience, her expertise, and her opinions. The crux of the matter was not that she was African American but that she was a woman operating within organizations where men dominated the decision making.

Clark weathered the transition to SCLC as best she could. Not long after arriving in Atlanta, she informed the Warings that "at last" she had reached a working base, at least for another year, having "been tossed around like a poor relative while a decision was being made." Part of the friction had emanated from Horton's attempt to protect his life's work, occasionally at Clark's expense. Part had stemmed from Clark's uncertainty about the changes in her role and responsibilities. Bureaucratic details concerning her salary had aggravated the situation. Still, she remained focused on the larger goal. By 1961, Clark recognized that black adults needed to "be brought up to the level of the action of the students." Her job now included training people to "use the rights and privileges the boycotters, picketers, and sit-inners have obtained for them." Everyday life confirmed what she learned from local people in workshops. Passing through Concord, North Carolina, on a bus, Clark had seen a pregnant African American woman refuse the only vacant seat because it would have meant sitting beside a white soldier. The educational work never ceased, so Clark propelled herself relentlessly forward. At the same time, constant travel and constant stress took their toll on her body. Clark's only regrets involved the physical limitations she occasionally confronted. "I'm not complaining," she insisted, "but wish I had longer to live and actively work in the movement."[88]

Clark received ongoing acknowledgment from Highlander supporters for her accomplishments. In 1963, Carl Tjerandsen of the Schwartzhaupt Foundation, which had provided the original funding for the Citizenship Schools, wrote to thank Clark for sending him materials on the program. "I am impressed by the ingenious methods you have worked out for relating the subject matter to the lives of your students," he observed. "The evidence of your success is most heartening and we are proud to have been a part of it." Clark's loyalty to HFS also endured. When approached by the Peace Division of the American Friends Service Committee to participate in its National Speakers' Series, she consented to give twelve talks. Then she wrote to Horton to ask if he would like for her to reserve one of them for a speech on the closing of Highlander.[89]

Shared success meant that Horton and Clark would continue to work together. Clark would soon be too engaged with her duties at SCLC to harbor a grudge. She would also be working more exclusively with African Americans. Yet Horton remained an important resource person, especially in the first days following the transfer. Clark thanked Horton for participating in a workshop by commenting, "It was good to have you in the circle once more." For his part, Horton conceded that HFS took great satisfaction in the fact that "you and your co-workers have been able to carry on the Citizenship program under other auspices." Even so, Clark occasionally ran interference on behalf of Bernice Robinson. After Horton decided that personnel and content changes might have to be made in a workshop and assumed that she would take up the slack, Robinson fired off a letter to Clark: "I cannot stand from 9 A.M. in the morning until 10:00 P.M. in the evening carrying on a workshop myself." Nor could she "keep the machinery rolling behind the scenes of the workshop and run the workshop too." Clark wrote to explain to Horton that Robinson needed help and to assure him that the resource person she and Robinson had in mind "can follow any plan you give him, but it is impossible for any of us to plan the things you have in your mind." With regard to the workshop's focus, she reminded him that "to be successful it must be tied to the life of the people and not what you want for them." In 1963, when Robinson could stand the situation no longer, she resigned from HFS.[90]

Almost thirty years later, Clark reflected on the ways she and Horton had complemented each other as adult educators by returning to the story of their heated argument over the methodology for the first Citizenship School. To his credit, Horton would "go back home and think about what I said; then he would come back the next day and get things typed up the way I suggested."[91] At times, he listened. Regardless of who received acclaim in narratives of the origins of Highlander's most successful program, Septima Clark came to appreciate exactly how Myles Horton had helped her forge one of the movement's most significant community organizing tools.

CHAPTER NINE

Similar and Yet Different

A teacher writes "Citizen" on a blackboard. Beside it, she adds "Constitution" and "Amendment." Then she asks her thirty adult students what the words mean. After the class establishes the link between constitutionally defined and protected citizenship, discussion will turn to what citizens do. In the course of a week, the African American adults in this Citizenship School teacher training class will learn how to tackle registration and voting in their communities by fostering practical, political, and economic literacy. They will also learn how to become "action-research minded" so that they can "discover how to make decisions about changes in the structure of government and all phases of life" they aim to improve. These teacher trainees are part of a larger national movement. Yet as Septima Clark recognized, "the place where things really count and where people really grow is at the local community level."[1]

The Citizenship Schools extended across the South after the Southern Christian Leadership Conference (SCLC) assumed responsibility for the venture in 1961 and renamed it the Citizenship Education Program (CEP). During the first year of SCLC's administration, Clark, along with Dorothy Cotton and Andrew Young, trained 291 CEP teachers who conducted 263 classes for 2,330 adults. A total of 13,266 black southerners registered to vote that year as a consequence of community canvassing and voter registration drives organized by CEP graduates. From July 1962 to June 1963, 395 new teachers undertook training, initiated 366 classes that enrolled 5,623 students, and, along with those students, influenced 17,575 people to obtain registration certificates. In 1964, 897 schools operated; a year later, the aggregate numbers stood at 1,600 teachers trained, 25,000 students taught, and more than 50,000 new African American names on southern registration books as a direct result of the program's stimulus. Between October 1966 and February 1968, 402 additional teachers received training, and a total of 26,686 students attended 7,280 classes. By 1969, more than 5,000 people had passed through the training sessions. Keeping track of the numbers inspired to register by the program had become nearly impossible because the lines between it and other civil rights organizing had become so blurred and because the movement itself had changed.[2]

As Clark's approach to citizenship education moved into this larger context, it also functioned through an institutional vehicle quite different from Highlander. Martin Luther King Jr. headed SCLC, and where King went, journalists and cameras followed. After the surprising successes of the 1960 student sit-ins and the 1961 Freedom Rides, SCLC developed a game plan for employing nonviolent direct action to provoke crises in local communities, with the goal of attracting federal support that would yield civil rights legislation. SCLC targeted particular communities and relied heavily on mass meetings to galvanize local action. Then a deliberate staging of a morality play — juxtaposing peaceful protests by dignified African Americans against the violent reprisals of white supremacists — began to take shape for national and international audiences. SCLC leaders moved rapidly from one community to the next to avoid becoming entangled in local quagmires and to keep the momentum moving forward.[3]

King spent very little if any time in CEP classes, though he did occasionally visit the Dorchester Center in Liberty County, Georgia, where SCLC conducted its CEP training workshops. Yet had not an educational organizing structure been in place before the visible drama began, no marchers would have followed King into the camera's glare. SCLC would not have generated the sustained protest that so starkly portrayed segregation's injustice in black and white and compelled the federal government to respond. Along with the church, the CEP provided SCLC's grassroots institutional base.

People do not decide to risk their lives and livelihoods because an organizer talks them into it. They choose to do so because something inside of them changes. For thousands of black southerners, the CEP fostered that transformation. As on the Sea Islands, the program's success depended on its ability to move quietly into a community and begin to attack the psychological ramparts created by a lifetime of living in a segregated society. "Until you free a person mentally, emotionally, and spiritually, you can't accomplish very much," CEP veteran Victoria Gray Adams remembered, "but as those things happen, oh my Lord, it just gets better."[4] Mass meetings and the singing of freedom songs yielded the emotional and spiritual release that fortified the collective will to confront white segregationists at the courthouse or in the streets. But in a tactical sense, this liberation remained temporary and fleeting, absolutely critical to the short term but unable to create lasting change on the ground. After SCLC representatives and the cameras turned their attention elsewhere, those left behind still had to find a way to negotiate concrete change in their hometowns. The CEP provided many of these people with the courage and practical proficiency required for that task, though that did not mean they always succeeded.

As had been the case in the Highlander-sponsored Citizenship Schools, black women predominated in the CEP. While the movement provided a framework for action, participation in the CEP offered these women the opportunity to think about community development from a female perspective and to act on it. CEP training sessions created the space in which women learned that their personal problems were shared by others across the South and across the generations, and in which women developed a political analysis grounded in everyday life. Linking everyday experience and social action, they made the personal political. In their home communities, these women became recognized as leaders because of their commitment to the struggle and the risks they took on its behalf. They pursued a broad agenda and in the process helped expand the civil rights movement's goals.[5]

In fact, the local activities of southern CEP women addressed many issues that also emerged in the broader women's movement before the end of the decade, including education, job opportunities and wage differentials, health care, child care, reproductive freedom, protection from sexual violence, and respect for womanhood. Yet unlike white women, black women felt no need to form a separate organization from their male counterparts because they viewed citizenship as a communal rather than an individual right to be wielded for the collective benefit. Sexism, both in SCLC and in the mainstream media, denied black women national recognition as leaders but did not hamper their ability to perform community work. Septima Clark acknowledged the comprehensive impact of women's activism when she asserted, "I think the civil rights movement would never have taken off if some women hadn't started to speak up."[6]

Involvement in the CEP also prepared black women at the local and regional levels for engagement with the federal Community Action Programs associated with Lyndon Johnson's War on Poverty, which invites a reconsideration of common conceptions of the civil rights movement's decline. CEP women adjusted to changing conditions after the passage of the Voting Rights Act of 1965, after calls for Black Power began to capture the nation's attention, and after King's assassination in 1968. In the latter half of the 1960s, some women ran for office, while others continued to attend to the needs of the young, the elderly, and the poor. Their movement did not end. Taking up the work in their communities, they kept going—some for months, some for years, some for decades. Their movement became a way of life.

⋅⊰✳⊱⋅

Soon after making the switch to SCLC, Septima Clark received a letter from one of her new coworkers, Andrew Young, in which he admitted that he had agreed to administer the Field Foundation grant for the CEP "even though I don't know very much about the program operation." Young had full confidence in its worth and believed that he could help make it more effective as it spread under the auspices of SCLC. Still, he asked Clark to help him understand "the full implications of my job," which included her "visions for this program . . . as well as some of the frustrations you encounter." The messiness of the transfer had put Young in an awkward position. He carefully accorded Clark the respect she deserved even as he asked her to train him to be her boss. That distinction was reflected in their salaries as well. The completely inexperienced Young earned nearly twelve hundred dollars more than Clark the first year; in the second, both received modest raises, but Young's salary exceeded Clark's by seventeen hundred dollars.[7]

Dorothy Cotton, a staff member at SCLC, met Clark and Young in Atlanta in July 1961. A veteran of the Petersburg, Virginia, movement, Cotton had followed her mentor, Wyatt T. Walker, to SCLC when he assumed the position of executive director. As the trio discussed how to build SCLC's new program, the idea for a road trip emerged. "Septima, Dorothy, and I really didn't know each other," Young remembered. "I figured if we were going to work together, instead of each of us going our separate ways, we ought to get in the same car." A few weeks prior to SCLC's annual August convention in Chattanooga, all three piled into Cotton's two-toned green Buick and hit the road in search of "people with Ph.D. minds who never had the chance to get an education who were the natural leaders in their communities." They stopped first at the Dorchester Center, where Clark and Bernice Robinson led SCLC's inaugural teacher training session. From there, Clark, Young, and Cotton traveled through Georgia to Alabama and Mississippi. "Between the three of us, we managed to find someplace to stay all along the way and also somebody to talk to," Young recalled. If a chapter of the National Association

Guy Carawan leads a group of Citizenship School teacher trainees in song,
ca, 1960–61. Seated on Carawan's right is Dorothy Cotton; Aimee Horton
is fourth from right; Septima Clark is seated on Carawan's left.
Courtesy of the Avery Research Center for African American
History and Culture, College of Charleston.

for the Advancement of Colored People (NAACP) existed, they approached its leader. Where they knew no one, "we went to the black beauty parlor or barbershop or the undertaker. Those were the people who were economically independent of the system of segregation."[8]

When recruits arrived at Dorchester, moss-covered oaks welcomed them. Most came in small groups by car, but some rode a bus that had been chartered to drive through the Black Belt and pick them up along the way. Inside the Reconstruction-era school building that had been refitted to accommodate sixty guests, women made their way to rooms on the first floor, while men headed upstairs. Each chose a bunk bed, and some inspected the communal showers. At mealtimes, everyone reconvened downstairs to eat in a large auditorium. They reported to class in high-ceilinged rooms with tall windows. In the summers, organizers provided handheld cardboard church fans to combat the lack of air-conditioning. Though the days were filled, staff reserved time for relaxation, usually an afternoon softball game or an evening dance and limbo contest.[9]

CEP training at Dorchester did not differ dramatically from that at Highlander. Students gathered the evening they arrived to get acquainted and to discuss some current movement activity in the South. The next morning's session focused on the first night in a Citizenship School; the afternoon was turned over to a reading demonstration class using voting and registration requirements as primary texts. On the third day, staff outlined teachers' and supervisors' duties and explained how to gauge pupils' educational levels. The evening featured instruction in how to lead discussions of current world events. Day 4 dealt with the details of scheduling classes, recruiting students, appropriating class time, and incorporating role-playing and educational films. The last day, participants learned how to assess the level of activist experience in their communities, and each group presented its follow-up plan for community action.[10] A celebratory banquet completed the week. Dorchester students opened and closed each day by singing freedom songs and offering prayers for the people back home.

As the CEP's educational director, Septima Clark taught workshop participants how to teach reading and writing to others. The instruction underscored the importance of preserving an individual's dignity. CEP teachers should busy themselves with something else while students read or wrote for the first time. Instructors should speak softly when asking people their ages and should not attempt to help students until asked. "Never say that the School is only for those who can't read and write," participants were advised, "but say it is for citizenship." Prospective teachers learned how to teach reading by emphasizing words that most people encountered in daily life. "Everybody knows Coca-Cola when they see it," Young remarked. "If they saw 'coc-a col-a,' anywhere they saw the 'coc' or the 'col' they knew the sounds." From there, he continued, it was only a matter of relating those sounds to words "on the voter registration application, on the application to get a job, social security application, driver's license applications, and how to write a check."[11]

Dorothy Cotton, the CEP's educational consultant, covered methodological instruction in "The Art of Recruiting Adults for Local Classes," "Demonstration in Uses of Teaching Aids," and "Teaching the U.S. Constitution." "We'd have a long discussion all morning about what the constitution was," Clark confirmed. Rather than providing answers, staff relied on what she referred to as a "non-directive approach" in which group members reached their own conclusions through guided discussion. Dorchester workshops always included local people from a wide range of educational and experiential backgrounds. Clark noted that staff surveyed participants' knowledge in the same nondirective way, asking, "Do you have an employment office in your town? Where is it located? What hours is it open? Have you been there to get work?"[12]

Andrew Young, whose title was executive secretary, taught classes on non-violence and social change and on the relationship between education and voting. "I remember one little exercise that everybody understood," he later commented. "If you go to any southern town, where rich white people live, the streets were paved with concrete; where poor white people live, they were blacktop; where black people live, they were dirt." Ensuing conversations linked an understanding of who decided which streets got paved to voting and civic responsibility. "We had to give them a plan of how these people were elected, of how people who had registered to vote could put these people in office, and how they were the ones who were over you," Clark explained. The purpose, as she pronounced on a different occasion, was to help local people realize "that the government of [their] state can be handled by blacks as well as whites. They didn't know it before."[13]

There was no such thing as an average recruit to a Dorchester workshop. Individuals came from both embattled areas and those that were just beginning to organize. They ranged in age from high school students to retirees, and staff intentionally grouped people from different parts of the South together as roommates so that they might learn more about their shared experiences. For many participants, the week in Liberty County provided breathing room amid the intensity of local movements. "Most of the young men of SNCC would come to our training camp because it was an opportunity for them to get away," Young averred. Bernice Johnson Reagon, a SNCC veteran of the Albany movement, arrived in early 1962. "It was an important week," she affirmed, "because we had just come through a period where we had been arrested." The education she received proved invaluable. "I had never heard anybody break down the different stages of where decisions are made, like where is it decided who the party is going to put up for what offices. That had never been a part of any civics course I'd taken."[14]

Through the years, staff members responded to what people wanted to learn and adapted the curriculum at Dorchester to new developments. In 1962, for example, they added "Negro history" to workbooks. A year later, they instituted a training session on "New Trends in Politics" that described how political machines and policymaking bodies worked and how CEP students could leverage that knowledge to advocate for civil rights, social security, or farm and labor legislation. As Cotton observed, "Being introduced to a political machine arouses a curiosity and desire for understanding that

Citizenship Education Program teacher trainees with SCLC and Highlander staff, ca. 1960–61. The group includes Andrew Young (back row, far left), Septima Clark (back row, fourth from left), Aimee Horton (back row, fifth from left), Candie Carawan (back row, fifth from right), Bernice Robinson (back row, fourth from right), Guy Carawan (back row, far right), and Dorothy Cotton (front row, far left). Courtesy of the Wisconsin Historical Society, Image #41219.

sends most citizenship school students scurrying to newspapers and other reading material that will help them see such machine in operation." Clark underscored the importance of literacy in equally practical terms, preaching, "Read newspapers and find meetings where [the] public is invited. Go to them." Soon after President Johnson signed the 1964 Civil Rights Act, CEP students studied it in class as well. Staff also developed a consumer education course that highlighted "good buying habits" and "family planning," defined consumer and housing cooperatives and credit unions, and explained how to access benefits offered by federal programs.[15]

Equally significant, when people began establishing their own local political organizations, training at Dorchester offered instructions on how to prepare precinct voting lists, publicize voter registration drives, contact absentee voters, and secure pledges of assistance from community residents. Some people could donate their time leafleting, transporting voters to the polls, or serving as poll watchers; others could make phone calls, babysit, or prepare food for election workers.[16] The CEP left no stone unturned and incorporated a job for everyone, particularly the black women who sustained the movement in spirit and in flesh by attending to what needed doing, including child care and cooking. Its genius lay in its flexibility, its specificity, and its reach. By 1963, citizenship education classes extended across the southern Black Belt from eastern Texas to the Virginia Tidewater.

In many respects, working for SCLC suited Septima Clark. A lifelong church member, she felt more comfortable with its faith-based approach than with Highlander's avowed secularism. She had the room to do what she did best with little interference or supervision. Even so, SCLC's organizational culture differed from what she had grown accustomed to in Tennessee. HFS had refocused her activist energies on developing the leadership potential of others. SCLC, by contrast, functioned as the "political arm" of the black church and reflected its top-down structure. Baptist ministers predominated as leaders and grounded their leadership style in personal charisma. They roused the masses with their oratorical talents, but very few had considered spreading leadership throughout a community, and they tended not to pay attention to the day-to-day upkeep of the movement that their words aimed to set in motion. They left such details to women. Clark estimated that the CEP "grew until there were something like fifteen women working to coordinate everything out of Atlanta . . . mimeographing teaching materials and keeping track of students."[17] Within SCLC, she worked in a familiar woman-centered environment.

In addition to her staff duties, Clark mentored her younger colleagues. When Cotton became discouraged about the lack of response in one community, she turned to Clark for advice. "You are troubled as I was many years ago about broken verbs," Clark responded. "Now I am deeply concerned about broken promises and in all my work and participation with civic organizations, the broken verb participant never becomes the broken promise participant." True to her vision of leadership, Clark gently counseled Cotton to look beyond the class chasm to find the potential in grassroots folk. Clark's mentoring extended to SNCC youth, too. "When I worked with the college students," she commented, "I would say to them, 'Don't go and cash the check for this woman at the A & P. Let her do it.'" Accompanying a person might boost her courage, but making "her cash her check and do her own talking" made her "have the feeling that she *can*."[18]

At the same time, class divisions within the movement continued to annoy Clark, and she did not refrain from criticizing her coworkers. "Andy was a highly middle-class black boy," she later remarked of Young; "We had to teach him how to work with our low-income people." She once chastised him for arriving at Dorchester by plane and bypassing folk who had just gotten off the bus on his way to get a snack. The bus riders had not eaten, she reminded him, and he should not eat unless food was available for all. On another occasion, Clark sent a scathing letter to Harriet Adams, a former social worker and SCLC administrator, who chartered a plane from Atlanta to reach Liberty County but would not budget money to cover food costs during travel for CEP recruits: "I know that we are in a movement and things are done at a moment's notice, but no workshop participant should be penalized for administrative procrastination," she fumed. The women had exchanged heated words when Adams arrived at Dorchester, and Clark accused Adams of "continuing with that white attitude though you are clothed in Negro skin." Clark offered no apology: "All the respect you have had or may lose can be placed in any garbage disposal. I will welcome that considering the source from which it comes."[19]

Septima Clark remained ever sensitive to the mundane but nuanced details that spoke volumes about what citizenship education meant to trainees. When two elderly women from Perry County, Alabama, grew distressed the first time they confronted a ten-cent charge to open the door to a toilet stall, Clark showed them what to do and used her own money. She noticed that some workshop participants collected sand and water to carry home as proof that they had been to the Atlantic Ocean; others folded their placemats from Howard Johnson's and tucked them into pocketbooks to prove to their children they had eaten in the restaurant. Clark used these examples to teach her colleagues that just bringing people "away from home gives learning experiences that they would never have" and that things "that we take for granted" mean "so much to deprived citizen[s]." Similarly, when a few organizers criticized poor people for installing TV antennas on the shacks in which they lived, Clark asked, "Would you deny these people that kind of enjoyment and exposure to the rest of the world just because they're poor?" She also encouraged both Cotton and Young to honor people's different responses to white repression. The two had closed their eyes during one singing session at Dorchester. As the group sang an "I love everybody" refrain, Clark saw "a young woman who was really crying." The woman subsequently explained to Clark that she had been arrested by white men who "called her a mulatto . . . to make her ashamed" and who "put cattle prods to her heels to make her jump up and down." Clark talked to her fellow staffers: "I said, 'You've got to open your eyes and see what's happening to this young woman. She can't sing that song. She can't love everybody when people treated her so mean.'"[20]

Workshop participants especially appreciated Clark's counsel. One movement worker recalled that when some of the older people complained about the noise and boisterousness of the youth in their midst, Clark "helped people see how important this time was and the importance of these young people being able to vent after all the things they had been through." Bernice Johnson Reagon, who returned over the years to help with singing sessions, judged Clark as "a real centering force in that program": "The thing I really remember about Septima Clark was the way in which she talked to people and how many different things she talked about." Topics ranged from Clark's affinity for what Marcus Garvey had preached after World War I to organizing strategies. Reagon remembered that Clark explained her understanding of the difficulty of knocking on doors and having people close them in your face by speaking about her own door-to-door canvassing in the 1919 campaign to get black teachers hired in Charleston's public schools. "You would just go, *What?!* Where did you come from?" The story might have been five decades old, but the message had not changed: "When you talked to Septima, you were rarely talking to her outside of something that she had not done."[21]

Aside from the received wisdom that education was women's work, the program attracted African American women because of the social and economic realities that they confronted. CEP teachers received stipends for their efforts. For those who were unemployed, the chance to earn thirty dollars a month teaching classes two nights a week looked much better than picking cotton for three dollars a day. Working and single women in female-headed households had long been used to relying on extended family to care for their children. Why not seize the opportunity to supplement the monthly budget? Where husbands had to work continuously to keep the bills paid and food on the table, wives could get away for a week to learn how to teach reading, writing, and community organizing. Moreover, becoming a CEP teacher appeared a relatively safe entry point for some mothers whose children had already joined the movement.[22]

Beyond learning about the technicalities of voting and registration, black women used CEP training to articulate their intimate concerns and to define what freedom meant to them. Women's health, particularly birth control, emerged as a topic of discussion. According to Reagon, Clark "said she was initially against birth control, because for her birth control was no sex and she didn't see how black people could survive, after all they went through, without holding on to each other." The birth of her last grandson, David, and the death of his mother (Nerie Clark Jr.'s second wife) shortly thereafter changed her mind. "She felt that women were not able to take care of themselves or space their children or recover from childbirth." Clark revealed this aspect of her private life to emphasize the importance of black women's ability to exercise reproductive choice with autonomy. Reagon remembered "the way I felt looking at Septima and hearing her talk about something that women needed that we were not getting from our culture. All of this had to do with desperation over not being able to take care of your family."[23]

Black women debated birth control in the context of a history of involuntary sterilization, personal experience, and current events. For example, when future CEP teacher and Mississippi civil rights leader Fannie Lou Hamer entered the Sunflower City Hospital in 1961 for the removal of a uterine tumor, her doctor performed a hysterectomy without informing her and without her permission. She later asserted that 60 percent of black women in Sunflower County had been victims of postpartum sterilizations without their consent. Annell Ponder, the CEP's recruiter in Mississippi, mentioned women's voicing the same complaint in one of her summaries from the field. At times, attacks on black women's reproductive freedom responded to their civil rights activism. Following a 1960 court order requiring New Orleans to desegregate its schools, the Louisiana state legislature considered a law that would have made unmarried women who gave birth to their second child subject to imprisonment. Four years later, the Mississippi state legislature introduced House Bill 180, which advocated one- to three-year prison terms for unmarried parents who had a second child together. In lieu of prison, mothers could "choose" to be sterilized. The bill did not pass, but poor women remained especially vulnerable. Over the next decade, sterilization became a common procedure for women who obtained medical care in federally funded programs. In 1973, a federal court found that an estimated 100,000 to 150,000 poor women had been sterilized *annually* since 1964, often under the threat of the elimination of their welfare benefits or because doctors refused to deliver their children unless mothers agreed to be sterilized afterward.[24]

As they had historically, southern African American women began conversations about reproductive freedom among themselves and framed the problems in terms of the health of both the mother and the broader community. CEP pedagogy reflected Septima Clark's long engagement in an educational world that underscored the necessity of tying learning to lived experience. By allowing southern grassroots women to connect personal issues to political realities, such CEP training sessions epitomized what would later become known as consciousness-raising, a defining organizational technique of the women's movement. Involvement in the civil rights movement transformed southern black women's perceptions of themselves and society. Yet as Reagon's recollections suggest, the CEP fostered the development of woman-centered discussions that focused on both individual prerogatives and community survival.[25] Black women soon brought their issues to local and national attention through their advocacy for impoverished black families and black children.

CEP training sessions occurred once a month. The rest of the time, Septima Clark traveled to places where help had been requested and convened meetings with teachers, students, and area supervisors, reminding local planners beforehand that "my idea is to work with the teachers and not be concerned about big meetings." Clark conferred with community leaders in crisis situations as well. During all of SCLC's major campaigns, "Septima met with women in the churches to explain what was going on," Young observed, "and it was far less threatening for her to do [so] than, say, for me to do it, or even for Martin Luther King to do it."[26] It was not so much that local women would have welcomed listening to a man less. Rather, as CEP training sessions and Clark's experiences had revealed, women spoke more frankly with other women. Circumstances changed rapidly, but Clark's focus reflected the continuity of her lifework. She remained an educational organizer at the grassroots.

Administrative problems plagued the CEP from the beginning. Money posed perennial trouble as SCLC barely remained solvent. Staff members regularly informed field workers that they would have to cut back expenses because local movements — and their need for bond money — drained the coffers. Clark actually declined a raise in 1963.[27] Financial shortfalls also affected the relationship between SCLC and the foundations that provided grant money to operate the CEP. In 1963, SCLC asked the Field Foundation to commit support for three to five years, eliminating the need to reapply for annual grants, and received a $250,000 two-year grant. Before the end of the first year, however, Young wrote to Maxwell Hahn to confess that the CEP had expended the entire $125,000 allotted for 1963–64 and to request a $20,000 supplement. Young stressed that SCLC had not violated the terms of its grant but had underestimated the number of people who would be trained and the number of schools that would run. "The increased activity of 1963 is by and large responsible for the boom in our program," Young explained, "but 64' promises to be just as 'hot a summer.'"[28]

Problems of representation developed between SCLC and the American Missionary Association (AMA) and its Division of the United Church Board of Homeland Ministries, the sponsoring organization that administered the Field Foundation grant to SCLC. Early on, Clark emphasized the CEP's potential. "It is evident that we have now within our grasp a new kind of society," she wrote during a recruiting trip to Georgia in the winter of 1962, "a learning society made up of educative communities." By 1964, CEP staff envisioned building a network of permanent learning centers across the South, not unlike the schools that the AMA had established one hundred years earlier. "My criticism of the AMA," Young wrote that summer, "has always been that it devoted itself to the theory of the 'talented tenth,' but did not develop an approach to aid the masses." Wesley Hotchkiss, the division's general secretary, conceded that the CEP was "well within the tradition of the AMA." Yet he insisted that "if we continue our relationship . . . there must be no question in the minds of the people that this *is* the work of the American Missionary Association." Young countered that such distinctions mattered little to grassroots activists and that adding "another set of initials" to the mix would not amount to much. From SCLC's perspective, the program's effectiveness depended on the association local people made between it and their confidence in Martin Luther King Jr. Still, Young agreed to begin using AMA stationery and publicizing its involvement in all CEP literature. Privately, he informed SCLC staff that the "mistake that the AMA made originally which we must avoid, was to assume that education was in itself an answer to the Negroes problems. Education must be related directly to social change and social action."[29]

At arm's length from this administrative wrangling, Septima Clark focused on SCLC's need to cultivate grassroots leaders. "I always felt that if you were going to develop other people, you don't talk for them. You train them to do their own talking," she contended. This philosophy lay completely outside the male-dominated executive staff's field of vision. While they — and the broader society — regarded King's celebrity as a key catalyst, Clark understood that the movement's momentum waxed and waned. The CEP rested fundamentally on the radical notion that its leaders — the staff who trained others — should work themselves out of their jobs. Empowering people to make their own decisions guaranteed forward motion. Only by involving as many as possible could local struggles sustain themselves and expand. When one leader's energy faltered, CEP training meant that another person could take up the slack. Or if the momentum slowed, a committed cadre of activists would not allow it to come to a complete stop; it might be less visible, but it would always be there.[30]

Clark repeatedly tried to persuade King to forgo the spotlight in SCLC's campaigns and let local people assume leadership positions, but the men of SCLC could not imagine others leading a march because they believed that "if you think another man should lead, then you are looking down on Dr. King." King grew distressed when Clark bestowed an SCLC certificate of affiliation in a town near Aiken, South Carolina: "He thought I presented it and didn't call his name," she remembered. Like other women in the movement, Clark felt comfortable with men occupying public positions of leadership, yet men's private disrespect for women irritated her. When King read to his male colleagues a letter from Clark suggesting that others might lead, "it just tickled them; they just laughed," she claimed. SCLC's organizational culture created an atmosphere that welcomed women's contributions as long as they remained invisible. According to Clark, Ralph Abernathy repeatedly inquired why she held a position on the executive staff, a rarity for a woman in SCLC, and what right she had to participate in any meetings. Each time King explained her work in the CEP, but "Rev. Abernathy'd come right back the next time and ask again."[31]

Septima Clark reasoned that these men generally disregarded women's opinions because of the way they had been raised: "I think about my mother, who had a feeling that black boys in the South could be conspired upon. She wanted to keep her boys right under her nose." The white South's denigration of black manhood compounded the situation, but Clark believed that black sons resented their mothers' caution and "grew up feeling that women should not have a say in anything." Young agreed. King's "mother was one of the strongest, most domineering women you'd want to meet, so part of his growing up was to shed himself of this dominant influence of women in his life and in his church." King flattered Clark, Young maintained, but remained unaware "of his tendency to ignore her substantive comments or undervalue her work." Clark and Cotton "would grumble privately about how women were treated in SCLC," he added. During the movement's heyday, however, Clark never publicly criticized King or his lieutenants. When King won the Nobel Peace Prize in 1964, she paid her own way to Oslo to witness the event: "I felt when a southern black man could win a Nobel Peace Prize, I wanted to be there."[32]

Behind the scenes, SCLC's poor administrative practices bothered Clark, particularly the habitual delays in reimbursing CEP teachers for costs they incurred. In 1963, for example, Barbara Gregg wrote from New Bern, North Carolina, explaining that she had already sent one monthly statement to Atlanta and was ready to send another, but she still awaited her first payment. The situation not only disappointed her students and her fellow teachers but also threatened to ruin Gregg's economic standing in her hometown because she had purchased materials on credit. "When I finish this class," she announced, "I don't believe I shall bother with another one, because I am not getting the full support promised me by the SCLC." Similarly, in Cleveland, Mississippi, Margaret Block had found a church that would let her hold classes for a small rental fee. "I would appreciate it very much if you all can find the time to drop my check in the mail so I won't have to keep lying to the people about the money I owe them," she wrote. Many other teachers returned home eager to begin classes but could not get started because the CEP failed to send student workbooks.[33]

Clark brought such matters to Young's attention in the summer of 1964. Noting that CEP office staff had fallen five months behind in sending out payment vouchers, she reminded him, "The people for whom we get the money are those in the most benighted areas and to whom $30 is a great blessing. These are the people on the first of the list to be paid in my estimation. If we fail to do this the great battle for rights is in vain." For Clark, building a movement meant paying attention to its practical details and its local warriors. She "felt terribly let down" when teachers reported that they had not received vouchers in time for the previous December's holidays, especially since she had specifically asked to have the payments made. Finally, she raised the issue of equal pay for equal work by suggesting that SCLC equalize salaries among CEP teaching and field staff. Evidently, Young had prioritized paying men with families over paying women. Clark said she understood this logic but added, "Women have great responsibilities also."[34]

As the CEP quickly expanded, bureaucratic entanglements could hardly be avoided. "I know I have to say this almost every time," Cotton told one teacher in Clarksdale, Mississippi, "but since SCLC has been printing our workbooks, we have difficulty. They have been promising us 10,000 books for about a month and a half now and we still do not have them." Additional confusion arose because many teachers and supervisors remained unclear about what the SCLC payments would cover. When Edward Banks included car repairs on his statement, which seemed reasonable since he used his vehicle to transport people to and from class, Cotton corrected his mistake. Some people apparently seized the opportunity to earn a little money, but lacked proper qualifications. Cotton warned Banks "that only persons who have been trained to teach adults at Dorchester Center" could lead classes. In addition, some participants liked the classes so much that they tried to sign up for multiple sessions. An office staffer had to remind Hosea Williams that, under the terms of the grant, his teachers should not duplicate their work among returning students.[35]

A few educational organizers failed to fulfill their obligations. Cotton censured a teacher in Birmingham for misappropriating CEP funds: "We were shocked to know that you have not been operating Citizenship Classes. The fair thing for you to do would be to return the money, but since you've probably spent it all, let's hope that some bit of it was put to good use." Clark remembered sending "four hundred and some dollars" so that one Alabama woman could get her group to Dorchester. "She had never seen that much money before, and she took that money and paid most of her debts," which meant that the members of her group had nothing to eat on the long trip to Georgia. Without judgment, Clark commented, "You have to work with people." Some trainees certainly did not live up to organizers' hopes. For some, the prospect of a weeklong "vacation" did not translate into genuine efforts to start classes back home. Others lacked sufficient literacy skills to teach reading and writing to their neighbors. In the margins of one Tennessee CEP teacher's report describing her friend's interest in joining the class, Clark wrote, "This is the blind leading [the blind]. I hope both will restore sight to each other." By 1963, Cotton counseled Annell Ponder, the CEP's Mississippi field secretary, that increased demand translated into the need to screen "much more carefully" the recruits sent to Dorchester.[36]

Federal government intervention had provided an unexpected springboard for spreading citizenship education across the South. Images of burned buses occupied by activists from the Congress of Racial Equality (CORE) on the Freedom Rides fueled the Kennedy administration's attempt to shift the focus of civil rights activism to less confrontational—and politically embarrassing—activities. The Justice Department spent the latter part of 1961 establishing the Voter Education Project and working to get all of the major civil rights groups under its umbrella. In exchange for abandoning direct action, they could expect financial assistance channeled through a generously funded tax-exempt organization. Along with SNCC, CORE, and the NAACP, SCLC targeted black-majority districts and hired five full-time field secretaries to get voter registration drives under way in eight southern states.[37]

Administratively, SCLC's voter education program was distinct from Septima Clark's department. Hosea Williams oversaw the Voter Education Project, which shared the same goals but lacked the CEP's emphasis on literacy training. Voter education targeted people who could already read but who needed to overcome apathy and fear. Williams's staff set up registration clinics to train volunteer organizers. CEP staff nonetheless assisted Voter Education Project efforts in various quarters. Clark spent nearly two weeks in the summer of 1962 in Albany, Georgia, standing at the courthouse door, "from morning until late afternoon," encouraging African Americans to register. "The white man would say, 'You can't vote in this election. It's no use for you to register.' And I would say to them, 'Registration is permanent in Georgia, so you go ahead and register now.'" Clark also used her time in Albany to revive the citizenship education classes that young people had begun in the spring but that had reached a standstill as direct action campaigns commanded their attention.[38]

Other organizations engaged with the Voter Education Project soon realized that mobilizing their communities en masse—especially reaching the rural poor—depended on laying an educational foundation. They turned to the CEP. "May I bring my NAACP members to a training session?" a North Carolina branch president inquired. "Do come over to Mississippi, and help us train these people to fill in the application blank for registration," a SNCC field secretary implored. "We also need help in the planning of a voter registration campaign," a CORE representative in New Orleans noted. Because the CEP offered a widely needed service, it functioned as a neutral space wherein competing civil rights groups' struggles for power, resources, and influence paled in comparison to acquiring the practical skills to get the job done. As Clark acknowledged in 1963, "The acceptance of these services by other civil rights organizations says that great designs are based on method not madness."[39]

Yet Clark harbored misgivings about how SCLC conducted its voter registration work. Unlike the Voter Education Project, the CEP did not receive federal funds. Clark believed that the CEP was better situated to generate the necessary follow-up but that it suffered from inattention. In late 1963, she prepared a memo for King that attempted to clarify the issues. Commenting that she was the only paid CEP staff member visiting classes in the field at that time, Clark railed, "It seems as if Citizenship Education is all mine, except when it comes time to pick up the checks." Clark contended that some of her colleagues felt "that the work is not dramatic enough to warrant their time." "Direct action is so glamorous and packed with emotion," she explained, "that most young people prefer demonstrations over genuine education." Gendered and generational differences distinguished Clark's perspective. Clark had come of age as an activist in a woman-centered educational culture that relied on a type of organizing distinct from the direct action strategies that began to be adopted during World War II. Like Ella Baker, Septima Clark recognized that the follow-up work could not be overlooked. King missed this point.

Clark also used this memo to provide her estimation of all of SCLC's CEP campaigns. Programs in Virginia, North Carolina, Florida, and Tennessee "have given very little in return for the amount spent on students who were trained," she maintained, while Louisiana had "sent many to be trained, but the follow-up has been lacking and no results have come from the output." Alabama completely lacked any supervision, which led Clark to assert that citizenship education there "is practically moot." She judged Mississippi recruits "full of smoldering hatred. They have been so depressed that they take this out on each other." In her view, southeastern and southwestern Georgia and South Carolina, where the Citizenship Schools had taken earliest root, were making the most progress. Such a frank assessment measured the distance between a frustrating reality and what Clark envisioned as the program's true promise if it received the support it deserved. "Dr. King, I believe that mass education and a federally financed program will eliminate the political fear and police brutality in the South, especially Mississippi," she concluded.[40]

If officials at the Justice Department had studied their history, they might have predicted that African American activists would select the Black Belt as a primary site for implementing the Voter Education Project. These officials undoubtedly knew that the region's most powerful white politicians and staunchest defenders of segregation hailed from these areas, as did the most hard-core white supremacists. However, Kennedy administration officials apparently failed to take into account the degree to which voter registration in the Black Belt amounted to a kind of direct action and provoked violent reprisals.

CEP teachers were not immune to the danger. One South Carolina woman reported that local whites had tried "to force her father's employer and landlord to fire him and put him off the land." She kept teaching. Carolyn Daniels in Georgia's Terrell County, known as "Terrible Terrell," had her home bombed. Fannie Lou Hamer returned home from her first Dorchester session and promptly started a class to teach her neighbors the basics of citizenship. When she led a group to the courthouse to register, she lost her job as a plantation timekeeper; when she took refuge with a family in Ruleville, white supremacists shot into the house. Ida Holland, the first CEP teacher in Greenwood, Mississippi, went to jail "several times" but "used the opportunities to 'teach citizenship' to the guard." Nearby, in the middle of the night, two masked men visited the owner of the plantation where CEP teacher Sallie Carthen and her husband worked to advise him to "get rid of her." Carthen talked to her landlord and convinced him that "anyone should do what they can to help their people," but she still moved to Ruleville. "Her husband will stay on the plantation, since they are not bothering him," CEP staff noted.[41]

Septima Clark encountered her share of trouble and saw considerable violence against civil rights workers. "The White Citizens' Council or the Ku Klux Klan would be surrounding us wherever we were," she asserted. In Marion, Alabama, a black youth intervened to keep his mother from being slapped by a white policeman. "They shot him in the groin. He died the next day," Clark recalled. In Greenwood, Mississippi, she watched as a white man threw a black teenager to the ground; volunteers had to take him to Clarksdale to obtain medical care for his broken leg. Soon thereafter, Clark found herself in a Baptist church in Grenada, Mississippi, discussing registration and voting: "Just as we finished up that meeting and walked out of the church, it caught fire in every corner. We hadn't been out of there five minutes before the whole thing was down." Clark stayed up until four in the morning collecting affidavits from witnesses. The Klan surrounded another meeting in a Natchez, Mississippi, church. "The Deacons for Defense from Louisiana had come over that night for the program," Clark remembered, adding that the nervous chief of police asked both the Klan and African Americans to disperse to preserve the peace. Clark nevertheless remained committed to nonviolence: "I worked with the students in Birmingham. Sometimes they wanted to fight back. I said to them: 'Do you think you can take the slaps? Because they will slap your face or they will knock you down.'" If the students did not think they could refrain from responding, she told them, "Stay up in this room with me."[42]

The sole exception was the time Clark attended the trial of the white policemen who had savagely beaten a group of black women for attempting to integrate a bus station lunch counter in Winona, Mississippi. The women were traveling home from a June 1963 CEP training session at the Sea Island Center on Johns Island. Annell Ponder, June Johnson, and Fannie Lou Hamer received the worst thrashings. So much blood gushed from Johnson's left eye that her cellmates thought it had fallen out of its socket; Ponder's face was so swollen that she could barely talk; and Hamer was blinded in her left eye and sustained permanent kidney damage. Clark went to Oxford for the trial but had to secure accommodations from a beautician in another town. "I couldn't get any of the black people in Oxford to give me a room to stay there. I had to go all the way [up] to Holly Springs, ride forty-six miles every morning and I did that for five days back and forth to that trial." In addition, SCLC made no attempt to show its support during the proceedings, which Clark judged "a terrible thing." The mockery of justice in the courtroom enraged her. "When I heard those men testifying," she later admitted, "I wished that a chandelier would drop on their heads and kill them. My mind wasn't non-violent."[43]

Most often, however, Clark relied on her spiritual convictions to see her through difficult times. "My *faith* in a *Supreme Being* has been built up through the years. I can't ever turn that *faith* loose," she testified to a movement supporter. Divine intervention had saved her life more than once. Traveling incessantly, she had been in a train wreck, a bus wreck, and an airplane accident. Each time, she emerged with only minor cuts and bruises. Attempted violence against Clark only strengthened her faith: "I'll never know how a sheriff caught up with three white boys, all teenagers, coming to bomb the house I slept in just in time to take away the dynamite while I lived in Monteagle, Tennessee. I said to myself, 'God kept me that night, so I'll put my body in His care each night thereafter' and I did."[44]

Clark's faith also sustained her belief in the efficacy of the CEP's work and bolstered her hope for what Dorchester trainees could accomplish in their local communities. As a pragmatist, Clark could concede failure, often as a way to argue for strengthening the CEP, without losing sight of the larger picture. At the same time, she could not predict how CEP training would affect the South's many local movements. Instead, she remained focused on training a corps of teachers to organize their communities. Septima Clark did not have to be everywhere at once, but her influence extended far and wide.

꿏꓇꙾

Perhaps nowhere were the results of citizenship education as dramatic as in the closed society of Mississippi, where even the least bit of civil rights organizing frequently meant losing one's job or one's home and sometimes one's life. Recognizing that survival in the Magnolia State depended on unity, civil rights activists joined together to establish the Council of Federated Organizations (COFO) in early 1962. The resulting cross-fertilization meant that grassroots organizers might learn of SCLC's program from CEP staff; from the Reverend James Bevel, a veteran of the Nashville sit-ins hired by SCLC to direct its Voter Education Project in Mississippi; from SNCC field workers, who first entered the state in late 1961; or from each other.

Left to right: Dorothy Cotton, Annell Ponder, and Septima Clark
on a trip to recruit Citizenship School teachers, Mississippi, 1963.
Courtesy of the Avery Research Center for African American
History and Culture, College of Charleston.

During their initial southern tour in the summer of 1961, Clark, Cotton, and Young encountered many of the people who would emerge as the movement's leaders there. In Clarksdale, located in the northwestern Delta's Coahoma County, they met Vera Pigee, a beautician. Clarksdale showed early promise. By November, black activists had begun boycotting downtown merchants, and in the last week of the month, Pigee traveled to Dorchester for a training session. Pigee's workshop performance led staff members to predict that "she will make an excellent supervisor of the schools in her area." Pigee inaugurated classes for adults, but she also headed the local NAACP youth chapter. Like Bernice Robinson on Johns Island, Pigee extended her training to African American teenagers so that they would be informed voters the first time they cast ballots. In 1965, Pigee, who had indeed become a CEP area supervisor, reported that she had conducted twenty citizenship education classes in the previous four years and that she had led "more than 100" people to register to vote in that year alone. Clark was so impressed by what she saw when she returned to Clarksdale that she decided to take her lifetime NAACP membership through its chapter "because they were really getting something done."[45]

Citizenship education took deeper root in Mississippi because of the organizing of SNCC field staff in the Delta and in the southwestern part of the state. SNCC differed from traditional civil rights organizations in several important ways. From the beginning, students preserved their autonomy, which gave them the freedom to chart their own course. According to one adult participant, SNCC constituted the "cutting edge of the movement," "the young people who dared to do the things their parents would not do." SNCC cultivated leadership among the most impoverished and dispossessed as well as the economically independent and independently minded. By the spring of 1962, COFO had targeted six Delta counties and selected Greenwood, a town where the population was two-thirds black and extremely poor, as the place to begin.[46]

SNCC members learned more about laying an educational foundation at a June 1962 Highlander workshop. There, they met Esau Jenkins and Bernice Robinson, who shared their experiences and tips for getting started. SNCC put what it had learned into practice almost immediately. At the end of the month, Bob Moses, SNCC's field director for the Voter Education Project, asked Robinson to conduct citizenship training workshops in Mississippi. In the course of her July travels, Robinson "found six citizenship school classes for adults being held in Ruleville and Cleveland."[47] More broadly, having been introduced to the Citizenship School idea, SNCC thereafter sent a steady stream of local people to Dorchester.

Lois Lee Rodgers was one of them. A resident of Shaw, Rodgers began teaching her first CEP class in March 1963. Over the next two months, she enrolled twenty people in a second class she taught out of her home and accompanied forty-seven would-be black voters to the registrar's office. When a white grocery store owner shot a black man, Rodgers participated in a boycott of his store, which gave her the opportunity to canvass among the nearly three hundred field laborers who shopped there each day. By June, CEP students in Shaw had decided to focus on a fund-raising project—making and selling quilts, throw rugs, and tablecloths—with plans to use the proceeds to assist people whose involvement in the struggle had cost them their jobs and homes. Shaw students also joined people from nearby Greenwood, Mound Bayou, and Shelby in establishing a community newsletter, the *Mississippi*

Free Press, to provide residents with information "that is kept out of the newspapers."[48]

Throughout the spring and summer of 1963, Rodgers worked closely with COFO and aided its activities. She helped distribute clothing, for example, until Septima Clark gently reminded her to keep her attention on the schools. "Do you know that picking up clothing is not in the CEP?," Clark asked. "This project should be done by community people." Clark did not want Rodgers to spread her energies too thin and recognized that simply dispensing relief represented another avenue by which more people could enter the movement. For her part, Rodgers helped to publicize and arrange transportation to a July 6 music festival because she understood that "it was a good way to influence new people." When whites learned of her Shelby CEP class, she had to suspend it temporarily because students became afraid to attend. Rodgers continued her classes in Shaw and Mound Bayou, however, and joined other CEP teachers to drum up support for the movement in Greenville, convinced an elderly black businesswoman to rent a furnished house that she owned to movement workers, and attended the trial of activists arrested in Itta Bena. Late in July, Rodgers helped lead a local workshop on "The Changing Southern Landscape."[49]

Along with other CEP teachers in the area, Rodgers sat on COFO canvassing committees and participated in tactical discussions. Perhaps the close proximity to the young organizers influenced her to start thinking about addressing the problems of local youth. "When I think beyond the ballot," she wrote in August 1963, "I cannot over look the major problems that exist most among young Negro people." For Rodgers, the lack of recreational programs and high dropout rates, especially among pregnant teenage girls, ranked as high priorities. Like countless black women activist educators before her, Rodgers went to talk to the high school principal about "beginning a Moral Education Program," and she visited the Bolivar County Health Center to inquire about material that could be used in classes. Rodgers also met with the school nurse, who said she agreed with the necessity of incorporating such issues into health education but was forbidden "to teach anything pertaining to moral." Still, the nurse consented to volunteer in her spare time and to ask the county doctor for pamphlets and films. Moreover, as had often been the case, educating teenagers meant educating their parents. The high school secretary promised to assist by providing Rogers with a list of parents' names and addresses.[50]

Lois Lee Rodgers and other CEP teachers helped transform Greenwood and its surrounding environs from a place where most people initially described the movement as a "mess" into a place where people realized that they had the ability to help themselves. Then they began to think beyond voter registration to addressing additional community problems. As one CEP supervisor later observed, "those who had been a part of the citizenship education process . . . are the people who formed the core of the local movements."[51] Young COFO activists could not have accomplished as much as they did without the CEP teachers and students who labored alongside them.

A similar conversion was under way in Hattiesburg, in the southwestern part of the state. African Americans comprised one-third of the population in this piney woods area, and the preponderance of small farms meant that black residents were not as indigent as those who worked the cotton plantations in the Delta. In the community of Palmer's Crossing, two SNCC field workers met Victoria Gray, a former schoolteacher and an independent businesswoman, head of the local parent-teacher association, and church leader, and recruited her to go to Dorchester. Gray later praised the CEP's comprehensive plan for community organizing. Granting that the curriculum depended on "what you were doing in the movement," she added, "You've got your format. You know what your approaches are. You know what your principles are, etc. And you tell those to the local community wherever it happened to be." When the young men from SNCC left to join their colleagues in Greenwood in the spring of 1963, Gray took up the work.[52]

From the outset, Gray sought other potential teachers. She looked for those who had "good, solid reasoning" and enrolled them in her class before sending them for training with Clark. She soon became an area supervisor with multiple classes running in the city and across Forrest County. "One of the things I learned early on," Gray recalled, "is never underestimate the intelligence of *anyone* in the community." Nor did she limit her view of the contributions average citizens could make: "Always try to meet people where they are and receive them at *whatever* point." When Gray needed a film projector, for example, she would "pick up that phone and call the principal." He responded, "Can you be in such-and-such a place at such-and-such a time? I won't be there, but it will be." Likewise, black men employed by whites visited Gray's house on payday. "You know I can't come out there and march," they told her as they handed over cash donations, but "take this and do whatever you need to do with it." When community women who "might not show up anywhere" learned that COFO organizers rarely got enough to eat, they responded, "Goodness sakes, we can't have the people hungry." Some donated home-canned food; others cooked meals at the Freedom House.[53] Keeping an open mind, Gray made room for people who feared being visibly involved in the movement, aware that her actions might lead them to make a stronger commitment.

Gray let it be widely known that she "ran a literacy program." She counseled her people to give a similar explanation of their activities if questioned by either whites or other African Americans. Only later, after the mass marches and protests began, did local white residents identify the classes as a source of the trouble. Harassment followed. On one occasion, Gray's uncle, a grocer, went to the wholesale warehouse in another town to pick up supplies. The white men there told him that "there's a woman down there in your community that's going to get in big trouble." Gray's uncle feigned ignorance and got the men to tell him the exact details, including where the targeted woman lived. Then he asked, "Are you prepared to leave anybody when you come for this woman? Because I can tell you, that house is under surveillance twenty-four hours a day. Anybody that comes down there and they are not recognized, they will probably not leave if they start anything." The men who patrolled Gray's neighborhood belonged to what she described as "the icehouse group. They sit up there at the center of the community, talk and lounge, if you will." However, "when the sun went down," she observed, "there was nobody at the icehouse."[54]

Hoping to shine the national spotlight on Mississippi and to awaken local people to the possibility of circumventing white chicanery by establishing an independent political structure, COFO decided to hold a mock election—with its own slate of candidates—in November 1963. CEP teachers rallied behind the Freedom Vote. Sallie Carthen "secured 1,500 freedom registrations from plantation workers" in Sunflower County. Lois Rodgers prepared leaflets explaining the campaign, visited churches to see if they could serve as polling places, invited other CEP teachers to serve as poll watchers, set up voting booths, and distributed ballot boxes in eighteen locations. On Election Day, she worked with the vote-mobile, a roving polling place that sought to reach people who might not have transportation or might be too afraid to vote publicly at the stationary polls. The next day, Rodgers collected ballot boxes and arranged for them to be sent to Jackson for the final tally.[55]

Despite threats and arrests, eighty-three thousand black Mississippians, the majority of them living in eight counties, voted. It was a respectable turnout for a mere two months of intensive effort. The Freedom Vote failed to garner national media attention, however, leading COFO strategists to plan a more intensive "Freedom Summer" for 1964 and to invite white volunteers from the North to participate. November 1963 also brought more discouraging developments. Washington officials overseeing the Voter Education

Project suspended funding for Mississippi work because it had not proven "cost effective."[56] Two weeks later, Lee Harvey Oswald assassinated President John Kennedy. Still, the Freedom Vote, a logical extension of citizenship education, had prepared the ground for 1964.

COFO began the new year by instituting "Freedom Days," in which large numbers of black Mississippians went to courthouses to register while supporters stood outside picketing. Though only a few added their names to the rolls, they did so amid a revival of the Ku Klux Klan and a wave of violence. Citizenship education strengthened their resolve. Ethel Shaw, a CEP teacher in Greenwood, led a discussion of nonviolence during which her students expressed "their willingness to endure whatever come that help bring our freedom." Incorporating the faith that sustained grassroots people, Shaw and other CEP teachers also taught a unit on "The Bible and the Ballot" that connected Jesus Christ's concern for humanity to the importance of accepting "the task he left for us" by registering and voting. The curriculum in Mississippi had evolved to include useful lessons from the past as well. Adults in Shaw's class learned that "Crispus [Attucks] was the first freedom fighter" and likened their movement to American Revolution. Students taught by Laura McGhee compared their situation to slavery, talked about women such as Sojourner Truth, and reached the conclusion that slaves' suffering "and ours today is somewhat alike but we will never turn back." CEP students "could see that this freedom fight has been brought over many centuries," a supervisor commented; "Now we must share in this struggle." CEP teachers' and alumni's perceptions of themselves as historical actors transformed how they viewed the present. "I think everyday should be freedom day," Ethel Shaw pronounced, "and any day one can go is freedom day."[57]

Local people expressed their newfound skills and self-respect most dramatically by contesting the seating of Mississippi's all-white delegation at the 1964 Democratic National Convention in Atlantic City. To do so, they and COFO organizers established the Mississippi Freedom Democratic Party (FDP) that April. The FDP had two interrelated goals. First, it served as a vehicle for affirming black political self-determination and offering black candidates for state offices. Second, by driving a wedge between southern white supremacists and white liberals in the national Democratic Party, the FDP sought to force white allies to take a stronger public stance on behalf of the civil rights movement.[58]

The FDP reflected the widespread impact of grassroots citizenship education. Though it bore a striking similarity to the challenge by South Carolina's Progressive Democratic Party twenty years earlier, black activists in

Mississippi avoided the mistakes made by that generation, most notably by organizing from the precinct up to the state level. CEP training, which emphasized the structure of state government, had taught black Mississippians what a precinct was. To prove that whites had systematically barred their participation in party politics, black activists arrived at 1,884 precinct meetings of the regular Democratic Party on June 16. With the exceptions of Greenville and Jackson, white Democrats turned the activists away both from those gatherings and from all later county, district, and state meetings. In late July, the FDP held its own precinct meetings to nominate delegates to travel to the county and district sessions that would culminate in a state convention on August 6. Organizers had trouble fostering participation in the rural areas where white violence and intimidation was the worst. Even so, twenty-five hundred people converged on Jackson to select the sixty-eight delegates who would go to Atlantic City.[59]

According to Victoria Gray, most of the people who filled the ranks of the FDP had been CEP students, "came right out there, absolutely." Given that citizenship education classes had served as a preeminent site for nurturing women's self-confidence, it should come as no surprise that women had significant visibility within the FDP. Half of its members were women, and as in SNCC, decision making was collective, which encouraged women to raise their voice at meetings. Women also expressed their opinions by writing articles and press releases for FDP newsletters. Twelve of the sixteen delegates elected from the Second Congressional District were women. There, FDP members elected Hamer, who had already announced her decision to run for Congress, to serve as vice chair in Atlantic City. Gray decided to launch a campaign for the U.S. Senate and was elected an FDP representative to the Democratic National Committee. More broadly, the preponderance of CEP graduates helped ensure that the FDP represented a cross-section of Mississippi's black population.[60]

The FDP arrived in Atlantic City with high expectations and left bitterly disappointed. With the passage of the 1964 Civil Rights Act, which prohibited segregation in public facilities and racial discrimination in employment and education, President Lyndon B. Johnson felt assured that he had secured the loyalty of the nation's enfranchised African Americans, especially since his opponent, Republican senator Barry Goldwater, had voted against the measure. Still, Johnson wanted to avoid the embarrassment of a fight for seating at the national convention. During the convention, Martin Luther King Jr. spoke on the FDP's behalf, but it was Fannie Lou Hamer's speaking for herself in an impassioned testimony that caused the president to interrupt live network coverage by calling an impromptu press conference. Meanwhile, negotiations between the Johnson administration and FDP representatives sputtered. In the end, the White House offered to tender FDP chair Aaron Henry and Ed King, a white chaplain, two at-large seats on the convention floor, admit the rest as guests, and seat only members of Mississippi's all-white delegation who pledged to support the Democratic nominee. After much internal wrangling, the FDP rejected the offer. Said Hamer, "We didn't come all this way for no two seats."[61]

Many FDP members felt betrayed by the Johnson administration and suspected that some of their own had sold them out during conferences with national party officials. Lessons in citizenship had not prepared the grassroots core of the FDP for the reality of backroom dealing that yielded limp compromises in lieu of clear justice. Most black activists ascertained that awakening white America was only one method for combating the white South's obstinacy. Failure in Atlantic City prompted local people to return home and apply themselves to the task of strengthening the FDP to wield more power in state and community affairs.[62]

CEP teachers and students continued to abet the FDP's mission by organizing more of their neighbors to support it. CEP area supervisor Pinkie Pilcher became the chair of all FDP block captains in Greenwood, while Alice Blackwell, another CEP teacher and supervisor there, served as an FDP vice president. Blackwell continued to teach citizenship education classes as well as to convene precinct workshops once a week. From Carroll County, Lou Emma Shipp said that she had shifted her focus away from formal CEP classes to FDP work and had taught people interested in the organization "not as a class but as personal help."[63]

CEP stalwarts also helped extend the FDP's agenda. As Tallahatchie County teacher Ethel Lee Thompson announced, "We have organized the Mississippi Freedom Labor Union." More than a thousand people joined the union within a few months and fashioned a set of demands that included a minimum wage, medical care, and social security benefits. By the mid-1960s, however, farming mechanization and other changes in agricultural production had contributed to the decline in jobs available for black farm laborers, and the union had little negotiating leverage. A farming cooperative movement proved similarly short-lived. Nevertheless, both organizations represented attempts by local people to put into practice what they had learned in SCLC's citizenship schools. They made better headway on public education issues. "We are working with the FDP this year in school desegregation," teacher Georgia Mae Dickerson wrote from Holmes County. Likewise, Victoria Gray reported in 1965, "Our classes have been active in every area of community activity, from voter registration to agitating the county school board regarding their actions and policies." Hattiesburg adult students had "forced the Board to hire 3 [black] teachers."[64]

A few CEP teachers took the same path as Hamer and Gray and sought electoral office. On April 8, 1965, Alice Blackwell and Pinkie Pilcher went to Greenwood's City Hall and registered as candidates for the upcoming municipal elections. Blackwell ran for mayor and Pilcher for city commissioner of sanitation. Mary B. Lane, a former SNCC project director, offered herself as a candidate for city commissioner of streets. The three women became the first African Americans to run for these offices in the history of the city. A year later, former CEP teacher Rathis Hayes ran for the U.S. House of Representatives in the Second Congressional District.[65]

In 1967, 108 African Americans ran for local and state offices in Mississippi, with 22 of them winning election. Hamer lost her bid for the state senate, but she and six other black candidates filed suit in court charging election irregularities. In Holmes County, former public school teacher Robert G. Clark became the first African American elected to the Mississippi state legislature since Reconstruction. For a recently enfranchised population that still confronted white violence and more subtle legislative maneuvering to dilute black voting strength, no political office was unimportant. Citizenship training in how local governments functioned meant that the reasonable place to begin building black political power was by electing African American constables, justices of the peace, and county supervisors. Not only did local campaigns cost less, but local victories included the practical benefit of more readily demonstrating the connection between the ballot and everyday life to the wider community. In the aftermath of Atlantic City, CEP and FDP alumni continued to walk the long, and still onerous, road to economic, social, and political equality. Yet they moved forward with the knowledge that henceforth they would have to wield power both to achieve desired goals and to prevent undesirable outcomes.[66]

Septima Clark participated in the last SCLC campaign that garnered a significant response from the federal government. The Johnson administration introduced the Voting Rights Act to Congress on March 17, 1965, just ten days after "Bloody Sunday," when news cameras captured white police and state troopers attacking a group of black marchers in the shadow of the Edmund Pettus Bridge in Selma, Alabama. The legislation, which suspended literacy tests and called for the appointment of federal registrars in areas where less than half the voting-age population was registered, became law the following August. Clark remembered having a difficult time in Selma and Dallas County in the aftermath of the springtime violence: "Dr. King sent six of us in to teach the people how to write their names in cursive writing so they could register when the Federal man came down in August," but the other five members of the group became so fed up with resistance by local ministers and members of the black professional class that they left. Clark stayed by herself in Selma for three months, canvassing "until I could find someone who listened" and then training others to help her organize handwriting clinics. Local women soon taught forty-five classes in their homes, churches, and at SCLC's office. To overcome fear, activists advertised that students would learn how to apply for jobs, sign checks, write letters, and use their penmanship for "Other Everyday Needs." Such educational camouflage yielded the desired results. "We had some ninety-one years of age learning to write their names," Clark declared, "and in August, 7,002 persons were registered."[67]

Participants in SCLC's ninth annual convention praised the CEP as "our most vital and positive program" and characterized the Dallas County handwriting clinics as the CEP's "major contribution" for 1965. Yet as Clark's description of the work in Selma suggests, the CEP's focus had begun to change. By eliminating literacy tests, the Voting Rights Act inadvertently undermined the CEP's raison d'être. "It made people think it was no longer necessary," Andrew Young remarked.[68] The same year, Young left the program to take over as SCLC's executive director. Clark prepared a five-year proposal for the CEP after his departure. She identified Alabama and Louisiana as sites for "priority projects" and noted that "Mississippi still needs more support than the rest of the Southern states." "From now on we need to work even harder to rid our states of illiterates," she concluded.[69] Clark's historic vision informed her reasoning. The prospect of more registered voters meant a greater need for citizenship education than ever before. But the tide of the struggle had begun to turn.

As early as 1964, civil rights activists recognized that the movement had reached a crossroads; by 1966, its center appeared to have shifted. SCLC executive staff met at the Penn Center on St. Helena Island that year to reassess what had been accomplished and where the future led. Martin Luther King Jr. identified the difficulties the movement confronted. SCLC had moved into Chicago at the end of 1965, and the campaign in the North had demonstrated that attacking the most visible signs of white supremacy yielded "surface changes" rather than "substantive changes" because it ignored the deeper problems of institutional racism. King urged his colleagues to "face the fact that progress had been limited mainly to the Negro middle class." Changing patterns of thought also had to be considered. "The two phrases we hear most during this particular period," he preached, "are White backlash and Black Power." Characterizing the latter as a "cry of pain," King argued, "White backlash is really White reaction to questions being raised by the Civil Rights Movement which demand a restructuring of the very architecture of American society." The answers to those questions would prove infinitely more expensive and therefore more troublesome. "We are now dealing with issues that relate to the privileged as against the underprivileged," King maintained, and white America "never intended to give on this anyway." Movement activists must continue to grapple with underemployment, inadequate housing, and schools, he charged, all the while insisting on interracial cooperation.[70]

Mississippi CEP state supervisor Victoria Gray, who had joined SCLC's national board by 1965, agreed. "As the struggle shifts from the overcoming of a common enemy to more diverse directions and objectives, the struggle for the minds of the masses presents quite a complicated and complex situation," she stated in her 1965–66 annual report. For Gray, the issue lay in relating abstract movement terms such as "freedom" and "self determination" to people's "daily lives and expectations" so that "they will be able to withstand the pressures and continue to fight for the things of value rather than trading their hard earned freedom for a mess of pottage." Gray's argument resembled Clark's, calling for "increased and extended" citizenship education because when classroom activity shifted to community action, education had proven to be an effective "nucleus for political organizing at the local level." In Mississippi, at least, "people now realize that more is required of them than marching and mass meetings, and this is where our labors pay off."[71]

The necessity of changing course in midstream, however, meant that SCLC reprioritized its spending and its programs. Campaigns in the rural South took a backseat to developing those in urban and northern locales, where the black community confronted more diffuse problems and proved less united. Perhaps because it was designed to be adapted to any local situation, SCLC's citizenship education outside of the South differed as a result. Training in the fundamentals of literacy and consumer education continued, but the overall content stressed preparing poor people for employment rather than preparing a new generation of community organizers.[72]

Throughout 1965 and 1966, SNCC also wrestled with the question of how to achieve fundamental social change. Septima Clark counseled those who had become disenchanted because they felt that other civil rights groups — and especially King — had reaped the glory of their hard work or too often compromised with white liberals. Bernice Johnson Reagon recalled one conversation where "Septima was trying to say to me that I was not seeing something in Dr. King's heart; that I was seeing the way he was being presented and I was responding to a culture that needed a leader." Clark explained to Reagon that King wielded that cultural expectation by lending his image to raise money and keep attention focused on the larger struggle. But her main point was "there was also a Martin Luther King who had another reason for doing what he was doing," and Reagon "wasn't seeing it."[73]

Clark was less successful in her conversations with Stokely Carmichael, who had gone into rural Alabama in 1965 to assist in a voter registration drive instigated by local people. After a deputy sheriff fired into a crowd, killing one of his friends and another white civil rights worker, Carmichael helped found the Lowndes County Freedom Organization, an independent political party that adopted a black panther as its symbol. A few women from Lowndes County visited Clark during her stay in Selma "to tell me that Stokely Carmichael was really overstepping his bounds" and that they "were afraid that all of them would be killed." Clark doubted that Carmichael would have much success until he laid an educational foundation. The people "weren't ready," she stated. "His thinking was up high, and theirs was down low."[74]

Soon thereafter, she met Carmichael and six other SNCC members in Atlanta and tried to talk to them about their frustrations and their growing impatience with nonviolence as a tactical strategy. Like the men of SCLC, "Stokely just laughed," Clark recollected; "he really didn't think well of my ideas, and some of the fellows with him were just hee-hawing at me." She agreed with some of Carmichael's ideas, however. After hearing him tell a group of students at Birmingham's Miles College that if the government wanted to send them to Vietnam, they should demand training at West Point, Clark declared, "I feel that is right." Moreover, she "understood why Stokely felt so angry." Too many arrests, beatings, and slain civil rights workers had led him and others "to feel that black people had to take more initiative," a feeling that ultimately manifested itself in a repudiation of nonviolence. "I don't believe they really wanted open and violent attacks on whites," Clark observed, "but at the very least they wanted blacks to defend themselves."[75]

Militant black radicals occasionally frightened Septima Clark. In 1967, she accompanied King to the National Conference for New Politics, held in Chicago. The gathering, which became the final 1960s attempt to build a radical interracial alliance, brought together a wide array of antiwar, New Left, and African American activists. "There, blacks and whites were against us," Clark remembered. "They were *tired* of this foolish stuff of nonviolence." As King addressed the convention, she continued, "they started parading with banners" that read "Down with nonviolence!" Clark remained after King left and attended smaller meetings with African American groups. "They just considered me a foolish old woman, but they didn't harm me. I expected them to, but they didn't." Before the end of the conference, some participants had even elected Clark to speak for them in the large meetings because they valued her ability to persuade others to listen to what she had to say. "She quiet everybody down," Johns Islander Bill Saunders asserted. "She had the ability to settle things. She was ordained to mediate and console." Years later, Clark confessed, "I feel that the Black Power boys were a little bit too radical. I think we needed just such people, but I think we needed to try to find out more about the facts."[76] Clark certainly grasped the links between black political and economic self-determination and community development articulated by Carmichael and others. It was not ideology that distanced her from them. It was a matter of methods.

Clark kept her eye primarily trained on the southern struggle. She spent more than a week in May 1966 in Wilcox County, Alabama, assisting get-out-the-vote efforts. Explaining local people's continuing difficulties in surmounting their fears, she reported, "It was hard for them to come off a plantation and be sworn in by the plantation boss who was a poll watcher." Admitting later that summer that the CEP's "administrative force is sadly depleted," Clark still found reason to be optimistic. After returning from helping CEP teachers start classes in Grenada, Mississippi, she described what she had witnessed: white state troopers assigned to guard picketing African Americans; "a 100% selective buying campaign in progress"; black Mississippians "registering in large numbers"; 170 black children attending formerly all-white schools; and "Negro school teachers taking an active part and marching every night to the courthouse." Participation by public school teachers she judged as evidence of "a new kind of courage." Clark lent her fund-raising talents to the Grenada activists by soliciting support from West Coast donors for a supermarket the black community hoped to build. "Such a venture," she wrote, "will mean jobs for Negroes and in turn will put money in the Negro community which will help them get better housing and improved education."[77]

Meanwhile, the Citizenship School teachers whom Clark had helped to train continued to carry forward the organizing torch. Addressing the intersection of racial discrimination and economic inequality that civil rights activism had exposed, President Johnson announced his plan to build a Great Society in early 1964 and then pushed a slew of antipoverty measures through Congress. The Office of Economic Opportunity (OEO), created that August and headed by Sargent Shriver, coordinated the network of federal programs that targeted employment, health care, and education. Through its most pioneering and contentious initiative, the Community Action Program (CAP), the OEO channeled one billion dollars to community-based antipoverty programs in its first year and double that amount during the following two years, seeking to provide people with a "hand up, not a handout." The Johnson administration's War on Poverty signaled the boldest expansion of federal social welfare initiatives since the New Deal. Aside from the considerable economic prosperity of the mid-1960s, "maximum feasible participation" by the poor in planning and administering community grants distinguished these programs from efforts launched three decades earlier.[78] In the South, that meant reserving a place for African Americans at the decision-making table.

CEP-trained women seized the opportunities stemming from the War on Poverty to establish community health and child care centers as well as job training and educational programs and to seek paid employment for the movement work they had been performing with little remuneration. As Septima Clark told one colleague, "Many of our Citizenship School teachers have jobs paying $125 a week in Mississippi in the OEO programs in the state." Others relied on OEO services to secure relief for those who continued to face reprisals for their political activism. Lorraine Howard, a CEP teacher from Taliaferro County, Georgia, testified, "We've helped people get back on welfare that was cut off unjust. We've helped needed families get clothes and surplus food. We've helped people to find houses to move in, after their landlord told them to move after they registered." As the nation's attention turned north and west and from civil rights to Black Power—and with individual and private contributions for southern civil rights initiatives decreasing as a result—local activists viewed these federal programs as a much-needed source of financial support. They also accrued new status from paid positions despite the fact that they remained concentrated in lower-paying jobs. In both the rural and urban South, the CAPs offered black women an avenue for extending and reaffirming their political and social welfare commitments.[79]

Many CEP teachers and alumni especially focused on addressing the needs of African American children through Head Start, which became the OEO's most successful and lasting CAP. Launched nationwide in the summer of 1965, when thirty-two states did not offer kindergarten programs, Head Start provided half a million poor children with two nutritious meals a day, basic medical services, and sought to instill in them the confidence they would need as future learners. Planners emphasized the importance of parental involvement for improving children's daily environments. Doing so not only offered a way to educate and to begin to empower parents alongside their children but also coincided with the OEO's goal of creating jobs for poor adults.

Reports from CEP teachers confirmed their recognition of Head Start as an arena in which they could practice what they had learned through citizenship education. They knew how to identify sources of federal funding and to apply for grants. They knew how to teach in an environment where the official pedagogical recommendations included maintaining a "flexible schedule," relying on role-playing to stimulate the imagination, and strengthening communication and verbal skills. In the summer of 1965, Keysville, Georgia, CEP teacher Emma Dean Roberson noted her membership on an executive committee that had secured an OEO grant to launch Head Start, "an integrated project, the *first* in Burke County." "We have brought Project Head Start into 5 centers in Dorchester County and we are now working on other Anti-[Poverty] Programs," the Reverend Lewis H. Simmons of Summerville, South Carolina, wrote. Ethel Grimball, the first Citizenship School teacher on Wadmalaw Island, became a director in a local Head Start center. From Shreveport, Earnestine Germany reported that she had helped people in Greenwood, Louisiana, get their Head Start program under way, while Mary L. Love confessed that she had suspended citizenship school classes in Gadsden, Alabama, to work "in the Head Start program for eight weeks."[80]

The Child Development Group of Mississippi (CDGM) initially spearheaded Head Start in the Magnolia State. In its first year, CDGM operated the nation's largest and best-funded Head Start program, employing 1,100 people in eighty-four centers that served 6,000 children. After the session officially ended and before the CDGM had secured its second grant, workers continued to operate classes for 3,000 children without pay, providing food and transportation at their own expense. CDGM administrators specifically concentrated staff recruiting efforts among those who had civil rights credentials. Grassroots activists who identified with the FDP and the CEP claimed the project as their own. Victoria Gray later stated that CEP alumni saw themselves "bringing citizenship education to Head Start, issues and all." In other words, these activists used Head Start as another educational organizing tool and a vehicle for passing on the lessons gleaned elsewhere in the movement to both a younger generation and their parents. Yet Gray reported in 1966, "Many of our citizenship teachers and/or students now hold key positions on most of these programs, but they are having to fight to retain their positions because of their knowledge of the intended context of the programs and their unwillingness to see them subverted."[81] She referred to the controversial provision that provided for "maximum feasible participation" by the poor in the CAPs, a requirement that had serious political ramifications both locally and nationally.

Mississippi's white leaders understood that in channeling federal money directly to the poor, the OEO had bypassed traditional patronage networks. White officials also saw that civil rights activists sought to use the "maximum feasible participation" clause to increase the political power of black Mississippians who advocated racial equality. Where white supremacists had always raised the banner of "local control" to preserve segregation in public education, they believed that the CAPs placed too much local control in the wrong hands. Threatened with political impotence, they established alternate CAP agencies to compete with black activists for OEO grants. Segregationist whites dominated these boards; the African Americans appointed were handpicked "moderates" from the professional class who disapproved of the movement and who went along with decisions made by white Mississippians. Mississippi senator John Stennis, who sat on the Senate Appropriations Committee, which funded both the War on Poverty and the war in Vietnam, launched an investigation to prove to OEO officials that the CDGM had mismanaged its funds.[82]

The quality of Head Start programs varied from place to place, but federal bureaucratization introduced fresh problems as well. CEP teachers had been trained to keep class records and encouraged to submit annual reports to provide evidence of the program's efficacy for the foundations funding the work. Some completed this task better than others. The rapid implementation of Head Start left little time to retrain community workers in new methods of record keeping. The original inability to navigate federal bureaucratic requirements might have been surmountable, however, had it not been for the OEO's acquiescence to considerable pressure at the national level from local politicians, powerful segregationist senators and congressmen, and traditional social service organizations, curtailing the "maximum feasible participation" by the poor.[83]

Involvement by CEP alumni with Head Start and other antipoverty programs had repercussions. On one hand, the preoccupation with new endeavors constituted a potential liability for the CEP's continued existence. On the other, it signaled that the CEP had achieved its goal of educating for individual and communal empowerment. In the last half of the 1960s, citizenship participation replaced citizenship education in many communities. Moreover, the fact that the black women who passed through the CEP had begun to concentrate on a plethora of community projects underscores the reality that local movements persisted.

For example, Septima Clark had first visited the piedmont town of Monroe, North Carolina, six months after local leader Robert F. Williams, who publicly eschewed nonviolence in favor of "armed self-reliance," had been forced to flee the country in the summer of 1961. Clark met Ethel Azalea Johnson, a loyal Williams supporter as well as a cofounder and columnist for *The Crusader*, the local movement's official organ, and recruited her to go to Dorchester. Citizenship School classes began in Monroe in 1962. Three years later, Johnson reviewed her annual activities: she had conducted two classes with a combined enrollment of thirty-nine students and helped four hundred people register to vote. Johnson conceded that "the majority of Citizenship work is done outside the classroom because many people will not take the time to attend, so we go to them." Her students led the way in promoting black representation in local government. "The Citizenship Adult Education classes sponsored the first woman candidate for local public office last May," Johnson wrote. Students had also sponsored the local Head Start project, enrolled more than five hundred people in President Johnson's Adult Education program, worked with the elderly to obtain social security benefits, and were in the process of establishing a local chapter of the interracial North Carolina Council on Human Relations. The task of community organizing had imbued Johnson with a long-haul vision of social change: "Citizenship work here never ceases."[84] Unfortunately much of CEP teachers' success remained tied to the Johnson administration's funding of social welfare reform, which became more untenable as costs for the war in Vietnam increased.

Nationally, the interracial civil rights coalition continued to unravel. Escalation of the conflict in Vietnam after 1965 prompted many white liberals to redirect their attention to building an antiwar movement. White women who had been involved in the southern civil rights struggle joined other white women, primarily in the North and among the middle class, in forging a women's liberation movement. Its initial focus on sexism as the predominant problem all women confronted distinguished this movement from the one in which southern black women were engaged. That some black feminists in the urban North and West embraced a nationalist ideology also reflected a repositioning with regard to the civil rights goal of integration. Though engagement with the civil rights movement constituted a seminal experience for both groups, black feminists challenged white women's failure to account for race and class in their analysis and thereby attempted to enlarge the women's movement's definition and agenda.[85]

White conservatives, by contrast, launched a counterrevolution. In his 1968 presidential bid, George Wallace first capitalized on the prevailing sense among urban ethnic minorities and working-class whites and suburban middle-class whites that the federal government had abandoned them. Republican candidate Richard Nixon grasped the significance of Wallace's message but employed more nuanced language on the campaign trail. Septima Clark recognized the Wallace movement and its offshoots for what they were, "evidence of the shift to the right in the attitudes of millions of white voters" informed by "the white man's hatred for the Negro." But she found no reason to be alarmed: "The people who comprise it have always been there, inarticulate and without the shrewd leadership which has now given them cohesiveness." Clark also explained the accompanying change in American political rhetoric. Where communism had been the "scare word" in the 1950s, by the late 1960s it had "been replaced by the phrase 'law and order,' another code for regression and repression, used as a justification for avoiding a constructive approach to the social problems which beset us." Commenting on the nation's sizable number of poor whites, she challenged the misrepresentation of federal poverty programs as primarily intended for and beneficial to African Americans. As proof, Clark observed, CEP staff had begun extending training to poor white communities by late 1967. Moreover, she denounced the "anti-intellectualism" that fueled conservative resentment of "any definition of American Society sharply at odds with its own."[86]

Just like the women she trained, Clark kept refining her ideas. Though she never shared the racial separatism that many black activists embraced after 1966, she thought long and hard about Black Power and incorporated its analyses into her own ruminations. Writing "The Nature of Current Revolts" in 1969, for example, Clark described the ghetto as "the main institution of confinement for the Black population" in the "post-slavery period," complete with a "police occupation force representing the State power of the colonial regime." She condemned "a government which is currently spending $75 billion a year on war and outer space efforts to put a man on the moon" but "has no intention of providing adequate funds to end joblessness, slum conditions, and [to] correct educational deprivation in the ghettos." She explained that if "large segments" of the black community "are not making their appeal" for freedom "by way of moral argument, it is because they have concluded . . . that the leadership of this nation is basically immoral in its dealing with non-white people, the world over." Like other militant activists at the end of the 1960s, Clark had connected her preoccupation with the lack of racial justice in local southern communities to global events.[87]

Clark had prescriptions for these problems. "Liberals rather than urging bigger slices of the education, political, and employment pies for Black Americans must begin to find ways to bake bigger pies," she suggested. Instead of focusing on issues that divided people, "a new coalition of the discontented" should strive to find common ground in "aspirations and concerns which we all share." Job creation had to be tied "not just [to] dead-end jobs, but [to] meaningful work that does not limit the future to the worn and despairing patterns of the past," while educational opportunity had to overcome "the stubborn and selfish unwillingness of the business and political leadership . . . to use our tax money to pay for the kind of schools our children deserve." People needed to see a guaranteed income not as "a give-away to the lazy, but a provision for the helpless, white and black, which is a mark of our compassion and our civilization." Clark considered ignorance another great obstacle: "We need to be taught to study rather than believe, to inquire rather than to affirm"[88]

In a time that witnessed the birth of black studies programs on many university campuses around the nation, Clark reserved a special responsibility for African American scholars to "speak truth about white America" and its systematic oppression. As much as these systems "do not exist apart from individuals," she added, "there is no escape from the fact that all those 'good' white people who support, acquiesce, and encourage Blacks to believe in these systems are the enemy." Finally, Clark urged African American intellectuals to identify the enemy within, to "speak the truth to our tendencies to place all responsibility for Black crime upon white people, to clarify our unspoken desire for white models, white recognition, white legitimization." She concluded, "For it is in the struggle to overcome those inner weaknesses that we generate much of the strength, the energies, and the commitment to move us toward the new building, the new society, the new men and women which are our ultimate goal."[89] Now in her seventh decade, Clark's longevity informed her view of struggle as a natural part of the human condition as well as her insistence that a committed cadre of activist educators must wage the continual battle to make American democracy a reality.

⌒⋆⌒

By the end of the 1960s, Septima Clark may have employed new language, but her radicalism remained grounded in four decades of experience as a black woman educator and civic organizer. Historically, black women had accorded their community's physical, emotional, and psychological well-being equal weight with its obtaining political power. For Clark, that view meant that practical solutions mattered more than ideological theories. "I have been trying all my days to solve problems," she observed, "and problems — bothersome ones at any rate — are annoyingly specific."[90] Clark's influence proved far-reaching because she devoted herself to educating and mobilizing southern black communities by training a new corps of black women to lead the endeavor.

Public recognition of black women's activities was another matter entirely. Clark later characterized "the way the men looked at the women" as "one of the weaknesses of the civil rights movement." The members of the predominantly male SCLC executive board "didn't have any faith in women, none whatsoever. They just thought that women were sex symbols and had no contribution to make," she reflected. Having grown up in a house where her mother was the boss and having spent more than three decades working with women in civic groups, Clark knew better. But within SCLC, she added, women "were never able to put ourselves on the agenda to speak to the group." Men's failure to listen did not stop Clark from pressing forward, and according to Andrew Young, Martin Luther King Jr. had gained a greater appreciation for her contributions to SCLC by the end of his life.[91] In the meantime, what black women *did* in their communities testified to what they had acquired personally from the CEP. Admitting the difficulty in launching a local movement, one citizenship education veteran asserted, "We were just existing then. If we had not done this, where would we be today?"[92] How many women teachers and graduates of the CEP could pose the exact same question?

Multiple factors beyond any single individual's control contributed to the fact that the CEP ceased operating in 1970. Yet these factors cannot be analyzed apart from the reality that the program represented a preeminent site of black women's activism, which itself underscores a deeper truth: had black women succeeded in putting their concerns on the SCLC's agenda, the organization might have adopted different priorities. For example, SCLC never established the permanent citizenship education centers that CEP staff identified in the mid-1960s as critical to equipping folk to anticipate and then overcome future impediments to the freedom struggle. On this issue alone, how much did it matter that Septima Clark's opinions carried less weight? The shift to northern and urban campaigns also affected the allocation of scarce resources within SCLC. If black women had had a voice in SCLC's financial decisions, funds might have been appropriated differently. Then, too, the Voting Rights Act's eradication of literacy requirements dovetailed with SCLC's concentration on economic inequality in the second half of the decade, reducing demand for a program that emphasized practical literacy as a necessary prerequisite for political and economic literacy. This change may have made black women's contributions within the CEP appear less valuable. Even the CEP's most sympathetic male observer failed to appreciate what had been accomplished by the end of the decade. Andrew Young lamented in 1969, "It is impossible to measure or to see the impact of this program on our overall efforts toward social change" because "we have left no visible evidence of our work and our presence in the community."[93] Young looked for confirmation of SCLC's institutional health rather than for an independent if occasionally beleaguered activism that persevered at the local level.

Septima Clark certainly read more promising outcomes when she claimed that black women moved from exerting "very little" local leadership at the beginning of the movement to "speaking out" by the mid-1960s. Clark saw the civil rights movement as a women's movement, one whose significance could be measured in black women's making their voices heard in the broader society as much as in their registering to vote.[94] The CEP became the forum in which Clark transferred to a new generation both the philosophy and the know-how of an earlier cohort of black women. As such, the ongoing activism of CEP alumni in the 1960s must be understood as reflecting an enduring political culture among southern black women, premised on answering a wide range of community needs. In comparison, SCLC arrived at that agenda rather late. Moreover, as the overwhelming presence of CEP teachers and students within Head Start and other OEO programs suggests, black women linked their local activism to national opportunities. Contemplating the life-long commitment that citizenship education inspired among the grassroots, Victoria Gray remarked, "Some people were in the movement, and that was wonderful. But for those people who the movement was in them, once it gets in you, it's there forever."[95]

Epilogue
A Right to the Tree of Life

It was an appetizing menu. Diners sipped "nonviolent vegetable juice" before munching on "community green salad" with "educated Thousand Island dressing." "Registered rice" and "stuffing with voting giblet gravy" accompanied half of a "citizenship roast chicken" as the entrée. Of course there were "equality and peace rolls with butter." "Love lemon pie" left only a hint of tartness on the sweet finish and complemented the "black and white coffee and tea."[1] Always one to enjoy a hearty meal, Septima Clark savored such tasty fare at her Southern Christian Leadership Conference (SCLC) retirement dinner in Charleston on June 19, 1970. Clark looked forward to moving home. It had been fourteen years since she had lived full time in her native city. Unlike most retirees, the seventy-two-year-old Clark did not spend her twilight years passing peaceful days with family and friends or vacationing. Rather, like the Citizenship School teachers she had trained, she kept organizing in her local community.

Throughout the 1970s and 1980s, Clark continued to focus on education and politics, black children, care for the elderly, and women's issues. In 1972, she won election to the Charleston County School Board, the same body that had fired her for belonging to the National Association for the Advancement of Colored People sixteen years earlier.[2] As the lone African American and first woman on the board, Clark promoted improvements for teachers and students and tried to ensure that African Americans had a representative place in the curriculum. When members evaluated a proposed booklet on American government, for example, Clark pointed out that it included no black people. "I wanted to know who the black children would have to look up to in that book." "There was nothing in there that would help black chil-

*Andrew Young and Septima Clark at her retirement celebration,
Charleston, 1970. Courtesy of the Avery Research Center for African
American History and Culture, College of Charleston.*

dren to feel that they had a right to the tree of life," she continued, "and I know how important that is." Behind the scenes, Clark worked to secure scholarships for black youth. As the superintendent noted, "few in the community, other than the donor or recipient, are aware of this great human service since she never seeks praise or publicity."[3]

Given the events of her career, Clark recognized the importance of school board policies that guaranteed teachers' right to speak freely both inside and outside of the classroom. On one occasion, Clark defended a teacher whom the board planned to fire because she had "been telling her children about standing up for their rights" and "because she will speak out." Clark judged other factors as more indicative of the woman's capabilities: "She has put on dramas. . . . She has gone down to Dafuskie Island with the children and carried gifts at Christmas time. These are the kinds of things you ought to note." Clark conceded that the businessmen who predominated on the school board were "not very concerned about teachers, so I'm still in the minority."[4] Meeting her associates where they were, she tried to persuade them to fill job vacancies and increase retention rates by offering bonuses to teachers.

Clark firmly believed in providing citizenship education to students. She prioritized teaching youth "how change comes about" and helping them "to develop their own thinking and not accept unjust things but . . . change them." In 1981, when President Ronald Reagan announced cuts in educational funding, she connected children's learning to political action that depended on parental involvement. "We need to have special money for handicapped kids," but politicians "are voting against those things," she declared. "We need to have physical education, art, and music in first grades. . . . [T]hey claim they want to cut these out. Now we've got to stand up in arms against those cuts, because [the] Reagan cuts haven't gone through Congress yet. And so, don't sit down and accept them. . . . [V]ote against them." Similarly, when her fellow board members argued that the schools should not be involved in health screening for first-grade children, Clark proclaimed, "I want the parents to stand up and say that's part of education." Viewing education in its broadest sense, Clark saw the potential long-term return on wise investments: "I want people to see children as human beings and not think of the money that it costs nor to think of the amount of time that it will take." Instead, society should "think of the lives that can be developed into Americans who will redeem the soul of America and will really make America a great country."[5]

"You bring a balance to the board that is needed," one of Clark's colleagues told her near the end of her first term. "Every time I talk about the importance of 'people helping people,' I think of you. You exemplify this in your actions each day," he wrote when she tendered her resignation in 1982. The superintendent agreed. "In the years that Mrs. Clark has served on the school board, she has had a calming effect on sometimes turbulent school affairs . . . and proved anew that a useful life does not end with retirement."[6]

Septima Clark did not limit her usefulness to the school board. After five children died in five separate Charleston house fires, she joined the city's clubwomen to raise money to build a day care center and to hire a qualified teacher for it. When a car accidentally killed a young girl as she crossed the street, Clark persuaded friends in her civic organizing circle to donate a dollar a month to employ fifteen women as crossing guards at busy intersections.[7] By 1975, Clark served on the Charleston Committee for Day Care; two years later, Alleen Brewer Wood, Bernice Robinson, and Ethel Grimball, the first three Citizenship School teachers on the Sea Islands, sat on the same board. As a member of the Advisory Council for the Aging, Clark voiced her concern with the lack of care for the elderly who lived alone. One woman had drowned when she left her house and walked into a marsh, another had spent two nights sleeping naked by the Ashley River, and another had fallen in her bathtub. Clark made a series of phone calls and composed

Septima Clark talking with students at the University of California at Santa Cruz, early 1970s. Courtesy of the Avery Research Center for African American History and Culture, College of Charleston.

a list of volunteers willing to call older people to check on them.[8] She also stayed active in her sorority, Alpha Kappa Alpha. By 1978, members had launched a program called Parental Involvement Now, designed to increase participation in school and community activities, for which they had secured federal funding. They anticipated using home visits to educate parents on how they might "strengthen their children's skills in reading, language, and arithmetic." Finally, Clark remained involved in the nonpartisan League of Women Voters and signaled her partisan affiliation by becoming a member of the Democratic Women of Charleston County.[9]

Clark's preoccupation with improving the plight of black women also expressed itself in her hometown. In 1969, she provided advice to employees at the Medical College Hospital who formed a union and went on strike for four months. At Clark's invitation, SCLC came to Charleston to assist the strikers. Strike leader Mary Moultrie estimated that "out of 500 or so members" in the newly formed Local 1199, "we had 16 or 17 men" and conceded that the women needed guidance. "We met with Mrs. Clark because of her leadership ability," Moultrie recalled. "Although she was a very quiet leader, she had a lot of experience in things that we knew nothing of. Mrs. Clark was one of the people we went to often." Moultrie claimed that strikers felt more comfortable talking to a woman: "We would just meet with her and talk about the problems we were having and she would tell us things we needed to do in terms of writing letters, that kind of stuff." Clark most likely had encouraged this new cohort of women leaders to think about how to preserve the gains they made during the struggle. After the strike ended, according to Moultrie, "we went out in the community; we went door-to-door and got people registered to vote, because there's power in voting."[10]

Clark aligned herself with national women's organizations as well. She accompanied Virginia Durr to a large meeting of the National Organization of Women in Washington, D.C. Durr wanted Clark "to talk about the women of the South who failed to speak up when they knew what they wanted." Clark also took a keen interest in national organizations formed by black women, such as the Black Women's Community Development Foundation (BWCDF). Founded in 1968, the BWCDF channeled funds to local, nonprofit black women's groups involved in direct action. The BWCDF's philosophic goals mirrored those of the Citizenship Education Program. Beyond bestowing grants to existing organizations, it aided the establishment of new ones by serving as a clearinghouse for funding and leadership training information, thereby enabling "low income women to serve the needs of their communities more effectively." Moreover, the BWCDF financed projects that bore a striking resemblance to those begun by many alumni of the Citizenship Education Program—for example, providing funds to build a day care center, community cannery, and woodcraft cooperative in rural northeastern Mississippi.[11]

In January 1972, Septima Clark joined many movement veterans, including Ella Baker and Fannie Lou Hamer, as well as the head of the Domestic Workers Union and members of the National Welfare Rights Organization, at the BWCDF-sponsored Chicago Symposium for black women. The gathering attracted people who would define the black feminist agenda throughout the decade. Tempers occasionally flared as women of all ages and socioeconomic backgrounds discussed topics that ranged from "adamant opposition to the infiltration of a Marxist-Leninist ideology into the Black community" to images of African Americans in the mass media to the "Black man question." More important, as a summary noted, the symposium served as a forum in which black women from across the nation came together and did not have to "tuck their true feelings and beliefs in the pit of their stomachs or a remote corner of their brains" as they hammered out "a program for action in the next stage of Black development."[12]

A year later, the BWCDF's executive director, Inez Smith Reid, wrote to ask Clark to serve as the national chair for a fund-raising campaign. "We have worked quietly over the past four years and, at our wish, our accomplishments have not been projected into the public eye," Reid observed. Now the BWCDF confronted new difficulties. National budget cuts to federal programs and the dismantling of the Office of Economic Opportunity, which had provided grassroots women with employment and a living wage, meant that many people would expect the BWCDF to fill the void. To make matters worse, the BWCDF's grant had expired in 1972. Having spent seventy-four thousand dollars helping local people to help themselves, the BWCDF apparently ceased to exist by 1975.[13]

Septima Clark discerned that seeds scattered sometimes disappear into the wind, but others take root and yield a bountiful harvest. In the long civil rights era, Clark directed her efforts toward building a radically democratic society by training everyday people to acquire a voice in the decisions that affected their daily lives. Her unceasing work behind the scenes in local civil rights movements, despite her status as an educational expert, reflected her commitment to building that society. Familiar with the tactical invisibility black women had historically used to achieve their goals, Clark also knew that the success of citizenship education depended on trained grassroots women assuming leadership roles in their communities. At the same time, her organizing approach has too often limited Clark and the women she influenced to a supporting role in narratives of the civil rights and women's movements.

One reason for black women's invisibility at the time was the media's expectation that black men or white women would lead. Looking for charismatic leaders, the press found them. Yet another explanation lies in the nature of these women's movement work. The transformative educational preparation that occurred in citizenship education classes proved nearly impossible to capture for newspaper photographs or television broadcasts. It made neither dramatic nor sexy copy. Ironically, this invisibility was precisely the key to the program's success. Clark realized the difference between the media's perspective and the movement she nurtured. "From one end of the South to the other, if you look at the black elected officials and the political leaders," she asserted regarding the earliest postmovement generation, "you find people who had their first involvement in the training program of the Citizenship School."[14]

Attention must also be paid to how leaders functioned within the black community and in broader public realms. Where SCLC privileged having men at the head of the organization and at the front of long lines of marchers, Clark prioritized increasing participation by everyone, thereby propagating a vision of leadership embraced by earlier generations of black activist educators. African American women involved in local civil rights movements relied on a variety of leadership skills to organize their neighbors.[15] Foremost among these skills was "meeting people where they were" and being a good listener. Only then could leaders recognize their community's strategic strengths and diffuse internal conflicts as events unfolded.

In her later years, Septima Clark began to receive recognition for her achievements. Charleston named a day care center and a portion of an expressway after her in 1978 and, as she averred, "I have gotten many plaques." She received the National Education Association's 1976 Race Relations Award; an honorary doctorate of humane letters awarded by the College of Charleston in 1978; a Living Legacy Award bestowed by President Jimmy Carter in 1979; and the Order of the Palmetto, South Carolina's highest honor for civilians, in 1982.[16] Clark believed that such accolades resulted from her ongoing efforts to assist people, particularly black students seeking to go to college. "I always say I don't want to refuse any [requests for help] because I might refuse the very one who's going to do well," she commented. "I see it comes back because of all that recognition I received." She had more personal reasons too. Referring to her grandchildren who shared her home,

Septima Clark shakes hands with President Jimmy Carter after receiving
the Living Legacy Award, 1979. Courtesy of the Avery Research Center for
African American History and Culture, College of Charleston.

Clark admitted, "I want somebody to be able to help them. So I have to keep helping so they will be helped."[17]

Johns Islander Bill Saunders testified to the assistance Clark gave his daughter, who enrolled in the College of Charleston but was unable to find a quiet place to study while living at home. Because of Saunders's political involvement, his friends turned him down as he hunted a room to rent for the girl on the mainland. When he called Clark, she responded, "Well, Bill, I have this spare room but I have just given it out." Then Clark suggested that if he bought a cot, she would let his daughter stay in her bedroom at no charge. "I started crying," Saunders remembered. "Here's this woman at her age, would take my child and put her in her *bedroom*! To stay." Clark's refusal of payment for what she considered service was typical, despite the fact that her financial situation remained shaky. To improve her financial security, she sought reimbursement from the state for the wages and the retirement she had lost when the school board fired her in 1956. She received the first installment in 1976 but had to wait to see if the General Assembly would have enough money in its budget to approve ongoing support thereafter. Thus, when Saunders sat on a local committee to recognize Clark with yet another certificate of appreciation, he reminded everyone, "She's got enough plaques. Let's show how much you love her, but give her some damn money." Speculating on Clark's weaknesses, Saunders remarked, "I told her one time, if God ever charged her for anything, it would have been [for being] too nice." Another movement colleague described her as "caring to a fault."[18]

Prior to her retirement from SCLC, Clark identified the issues that continued to plague the black community and the nation at large:

- "Political systems which have code words like 'bussing' and 'welfare,' 'no quota systems' and 'crime in the streets' to signal their fear of Black people."
- "Economic systems which reject so many of the basic human needs of the poor and the weak in favor of the wealthy."
- "Health care systems which provide neither health nor care for the powerless."
- "Legal and penal systems which persistently place large overwhelming numbers behind bars and which place whites in almost all seats of authority."
- "Energy conservation systems which give our needs the lowest priority and literally leave us out in the cold."
- And a "military system which serves as the only respectable alternative available to Black Youth who have been manacled and rejected by America's other systems."[19]

That this checklist from the late 1960s could still apply to the twenty-first century—perhaps suggesting that such problems have only become more entrenched in the ensuing decades—is sobering.

Equally troubling is the reality that the Johns Island Progressive Club is now deteriorating, its roof long ago collapsed, the breeze prompting tall weeds to dance silently inside what remains of the building. In 2005, Hurricane Katrina and its aftermath exposed the continuing economic and physical vulnerability of black women, children, the elderly, and families and communities on the Gulf Coast as well as the absolute poverty of our government's moral compass and spiritual compassion. The United States currently imprisons more people than any other country in the world, a disproportionate number of them young black men. Moreover, new issues of sustainability in our time complicate the search for solutions and render Clark's idea of baking bigger pies tactically obsolete.

But here again, Septima Clark's life offers guidance. The freedom struggle in which she engaged did not proceed down a straight path. The way took twists and turns and detours and hit dead ends. Clark assumed personal risks and paid personal costs. The significance of what she achieved lies in her choices as she formulated a response to these setbacks. She remained a learner as she matured and with increasing conviction found ways to apply her accumulated wisdom to benefit her community. Nor did she lose faith in her belief that individuals had the wherewithal to find the answers within themselves and the community and to set aside differences to work together to implement them. Clark recognized the need to approach the task imaginatively as well as practically and flexibly. Her personal development as an activist illustrated her awareness that each generation must adapt previous strategies to its particular circumstances. Looking back, Clark asserted that if she had the chance to retrace her steps, "I'd do the same things over and over again." Clark lived to see many of her dreams come true, even as she witnessed the persistence of some problems. Where others bemoaned social and political chaos, she saw an opportunity for new ideas to emerge. "I have a great belief in the fact that whenever there is chaos, it creates wonderful thinking. I consider chaos a gift and this has come during my old age."[20]

As age took its toll on her body, family members moved Septima Clark to the Sea Islands Health Care Center on Johns Island, the health facility established by graduates of the Citizenship Schools. She passed away there on December 15, 1987. Her baby sister, Lorene, stricken by Parkinson's disease, lay in the bed next to her and lived only another month without her Seppie.[21]

⤞❦⤝

A massive oak tree occupies the grounds next door to the Sea Islands Health Center. Locals say it has been there more than fourteen hundred years. It appears stooped, bent, arthritic yet still rises sixty-five feet into the air. Its trunk measures twenty-five-and-a-half feet around, and its largest limb stretches eighty-nine feet. Additional limbs have been supported by wooden boards and coiled wires, while others dip underground and then reemerge. Its shade encompasses seventeen thousand square feet. It does not fit into one photograph, and looks different from every angle. It can tolerate drought. It has survived the wrath of hurricanes and the curse of ever-encroaching development. It has survived ownership. It carries scars on its bark and ancient memories tucked in knobby creases. Some say that this *Quercus vir-*

giniana recalls the Old South. Island women weave sea grass baskets under its canopy. Elderly island people — grandmothers and grandfathers — take youngsters to stand beside the Angel Oak, not so they will feel small but so they might imagine, staring up and out as far as they can see, how deep its roots go.[22]

$$\mathscr{Appendix}$$

South Carolina Educational Statistics

TABLE 1. South Carolina Expenditures on Pupils and Teacher Salaries

Year	Average per Pupil Spent*	Average Teacher Salary	Differential
1920–21	White: $39.26 Black: $4.84	White: $773.33 Black: $225.47	State spends 8.1 times more per white pupil; white teachers earn 3.4 times more
1924–25	White: $56.32 Black: $7.25	White: $950.37 Black: $296.84	State spends 7.8 times more per white pupil; white teachers earn 3.2 times more
1931–32	White: $37.62 Black: $6.12	White: $868.00 Black: $272.00	State spends 6 times more per white pupil; white teachers earn 3.2 times more
1938–39	White: $45.67 Black: $10.49	White: $937.00 Black: $380.00	State spends 4.4 times more per white pupil; white teachers earn 2.5 times more
1942–43**	White: $68.00 Black: $23.00	White: $1,091.00 Black: $538.00	State spends approx. 3 times more per white pupil; white teachers earn 2 times more
1949–50	White: $113.00 Black: $54.00	White: $2,131.00 Black: $1,498.00	State spends 2.1 times more per white pupil; white teachers earn 1.4 times more

Sources: All figures from the *Annual Report of the State Superintendent of Education of the State of South Carolina*. 1920–21: *Fifty-Third Annual Report*, 289 and 291. 1924–25: *Fifty-Seventh Annual Report*, 7 and 8. 1931–32: *Sixty-Fourth Annual Report*, 80 and 81. 1938–39: *Seventy-First Annual Report*, 154 and 155. 1942–43: *Seventy-Fifth Annual Report*, 171. 1949–50: *Eighty-Second Annual Report*, 232 and 235.

* All per-pupil expenditures are according to enrollment, with the exception of 1942–43. Spending in that school year is based on "annual cost per pupil in average daily attendance for current expenses," as figures according to enrollment were not provided.

** Salary figures follow the Supreme Court's *Alston v. City School Board of Norfolk* ruling that states must equalize black and white teachers' salaries.

TABLE 2. Suspects Apprehended by Juvenile Officers in Charleston, S.C., 1916

Age	Black Male	White Male	Black Female	White Female
10 years and under	23	6	1	6
11 to 14 years	77	10	4	0
15 to 19 years	48	18	4	4
20 years+	3	1	1	1
No age given	16	2	1	N/A
Total*	167	37	11	11

Source: "Police Reports, February 22, 1916 to December 27, 1916, Complete Year: Juvenile Cases," box 2, folder 141, Hyde Papers.
* The race of offenders was unclear in 31 cases. These are not included in the total.

TABLE 3. 1940–41 and 1941–42 Annual Salary Increases Signed by South Carolina Governor Burnet R. Maybank Jr.

Teacher Group	1940–41 Salary	1941–42 Salary and (No. of Teachers)	Amount Increase
Elementary: white men	$998.00	$1,084.00 (442)	$86.00
Elementary: black men	$411.00	$525.00 (641)	$114.00
Elementary: white women	$856.00	$928.00 (5,931)	$72.00
Elementary: black women	$372.00	$423.00 (4,520)	$51.00
High School: white men	$1,433.00	$1,634.00 (888)	$201.00
High School: black men	$600.00	$669.00 (355)	$69.00
High School: white women	$960.00	$1,021.00 (2,178)	$61.00
High School: black women	$506.00	$575.00 (340)	$69.00

Sources: For 1940–41 school year, *Seventy-Third Annual Report of the State Superintendent of Education of the State of South Carolina, 1941*, 178. For 1941–42 school year: *Seventy-Fourth Annual Report of the State Superintendent of Education of the State of South Carolina, 1942*, 202–3.

TABLE 4. Changes to South Carolina's Teacher Certification Requirements, 1945

Class	Educational Requirement	Grade (NTE Score)
1	M.A.	A or B
2	B.A. +18 hours graduate credit	A, B, C
3	B.A.	A, B, C, D
4	60 hours college credit	A, B, C, D
5	Less than 60 hours college credit	A, B, C, D

Source: *Requirements for Teacher Education and Certification Adopted by State Board of Education 1945*, rev. ed. (Columbia: State of South Carolina Department of Education, 1948), 46–50. Though this is a revised edition, the categories in the table above did not change from the original 1945 proposal. Instead, additional categories, which I have not included, were eliminated from the original plan.

TABLE 5. South Carolina Teachers' Salary Figures
Following Recertification, 1945–46

	Total Number of Teachers	Class					Grade: Based on NTE Score			
		1	2	3	4	5	A	B	C	D
White	10,312	606	285	6,453	1,932	1,036	4,113	5,720	437	42
		6%	3%	63%	19%	10%	40%	55%	4%	<1%
Black	5,967	42	54	2,055	2,065	1,751	250	2,313	1,938	1,466
		<1%	<1%	34%	35%	29%	4%	39%	32%	25%

Source: *Seventy-eighth Annual Report of the State Superintendent of Education of the State of South Carolina* (1945–46), 174.
Note: Class 1 and Class 2 were reserved for teachers with postundergraduate educational training. Ninety-one percent of all white and 98 percent of all black teachers in South Carolina held Class 3 certificates or lower following recertification. Yet a disproportionate number of black teachers remained clustered in the lowest salary range due to their scores on the NTE. For example, all teachers in Class 3 had earned B.A. degrees, but those who held 3A certificates received a higher salary than those who held 3B; 3B holders were paid more than 3C; and 3C more than 3D.

Notes

Abbreviations

The following abbreviations are used throughout the notes.

AR	*Annual Report of the State Superintendent of Education of the State of South Carolina.* Various publishers, 1915–59
ARC	Avery Research Center for the Study of African American History and Culture, College of Charleston, Charleston, S.C.
CBC Minute Books	City Board of Commissioners Minute Books, Charleston County School District, Office of Archives and Records, Charleston, S.C.
CCSD	Charleston County School District, Office of Archives and Records, Charleston, S.C.
Clark Papers	Septima Poinsette Clark Papers, Avery Research Center for the Study of African American History and Culture, College of Charleston, Charleston, S.C.
CNC	*Charleston News and Courier*
CPL	*Columbia Palmetto Leader*
Cornwell Collection	Ruby Cornwell Collection, Avery Research Center for the Study of African American History and Culture, College of Charleston, Charleston, S.C.
CRC	Septima Clark and Bernice Robinson Collection, Avery Research Center for the Study of African American History and Culture, College of Charleston, Charleston, S.C.
CS	*Columbia State*
F. P. Adams Interview	Fannie Phelps Adams, interview by author, Columbia, S.C., April 16, 2002, in author's possession
Gray Papers	Wil Lou Gray Papers, South Caroliniana Library, University of South Carolina, Columbia
Grimball Interview	Ethel Grimball, interview by author, Wadmalaw Island, S.C., February 26, 2002, in author's possession
Hall Interview	Septima Poinsette Clark, interview by Jacquelyn Hall, Charleston, S.C., July 25, 1976, Southern Oral History Project, Wilson Library, University of North Carolina, Chapel Hill
Harleston Papers	Edwin Augustus Harleston Papers, South Carolina Historical Society, Charleston

HERC	Highlander Education and Research Center, New Market, Tenn.
Highlander Papers	Highlander Research and Education Center Papers, 1917–1978, Social Action Collection, Wisconsin Historical Society, Madison
H. S. Simons Collection	Harriet Stoney Simons Collection, South Carolina Historical Society, Charleston
McCray Papers	John Henry McCray Papers, microfilm, Sterling Memorial Library, Yale University, New Haven, Conn.
NAACP Papers	Papers of the National Association for the Advancement of Colored People (microfilm), Sterling Memorial Library, Yale University, New Haven, Conn.
Poinsette-Fisher Interview	Elizabeth Poinsette-Fisher, interview by author, Charleston, S.C., May 27, 2002, in author's possession
Robinson Interview	Bernice Robinson, interview by Sue Thrasher and Eliot Wigginton, New Market, Tenn., November 9, 1980, HERC
SCLC Papers	Southern Christian Leadership Conference Papers, King Center, Atlanta, Ga.
SEB Papers	Southern Education Board Papers, Wilson Library, University of North Carolina, Chapel Hill
SOCAR	South Caroliniana Library, University of South Carolina, Columbia
SPC Interview	Septima Poinsette Clark, interview, Johns Island, S.C., n.d., box 1a, folder 4, Septima Poinsette Clark Papers, Avery Research Center for the Study of African American History and Culture, College of Charleston, Charleston, S.C.
Thrasher Interview	Septima Clark, interview by Sue Thrasher, New Market, Tenn., June 20, 1981, Highlander Education and Research Center, New Market, Tenn.
T. R. Waring Papers	Thomas R. Waring Jr. Papers, South Carolina Historical Society, Charleston
J. W. Waring Papers	Judge Julius Waties Waring Papers, Moorland-Spingarn Research Center, Howard University, Washington, D.C.
Wood Interview	Septima P. Clark, interview by Peter H. Wood, Charleston, S.C., February 3, 1981, Avery Research Center for the Study of African American History, College of Charleston, Charleston, S.C.

Introduction

1. Bernice Robinson, "Report from the Field, April 18, 1964," ser. 3, box 155, folder 30, SCLC Papers.

2. Studies that have located the civil rights movement's origins in the World War II years often discuss the war's impact on the deeds of male veterans without considering

how home front battles radicalized black women. See Dittmer, *Local People*; Tyson, *Radio Free Dixie*.

3. Andrew Young, interview by author, Atlanta, Ga., January 29, 2002, in author's possession; "Citizenship Education Report," January 1968, box 23, folder 24, Clark Papers.

4. Bernice Robinson, "Report from the Field, April 18, 1964," ser. 3, box 155, folder 30, SCLC Papers.

5. Most studies credit Highlander and its radical pedagogy for shaping the program's success. See, for example, Aimee Isgrig Horton, *Highlander Folk School*; Morris, *Origins*. Both authors concede Clark's importance in establishing the program. Additional published articles on Clark and the Citizenship Schools include Brown-Nagin, "Transformation"; Cuthbert-Kerr, "'You Don't Have to Make the X'"; Rouse, "'We Seek to Know.'"

6. See Brown, "Negotiating and Transforming"; Hahn, *Nation*, esp. pt. 2.

7. On the church, see, for example, Branch, *Parting the Waters*; Branch, *Pillar of Fire*; Branch, *At Canaan's Edge*; Fairclough, *To Redeem the Soul*; Garrow, *Bearing*. On key debates in the movement's historiography, including its institutional foundations, mobilization strategies, definitions of leadership, and gender dynamics, see Lawson, "Freedom Then, Freedom Now," esp. 459.

8. Lu Ann Jones makes a similar point about teachers in her study of southern rural farm women (*Mama Learned Us*, 143). On Progressive Era black women's activism more broadly, see Gilmore, *Gender and Jim Crow*; White, *Too Heavy a Load*; Higginbotham, *Righteous Discontent*; Shaw, *What a Woman Ought to Be*.

9. See, for example, James D. Anderson, *Education of Blacks*; Chirhart, *Torches of Light*; Walker, *Their Highest Potential*; Heather Andrea Williams, *Self-Taught*; Michele Foster, "Constancy."

10. For critiques of black teachers during the civil rights movement, see Fairclough, "'Being in the Field'"; Payne, *I've Got the Light*, chap. 5, esp. 177. Fairclough has amended his original view somewhat but still falls short in his attention to gender; see Fairclough, *Class of Their Own*; Fairclough, "Costs of *Brown*."

11. Kluger, *Simple Justice*, reveals how pressure from the bottom up generated structural change through the courts but does not position white retaliation in relation to both local and national educational trends. See also Baker, *Paradoxes*.

12. For examples of the class bias often inherent in African American notions of uplift, see Gaines, *Uplifting*; Hunter, *To 'Joy My Freedom*.

13. Clark's literacy-focused approach represents a practical expression of Paulo Freire's theory of critical literacy, which links the ability to read with reconstituting one's relationship to the wider society. See, for example, Freire and Maceo, *Literacy*, esp. 1–27; Freire, *Education*; Freire, *Pedagogy*. See also Clark, "Literacy and Liberation."

14. Clark, *Ready from Within*, 126.

15. Ibid.

16. A closer look inside local classrooms and communities accentuates the emerging consensus that there were many civil rights movements rather than one monolithic struggle. See, for example, Dittmer, *Local People*; Payne, *I've Got the Light*; Tyson, *Radio Free Dixie*. A number of local studies make this point obliquely. See, for example, Chafe,

Civilities and Civil Rights; Eskew, *But for Birmingham*; Fairclough, *Race and Democracy*; Norrell, *Reaping the Whirlwind*. For a more recent work that self-consciously discusses civil right movements, see the essays collected in Theoharis and Woodard, *Groundwork*.

17. See Payne, *I've Got the Light*.

18. Woman-centered studies of the movement include Collier-Thomas and Franklin, *Sisters in the Struggle*; Crawford, Rouse, and Woods, *Women*; Greene, *Our Separate Ways*; Olsen, *Freedom's Daughters*. Useful memoirs and biographies include Bates, *Long Shadow*; Fleming, *Soon We Will Not Cry*; Lee, *For Freedom's Sake*; Moody, *Coming of Age*; Ransby, *Ella Baker*; Robinson, *Montgomery Bus Boycott*. For exciting new scholarship, see Frystak, *Our Minds on Freedom*; Hamlin, "'Book Hasn't Closed.'"

19. Clark, *Ready from Within*, 83. Clark then went on to discuss women's contributions to the 1955 Montgomery Bus Boycott.

20. See Standley, "Role of Black Women," esp. 198, 201. Robnett, *How Long? How Long?*, argues that the civil rights movement succeeded as a consequence of its gendered divisions of leadership.

21. Many scholars have demonstrated that the white and black women who founded the first explicitly feminist organizations experienced their ideological awakenings through their involvement in the civil rights movement. Most often, however, such studies identify SNCC as a point of origin and then discuss groups founded by women in the urban North and West. See Breines, *Trouble between Us*; Evans, *Personal Politics*; Springer, *Living*; Baxandall, "Re-Visioning"; Williams, "Black Women, Urban Politics." Greene's *Our Separate Ways*, a southern-based study, is a notable exception.

22. Roth, whose work focuses on women outside of the South, has argued that black, white, and Chicana feminist groups emerged simultaneously. She advocates a conceptual framework of "feminisms" (*Separate Roads*). See also Thompson, "Multiracial Feminism."

23. See Nasstrom, "Down to Now"; Payne's bibliographic essay in *I've Got the Light*, 413–41. See also Hall, "Long Civil Rights Movement." On the issue of sexism within SNCC, see Robnett, "Women"; Breines, *Trouble between Us*, esp. chap. 1.

24. Victoria Gray Adams, interview by author, Petersburg, Va., April 22, 2002, in author's possession. For a recent study that explicitly takes up similar issues, see Romano and Raiford, *Civil Rights Movement*.

25. See, for example, Andrews, *To Tell a Free Story*; Braxton, *Black Women*; Butterfield, *Black Autobiography*; Foster, *Written by Herself*.

26. Clark, *Ready from Within*, 82.

27. Ruby Cornwell, interview by author, James Island, S.C., April 11, 2002, in author's possession.

28. Stephanie Gilmore has ruminated on the relationship between women's life stages and their activism ("Regenerating Women's History").

29. Young, interview.

30. Clark, *Ready from Within*, 114.

31. See Ling, "Gender and Generation," esp. 103.

32. Clark's willingness to discuss private matters in Citizenship School training sessions differed from her choosing to conceal them from an interracial public. In this, she engaged black women's "culture of dissemblance" in the broader world. See Hine, "Rape." Clark also differed from Ella Baker, who kept her marriage a secret from movement coworkers (Ransby, *Ella Baker*, 8–9). For an alternative view of black women's tradition of speaking out, particularly in relation to sexual violence, see McGuire, "'It Was Like All of Us.'"

33. Russell Brown, president of the Charleston NAACP branch, provided this characterization to bureau agents. See document dated September 21, 1967, in U.S. Department of Justice, Federal Bureau of Investigation, Subject: Clark, Septima Poinsette, File. 157-4505, section 1, in author's possession.

34. Clark, *Ready from Within*, 124.

Chapter One

1. Wood Interview. Additional information here is drawn from Clark, *Echo*, 13–16; Clark, *Ready from Within*, 87–89. A note on naming: when referring to Clark in "real time" as a young girl, I call her Septima Poinsette; when referring to an older Clark remembering her childhood, I call her Septima Clark. On black washerwomen's autonomy, see Hunter, *To 'Joy My Freedom*, esp. chap. 4.

2. On South Carolina's Reconstruction-era black leadership, see Holt, *Black over White*, esp. 9–22, 122–34. More broadly, see Foner, *Reconstruction*; Hahn, *Nation*, esp. pts. 1 and 2.

3. See Kantrowitz, *Ben Tillman*, esp. chap. 2. See also Holt, *Black over White*, 211–17.

4. Kantrowitz, *Ben Tillman*, 64–70, 206–9, 216, 221–28. See also Tindall, *South Carolina Negroes*, 81–91. On the streetcars, see Powers, *Black Charlestonians*, 265.

5. Clark, *Echo*, 147. Edward Ball's national best seller underscores Charleston's long memory (*Slaves in the Family*, 8–9).

6. On the South Carolina–Barbadian connection, see Dunn, *Sugar and Slaves*, chap. 3, esp. 111–16. See also Berlin, *Many Thousands Gone*, chaps. 3, 6, 11; Fraser, *Charleston! Charleston!*, 135–68, chap. 4, esp. 244.

7. See Gomez, *Exchanging*, 21–23; Wood, *Black Majority*; Raphael, *People's History*, chap. 6; Drago, *Initiative*, chap. 1, esp. 29–36; Fields, *Lemon Swamp*, 5, 29, 36–37; Fraser, *Charleston! Charleston!*, 63; *Charleston South Carolina*, 59. Drago argues that Charleston's antebellum free black population was "too small to sustain" the three-tier system. Still, many local attitudes and practices — including caste-based segregation within Charleston's black community — reflected its ideology.

8. Blight, *Race and Reunion*. See also Connerton, *How Societies Remember*; Foucault, *Language*; Morrison, *Playing*; Balibar and Wallerstein, *Race, Nation, Class*, chap. 5.

9. Glymph, "'Liberty Dearly Bought,'" 114, 117, 126, 132 n. 11; Balibar and Wallerstein, *Race, Nation, Class*, chap. 5. I borrow the term "memory-work" from Glymph, whose observations regarding the shortcomings of the term "counter-memory," which presupposes a white norm as a point of reference, are particularly relevant. See also Barbara Jeanne Fields, "Ideology and Race"; Higginbotham, "African-American Women's History."

10. H. White, *Tropics*, 94. Adding another level of interpretation to White's, I argue that events cannot be understood apart from the process of remembering them, through which they acquire meaning.

11. Alvin Anderson, interview by author, Atlanta, Ga., January 27, 2002, in author's possession. Born in 1936, Anderson was a neighbor and close family friend of the Poinsettes. See also Fields, *Lemon Swamp*, 11; Ball, *Slaves in the Family*; Ball, *Sweet Hell Inside*.

12. Drago, *Initiative*, 16–17, 24. Drago notes that 132 of Charleston's 1,845 free blacks owned slaves. See also Berlin, *Slaves without Masters*.

13. Fields, *Lemon Swamp*, 24.

14. Brundage, "White Women," esp. 115–16. See also Brundage, *Southern Past*, esp. chap. 4; Cox, *Dixie's Daughters*; Yuhl, *Golden Haze*; Blight, "W. E. B. Du Bois," esp. 51–52; Glymph, "'Liberty Dearly Bought.'"

15. Alvin Anderson, interview. See also Verner, *Mellowed by Time*, 67.

16. Victoria Poinsette quoted in Alvin Anderson, interview.

17. Ibid.; Yvonne Clark, interview by author, Atlanta, Ga., January 26, 2002, in author's possession. Yvonne Clark is Septima Clark's granddaughter and grew up in Charleston.

18. See Freeman, *Rewriting the Self*, chap. 2, esp. 46–49, chap. 7, esp. 185–98; Brown, "Negotiating and Transforming."

19. Septima Clark estimated that at the end of the Civil War, her father was between fifteen and eighteen years old, meaning he would have been born ca. 1847–50. His tombstone reads 1849. The 1850 census valued White House at fifty thousand dollars and listed 103 slaves belonging Joel Poinsett. Of these, ten male children were between the ages of eight months and four years; another child was five. See Seventh Census of the United States, 1850 (microfilm), South Carolina Population and Slave Schedule.

20. See "List of Negroes at the White House Plantation, May 1858," White House Plantation Book, 1857, R. F. W. Allston Papers: Pringle Family Papers: Julius Izard Pringle, South Carolina Historical Society, Charleston; Berlin, *Many Thousands Gone*, 146–47, chap. 11. Bremer, a Swedish feminist and writer, visited White House in April 1850 and later described slave food, clothing, and housing (*Homes*, 285, 292–93). For a more in-depth discussion of the task system unique to rice production, see Joyner, *Down by the Riverside*, chap. 2, esp. 43–53, 65–68.

21. Bremer, *Homes*, 288–90, 297; Pringle, *Woman Rice Planter*, 13–14, 19, 142–43, 165, 167.

22. Alford, *Joel Roberts Poinsett*, 1.

23. Dumas Malone, "Joel Roberts Poinsett," in *Dictionary of American Biography*, 32. See also Bremer, *Homes*, 283–85; Pulley, "Introduction." As a U.S. representative during the 1820s, Poinsett undoubtedly gained familiarity with the political movement, driven by expanding white settlement, that preceded Indian removal.

24. Linder and Thacker, *Historical Atlas*, 251–57; Bremer, *Homes*, 285–87, 298–99, 301.

25. See Alford, *Joel Roberts Poinsett*, 1; Bremer, *Homes*, 288.

26. See "Will of Joel R. Poinsett," Record of Wills, 1851–56, Charleston County, S.C., Charleston County Public Library, Charleston, S.C. John Julius Izard Pringle owned 49

slaves in 1850; ten years later, he owned 198, including those at White House. In all probability, Septima Clark's father was one of the ten males listed in the 1860 Census between
the ages of ten and thirteen. See Seventh Census of the United States, 1850, South Carolina Population and Slave Schedule; Eighth Census of the United States, 1860, South Carolina Population and Slave Schedule; "Descendants of Judge Robert Pringle," in *South
Carolina Genealogies*, 340–41.

27. See Clark, *Echo*, 14; Clark, *Ready from Within*, 87; Wood Interview; Thrasher Interview; Hall Interview. Clark provided many different versions of her father's origins. In
one, she claimed that her grandmother had come from the Bahamas and that her father
had been born there as well. In another, she stated, "My father's mother was pregnant
with him when she was brought from Africa" and estimated that Joel Poinsett bought
her grandmother around 1846. These versions seem highly unlikely, given that the legal
Atlantic slave trade ended in 1808. In yet another iteration, she proposed that he had come
on the *Wanderer*, a ship that smuggled African slaves into the Low Country in 1858. While
possible, that means Peter Poinsette would have lived at White House only three years;
and sometime in the late 1850s, the Pringle sons traveled to Europe for further education.
They were in Heidelberg, Germany, when the Civil War broke out in 1861. See Gomez,
Exchanging, 175; Linder and Thacker, *Historical Atlas*, 255.

28. Thrasher Interview; Wood Interview. See also Clark, *Ready from Within*, 87; Clark,
Echo, 14 (where Clark says she remembered two of Peter Poinsette's brothers, Thomas and
Samuel); Marguerite Moseley, interview by author, Charleston, S.C., February 22, 2002, in
author's possession.

29. Hall Interview.

30. Wood Interview.

31. Clark, *Ready from Within*, 87. In *Echo in My Soul*, Clark claims that her father
took only one child to school and that it was Mary Poinsett's child from her first marriage
(Clark, *Echo*, 15). However, any children in the family that Peter Poinsett accompanied
to school would have been Mary Poinsett's grandchildren, the offspring of her son, John
Julius Izard Pringle: John Julius, Joel Roberts Poinsett, Dominick Lynch, and Mary. The
oldest, John, was nineteen in 1861 ("Descendants of Judge Robert Pringle," in *South Carolina Genealogies*, 340–41). Clark also mistakenly thought that Mary Poinsett's first husband had been named McGuire (Thrasher Interview; Hall Interview).

32. Clark, *Echo*, 15. See also Hall Interview.

33. In the spring of 1862, the Pringle boys hurried home from Europe, making their
way through a federal blockade, to aid the Confederate cause (*Index to Records of Confederate Soldiers* [microfilm]; Hewett, *South Carolina Confederate Soldiers*, 35–36; Wells,
Sketch, 8, 27, 32, 97).

34. Wood Interview; Clark, *Ready from Within*, 88; Clark, *Echo*, 15; Sifakis, *Compendium*, 42–43.

35. Poinsette-Fisher Interview. On the federal bombardment of the city, see Fraser,
Charleston! Charleston!, 265. For a broader view of wartime conditions in Beaufort, see
Rose, *Rehearsal for Reconstruction*.

36. See Comptroller General, Pension Department, Confederate Pension Applications,

nos. 1636–1940, (Berkeley–Charleston Counties): 1919–26 (microfilm), South Carolina State Archives, Columbia. The board approved Poinsette's pension application less than a week later. See also Wells, *Sketch*, 97. Clark recorded the amount of the annual pension (Clark, *Echo*, 15). She also claimed that he had learned to sign his name by this time, which invites much speculation about why he signed the pension application with an "X."

37. Hall Interview. See also Linder and Thacker, *Historical Atlas*, 255–56; Pringle, *Woman Rice Planter*; "Colonial Mansion Burns," *CNC*, January 2, 1926.

38. Wood Interview. In 1891, two of Peter Poinsette's brothers, Henry and Thomas W., worked in Charleston as bakers, and his other brother, Samuel, worked as a carpenter in the city. Thomas disappears from the city directory after 1908, apparently because he moved out west (*Charleston City Directory*, 1891–1908; Hall Interview).

39. Sherman quoted in Fraser, *Charleston! Charleston!*, 268; see also 272–73. For a more detailed account of the parade, held on March 29, 1865, and the Fort Sumter ceremony, see Jenkins, *Seizing*, 36, 38–39.

40. Jenkins, *Seizing*, 48–49, 52–55. Charleston's black population increased from 17,146 in 1860 to 26,173 in 1870. Former slave and free black alike understood the Black Codes as both race and class legislation. See Foner, *Reconstruction*, 208–9; Litwack, *Been in the Storm*, 367–68. According to Powers, 52.2 percent of Charleston's black men labored as unskilled workers in 1870 (*Black Charlestonians*, 105, chap. 6). On federal complicity in returning former slaves to plantations, sometimes by force, see Saville, *Work*, chap. 3. On organizational work done by Charleston's postwar black community, see Drago, *Initiative*, chap. 2.

41. Jenkins, *Seizing*, 41–42, 134–39, 140–42; Fraser, *Charleston! Charleston!*, 275.

42. Cain quoted in Powers, *Black Charlestonians*, 229. See also Holt, *Black over White*, 218.

43. For other examples of early autonomous black political organizing, see Hahn, *Nation*, pt. 2; Elsa Barkley Brown's study of Richmond, Virginia, "Negotiating and Transforming"; Cecelski's study of North Carolina, "Abraham H. Galloway."

44. Holt, *Black over White*, 1, 4, 38–39, 73, 109–11, 120. Of the 487 men elected to state or federal office between 1867 and 1876, 255 were African American.

45. For elaborations of the white supremacist counterrevolution that culminated in the 1876 Hamburg Massacre, see Kantrowitz, *Ben Tillman*, chap. 2; Jenkins, *Seizing*, 147–56.

46. Hall Interview; Clark, *Ready from Within*, 88; Wood Interview.

47. Hall Interview; Clark, *Echo*, 15. Peter P. Poinsette does not appear in the federal census as residing anywhere in South Carolina in 1870 or 1880, and the 1890 records for the state burned. Neither Septima Clark nor any surviving family members know the name of his first wife. The 1900 census records Alice Poinsette as born in January 1880 and living in Charleston. A few years later, she moved to New York City, where she married a man named Gray and lived until her death. Clark's niece and granddaughter visited "Aunt Alice" in New York annually. See Ninth Census of the United States, 1870, South Carolina Population; Tenth Census of the United States, 1880, South Carolina Population; Twelfth Census of the United States, 1900, South Carolina Population; Poinsette-Fisher Interview; Yvonne Clark, interview.

48. See Clark's comments in McFadden, "Septima P. Clark," 85. Clark usually claimed her maternal grandmother was part Santee Indian and that she knew nothing of her maternal grandfather. On one occasion, however, she said he was a member of the Muskhogean tribe who lived on the Sea Islands. See Hall Interview; Wood Interview; Clark, *Ready from Within*, 89.

49. Tenth Census of the United States, 1880, South Carolina Population. Masaline appears as Masalin, age thirteen; Victoria is ten, and Martha is eight.

50. Clark, *Ready from Within*, 89; Septima P. Clark, interview by Joan Mack, Charleston, S.C., March 18, 1987, videotape recording, ARC. Bernice Robinson, Clark's maternal first cousin, claimed that the family line in Jacksonville began with her great-grandmother, a Seminole Indian who married an Italian sailmaker and relocated there. See Robinson Interview.

51. Hall Interview. The 1880 Census shows Victoria Anderson's siblings as seventeen-year-old Anna Eliza Poinsett, a seamstress, with a four-month-old son, Edmond, whose father was Samuel Poinsett. Others included thirty-year-old Septima and twenty-seven-year-old Frederick, in all likelihood half–siblings (Tenth Census of the United States, 1880, South Carolina Population). The family's spellings of "Poinsett/e" vary. According to Septima Clark, her mother talked about Robinson for the rest of her life: "She and her sister had many words about it, but the children, we became great friends." Martha and Fletcher Robinson's ninth daughter, born in 1914, was Bernice Robinson, later the teacher of the first Citizenship School on Johns Island. See Robinson Interview and Wood Interview.

52. Clark, *Echo*, 14. According to Clark, her name meant "seven" as well as "sufficient." The Poinsettes' first daughter, Etheline R., had been born in June 1894; Peter T. Poinsette was born in December 1899. See Twelfth Census of the United States, 1900, South Carolina Population; *Charleston City Directory*, 1895.

53. Clark, *Ready from Within*, 97; Wood Interview; *Charleston City Directory*, 1902. Clark believed that her father's restaurant was on Tradd Street; actually, it was at 3 State Street, near the corner where State intersects with Broad Street.

54. Peter and Victoria Poinsette's other children included Ruby A., who was born in 1905; Harold R., who was born in 1906 and died young; another unnamed infant who died shortly after birth; Lorene R, who was born in 1908; and Wilfred, who was born in 1914. (Thirteenth Census of the United States, 1910, South Carolina Population Schedule; Fourteenth Census of the United States, 1920, South Carolina Population Schedule).

55. Alvin Anderson, interview. See also Poinsette-Fisher Interview.

56. See Wood Interview; Hall Interview; Thrasher Interview.

57. Alvin Anderson, interview.

58. Hall Interview. See also Thrasher Interview.

59. Clark, *Echo*, 13, 48; Septima P. Clark, interview by Mack. Clark suspected that part of the reason his lunchroom failed stemmed from Peter Poinsette's inability to turn away those who could not pay.

60. Clark, *Ready from Within*, 97–98; Septima Clark, interview by Cynthia Brown, Charleston, S.C., August 1979, tape 2, side B, in author's possession; Alvin Anderson, interview.

61. Hall Interview.

62. Thrasher Interview; Clark, *Ready from Within*, 94–95; Poinsette-Fisher Interview; Hall Interview.

63. Thrasher Interview. See also Hall Interview; Wood Interview.

64. Clark, *Ready from Within*, 89, 91. See also Wood Interview.

65. Hall Interview. See also Poinsette-Fisher Interview; Alvin Anderson, interview.

66. Hall Interview. Michael Barry lived at 31 Henrietta Street, almost directly across from the Poinsettes (Fourteenth Census of the United States, 1920, South Carolina Population Schedule).

67. Clark, *Ready from Within*, 96.

68. *Charleston City Directory*, 1898, 1904, 1908, 1916; S. W. Bennett to Dr. A. C. McClennan, March 21, 1904, box 12, folder 30, SEB Papers; Meffert, Pyatt, and Avery Research Center, *Black America Series*, 60. See also Poinsette-Fisher Interview.

69. See, for example, *Charleston City Directory*, 1898, 1904, 1908, 1916. The 1916 edition lists Edward B. Burroughs, minister of Wesley African Methodist Church, as the editor of the *Southern Reporter*. This paper apparently was short-lived, for this is the only year it appears, and no editions have been preserved.

70. Fields, *Lemon Swamp*, 9–10, 29–30. Fields claims that the city halted the parade after African American workers outperformed whites, but other residents recalled attending annually. See Geneva B. Dansby, interview by author, Charleston, S.C., May 22, 2002, in author's possession. On the benefits of urban living in the segregated South, see, for example, Hale, *Making Whiteness*; Hunter, *To 'Joy My Freedom*; Kelley, "'We Are Not What We Seem.'"

71. Fields, *Lemon Swamp*, 19, 51–52.

72. See Dansby, interview; Ball, *Sweet Hell Inside*; Meffert, Pyatt, and Avery Research Center, *Black America Series*, 75.

73. See Clark, *Ready from Within*, 94; Wood Interview.

74. On the family's church attendance, see Hall Interview; Poinsette-Fisher Interview; Alvin Anderson, interview. For a broader view of the United Methodists, see Bennett, *Religion*.

75. Holt, *Black over White*, 9–22.

76. Ibid., 74–76, 105; Jenkins, *Seizing*, 73, 78–79, 116, 128–32; Powers, *Black Charlestonians*, 149, 152.

77. Miller quoted in Gordon, *Sketches*, 67–68. See also James D. Anderson, *Education of Blacks*, 20–30.

78. Alvin Anderson, interview. A sense of Christian duty occasionally led Victoria Poinsette to abandon her rule against associating with "kept" black women on Henrietta Street. She once sent her daughter to read the Bible to one of these women suffering from a terminal illness (Clark, *Ready from Within*, 90).

79. See Thrasher Interview; Clark, *Ready from Within*, 97.

80. Jenkins, *Seizing*, 72; Powers, *Black Charlestonians*, 137–39, 146. Despite its interracial student body, the Morris Street School practiced internal segregation: whites studied on the second floor, while African Americans used the first and third.

81. See Drago, *Initiative*, 44–52; Powers, *Black Charlestonians*, 145–46; Jenkins, *Seizing*, 84. See also Hahn, *Nation*, 260.

82. See James D. Anderson, *Education of Blacks*, chap. 1, esp. 5–10. See also Fields, *Lemon Swamp*, 2–3; Heather Andrea Williams, *Self-Taught*; Jenkins, *Seizing*, 73–77.

83. Balibar and Wallerstein, *Race, Nation, Class*, chap. 5, esp. 100–103; Walker, *Their Highest Potential*. While Balibar concedes the inherence of sexism and racism in nationalism, he fails to pay sufficient attention to how the reproduction of nationalist discourses — which he argues begins with the family and the school — are gendered, or, rather, who performs the labor of disseminating notions of the ideal national citizen to children. Adapting his argument to my own, I contend that because women, as mothers and teachers, played central educating roles in the home and school, they were critical to both the perpetuation and possible disruption of social and political formations in the Jim Crow South.

84. Hall Interview. Clark told this version of the story in numerous interviews. Only in her first autobiography did she reverse the facts and claim that she began her education by attending a private school operated by two black women (Clark, *Echo*, 17). See also Drago, *Initiative*, 36–39; Powers, *Black Charlestonians*, 139, 150, 158; Birnie, "Education"; Fields, *Lemon Swamp*, 44–45.

85. Clark, *Ready from Within*, 99; Clark, *Echo*, 19.

86. Clark, *Echo*, 18, 20; Hall Interview.

87. Clark, *Echo*, 18; see also 17; Drago, *Initiative*, 127.

88. See Fields, *Lemon Swamp*, 45, 53, 55. See also Brundage, "White Women," esp. 115–16.

89. See Meffert, Pyatt, and Avery Research Center, *Black America Series*, 50. The school opened in January 1911 and was renamed Burke in 1925. In all likelihood, Septima Poinsette returned to Shaw before attending Burke. According to my calculations, she completed the eighth grade in the 1911–12 school year, though some confusion exists because she skipped one grade. Knowing that she went to Burke for one year and Avery for four, graduating in the spring of 1916, it is possible to count backward and determine that she entered Avery in the fall of 1912. See Clark, *Echo*, 20; Clark, *Ready from Within*, 101.

90. Clark, *Echo*, 21–22.

91. Ibid., 24; Clark, *Ready from Within*, 101; Drago, *Initiative*, 88, 129–30, 134.

92. Thrasher Interview. Septima Clark's granddaughter testified that such practices endured into her own teenage years. "I remember going to one of my classmates' house for her sixteenth birthday and her father shunning us off his property with a shotgun because we were too dark" (Yvonne Clark, interview). See also Drago, *Initiative*, chaps. 2–3. My argument differs from that of Drago, who uses Septima Poinsette's extracurricular involvement to argue that Avery provided her with "upward mobility." I suggest instead that lessons from home, church, and her private elementary school first inculcated the attitude of social striving necessary to sustain such upward mobility as well as the practice of distinguishing oneself socially in the community. Drago also contends that Avery's reputation for excluding dark-skinned students is historically inaccurate because it is premised on anecdotes that reflected personal biases. Whatever merit this idea holds, Septima Clark perceived discrimination at Avery because of her parents' status, and the frequency with

which she told stories of her social rejection seems indicative of the great pain it caused her. See also Fields, *Lemon Swamp*, 13.

93. Clark, *Echo*, 23–24. In 1920, Daniel and Ella Sanders and their two children, Daniel Jr. (b. 1911) and Sadie (b. 1913) lived on Henrietta Street (Fourteenth Census of the United States, 1920, South Carolina Population Schedule).

94. Drago, *Initiative*, 82–83.

95. See James D. Anderson, *Education of Blacks*, chap. 3, 102.

96. Thrasher Interview. Clark later "found out from people like Zilphia Horton [at Highlander] the two great lessons of the spirituals: how they carried a message, and how they told of the sufferings of the people. When I found those things out, then I felt better about singing them." See also Drago, *Initiative*, 94–95, 139–40, 163; Meffert, Pyatt, and Avery Research Center, *Black America Series*, 14.

97. Clark, *Echo*, 25. See also Drago, *Initiative*, 104, 170–71. On training for African American nurses, see Hine, *Black Women*.

98. Cooper, *Voice*, 21, 131. For examples of contemporary scholarly works that examine the thoughts and deeds of Progressive Era black women feminists, see Higginbotham, *Righteous Discontent*; Gilmore, *Gender and Jim Crow*; White, *Too Heavy a Load*; Brown, "Womanist Consciousness."

99. Dansby, interview. See also Drago, *Initiative*, 148.

100. U.S. Bureau of the Census, *Census of the Population, 1920*, 4:1016; *AR* (1920–21), 291; Clark, *Echo*, 28. See also Wood Interview.

101. Clark, *Echo*, 26–27.

102. Elbert M. Stevens quoted in Drago, *Initiative*, 87.

103. See Holt, *Black over White*, 10–11; Saville, *Work*, 73–74, 82–85, 87–95, 125–27; Foner, *Reconstruction*, 163–64.

104. On the crucial role of black landowners in the modern civil rights movement, see Dittmer, *Local People*; Payne, *I've Got the Light*.

105. McFadden, "Septima P. Clark," 85; Thrasher Interview; Hall Interview; Clark, *Echo*, 13.

106. Wood Interview; Septima P. Clark, interview by Mack.

107. Wood Interview.

108. The Aztecs called the plant Cuetlayochitl. Historian and horticulturalist William Prescott named the plant in honor of Joel Poinsett shortly after completing a book, *The Conquest of Mexico*. For the Mexican legend regarding the plant, see University of Illinois Extension, "Poinsettia Pages"; Ecke Ranch, "The History of the Poinsettia."

Chapter Two

1. Clark, *Echo*, 32–35; Wood Interview; SPC Interview; weather reports in *CNC*, September 9, September 10, 1916.

2. Wood Interview.

3. See *AR* (1915–16), 12–13, 141. All per-pupil expenditures, unless otherwise noted, are according to enrollment. However, the $13.45 figure reflects average attendance for pur-

poses of comparison with national per-pupil average expenditures, which stood at $41.73. See U.S. Bureau of the Census, *Historical Statistics*, 374.

4. Eighty-three percent of white teachers and 75 percent of black teachers were female; only 51 percent of all whites taught in one-teacher schools, while 91 percent of all black teachers did so (*AR* [1916–17], 7, 10; for average length of school term and average number of pupils, see 9). On white county teaching supervisors, all but one of whom worked upstate, see *AR* (1915–16), 45–69. For a description of district trustee jobs, see "Reports for South Carolina, 1904–1911," box 5, folder 106, SEB Papers.

5. *AR* (1916–17), 9.

6. Dorothy Robinson, *Bell Rings at Four*, 3; Singleton, *Recollections*, 31.

7. W. K. Tate, "Statement of the Rural School Problem in South Carolina, 1910–1911," box 5, folder 106, SEB Papers; Blease quoted in Lewis K. McMillan, *Negro Higher Education*, 258.

8. See appendix, table 1.

9. See Anderson and Moss, *Dangerous Donations*, 4–5. See also Fairclough, *Class of Their Own*; Fairclough, *Teaching Equality*, esp. 56–58. My analysis differs significantly from Fairclough's in its use of gender. Where he defines anyone engaged in education as a teacher, I make a crucial distinction between black administrators and educational leaders, the majority of whom were men, and black women teachers at the grassroots. For broader overviews, see, for example, James D. Anderson, *Education of Blacks*; Leloudis, *Schooling*; Walker, *Their Highest Potential*.

10. Rose Butler Browne makes this observation in Browne, *Love My Children*, 121.

11. See, for example, Jones, *Jeanes Teacher*, 77.

12. School revenue consisted of funds appropriated by the General Assembly, poll taxes, and "voluntary local taxation" (Tindall, *South Carolina Negroes*, 209–11). Holt notes that while the 1868 state constitution did not explicitly forbid segregation in public education, it did preserve a "freedom of choice" plan that relied on demographics in lieu of mandating integration by law (*Black over White*, 122–34). See also Kantrowitz, *Ben Tillman*, 51.

13. Tindall, *South Carolina Negroes*, 212–19. See also McCurry, *Masters*.

14. See Kantrowitz, *Ben Tillman*, 5, 7, 110–11.

15. Tindall, *South Carolina Negroes*, 221–22. A resolution to provide free textbooks to all students also failed (Kantrowitz, *Ben Tillman*, 215–16).

16. Kantrowitz, *Ben Tillman*, 242.

17. The State Board of Education comprised the governor, the state superintendent of education, and one member from each congressional district selected by the governor to serve a four-year term. The board exerted its influence most by appointing two members to county school boards ("Organization of South Carolina's Public Schools," September 1904, box 5, folder 106, SEB Papers). See also Tindall, *South Carolina Negroes*, 213–15, 219. The gap in per-pupil spending between black and white students began to widen in 1880.

18. See Carlton, *Mill and Town*. Progressive Era educational reform arrived in South Carolina in 1902, when reformers first targeted the elimination of child labor in the mills. The success of their strategy depended on the passage of compulsory education legislation.

For a broader view of Progressivism, see Wiebe, *Search for Order*; Flanagan, *America Reformed*.

19. For an in-depth discussion of how anxieties of gender, race, sexuality, and class informed Bleasism, see Simon, *Fabric of Defeat*, 11–35; Carlton, *Mill and Town*, chap. 6. For a view of how Tillman changed his opinion of his former protégé, see Kantrowitz, *Ben Tillman*, 296–99.

20. Blease quoted in Lewis K. McMillan, *Negro Higher Education*, 257. The state passed its first compulsory attendance law in 1915, but enforcement remained purely a local option. The situation changed little in 1919, when lawmakers adopted a statewide requirement, because it was not effectively enforced until the 1930s (Carlton, *Mill and Town*, 185, 212).

21. Browne, *Love My Children*, 121. For an example of working-class black parents prioritizing "financial imperatives" over "book learning," see Mack, *Parlor Ladies*, 129–42. For examples of black families sacrificing to educate their children, see Chirhart, *Torches of Light*, 43–55; Charles S. Johnson, *Growing Up*, 114–19.

22. See *AR* (1915–16), 8, 10.

23. W. K. Tate, "Statement of the Rural School Problem." County boards appointed district trustees for two-year terms to manage school property, to levy taxes in their districts, and to employ teachers and to determine their salaries ("Organization of the Public School System," box 5, folder 106, SEB Papers; *AR* [1916–17], 98). On politics and the home rule of county delegates, see Littlejohn, *Littlejohn's Political Memoirs*.

24. See, for example, *AR* (1916–17), 164, 172, 175.

25. Ibid., 164, 177–78. On average, Charleston County paid white men $1,143.99, white women $530.80, black men $751.70, and black women $348.88.

26. Ibid., 7. Only 9 percent of South Carolina's African American teachers and 15 percent of its white teachers taught in urban schools.

27. Ibid., 99–100. In his annual report, Hand, the state high school inspector, estimated that "at least five hundred white teachers holding legal certificates to teach" would "not make a grade of 50 per cent on the studies of the eighth and ninth grades . . . if examined as rigidly as are the pupils" in the state's top schools. A state board of examiners was established in 1921.

28. See W. K. Tate, "Statement of the Rural School Problem." In an effort to provide desperately needed state aid for rural schools, the General Assembly passed the Rural Graded School Law in 1912, but legislative appropriations did not keep pace with the rapidly increasing demand (*AR* [1915–16], 11–12). At best, reform efforts were uneven. Consolidation, for example, was a district-by-district affair. Thus, consolidating 55 districts in one year was a small achievement in a state with a total of 1,903 districts (ibid., 31–45).

29. See J. H. Brannon, "Report of the State Agent for Negro Schools," *AR* (1917–18), 95–103; *AR* (1916–17), 7–9.

30. For descriptions of Promise Land, see Clark, *Echo*, 36, 38–39; Clark, *Ready from Within*, 104–6; Septima Poinsette Clark, interview by Sandra Brenneman Oldendorf, Charleston, S.C., January 17, 1986, HERC; SPC Interview. See also Charleston County Board of Education Minute Book, June 1878–April 1920, box 1, CCSD.

31. Clark, *Echo*, 34, 36, 39, 108; Septima Poinsette Clark, interview by Judy Barton, Charleston, S.C., November 9, 1971, box 1a, folder 5, Clark Papers. See also Grimball Interview.

32. See J. B. Felton, "Folder about Colored Schools in South Carolina," 3, 4, SOCAR.

33. J. E. Swearingen to E. D. Smith and W. P. Pollock, November 13, 1918, box 891, folder "Federal Department of Education, 1919–1943," CCSD. See also Lu Ann Jones, *Mama Learned Us*, 141–42.

34. See Brannon, "Report," *AR* (1917–18), 95–103; Felton, "Folder about Colored Schools," 5, which notes that in 1922 fifty-one schools in twenty-four counties had been built with Rosenwald funds. Prospective teachers attended county training schools, as did those already employed. See also Anderson and Moss, *Dangerous Donations*, 4, 6, 9; James D. Anderson, *Education of Blacks*.

35. *AR* (1917–18), 95–103, 108. Counties had only to supplement Jeanes teachers' salaries rather than pay their entire salaries.

36. Anderson and Moss, *Dangerous Donations*, 4–5, 9, 10, 61; Felton, "Folder about Colored Schools," 6. See also Gordon, *Sketches*, 108. No organization was as influential as the General Educational Board, but Anderson and Moss observe that although the board had been established primarily for African Americans, "in the end only 19 percent of the board's gifts went to black education."

37. Anderson and Moss, *Dangerous Donations*, 217; Carlton, *Mill and Town*, 243–44. Booker T. Washington had perfected the local-accommodation strategy by 1895, and these developments constituted attempts to apply his model to the primary and secondary public school level. On Washington, see *Up from Slavery*, esp. vii–xlviii.

38. See Chirhart, *Torches of Light*, esp. chap. 4, 128–47; Lu Ann Jones, *Mama Learned Us*, chaps. 3, 4. The Smith-Hughes Act channeled federal aid for agricultural and vocational education to public secondary schools.

39. See Jones, *Jeanes Teacher*, 73, 93; Littlefield, "'I Am Only One'"; Brannon, "Report," *AR* (1917–18), 97–98. On black women serving as racial diplomats to the white state to secure improved social services, see Gilmore, *Gender and Jim Crow*, chap. 6.

40. See "The South Carolina Sea Islands," *CNC*, January 1, 1910. This "Jubilee Edition" of the newspaper is indicative of Charleston's distinctive brand of New South boosterism in that it blends nostalgia for the Old South with the necessity of bringing New South economic progress to the region. Yuhl makes a similar point in *Golden Haze*. The boll weevil arrived in the state in 1917; in 1919, the pest destroyed 90 percent of the cotton crop on the Sea Islands, thus ending its widespread commercial production (Guion Griffis Johnson, *Social History*, 202; Rogers and Taylor, *South Carolina Chronology*, 123–24).

41. "The South Carolina Sea Islands," *CNC*, January 1, 1910. See also Fields, *Lemon Swamp*, 133. Fields taught on Johns Island from 1909 to 1913.

42. "The South Carolina Sea Islands," *CNC*, January 1, 1910; Carawan and Carawan, *Ain't You Got a Right*, 26, 27, 31, 34; Clark, *Echo*, 37, 50; Clark, *Ready from Within*, 108–9.

43. Clark, *Echo*, 33, 35; SPC Interview.

44. Clark, *Echo*, 33, 35, 37, 50; Clark, *Ready from Within*, 108–9.

45. Clark, *Ready from Within*, 105, 108; SPC Interview.

46. See Clark, *Echo*, 40–42, 49; SPC Interview. See also Fields, *Lemon Swamp*, 118–21, 130. Bill Saunders confirmed Clark's skepticism of Johns Island superstitions in a conversation with the author.

47. Carawan and Carawan, *Ain't You Got a Right*, 45. See also Thrasher Interview.

48. Clark, *Echo*, 49, 50. Clark likely distinguished between "immoral" and "unmoral" with a white and/or middle-class audience in mind. Rural teacher Ella Earls Cotton makes the same contrast in her autobiography (*Spark*, 220).

49. Thrasher Interview; Wood Interview. Clark used almost identical language to tell this story in two different interviews. Beyond the profound effect it had on her, it became one of the stock narratives Clark relied on to describe conditions when she first went to Johns Island.

50. See Clark, *Ready from Within*, 107; Clark, *Echo*, 38, 54. Many autobiographies of black teachers in the rural South discuss the problem of classifying students; see, for example, Rice, *He Included Me*, chap. 4.

51. Clark, *Echo*, 39.

52. Dorothy Robinson, *Bell Rings at Four*, 33.

53. Fields, *Lemon Swamp*, 125–26. It is unlikely that Clark and Fields knew each other at this time. Both were from Charleston but did not live in the same neighborhood or attend the same church. Fields received her teacher training at Claflin University in Orangeburg.

54. Quoted in Michele Foster, *Black Teachers*, 38; Walker, *Their Highest Potential*. See also Chirhart, *Torches of Light*, 120–21, 132.

55. Grimball Interview. Grimball is Esau Jenkins's daughter; she became a Citizenship School teacher on Wadmalaw Island.

56. Ibid.

57. Clark, *Ready from Within*, 107 (emphasis added). See also Clark, *Echo*, 36–39.

58. Grimball Interview; Dorothy Robinson, *Bell Rings at Four*, 3; Browne, *Love My Children*, 200, 231.

59. Clark, *Ready from Within*, 106.

60. Melville Herskovits quoted in Gomez, *Exchanging*, 177. The discussion here is not limited strictly to Gullah, but it proves a useful point. As Gomez asserts, "African Americans continued to tinker with the language in order to maintain distance, distinctiveness, and some sense of ownership." See also Gomez, *Exchanging*, 102–5; Guy B. Johnson, *Folk Culture*, 17; Turner, *Africanisms*.

61. According to Bill Saunders, "There's a feeling that only blacks speak Gullah. And blacks *and* whites that live in the area speak Gullah. Lots of the whites' Gullah is just thick, more than blacks, simply because the folk that took care of the child was a black woman. But there would never be anything that you would read, especially around Charleston, that say that whites speak Gullah because that would be degrading to whites" (interview by author, Charleston, S.C., March 23, 2002, in author's possession). See also Verner, *Mellowed by Time*, 43.

62. Clark, *Echo*, 43–45, chap. 4. Clark recognized the similarities between the dialect

of aristocratic Charlestonians and that of Gullah speakers, dubbing it "Charlestonese." See also Joyner, *Down by the Riverside*, 196–224.

63. Cotton, *Spark*, 274. Rose Butler Browne stresses the need to motivate parents as well as children (Browne, *Love My Children*, 136, 239).

64. Cotton, *Spark*, 230; Fields, *Lemon Swamp*, 100.

65. Dorothy Robinson, *Bell Rings at Four*, 14; Cotton, *Spark*, 174–75; Fields, *Lemon Swamp*, 112–13.

66. Fields, *Lemon Swamp*, 100; Clark, *Echo*, 54; Cotton, *Spark*, 180, 230.

67. Fredrick Celestine Jenkins-Andrews, "The Responsibilities of a Teacher," paper presented to the Edisto Island Teachers' Association, ca. 1934, box 1, folder 2, Frederick Celestine Jenkins-Andrews Collection, ARC; Clark, *Ready from Within*, 109.

68. See Hicks, *Golden Apples*, 13, 14; Cotton, *Spark*, 182. To her list of qualifications of a good teacher, Hicks added, "neat in personal appearance" and "open-minded, ready for changes in locations, curricula, daily programs." See also Lillie Gayle Smith, "Unearthing Hidden Literacy."

69. Cotton, *Spark*, 250. People "had studied me well and long to be sure they could trust me," and her darker skin proved an asset (231–33, 215).

70. Dorothy Robinson, *Bell Rings at Four*, 25. Lura Beam, a northern white woman who arrived in Wilmington, North Carolina, to teach in 1908, included in her teaching memoir black parents' accounts of the 1898 racial massacre (*He Called Them*, 28).

71. Fields, *Lemon Swamp*, 108; Clark, *Echo*, 56–57.

72. Dorothy Robinson, *Bell Rings at Four*, 23; Fields, *Lemon Swamp*, 126; Cotton, *Spark*, 100.

73. See Fields, *Lemon Swamp*, 115; Grimball Interview; Clark, *Echo*, 57, 60.

74. Clark, *Echo*, 54; Dorothy Robinson, *Bell Rings at Four*, 29, n.p.; Jones, *Jeanes Teacher*, 82.

75. See William McKinley Robinson, "Rural Point of View," 104. My argument here is similar to Lu Ann Jones's (*Mama Learned Us*, 153–54, 168).

76. Felton, "Folder about Colored Schools," 5; J. H. Brannon in *AR* (1917–18), 99; Dorothy Robinson, *Bell Rings at Four*, 16–17; Browne, *Love My Children*, 152.

77. It seems likely that Clark did not altogether approve of the secret society or questioned its usefulness as a real vehicle for self-improvement. After remarking that "they loved the mystery and rituals," she subtly changed her tone to assert, "*But this was the good thing about it*: in order to be functioning members of these lodges," they had to acquire rudimentary literacy skills (Clark, *Echo*, 51 [emphasis added]). The group probably took its name from the national Independent Order of the Odd Fellows lodge. Because of the island's geographical isolation, however, it is unlikely that they were active in the national organization.

78. Clark, *Ready from Within*, 107; Clark, *Echo*, 52; Septima Poinsette Clark, interview by Barton. See also Dorothy Robinson, *Bell Rings at Four*, 57.

79. See Felton, "Folder about Colored Schools," 7; U.S. Bureau of the Census. *Census of the Population, 1920*, 3:930. For the beginnings of formal adult literacy education in the state, see chap. 4.

80. See Browne, *Love My Children*, 116; *AR* (1933–34), 59.

81. See Saunders, interview; Grimball Interview. Saunders emphasizes the point about property taxes and loss of land, which remains a critical problem for African Americans on the Sea Islands. See also Devlin, "South Carolina," chap. 5.

82. See *AR* (1916–17), 16; Cotton, *Spark*, 89; Jenkins-Andrews, "Responsibilities."

83. Clark, *Echo*, 53. See also Browne, *Love My Children*, 124, 125; Jones, *Jeanes Teacher*, 110–12.

84. Clark, *Echo*, 75; Cotton, *Spark*, 278.

85. Narvie J. Harris, interview by Kathryn Nasstrom, Atlanta, Ga., June 11, 1992, Southern Oral History Project, Wilson Library, University of North Carolina, Chapel Hill; Dorothy Robinson, *Bell Rings at Four*, 38.

86. Clark, *Echo*, 52.

Chapter Three

1. Clark, *Ready from Within*, 110.

2. Ibid.; Clark, *Echo*, 59.

3. See, for example, Miller, "Negro." See also Lentz-Smith, *Freedom Struggles*.

4. Du Bois quoted in "Now or Never," *The Crisis*, November 1918, 11. See also Paula Baker, "Domestication." Because black male leaders continued to ideologically link manhood and suffrage, Baker's model seems more tenuous when applied to an African American context. See, for example, Gilmore, *Gender and Jim Crow*, chap. 8; Kantrowitz, *Ben Tillman*.

5. See Deborah Gray White's discussion of black feminists and clubwomen in *Too Heavy a Load*, chaps. 1–3; Hunter's discussion of class divisions separating clubwomen and the working class in the black community in *To 'Joy My Freedom*, chaps. 6–9; Carby's similar point about contesting representative voices in New Negro Renaissance in *Reconstructing Womanhood*, 164–65. On blueswomen, see Carby, "Sexual Politics"; Davis, *Blues Legacies*; Harrison, *Black Pearls*. On black women's silence with regard to sexuality, see Hine, "Rape."

6. Luther Richard Simms quoted in Meffert, Pyatt, and Avery Research Center, *Black America Series*, 13; see also photographs, 14–24; Drago, *Initiative*, chap. 4, esp. 140–50.

7. Lois Averetta Simms, interview by author, Charleston, S.C., April 9, 2002, in author's possession.

8. Clark, *Echo*, 59–60.

9. Thrasher Interview; Clark, *Echo*, 59.

10. See Fraser, *Charleston! Charleston!*, 344–63.

11. Ibid., 359–60; "Who's Who in Colored America Questionnaire," box 62, folder 13, Harleston Papers; Ball, *Sweet Hell Inside*, 75–89, 108–23, 192.

12. On charter members, see Drago, *Initiative*, 172–73; Simms, *Profiles*, 15. See also Harleston's 1920 poll tax receipt for $3.57, June 22, 1921, box 61, folder 7, Harleston Papers; Ball, *Sweet Hell Inside*, 192–93.

13. Edwina Harleston quoted in Ball, *Sweet Hell Inside*, 190; see also 110.

14. Hall Interview. See also Higginbotham, *Righteous Discontent*, 1.

15. See "Du Bois Visit to Charleston," *Crisis*, April 1917, 270.

16. Fields, *Lemon Swamp*, 31.

17. See Ball, *Sweet Hell Inside*, 193; Drago, *Initiative*, 174–75. On the 1898 Wilmington racial massacre, see essays collected in Cecelski and Tyson, *Democracy Betrayed*.

18. See, for example, Burts, *Richard Irvine Manning*, 158–62; Newby, *Black Carolinians*, 187.

19. See Ball, *Sweet Hell Inside*, 193–94; Hall, "'Mind That Burns'"; Hall, *Revolt*; Hine, "Rape"; Carby, "'On the Threshold'"; Feimster, *Southern Horrors*.

20. Thrasher Interview.

21. See Litwack, *Trouble in Mind*, 246–70, esp. 247–48, 258; Fraser, *Charleston! Charleston!*, 327, 262. See also, for example, "Might Have Been Lynched," and "A Negro Row," *CNC*, December 14, 1909.

22. See Mays, *Born to Rebel*, 22; "Police Reports, February 22, 1916 to December 27, 1916, Complete Year: Juvenile Cases," box 2, folder 141, Tristram T. Hyde Papers, City of Charleston Archives, Charleston, S.C. Documents in this file suggest that police intervention in juvenile delinquency cases originated in February 1916, though this is the only year that such reports appear. See also appendix, table 2.

23. Clark, *Ready from Within*, 100. A black YMCA had been established in 1907, and its sister YWCA in 1911. See Eugene C. Hunt's historical play, "A Journey in Faith and Courage: The Story of the Coming Street YWCA," box 11, folder 39, Clark Papers. See also Fields, *Lemon Swamp*, 58; A. J. Clement Sr., T. R. Blanchard, and William Johnson to Tristram T. Hyde, February 5, 1916, box 1, folder "Complaints," Hyde Papers; box 2, folder "Police Reports," Hyde Papers.

24. See "Asks for Negro Teachers," *CNC*, January 15, 1919; Thrasher Interview. In 1896, 1913, and 1916, local black leaders had argued for the need to revise Charleston's teacher hiring policy. See "Negroes in City Schools Once Had White Teachers," *CNC*, April 22, 1954.

25. Fultz, "Charleston, 1919–1920," esp. 633–35.

26. See Clark, *Echo*, 60; Fraser, *Charleston! Charleston!*, 363; "Colored Teachers in Charleston Schools," *Crisis*, June 1921, 59.

27. See J. M. T., "A Professional Colored Citizen," *Charleston Messenger*, November 23 (?), 1918, clipping, box 62, folder 9, Harleston Papers. The author was likely Dr. John M. Thompson, whose signature appeared on the formal petition to the city school board.

28. See *Charleston Messenger*, [November 21, 1918?], clipping, box 62, folder 9, Harleston Papers. Jenkins did not enjoy a good relationship with the Harlestons. See Ball, *Sweet Hell Inside*, 64, 92–93. On funding for the orphanage, see Fraser, *Charleston! Charleston!*, 354–55.

29. See "Asks for Negro Teachers," *CNC*, January 15, 1919. The paper reprinted the full petition with its original November 30, 1918, date after the city school board acted on it.

30. Ibid.; "Negro Teachers Favored," *CNC*, January 31, 1919.

31. Clark, *Echo*, 60–61. Only 48 of the city's 150 white teachers faced replacement. Still, a change would have increased competition for jobs among graduates of Memminger, the local white teacher training institute. On employment numbers, see *Yearbook, 1919*, 400.

32. Fields, *Lemon Swamp*, 203; Thrasher Interview. Cox was a founding member of the NAACP's Executive Committee, and Avery was an ongoing source of support for the NAACP, so it seems unlikely that Cox would have been absolutely against the campaign. Nor did Clark ever mention being reprimanded or fired for her actions. See also "Colored Teachers in Charleston Schools," *Crisis*, June 1921, 59.

33. Hall Interview. See also Clark, *Echo*, 61; Clark, *Ready from Within*, 110.

34. See "Affidavit by Chairman of Board of Registers," unidentified clipping, n.d., box 62, folder 9, Harleston Papers. See also "Colored Teachers in Charleston Schools," *Crisis*, June 1921, 59.

35. See William C. Hine, "Thomas E. Miller," 8–10; "Miller, Thomas Ezekiel," in *Biographical Dictionary*, 1114–16. See also "The Ousting of Miller," *CNC*, January 30, 1911, reprinted in Lewis K. McMillan, *Negro Higher Education*, 246.

36. See "Miller's Dismissal," *CNC*, January 28, 1911; *CS*, January 28, 1911, "Miller's Letter of Resignation," *CS*, January 29, 1911, all reprinted in Lewis K. McMillan, *Negro Higher Education*, 243–44, 245. See also William C. Hine, "Thomas E. Miller," 11–12.

37. See Drago, *Initiative*, 176; Ball, *Sweet Hell Inside*, 195; "Colored Teachers in Charleston Schools," *Crisis*, June 1921, 59–60; "Colored Teachers' Bill," *CNC*, January 22, 1919; "The Negro Teachers Bill," *CNC*, January 29, 1919. The petition officially had only 4,551 signatures, but both participants and the white press fixed on the 10,000 number; see, for example, Clark, *Echo*, 61.

38. "Colored Teachers in Charleston Schools," *Crisis*, June 1921, 58–59; "Colored Teachers' Bill," *CNC*, January 22, 1919; "The Negro Teachers Bill," *CNC*, January 29, 1919; "Affidavit by Chairman of the Board of Registers," *Charleston Messenger*, n.d., clipping, box 62, folder 9, Harleston Papers.

39. See "Colored Teachers in Charleston Schools," *Crisis*, June 1921, 60; Fields, *Lemon Swamp*, 203. Although this story may be apocryphal, it illuminates how black Charlestonians used memory to capture the political drama of this moment. Retelling it years later, Fields cast it as a performance that highlighted Miller's ability to outmaneuver his opponents. Thus, the story asserted both black pride and political adroitness in the era of disfranchisement.

40. See "Colored Teachers in Charleston Schools," *Crisis*, June 1921, 60. The NAACP compromised by agreeing to delay full implementation until 1920. On Rhett's notice, see unidentified clipping, box 62, folder 9, Harleston Papers. See also "Bill to Be Withdrawn," *CNC*, February 5, 1919. On employment figures, see *Yearbook, 1920*, 435; *Yearbook, 1921*, 398.

41. See Mays, *Born to Rebel*, 2; Ball, *Sweet Hell Inside*, 196; "An Objection Cured," *Charleston Messenger*, n.d., clipping, box 62, folder 9, Harleston Papers.

42. Forsythe quoted in Michele Foster, *Black Teachers*, 25. Forsythe credited Septima Clark with leadership in the campaign for black teachers.

43. Rhett quoted in Drago, *Initiative*, 177; see also 179–81. See also Fields, *Lemon Swamp*, 204; Fraser, *Charleston! Charleston!*, 364; "Colored Teachers in Charleston Schools," *Crisis*, June 1921, 58.

44. Hall Interview.

45. See "Lincoln-Douglass Memorial Meeting Programme," February 12, 1919, box 62, folder 11, Harleston Papers; "Negro Soldiers to Meet," *CNC*, May 15, 1919.

46. See Lewis, *W. E. B. Du Bois*, 1; Tuttle, *Race Riot*, 11–22; Franklin and Moss, *From Slavery to Freedom*, 348–52.

47. See *CNC*, May 11, 12, 16, 1919; "Charleston Riot Costs Two Lives," *CS*, May 12, 1919.

48. Wood Interview; Tuttle, *Race Riot*, 24; "Race Riots Occur Here," *CNC*, May 11, 1919.

49. Wood Interview. Clark recalled that "the mob killed quite a few that night." On Ed Mitchell, see "Race Riots Occur Here," *CNC*, May 11, 1919. The reported number of casualties, however, did not represent an accurate final tally. See *CNC*, May 11, 12, 16, 1919. See also "Riot Trouble Is Followed by a Quiet Sunday," *Charleston Evening Post*, May 12, 1919; "Charleston Riot Costs Two Lives," *CS*, May 12, 1919.

50. Hyde quoted in "2 Dead; 27 Wounded in Street Rioting," *CNC*, May 12, 1919. See also "Verdict Returned on Street Rioting," *CNC*, May 16, 1919.

51. See "Race Riots Occur Here," *CNC*, May 11, 1919; "2 Dead; 27 Wounded in Street Rioting," *CNC*, May 12, 1919; "Riot Trouble Is Followed by Quiet on Sunday," *Charleston Evening Post*, May 12, 1919.

52. "Verdict Returned on Street Rioting," *CNC*, May 16, 1919. See also *CNC*, May 11, 1919, for initial reports of the riot's cause.

53. Wood Interview. See also Fraser, *Charleston! Charleston!*, 325–26, 347, 361; Burts, *Richard Irvine Manning*, 57, 73, 99, 105, 140. State liquor laws in Progressive Era South Carolina were preceded by the rise and fall of a state liquor monopoly, known as the Dispensary system, with uneven enforcement of state Prohibition. In 1915, South Carolina voters passed Prohibition by a margin of two to one; drinking in Charleston continued.

54. See "Negroes Deplore the Mob Spirit," unidentified clipping, n.d., box 62, folder 9, Harleston Papers; "Who's Who in Colored America Questionnaire," box 62, folder 13, Harleston Papers; the 1926 correspondence from Clelia McGowan in box 62, folder 1, Harleston Papers; Clelia McGowan to Harriet Stony Simons, July 15, 1946, box 75, folder 3, H. S. Simons Collection. Throughout the South, the racial violence of 1919 led to the formation of similar interracial committees. See Hall, *Revolt*, 60–65; Dykeman and Stokely's biography of Will W. Alexander, *Seeds*. For a view of living conditions for the majority of black Charlestonians in this era, see "Charleston Negro Housing," n.d., box 27, folder 11, Albert Simons Collection, South Carolina Historical Society, Charleston; Albert Simons to J. M. Hamilton, September 7, 1933, box 27, folder 13, Albert Simons Collection. The overall death rate for black Charlestonians was 2.5 times higher than whites.

55. "More Women Qualified," *CNC*, September 10, 1920; Terborg-Penn, "Discontented Black Feminists," 492; "Democrats Given Large Majorities," *CNC*, November 3, 1920; "Election Returns throughout the State," *CNC*, November 4, 1920. See also "Liberty Limited," *The Survey*, December 4, 1920, 350. South Carolina legislators did not formally ratify the Nineteenth Amendment until 1969 (Hine and Farnham, "Black Women's Culture," 214).

56. See Baker, "Domestication," 622; Higginbotham, "In Politics to Stay." For a characteristic example of black women's efforts to secure interracial cooperation, see "Colored

Women's Statement," 458–59; see also 461–67. More broadly, see Kraditor, *Ideas*, esp. chaps. 3, 5, 7; Green, *Southern Strategies*; Wheeler, *New Women*; Terborg-Penn, *African American Women*; Gilmore, "False Friends"; Gilmore, *Gender and Jim Crow*, chap. 8, esp. 203–13.

57. Clark, *Echo*, 61, 64, 63. Septima Clark remembered Nerie's arriving on the USS *Umpqua*. According to naval records, the *Umpqua* was a Bagaduce Class fleet tug, launched in September 1919; it operated out of Charleston Harbor through the end of World War II. Thus, Clark could not have been aboard the *Umpqua* in January 1919, though he may have served on it during one of his naval seagoing voyages a year later. See NavSource On-Line, Service Ship Photo Archive.

58. See Thrasher Interview. On the distinction between Charleston's own and strangers, see Fields, *Lemon Swamp*, 194.

59. Clark, *Echo*, 62.

60. Ibid.

61. See Clark, *Ready from Within*, 110–11; Clark, *Echo*, 63; Alvin Anderson, interview by author, Atlanta, Ga., January 27, 2002, in author's possession; Poinsette-Fisher Interview.

62. Clark, *Echo*, 65.

63. Hall Interview; Clark, *Ready from Within*, 111. In *Ready from Within*, Clark says that she went to McClellanville in the fall of 1920, but her résumé indicates otherwise ("Biographical [Sketch] of Mrs. Septima Poinsette Clark," box 1a, folder 20, Clark Papers).

64. "Biographical [Sketch]," box 1a, folder 20, Clark Papers. Clark, *Echo*, 66, and other sources (e.g., Thrasher Interview) give the year of her marriage as 1922, but she apparently misremembered and substituted her age at the time for the year.

65. Clark, *Ready from Within*, 112; Hall Interview. See also Tate's discussion of marriage and sexuality as an avenue toward "self-authority" in Zora Neale Hurston's *Their Eyes Were Watching God* (*Domestic Allegories*, 71–73). Collins has also theorized on marriage and black women's journey toward self-definition as well as on the need for black mothers to socialize daughters for survival in a racist and sexist society (*Black Feminist Thought*, 104–5, chap. 6, esp. 123–29).

66. Fields, *Lemon Swamp*, 153; Hall Interview; Alvin Anderson, interview. In 1930, Peter T. Poinsette married Lucille Mears, whose grandfather had been involved in Reconstruction politics as a Democrat and whose father served as the captain of the city's only African American fire department for forty-two years prior to his death in 1952 (Poinsette-Fisher Interview).

67. James R. Logan, "The Essentials of True Womanhood," speech delivered to the Zion Presbyterian Church's Women's Bible Class, January 26, 1930, box 3, James R. Logan Collection, ARC. See also Deborah Gray White's discussion of black clubwomen in *Too Heavy a Load*, chaps. 1–3; Claudia Tate's discussion of literary representations of black feminists in *Domestic Allegories*, introduction, esp. 13; Hazel Carby's discussion of cultural representations of black women's sexuality in "Sexual Politics," 10; Darlene Clark Hine's discussion of black women's culture of dissemblance in "Rape."

68. See Jeannette Keeble Cox, "A History — by Administration — of the Phyllis Wheatley Literary and Social Club [1934]," 1, Phillis Wheatley Literary and Social Club Collection, box 1, folder 3, ARC. "Phyllis" is the spelling that the club used. Apparently, an archivist who organized the club's papers decided, however, to change the spelling to the way Wheatley's first name is traditionally given. See also Drago, *Initiative*, 148–50.

69. Cox, "History," 2.

70. Ibid., 46–47. See also Hine, "Corporeal," 6–10.

71. Cox, "History," 46. See also Gilmore, *Gender and Jim Crow*; Shaw, *What a Woman Ought to Be*.

72. Clark, *Ready from Within*, 113. Detailing this most difficult time of her personal life — which included an implied confession of failing as a mother to protect her infant daughter's health — the difference between Clark's narrative posture as a black woman autobiographer in 1962 and 1986 emerges dramatically. Though her first autobiography offers much richer details about her courtship with Nerie Clark, propriety at the time kept her from explicitly naming female genitalia. She wrote simply that "the baby only lived a month; an operation performed for the repair of a hernia was not successful" (Clark, *Echo*, 67). The baby's middle name, Irma, honored Nerie Clark's sister in Hickory.

73. Thrasher Interview.

74. Ibid. See also Clark, *Echo*, 67–68.

75. See *Miller's City Directory*, 12, 236–38, 241, 245, 251, 253, 260, 265, 267–68, 270. Only 21 percent of Hickory's population was African American; in all of Catawba County, the black population was less than 12.5 percent. By contrast, black people comprised 47.6 percent of Charleston's population (U.S. Bureau of the Census. *Census of the Population, 1920*, 3:747, 750, 934).

76. See Clark, *Echo*, 68, 69, 84; Hall Interview; "Biographical [Sketch]." Septima Clark's granddaughter, Yvonne, remembered Nerie Clark's parents as Albert and Matilda. No African American Clarks with these names appear in the 1920 Hickory City Directory, which means they could have resided outside of the city limits at that time. In the remaining extant city directories, the only Matilda Clark listed was married to George W. (*Hickory, North Carolina City Directory*; *Miller's City Directory*, 124–25, 253, 260, 265, 267–68, 270; Yvonne Clark, interview by author, Atlanta, Ga., January 26, 2002, in author's possession).

77. See Hall Interview. Discussing her years in Dayton, Clark never said "we"; instead, she said, "I went to our church" and described the other things she did alone.

78. Clark, *Ready from Within*, 113. See also Clark, *Echo*, 71; Hall Interview. Clark's inclusion of this detail of her marriage in her 1986 autobiography offers perhaps the most glaring difference between it and her 1962 text. Writing in 1962, at the height of her involvement in the civil rights movement — and to persuade an interracial audience of the inherent justice of that movement — Clark could not characterize her husband as a less than admirable black man and/or father. Doing so would have provided white supremacists with too much ammunition to impugn black men more broadly and might have given white moderate supporters pause. Instead, she described Nerie Clark as "a generous, good man" and claimed that she left Dayton to show the baby off to his grandparents in both

Hickory and Charleston (Clark, *Echo*, 64, 69). Clark's honesty two decades later reflects the difference in consciousness she gained through the women's movement of the 1970s. Still, it took tremendous courage to share this painful detail from her private life. Barbara Ransby makes a similar point about Ella Baker's protecting her privacy, particularly her reluctance to discuss her marital status (*Ella Baker*, 8–9). Nerie Clark may not have legally separated from his first wife, since divorces were expensive and hard to come by, particularly for a sailor constantly on the move.

79. Clark, *Echo*, 70. See also Hine, "Corporeal," 15–17.

80. See Clark, *Ready from Within*, 113–14.

81. Alvin Anderson, interview.

82. Bessie Smith, "Used to Be Your Sweet Mama." See also Collins, *Black Feminist Thought*, 104; Carby, "Sexual Politics," 10–17; Ellison, *Shadow and Act*, 77–94; Werner's elaboration of the "blues impulse" in *Change*, 68–72.

83. Septima Poinsette Clark, interview by Judy Barton, Charleston, S.C., November 9, 1971, box 1a, folder 5, Clark Papers; Hall Interview.

84. Hall Interview. Clark lived in Columbia from 1929 to 1947, but Nerie Jr. only lived there for a short time in 1936–37. See also Clark, *Echo*, 84.

85. Clark, *Echo*, 71–72.

86. Ibid.

87. See "The [NAACP] Branch Bulletin," November 1922, box 62, folder 11, Harleston Papers; Hine, "Corporeal," 8.

88. See Collins, *Black Feminist Thought*, 105; Lorde, "Transformation," 40, 42.

Chapter Four

1. Clark, *Echo*, 73–74.

2. Ibid.; Hall Interview. See also Poinsette-Fisher Interview.

3. Robert Reynolds quoted in Edwards, "Booker T. Washington High School," 102.

4. Clark, *Echo*, 76.

5. Ibid., 77. Excellent studies on the civil rights movement in South Carolina and its local leaders include Lau, *Democracy Rising*; Aba-Mecha, "Black Woman Activist"; Richards, "Osceola E. McKaine"; Roefs, "Leading."

6. The historians who wrote the earliest studies of interwar civil rights activism in South Carolina took this view; they concede, however, that activists in the 1930s laid important groundwork. See Hoffman, "Genesis"; Newby, *Black Carolinians*, esp. chaps. 4–6; Lofton, "Columbia Black Community," esp. 86–87.

7. See Sitkoff, *New Deal*; Sullivan, *Days of Hope*; Weiss, *Farewell*; Bartley, "Era."

8. For recent works that have shifted our attention to the "long civil rights movement," see Chafe, "Gods Bring Threads"; Hall, "Long Civil Rights Movement"; Hine, "Black Professionals."

9. See Brown, "To Catch the Vision"; Brown, "Negotiating and Transforming." For additional perspectives on 1930s southern black radical activism, see Gilmore, *Defying Dixie*; Kelley, *Hammer and Hoe*; Korstad, *Civil Rights Unionism*; Korstad and Lichtenstein, "Opportunities Found and Lost."

10. See Newby, *Black Carolinians*, 199–200; Hayes, *South Carolina*, 7–8, 121–22.

11. See Lofton, "Social and Economic History," vi–vii, 17; Moore, *Columbia*, 336–40. On starvation, see Hayes, *South Carolina*, 8.

12. U.S. Bureau of the Census, *Census of the Population, 1930*, 795, 805.

13. F. P. Adams Interview. Clark first moved to Heidt Street in the Waverly neighborhood in 1934, but a year later she resettled in the southwestern part of the city on Assembly Street. She returned to Waverly in 1936, living at 2118 Washington Street for two years before moving to 2117. See *Hill's Columbia City Directory*, 1931–47. For discussions of African American neighborhoods in Columbia, see Lofton, "Columbia Black Community," 86; Moore, *Columbia*, 329, 385.

14. See Johnson and Dunn, *True Likeness*, 4, 24 (photograph); John McCray, "The Passing of Congo Square," *Charleston Chronicle*, August 22, 1981; *Hill's Columbia City Directory*, 1930–45. See also Lofton, "Columbia Black Community," 89; Moore, *Columbia*, 382.

15. Quoted in Johnson and Dunn, *True Likeness*, 4.

16. Clark, *Echo*, 80.

17. Hayes, *South Carolina*, 17; Lisio, *Hoover*; Franklin and Moss, *From Slavery to Freedom*, 385.

18. Corrie Wingard interview, December 12, 1938, box 25, folder 869, Federal Writers Project Papers, Southern Historical Collection, Wilson Library, University of North Carolina, Chapel Hill. By 1935, 54 percent of the people on Richland County relief rolls were African American, though they comprised only 52 percent of the population. See Lofton, "Columbia Black Community," 90. See also Sullivan, *Days of Hope*, 3, 43–45; Frederickson, *Dixiecrat Revolt*, 11, 17.

19. Roosevelt quoted in Sitkoff, *New Deal*, 46. See also John P. Davis, "New Deal." On resistance to the New Deal by South Carolina Senator Ellison Durant "Cotton Ed" Smith, chair of the Senate Agricultural Committee, see Hayes, *South Carolina*, 19, 21–23; Egerton, *Speak Now*, 86–87.

20. See Sullivan, *Days of Hope*; Franklin and Moss, *From Slavery to Freedom*, 391–94.

21. "C. A. Johnson to Supervise Negro Schools," *CPL*, May 17, 1930; Leake, "Survey," 14, 21–23, 28–30, 50–51, 54, 63. City spending on white schools averaged $138.99 per student; on black schools, $20.63 per student. See also Beale, "Needs," 13.

22. Robinson (class of 1931) quoted in Edwards, "Booker T. Washington High School," 102, 103, 104. On Saxon, see "Dies after Fifty-Five Years of Service," and "Mrs. Celia Dial Saxon" (editorial), *CPL*, February 2, 1935. Saxon received an honorary master's degree from South Carolina State in 1926. See also Newby, *Black Carolinians*, 225.

23. Esther B. Sims (class of 1946) quoted in Edwards, "Booker T. Washington High School," 105. Students had to pass an entrance exam to attend Booker T. (109). For additional views of how black educational institutions affected individual and community life, see Walker, *Their Highest Potential*; Hathaway, "Class of 1944"; and, in the context of integration, Cecelski, *Along Freedom Road*.

24. F. P. Adams Interview. Adams graduated from Booker T. in 1934. On the athletics program, see Edwards, "Booker T. Washington High School," 99.

25. Clark, *Echo*, 76.

26. F. P. Adams Interview. See also "C. A. Johnson to Supervise Negro Schools," *CPL*, May 17, 1930.

27. Leake, "Survey," 30, 54–55.

28. In 1935, Clark noted that she had attended summer training sessions in 1918, 1922, 1926, 1929, and 1930 and that she held a first-grade general elementary teaching certificate. See S. P. Clark, "Annual Report of Booker T. Washington Adult School, March 25 to May 24, 1935," box 3, folder 201, Gray Papers; Clark, *Echo*, 69. On Clark's New York classes, see "Biographical [Sketch] of Mrs. Septima Poinsette Clark," box 1a, folder 20, Clark Papers. Myles Horton later credited Clark's interest in "rural problems" to her having studied with Mabel Carney at Columbia's Teachers College (Myles Horton, "Report on the February 28–March 4 Trip to Charleston and Johns Island," March 4, 1955, box 67, folder 3, Highlander Papers). On Carney, see Weiler, "Mabel Carney." See also Edwards, "Booker T. Washington High School," 102.

29. Hall Interview. See also Clark, *Echo*, 84, 86.

30. Clark, *Echo*, 84; *Hill's Columbia City Directory*, 1935, 1936.

31. Clark, *Echo*, 84, 85.

32. Ibid.

33. *Hill's Columbia City Directory*, 1938–47; Poinsette-Fisher Interview. According to Poinsette-Fisher, Lorene Poinsette met Susie Lane Bailey while studying at Benedict College, and Bailey became a friend to the entire Poinsette family. Clark lived with Bailey and worked at Saxon until she left Columbia in 1947.

34. See Fultz, "Teacher Training," 199, 197. The number of teachers with six or more years of training rose from 16.8 to 39.1 percent between 1930 and 1935, while the number teaching in rural one-teacher schools with four years or less of education beyond elementary school fell from 71.6 percent to 41.2 percent. Although many teachers remained undereducated and horrible conditions persisted within most black southern schools, scholars have too often emphasized how far there was to go rather than how much improvement was made in a relatively short period.

35. Leake, "Survey," 57. Leake notes that all of Columbia's African American teachers belonged to the PSTA and subscribed to professional magazines.

36. See Potts, *History*, 31–50.

37. Quoted in ibid., 47. See also Leloudis, *Schooling*, esp. xii, chaps. 4–6.

38. C. A. Johnson to A. C. Flora, February 9, 1931, box 1, folder "School Board, 1931," A. C. Flora Papers, SOCAR.

39. F. P. Adams Interview; Edwards, "Booker T. Washington High School," 98.

40. Modjeska Simkins, interview by Jacquelyn Dowd Hall, Columbia, S.C., July 28–31, 1976, Southern Oral History Project, Wilson Library, University of North Carolina, Chapel Hill.

41. See James D. Anderson, *Education of Blacks*, 249–51; Edwards, "Booker T. Washington High School," 91–94; *Teachers' Bulletin* 15 (March 1935): 2, SOCAR. By the early 1930s, South Carolina had two systems for accrediting black schools, one conducted by the State Department of Education and the more prestigious regional evaluation by the

Southern Association of Colleges and Secondary Schools, which was founded in 1895. It did not begin inspecting black colleges until 1930.

42. See Fultz, "Teacher Training," 200; Johnson quoted in Potts, *History*, 53; Newby, *Black Carolinians*, 223.

43. Potts, *History*, 54–58. In 1920, the PSTA had 323 members; a decade later, it had 2,385. Membership rose to 5,488 by the end of the 1930s. Moreover by the mid-1930s, the organization provided financial support for "nine district summer schools which were upgrading teacher certification."

44. See "Constitution of the Charleston County Education Association," n.d., folder 19, Albertha Johnston Murray Collection, ARC. See also E. Philip Ellis, "The 'Old Gray' and the New Rider," *CPL*, April 5, 1930.

45. On the national NAACP's internal battles, particularly in the early to mid-1930s, see Holloway, *Confronting the Veil*, 8, 93–101; Lewis, *W. E. B. Du Bois*, chap. 9. See also Tushnet, *NAACP's Legal Strategy*, chaps. 1–3.

46. See *Teachers' Bulletin* 15 (March 1935): 16–17. See also "Teachers Note Achievements as Convention Closes Here," *CPL*, April 11, 1931.

47. Findings of the Citizenship Committee of the National Conference on Fundamental Problems in the Education of Negroes, reprinted in *Journal of Negro Education* 3 (October 1934): 650–51.

48. Ibid.

49. See "Palmetto State Teachers Close Successful Convention in Capital City," *CPL*, March 23, 1935; *Teachers' Bulletin* 15 (March 1935): 12. Clark's name appears on the "Roll of Teachers"; see 33. Such emphases were part of national trends in curriculum development that bore direct relation to the rise of the social sciences. See, for example, "Report of Special Summer Session of a Demonstration in Elementary Education Conducted at Booker T. Washington High School, East Chattanooga, 1936," box 81, folder 1285, Guy B. Johnson Papers, Southern Historical Collection, Wilson Library, University of North Carolina, Chapel Hill; "Recommendations on Teacher-Training for Negro Schools," box 11, folder 99, Penn School Papers, Southern Historical Collection, Wilson Library, University of North Carolina, Chapel Hill.

50. *Teachers' Bulletin* 15 (March 1935): 3. For a broader discussion of southern radicals, see Gilmore, *Defying Dixie*, pt. 2.

51. Quoted in *AR* (1921–22), 180.

52. *AR* (1931–32), 28; for achievements and ongoing challenges, see also 27–30, 35, 78–81. See also U.S. Department of the Interior, Office of Education, "Facts about Negro Education," 1–2.

53. Clark, *Echo*, 78–79 (emphasis added). In terms of generating a movement culture, Goodwyn argues that the act of seeing oneself "experimenting in democratic forms" is an important first step in organization that will later propel itself into broader political spheres (*Populist Revolt*, introduction, 122–23).

54. Clark, *Echo*, 76.

55. See *South Carolina Federation of Colored Women's Clubs*, 6–7, 9, SOCAR. See also

"Constitution of the SCFCW," Article III, box 2, Ethelyn Parker Collection, ARC; Gordon, *Sketches*, 185.

56. On Wilkinson, see Gordon, *Sketches*, 179–82. On Saxon, see "The Colored YWCA," *CPL*, September 25, 1926; *South Carolina Federation of Colored Women's Clubs*, 42. On Vincent, see "Outline Program for Next Two Years," *CPL*, May 17, 1930; "YWCA Worker Coming," *CPL*, February 7, 1931; Papers of the National Association for the Advancement of Colored People (microfilm), ser. A, pt. 12, reel 19, Sterling Memorial Library, Yale University, New Haven, Conn.; Aba-Mecha, "Black Woman Activist," 160.

57. Clark, *Echo*, 79. See also "Coastal District Scrapbook," n.d., box 8, Mamie Garvin Fields Collection, ARC.

58. Etta B. Rowe, "Our Heritage," 2–5, box 2, Ethelyn Parker Collection; *South Carolina Federation of Colored Women's Clubs*, 9; Clark, *Echo*, 79.

59. Fields, *Lemon Swamp*, 199. Fields served as the state president of the SCFCW from 1948 to 1950 and from 1958 to 1964. See "Federated Clubs & NCNW from Charleston, Many Places in South Carolina to Washington D.C." (scrapbook), box 8, Fields Collection. See also "Outline Program for Next Two Years," *CPL*, May 17, 1930. On the tensions that sometimes erupted between black middle-class reformers and the lower-class constituency they served, see Hunter, *To 'Joy My Freedom*, chaps. 6–8; Gaines, *Uplifting*.

60. "Palmetto Teachers to Invade Columbia," *CPL*, March 28, 1931; Clark, *Echo*, 78.

61. A total of 1,344 teachers attended the eighteen summer institutes led by Simkins. See Aba-Mecha, "Black Woman Activist," 103–6. Modjeska Simkins never joined the SCFCW, but her work for the Tuberculosis Association radicalized her (Simkins, interview). Columbia's Dr. Matilda Evans used identical methods to mobilize support for a public health clinic in that city (Hine, "Corporeal," 28).

62. Newby, *Black Carolinians*, 214–18.

63. Clark, *Echo*, 84; "Biographical [Sketch]."

64. Clark, *Ready from Within*, 116. Du Bois had changed as well (Holloway, *Confronting the Veil*, 72–73, 94; Lewis, *W. E. B. Du Bois*, 334–48, esp. 334–36).

65. Clark, *Ready from Within*, 116. See also Septima Clark, interview by Eliot Wigginton, New Market, Tenn., June 20, 1981, HERC. Much of this interview has been published. See Wigginton, *Refuse to Stand*, 3–21, 236–54, 302–14, 396–99.

66. Rowe, "Our Heritage," 5.

67. For an example of a Bethune speech in this era, see Mary McLeod Bethune, "How Fare Negro Youth?," address to Louisiana Negro State Teachers Convention, Shreveport, La., n.d., 7–8, 10, box 40, subject file "Negro Youth, 1937–1939," Alliance for Guidance of Rural Youth Papers, Rare Book, Manuscript, and Special Collections Library, Duke University, Durham, N.C. For a brief biography of Bethune, see Elaine M. Smith, "Bethune, Mary McLeod." For an earlier piercing critique of discrimination in the distribution of federal funds, see "Editorial Comment," *Journal of Negro Education* 3 (October 1934): 565–72.

68. Septima Clark, interview by Wigginton.

69. Hall Interview. On black women's insistence that white allies treat them as equals,

see Bethune, "How Fare Negro Youth?," 10; Reim, "Dorothy Tilly," 28. On the founding of other important interracial organizations in the South during the 1930s, see Hall, *Revolt*; Reed, *Simple Decency*.

70. See *Teachers' Bulletin* 15 (March 1935): 6; S. P. Clark, "Annual Report."

71. See Fink, "Teaching the People," esp. 243–50, 256, 263–64. See also Synott, "Crusaders and Clubwomen," 55, 67; "1934 Enrollment in Opportunity School by County and Race," box 3, folder 178, Gray Papers. For additional biographical information on Gray, see Montgomery, *South Carolina's Wil Lou Gray*, esp. 1–23; Ayres, *Let My People Learn*. On the growth of adult education in South Carolina, see Carlton, *Mill and Town*, 261–69.

72. Fink, "Teaching the People." The antielitism of nineteenth-century philosopher Nikolai Grundtvig inspired folk school founders. On Grundtvig and the Danish folk schools in the South, see Rodgers, *Atlantic Crossings*, chap. 8, esp. 354–62; Whisnant, *All That Is Native and Fine*.

73. Gray's report in *AR* (1937–38), 74–76; "Announcement," June 18, 1932, box 3, folder 144, Gray Papers; "Information Sheet: Why an Opportunity School?," n.d., box 3, folder 145, Gray Papers; Vernice Saunders to Wil Lou Gray, February 3, 1933, box 3, folder 151, Gray Papers.

74. See "Recruiting Program—September–October 1935," box 3, folder 192, Gray Papers; Montgomery, *South Carolina's Wil Lou Gray*, 2, 23, 33, 91. See also Carlton, *Mill and Town*, 263; Fink, "Teaching the People," 249–50.

75. James H. Hammond quoted in Montgomery, *South Carolina's Wil Lou Gray*, 39.

76. *AR* (1937–38), 74. See also Fink, "Teaching the People," 244, 259–60. The Jeanes Fund and the Rosenwald Foundation contributed to adult education classes for African Americans.

77. Reid, *Adult Education*, 5–12, 19, 17. The American Adult Education Association first turned its attention to African Americans in 1931. See also Grant, "Adult Education"; Rodgers, *Atlantic Crossings*, 415.

78. Reid, *Adult Education*, 8. Sullivan makes the last point in relation to other forms of New Deal relief (*Days of Hope*).

79. See Atkins, "Participation," 346.

80. See "Annual Report of Mrs. Sarah Ballentine," Richland County, box 3, folder 195, Gray Papers; S. P. Clark, "Annual Report."

81. S. P. Clark, "Annual Report."

82. Hall Interview.

83. Clark, *Echo*, 148–49; S. P. Clark, "Annual Report." See also Hall Interview.

84. See examples of "My Trip to Columbia" essays, box 3, folder 201a, Gray Papers.

85. Fink, "Teaching the People," 260–62; S. P. Clark, "Annual Report."

86. Hall Interview. On Bethune, see Synott, "Crusaders and Clubwomen," 55.

87. See "Findings of Adult Education and the Negro," copy at SOCAR, 41–42. See also Dennis, *Luther P. Jackson*.

88. "Findings of Adult Education and the Negro," 2–3, 67, 71.

89. Ibid., 38.

90. Gray quoted in Fink, "Teaching the People," 258.

91. Epps quoted in Hayes, *South Carolina*, 174; see also 168; Frederickson, *Dixiecrat Revolt*, 23–25.

92. See "Record Registration of Race Voters in S.C. Raises Query on Who Will Be Benefited," *Pittsburgh Courier*, September 5, 1936. Southern white conservatives also worried about the implications of federal intervention in education. In 1937, attendees at the National Governor's Conference in Atlantic City devoted an entire session to debating the question, "Shall we turn the control of our schools over to the Federal government?" (*AR* [1938–39], 22–23).

93. See "Church and Social Workers," speech 4, n.d., folder 6, Murray Collection.

94. See "Findings of Adult Education and the Negro," 67.

95. Studying Dr. Matilda Evans's efforts to establish a public health clinic in Columbia, Darlene Clark Hine has theorized the links between black community mobilization and raising black political consciousness ("Corporeal," 29).

Chapter Five

1. Clark, *Echo*, 80.

2. See Dalfiume, "'Forgotten Years,'" esp. 98–99; Sitkoff, "Racial Militancy," esp. 663; Egerton, *Speak Now*, 213–16. On the Washington, D.C., sit-ins in April 1943 and April 1944, see Murray, *Autobiography*, 200; on *Smith v. Allwright*, see Kluger, *Simple Justice*, 234–37. See also Gilmore, *Defying Dixie*, chaps. 6–8.

3. More broadly, the politics of salary equalization played out differently in southern states depending on the willingness of the leaders of black teachers' associations to align with the NAACP. See, for example, Chirhart, *Torches of Light*, chap. 6.

4. Clark, *Echo*, 82; Harvey quoted by John McCray in "Address before the Barnwell County Teachers Association," March 30, 1945, 8, McCray Papers, reel 7.

5. Clark, *Ready from Within*, 23; F. P. Adams Interview.

6. See Tushnet, *NAACP's Legal Strategy*, 13–14, 29, 34, 42–45, 47.

7. See *Teachers' Salaries in Black and White: A Pamphlet for Teachers and Their Friends* (New York: NAACP Legal Defense and Educational Fund, 1942), 2, 4–9, Social Ethics Collection, Yale Divinity School, Yale University, New Haven, Conn. More broadly, see Klarman, *From Jim Crow to Civil Rights*.

8. *AR* (1938–39), 135, 153–55; *AR* (1937–38), 81; *AR* (1940–41), 175.

9. *AR* (1940–41), 106–9, 175, 178–79. As late as 1948, the number of school districts in South Carolina remained 47 percent greater than the combined number in eight other southern states (*Public Schools of South Carolina*, 19, 59, SOCAR). South Carolina's 1,680 school districts far outstripped those of the next-highest state, Kentucky, which had 246.

10. See Clark, *Echo*, 79; and "Sketch of Septima Clark's Career," box 1, folder 1, CRC. On the NAACP, see Lau, *Democracy Rising*, chap. 4, esp. 108–24; Aba-Mecha, "Black Woman Activist," 165–70; Woods, "South Carolina Conference of the NAACP," 2–3; Richards, "Osceola E. McKaine," 107–9.

11. On McCray, see Roefs, "Leading," 462–91; on McKaine, see Richards, "Osceola E. McKaine," 97–98; Sullivan, *Days of Hope*, 196.

12. L. Raymond Bailey to Thurgood Marshall, November 28, 1940, Thurgood Marshall to L. Raymond Bailey, December 11, 1940, both in NAACP Papers, pt. 3, ser. B, reel 9. (All documents from pt. 3, ser. B, reel 9 hereafter cited as NAACP Papers, 3:B:9.)

13. Joseph Murray to Thurgood Marshall, July 30, 1941, NAACP Papers, 3:B:9. On the Columbia school board's recommendation, see "Report of the Salary Schedule Committee, Columbia City Schools," December 14, 1941, box 2, folder "Columbia School Board, 1941," A. C. Flora Papers, SOCAR. See also Baker, *Paradoxes*, chaps. 3, 7.

14. See "Interesting Viewpoint," *CS*, May 28, 1941.

15. *AR* (1940–41), 103, 178; *AR* (1941–42), 152–53, 202–3; "New Teacher Salary Base Is Approved," *CS*, August 6, 1941, clipping, NAACP Papers, 3:B:9. See also appendix, table 3.

16. See "New Teacher Salary Base Is Approved," *CS*, August 6, 1941; Potts, *History*, 62–63; see also 104, 144, 190; Aba-Mecha, "Black Woman Activist," 180, 185.

17. John P. Burgess to Joseph Murray, July 16, 1941, NAACP Papers, 3:B:9; *AR* (1938–39), 109.

18. See "Comments by Osceola McKaine," *Lighthouse and Informer*, ca. August 1941, clipping, NAACP Papers, 3:B:9; Richards, "Eminent Lieutenant McKaine," 49. See also relevant minutes in NAACP, Sumter Branch Minute Book, April 12, 1942–September 28, 1952, SOCAR.

19. See "Your Salary, Our Fight," 1–2, n.d., NAACP Papers, 3:B:9; Richards, "Osceola E. McKaine," 115–16; Aba-Mecha, "Black Woman Activist," 176–77; *AR* (1942–43), 123. African American schools faced a 15.6 percent teaching shortage, and more black educators abandoned the profession to seek commercial and industrial jobs (17 percent) and to enlist in the armed forces (13 percent) than did whites (16 percent and 9 percent, respectively).

20. Unnamed PSTA official to B. W. Gallman, a member of the PSTA executive committee who supported filing suit, quoted in Richards, "Osceola E. McKaine," 122.

21. F. P. Adams Interview; Clark, *Echo*, 81. Clark knew Simmons personally because he had served as an usher at her brother's wedding (Poinsette-Fisher Interview). See also Drago, *Initiative*, 177–79.

22. Osceola McKaine to Thurgood Marshall, February 10, 1943, James M. Hinton to NAACP, March 5, 1943, both in NAACP Papers, 3:B:9. See also Aba-Mecha, "Black Woman Activist," 181–82. On J. Arthur Brown, see Drago, *Initiative*, 179, 239–40.

23. Potts, *History*, 63–66. The House of Delegates, which became the PSTA's governing body in 1939, was composed of one to three delegates from county teachers' associations and representatives from the state's black colleges and private schools.

24. McCray quoted in Roefs, "Leading," 473; Simkins quoted in Aba-Mecha, "Black Woman Activist," 185. See also Richards, "Osceola E. McKaine," 129.

25. Kluger, *Simple Justice*, 195.

26. Septima Clark, interview by Cynthia Brown, Charleston, S.C., August 1979, tape 6, side B, in author's possession.

27. Ibid.; Hall Interview.

28. Clark, *Echo*, 148–49. See also *AR* (1940–41), 31, in which Gray discusses organizing classes for soldiers at Fort Jackson; *AR* (1941–42), 46.

29. Septima Clark, interview by Brown, tape 2, side B.

30. Hall Interview.

31. A. B. Rhett in "Minutes of the Regular Meeting, April 1, 1942," H. L. Erckmann to Charleston City Board of School Commissioners, July 22, 1943, both in CBC Minute Books: April 1940–July 1946, box 603, CCSD (emphasis added).

32. See Harold R. Boulware to National NAACP Office, January 10, 1943, Harold R. Boulware to Leon A. Ransom, May 12, 1943, James M. Hinton to Thurgood Marshall, October 16, 1943, Osceola McKaine to Thurgood Marshall, November 2, 1943, all in NAACP Papers, 3:B:9. At this time, Marshall was preparing to argue *Smith v. Allwright* before the Supreme Court.

33. "Minutes from the Regular Meeting, October 6, 1943," CBC Minute Books: April 1940–July 1946, box 603, CCSD; H. R. Erckmann to Charleston City Board of School Commissioners, October 11, 1943, Superintendent Files, box 902, folder "Melissa [*sic*] T. Smith, 1943," CCSD.

34. Drago, *Initiative*, 241; Harold R. Boulware to Thurgood Marshall, October 10, 1943, NAACP Papers, 3:B:9.

35. See "Court Refuses to Dismiss Negro Teacher Suit," *CNC*, n.d., clipping in NAACP Papers, 3:B:9. On Waring's background and political connections, see Yarbrough, *Passion*, chap. 1, esp. 16–20.

36. McCray, "South Carolina—The Way It Was," n.d., *The Chronicle* (Charleston, S.C.), clipping, box 1, folder "Charleston," James R. Logan Collection, ARC. Marshall and school board attorneys agreed that officials should begin to close the pay gap in the next school year, with full salary equalization beginning in 1946 (Yarbrough, *Passion*, 43).

37. See "Negroes Plan Equalization Suits against Other Cities," unidentified clipping, February 15, 1944, NAACP Papers, 3:B:9; "The Submissive South," *CNC*, February 16, 1944, clipping, NAACP Papers, 3:B:9.

38. See "New School Control Up to Fix Pay: Measure in House Would Decentralize System, Create 'Managers,'" unidentified clipping, n.d., NAACP Papers, 3:B:9 (emphasis added). Members of the State House of Representatives also "voted unanimously" for "a recertification plan for teachers," but it too failed to pass ("House Votes Secretly to Re-Certify," unidentified clipping, n.d., NAACP Papers, 3:B:9). See also "In the Open" (editorial), *Columbia Record*, February 22, 1944.

39. See "Transcript of Proceedings at Hearing of R. Rebecca Monteith, individually and on behalf of other Negro teachers and Principals . . . vs. W. H. Cobb, County Superintendent of Education, Richland County, South Carolina, and the County Board of Richland County," September 25, 1944, NAACP Papers. Monteith was Modjeska Simkins's sister; her case was dismissed on November 11, 1944, on the basis of the new law. By attaching the proviso to the Deficiency Appropriations Act, proponents exploited a legal loophole to circumvent the state constitutional requirement that all proposed legislation receive three separate readings in the House and Senate on different days (Littlejohn, *Littlejohn's Political Memoirs*, 44–46).

40. "Second Step—Grievance Procedure" (copy of the General Assembly's law), n.d.,

NAACP Papers, 3:B:9 (emphasis added). See also Yarbrough, *Passion*, 43, 45. Because it was attached to an appropriations bill, the statute "was only binding for one fiscal year."

41. "Teacher Grievance Clause to Aid S.C., Brown Says," unidentified clipping, n.d., NAACP Papers, 3:B:9; "Press Release," March 23, 1944, NAACP Papers, 3:B:9.

42. Aba-Mecha, "Black Woman Activist," 188; Browne, *Love My Children*, 239. See also Clark, *Echo*, 80–81.

43. Clark, *Echo*, 81–82.

44. See "Copy, Letter of Atty. Frank A. Graham, Attorney for Richland Co.," June 14, 1944; "Respondent's Argument," n.d.; and James M. Hinton to Thurgood Marshall, December 7, 1944, all in NAACP Papers, 3:B:9.

45. See *Journal of the Senate*, 3, 4. Black activists in Columbia had initially believed that they would lead the legal attack on the all-white primary (Committee from the Colored Enrolees to the Board of Election Commissioners, April 21, 1942; "Negro Voting in Primaries Rejected Here," unidentified clipping, [May 4, 1942?]; and James Hinton to Thurgood Marshall, May 4, 1942, all in NAACP Papers, pt. 4, reel 10. On the South Carolina Plan, see Richards, "Osceola E. McKaine," 166.

46. McKaine quoted in "The Progressive Democratic Meeting," May 24, 1944, McCray Papers, reel 7; Hinton in "Negro Willing to Shed Blood for Rights," Associated Press clipping, May 24, 1944, Black History Collection, James M. Hinton File, SOCAR. The PDP had representatives from thirty-eight of the state's forty-six counties.

47. See "A Report from the State Chairman," July 26, 1944, McCray Papers, reel 7; Richards, "Osceola McKaine," 182–87; Sullivan, *Days of Hope*, 170; Frederickson, *Dixiecrat Revolt*, 43.

48. Richards, "Osceola McKaine," 189–92, 204–5. See also Sullivan, *Days of Hope*, 192.

49. Hall Interview; Clark, *Echo*, 81. Clark does not mention the PDP in either of her two autobiographies or in any interview, omissions that indicate her lack of involvement. Marshall spent two days in Columbia for a strategy session in March but was not in the courtroom during the trial itself. See Thurgood Marshall to James M. Hinton, February 9, 1945; James M. Hinton to Thurgood Marshall, February 12, May 10, 1945; and Shadrack Morgan to Robert L. Carter, March 27, 1945, all in NAACP Papers, 3:B:9. On Boulware's enlistment, see Thurgood Marshall to Osceola McKaine, March 24, 1944, NAACP Papers, 3:B:9.

50. "'Race' Factor in Teachers' Pay Denied," unidentified clipping, n.d., and James M. Hinton to Thurgood Marshall, May 10, 1945, both in NAACP Papers, 3:B:9.

51. Quoted in "'Race' Factor in Teachers' Pay Denied," unidentified clipping, n.d., NAACP Papers, 3:B:9. On Simmons's experience and training, see "Decision in South Carolina Teachers' Salary Case Pending" (press release), May 17, 1945, NAACP Papers, 3:B:9.

52. Flora quoted in "'Race' Factor in Teachers' Pay Denied," unidentified clipping, n.d., NAACP Papers, 3:B:9; Waring quoted in Yarbrough, *Passion*, 46; Clark, *Echo*, 82.

53. Waring quoted in Yarbrough, *Passion*, 46.

54. *AR* (1944–45), 170; Brown quoted in McCray, "Address," 9. Mandatory recertifica-

tion placed a tremendous burden on the state's Division of Teacher Education and Certification, forcing it to hire additional staff and run on the night shift. See, for example, "Minutes from the Regular Meeting, May 2, 1945," CBC Minute Books: April 1940–July 1946, box 603, CCSD. See appendix, table 4.

55. See *AR* (1944–45), 171; *Requirements for Teacher Education*, 46–50; Rhett quoted in "Regular Meeting, November 14, 1944," CBC Minute Books: April 1940–July 1946, box 603, CCSD. This revised 1948 edition eliminated some categories from the original plan. See also "Preliminary Explanation to Teachers and School Officials," NAACP Papers, 3:B:9.

56. Clark, *Echo*, 83. See also McCray, "Address," 7.

57. Lois Averetta Simms, interview by author, Charleston, S.C., April 9, 2002, in author's possession; F. P. Adams Interview. See also Simms, *Chalk and Chalkboard Career*, 10.

58. Edward R. Dudley to James M. Hinton, May 29, 1945, NAACP Papers, 3:B:9; *AR* (1945–46), 174; appendix, table 5.

59. F. P. Adams Interview.

60. See Edward R. Dudley to James M. Hinton, May 29, 1945, NAACP Papers, B:3:9; Smith's comments appear in *AR* (1946–47), 141–42; on the PSTA, see Potts, *History*, 72, 191; see also 79, which mentions that "the only dark cloud on the horizon" for the PSTA was when a number of African American teachers were caught cheating on the NTE in the late 1940s; F. P. Adams Interview.

61. McCray, "Address," 12; Potts, *History*, 72. See also "The *Lighthouse and Informer* 1944 Policies and Programs," McCray Papers, reel 1.

62. Potts, *History*, 192. The PSTA allotted five hundred dollars for Delaine and Wrighten's suits. See also Thurgood Marshall to Osceola McKaine, March 24, 1944, NAACP Papers, 3:B:9; Richards, "Eminent Lieutenant McKaine," 50; Richards, "Osceola E. McKaine," 117. On *Briggs v. Elliott*, which became one of the cases in *Brown v. Board*, see Kluger, *Simple Justice*, chap. 1.

63. Clark, *Echo*, 82. On voting, see B. W. Gallman to John H. McCray, May 5, 1946, McCray Papers, reel 13; McCray quotes Duvall in Richards, "Osceola E. McKaine," 142; on Thompson, see "Minutes from the July 17, 1946 Meeting," box 2, folder "Columbia School Board, 1946–47," Flora Papers. For examples of others who lost their jobs, see Potts, *History*, 66–67.

64. Aba-Mecha, "Black Woman Activist," 212; "Minutes from the Regular Meetings, April 17, 1945 and July 25, 1945," County Board of Education Minute Book: July 1944–June 1949, box 2, CCSD. See also Martin, *History and Development*, 19, SOCAR.

65. See, for example, "An Affadavit," November 20, 1944, McCray Papers, reel 7.

66. Septima Clark, interview by Brown, tape 5, side A. See also F. P. Adams Interview. More than sixty years later, Adams would still not reveal the name of the person who collected teachers' donations for the NAACP.

67. F. P. Adams Interview; Clark, *Echo*, 82.

68. Carter quoted in Edwards, "Booker T. Washington High School," 104, 108.

69. Clark, *Echo*, 86–87.

70. Ibid., 82–83, 87.

71. Alpha Kappa Alpha Sorority, telephone interview by author, March 10, 2005, in author's possession.

Chapter Six

1. See Clelia McGowan to Harriet Stoney Simons, July 15, 1946, box 75, folder 3, H. S. Simons Collection. Portions of this chapter have appeared in Charron, "We've Come a Long Way."

2. See, for example, "Minutes of Committee on Administration, January 18, 1954 to April 17, 1967," Young Women's Christian Association, Coming Street Branch, Charleston, S.C. As late as 1956, the Coming Street YWCA depended on the local Community Chest for more than half of its budget. See also Brown, "Civil Rights Activism," 21–22; O'Neill, "From the Shadow of Slavery"; Fields, *Lemon Swamp*, 192–96.

3. See Yarbrough, *Passion*, 64–66.

4. Clark, *Echo*, 95.

5. Septima Clark to the Warings, January 7, 1958, box 9, folder 230, J. W. Waring Papers. When she wrote to the couple, Clark used the salutation "My dear, dear friends."

6. On more aggressive African American groups, such as the Veterans Civic Organization, see Millicent Ellison Brown, "Civil Rights Activism," 45–47, 138–48; Yarbrough, *Passion*, 115.

7. See Fraser, *Charleston! Charleston!*, 373–74, 387–88, 390, 392; *Charleston Grows*, xii, 35–64, esp. 43–44, 62–63.

8. See *Charleston Grows*, 47, 49, 52–56, 58–59, 62–63, 88, 103, 118; Septima Clark, interview by Cynthia Brown, Charleston, S.C., August 1979, tape 3, side B, in author's possession. Clark related the bus story in the context of discussing Rosa Parks's training at Highlander four months before the Montgomery Bus Boycott began.

9. See "Report of Superintendent in November [1946] Meeting," CBC Minute Books: August 1946–February 1951, box 604. Archer, built in 1936, served 1,303 pupils in a facility originally designed for 680. Buist, constructed in 1921 to house 520 students, had 878. Archer ran on a double session, and Buist and Simonton ran on triple sessions every day.

10. Minutes of the Regular Meetings, November 13, 1946, April 7, 1947, CBC Minute Books: August 1946–February 1951, box 604; "Report of the Education Sub-Committee," A-6, in *Charleston Looks at Its Services for Negroes: A Condensed Report of the Findings and Recommendations of the Inter-Racial Study Committee of the Charleston Welfare Council in Cooperation with the Community Relations Project of the National Urban League*, in box 19, folder "Charleston," William D. Workman Jr. Papers, Modern Political Collection, University of South Carolina, Columbia. The city hired its first black supervisor for African American schools, Wilmot Frasier, in 1944.

11. See "The Setting" (introduction) and "Report of the Health Sub-Committee," B-2, B-11–B-12, in *Charleston Looks at Its Services for Negroes*. In 1944, black and white death rates stood at 21.2 and 13.2 per 1,000, respectively, and the black infant mortality rate was

almost double that of whites. In 1946, only 232 hospital beds served approximately 66,000 black people in Charleston County, and three times more African Americans died from tuberculosis than whites.

12. See Clark, *Echo*, 90–91; Thrasher Interview; "Report of the Health Sub-Committee," B-4, in *Charleston Looks at Its Services for Negroes*. On the activities of the African American parent-teacher association, see Peter Poinsette Papers, ARC.

13. In 1951, Clark also served as chair of the Civic Committee of her federated club and chair of the Coordinating Committee of the local NAACP (Septima Clark to Robert Vann, November 2, 1951, box 9, folder 224, J. W. Waring Papers). On the Charleston chapter of the National Council of Negro Women, established in 1949, and Alpha Kappa Alpha, see "National Council of Negro Women Souvenir Yearbook," 105, box 11, folder 38, Clark Papers. For Clark's involvement in the local and state Federated Women's Clubs, see "Fortieth Anniversary of the South Carolina Federation of Colored Women's Clubs, 1909–1949" and "Minutes of the Forty-second Anniversary of the South Carolina Federation of Colored Women's Clubs, May 4–5, 1951," box 2, Ethelyn Parker Collection, ARC. Clark is listed as the chair of the Coming Street YWCA in the 1949 publication *Charleston Grows*, 249. See also Septima Clark to the Warings, March 10, 1952, box 9, folder 224, J. W. Waring Papers.

14. I have culled this information from membership rosters of the various organizations. For LaSaine's involvement with the NAACP, see Septima Clark, interview by Brown, tape 3, side B. See also Fields, *Lemon Swamp*, 187.

15. Clark, *Ready from Within*, 27. Clark stated that she would have never been invited to Irma Clement's house to play bridge (Yarbrough, *Passion*, 111).

16. Clark quoted in Poinsette-Fisher Interview. See also Septima Clark, interview by Brown, tape 5, side A; Charleston County Auditor Ward Books 1–9, 1950–53 (microfilm), O. T. Wallace County Office Building, Charleston, S.C.

17. My account is drawn from Eugene C. Hunt's historical play, "A Journey in Faith and Courage," copy in box 11, folder 39, Clark Papers.

18. Ibid. The conservatism of Charleston's white Y only increased as the civil rights era progressed. In 1967, white members voted to disaffiliate from the national organization because they abhorred the group's "socialistic" stance on a wide range of issues, including civil rights. Charleston's black women immediately set about reorganizing and 1969 established the YWCA of Greater Charleston. The day after black women received a state charter, the National YWCA revoked the white Y's charter and sued a year later to prevent that group from using the YWCA name or symbol. Today, what was once the central white YWCA is known as the Family Christian Y. On white southern progressive women more broadly, see Scott, *Southern Lady*, chaps. 7, 8, esp. 186–99; Gilmore, *Gender and Jim Crow*, esp. chaps. 6–8.

19. Harriet Simons to Caroline Wagner, July 17, 1946, box 75, folder 3, H. S. Simons Collection. See also Egerton, *Speak Now*, 47–51; Yuhl, *Golden Haze*.

20. Clark, *Echo*, 91–94. See also Septima Clark, interview by Brown, tape 5, side A.

21. Clark, *Echo*, 91–94. A few months later, a YMCA program was established for boys.

22. Yarbrough, *Passion*, 57–60; Kluger, *Simple Justice*, 299. For biographical information on Wrighten, see Millicent Ellison Brown, "Civil Rights Activism," 44–45.

23. Yarbrough, *Passion*, 64; NAACP Papers, pt. 4, reel 10. See also Frederickson, *Dixiecrat Revolt*, 109.

24. For a broader discussion of the onset of the Cold War, see Gilmore, *Defying Dixie*, chap. 9; Sullivan, *Days of Hope*, 223–27, 237–40; Egerton, *Speak Now*, 410–13, 452–53; Bailey, *Diplomatic History*, 796–99.

25. Egerton, *Speak Now*, 361–69, 415–16, 476; Frederickson, *Dixiecrat Revolt*, 52–66; O'Brien, *Color*; Savage, *Broadcasting Freedom*, 227.

26. Frederickson, *Dixiecrat Revolt*, esp. 76–81, 104–6; Key, *Southern Politics*, 329–44. R. Beverly Herbert, a white moderate, publicly insisted that segregation was necessary to fight communism but privately advised Johnston that outsiders would be more sympathetic to this argument "if the matter was not referred to as 'White Supremacy,' but as one of 'Orderly Government'" (Herbert to Johnston, July 29, 1948, box 13, folder 14, Olin D. Johnston Papers, Modern Political Collection, University of South Carolina, Columbia; Herbert, *What We Can Do*).

27. A. G. Kennedy to J. Howard McGrath, February 27, 1948, box 1, folder "Legislative, 1948, Civil Rights," Joseph R. Bryson Papers, Modern Political Collection, University of South Carolina, Columbia.

28. Kluger, *Simple Justice*, 300.

29. "How to Stop Club Enrolling," *CNC*, July 17, 1948; Thurmond quoted in Frederickson, *Dixiecrat Revolt*, 140.

30. "Vote Is Heavy; Order Prevails," *Columbia Record*, August 10, 1948; Fraser, *Charleston! Charleston!*, 398; *Elmore v. Rice* file, NCAA Papers, pt. 4, reel 10; Kluger, *Simple Justice*, 300; Sullivan, *Days of Hope*, 256; Clark, *Ready from Within*, 25. Figures for statewide black voter turnout that day vary.

31. Yarbrough, *Passion*, 108–10. See also Miriam DeCosta Willis to author, April 30, 2002, in author's possession.

32. Ruby Cornwell, interview by author, James Island, S.C., April 11, 2002, in author's possession; "A Memorial Service of Worship for the Late Ruby Madeline Pendergrass Cornwell, March 9, 2003," in author's possession. See also "Minutes of the Phyllis Wheatley Literary and Social Club, 1928–29 and 1931–32," Phillis Wheatley Literary and Social Club Collection, box 1, folder 1, ARC; *Charleston Grows*, 242; Yarbrough, *Passion*, 110–13. When I visited Cornwell, she still had photographs of the Warings adorning her walls.

33. Cornwell, interview.

34. Yarbrough, *Passion*, 29–41, 113. Septima Clark believed that Annie Waring could not abide her husband's change of heart with regard to civil rights (Thrasher Interview).

35. As Harriet Simons observed, "The people of Charleston who have known Judge Waring all of his life find it hard to accept his extraordinary conversion in later life, particularly when his attitude had formerly been one of complete disregard, to the whole bi-racial problem." Charlestonians claimed to be ostracizing Judge Waring because of his "treatment of his first wife and the manner in which he handled his divorce," prior to

any of his controversial civil rights rulings. She added, "We also resent very bitterly the speech which his second wife made to the YWCA Coming Street branch" (Harriet Simons to South Carolina Council on Human Relations, February 7, 1955, box 76, folder 2, H. S. Simons Collection).

36. For Clark's version of the YWCA fiasco, see Clark, *Echo*, 95–99. See also Clark, *Ready from Within*, 25–26; Yarbrough, *Passion*, 127–35; Rowan, *South of Freedom*, 87–100; West, "Saga."

37. Clark, *Echo*, 97.

38. Elizabeth Waring to Bicknell Eubanks, January 3, 1951, box 4, folder 12, Cornwell Collection. On the evening, see Clark, *Echo*, 99–100.

39. See Elizabeth Waring, "YWCA Speech," NAACP Papers, pt. 4, reel 11; anonymous Charleston resident, interview by author, May 16, 2002, Charleston, S.C., in author's possession.

40. Waring, "YWCA Speech."

41. Clark, *Echo*, 100. Waring would hear preliminary arguments in *Briggs v. Elliott* on November 17, 1950 (Kluger, *Simple Justice*, 23, 301, 345).

42. Yarbrough, *Passion*, 132–33; see also 135–39, 141, 143, 145. For a more in-depth analysis of the Warings and racial and gender hierarchies, see Frederickson, "'As a Man.'"

43. Charles T. Dixon to Dan Henderson, May 28, 1950, box 432, folder 3, T. R. Waring Papers; Yarbrough, *Passion*, 147, 154, 157–63; Harriet Simons to South Carolina Council on Human Relations, February 7, 1955, box 76, folder 2, H. S. Simons Collection.

44. Waties Waring quoted in Yarbrough, *Passion*, 158, 176; see also 154; Elizabeth Waring to Ruby Cornwell, September 9, 1950, box 1, folder 1, Cornwell Collection.

45. Walter White to John McCray, January 24, 1950, NAACP Papers, pt. 4, reel 11; Elizabeth Waring quoted in Clark, *Echo*, 104.

46. Septima Clark to Elizabeth Waring, March 11, 1950, box 4, folder 52, J. W. Waring Papers.

47. Elizabeth Waring to Ruby Cornwell, July 31, 1951, box 1, folder 2, Cornwell Collection; Elizabeth Waring to Ruby Cornwell, February 4, 1954, box 1, folder 15, Cornwell Collection; Elizabeth Waring to Ruby Cornwell, May 18, 1955, box 2, folder 2, Cornwell Collection. See also Septima Clark to the Warings, June 1, 1955, box 9, folder 227, J. W. Waring Papers.

48. See, for example, Hubert Delany to Ruby Cornwell, October 30, 1951, box 4, folder 25, Cornwell Collection; Yarbrough, *Passion*, 245; Miriam DeCosta Willis to author, April 30, 2002, in author's possession.

49. Septima Clark to the Warings, June 14, 1959, box 9, folder 231, J. W. Waring Papers; Clark, *Echo*, 102, 103; Clark, *Ready from Within*, 27. See also Yarbrough, *Passion*, 149; Miriam DeCosta Willis to author, April 30, 2002, in author's possession.

50. Septima Clark to Elizabeth Waring, July 30, 1950, box 4, folder 52, J. W. Waring Papers; Johnston quoted in Yarbrough, *Passion*, 153. See also Frederickson, *Dixiecrat Revolt*, 207–8. On a more practical level, the judge tutored his black friends in safeguarding against possible white reprisals, specifically warning them of the dangers of outstanding debt (Cornwell, interview).

51. Septima Clark to the Warings, November 7, 1955, box 9, folder 227, J. W. Waring Papers; Septima Clark to Elizabeth Waring, October 12, 1962, box 4, folder 53, J. W. Waring Papers; Septima Clark, interview by Brown, tape 5, side A.

52. Clark, *Echo*, 104, 105; Clark, *Ready from Within*, 27; Hall Interview; Cornwell, interview.

53. Septima Clark, interview by Brown, tape 3, side B.

54. Poinsette-Fisher Interview.

55. Septima Clark to the Warings, February 12, 1951, box 9, folder 223, J. W. Waring Papers.

56. Poinsette-Fisher Interview; Waring quoted by Septima Clark, interview by Brown, tape 5, side A.

57. Septima Clark to the Warings, March 10, 1952, box 9, folder 224, J. W. Waring Papers; Septima Clark, interview by Brown, tape 5, side A; Yarbrough, *Passion*, 131. See also Cornwell, interview.

58. Clark, *Ready from Within*, 27–28; Clark, *Echo*, 105–7.

59. Septima Clark to Elizabeth Waring, March 4, 1950, box 4, folder 52, J. W. Waring Papers.

60. See Septima Clark to the Warings, September 3, 1951, box 9, folder 223, J. W. Waring Papers; Septima Clark to the Warings, July 2, 1952, box 9, folder 224, J. W. Waring Papers; Clark, *Echo*, 107–8.

61. Septima Clark to the Warings, November 1, 1952, box 9, folder 224, J. W. Waring Papers; Septima Clark to the Warings, July 16, 1953, box 9, folder 225, J. W. Waring Papers. Clark and the more integrationist-minded women did not give up. By November 1952, they had convinced Halsey that the Tuberculosis Association's segregated auxiliary had outgrown its usefulness and urged that the organization's constitution be revised to prevent discrimination. By October 1953, the Community Chest no longer had a segregated auxiliary. Amending constitutions proved easier than changing attitudes and practices, however.

62. Brown, "Civil Rights Activism," 261; Yarbrough, *Passion*, 111.

63. Brown, "Civil Rights Activism," 259–64.

64. Septima Clark to the Warings, March 10, November 30, 1952, box 9, folder 224, J. W. Waring Papers; Elizabeth Waring to Ruby Cornwell, June 29, 1953, box 1, folder 8, Cornwell Collection.

65. See "Minutes of the Meeting of Presidents of the Southern States Held in Atlanta Georgia, July 27–28, 1954," box 75, folder 16, H. S. Simons Collection. On black women's exclusion from the Maybank dinner, see Septima Clark to the Warings, January 12, 1954, box 9, folder 226, J. W. Waring Papers.

66. See Etheline M. Parker to John McCray, September 27, 1947, McCray Papers, reel 14; Marion Wilkinson to Mamie Fields, May 23, 1949, box 3, folder 5, Mamie Garvin Fields Collection, ARC. Between 1945 and 1949, the number of clubs in the Charleston federation grew from three to twelve.

67. Septima Clark to Elizabeth Waring, March 26, July 9, 1950, box 4, folder 52, J. W. Waring Papers.

68. A. J. Tamsberg to William McGillivray Morrison, June 13, 1949, William McGillivray Morrison Papers, box 1, City of Charleston Archives, Charleston, S.C.; "Renominated Mayor Veteran of 25 Years in Politics," *CNC*, July 25, 1951; Fraser, *Charleston! Charleston!*, 397, 405; copy sheet from the *Lighthouse and Informer*, July 22, 1951, box 432, folder 2, T. R. Waring Papers.

69. Elizabeth Waring to Ruby Cornwell, February 25, 1951, Cornwell Collection; "Both Political Camps Foresee Victory Today," *CNC*, July 24, 1951; *Lighthouse and Informer*, July 22, 1951, box 432, folder 2, T. R. Waring Papers; Septima Clark to the Warings, June 23, July 23, 1951, box 9, folder 223, J. W. Waring Papers.

70. Septima Clark to the Warings, July 23, 1951, box 9, folder 223, J. W. Waring Papers; "Morrison Renominated," *CNC*, July 25, 1951.

71. Septima Clark to the Warings, July 23, 1951, box 9, folder 223, J. W. Waring Papers; A. J. Tamsberg to William McGillivray Morrison, June 13, 1949.

72. Septima Clark to Elizabeth Waring, July 24, 1951, box 4, folder 53, J. W. Waring Papers; Septima Clark to the Warings, August 2, 1951, box 9, folder 223, J. W. Waring Papers; "Both Political Camps Foresee Victory Today," *CNC*, July 24, 1951; "Morrison Renominated," *CNC*, July 25, 1951.

73. Elizabeth Waring to Ruby Cornwell, July 13, 1951, box 1, folder 2, Cornwell Collection; Elizabeth Waring to Ruby Cornwell, August 12, 1951, box 1, folder 3, Cornwell Collection.

74. Septima Clark to the Warings, July 2, 1952, box 9, folder 224, J. W. Waring Papers; "Veal Letter Says White Bosses Ruled Leaders," *Lighthouse and Informer*, July 26, 1952; "Negro Candidates Deny Report They Cried 'Sellout,'" *CNC*, July 24, 1952, clipping, box 432, folder 2, T. R. Waring Papers.

75. Kluger, *Simple Justice*, 268, 282–84.

76. Littlejohn, *Littlejohn's Political Memoirs*, 158–59; Robertson, *Sly and Able*; Frederickson, *Dixiecrat Revolt*, 205.

77. James Byrnes to Thomas R. Waring, June 28, 1952, box 390, folder 5, T. R. Waring Papers; Byrnes quoted in Kluger, *Simple Justice*, 334.

78. Hollings quoted in Yarbrough, *Passion*, 190.

79. James Byrnes to Thomas R. Waring, June 27, 1951, box 390, folder 5, T. R. Waring Papers. See also James F. Byrnes, "Speech before the South Carolina Educational Association, March 1954," 7, SOCAR, in which Byrnes claimed that NAACP officials had misinterpreted his statement about abandoning public education.

80. Yarbrough, *Passion*, 174–75; Kluger, *Simple Justice*, 303.

81. Yarbrough, *Passion*, 179, 193, 196, 181. For details of the hearing, see Kluger, *Simple Justice*, chap. 15. Roderick Elliott, the chair of the Board of Trustees in District 22, admitted on the stand that he "did not know the geographical boundaries of the school district . . . though he had been its chairman for 25 years" (ibid., 349).

82. The Gressette Committee consisted of five state senators, five state representatives, and five citizens appointed by the governor ("Memorandum, May 3, 1983," David W. Robinson Papers [microfilm], Desegregation Files, reel 1, Law School Library, University of South Carolina, Columbia).

83. The referendum specifically referred to Article XI, Section 5, of the state constitution, a statutory law. If the repeal passed, as the LWV explained, "it would not change a single law governing the public schools in the state. These statutory laws are subject only to change by the General Assembly" (League of Women Voters, Bulletin 3, vol. 3, September 19, 1952, box 19, folder "Civil Rights, General," Workman Papers). For a summary of the *Brown* cases and Byrnes's monitoring of the Supreme Court, see Kluger, *Simple Justice*, chap. 21, esp. 525, 535. See also Frederickson, *Dixiecrat Revolt*, 219.

84. Septima Clark to the Warings, November 1, 1952, box 9, folder 224, J. W. Waring Papers.

85. Septima Clark to the Warings, March 30, 1953, box 9, folder 225, J. W. Waring Papers. A committee of white women from the state chapter of the LWV preferred that the state would "show leadership in a positive and not a negative manner." Nevertheless, very few league women supported desegregation in elementary and secondary schools (Harriet Simons to Kit, November 21 [no year], box 75, folder 16, H. S. Simons Collection).

86. "Negroes Seek New Schools in City," *CNC*, January 23, 1952.

87. Modjeska Simkins, interview by Jacquelyn Dowd Hall, Columbia, S.C., July 28–31, 1976, Southern Oral History Project, Wilson Library, University of North Carolina, Chapel Hill. Frederickson provides good in-depth discussion of the Woodard and Earle cases (*Dixiecrat Revolt*, 54–64). On Winn, see Yarbrough, *Passion*, 154.

88. Septima Clark to the Warings, October 13, 1953, box 9, folder 226, J. W. Waring Papers.

89. Septima Clark to the Warings, August 2, 1951, box 9, folder 223, J. W. Waring Papers; Septima Clark to the Warings, January 26, 1952, Septima Clark to J. W. Waring, July 6, 1952, both in box 9, folder 224, J. W. Waring Papers.

90. Septima Clark to Elizabeth Waring, July 30, 1950, box 4, folder 52, J. W. Waring Papers; Septima Clark to J. W. Waring, July 6, 1952, Septima Clark to the Warings, November 1, 1952, both in box 9, folder 224, J. W. Waring Papers.

91. Septima Clark to the Warings, March 10, May 23, 1952, box 9, folder 224, J. W. Waring Papers.

92. Septima Clark to the Warings, July 16, 1953, box 9, folder 225, J. W. Waring Papers.

Chapter Seven

1. There are a number of book-length studies of HFS. See Adams, *Unearthing Seeds*; Aimee Isgrig Horton, *Highlander Folk School*; Glen, *Highlander*. See also J. Herman Blake, "Citizenship Participation, Democracy and Social Change: A Report to the Emil Schwarzhaupt Foundation," 11–12, box 10, folder 41, Clark Papers; Morris, *Origins*, 142. Portions of this chapter have appeared in Charron, "We've Come a Long Way."

2. Years later, Bernice Robinson remarked, "It seems ironic that the successful work on Johns Island should have been so deeply involved in the teaching of the 3Rs. The very activity that Myles had excluded from his statement about Highlander's mission, but the irony is peripheral because [on] Johns Island, and later throughout the south, the 3Rs be-

came a [means] to achieve that which was essential to Highlander, which was development of effective leadership" ("South Carolina Voices of the Civil Rights Movement Conference: A Conference on the History of the Civil Rights Movement in South Carolina, 1940–1970," 164, ARC).

3. See Adams, *Unearthing Seeds*, 26–27; Langston, "Women," 146; Glen, *Highlander*, 17; Clark, *Echo*, 123–24, 128; Mary Johnson Lee to Thomas R. Waring, April 1, 1959, box 405, folder 6, T. R. Waring Papers.

4. Horton quoted in Aimee Isgrig Horton, *Highlander Folk School*, 16; see also 11–12, 17–18; Adams, *Unearthing Seeds*, 1–6; Glen, *Highlander*, 6–7.

5. Adams, *Unearthing Seeds*, 11–12.

6. Ibid., 23. See also Aimee Isgrig Horton, *Highlander Folk School*, 24–25.

7. Myles Horton quoted in Adams, *Unearthing Seeds*, 27. Lilian Johnson deeded the property to HFS in 1935. See also Glen, *Highlander*, 15–17.

8. On West's departure and early goals, see Glen, *Highlander*, 21, 26, 33. On Highlander's involvement with the labor movement, particularly the Congress of Industrial Organizations, see Glen, *Highlander*, 2, chaps. 4–5; Sullivan, *Days of Hope*, 94–96, 172–74, 208–9, 235, 250–55. On Zilphia Horton and the influence of women in HFS's early years, see Langston, "Women," 145–47. See also Clark, *Echo*, 126; Adams, *Unearthing Seeds*, 29–30.

9. Glen, *Highlander*, 129–30; Egerton, *Speak Now*, 161.

10. Myles Horton, "Materials on a Highlander Workshop, 1958," box 82, folder 2, Highlander Papers. See also Tjerandsen, *Education*, 141–49; Blake, "Citizenship Participation," 24–28. Between 1952 and 1954, HFS launched programs in four locations to develop rural community leadership, but all failed.

11. Kelly quoted in "South Carolina Voices," 159–60; Clark, *Echo*, 119–20.

12. Wood Interview; Clark, *Ready from Within*, 42; "Report of Myles Trip to the Sea Islands, January 1958," ser. 3, box 154, folder 9, SCLC Papers; Septima Clark to the Warings, July 11, 1954, box 9, folder, 226, J. W. Waring Papers. See also Aimee Isgrig Horton, *Highlander Folk School*, 207–9.

13. See Septima Clark to Betty Shipherd, May 17, 1955, box 9, folder 12, Highlander Papers; *A Guide to Community Action for Public School Integration* (Monteagle, Tenn.: HFS, October 1955), box 253, folder 5, J. B. Matthews Papers, Rare Book, Manuscript, and Special Collections Library, Duke University, Durham, N.C.; "Purpose of a Workshop," July 12, 1954, box 9, folder 52, Clark Papers. See also Clark, *Echo*, 120.

14. See Septima Clark to the Warings, July 11, 1954, box 9, folder 226, J. W. Waring Papers; Septima Clark to Myles Horton, July 22, 1954, box 9, folder 12, Highlander Papers. On Hodges and German, see Henry F. Shipherd, "Report on Field Trip to Charleston, Moncks Corner, and Columbia," January 1955, box 67, folder 3, Highlander Papers; Septima Clark to Myles Horton, November 11, 1955, box 65, folder 14, Highlander Papers. Within a year, Hodges had organized a group of black parents to meet with the Charleston school board.

15. Clark, *Echo*, 121; Blake, "Citizenship Participation," 68; "Report of Myles Trip."

16. Carawan and Carawan, *Ain't You Got a Right*, 162–63; "Esau Jenkins Engineers

Change for Negro People," *CNC*, July 28, 1968. For additional biographical information, see box 1, folder 4, Esau Jenkins Collection, ARC; Grimball Interview. See also Clark, *Echo*, 135.

17. Jenkins obliquely referred to African American self-defense as he retold these stories in Carawan and Carawan, *Ain't You Got a Right*, 163–64. See also "Materials on a Highlander Workshop, 1958," box 82, folder 2, Highlander Papers.

18. Jenkins quoted in "Esau Jenkins Engineers Change for Negro People," *CNC*, July 28, 1968; Bill Saunders, interview by author, Charleston, S.C., March 23, 2002, in author's possession. See also Esau Jenkins statement, September 9, 1966, box 1, folder 1, Jenkins Collection; Tjerandsen, *Education*, 151.

19. Clark, *Echo*, 136; Clark, *Ready from Within*, 46. See also Kelley, "'We Are Not What We Seem.'"

20. Jenkins quoted in Tjerandsen, *Education*, 152.

21. Poinsette-Fisher Interview; Clark, *Echo*, 137–38.

22. Septima Clark to the Warings, October 6, 1955, box 4, folder 53, J. W. Waring Papers; Tjerandsen, *Education*, 150, 151; Clark, *Echo*, 143.

23. Yarbrough, *Passion*, 227; Septima Clark to the Warings, August 31, 1954, box 9, folder 226, J. W. Waring Papers. In 1953, the Schwartzhaupt Foundation granted HFS $44,100 for three years; it renewed the grant at $56,150 for another three years in April 1956 (Blake, "Citizenship Participation," 25).

24. See Richard Borden, "Field Trip, December 1954," Myles Horton, "Field Trip Report, Dec. 11–13, 1954," both in box 67, folder 3, Highlander Papers. The literacy obstacle to registration apparently did not register with Horton, who did not mention this detail and merely noted that "the probability of follow-up through Septima and through the county supervisor—Mr. Sain" existed. He was referring to Alice LaSaine, longtime Charleston County Jeanes Teacher.

25. Myles Horton, "Field Trip Report, Dec. 11–13, 1954." Horton visited John McCray and Modjeska Simkins in Columbia as well. See also Henry Shipherd, "Report on Field Trip, January 28, 1955," box 67, folder 3, Highlander Papers.

26. Horton quoted in an untitled Highlander document, n.d., 5, box 1, folder 5, CRC; for Clark, see Poinsette-Fisher Interview. See also Tjerandsen, *Education*, 153–54; Morris, *Origins*, 151. Overall, Morris assigns entirely too much credit to Horton in laying the foundation for the Citizenship School program (149–52).

27. Myles Horton to Septima Clark, March 5, 1955, box 67, folder 5, Highlander Papers; Septima Clark, "Services Rendered," box 67, folder 3, Highlander Papers; Septima Clark, "Trips to Johns Island," Summer 1955, box 67, folder 5, Highlander Papers; Myles Horton, "Notes on Trip to Charleston and Johns Island," May 24, 1955, box 67, folder 3, Highlander Papers; Blake, "Citizenship Participation," 31–32. Robnett has accurately characterized Clark as a civil rights movement "bridge leader," but her study limits its focus to 1954–65 (*How Long? How Long?*, esp. 88–93).

28. Septima Clark to Myles Horton, June 1, 1955, box 67, folder 3, Highlander Papers; "Demonstration of Use of Soundless Highlander Movie," box 67, folder 5, Highlander Papers.

29. Septima Clark to the Warings, August 30, 1955, box 9, folder 227, J. W. Waring Papers.

30. See Glen, *Highlander*, 175–79; Horton quoted in Septima Clark to the Warings, May 16, 1955, box 9, folder 227, J. W. Waring Papers. On McCarthyism, see Oshinsky, *Conspiracy*; Schrecker, *Many Are the Crimes*. For a broader view of the radicalism of the 1930s and early 1940s and how the Cold War contributed to its eclipse, see Von Eschen, *Race against Empire*; Gilmore, *Defying Dixie*, chap. 9.

31. Septima Clark to the Warings, May 16, June 1, 1955, box 9, folder 227, J. W. Waring Papers; Horton quoted in Tjerandsen, *Education*, 154. The Warings' skepticism persisted much longer; see Elizabeth Waring to Ruby Cornwell, April 15, 1956, box 2, folder 10, Cornwell Collection. See also Myles Horton to Septima Clark, May 30, 1955, box 9, folder 12, Highlander Papers.

32. "Summary of Community Leadership Training Activities Involving Esau Jenkins, Johns Island, S.C. through March 1955," box 67, folder 3, Highlander Papers. See also Tjerandsen, *Education*, 153. In 1950, Johns Island had 2,702 African American and 1,302 white residents (Blake, "Citizenship Participation," 15).

33. Jenkins quoted in Tjerandsen, *Education*, 156–57. See also "Conference on Leadership Training, Charleston, March 19, 1955," box 67, folder 3, Highlander Papers; Septima Clark, "Report of Civic Club, Johns Island," September 6, 1955, box 67, folder, 9, Highlander Papers. See also Blake, "Citizenship Participation," 32–34; Aimee Isgrig Horton, *Highlander Folk School*, 219.

34. "Index of Developments on Johns Island," July 22, 1955, box 67, folder 3, Highlander Papers; Septima Poinsette Clark, interview by Sandra Brenneman Oldendorf, Charleston, S.C., January 17, 1986, HERC.

35. Septima Clark to Myles Horton, August 14, 1955, box 9, folder 12, Highlander Papers.

36. Septima Clark to the Warings, June 30, 1955, box 9, folder 227, J. W. Waring Papers.

37. See Septima Clark, "Interview with Mr. Geo. Bellinger," June 23, 1955, Jenkins quoted in "Conference on Leadership Training, Charleston," March 19, 1955, both in box 67, folder 3, Highlander Papers; Horton quoted in "Index of Developments on Johns Island."

38. See "Buddy Freeman's Talk, Johns Island," July 1955, box 67, folder 9, Highlander Papers.

39. Robinson Interview. Much of this material has been published. See Wigginton, *Refuse to Stand*, 171–90, 236–54, 264–72, 297–301, 368–70. While growing up in Charleston, Robinson did not know Clark.

40. Clark quoting Jenkins in Morris, *Origins*, 150. See also "The United Nations and You Workshop, July 3–9, 1955," box 78, folder 6, Highlander Papers. More broadly, see Anderson, *Eyes off the Prize*.

41. Robinson Interview.

42. See Clark, *Ready from Within*, 32. For biographical information on Durr, see her

autobiography, *Outside the Magic Circle*. For a brief history of black women's organizing in Montgomery, see McGuire, "'It Was Like All of Us.'"

43. Wood Interview; Clark, *Ready from Within*, 33.

44. Wood Interview; Septima Clark to the Warings, May 3, 1956, box 9, folder 228, J. W. Waring Papers. On the boycott, see Robinson, *Montgomery Bus Boycott*.

45. Thrasher Interview.

46. Septima Clark to the Warings, June 21, 1954, box 9, folder 226, J. W. Waring Papers.

47. See "The Association of Citizens' Councils of South Carolina: The First Half-Year," box 19, folder "Citizens Councils," William D. Workman Jr. Papers, Modern Political Collection, University of South Carolina, Columbia; "S.C. Congressmen Give Strong Replies to Query by Council," *CNC*, May 27, 1956. Rivers, Thurmond, and Lieutenant Governor Ernest Hollings shared the stage with Low Country CC leaders shortly after the two-year anniversary of *Brown* ("Southern People and Leaders March Together in Resisting Court Rule," *CNC*, May 19, 1956). For broader overviews, see McMillan, *Citizen's Council*; Bartley, *Rise*. On *Brown I* and *Brown II*, see Kluger, *Simple Justice*, chap. 26.

48. See "Roster of Citizens' Councils, February 15, 1956," Micah Jenkins to Citizens Council Members, January 12, 1957, both in box 19, folder "Citizens Councils," Workman Papers; "Report on Citizen's Council Movement in South Carolina," *Citizens Council*, vol. 1, no. 2 (November 1955), Waring, unpublished musings, n.d., both in box 393, folder 2, T. R. Waring Papers; Joe Brown quoted in "South Carolina Voices," 112–13.

49. Speech to Greenville Citizens' Council, February 3, 1961, L. Marion Gressette Papers, Modern Political Collection, University of South Carolina, Columbia. For other speeches by Gressette to these organizations from 1956 through 1963, see box 1, folders 12 and 13, and box 6, folder 13,

50. See Speech to Latta Rotary Club, October 16, 1956, box 1, folder 12, Gressette Papers. See also "Address of L. Marion Gressette to the State and Local Officers of the Citizens' Councils of South Carolina," June 23, 1959, "Fifth Interim Report, 1958," "Statement of Wayne W. Freeman, Secretary, South Carolina Special School Committee, Delivered in Closed Session of the Committee, May 2, 1960," all in box 20, folder "Gressette Committee," Workman Papers; Baker, *Paradoxes*.

51. *Dixie Dynamite: The Inside Story of the White Citizens Councils* (reprinted from the *New York Post*) (New York: NAACP, 1957), 12, 15, 17, J. Arthur Brown Papers, box 5, ARC. See also Tyson, "Dynamite and the 'Silent South.'"

52. *Highlander Reports, 24th Annual Report, September 1, 1955–October 30, 1956*, 1–2, box 253, folder 1, Matthews Papers; Septima Clark to the Warings, March 20, 1957, box 9, folder 229, J. W. Waring Papers; "Negroes Can Smash the Klan," *Lighthouse and Informer*, October 21, 1950, box 410, folder 13, T. R. Waring Papers; Modjeska Simkins, interview by Jacquelyn Dowd Hall, Columbia, S.C., July 28–31, 1976, Southern Oral History Project, Wilson Library, University of North Carolina, Chapel Hill.

53. "Conversation at Septima Clark's Home, Charleston, 1955," tape 515A, reel 43, Highlander Papers. In all likelihood, the increased militancy in Miami resulted partly

from the 1951 deaths of local NAACP leader Harry T. Moore and his wife on Christmas Day (James C. Clark, "Civil Rights Leader Harry T. Moore"). For an elaboration, see Tyson, *Radio Free Dixie*, esp. chaps. 3, 6; Hill, *Deacons*.

54. Septima Poinsette Clark, interview by Judy Barton, Charleston, S.C., November 9, 1971, box 1a, folder 5, Clark Papers; on her work with auditors, see Septima Clark to the Warings, January 8, 1956, box 9, folder 228, J. W. Waring Papers. On attacks on the NAACP, see Morris, *Origins*, 30–33. More broadly, see Dudziak, *Cold War Civil Rights*; Borstelmann, *Cold War*; Tyson, *Radio Free Dixie*, chap. 5.

55. Septima Clark to the Warings, October 6, 1955, box 4, folder 53, J. W. Waring Papers; "The Orangeburg Story," in *Champions of Democracy* (pamphlet), box 38, folder 13, Highlander Papers; *Dixie Dynamite*, 4, 12, 13; "South Carolina Voices," 113.

56. Septima Clark to the Warings, November 7, 1955, box 9, folder 227, J. W. Waring Papers. See also Septima Poinsette Clark, "The Movement I Remember," 27, box 1a, folder 52, Clark Papers; related documents in box 393, folder 2, T. R. Waring Papers; "'Touch Not,' Says Orangeburg," *Columbia South Carolina Independent*, October 15, 1955, box 7, folder 7, Cornwell Collection. For another overview of the boycott, including photographs, see Williams, *Freedom and Justice*, 97–121.

57. Timmerman quoted in Yarbrough, *Passion*, 229; Septima Clark to the Warings, October 31, 1955, box 9, folder 227, J. W. Waring Papers. See also "Negro Students at Orangeburg Set Up Pickets," *CNC*, March 31, 1956; Alvin Anderson, interview by author, Atlanta, Ga., January 27, 2002, in author's possession.

58. Septima Clark to the Warings, October 31, 1955, box 9, folder 227, J. W. Waring Papers; Clark quoted in untitled HFS document, n.d., box 1, folder 5, CRC.

59. Septima Clark to the Warings, January 22, February 23, 1955, box 9, folder 227, J. W. Waring Papers; Septima Clark to Betty Shipherd, May 17, 1955. On the credit union, see Hall Interview. According to Clark, organizers battled for four months to keep segregation out of the new credit union's constitution and bylaws.

60. Septima Clark to the Warings, June 1, 1955, box 9, folder 227, J. W. Waring Papers; Minutes of the Committee on Administration, January 18, 1954, to April 17, 1957, Young Women's Christian Association, Coming Street Branch, Charleston, S.C.; *Nelsons' Baldwin Charleston South Carolina City Directory*. Cross-referencing the available lists of officers and information in the city directory, I counted ten teachers among twenty-seven women. Another woman was married to a principal.

61. Septima Clark to the Warings, October 6, 1955, box 4, folder 53, J. W. Waring Papers; Septima Clark to the Warings, October 31, 1955, box 9, folder 227, J. W. Waring Papers; Septima Clark to the Warings, May 3, 1956, box 9, folder 228, J. W. Waring Papers. On the Till case, see Whitfield, *Death*.

62. See Septima Clark to the Warings, October 6, 1955, box 4, folder 53, J. W. Waring Papers; Septima Clark to the Warings, May 3, 1956, box 9, folder 228, J. W. Waring Papers; Robinson Interview.

63. Septima Clark to the Warings, October 6, 1955, box 4, folder 53, J. W. Waring Papers; Septima Clark to the Warings, May 3, 1956, box 9, folder 228, J. W. Waring Papers; Septima Clark to the Warings, October 31, 1955, box 9, folder 227, J. W. Waring Papers.

64. Septima Clark to the Warings, January 22, October 31, 1955, box 9, folder 227, J. W. Waring Papers.

65. Septima Clark to the Warings, May 3, 1956, box 9, folder 228, J. W. Waring Papers; Lorene Poinsette quoted in Clark, *Echo*, 118; Elizabeth Waring to Ruby Cornwell, April 29, 1956, box 2, folder 10, Cornwell Collection. See also Elizabeth Waring to Ruby Cornwell, May 6, 1956, box 2, folder 11, Cornwell Collection; Clark, *Ready from Within*, 36.

66. For this and other examples of how Clark "had called attention" to herself, see Clark, *Echo*, 112–15. See also Clark, *Ready from Within*, 37; Septima Clark to the Warings, February 12, 1956, box 9, folder 228, J. W. Waring Papers.

67. Clark, *Ready from Within*, 36; Hall Interview; Simms, *Profiles*, 11–12; "House Acts Swiftly on Bill Banning NAACP Members," *CNC*, February 22, 1956; "Timmerman Signs NAACP Employe Bill," *CNC*, March 18, 1956.

68. "21 Elloree Negro Teachers Not to Return in September," *CNC*, May 17, 1956; "3 Federal Judges Defer Decision in Elloree Case," *CNC*, October 23, 1956. By the time the case was heard again, South Carolina had changed its law to remove the NAACP-specific prohibition.

69. Clark, *Echo*, 114, 117, 116; "Meeting of May 9, 1956," CBC Minute Books: March 1951–September 1957; Septima Clark to the Warings, June 8, 1956, box 9, folder 228, J. W. Waring Papers.

70. "Reports on Teachers" folders, 1947–48, 1951–52, 1953–54, "Reports on Teachers, Archer, n.d.," Superintendent Files, box 848, CCSD; Virginia Kinnaird to Septima Clark, October 10, 1956, box 3, folder 115, Clark Papers; W. E. Solomon to H. P. Hutchinson, November 8, 1956, W. E. Solomon to Septima Clark, December 6, 1956, both in box 3, folder 108, Clark Papers; Septima Clark to the Warings, October 15, 1956, box 9, folder 228, J. W. Waring Papers; Hall Interview.

71. Clark, *Ready from Within*, 37–39.

72. Clark, *Echo*, 168–71; Septima Clark to the Warings, August 6, 1956, box 9, folder 228, J. W. Waring Papers. Clark also refused a job offer from Alice Spearman Wright of the South Carolina Council on Human Relations (Hall Interview).

73. "Minutes Covering an Emergency Meeting of the Executive Council of the Highlander Folk School," April 21, 1956, box 2, folder 1, Highlander Papers; "Official Statement Mutually Agreed upon Regarding the Shipherds' Resignation April 30, 1956 from the Highlander Folk School," box 26, folder 5, Highlander Papers.

74. Septima Clark to the Warings, June 6, 1956, box 9, folder 228, J. W. Waring Papers; Clark, *Ready from Within*, 41–42, 38–39; Clark, *Echo*, 169–70, 174–76; Alvin Anderson, interview; Poinsette-Fisher Interview. On antiblack sentiment among HFS's white neighbors, see testimony in *Highlander Folk School, Myles Horton and May Justus, and Septima Clark v. the State of Tennessee, Assignments of Error, Brief, and Argument of Plaintiffs-in-Error*, 26, n. 26, in David Underdown Papers, in author's possession.

75. Clark, *Ready from Within*, 39.

76. Guy Carawan and Candie Carawan, interview by author, New Market, Tenn., November 12, 2001, in author's possession; "Staff Job Descriptions," Highlander Folk School, box 21, folder 3, Department of United Church Board for Homeland Ministries

Collection, Amistad Research Center, Tulane University, New Orleans, La.; Clark, *Echo*, 156.

77. Septima Clark to the Warings, March 22, 1956, box 9, folder 228, J. W. Waring Papers; Saunders, interview.

78. Wood Interview; "Notes on Conversation between Septima Clark and Maxwell Hahn," February 16, 1959, box 67, folder 9, Highlander Papers. On the project, which had originally been developed at Columbia University while Eisenhower served as its president, see "Students Learn How to Be Good Citizens," *Charleston Evening Post*, May 27, 1952; "Minutes of the Regular Meeting," July 30, November 7, 1951, CBC Minute Books: March 1951–September 1957, box 604.

79. Clark, *Ready from Within*, 51–52; Tjerandsen, *Education*, 160; Glen, *Highlander*, 161; "Notes on Johns Island Workshop," February 5, 1956, box 67, folder 3, Highlander Papers; Payne, *I've Got the Light*, 75.

80. Clark quoted in Tjerandsen, *Education*, 160. See also "Highlander Citizenship Discussion, July 1957," tape 515A, reel 44, Highlander Papers; Clark, *Ready from Within*, 47.

81. Saunders, interview. In contrast, Carawan and Carawan document the rural poverty of Johns Island residents (*Ain't You Got a Right*). On why Clark could not teach, see Clark, *Ready from Within*, 48.

82. See Clark, *Ready from Within*, 49; Septima Clark, interview by Eugene Walker, Atlanta, Ga., July 30, 1976, box 1a, folder 6, Clark Papers. Of course, many would probably disagree with Clark's assessment.

83. Bernice Robinson, interview by Sandra Brenneman Oldendorf, Charleston, S.C., January 15, 1986, HERC.

84. Septima Poinsette Clark, interview by Oldendorf; Tjerandsen, *Education*, 161.

85. Bernice Robinson, interview by Oldendorf. Clark remembered that there were eleven women and three men in the class (Clark, *Ready from Within*, 51).

86. Robinson Interview. See also Adams, *Unearthing Seeds*, 116–17. Myles Horton had sent a copy of the United Nations document down from Highlander.

87. Bernice Robinson, interview by Oldendorf; Clark, *Echo*, 147–48; Tjerandsen, *Education*, 163.

88. Septima Clark to Myles Horton, September 24, 1963, box 9, folder 12, Highlander Papers; "My Reading Booklet," box 38, folder 13, Highlander Papers.

89. Bernice Robinson, interview by Oldendorf.

90. Robinson quoted in Adams, *Unearthing Seeds*, 117.

91. Clark quoted in Bernice Robinson, interview by Oldendorf; Myles Horton to Carl Tjerandsen, February 16, 1957, box 67, folder 3, Highlander Papers; Myles Horton to Bernice Robinson, January 26, 1957, box 1, folder 19, Bernice Robinson Collection, ARC. On Clark's first visit to the class, in its last week, see Clark, *Ready from Within*, 51.

92. Jenkins quoted in Saunders, interview; Clark, *Ready from Within*, 51; "Statistical Reports for the Citizenship Schools," box 18, folder 4, Highlander Papers.

93. Clark, *Ready from Within*, 54; Wood Interview; Septima Clark to Ann Lockwood, n.d., box 9, folder 12, Highlander Papers; "Selection of Teachers for Citizenship Schools," n.d., box 38, folder 13, Highlander Papers; Morris, *Origins*, 153.

94. Grimball Interview; Clark, *Echo*, 157. On family and community networks leading to civil rights activism, see Payne, *I've Got the Light*, esp. chap. 7.

95. Clark, *Echo*, 158–60; Abraham Jenkins (no relation to Esau) comments about Brewer in Carawan and Carawan, *Ain't You Got a Right*, 186; Septima Clark to Mickii Marlowe and Myles Horton, February 23, 1959, box 9, folder 12, Highlander Papers; Oldendorf, "South Carolina Sea Island Citizenship Schools," 173. Brewer was a charter member of Clark's Alpha Kappa Alpha chapter ("Alpha Kappa Alpha Handbook" and "Year Book, 1976," box 8, folder 11, Clark Papers). Bernice Robinson observed that Brewer "had been to Highlander ever since the first time I went up there" (interview by Oldendorf).

96. Clark, *Echo*, 161, 162; Wood Interview. See also Bernice Robinson's description of the class in her interview by Oldendorf.

97. "Trip to Charleston, Wadmalaw, St. Helena's and Hilton Head, April 20–27, 1958," box 67, folder 4, Highlander Papers. More broadly, HFS relied on technology — filmstrips, movies, and tape recordings — to document its activities as well as to attract rural people.

98. "Charleston and Sea Island Activities, 1960–1961," box 1, folder 7, Highlander Papers; Tjerandsen, *Education*, 167; Glen, *Highlander*, 165–66.

99. Wigfall's and Reed's testimonies appear in Blake, "Citizenship Participation," 51, 52–54. Reed owned fifty acres of land and had obtained her registration certificate prior to enrolling in a Citizenship School class.

100. Ibid., 51, 55–56; Solomon Brown to Myles Horton and Septima Clark, March 6, 1959, box 67, folder 9, Highlander Papers.

101. Blake, "Citizenship Participation," 49–51.

102. Saunders, interview; Robinson, interview by Oldendorf; Mack quoted in Blake, "Citizenship Participation," 52. See also Cuthbert-Kerr, "'You Don't Have to Make the X.'"

103. Clark, *Echo*, 162; Grimball Interview; Laura Johnson to Septima Clark, March 8, 1959, box 67, folder 9, Highlander Papers; untitled document, [1957?], box 67, folder 3, Highlander Papers; Blake, "Citizenship Participation," 57.

104. Minutes, 1955–63, Citizens Committee and Palmetto State Voters Association of Johns Island, and Voters Association of Edisto Island, box 67, folder 9, Highlander Papers.

105. Ibid., esp. "Minutes of the Voters Association, Edisto Island, July 5, 1959"; Septima Clark, interview by Cynthia Brown, Charleston, S.C., August 1979, tape 5, side B, in author's possession.

106. Saunders, interview; Tjerandsen, *Education*, 167.

107. "Highlander School's Influence Felt among Charleston County Negroes," *CNC*, March 12, 1959; Septima Clark to Myles Horton, February 27, 1959, box 9, folder 12, Highlander Papers. See also "Classes Here Sponsored by Folk School," *CNC*, March 11, 1959.

108. Septima Clark, interview by Brown, tape 5, side B.

109. Tjerandsen, *Education*, 164, 167; Blake, "Citizenship Participation," 58–59.

110. Quoted in Carawan and Carawan, *Ain't You Got a Right*, 66.

Chapter Eight

1. Septima Clark, interview by Cynthia Brown, Charleston, S.C., August 1979, tape 6, side A. Clark did not pinpoint when and where she first met Baker, commenting only, "I knew Ella Baker before."

2. Septima Clark to the Warings, May 3, 1956, box 9, folder 228, J. W. Waring Papers; see also June 22, November 23, 1956; Clark, *Ready from Within*, 62. For additional examples of Clark's expanding network, see "Island Program," January–July 1959, box 67, folder 4, Highlander Papers; Septima Clark schedule, March 12, 1959, box 67, folder 9, Highlander Papers.

3. Septima Clark to the Warings, August 9, 1958, box 9, folder 230, J. W. Waring Papers; "Report of Septima Clark, Mostly on Trip to Charleston," October 13–20, 1958, box 67, folder 9, Highlander Papers.

4. Septima Clark to Myles Horton, Eugene Kayden, and May Justus, April 12, 1959, box 3, folder 104, Clark Papers.

5. Septima Clark to the Warings, May 19, 1961, box 9, folder 232, J. W. Waring Papers.

6. See Glen, *Highlander*, 181–84; Adams, *Unearthing Seeds*, 122–27.

7. See *Highlander Folk School, Myles Horton and May Justus, and Septima Clark v. the State of Tennessee, Assignments of Error, Brief, and Argument of Plaintiffs-in-Error*, 4–6, in David Underdown Papers, in author's possession. Nearby white residents had aired their grievances at a public hearing in Tracy City on February 26. See also Glen, *Highlander*, 188–90, 192.

8. "Tennessee Probe Casts Light on Trouble Spot," *CNC*, March 28, 1959; "Myles Horton Outlines His Objectives," *CNC*, March 24, 1959. Both articles are part of a series, "A Look at Highlander." See also "Myles Horton: 'An Attractive Nuisance,'" *CNC*, March 25, 1959; "'Poor Judgment' Charged Against 14 Professors," *CNC*, March 27, 1959; "A Tempest Blows in Tennessee," *CNC*, March 29, 1959.

9. Robinson Interview; U.S. Department of Justice, Federal Bureau of Investigation, Subject: Septima Poinsette Clark, File 44-14876, in author's possession; Bill Saunders, interview by author, Charleston, S.C., March 23, 2002, in author's possession; Voters Association Minutes, Edisto Island, August 2, 1959, box 67, folder 9, Highlander Papers.

10. Yvonne Clark, interview by author, Atlanta, Ga., January 26, 2002, in author's possession; Clark, *Ready from Within*, 42; Septima Clark to the Warings, August 1, 1958, box 9, folder 230, J. W. Waring Papers.

11. Clark, *Echo*, 3–5.

12. Guy Carawan and Candie Carawan, interview by author, New Market, Tenn., November 12, 2001, in author's possession; Adams, *Unearthing Seeds*, 131; Glen, *Highlander*, 193.

13. Robinson Interview; Saunders, interview; Adams, *Unearthing Seeds*, 132; Glen, *Highlander*, 194; Alice Cobb, "The Trial and Charges against Highlander," *Concern: A Biweekly Journal of Social and Political Comment*, October 23, 1959, Underdown Papers.

14. Clark, *Ready from Within*, 57; Clark, *Echo*, 7.

15. Clark, *Echo*, 8–9; Clark, *Ready from Within*, 58. See also Cobb, "Trial and Charges," 4; Robinson Interview; Carawan and Carawan, interview; Glen, *Highlander*, 193–94.

16. Branstetter quoted in "Friends of Highlander," August 27, 1959, 2, Underdown Papers; Glen, *Highlander*, 194–95; *Highlander Folk School et al. v. Tennessee*, 7. After being contacted by the American Civil Liberties Union, U.S. senator Hubert Humphrey asked the Civil Rights Division of the Justice Department to investigate whether officials had engaged in illegal search and seizure during the raid (U.S. Department of Justice, Federal Bureau of Investigation, Subject Septima Poinsette Clark, File 44-14876). The search warrant issued by a Grundy County magistrate was later held to be illegal.

17. Horton quoted in *Highlander Folk School et al. v. Tennessee*, 9 n. 10, 60–61; Clark, *Ready from Within*, 56; Glen, *Highlander*, 195–99; Cobb, "Trial and Charges," 4, 8.

18. Yvonne Clark, interview; Clark, *Echo*, 9–10; A. J. Clement Jr. to Thomas R. Waring Jr., August 20, 1959, Thomas R. Waring Jr. to A. J. Clement Jr., August 24, 1959, box 405, folder 6, T. R. Waring Papers.

19. King quoted in "News from Highlander Folk School," October 8, 1959, box 21, folder 4, Department of United Church Board for Homeland Ministries Collection, Amistad Research Center, Tulane University, New Orleans, La.; letters to Septima Clark in Underdown Papers.

20. "Conversation between Justine Wise, Septima Clark and Myles Horton," May 1959, box 67, folder 11, Highlander Papers.

21. Septima Clark to the Warings, January 7, 1958, box 9, folder 230, J. W. Waring Papers; Elizabeth Waring to Ruby Cornwell, August 11, 1959, box 3, folder 10, Cornwell Collection.

22. Quoted in Wakefield, "Siege," 325. At least one letter that Clark penned to raise funds to defend the school landed in the wrong hands (Septima P. Clark to Gilbert Wilkes, July 30, 1959, Gilbert Van B. Wilkes to Thomas R. Waring Jr., n.d., both in box 405, folder 6, T. R. Waring Papers).

23. Septima Clark to Myles Horton, ca. October 1960, box 38, folder 2, Highlander Papers; untitled HFS document, n.d., box 1, folder 5, CRC.

24. Glen, *Highlander*, 189, 200–209; *Highlander Folk School et al. v. Tennessee*, 10–11 n. 11, 15 n. 17.

25. Glen, *Highlander*, 203; Adams, *Unearthing Seeds*, 133, 140–41.

26. Horton quoted in Morris, *Origins*, 154–55.

27. James L. Macanic to Septima Clark, "Report of a Workshop," March 4, 1961, box 67, folder 4, Highlander Papers; *Highlander Reports, 28th Annual Report, October 1, 1959–September 30, 1960*, ser. 3, box 154, folder 9, SCLC Papers; Myles Horton to Jane Lee J. Eddy, n.d., box 38, folder 12, Highlander Papers; *Highlander Reports, 29th Annual Report, October 1, 1960–September 30, 1961*, box 21, folder 16, Department of United Church Board for Homeland Ministers Collection.

28. Septima Clark, interview by Brown, tape 4, side A.

29. "Septima Clark Extension Report to Highlander Executive Council," January 1957, box 67, folder 3, Highlander Papers; Septima Clark to the Warings, January 27, 1957, box 9, folder 299, J. W. Waring Papers; Clark, *Ready from Within*, 66.

30. Fairclough, *To Redeem the Soul*, 94; Young, *Easy Burden*, 258–59. Williams also served as the vice president of the Savannah NAACP.

31. Septima Clark to Myles Horton, [ca. October 1960], box 38, folder 2, Highlander Papers; Hosea Williams to Septima Clark, February 9, 1961, box 38, folder 12, Highlander Papers. Robinson first spoke about HFS in Savannah in the fall of 1959, apparently prior to the organization of the Chatham County Crusade for Voters (Tjerandsen, *Education*, 178; *Highlander Reports, 28th Annual Report*).

32. "Progress Report, Highlander Folk School, April 26, 1961," box 38, folder 2, Highlander Papers; Septima P. Clark and Bernice V. Robinson, "Report of Training Leaders for Citizenship Schools," April 10–16, 1961, box 80, folder 5, Highlander Papers; "Memorandum on Citizenship Program, June 26, 1961," 4–5, ser. 1, box 136, folder 28, SCLC Papers.

33. Williams quoted in Tjerandsen, *Education*, 180. By September, there were twenty-seven classes.

34. Ibid. Clark, *Ready from Within*, 66–67. See also First Baptist Church, Huntsville, Alabama, "Our History." On Clark's earlier YWCA organizing, see Septima Clark to Betty Shipherd, May 17, 1955, box 9, folder 12, Highlander Papers.

35. "Memorandum on Citizenship Program," 5–6; "Hours Spent in Preparation, Teaching and Travel of Teachers and Supervisors," n.d., box 38, folder 2, Highlander Papers.

36. "Tent City: Home of the Brave," Industrial Union Department, AFL-CIO Publication 36, n.d., "News from the Southern Conference Education Fund, Inc., June 15, 1960," both in box 38, folder 8, Highlander Papers; "Report on a Visit to Fayette and Haywood Counties, Tennessee," January 3–5, 1961, box 65, folder 13, Highlander Papers. See also "Tent City Timeline"; Winn, "Tent Cities." This local movement occurred in both Fayette and Haywood Counties, but I am limiting my discussion here to Fayette.

37. "Viola McFerren Remembers."

38. "Tent City: Home of the Brave"; "Tent City Timeline." Referring to the shooting incident at Tent City, the AFL-CIO pamphlet noted, "Some Tent City residents fired on the intruders and gave chase."

39. Septima P. Clark and Robinson, "Report"; "Memorandum on Citizenship Program," 5.

40. Mary E. Dowdy, Mattie M. Shaw, and Fannie Puckett to Septima Clark, n.d., box 38, folder 8, Highlander Papers. These women apparently had attended their first workshop in March 1961; Dowdy and Puckett returned again in April.

41. Septima Clark to the Warings, August 8, 1958, box 9, folder 230, J. W. Waring Papers; "Notes on Conversation between Septima Clark and Maxwell Hahn," February 16, 1959, box 67, folder 9, Highlander Papers; Septima Clark to the Warings, June 6, 1956, box 9, folder 228, J. W. Waring Papers. Robinson, who joined the HFS staff in April 1961, offered the same benefits of her connection to black women (Bernice Robinson to Maxwell Hahn, January 10, 1964, box 4, folder 19, Clark Papers).

42. "Citizenship School Program: Fayette and Haywood Counties, Tennessee, 1960–1961," box 38, folder 8, Highlander Papers. Shaw neither participated in the April training workshop nor led a class.

43. Press Release, January 17, 1961, box 80, folder 10, Highlander Papers; Myles Horton to Septima Clark, October 10, 1962, box 26, folder 27, Highlander Papers. Horton noted that "Lillian Robinson did a wonderful job last night telling about your first beauticians'

workshop at Highlander." Lillian Robinson was a board member of the Volunteer Health Center.

44. "Beauticians Meeting, February 26 and 27, 1961," untitled document, February 27, 1961, "Minutes from a Meeting at McFerren Store, March 26, 1961," Septima Clark to Eva Bowman, n.d., all in box 38, folder 8, Highlander Papers.

45. "News from the Original Fayette County Civic and Welfare League, Inc., March 14, 1961," box 38, folder 8, Highlander Papers. In January 1961, a falling out occurred between various members of the league's board of directors; on March 1, McFerren renamed his faction the Original Fayette County Civic and Welfare League.

46. Septima Clark to Eva Bowman, n.d., box 38, folder 8, Highlander Papers.

47. Press Release, February 28, 1961, box 65, folder 13, Highlander Papers; "Fayette County Work Camp," March 25–April 14, 1963, Virgie Hortenstine to Myles and Aimee Horton, February 7, 1963, both in box 15, folder 12, Highlander Papers.

48. Untitled documents in box 38, folder 8, Highlander Papers; "Tent City Timeline."

49. "Fayette County Work Camp"; "Operation Freedom Expands Its Aid Program," 1963, Minutes of Operation Freedom Board Meeting, May 1, 1965, box 65, folder 13, Highlander Papers. Operation Freedom began sending aid to activists in Georgia and in Selma, Alabama, as well. See also Forman, *Making*, chap. 17.

50. Septima Clark, Memo of Meeting with the MIA, January 23, 1961, 1, box 38, folder 13, Highlander Papers.

51. For Clark's condemnation of Abernathy's sexism and his belief that women should not challenge men, see Septima Clark, interview by Brown, tape 6, side A. See also Ransby's discussion of SCLC and women in the church in *Ella Baker*, 184–85.

52. Septima Clark, Memo of Meeting with the MIA.

53. Ibid.; "Progress Report"; "Memorandum on Citizenship Program," 6.

54. Septima P. Clark and Robinson, "Report."

55. *MIA Newsletter*, March 15, 1961, box 64, folder 12, Highlander Papers.

56. Clark, *Ready from Within*, 60–61.

57. Bernice Robinson to Myles Horton, June 25, 1961, box 1, folder 3, CRC; Bernice Robinson, "Report of Training Leaders for Citizenship Schools," June 16–18, 1961, box 80, folder 5, Highlander Papers; Septima P. Clark and Robinson, "Report." See also Anne Lockwood to Bernice Robinson, February 27, 1961, Bernice Robinson to Anne Lockwood, March 8, 1961, box 3, folder 14, Bernice Robinson Collection. Lockwood wrote on behalf of HFS to offer Robinson a position as a full-time staff member to meet increased need as the Citizenship Schools spread; Robinson cited her hospitalization and replied that she would need to think more about the proposal.

58. Carawan and Carawan, interview.

59. Septima Clark to Myles Horton, n.d., box 38, folder 2, Highlander Papers.

60. Septima Clark to Anne, Myles, Alice, "Re: Nov 18–20, 1960 Workshop," box 80, folder 5, Highlander Papers.

61. Septima Clark to Myles Horton, May 4, 1961, box 1, folder 4, CRC.

62. "Notes for a Ralph Tyler Memo," [summer 1961?], box 38, folder 2, Highlander Papers.

63. Septima Clark to the Warings, August 1, 1958, box 9, folder 230, J. W. Waring Papers; Septima Clark schedule, March 1959, box 67, folder 9, Highlander Papers; Myles Horton to Dorothy Cotton, June 28, 1962, Myles Horton to Septima Clark, November 17, 1962, Septima Clark to Myles Horton, November 26, 1962, all in box 26, folder 27, Highlander Papers; *Highlander Reports, 28th Annual Report*. She was also named 1959 Woman of the Year by the Utility Club in New York City.

64. "Notes to Ralph Tyler Memo"; Clark, *Ready from Within*, 53.

65. Septima Clark to Perry MacKay Sturges, June 10, 1960, box 27, folder 10, Highlander Papers.

66. Septima Clark to the Warings, June 14, July 1, 1959, box 9, folder 231, J. W. Waring Papers. For an elaboration, see Charron, "We've Come a Long Way."

67. Septima Clark, interview by Brown, tape 5, side A.

68. Carawan and Carawan, interview; Septima Clark to the Warings, March 31, 1957, box 9, folder 229, J. W. Waring Papers. See also *Highlander Reports, 26th Annual Report, October 1, 1957–September 30, 1958*, 3, Underdown Papers; "Report of Myles Trip to the Sea Islands, January 1958," ser. 3, box 154, folder 9, SCLC Papers.

69. Carawan and Carawan, interview; Septima Clark to Ella Baker, March 24, 1960, box 3, folder 12, Clark Papers.

70. *Highlander Reports, 28th Annual Report*; "The New Generation Fights for Equality (Report of the 7th Annual Highlander Folk School College Workshop, April 1–3, 1960)," box 78, folder 9, Highlander Papers.

71. *Highlander Reports, 28th Annual Report*. See also Carson, *In Struggle*, 19–25; 144–45; 236–43. Carson does not raise the issue of debates about white participation at the founding conference, though he writes that an increase in the number of white staff members in 1963–64 brought it to the surface.

72. Ella Baker to Septima Clark, April 14, 1960, Septima Clark to Ella Baker, April 9, 1960, both in box 3, folder 12, Clark Papers. By this time, Baker was in the process of leaving the SCLC and told Clark that "the cooperation you suggested may not be feasible."

73. Ransby, *Ella Baker*, 175–80; for a view of Baker's extensive organizing background that made her the ideal candidate for the job, see chaps. 3–5. See also Morris, *Origins*, 92–94, chap. 5; Branch, *Parting the Waters*, 228, 231–32; Septima Clark to the Warings, May 20, 1957, box 9, folder 229, J. W. Waring Papers.

74. Baker quoted in Ransby, *Ella Baker*, 181; Morris, *Origins*, 109–12.

75. Ella J. Baker to Committee on Administration, October 23, 1959, ser. 1, box 32, folder 43, SCLC Papers.

76. Ella Baker, "Developing," 352. On the SCLC's strategy, see Wyatt T. Walker, "Report of the Director: Semi-Annual Report, November 1–April 30, 1960," 6, ser. 13, box 129, folder 6, SCLC Papers; Ransby, *Ella Baker*, 183–89; Thrasher Interview. See also Hall Interview.

77. "Memorandum on: SCLC-Highlander Financial Arrangements," December 1, 1960, ser. 1, box 136, folder 9; "Public Relations Report by James Wood," November 23, 1960,

ser. 1, box 138, folder 8, SCLC Papers. Similarly, Rustin, Levinson, and King had negotiated Baker's SCLC employment without consulting her (Ransby, *Ella Baker*, 180).

78. Andrew Young to Robert Spike, April 25, 1961, box 30, folder 5, Highlander Papers; Andrew Young, interview by author, Atlanta, Ga., January 29, 2002, in author's possession; Young, *Easy Burden*, 131.

79. Maxwell Hahn to Charles M. Jones, April 28, 1961, ser. 1, box 136, folder 4, SCLC Papers; "Report to Citizenship School Committee from Myles Horton," June 30, 1961, ser. 1, box 136, folder 10, SCLC Papers; Myles Horton to Citizenship School Program Committee, June 21, 1961, ser. 3, box 154, folder 3, SCLC Papers. In the June 30 report, Horton noted that after consulting with Jim Wood, he "took the liberty" of asking Young to serve as a paid administrative staff member. See also Young, *Easy Burden*, 133–34.

80. Myles Horton to Citizenship School Program Committee, June 21, 1961, box 1, folder 4, CRC. Other members included Wood and Herman Long of Fisk University's Race Relations Institute.

81. Septima P. Clark and Bernice V. Robinson to Myles Horton, June 19, 1961, box 1, folder 4, CRC; "Highlander School's Septima Clark among 7 Taking Peace Corps Test," *Chattanooga News Free Press*, May 29, 1961, clipping, box 1, folder 5, CRC; Myles Horton to Septima Clark, June 21, 1961, box 3, folder 103, Clark Papers.

82. Myles Horton to Septima Clark, June 21, 1961, box 3, folder 103, Clark Papers; Myles Horton to Bernice Robinson, June 21, 1961, ser. 3, box 154, folder 3, SCLC Papers.

83. Septima Clark to Myles Horton, June 29, July 3, 1961, box 1, folder 4, CRC. Over the next few months, additional confusion arose over who bore the responsibility for paying Clark's medical insurance premiums. See, for example, Septima Clark to Myles Horton, August 6, 1961, box 1, folder 3, CRC; Septima Clark to Myles Horton, August 22, 1961, box 1, folder 5, CRC.

84. Myles Horton to Maxwell Hahn, June 19, 1961, box 38, folder 2, Highlander Papers; Anne Lockwood to B. R. Brazeal, August 30, 1961, record group 2, ser. 1, box 1, Myles Horton Papers, HERC. Clark and Robinson had indicated that they would "talk first-hand to Mr. Hahn" if the committee continued to disregard their wishes (Septima P. Clark and Bernice V. Robinson to Myles Horton, June 19, 1961, box 1, folder 4, CRC).

85. Alice Cobb to Scott Bartlett, November 8, 1960, box 9, folder 12, Highlander Papers. Cobb ended by suggesting that Bartlett might "want to correspond directly with Mrs. Clark" and that "you will probably find the Highlander associates more excited than she is" about the project.

86. Clark, *Echo*, 11–12. On Blythe, see North Carolina Writers' Network, "Literary Hall of Fame." In a gesture reminiscent of the practice of having white abolitionists authenticate nineteenth-century slave narratives, Harry Golden, a prominent Jewish liberal from Charlotte, wrote the foreword to the first edition.

87. Clark, *Echo*, 123; Myles Horton to Septima Clark, October 30, 1962, box 26, folder 27, Highlander Papers.

88. Septima Clark to the Warings, August 15, 1961, box 9, folder 232, J. W. Waring Papers.

89. Carl Tjerandsen to Septima Clark, May 22, 1963, Septima Clark to Myles Horton, December 1, 1962, both in box 9, folder 12, Highlander Papers.

90. Myles Horton to Septima Clark, October 15, 1962, Septima Clark to Myles Horton, November 26, 1962, both in box 26, folder 27, Highlander Papers; Septima Clark to Myles Horton, July 20, 1963, box 9, folder 12, Highlander Papers; Bernice Robinson to Septima Clark, July 22, 1963, box 24, folder 13, Highlander Papers. The resource person in question was Benjamin Mack, an area supervisor in the SCLC's Citizenship Education Program. On Robinson's resignation, which she attributed her inability to "endure the frustration ever present at Highlander and the continued reference to 'Have to raise funds for Bernice's salary,'" see Bernice Robinson to Maxwell Hahn, January 10, 1964, box 4, folder 19, Clark Papers.

91. Clark, *Ready from Within*, 53.

Chapter Nine

1. See Clark, "Literacy and Liberation," esp. 113, 117, 122.

2. Andrew Young to Maxwell Hahn, October 25, 1962, ser. 1, box 136, folder 5, SCLC Papers; "Statistical Report, July 1, 1962–June 30, 1963," ser. 3, box 129, folder 39, SCLC Papers; "Southern Christian Leadership Conference Citizenship Education Program," from a taped report by Septima Clark at the Highlander Board of Directors Meeting, May 14, 1965, box 2, folder 3, Highlander Papers; "Citizenship Education Report," January 1968, box 23, folder 24, Clark Papers; "Proposed SCLC Program — September 1969 to July 1970," ser. 4, box 48, folder 9, SCLC Papers.

3. Fairclough, *To Redeem the Soul*; Morris, *Origins*, 94–99; Ransby, *Ella Baker*, 175–77. On the Freedom Rides, see Arsenault, *Freedom Riders*.

4. Victoria Gray Adams, interview by author, Petersburg, Va., April 22, 2002, in author's possession.

5. Gilkes, "Building"; Sacks, "Gender"; Ackelsburg, "Communities." See also Naples, *Grassroots Warriors*; Greene, *Our Separate Ways*; Orelick, *Storming Caesar's Palace*; Collins, *Black Feminist Thought*. On the numerical dominance of black women in the CEP, see, for example, "Teachers Paid December 1969," box 6, folder 50, Clark Papers.

6. Clark, *Ready from Within*, 83. See also Naples, *Grassroots Warriors*, esp. 141–42; Robnett, *How Long? How Long?*; Robnett, "Women." My argument with regard to sexism is specific to the SCLC. For an example of how sexual violence informed black women's activism in Montgomery, Alabama, nearly a decade prior to the bus boycott, see McGuire, "'It Was Like All of Us.'" See also Roth, *Separate Roads*; Breines, *Trouble between Us*. On citizenship as a communal possession in an earlier period, see Brown, "Negotiating and Transforming."

7. Andrew Young to Septima Clark, n.d., ser. 1, box 136, folder 10, SCLC Papers; "Statement of Expenditures, July 1, 1961–June 22, 1962," ser. 1, box 136, folder 3, SCLC Papers; "Statement of Expenditures, July 1, 1962–June 30, 1963," ser. 1, box 136, folder 12, SCLC Papers.

8. Andrew Young, interview by author, Atlanta, Ga., January 29, 2002, in author's pos-

session; Young, *Easy Burden*, 140–43; "Report on Training Workshop, July 17–21, 1961," ser. 3, box 155, folder 21, SCLC Papers.

9. Young, interview; Young, *Easy Burden*, 144–45.

10. Dorothy Cotton, "Report of Citizenship School . . . December 11, 1961," ser. 1, box 29, folder 10, SCLC Papers; "Schedule: Training Leaders for Citizenship Schools," ser. 3, box 155, folder 15, SCLC Papers; Young, interview. CEP training also occurred at both Esau Jenkins's Sea Island Center on Johns Island and at the Penn Center on St. Helena Island.

11. "Report on Teacher Training Workshop, July 17–21, 1961," ser. 3, box 155, folder 21, SCLC Papers; Young, interview.

12. Clark, *Ready from Within*, 63–64; "Job Description, Dorothy Cotton," in Septima Clark to Wesley Hotchkiss, August 25, 1964, ser. 1, box 136, folder 24, SCLC Papers.

13. Clark, *Ready from Within*, 64; Morris, *Origins*, 239; Young, interview. On job titles, see "Citizenship Education Program in the South, Field Foundation: Statement of Expenditures July 1, 1961 through June 22, 1962," ser. 1, box 136, folder 3, SCLC Papers.

14. Young, interview; Bernice Johnson Reagon, interview by author, Washington, D.C., July 12, 2002, in author's possession; Young, *Easy Burden*, 143–46.

15. Dorothy Cotton to Hosea Williams, April 5, 1962, ser. 3, box 160, folder 27, SCLC Papers; Dorothy Cotton, "Citizenship School Report, November 1963," ser. 3, box 153, folder 19, SCLC Papers. Clark's comments appear in "Civil Rights Struggle," ca. 1963, box 1a, folder 29, Clark Papers. On the Civil Rights Act as a reading text, see "Annual Report, Citizenship Education Program . . . 1963–1964," ser. 1, box 29, folder 13, SCLC Papers; on Consumer Education, see "Consumer Education," box 2, Bernice Robinson Collection, ARC.

16. "Instructions on the Administration of Your Political Organization," n.d., box 25, folder 1, Clark Papers.

17. Thrasher Interview; Morris, *Origins*, 86, 91–94; Branch, *Parting the Waters*, 232–33. Elsewhere, Clark compared herself to Ella Baker, noting "she was concerned about not being recognized in a man-made world, and it didn't bother me. It really didn't" (Hall Interview).

18. Septima Clark to Dorothy Cotton, March 19, 1961, box 38, folder 3, Highlander Papers; SNCC, see Thrasher Interview.

19. Clark's comments on Young appear in Couto, *Ain't Gonna Let Nobody*, 128; on Adams, see Septima P. Clark to Harriet Adams, n.d., box 2, folder 20, Clark Papers. See also Branch, *Parting the Waters*, 577–78; Hall Interview; Septima Clark, interview by Eugene Walker, Atlanta, Ga., July 30, 1976, box 1a, folder 6, Clark Papers.

20. Septima P. Clark to Leslie Dunbar, November 7, 1966, box 3, folder 67, Clark Papers; Victoria Gray Adams, telephone interview by author, June 27, 2002, in author's possession. The sand/water and the Howard Johnson tales became stock stories that Clark repeated. See, for example, Thrasher Interview; Septima Clark, interview by Walker.

21. Reagon, interview; Victoria Gray Adams, telephone interview.

22. Young, interview; Victoria Gray Adams, interview; Payne, *I've Got the Light*, 270–71.

23. Reagon, interview. Clark eventually assumed care for her grandson.

24. Solinger, *Pregnancy and Power*, 187; Dittmer, *Local People*, 229; Orelick, *Storming*, 228; Annell Ponder, "Mississippi Report to the Annual Convention of the Southern Christian Leadership Conference," ca. 1963, ser. 3, box 155, folder 26, SCLC Papers; Roberts, *Killing*, chap. 2, esp. 89–93 and 98–103; Davis, *Women*, 217. Decades-old debates in the black community over birth control assumed new resonance during the civil rights and Black Power eras, when it was frequently associated with state-sponsored genocide. See, for example, Cade, "The Pill."

25. Southern black women were not alone. In New York, the Black Women's Liberation Group of Mount Vernon/New Rochelle, founded in 1960, debated the same issues and framed them similarly. See Baxandall, "Re-Visioning," 226, 233–40; Roth, *Separate Roads*, chap. 3, esp. 87.

26. Septima P. Clark to L. Francis Griffin, December 11, 1961, box 3, folder 86, Clark Papers; Young, interview.

27. For examples of memos urging field workers and staff to cut back expenses, see Andrew Young to SCLC Field Staff, September–October 1965, ser. 1, box 56, folder 16, SCLC Papers; Ralph David Abernathy to Martin Luther King Jr., January 21, 1966, ser. 2, box 62, folder 21, SCLC Papers. See also Young, interview. On Clark's refusing a raise, see Francis Covington to Andrew Young, December 3, 1964, ser. 1, box 56, folder 14, SCLC Papers.

28. Wyatt T. Walker, "Report of the Director, Annual Report, October 1960–September 1961," 11, ser. 13, box 129, folder 14, SCLC Papers; Martin Luther King Jr. to Maxwell Hahn, February 13, 1963, ser. 1, box 136, folder 6, SCLC Papers; Andrew Young to Maxwell Hahn, May 4, 1964, ser. 1, box 136, folder 7, SCLC Papers.

29. Septima Clark, "Report from the Field, Telfair County, Jacksonville, Georgia," n.d., box 160, folder 49; Wesley A. Hotchkiss to Andrew J. Young, June 17, 1964, ser. 1, box 136, folder 13, SCLC Papers; Andrew J. Young to Truman Douglas and Wesley A. Hotchkiss, June 10, 1964, Andrew J. Young to Wesley A. Hotchkiss, July 20, 1964, Wesley A. Hotchkiss to. Truman B. Douglass, August 14, 1964, all in ser. 1, box 136, folder 14, SCLC Papers; Andrew Young to Septima Clark, Dorothy Cotton, and Martin Luther King Jr., December 17, 1963, ser. 1, box 29, folder 13, SCLC Papers. The idea for permanent Citizenship School area centers persisted. See, for example, CEP to Officers of the SCLC Board, November 8, 1965, ser. 1, box 29, folder 14, SCLC Papers. Staff apparently never secured a foundation grant for this purpose.

30. Thrasher Interview. See also Tjerandsen, *Education*, 185; Victoria Gray Adams, telephone interview.

31. Clark, *Ready from Within*, 77–78; Septima Clark, interview by Cynthia Brown, Charleston, S.C., August 1979, tape 6, side A, in author's possession. For an example of a letter, see Septima P. Clark to Martin Luther King Jr., June 12, 1967, ser. 1, box 29, folder 15, SCLC Papers. On SCLC and gender, see Ling, "Gender and Generation." On women's leadership more broadly, see Sacks, "Gender"; Robnett, "Women"; Greene, *Our Separate Ways*.

32. Clark, *Ready from Within*, 77, 79; Thrasher Interview; Young, interview; Young,

Easy Burden, 139. See also Septima P. Clark to Martin Luther King Jr. and Coretta Scott King, October 15, 1964, ser. 1, box 29, folder 18, Martin Luther King Jr. Papers, King Center, Atlanta, Ga.

33. Barbara Gregg to Whom It May Concern, September 4, 1963, ser. 1, box 164, folder 18, SCLC Papers; Margaret Block to SCLC Staff, May 26, 1964, ser. 3, box 161, folder 54, SCLC Papers. For examples of delay receiving materials, see Samuel Block [Cleveland, Miss.] to Andrew Young or Septima Clark, May 28, 1962, ser. 3, box 161, folder 53, SCLC Papers; Lorraine Bowman Howard [Taliaferro County, Ga.], "Teacher Survey, July 1964 to June 1965," box 154, folder 24, SCLC Papers; A. Edward Banks [Marion, Ala.] to Andrew Young, December 31, 1962, ser. 3, box 156, folder 57, SCLC Papers.

34. Septima Clark to Andrew Young, July 12, 1964, Andrew Young to Septima Clark, July 9, 20, 1964, both in box 4, folder 117, Clark Papers.

35. Dorothy Cotton to Susie Jones, August 2, 1965, ser. 3, box 162, folder 45, SCLC Papers; Dorothy F. Cotton to A. Edward Banks, March 26, 1963, ser. 3, box 156, folder 57, SCLC Papers; Annemarie Quiring to Hosea Williams, October 11, 1963, ser. 3, box 160, folder 30, SCLC Papers.

36. Hall Interview; Ethel Britton to Septima Clark, June 30, 1964, ser. 3, box 164, folder 32, SCLC Papers; Dorothy Cotton to Henry Burrell, October 16, 1964, ser. 3, box 156, folder 5, SCLC Papers; Dorothy Cotton to Annell Ponder, September 11, 1963, ser. 3, box 155, folder 24, SCLC Papers.

37. Branch, *Parting the Waters*, 478–82; Jack O'Dell, "Report on Voter Registration Work, February 15–September 1, 1962," box 6, folder 42, Clark Papers.

38. Septima Clark, interview by Walker. Elsewhere, Clark recalled that she "had some trouble" in Albany (Wood Interview). See also Fairclough, *To Redeem the Soul*, chap. 4, esp. 86, 89–90, 100–109. For a report on CEP organizing in Albany, see Annell Ponder, "Citizenship Education Program, Albany, Georgia, (Summer and Fall, 1962)," ser. 3, box 158, folder 11, SCLC Papers.

39. Septima P. Clark, "Success of SCLC Citizenship School Seen in 50,000 New Registered Voters," *SCLC Newsletter*, September 1963, box 82, folder 7, Highlander Papers. The tensions, particularly between SNCC and SCLC and between SCLC and the NAACP, are well documented. See, for example, Branch, *Parting the Waters*; Payne, *I've Got the Light*; Fairclough, *To Redeem the Soul*.

40. Septima Clark to Martin Luther King Jr., n.d., box 3, folder 122, Clark Papers. The latest date mentioned in the memo is November 26, 1963. By this time, activists in South Carolina had organized 40 of 46 counties; Hosea Williams's efforts in southern Georgia extended to 50 of 159 counties. See also Ling, "Gender and Generation," esp. 103.

41. Bernice V. Robinson, "Report from the Field (1964)," ser. 3, box 155, folder 30, SCLC Papers; Andrew Young to Wesley Hotchkiss, May 19, 1964, ser. 1, box 136, folder 13, SCLC Papers; "Citizenship School Report, March–May 1963," ser. 3, box 162, folder 24, SCLC Papers; "Report of Harassment and Intimidation," ser. 3, box 155, folder 24, SCLC Papers; Young, *Easy Burden*, 151.

42. Clark, *Ready from Within*, 71–73; Septima Clark, interview by Walker; Septima P. Clark memo to Dr. Green and Mr. Blackwell, November 5, 1965, ser. 3, box 154, folder 8,

SCLC Papers; Septima Clark to Josephine Carson, January 31, 1967, box 4, folder 18, Clark Papers. Carson was the author of *Silent Voices: The Southern Negro Woman Today*, a fictional work published in 1969 in which the character of Charity Simmons is based on Clark. Correspondence between the two women indicates that Clark was in Grenada in late 1966 and early 1967.

43. Septima Clark, interview by Walker; Thrasher Interview. See also Lee, *For Freedom's Sake*, chap. 3, esp. 46–47, 49–53; Young, *Easy Burden*, 253–58.

44. Septima Clark to Josephine Carson, August 31, 1966, box 4, folder 18, Clark Papers.

45. Septima Clark, interview by Brown, tape 3, side B; "Report of the Citizenship School, December 11, 1961," ser. 1, box 29, folder 10, SCLC Papers; Vera Mae Pigee, "Citizenship School Report: July, 1964–June, 1965," ser. 3, box 155, folder 2, SCLC Papers. See also Dittmer, *Local People*, 85, 121–22, 176–77; Hamlin, "Vera Mae Pigee"; Hamlin, "Book Hasn't Closed"; Young, *Easy Burden*, 141–43.

46. Victoria Gray Adams, interview. For a broader overview of SNCC and its early days in Mississippi, see Ransby, *Ella Baker*, 239–81; Carson, *In Struggle*, chaps. 1–2, 4; Payne, *I've Got the Light*, chaps. 3–5; Dittmer, *Local People*, chaps. 6–7. For a personal account of the movement in Greenwood, see Holland, *From the Mississippi Delta*. Sam Block, the first SNCC activist to arrive in Greenwood in the spring of 1962, had just finished conducting CEP classes in his hometown of Cleveland, Mississippi.

47. Bernice Robinson to Bob Moses, July 13, 1962, Bernice Robinson to Myles Horton, July 30, 1962, Bernice Robinson, "Confidential Mississippi Voter-Education Report," n.d., all in box 38, folder 6, Highlander Papers; Bernice Robinson, "Summary of Mississippi and Louisiana Extension Report, August 1962," box 253, folder 6, J. B. Matthews Papers, Rare Book, Manuscript, and Special Collections Library, Duke University, Durham, N.C. Robinson and Anell Ponder arrived in Greenwood in March 1963 to organize CEP classes and recruit teachers. Robinson returned in June to conduct three week-long workshops — with a total of eight hundred participants — with Bob Moses (Bernice Robinson, "Summary of Activities, 1963–1964," box 21, folder 26, Highlander Collection, Amistad Research Center, Tulane University, New Orleans, La.).

48. Lois Lee Rodgers, "Report for the Month of March 1963," "Report for April 1963," "Report for May 1963," ser. 3, box 161, folder 57, SCLC Papers; Lois Lee Rodgers, "Report for June 1963," ser. 3, box 162, folder 1, SCLC Papers.

49. Septima Clark to Lois Rodgers, October 17, 1963, ser. 3, box 162, folder 2, SCLC Papers; Lois Lee Rodgers, "Report for July 1963," ser. 3, box 162, folder 1, SCLC Papers.

50. Lois Lee Rodgers, "Report for August 1963," ser. 3, box 162, folder 1, SCLC Papers. See also Robnett, "Women," 134–35. Robnett notes that along with Rodgers, Willie Ester McGee worked alongside Stokely Carmichael as a SNCC project director in Itta Bena. McGee's CEP class reports appear in ser. 3, box 163, folder 3, SCLC Papers.

51. Victoria Gray Adams, interview. See also Payne, *I've Got the Light*, 132.

52. Victoria Gray Adams, interview. See also Dittmer, *Local People*, 179–83.

53. Victoria.Gray Adams, interview.

54. Ibid. Gray claimed she learned of the patrol only much later. On how CEP training promoted openness with whites, see also Young, interview.

55. Lois Lee Rodgers, "Report for October 1963" and "Report for November 1963," ser. 3, box 162, folder 2, SCLC Papers. On Carthen and the reprisals she faced for her activism, see "Annual Report, Citizenship Education Program"; Septima Clark to Martin Luther King Jr., n.d., box 3, folder 122, Clark Papers; See also Dittmer, *Local People*, 200–203.

56. Dittmer, *Local People*, 205–12. For personal accounts of Freedom Summer, see, for example, Belfrage, *Freedom Summer*; McAdam, *Freedom Summer*; McAdam, "Gender."

57. Pinkie Pilcher, "Mrs. Ethel Shaw Report, February 21, 1964," "Mrs. Ethel Shaw, Citizenship Class Report from December 18, 1963," both in ser. 3, box 162, folder 35, SCLC Papers; Ethel Shaw, "Report," n.d., ser. 3, box 155, folder 2, SCLC Papers; Laura McGhee, "Report March 10, 1964," ser. 3, box 162, folder 35, SCLC Papers; "Report of Mrs. Laura McGhee, January 14, 1964," ser. 3, box 162, folder 36, SCLC Papers. On violence, see Dittmer, *Local People*, 219–24; for an excellent account of McGhee's role in the Greenwood struggle, see Payne, *I've Got the Light*, 208–18, 234–39.

58. Dittmer, *Local People*, 237. See also Ransby, *Ella Baker*, 331–34.

59. Dittmer, *Local People*, 272–73, 280–83.

60. Victoria Gray Adams, interview. See also Robnett, "Women," 143–44; Dittmer, *Local People*, 281; Lee, *For Freedom's Sake*, 69.

61. Hamer quoted in Dittmer, *Local People*, 302; for an in-depth discussion, see 285–302; Lee, *For Freedom's Sake*, 86–87, chap. 5; Ransby, *Ella Baker*, 336–42. For a view of divisions as a consequence of class and national versus local perspectives, see Robnett, "Women," 145–50.

62. Dittmer, *Local People*, 409–11; Carson, *In Struggle*, 126–29.

63. Alice Blackwell, "CEP Report, April 9, 1965," ser. 3, box 162, folder 19, SCLC Papers; Lou Emma Shipp, "Citizenship School Report, June 1964–July 1965," ser. 3, box 155, folder 3, SCLC Papers.

64. Dittmer, *Local People*, 364–66; Georgia Mae Dickerson, "Citizenship School Report, July 1964–June 1965," ser. 3, box 155, folder 2, SCLC Papers; Victoria Gray, "Citizenship School Report, July 1964–June 1965," ser. 3, box 155, folder 2, SCLC Papers; Ethel Lee Thompson, "Citizenship School Report, July 1964–June 1965," ser. 3, box 155, folder 3, SCLC Papers. See also Lee, *For Freedom's Sake*, chaps. 7–8.

65. Alice Blackwell, "CEP Report, April 9, 1965," ser. 3, box 162, folder 19, SCLC Papers; Pinkie Pilcher, "Biography," ser. 3, box 161, folder 34, SCLC Papers; Robnett, "Women," 134; Victoria Gray, "Mississippi CEP Report," 1966, ser. 13, box 131, folder 10, SCLC Papers.

66. *Highlander Reports*, ca. March 1968, box 253, folder 7, Matthews Papers; Dittmer, *Local People*, chap. 18, esp. 408–16; Hollis Watkins, comments at the Conference on Religion in the Civil Rights Movement, April 4, 2009, Princeton University, Princeton, N.J. Dittmer dismisses some of the local victories as of relatively minor importance. For an alternative view of the importance black activists attached to winning local elections during Reconstruction, see Hahn, *Nation*, chap. 5. On white backlash more broadly, see Crespino, *In Search*, esp. 135–36.

67. Thrasher Interview; Clark, *Ready from Within*, 68–69; Wood Interview; "CEP

News, September 1965," ser. 1, box 29, folder 14, SCLC Papers; "Attention! Free Handwriting Clinics Being Offered" (flyer), ser. 3, box 155, folder 26, SCLC Papers. The clinics ran from May 18 to July 3, 1965. On Selma more broadly, see Garrow, *Protest*; Fairclough, *To Redeem the Soul*, chap. 9, esp. 249.

68. "Summary of Ninth Annual Convention, August 9–13, 1965," 6, ser. 13, box 130, folder 28, SCLC Papers; Young, interview. The author who lavished compliments on the CEP misspelled Clark's name, adding an "e" to the end.

69. Septima P. Clark, "Citizenship Education Proposal for 1965–1970," ser. 3, box 154, folder 14, SCLC Papers. Dr. Robert L. Green, a thirty-one-year-old former consultant on President Johnson's War on Poverty task force, replaced Young as the CEP's administrator for one year ("CEP News, September 1965"). Cotton became the CEP director after Green's departure.

70. "Dr. King's Speech, Frogmore 11/14/66," ser. 4, box 49, folder 12, SCLC Papers. See also "Resolutions of the Eight [*sic*] Annual Convention of the Southern Christian Leadership Conference, September 29–October 2, 1964," box 6, folder 14, Clark Papers. On the SCLC's northern campaigns and later battles, see Fairclough, *To Redeem the Soul*, chaps. 11–14; Branch, *At Canaan's Edge*, chaps. 21–23, pt. 3; Garrow, *Bearing*, chaps. 8–9.

71. Victoria Gray, "Mississippi CEP Report," 1966, ser. 13, box 131, folder 10; Ninth Annual SCLC Convention Program, 1965, ser. 3, box 130, folder 27, SCLC Papers.

72. See, for example, "Proposal to Ford Foundation, Part II: A Program for Citizenship Training for Neighborhood Leaders of Five Major Cities," 1966, ser. 1, box 56, folder 18, SCLC Papers; "SCLC Starts Adult Education Project for 1,000 Jobs in Chicago Ghettoes" (press release), 1968, ser. 4, box 46, folder 11, SCLC Papers. In its Ford proposal, the SCLC targeted Chicago, Cleveland, Houston, Atlanta, and St. Louis.

73. Reagon, interview. On SNCC's trajectory in the latter half of the 1960s, see Carson, *In Struggle*, chaps. 13–16, 18; Payne, *I've Got the Light*, chap. 13.

74. Hall Interview; Septima Poinsette Clark, interview by Judy Barton, Charleston, S.C., November 9, 1971, box 1a, folder 5, Clark Papers. See also Carson, *In Struggle*, 164; Jeffries, "Organizing." In all likelihood, SNCC's political education workshops in Lowndes County were based on the CEP model; these local activists pursued the same goals as CEP graduates elsewhere.

75. Clark, *Ready from Within*, 74, 75; Septima Clark to Josephine Carson, n.d., box 4, folder 18, Clark Papers.

76. Septima Clark, interview by Brown, tape 4, side A; Hall Interview; Bill Saunders, interview by author, Charleston, S.C., March 23, 2002, in author's possession. On the Chicago convention, see Simon Hall, "On the Tail of the Panther"; Carson, *In Struggle*, 170; Victoria Gray Adams, telephone interview. On Black Power more broadly, see Joseph, *Waiting*; Joseph, *Black Power Movement*.

77. Septima Clark to Josephine Carson, May 20, 1966, box 4, folder 18, Clark Papers; Septima Poinsette Clark, "The Movement I Remember," 33–34, box 1a, folder 52, Clark Papers; Septima Clark to Josephine Carson, August 31, September 26, 1966, Septima Clark to Mrs. M. Rider, September 23, 1966, all in box 4, folder 18, Clark Papers.

78. Faragher et al., *Out of Many*, 912–14; Brinkley, "Great Society." By 1966, the OEO

funded more than one thousand CAPs; eight years later it closed. For a more in-depth analysis, see Quadagno, *Color*.

79. Septima Clark to Josephine Carson, August 31, 1966, box 4, folder 18, Clark Papers; Lorraine Howard, "Teacher Survey, June 1964–July 1965," ser. 3, box 154, folder 25, SCLC Papers. For a broader view of how the OEO's "New Careers" program created entry-level jobs for women community workers but also of how gender limited their advancement, see Naples, *Grassroots Warriors*, esp. 1–12. Naples's book is a comparative study on how CAP involvement politicized grassroots women in Philadelphia and New York. I make an important regional distinction by arguing that in the South, black women joined CAPs having already been politicized by their involvement in the CEP and in local civil rights movements.

80. "Citizenship School Report, July 1964–June 1965." On Roberson, see ser. 3, box 154, folder 24, SCLC Papers; on Simmons, see ser. 3, box 155, folder 7, SCLC Papers; on Germany, see ser. 3, box 154, folder 27, SCLC Papers; on Love, see ser. 3, box 154, folder 18, SCLC Papers. In all likelihood, these teachers sent their reports in late. Grimball worked with Head Start from 1966 to 1980 (Grimball Interview). For an overview of Head Start, see Zigler and Muenchow, *Head Start*, chaps. 1–2, esp. 39–46.

81. Victoria Gray Adams, telephone interview; Victoria Gray, "Mississippi CEP Report," 1966, ser. 13, box 131, folder 10, SCLC Papers.

82. Quadagno, *Color*, 11, 37–44; Dittmer, *Local People*, 368–82.

83. Dittmer, *Local People*, 373, 377–82. See also Payne, *I've Got the Light*, 345; Naples, *Grassroots Warriors*, chap. 2, esp. 44.

84. "Itineraries, 1961–62," ser. 1, box 136, folder 23, SCLC Papers; U.S. Department of Justice, Federal Bureau of Investigation, Subject: Clark, Septima Poinsette, File 157-4505, Section 1, in author's possession; Ethel Azalea Johnson, "Citizenship School Report, July 1964–June 1965," ser. 3, box 155, folder 5, SCLC Papers. On the Monroe movement up to 1961, see Tyson, *Radio Free Dixie*, esp. chaps. 4–7, 10.

85. On the development and ideology of the women's movement, see, for example, Evans, *Personal Politics*; Breines, *Trouble between Us*; Roth, *Separate Roads*; Springer, *Living*, esp. chap. 1; Thompson, "Multiracial Feminism." See also Naples, *Grassroots Warriors*, chap. 6, esp. 138–41.

86. Septima P. Clark, "The Nature of Current Revolts," May 8, 1969, box 1a, folder 53, Clark Papers.

87. Ibid. On Wallace and the conservative counterrevolution, see Carter, *Politics of Rage*; Carter, *From George Wallace to Newt Gingrich*, chaps. 1–2, esp. 42. The literature on the ghetto underclass is vast. See, for example, Wilson, *Declining Significance*; Wilson, *Ghetto Underclass*; Katz, *Underclass Debate*.

88. Septima Clark, "The Challenge to Black and White," n.d., box 1a, folder 22, Clark Papers. On incorporating poor whites into the CEP, see Citizenship Education Department Report, December 27, 1967, ser. 4, box 49, folder 11, SCLC Papers; Boyte, "Dorchester Center."

89. Septima P. Clark, "The Vocation of Black Scholarship: Identifying the Enemy," n.d., box 1b, folder 74, Clark Papers.

90. Clark, *Echo*, 234.

91. Clark, *Ready from Within*, 79, 77; Hall Interview; Young, interview. By 1967, Annie Devine had joined Gray on the SCLC executive board (Eleventh Annual SCLC Convention Program, 1967, ser. 3, box 133, folder 10, SCLC Papers).

92. "Viola McFerren Remembers." See also Hillman, "Born into Poverty." Part of the Highlander-based Citizenship Schools in Fayette County, McFerren followed an activist trajectory that paralleled that of other CEP women. She went from being a reluctant joiner in 1960 to drafting Fayette County's first Head Start proposal in 1964. A year later, she served as the plaintiff in a school desegregation case on behalf of her son. In 1966, President Johnson appointed her a member of the OEO's National Advisory Committee. When the County Board of Education dismissed thirteen black teachers as part of its desegregation plan in 1970, McFerren participated in a federal court challenge to preserve black educators' jobs. Soon thereafter, African Americans gained representation on the board itself.

93. Andrew J. Young, "Proposed SCLC Program, September 1969 to July 1970," ser. 4, box 48, folder 9, SCLC Papers. As Nasstrom has observed, "The gendered nature of leadership in the movement may have had less to do with the differential activities of women and men than with their relative success in defining what goals and objectives defined the movement" ("Francis Freeborn Pauley," 96). See also Nasstrom, *Everybody's Grandmother*.

94. Hall Interview; Clark, *Ready from Within*, 83. McFadden makes the same argument regarding black women's raising their voices ("Septima P. Clark," esp. 94).

95. Victoria Gray Adams, telephone interview.

Epilogue

1. Septima Poinsette Clark SCLC Retirement Dinner Invitation, June 19, 1970, box 5, folder 1, Clark Papers.

2. In her second autobiography, Clark states that she won the election in 1976. A curriculum vita that she composed in 1979, however, confirms that it was 1972 (*Ready from Within*, 121; "Biographical [Sketch] of Mrs. Septima Poinsette Clark," box 1a, folder 20, Clark Papers). See also "Elect Septima Clark," Alpha Kappa Alpha poster, n.d., box 8, unnumbered folder, Clark Papers. This document appears to be part of a scrapbook.

3. Thrasher Interview; Alton Crews to Keith Davis, November 3, 1976, box 5, folder 21, Clark Papers.

4. Septima Clark, interview by Eliot Wigginton, New Market, Tenn., June 20, 1981, HERC; Clark, *Ready from Within*, 121.

5. Thrasher Interview; Septima Clark, interview by Wigginton; Clark, *Ready from Within*, 121.

6. Ronald A. McWhirt to Septima Poinsette Clark, December 15, 1977, July 6, 1982, box 4, folder 12, Clark Papers; Alton Crews to Keith Davis, November 3, 1976, box 5, folder 21, Clark Papers.

7. Septima P. Clark, interview by Joan Mack, Charleston, S.C., March 18, 1987, videotape recording, ARC; Fields, *Lemon Swamp*, 243–44.

8. Septima Clark, interview by Sandra Brenneman Oldendorf, Charleston, S.C., January 17, 1986, HERC. On the Day Care Committee, see box 11, folders 8, 10, Clark Papers.

9. Alpha Kappa Alpha, Gamma Xi Omega Chapter, "1978 Founder's Day Program," box 8, folder 4, Clark Papers; on the political organizations, see box 11, folders 17, 25, Clark Papers.

10. Mary Moultrie, interview by author, Charleston, S.C., April 15, 2002, in author's possession. See also Andrew Young, interview by author, Atlanta, Ga., January 29, 2002, in author's possession; Fink, "Union Power"; Estes, "'I Am Somebody.'"

11. Clark, *Ready from Within*, 80; "The Black Women's Community Development Foundation, Inc." (pamphlet), ca. 1971–72, box 11, folder 4, Clark Papers. See also Carden, *Feminism*, 12.

12. Black Women's Community Development Foundation, "The Chicago Symposium: A Revisit and Future Projection," September 1972, box 11, folder 5, Clark Papers. Additional attendees included Toni Cade Bambara, Unita Blackwell, Eva Clayton, Mari Evans, Nikki Giovanni, Audre Lorde, Pauli Murray, and Ida B. Wells's granddaughter, Alfreda Duster ("Participant Roster," January 7–8, 1972, box 11, folder 5, Clark Papers).

13. Inez Smith Reid to Septima Clark, February 15, 1973, box 4, folder 49, Clark Papers; Carden, *Feminism*. Nothing in Clark's papers indicates whether she gave Reid a favorable reply.

14. Clark, *Ready from Within*, 70.

15. The gendered distinction between organizing and leading essentially is not viable. See Payne, "Men Led."

16. Clark, *Ready from Within*, 120. See also "Funeral Services for the Late Septima Earthaline Poinsette Clark," December 19, 1987, Septima Poinsette Clark File, ARC.

17. Septima Clark, interview by Cynthia Brown, Charleston, S.C., August 1979, tape 5, side A, in author's possession.

18. Bill Saunders, interview by author, Charleston, S.C., March 23, 2002, in author's possession; Victoria Gray Adams, telephone interview by author, June 27, 2002, in author's possession. On Clark's battle to receive her retirement, see Clark, *Ready from Within*, 124, which notes that the state legislature voted to pay Clark her full lost wages in 1981; James B. Edwards to Septima Clark, July 14, 1976, R. W. Burnette to Charles T. Ferillo, February 21, 1979, both in box 4, folder 33, Clark Papers.

19. Septima P. Clark, "The Vocation of Black Scholarship: Identifying the Enemy," n.d., box 1b, folder 74, Clark Papers.

20. Clark, *Ready from Within*, 124–25.

21. Yvonne Clark, interview by author, Atlanta, Ga., January 26, 2002, in author's possession.

22. "Angel Oak"; U.S. Department of Agriculture, Natural Resources Conservation Service, "Live Oak"; Saunders, interview.

Bibliography

Primary Sources

Manuscript Collections

Atlanta, Ga.
    The King Center
        Martin Luther King Jr. Papers
        Southern Christian Leadership Conference Papers
Chapel Hill, N.C.
    Southern Historical Collection, Wilson Library, University of North Carolina
        Federal Writers Project Papers
        Guy B. Johnson Papers
        Penn School Papers
        Southern Education Board Papers
    Southern Oral History Project, Wilson Library, University of North Carolina
        Clark, Septima Poinsette. Interview by Jacquelyn Hall,
            Charleston, S.C., July 25, 1976. Transcript #G-16
        Harris, Narvie J. Interview by Kathryn Nasstrom, Atlanta, Ga.,
            June 11, 1992. Transcript #G-084
        Simkins, Modjeska. Interview by Jacquelyn Dowd Hall, Columbia, S.C.,
            July 28–31, 1976. Transcript #G-056-2
Charleston, S.C.
    Avery Research Center for the Study of African American History and Culture,
            College of Charleston
        J. Arthur Brown Papers
        Clark, Septima. Interview by Joan Mack, March 18, 1987 (videotape)
        Septima Poinsette Clark File
        Septima Poinsette Clark Papers
        Septima Clark and Bernice Robinson Collection
        Ruby Cornwell Collection
        Mamie Garvin Fields Collection
        Esau Jenkins Collection
        Frederick Celestine Jenkins-Andrews Collection
        James R. Logan Collection
        Albertha Johnston Murray Collection
        Ethelyn Parker Collection
        Peter T. Poinsette Papers
        Bernice Robinson Collection

"South Carolina Voices of the Civil Rights Movement Conference:
A Conference on the History of the Civil Rights Movement in
South Carolina, 1940–1970" (transcript)
Phillis [Phyllis] Wheatley Literary and Social Club Collection
Clark, Septima P. Interview by Peter H. Wood, Charleston, S.C.,
February 3, 1981. Transcript #G-17
Charleston County Public Library
*Index to Records of Confederate Soldiers Who Served in Organizations from
South Carolina* (microfilm). Washington, D.C.: National Archives, 1962
Record of Wills, 1851–56, Charleston County
Charleston County School District, Office of Archives and Records
Charleston City Board of Commissioners Minute Book: April 1940–July 1946
Charleston City Board of Commissioners Minute Book: August 1946–February 1951
Charleston City Board of Commissioners Minute Book:
March 1951–September 1957
Charleston County Board of Education Minute Book: June 1878–April 1920
Charleston County Board of Education Minute Book: July 1944–June 1949
Superintendent Files
City of Charleston Archives
Tristram T. Hyde Papers
William McGillivray Morrison Papers
South Carolina Historical Society
R. F. W. Allston Papers: Pringle Family Papers
Edwin A. Harleston Papers
Albert Simons Collection
Harriet Stony Simons Collection
Thomas R. Waring Jr. Papers
O. T. Wallace County Office Building
Charleston County Auditor Ward Books 1–9, 1950–53 (microfilm)
Young Women's Christian Association, Coming Street Branch
Minute Book, Committee on Administration: January 18, 1954–April 17, 1967
Columbia, S.C.
Law School Library, University of South Carolina
David W. Robinson Papers (microfilm)
Modern Political Collection, University of South Carolina
Joseph R. Bryson Papers
L. Marion Gressette Papers
Olin D. Johnston Papers
William D. Workman Jr. Papers
South Carolina State Archives
Comptroller General, Pension Department, Confederate Pension Applications,
1636–1940 (Berkeley-Charleston Counties): 1919–1926

South Caroliniana Library, University of South Carolina
James F. Byrnes, "Speech before the South Carolina Educational Association, March 1954"
Abram Cline Flora Papers
Wil Lou Gray Papers
James M. Hinton File
James Allen Hoyt Papers
NAACP, Sumter Branch Minute Book, April 12, 1942–September 28, 1952
The Teachers' Bulletin: Official Organ of the Palmetto State Teachers' Association
Durham, N.C.
Rare Book, Manuscript, and Special Collections Library, Duke University
Alliance for Guidance of Rural Youth Papers
J. B. Matthews Papers
Madison, Wis.
Wisconsin Historical Society, Social Action Collection
Highlander Research and Education Center Papers, 1917–78
New Haven, Conn.
Sterling Memorial Library, Yale University
Papers of the National Association for the Advancement of
Colored People (microfilm)
John Henry McCray Papers (microfilm)
Yale Divinity School, Yale University
Social Ethics Collection
New Market, Tenn.
Highlander Education and Research Center
Clark, Septima. Interview by Sandra Brenneman Oldendorf, Charleston, S.C., January 17, 1986
Clark, Septima. Interview by Sue Thrasher, New Market, Tenn., June 20, 1981
Clark, Septima. Interview by Eliot Wigginton, New Market, Tenn., June 20, 1981
Myles Horton Papers
Robinson, Bernice. Interview by Sandra Brenneman Oldendorf, Charleston, S.C., January 15, 1986
Robinson, Bernice. Interview by Sue Thrasher and Eliot Wigginton, New Market, Tenn., November 9, 1980
New Orleans, La.
Amistad Research Center, Tulane University
Department of United Church Board for Homeland Ministries Collection
Highlander Collection
Washington, D.C.
Mooreland-Spingarn Research Center, Howard University
Judge Julius Waties Waring Papers

Interviews and Documents in Author's Possession

Adams, Fannie Phelps. Interview by author, Columbia, S.C., April 16, 2002

Adams, Victoria Gray. Interview by author, Petersburg, Va., April 22, 2002

Adams, Victoria Gray. Telephone interview by author, June 27, 2002

Alpha Kappa Alpha Sorority Inc. Telephone conversation with author, March 10, 2005

Anderson, Alvin. Interview by author, Atlanta, Ga., January 27, 2002

Anonymous Charleston resident. Interview by author, Charleston, S.C., May 16, 2002

Carawan, Guy, and Candie Carawan. Interview by author, New Market, Tenn., November 12, 2001

Clark, Septima. Interview by Cynthia Stokes Brown, Charleston, S.C., August 1979

Clark, Yvonne. Interview by author, Atlanta, Ga., January 26, 2002

Cornwell, Ruby. Interview by author, James Island, S.C., April 11, 2002

Dansby, Geneva B. Interview by author, Charleston, S.C., May 22, 2002

Grimball, Ethel. Interview by author, Wadmalaw Island, S.C., February 26, 2002

"A Memorial Service for the Late Ruby Madeline Pendergrass Cornwell" (program), March 9, 2003

Moseley, Marguerite. Interview by author, Charleston, S.C., February 22, 2002

Moultrie, Mary. Interview by author, Charleston, S.C., April 15, 2002

Poinsette-Fisher, Elizabeth. Interview by author, Charleston, S.C., May 27, 2002

Reagon, Bernice Johnson. Interview by author, Washington, D.C., July 12, 2002

Saunders, Bill. Interview by author, Charleston, S.C., March 23, 2002

Simms, Lois Averetta. Interview by author, Charleston, S.C., April 9, 2002

Underdown, David. Papers pertaining to the Highlander Folk School, unprocessed private collection

U.S. Department of Justice, Federal Bureau of Investigation, Subject: Clark, Septima Poinsette. File 157-4505, section 1

U.S. Department of Justice, Federal Bureau of Investigation, Subject: Septima Poinsette Clark File 44-14876

Willis, Miriam DeCosta. Letter to author, April 30, 2002

Young, Andrew. Interview by author, Atlanta, Ga., January 29, 2002

Newspapers and Periodicals

Charleston Evening Post
Charleston News and Courier
Chicago Defender
Columbia Palmetto Leader
Columbia Record
Columbia State

Crisis (New York)
Journal of Negro Education
New York Times
Pittsburgh Courier
The Survey (New York)

Published Primary Sources

Annual Report of the State Superintendent of Education of the State of South Carolina. Various publishers, 1915–59.

Atkins, James A. "The Participation of Negroes in Adult Schools and Adult Education Programs." *Journal of Negro Education* 7 (July 1938): 345–56.

Beale, Howard K. "The Needs of Negro Education in the United States." *Journal of Negro Education* 3 (January 1934): 8–19.

Birnie, C. W. "Education of the Negro in Charleston, South Carolina prior to the Civil War." *Journal of Negro History* 12 (January 1927): 13–21.

Bremer, Frederika. *The Homes of the New World: Impressions of America.* Vol. 1. Translated by Mary Howitt. New York: Harper, 1853.

Charleston City Directory. Charleston, S.C.: Walsh, 1891–1908, 1916.

Charleston Grows: An Economic, Social, and Cultural Portrait of an Old Community in the New South. Charleston, S.C.: Carolina Art Association, 1949.

"The Colored Women's Statement to the Women's Missionary Council, American Missionary Association." 1919. Reprinted in *Black Women in White America: A Documentary History*, edited by Gerda Lerner, 461–67. New York: Vintage, 1973.

Cooper, Anna Julia. *A Voice from the South.* 1892. Reprint, New York: Oxford University Press, 1988.

Davis, John P. "The New Deal: Slogans for the Same Raw Deal." 1935. Reprinted in *New Deal Thought*, edited by Howard Zinn, 316–24. New York: Bobbs-Merrill, 1966.

Dictionary of American Biography. Vol. 15. Edited by Dumas Malone. New York: Scribner's, 1935.

"Editorial Comment." *Journal of Negro Education* 3 (October 1934): 565–72.

Felton, J. B. *Folder about Colored Schools in South Carolina: Facts about the Scholastic Year 1921–22 with Suggestions for the Session 1922–23.* Columbia, S.C.: n.p., 1922.

Findings of the First Annual Conference on Adult Education and the Negro, Held at Hampton Institute, Virginia, October 20–22, 1938. Washington, D.C.: American Association for Adult Education, [1939?].

Gordon, Asa H. *Sketches of Negro Life and History in South Carolina.* 1929. Reprint, Columbia: University of South Carolina Press, 1971.

Herbert, R. Beverly. *What We Can Do about the Race Problem.* Columbia, S.C.: 1948.

Hickory, North Carolina City Directory. Vol. 2. Statesville, N.C.: Brady, 1920–21.

Hill's Columbia City (South Carolina) Directory. Richmond, Va.: Hill's, 1931–47.

Johnson, Charles S. *Growing Up in the Black Belt: Negro Youth in the Rural South.* Washington, D.C.: American Council on Education, 1941.

Johnson, Guion Griffis. *A Social History of the Sea Islands, with Special Reference to St. Helena Island, South Carolina.* Chapel Hill: University of North Carolina Press, 1930.

Johnson, Guy B. *Folk Culture on St. Helena Island, South Carolina.* Chapel Hill: University of North Carolina Press, 1930.

Jones, Lance G. E. *The Jeanes Teacher in the United States, 1908–1933: An Account of Twenty-five Years' Experience in the Supervision of Negro Rural Schools.* Chapel Hill: University of North Carolina Press, 1937.

Journal of the Senate of the Second Session of the 85th General Assembly of the State of South Carolina, Being the Extraordinary Session Beginning Friday, April 14, 1944.

Columbia: Joint Committee on Printing, General Assembly of South Carolina, [1944?].

Martin, C. J. *History and Development of Negro Education in South Carolina*. Columbia, S.C.: State Department of Education, Division of Instruction, 1949.

Miller, Kelly. *The Negro in the New Reconstruction*. Washington, D.C.: Howard University, [1919?].

Miller's City Directory, Hickory, North Carolina, 1928–1929. Vol. 4. Asheville, N.C.: Miller, [1928–29?].

Nelsons' Baldwin Charleston South Carolina City Directory. Charleston: Nelsons' Baldwin, 1958.

Public Schools of South Carolina: A Report of the South Carolina Education Survey Committee. Nashville, Tenn.: Division of Surveys and Field Services, George Peabody College for Teachers, 1948.

Reid, Ira De A. *Adult Education among Negroes*. Washington, D.C.: Associates in Negro Folk Education, 1936.

Requirements for Teacher Education and Certification Adopted by State Board of Education 1945. Rev. ed. Columbia: South Carolina Department of Education, 1948.

Robinson, William McKinley. "A Rural Point of View." In *The Parent-Teacher Organization: Its Origins and Development*, 104–11. Chicago: National Congress of Parents and Teachers, 1944.

Rowan, Carl T. *South of Freedom*. New York: Knopf, 1952.

South Carolina Federation of Colored Women's Clubs, 1909–1949 [fortieth anniversary pamphlet]. [South Carolina: Federation of Colored Women's Clubs], 1949.

U.S. Bureau of the Census. *Census of the Population, 1920*. Vol. 3, *Population*. Washington, D.C.: U.S. Government Printing Office, 1922.

————. *Census of the Population, 1920*. Vol. 4, *Characteristics of the Population: Occupations*. Washington, D.C.: U.S. Government Printing Office, 1922.

————. *Census of the Population, 1930*. Vol. 3, Part 2, *Population*. Washington, D.C.: U.S. Government Printing Office, 1932.

————. *Census of the Population, 1940*. Vol. 2, Part 4, *Characteristics of the Population*. Washington, D.C.: U.S. Government Printing Office, 1943.

U.S. Bureau of the Census. *Historical Statistics of the United States: Colonial Times to 1970*. Part 1. Washington, D.C.: U.S. Government Printing Office, 1975.

————. *Manuscript Census*, 1850, 1860, 1870, 1880, 1900, 1910, 1920.

U.S. Department of the Interior, Office of Education. "Facts about Negro Education" [press release]. Washington, D.C.: May 7, 1934.

Wakefield, Dan. "The Siege at Highlander." *The Nation*, November 7, 1959, 323–25.

Washington, Booker T. *Up from Slavery: An Autobiography*. 1902. Reprint, New York: Viking Penguin, 1986.

Wells, Edward L. *A Sketch of the Charleston Light Dragoons, from the Earliest Formation of the Corps*. Charleston, S.C.: Lucas, Richardson, 1888.

Yearbook, 1919: City of Charleston, South Carolina. Charleston: Walker, Evans, and Cogswell, 1919.

Yearbook, 1920: City of Charleston, South Carolina. Charleston: Walker, Evans, and Cogswell, 1920.

Yearbook, 1921: City of Charleston, South Carolina. Charleston: Furlong, Charleston Printing House, 1922.

Published Secondary Sources

Ackelsberg, Martha A. "Communities, Resistance, and Women's Activism: Some Implications for a Democratic Polity." In *Women and the Politics of Empowerment*, edited by Ann Bookman and Sandra Morgen, 297–313. Philadelphia: Temple University Press, 1998.

Adams, Frank, with Myles Horton. *Unearthing Seeds of Fire: The Idea of Highlander.* Winston-Salem, N.C.: Blair, 1975.

Alford, Robbie L. *Joel Roberts Poinsett: Versatile American.* Georgetown, S.C.: Rice Museum, 1975.

Anderson, Carol. *Eyes off the Prize: The United Nations and the African American Struggle for Human Rights.* New York: Cambridge University Press, 2003.

Anderson, Eric, and Alfred A. Moss Jr. *Dangerous Donations: Northern Philanthropy and Southern Black Education, 1902–1930.* Columbia: University of Missouri Press, 1999.

Anderson, James D. *The Education of Blacks in the South, 1860–1935.* Chapel Hill: University of North Carolina Press, 1988.

Andrews, William L. *To Tell a Free Story: The First Century of Afro-American Autobiography, 1760–1865.* Urbana: University of Illinois Press, 1986.

"Angel Oak, Johns Island, South Carolina." ⟨http://www.angeloaktree.org/history.htm⟩. July 30, 2007.

Arsenault, Raymond. *Freedom Riders: 1961 and the Struggle for Racial Justice.* New York: Oxford University Press, 2006.

Ayres, DaMaris. *Let My People Learn: The Biography of Dr. Wil Lou Gray.* Greenwood, S.C.: Attic, 1988.

Bailey, Thomas A. *A Diplomatic History of the American People.* 9th ed. Englewood Cliffs, N.J.: Prentice-Hall, 1974.

Baker, Ella. "Developing Community Leadership." 1970. Reprinted in *Black Women in White America: A Documentary History*, edited by Gerda Lerner, 346–52. New York: Vintage, 1973.

Baker, Paula. "The Domestication of Politics: Women and American Political Society, 1780–1920." *American Historical Review* 89 (June 1984): 620–47.

Baker, R. Scott. *Paradoxes of Desegregation: African American Struggles for Educational Equity in Charleston, South Carolina, 1926–1972.* Columbia: University of South Carolina Press, 2006.

Balibar, Etienne, and Immanuel Wallerstein. *Race, Nation, Class: Ambiguous Identities.* New York: Verso, 1991.

Ball, Edward. *Slaves in the Family.* New York: Ballantine, 1998.

———. *The Sweet Hell Inside: A Family History.* New York: Morrow, 2001.

Bartley, Numan V. "The Era of the New Deal as a Turning Point in Southern History."

In *The New Deal and the South*, edited by James C. Cobb and Michael V. Namorato, 135–46. Jackson: University Press of Mississippi, 1984.

———. *The Rise of Massive Resistance: Race and Politics in the South during the 1950s.* Baton Rouge: Louisiana State University Press, 1969.

Bates, Daisy. *The Long Shadow of Little Rock.* New York: McKay, 1962.

Baxandall, Rosalyn. "Re-Visioning the Women's Liberation Movement's Narrative: Early Second Wave African American Feminists." *Feminist Studies* 27 (Spring 2001): 225–45.

Beam, Lura. *He Called Them by Lightning: A Teacher's Odyssey in the Negro South, 1908–1919.* Reprint, New York: Bobbs-Merrill, 1967.

Belfrage, Sally. *Freedom Summer.* Charlottesville: University Press of Virginia, 1965.

Bennett, James B. *Religion and the Rise of Jim Crow.* Princeton: Princeton University Press, 2005.

Berlin, Ira. *Many Thousands Gone: The First Two Centuries of Slavery in North America.* Cambridge: Harvard University Press, 1998.

———. *Slaves without Masters: The Free Negro in the Antebellum South.* New York: Vintage, 1976.

Biographical Dictionary of the South Carolina Senate, 1776–1985. Vol. 2. Columbia: University of South Carolina Press, 1986.

Blight, David W. *Race and Reunion: The Civil War in American Memory.* Cambridge: Harvard University Press, 2001.

———. "W. E. B. Du Bois and the Struggle for American Historical Memory." In *History and Memory in African American Culture*, edited by Genevieve Fabre and Robert O'Meally, 45–71. New York: Oxford University Press, 1993.

Borstelmann, Thomas. *The Cold War and the Color Line.* Cambridge: Harvard University Press, 2001.

Boyte, Harry. "The Dorchester Center: An Interview with Dorothy Cotton, 1991." ⟨http://www.publicwork.org/pdf/interviews/Citizenship%20Education,%201991.pdf⟩. July 27, 2007.

Branch, Taylor. *At Canaan's Edge: America in the King Years, 1965–1968.* New York: Simon and Schuster, 2006.

———. *Parting the Waters: America in the King Years, 1954–1963.* New York: Simon and Schuster, 1988.

———. *Pillar of Fire: America in the King Years, 1963–1965.* New York: Simon and Schuster, 1998.

Braxton, Joanne M. *Black Women Writing Autobiography: A Tradition within a Tradition.* Philadelphia: Temple University Press, 1989.

Breines, Winifred. *The Trouble between Us: An Uneasy History of White and Black Women in the Feminist Movement.* New York: Oxford University Press, 2006.

Brinkley, Alan. "Great Society." In *The Reader's Companion to American History*, edited by Eric Foner and John A. Garraty, 470–72. Boston: Houghton-Mifflin, 1991.

Brown, Elsa Barkley. "Negotiating and Transforming the Public Sphere: African American Political Life in the Transition from Slavery to Freedom." In *Jumpin' Jim*

Crow: Southern Politics from Civil War to Civil Rights, edited by Jane Dailey, Glenda Elizabeth Gilmore, and Bryant Simon, 28–66. Princeton: Princeton University Press, 2000.

———. "To Catch the Vision of Freedom: Reconstructing Southern Black Women's Political History, 1865–1880." In *Unequal Sisters: An Inclusive Reader in U.S. Women's History*, 4th ed., edited by Vicki L. Ruiz with Ellen Carol DuBois, 156–77. New York: Routledge, 2008.

———. "Womanist Consciousness: Maggie Lena Walker and the Independent Order of Saint Luke." In *Unequal Sisters: A Multi-Cultural Reader in U.S. Women's History*, 3rd ed., edited by Ellen Carol DuBois and Vicki L. Ruiz, 208–23. New York: Routledge, 1990.

Browne, Rose Butler, with James W. English. *Love My Children: An Autobiography*. New York: Meredith, 1969.

Brown-Nagin, Tomiko. "The Transformation of a Social Movement into Law?: The SCLC and NAACP's Campaigns for Civil Rights Reconsidered in Light of the Educational Activism of Septima Clark." *Women's History Review* 8, no. 1 (1999): 81–137.

Brundage, W. Fitzhugh. *The Southern Past: A Clash of Race and Memory*. Cambridge: Belknap Press of Harvard University Press, 2005.

———. "White Women and the Politics of Memory in the New South, 1880–1920." In *Jumpin' Jim Crow: Southern Politics from Civil War to Civil Rights*, edited by Jane Dailey, Glenda Elizabeth Gilmore, and Bryant Simon, 115–39. Princeton: Princeton University Press, 2000.

Burts, Robert Milton. *Richard Irvine Manning and the Progressive Movement in South Carolina*. Columbia: University of South Carolina Press, 1974.

Butterfield, Stephen. *Black Autobiography in America*. Amherst: University of Massachusetts Press, 1974.

Cade, Toni. "The Pill: Genocide or Liberation?" In *The Black Woman: An Anthology*, edited by Toni Cade, 162–69. New York: Mentor, 1970.

Carawan, Guy, and Candie Carawan. *Ain't You Got a Right to the Tree of Life?: The People of Johns Island, South Carolina, Their Faces, Their Words, and Their Songs*. New York: Simon and Schuster, 1966.

Carby, Hazel V. "'On the Threshold of Woman's Era': Lynching, Empire and Sexuality in Black Feminist Theory." In *"Race," Writing and Difference*, edited by Henry Louis Gates Jr., 301–16. Chicago: University of Chicago Press, 1986.

———. *Reconstructing Womanhood: The Emergence of the Afro-American Woman Novelist*. New York: Oxford University Press, 1987.

———. "The Sexual Politics of Women's Blues." In *Cultures in Babylon: Black Britain and African America*, 7–21. New York: Verso, 1999.

Carden, Maren Lockwood. *Feminism in the Mid-1970s: The Non-Establishment, the Establishment, and the Future: A Report to the Ford Foundation*. New York: Ford Foundation, 1977. ⟨http://www.fordfound.org/archives/item/0111/original/1⟩. March 20, 2009.

Carlton, David. *Mill and Town in South Carolina, 1880–1920*. Baton Rouge: Louisiana State University Press, 1982.

Carson, Clayborne. *In Struggle: SNCC and the Black Awakening of the 1960s*. Rev. ed. Cambridge: Harvard University Press, 1995.

Carter, Dan T. *From George Wallace to Newt Gingrich: Race in the Conservative Counterrevolution, 1963–1994*. Baton Rouge: Louisiana State University Press, 1996.

———. *The Politics of Rage: George Wallace, the Origins of the New Conservatism, and the Transformation of American Politics*. Baton Rouge: Louisiana State University Press, 1995.

Cecelski, David S. "Abraham H. Galloway: Wilmington's Lost Prophet and the Rise of Black Radicalism in the American South." In *Democracy Betrayed: The Wilmington Race Riot of 1898 and Its Legacy*, edited by David S. Cecelski and Timothy B. Tyson, 43–72. Chapel Hill: University of North Carolina Press, 1998.

———. *Along Freedom Road: Hyde County, North Carolina, and the Fate of Black Schools in the South*. Chapel Hill: University of North Carolina Press, 1994.

Cecelski, David S., and Timothy B. Tyson, eds. *Democracy Betrayed: The Wilmington Race Riot of 1898 and Its Legacy*. Chapel Hill: University of North Carolina Press, 1998.

Chafe, William H. *Civilities and Civil Rights: Greensboro, North Carolina, and the Black Struggle for Freedom*. New York: Oxford University Press, 1980.

———. "The Gods Bring Threads to Webs Begun." *Journal of American History* 86 (March 2000): 1531–51.

Charleston South Carolina and the Lowcountry: A Photographic Portrait. Rockport, Mass.: Twin Light, 2002.

Charron, Katherine Mellen. "We've Come a Long Way: Septima Clark, the Warings, and the Changing Civil Rights Movement." In *Groundwork: Local Black Freedom Movements in America*, edited by Jeanne Theoharis and Komozi Woodard, 116–39. New York: New York University Press, 2005.

Chirhart, Ann Short. *Torches of Light: Georgia Teachers and the Coming of the Modern South*. Athens: University of Georgia Press, 2005.

Clark, James C. "Civil Rights Leader Harry T. Moore and the Ku Klux Klan in Florida." *Florida Historical Quarterly* 72 (October 1994): 166–83.

Clark, Septima P. "Literacy and Liberation." *Freedomways* 4 (Winter 1964): 113–24.

———. *Ready from Within: Septima Clark and the Civil Rights Movement*. Edited by Cynthia Stokes Brown. Navarro, Calif.: Wild Tree, 1986.

Clark, Septima Poinsette, with LeGette Blythe. *Echo in My Soul*. New York: Dutton, 1962.

Collier-Thomas, Bettye, and V. P. Franklin, eds. *Sisters in the Struggle: African American Women in the Civil Rights–Black Power Movement*. New York: New York University Press, 2001.

Collins, Patricia Hill. *Black Feminist Thought: Knowledge, Consciousness, and the Politics of Empowerment*. New York: Routledge, 1990.

Connerton, Paul. *How Societies Remember.* New York: Cambridge University Press, 1989.

Cotton, Ella Earls. *A Spark for My People: A Sociological Autobiography of a Negro Teacher.* New York: Exposition, 1954.

Couto, Richard A. *Ain't Gonna Let Nobody Turn Me Round: The Pursuit of Racial Justice in the Rural South.* Philadelphia: Temple University Press, 1991.

Cox, Karen L. *Dixie's Daughters: The United Daughters of the Confederacy and the Preservation of Confederate Culture.* Gainesville: University Press of Florida, 2003.

Crawford, Vicki L., Jacqueline Anne Rouse, and Barbara Woods, eds. *Women in the Civil Rights Movement: Trailblazers and Torchbearers, 1941–1965.* Bloomington: Indiana University Press, 1990.

Crespino, Joseph. *In Search of Another Country: Mississippi and the Conservative Counterrevolution.* Princeton: Princeton University Press, 2007.

Cuthbert-Kerr, Simon. "'You Don't Have to Make the X for Me, Because I Can Write My Own Name': Septima Clark, Citizenship Education, and Voter Registration in the South Carolina Sea Islands, 1954–1963." *Avery Review* 2 (Spring 2000): 56–80.

Dailey, Jane, Glenda Elizabeth Gilmore, and Bryant Simon, eds. *Jumpin' Jim Crow: Southern Politics from Civil War to Civil Rights.* Princeton: Princeton University Press, 2000.

Dalfiume, Richard M. "The 'Forgotten Years' of the Negro Revolution." *Journal of American History* 55 (June 1968): 90–106.

Davis, Angela Y. *Blues Legacies and Black Feminism: Gertrude "Ma" Rainey, Bessie Smith, and Billie Holiday.* New York: Pantheon, 1998.

———. *Women, Race, and Class.* New York: Vintage, 1983.

Dennis, Michael. *Luther P. Jackson and a Life for Civil Rights.* Gainesville: University Press of Florida, 2004.

Dittmer, John. *Local People: The Struggle for Civil Rights in Mississippi.* Urbana: University of Illinois Press, 1994.

Drago, Edmund L. *Initiative, Paternalism, and Race Relations: Charleston's Avery Normal Institute.* Athens: University of Georgia Press, 1990.

Dudziak, Mary. *Cold War Civil Rights: Race and the Image of American Democracy.* Princeton: Princeton University Press, 2000.

Dunn, Richard S. *Sugar and Slaves: The Rise of the Planter Class in the British West Indies, 1624–1713.* New York: Norton, 1973.

Durr, Virginia Foster. *Outside the Magic Circle: The Autobiography of Virginia Foster Durr.* Edited by Hollinger F. Barnard. New York: Simon and Schuster, 1987.

Dykeman, Wilma, and James Stokely. *Seeds of Southern Change.* Chicago: University of Chicago Press, 1962.

Egerton, John. *Speak Now against the Day: The Generation before the Civil Rights Movement in the South.* Chapel Hill: University of North Carolina Press, 1994.

Ecke, Paul, Ranch. "The Legend of the Poinsettia." ⟨http://www.ecke.com/html/h_corp/corp_legend.html⟩. October 9, 2003.

Ellison, Ralph. *Shadow and Act.* 1953. Reprint, New York: Vintage, 1972.

Eskew, Glenn T. *But for Birmingham: The Local and National Movements in the Civil Rights Struggle*. Chapel Hill: University of North Carolina Press, 1997.

Estes, Steve. "'I Am Somebody': The Charleston Hospital Strike of 1969." *Avery Review* 3 (Spring 2000): 8–32.

Evans, Sara. *Personal Politics: The Roots of the Women's Liberation in the Civil Rights Movement and the New Left*. New York: Vintage, 1979.

Fairclough, Adam. "'Being in the Field of Education and Also Being a Negro . . . Seems . . . Tragic': Black Teachers in the Jim Crow South." *Journal of American History* 87 (June 2000): 65–91.

———. *A Class of Their Own: Black Teachers in the Segregated South*. Cambridge: Harvard University Press, 2007.

———. "The Costs of *Brown*: Black Teachers and School Integration." *Journal of American History* 91 (June 2004): 43–55.

———. *Race and Democracy: The Civil Rights Struggle in Louisiana, 1915–1972*. Athens: University of Georgia Press, 1995.

———. *Teaching Equality: Black Schools in the Age of Jim Crow*. Athens: University of Georgia Press, 2001.

———. *To Redeem the Soul of America: The Southern Christian Leadership Conference and Martin Luther King Jr.* Athens: University of Georgia Press, 1987.

Faragher, John Mack, Mari Jo Buhle, Daniel Czitrom, and Susan H. Armitage. *Out of Many: A History of the American People*. Vol. 2. 4th ed. Upper Saddle River, N.J.: Pearson Education, 2003.

Feimster, Crystal N. *Southern Horrors: Women and the Politics of Rape and Lynching*. Cambridge: Harvard University Press, forthcoming.

Fields, Barbara Jeanne. "Ideology and Race in American History." In *Region, Race, and Reconstruction: Essays in Honor of C. Vann Woodward*, edited by J. Morgan Kousser and James M. McPherson, 143–77. New York: Oxford University Press, 1992.

Fields, Mamie Garvin, with Karen Fields. *Lemon Swamp and Other Places: A Carolina Memoir*. New York: Free Press, 1983.

Fink, Leon. "Teaching the People: Wil Lou Gray and the Siren of Educational Opportunity." In *Progressive Intellectuals and the Dilemmas of Democratic Commitment*, 242–74. Cambridge: Harvard University Press, 1997.

———. "Union Power, Soul Power: The Story of 1199B and Labor's Search for a Southern Strategy." *Southern Changes* 5 (March–April 1983): 9–20.

First Baptist Church, Huntsville, Alabama. "Our History." ⟨http://www.fmbc.org/history.htm⟩. June 5, 2005.

Flanagan, Maureen. *America Reformed: Progressives and Progressivisms, 1890s–1920s*. New York: Oxford University Press, 2006.

Fleming, Cynthia Griggs. *Soon We Will Not Cry: The Liberation of Ruby Doris Smith Robinson*. Lanham, Md.: Rowman and Littlefield, 1998.

Foner, Eric. *Reconstruction: America's Unfinished Revolution, 1863–1877*. New York: Harper and Row, 1988.

Forman, James. *The Making of Black Revolutionaries*. Seattle: University of Washington Press, 1997.

Foster, Frances Smith. *Written by Herself: Literary Production by African American Women, 1746–1892*. Bloomington: Indiana University Press, 1993.

Foster, Michele. *Black Teachers on Teaching*. New York: Free Press, 1997.

———. "Constancy, Connectedness, and Constraints in the Lives of African American Teachers." *NWSA Journal* 3 (Spring 1991): 233–61.

Foucault, Michel. *Language, Counter-Memory, Practice: Selected Essays and Interviews*. Edited by Donald F. Bouchard. Ithaca: Cornell University Press, 1977.

Franklin, John Hope, and Alfred A. Moss Jr. *From Slavery to Freedom: A History of African Americans*. 7th ed. New York: McGraw-Hill, 1994.

Fraser, Walter, Jr. *Charleston! Charleston!: The History of a Southern City*. Columbia: University of South Carolina Press, 1989.

Frederickson, Kari. "'As a Man, I Am Interested in States' Rights': Gender, Race and Family in the Dixiecrat Party, 1948–1950." In *Jumpin' Jim Crow: Southern Politics from Civil War to Civil Rights*, edited by Jane Dailey, Glenda Elizabeth Gilmore, and Bryant Simon, 260–74. Princeton: Princeton University Press, 2000.

———. *The Dixiecrat Revolt and the End of the Solid South, 1932–1968*. Chapel Hill: University of North Carolina Press, 2001.

Freeman, Mark. *Rewriting the Self: History, Memory, Narrative*. New York: Routledge, 1993.

Freire, Paulo. *Education: The Practice of Freedom*. London: Writers and Readers, 1976.

———. *Pedagogy of the Oppressed*. New York: Penguin, 1972.

Freire, Paulo, and Donaldo Maceo. *Literacy: Reading the Word and the World*. Boston: Bergin and Garvey, 1987.

Frystak, Shannon L. *Our Minds on Freedom: Women and the Black Struggle for Equality in Louisiana, 1924–1967*. Baton Rouge: Louisiana State University Press, forthcoming.

Fultz, Michael. "Charleston, 1919–1920: The Final Battle in the Emergence of the South's Urban African American Teaching Corps." *Journal of Urban History* 27 (July 2001): 633–49.

———. "Teacher Training and African American Education in the South, 1900–1940." *Journal of Negro Education* 64 (Spring 1995): 196–210.

Gaines, Kevin K. *Uplifting the Race: Black Leadership, Politics, and Culture in the Twentieth Century*. Chapel Hill: University of North Carolina Press, 1996.

Garrow, David. *Bearing the Cross: Martin Luther King Jr. and the Southern Christian Leadership Conference*. New York: Morrow, 1986.

———. *Protest at Selma: Martin Luther King Jr. and the Voting Rights Act of 1965*. New Haven: Yale University Press, 1978.

Gilkes, Cheryl Townsend. "Building in Many Places: Multiple Commitments and Ideologies in Black Women's Community Work." In *Women and the Politics of Empowerment*, edited by Ann Bookman and Sandra Morgen, 53–76. Philadelphia: Temple University Press, 1988.

Gilmore, Glenda Elizabeth. *Defying Dixie: The Radical Roots of Civil Rights, 1919–1950*. New York: Norton, 2008.

———. "False Friends and Avowed Enemies: Southern African Americans and Party Allegiances in the 1920s." In *Jumpin' Jim Crow: Southern Politics from Civil War to Civil Rights*, edited by Jane Dailey, Glenda Elizabeth Gilmore, and Bryant Simon, 219–38. Princeton: Princeton University Press, 2000.

———. *Gender and Jim Crow: Women and the Politics of White Supremacy in North Carolina, 1896–1920*. Chapel Hill: University of North Carolina Press, 1996.

Gilmore, Stephanie. "Regenerating Women's History." *Journal of Women's History* 15 (Spring 2003): 178–82.

Glen, John M. *Highlander: No Ordinary School, 1932–1962*. Lexington: University Press of Kentucky, 1988.

Glymph, Thavolia. "'Liberty Dearly Bought': The Making of Civil War Memory in Afro-American Communities in the South." In *Time Longer Than Rope: A Century of African-American Activism, 1850–1950*, edited by Charles M. Payne and Adam Green, 111–39. New York: New York University Press, 2003.

Gomez, Michael A. *Exchanging Our Country Marks: The Transformation of African Identities in the Colonial and Antebellum South*. Chapel Hill: University of North Carolina Press, 1998.

Goodwyn, Lawrence. *The Populist Revolt: A Short History of the Agrarian Revolt in America*. New York: Oxford University Press, 1978.

Grant, Nancy L. "Adult Education for Blacks during the New Deal and World War II: The Federal Programs." In *Education of the African American Adult: An Historical Overview*, edited by Harvey G. Neufeldt and Leo McGee, 211–31. Westport, Conn.: Greenwood, 1990.

Green, Elna C. *Southern Strategies: Southern Women and the Woman Suffrage Question*. Chapel Hill: University of North Carolina Press, 1997.

Greene, Christina. *Our Separate Ways: Women and the Black Freedom Movement in Durham, North Carolina*. Chapel Hill: University of North Carolina Press, 2005.

Grossman, James R. *Land of Hope: Chicago, Black Southerners, and the Great Migration*. Chicago: University of Chicago Press, 1989.

Hahn, Steven. *A Nation under Our Feet: Black Political Struggles in the Rural South from Slavery to the Great Migration*. Cambridge: Harvard University Press, 2003.

Hale, Grace Elizabeth. *Making Whiteness: The Culture of Segregation in the South*. New York: Pantheon, 1998.

Hall, Jacquelyn Dowd. "The Long Civil Rights Movement and the Political Uses of the Past." *Journal of American History* 91 (March 2005): 1233–64.

———. "'The Mind That Burns in Each Body': Women, Rape, and Racial Violence." *Southern Exposure* 21 (November–December 1984): 61–72.

———. *Revolt against Chivalry: Jesse Daniel Ames and the Women's Campaign against Lynching*. New York: Columbia University Press, 1974.

Hall, Simon. "On the Tail of the Panther: Black Power and the 1967 Convention of the

National Conference for New Politics." *Journal of American Studies* 37 (April 2003):
59–78.

Hamlin, Françoise Nicole. "Vera Mae Pigee (1925–): Mothering the Movement."
In *Mississippi Women: Their Histories, Their Lives*, edited by Martha H. Swain,
Elizabeth Anne Payne, Marjorie Spruill Wheeler, and Susan Ditto, 281–98. Athens:
University of Georgia Press, 2003.

Harrison, Daphne Duval. *Black Pearls: Blues Queens of the 1920s*. New Brunswick, N.J.:
Rutgers University Press, 1990.

Hayes, Jack Irby, Jr. *South Carolina and the New Deal*. Columbia: University of South
Carolina Press, 2001.

Hewett, Jane B., ed. *South Carolina Confederate Soldiers, 1861–1865, Unit Roster*. Vol. 2.
Wilmington, N.C.: Broadfoot, 1998.

Hicks, Estelle Bell. *The Golden Apples: Memoirs of a Retired Teacher*. New York:
Exposition, 1959.

Higginbotham, Evelyn Brooks. "African-American Women's History and the
Metalanguage of Race." *Signs* 17 (Winter 1992): 251–74.

———. "In Politics to Stay: Black Women Leaders and Party Politics in the 1920s." In
Women, Politics and Change, edited by Louise A. Tilly and Patricia Gurin, 199–220.
New York: Sage Foundation, 1990.

———. *Righteous Discontent: The Women's Movement in the Black Baptist Church,
1880–1920*. Cambridge: Harvard University Press, 1993.

Hill, Lance. *The Deacons for Defense: Armed Resistance and the Civil Rights Movement*.
Chapel Hill: University of North Carolina Press, 2004.

Hillman, Jacque. "Born into Poverty, She Led Fight for Civil Rights." ⟨http://www
.jacksonsun/civilrights/sec4_sheledfight_mcferren.shtml⟩. March 1, 2005.

Hine, Darlene Clark. "Black Professionals and Race Consciousness: Origins of the Civil
Rights Movement, 1890–1950." *Journal of American History* 89 (March 2003): 1279–
94.

———. *Black Women in White: Racial Conflict and Cooperation in the Nursing
Profession, 1890–1950*. Bloomington: Indiana University Press, 1989.

———. "The Corporeal and the Ocular Veil: Dr. Matilda A. Evans (1872–1935) and the
Complexity of Southern History." *Journal of Southern History* 70 (February 2004):
3–34.

———. "Rape and the Inner Lives of Black Women in the Middle West: Preliminary
Thoughts on the Culture of Dissemblance." In *Unequal Sisters: A Multi-Cultural
Reader in U.S. Women's History*, 3rd ed., edited by Ellen Carol DuBois and Vicki L.
Ruiz, 292–97. New York: Routledge, 1990.

Hine, Darlene Clark, and Christie Anne Farnham. "Black Women's Culture of
Resistance and the Right to Vote." In *Women of the American South: A Multicultural
Reader*, edited by Christie Anne Farnham, 204–19. New York: New York University
Press, 1997.

Hine, William C. "Thomas E. Miller and the Early Years of South Carolina State

University." *Carologue: A Publication of the South Carolina Historical Society* (Winter 1996): 8–12.

Hoffman, Edwin D. "The Genesis of the Modern Movement for Equal Rights in South Carolina, 1930–1939." *Journal of Negro History* 44 (October 1959): 349–69.

Holland, Endesha Ida Mae. *From the Mississippi Delta: A Memoir.* New York: Simon and Schuster, 1997.

Holloway, Jonathan Scott. *Confronting the Veil: Abram Harris Jr., E. Franklin Frazier, and Ralph Bunche, 1919–1941.* Chapel Hill: University of North Carolina Press, 2002.

Holt, Thomas. *Black over White: Negro Political Leadership in South Carolina during Reconstruction.* Chicago: University of Illinois Press, 1977.

Horton, Aimee Isgrig. *The Highlander Folk School: A History of Its Major Programs, 1932–1961.* New York: Carlson, 1989.

Hunter, Tera W. *To'Joy My Freedom: Southern Black Women's Lives and Labors after the Civil War.* Cambridge: Harvard University Press, 1997.

Jeffries, Hasan Kwame. "Organizing for More Than the Vote: The Political Radicalization of Local People in Lowndes County, Alabama, 1965–1966." In *Groundwork*, edited by Jeanne Theoharis and Komozi Woodard, 140–63. New York: New York University Press, 2005.

Jenkins, Wilbert L. *Seizing the New Day: African Americans in Post–Civil War Charleston.* Bloomington: Indiana University Press, 1998.

Johnson, Thomas L., and Phillip C. Dunn, eds. *A True Likeness: The Black South of Richard Samuel Roberts, 1920–1936.* Columbia, S.C.: Bruccoli Clark, 1986.

Jones, Jacqueline. *Labor of Love, Labor of Sorrow: Black Women, Work, and the Family from Slavery to the Present.* New York: Basic Books, 1985.

Jones, Lu Ann. *Mama Learned Us to Work: Farm Women in the New South.* Chapel Hill: University of North Carolina Press, 2002.

Joseph, Peniel E., ed. *The Black Power Movement: Rethinking the Civil Rights–Black Power Era.* New York: Routledge, 2006.

———. *Waiting 'til the Midnight Hour: A Narrative History of Black Power in America.* New York: Holt, 2006.

Joyner, Charles. *Down by the Riverside: A South Carolina Slave Community.* Urbana: University of Illinois Press, 1984.

Kantrowitz, Stephen. *Ben Tillman and the Reconstruction of White Supremacy.* Chapel Hill: University of North Carolina Press, 2000.

Katz, Michael B., ed. *The Underclass Debate.* Princeton: Princeton University Press, 1993.

Kelley, Robin D. G. *Hammer and Hoe: Alabama Communists during the Great Depression.* Chapel Hill: University of North Carolina Press, 1990.

———. "'We Are Not What We Seem': Rethinking Black Working-Class Opposition in the Jim Crow South." *Journal of American History* 81 (June 1993): 75–112.

Key, V. O. *Southern Politics in State and Nation.* New York: Knopf, 1949.

Klarman, Michael J. *From Jim Crow to Civil Rights: The Supreme Court and the Struggle for Racial Equality.* New York: Oxford University Press, 2004.

Kluger, Richard. *Simple Justice: The History of Brown v. Board of Education and Black America's Struggle for Equality*. New York: Vintage, 1977.

Korstad, Robert Rogers. *Civil Rights Unionism: Tobacco Workers and the Struggle for Democracy in the Mid–Twentieth Century South*. Chapel Hill: University of North Carolina Press, 2003.

Korstad, Robert Rogers, and Nelson Lichtenstein. "Opportunities Found and Lost: Labor, Radicals, and the Early Civil Rights Movement." *Journal of American History* (December 1988): 787–811.

Kraditor, Aileen S. *The Ideas of the Woman Suffrage Movement, 1890–1920*. New York: Norton, 1981.

Langston, Donna. "The Women of Highlander." In *Women in the Civil Rights Movement: Trailblazers and Torchbearers, 1941–1965*, edited by Vicki L. Crawford, Jacqueline Anne Rouse, and Barbara Woods, 145–67. Bloomington: Indiana University Press, 1990.

Lau, Peter F. *Democracy Rising: South Carolina and the Fight for Black Equality since 1865*. Lexington: University Press of Kentucky, 2006.

Lawson, Steven F. "Freedom Then, Freedom Now: The Historiography of the Civil Rights Movement." *American Historical Review* 96 (April 1991): 456–71.

Lee, Chana Kai. *For Freedom's Sake: The Life of Fannie Lou Hamer*. Urbana: University of Illinois Press, 1999.

Leloudis, James L. *Schooling in the New South: Pedagogy, Self, and Society in North Carolina, 1880–1920*. Chapel Hill: University of North Carolina Press, 1996.

Lentz-Smith, Adriane. *Freedom Struggles: African Americans in World War I*. Cambridge: Harvard University Press, forthcoming.

Lewis, David Levering. *W. E. B. Du Bois, 1919–1963: The Fight for Equality and the American Century*. New York: Holt, 2000.

Linder, Suzanne Cameron, and Marta Leslie Thacker. *Historical Atlas of the Rice Plantations of Georgetown County and the Santee River*. Columbia: South Carolina Department of Archives and History, 2001.

Ling, Peter L. "Gender and Generation: Manhood at the Southern Christian Leadership Conference." In *Gender and the Civil Rights Movement*, edited by Peter L. Ling and Sharon Monteith, 101–29. New Brunswick, N.J.: Rutgers University Press, 2004.

Lisio, Donald. *Hoover, Blacks, and Lily Whites: A Study of Southern Strategies*. Chapel Hill: University of North Carolina Press, 1985.

Littlejohn, Bruce. *Littlejohn's Political Memoirs (1934–1988)*. Spartanburg, S.C.: Littlejohn, 1989.

Litwack, Leon F. *Been in the Storm So Long: The Aftermath of Slavery*. New York: Vintage, 1980.

———. *Trouble in Mind: Black Southerners in the Age of Jim Crow*. New York: Knopf, 1998.

Lofton, Paul Strohman, Jr. "The Columbia Black Community of the 1930s." *Proceedings of the South Carolina Historical Association* (1984): 86–95.

Lorde, Audre. "The Transformation of Silence into Language and Action." In *Sister Outsider: Essays and Speeches*, 40–44. Trumansburg, N.Y.: Crossing, 1984.

Mack, Kibibi Voloria C. *Parlor Ladies and Ebony Drudges: African American Women, Class, and Work in a South Carolina Community*. Knoxville: University of Tennessee Press, 1999.

Mays, Benjamin. *Born to Rebel: An Autobiography*. New York: Scribner's, 1971.

McAdam, Doug. *Freedom Summer*. New York: Oxford University Press, 1988.

———. "Gender as a Mediator of the Activist Experience: The Case for Freedom Summer." *American Journal of Sociology* 97 (March 1992): 1211–40.

McCurry, Stephanie. *Masters of Small Worlds: Yeoman Households, Gender Relations, and the Political Culture of the Antebellum South Carolina Low Country*. New York: Oxford University Press, 1995.

McFadden, Grace Jordan. "Septima P. Clark and the Struggle for Human Rights." In *Women in the Civil Rights Movement: Trailblazers and Torchbearers, 1941–1965*, edited by Vicki L. Crawford, Jacqueline Anne Rouse, and Barbara Woods, 85–97. Bloomington: Indiana University Press, 1990.

McGuire, Danielle L. "'It Was Like All of Us Had Been Raped': Sexual Violence, Community Mobilization, and the African American Freedom Struggle." *Journal of American History* 74 (December 2004): 906–31.

McMillan, Lewis K. *Negro Higher Education in the State of South Carolina*. N.p.: McMillan, 1952.

McMillan, Neil. *The Citizen's Council: Organized Resistance to the Second Reconstruction, 1954–1964*. Urbana: University of Illinois Press, 1971.

Meffert, John, Sherman E. Pyatt, and the Avery Research Center. *Black America Series: Charleston, South Carolina*. Charleston, S.C.: Arcadia, 2000.

Montgomery, Mabel. *South Carolina's Wil Lou Gray: Pioneer in Adult Education, a Crusader, a Modern Model*. Columbia, S.C.: Opportunity School, 1963.

Moody, Ann. *Coming of Age in Mississippi*. 1968. Reprint, New York: Dell, 1992.

Moore, John Hammond. *Columbia and Richland County: A South Carolina Community, 1740–1990*. Columbia: University of South Carolina Press, 1993.

Morris, Aldon. *Origins of the Civil Rights Movement: Black Communities Organizing for Change*. New York: Free Press, 1984.

Morrison, Toni. *Playing in the Dark: Whiteness and the Literary Imagination*. New York: Vintage, 1992.

Murray, Pauli. *The Autobiography of a Black Activist, Feminist, Lawyer, Priest, and Poet*. Knoxville: University of Tennessee Press, 1989.

Naples, Nancy A. *Grassroots Warriors: Activist Mothering, Community Work, and the War on Poverty*. New York: Routledge, 1998.

Nasstrom, Kathryn L. "Down to Now: Memory, Narrative, and Women's Leadership in the Civil Rights Movement in Atlanta, Georgia." *Gender and History* 11 (April 1999): 113–44.

———. *Everybody's Grandmother and Nobody's Fool: Francis Freeborn Pauley and the Struggle for Social Justice*. Ithaca: Cornell University Press, 2000.

———. "Francis Freeborn Pauley: Using Autobiography and Biography to Interpret a White Woman's Activist Identity." In *Throwing off the Cloak of Privilege: White Southern Women Activists in the Civil Rights Era*, edited by Gail S. Murray, 77–100. Gainesville: University Press of Florida, 2004.

NavSource On-Line. Service Ship Photo Archive. ⟨http://www.navsource.org/archives/09/47025.htm⟩. July 6, 2004.

Neufeldt, Harvey G., and Leo McGee, eds. *Education of the African American Adult: An Historical Overview*. Westport, Conn.: Greenwood, 1990.

Newby, I. A. *Black Carolinians: A History of Blacks in South Carolina from 1895 to 1968*. Columbia: University of South Carolina Press, 1973.

Norrell, Robert J. *Reaping the Whirlwind: The Civil Rights Movement in Tuskegee*. New York: Vintage, 1986.

North Carolina Writers' Network. "Literary Hall of Fame." ⟨http://www.ncwriters.org/services/lhof/induct2002.html⟩. June 13, 2005.

O'Brien, Gail Williams. *The Color of the Law: Race, Violence, and Justice in the Post–World War II South*. Chapel Hill: University of North Carolina Press, 1999.

Oldendorf, Sandra B. "The South Carolina Sea Island Citizenship Schools, 1957–1961." In *Women in the Civil Rights Movement: Trailblazers and Torchbearers, 1941–1965*, edited by Vicki L. Crawford, Jacqueline Anne Rouse, and Barbara Woods, 169–82. Bloomington: Indiana University Press, 1990.

Olsen, Lynne. *Freedom's Daughters: The Unsung Heroines of the Civil Rights Movement from 1830 to 1970*. New York: Scribner, 2001.

Orelick, Annelise. *Storming Caesar's Palace: How Black Mothers Fought Their Own War on Poverty*. Boston: Beacon, 2005.

Oshinsky, David M. *A Conspiracy So Immense: The World of Joe McCarthy*. New York: Free Press, 1983.

Payne, Charles M. *I've Got the Light of Freedom: The Organizing Tradition and the Mississippi Freedom Struggle*. Berkeley: University of California Press, 1995.

———. "Men Led, but Women Organized: Movement Participation of Women in the Mississippi Delta." In *Women in the Civil Rights Movement: Trailblazers and Torchbearers, 1941–1965*, edited by Vicki L. Crawford, Jacqueline Anne Rouse, and Barbara Woods, 1–11. Bloomington: Indiana University Press, 1990.

Potts, John F., Sr. *A History of the Palmetto Educational Association*. Washington, D.C.: National Education Association, 1978.

Powers, Bernard E., Jr. *Black Charlestonians: A Social History, 1822–1885*. Fayetteville: University of Arkansas Press, 1994.

Pringle, Elizabeth Waties Allston [Patience Pennington]. *A Woman Rice Planter*. Edited by Cornelius O. Cathey. Cambridge: Harvard University Press, 1961.

Pulley, Angela. "Introduction to the Southeastern Indians." Southeastern Native American Documents, 1730–1842, Digital Library of Georgia. ⟨http://www.dlg.galileo.usg.edu⟩. March 27, 2004.

Quadagno, Jill S. *The Color of Welfare: How Racism Undermined the War on Poverty*. New York: Oxford University Press, 1994.

Ransby, Barbara. *Ella Baker and the Black Freedom Movement: A Radically Democratic Vision*. Chapel Hill: University of North Carolina Press, 2003.

Raphael, Ray. *A People's History of the American Revolution: How Common People Shaped the Fight for Independence*. New York: New Press, 2001.

Reed, Linda. *Simple Decency and Common Sense: The Southern Conference Movement, 1938–1963*. Bloomington: Indiana University Press, 1991.

Reim, Edith Holbrook. "Dorothy Tilly and the Fellowship of the Concerned." In *Throwing off the Cloak of Privilege: White Southern Women Activists in the Civil Rights Era*, edited by Gail S. Murray, 23–48. Gainesville: University Press of Florida, 2004.

Rice, Sarah. *He Included Me: The Autobiography of Sarah Rice*. Transcribed and edited by Louise Westling. Athens: University of Georgia Press, 1989.

Richards, Miles S. "The Eminent Lieutenant McKaine." *Proceedings of the South Carolina Historical Association* (1992): 46–54.

Roberts, Dorothy. *Killing the Black Body: Race, Reproduction, and the Meaning of Liberty*. New York: Pantheon, 1997.

Robertson, David. *Sly and Able: A Political Biography of James F. Byrnes*. New York: Norton, 1994.

Robinson, Dorothy Redus. *The Bell Rings at Four: A Black Teacher's Chronicle of Change*. Austin, Tex.: Madrona, 1978.

Robinson, Jo Ann Gibson. *The Montgomery Bus Boycott and the Women Who Started It*. Edited by David Garrow. Knoxville: University of Tennessee Press, 1987.

Robnett, Belinda. *How Long? How Long?: African American Women in the Struggle for Civil Rights*. New York: Oxford University Press, 1997.

————. "Women in the Student Non-Violent Coordinating Committee: Ideology, Organizational Structure, and Leadership." In *Gender and the Civil Rights Movement*, edited by Peter L. Ling and Sharon Monteith, 131–68. New Brunswick, N.J.: Rutgers University Press, 2004.

Rodgers, Daniel T. *Atlantic Crossings: Social Politics in a Progressive Age*. Cambridge: Harvard University Press, 1998.

Roefs, Wim. "Leading the Civil Rights Vanguard in South Carolina: John McCray and the *Lighthouse and Informer*." In *Time Longer Than Rope: A Century of African American Activism*, edited by Charles M. Payne and Adam Green, 462–91. New York: New York University Press, 2003.

Rogers, George C., Jr., and C. James Taylor. *A South Carolina Chronology, 1497–1992*. 2nd ed. Columbia: University of South Carolina Press, 1994.

Romano, Renee C., and Leigh Raiford, eds. *The Civil Rights Movement in American Memory*. Athens: University of Georgia Press, 2006.

Rose, Willie Lee. *Rehearsal for Reconstruction: The Port Royal Experiment*. New York: Vintage, 1967.

Roth, Benita. *Separate Roads to Feminism: Black, Chicana, and White Feminist Movements in America's Second Wave*. New York: Cambridge University Press, 2004.

Rouse, Jacqueline A. "'We Seek to Know . . . in Order to Speak the Truth': Nurturing

Seeds of Discontent—Septima P. Clark and Participatory Leadership." In *Sisters in the Struggle: African American Women in the Civil Rights–Black Power Movement*, edited by Bettye Collier-Thomas and V. P. Franklin, 95–120. New York: New York University Press, 2001.

Sacks, Karen Brodkin. "Gender and Grassroots Leadership." In *Women and the Politics of Empowerment*, edited by Ann Bookman and Sandra Morgen, 77–94. Philadelphia: Temple University Press, 1988.

Savage, Barbara Dianne. *Broadcasting Freedom: Radio, War, and the Politics of Race, 1938–1948*. Chapel Hill: University of North Carolina Press, 1999.

Saville, Julie. *The Work of Reconstruction: From Slave to Wage Laborer in South Carolina, 1860–1870*. New York: Cambridge University Press, 1996.

Schrecker, Ellen. *Many Are the Crimes: McCarthyism in America*. Princeton: Princeton University Press, 1999.

Scott, Anne Firor. *The Southern Lady: From Pedestal to Politics, 1830–1930*. Chicago: University of Chicago Press, 1970.

Shaw, Stephanie J. *What a Woman Ought to Be and to Do: Black Women Professional Workers during the Jim Crow Era*. Chicago: University of Chicago Press, 1996.

Sifakis, Stewart. *Compendium of Confederate Armies: South Carolina and Georgia*. New York: Facts on File, 1995.

Simms, Lois Averetta. *A Chalk and Chalkboard Career in Carolina*. New York: Vantage, 1995.

———. *Profiles of African-American Females in the Low Country of South Carolina*. Charleston, S.C.: Avery Research Center for the Study of African-American History and Culture, 1992.

Simon, Bryant. *A Fabric of Defeat: The Politics of South Carolina Millhands, 1910–1948*. Chapel Hill: University of North Carolina Press, 1998.

Singleton, William Henry. *Recollections of My Slavery Days*. Edited by Katherine Mellen Charron and David S. Cecelski. Raleigh: North Carolina Department of Cultural Resources, Division of Archives and History, 1999.

Sitkoff, Harvard. *A New Deal for Blacks: The Emergence of Civil Rights as a National Issue*. Vol. 1, *The Depression Decade*. New York: Oxford University Press, 1978.

———. "Racial Militancy and Interracial Violence in the Second World War." *Journal of American History* 58 (June 1971): 662–63.

Smith, Bessie. "Used to Be Your Sweet Mama." *Bessie Smith: Empty Bed Blues*, Columbia Records, G30450.

Smith, Elaine M. "Bethune, Mary McLeod." In *Black Women in White America: An Historical Encyclopedia*, edited by Darlene Clark Hine, Elsa Barkley Brown, and Rosalyn Terborg-Penn, 113–27. Bloomington: Indiana University Press, 1993.

Smith, Lillie Gayle. "Unearthing Hidden Literacy: Seven Lessons I Learned in a Cotton Field." In *Readers of the Quilt: Essays on Being Black, Female, and Literate*, edited by Joanne Kilgour Dowdy, 37–47. Cresskill, N.J.: Hampton, 2005.

Solinger, Rickie. *Pregnancy and Power: A Short History of Reproductive Politics in America*. New York: New York University Press, 2005.

South Carolina Genealogies: Articles from the South Carolina Historical (and Genealogical) Magazine. Vol. 3, Jenkins–Quattlebaum. Spartanburg, S.C.: Reprint Company, 1983.

Springer, Kimberly. *Living for the Revolution: Black Feminist Organizations, 1968–1980.* Durham, N.C.: Duke University Press, 2005.

Standley, Anne. "The Role of Black Women in the Civil Rights Movement." In *Women in the Civil Rights Movement: Trailblazers and Torchbearers, 1941–1965,* edited by Vicki L. Crawford, Jacqueline Anne Rouse, and Barbara Woods, 183–202. Bloomington: Indiana University Press, 1990.

Sullivan, Patricia. *Days of Hope: Race and Democracy in the New Deal Era.* Chapel Hill: University of North Carolina Press, 1996.

Synott, Marcia G. "Crusaders and Clubwomen: Alice Norwood Spearman Wright and Her Women's Network." In *Throwing off the Cloak of Privilege: White Southern Women Activists in the Civil Rights Era,* edited by Gail S. Murray, 49–76. Gainesville: University Press of Florida, 2004.

"Taft-Hartley Act." In *The Reader's Companion to American History,* edited by Eric Foner and John A. Garraty, 1057. Boston: Houghton-Mifflin, 1991.

Tate, Claudia. *Domestic Allegories of Political Desire: The Black Heroine's Text at the Turn of the Century.* New York: Oxford University Press, 1992.

"Tent City Timeline: The Civil Rights Struggle in Fayette County." ⟨http://www.jacksonsun.com/civilrights/sec4_timeline.shtml⟩. March 1, 2005.

Terborg-Penn, Rosalyn. *African American Women in the Struggle for the Vote, 1850–1920.* Bloomington: Indiana University Press, 1998.

———. "Discontented Black Feminists: Prelude and Postscript to the Passage of the Nineteenth Amendment." In *We Specialize in the Wholly Impossible: A Reader in Black Women's History,* edited by Darlene Clark Hine, Wilma King, and Linda Reed, 487–503. New York: Carlson, 1995.

Theoharis, Jeanne, and Komozi Woodard, eds. *Groundwork: Local Black Freedom Movements in America.* New York: New York University Press, 2005.

Thompson, Becky. "Multiracial Feminism: Recasting the Chronology of Second Wave Feminism." *Feminist Studies* 28 (Summer 2002): 336–60.

Tindall, George. *South Carolina Negroes, 1877–1900.* Baton Rouge: Louisiana State University Press, 1966.

Tjerandsen, Carl. *Education for Citizenship: A Foundation's Experience.* Santa Cruz, Calif.: Schwarzhaupt Foundation, 1980.

Turner, Lorenzo D. *Africanisms in the Gullah Dialect.* New York: Arno, 1969.

Tushnet, Mark V. *The NAACP's Legal Strategy against Segregated Education, 1925–1950.* Chapel Hill: University of North Carolina Press, 1987.

Tuttle, William M., Jr. *Race Riot: Chicago in the Red Summer of 1919.* New York: Atheneum, 1970.

Tyson, Timothy B. "Dynamite and 'The Silent South': A Story from the Second Reconstruction in South Carolina." In *Jumpin' Jim Crow: Southern Politics from Civil*

War to Civil Rights, edited by Jane Dailey, Glenda Elizabeth Gilmore, and Bryant Simon, 275–97. Princeton: Princeton University Press, 2000.

———. *Radio Free Dixie: Robert F. Williams and the Roots of Black Power*. Chapel Hill: University of North Carolina Press, 1999.

University of Illinois Extension. "The Poinsettia Pages: History and Legends." ⟨http://www.urbanext.uiuc.edu/poinsettia⟩. October 9, 2003.

U.S. Department of Agriculture, Natural Resources Conservation Service. "Live Oak: Quercus virginiana P. Mill., Plant Fact Sheet." ⟨http://plants.usda.gov/factsheet/pdf/fs_quvi.pdf⟩. July 27, 2007.

Verner, Elizabeth O'Neill. *Mellowed by Time: A Charleston Notebook*. Columbia, S.C.: Bostick and Thornley, 1959.

"Viola McFerren Remembers." ⟨http://www.jacksonsun.com/civilrights/sec4_mcferren_remembers.shtml⟩. March 1, 2005.

Von Eschen, Penny M. *Race against Empire: Black Americans and Anticolonialism, 1937–1957*. Ithaca: Cornell University Press, 1997.

Walker, Vanessa Siddle. *Their Highest Potential: An African American School Community in the Segregated South*. Chapel Hill: University of North Carolina Press, 1996.

Weiler, Kathleen. "Mabel Carney at Teachers College: From Home Missionary to White Ally." *Teachers College Record* 107 (December 2005): 2599–2633.

Weiss, Nancy J. *Farewell to the Party of Lincoln: Black Politics in the Age of FDR*. Princeton: Princeton University Press, 1983.

Werner, Craig. *A Change Is Gonna Come: Music, Race, and the Soul of America*. New York: Plume, 1999.

West, Keith Franklin. "The Saga of J. Waties Waring." *Charleston Magazine*, November–December 2001, 62–69.

Wheeler, Marjorie Spruill. *New Women of the New South: The Leaders of the Woman Suffrage Movement in Southern States*. New York: Oxford University Press, 1993.

Whisnant, David E. *All That Is Native and Fine: The Politics of Culture in an American Region*. Chapel Hill: University of North Carolina Press, 1983.

White, Deborah Gray. *Too Heavy a Load: Black Women in Defense of Themselves, 1894–1994*. New York: Norton, 1999.

White, H. *Tropics of Discourse*. Baltimore: Johns Hopkins University Press, 1978.

Whitfield, Stephen J. *A Death in the Delta: The Story of Emmett Till*. Baltimore: Johns Hopkins University Press, 1991.

Wiebe, Robert H. *The Search for Order, 1877–1920*. New York: Hill and Wang, 1967.

Wigginton, Eliot. *Refuse to Stand Silently By: An Oral History of Grass Roots Social Activism in America, 1921–1964*. New York: Doubleday, 1991.

Williams, Cecil J. *Freedom and Justice: Four Decades of the Civil Rights Struggle as Seen by a Black Photographer of the Deep South*. Macon, Ga.: Mercer University Press, 1995.

Williams, Heather Andrea. *Self-Taught: African American Education in Slavery and Freedom*. Chapel Hill: University of North Carolina Press, 2005.

Williams, Rhonda Y. "Black Women, Urban Politics, and Engendering Black Power." In
    Black Power Movement: Rethinking the Civil Rights–Black Power Era, ed. Peniel E.
    Joseph, 79–104. New York: Routledge, 2006.
Wilson, William J. *The Declining Significance of Race: Blacks and Changing American
    Institutions*. Chicago: University of Chicago Press, 1978.
———, ed. *The Ghetto Underclass: Social Science Perspectives*. Newbury Park, Calif.:
    Sage, 1989.
Winn, Linda T. "Tent Cities of Fayette and Haywood Counties (1960–1962)." ⟨http://
    www.tnstate.edu/library/digital/tent.htm⟩. March 1, 2005.
Wood, Peter. *Black Majority: Negroes in Colonial South Carolina from 1670 through the
    Stono Rebellion*. New York: Norton, 1974.
Woods, Barbara A., "South Carolina Conference of the NAACP: Origin and Major
    Accomplishments, 1939–1954," *Proceedings of the South Carolina Historical
    Association* (1981): 2–3.
Yarbrough, Tinsley E. *A Passion for Justice: J. Waties Waring and Civil Rights*. New York:
    Oxford University Press, 1987.
Young, Andrew. *An Easy Burden: The Civil Rights Movement and the Transformation of
    America*. New York: HarperCollins, 1996.
Yuhl, Stephanie. *A Golden Haze of Memory: The Making of Historic Charleston*. Chapel
    Hill: University of North Carolina Press, 2005.
Zigler, Edward, and Susan Muenchow. *Head Start: The Inside Story of America's Most
    Successful Educational Experiment*. New York: Basic Books, 1992.

Unpublished Secondary Sources

Aba-Mecha, Barbara Woods. "Black Woman Activist in Twentieth Century South
    Carolina: Modjeska Monteith Simkins." Ph.D. diss., Emory University, 1978.
Brown, Millicent Ellison. "Civil Rights Activism in Charleston, South Carolina, 1940–
    1970." Ph.D. diss., Florida State University, 1997.
Devlin, George Alfred. "South Carolina and Black Migration, 1865–1940: In Search of
    the Promised Land." Ph.D. diss., University of South Carolina, 1984.
Edwards, Anthony L. "Booker T. Washington High School (1916–1974): Voices of
    Remembrance." Ph.D. diss., University of South Carolina, 1998.
Hamlin, Françoise Nicole. "The Book Hasn't Closed, the Story Isn't Finished:
    Continuing Histories of the Civil Rights Movement." Ph.D. diss., Yale University,
    2004.
Hathaway, Joseph Michael. "The Class of 1944 of Lincoln High School: Finding
    Excellence in a Black Segregated School." Ph.D. diss., University of South Carolina,
    1997.
Leake, Janet Scott. "Survey of the Negro Public Schools of Columbia, South Carolina."
    Master's thesis, Winthrop College, 1932.
Littlefield, Valinda W. "'I Am Only One, but I Am One': Southern African American
    Women Schoolteachers, 1884–1954." Ph.D. diss., University of Illinois at Urbana-
    Champaign, 2003.

Lofton, Paul Strohman, Jr. "A Social and Economic History of Columbia, South Carolina, during the Great Depression, 1929–1940." Ph.D. diss., University of Texas at Austin, 1977.

O'Neill, Steve. "From the Shadow of Slavery: The Civil Rights Years in Charleston." Ph.D. diss., University of Virginia, 1990.

Richards, Miles S. "Osceola E. McKaine and the Struggle for Black Civil Rights, 1917–1946." Ph.D. diss., University of South Carolina, 1994.

Index

Black private schools, 41–42, 63, 131. *See also* Avery Normal Institute

Black public schools in South Carolina, 38, 40–41, 52–53, 56, 58, 59, 70, 96, 123, 124, 130, 152–53, 182, 211, 213; and white supervision, 4, 59, 83, 93, 96, 125, 386 (n. 41), 400 (n. 81)

Black soldiers. *See* Black veterans; World War I; World War II

Black teachers (public and private schools), 18, 38, 40, 45, 52, 58, 59, 74, 123, 130, 152–53, 218, 227, 335, 346; activist organizing tradition of, 3, 4, 6, 10, 46–47, 54, 69, 78–79, 80, 86, 133, 222, 250, 251, 253, 262–63, 325, 343; pedagogy of, 3, 41–42, 70–71, 79, 132; as community organizers, 4, 63, 72–76, 91–92, 124, 136, 140; and NAACP, 4–5, 92, 96, 175–76; and black history, 42, 70, 123–24, 176; white reprisals to activism of, 96, 165, 171, 174–75; and professional development, 125, 127–28, 129, 131, 147, 177, 386 (n. 34); and voting, 138, 145, 174, 206, 208, 214; and salary equalization, 150, 152, 154, 155, 156, 163, 166, 177; and recertification, 171, 172–73; timidity of, 240, 241, 248, 249, 276. *See also* Citizenship Schools — teachers

Black veterans, 38, 97, 153, 175, 189, 190, 238, 275, 277

Blackwell, Alice, 330, 331

Black women: and freedom struggle, 3, 4, 7, 8, 12, 119, 134, 148, 178; and employment, 13, 45–46, 86, 161; and uplift and respectability, 18, 45, 82, 83, 86, 104, 106, 114, 115, 134, 221; and rape, 22, 46, 87; and voting, 82, 100, 205; and interracial organizing, 107, 186, 188; and health care issues, 136; and integration, 181, 201, 202, 203–4, 240, 279; and civil rights movement, 293. *See also* Citizenship Schools

Black women blues singers, 83, 112

Black Women's Community Development Foundation, 349–50

Black youth: and civil rights movement, 12, 239, 252–53, 323. *See also* Student Nonviolent Coordinating Committee

Blake, Jerry and Queen, 65

Blease, Coleman, 53, 57, 93

Booker T. Washington School (Columbia, S.C.), 117, 123–24, 125, 131, 142

Boulware, Harold R., 163, 164, 169

Bowman, Eva, 280

Brannon, J. H., 59, 60, 61

Branstetter, Cecil, 271

Brewer, Alleen, 256–57, 347

Briggs v. Elliott, 174, 210–11, 227

Broad Street (Charleston, S.C), 16, 28, 180, 192, 193, 198, 207, 215

Brown, Edgar, 166, 171

Brown, J. Arthur (Joe), 157, 208, 236, 238, 241, 243, 272

Brown v. Baskin, 191, 205

Brown v. Board of Education, 4, 165, 212, 216, 235, 273

Burgess, John P., 155

Burke High School (Charleston, S.C.), 42, 70, 157, 163, 175, 182, 223

Burroughs, Edward B., 46, 370 (n. 69)

Byrnes, James F., 154, 163, 209–10, 211–12, 213

Cain, Richard Harvey, 26

Carawan, Candie, 284, 290

Carawan, Guy, 246, 269, 270, 271, 290

Cardozo, Francis L., 38, 43, 44

Carmichael, Stokely, 334

Charleston, S.C., 31, 38, 84, 121, 181–82; black community in, 5, 14, 15–16, 17–19, 25–26, 35, 36–37, 45, 48, 82, 85, 86, 92, 95, 98–99, 101, 104, 106, 110, 112, 183–85, 191, 195, 207, 212–13, 227; white community in, 15, 28, 35, 89, 91, 96, 98, 194, 195; interracial relations in, 26, 90, 100, 107, 179–80, 186, 187, 188–89, 192–93, 197, 201, 202, 206–7; race riot in, 82, 97–100; 1969 hospital strike, 349

Charleston City School Board, 90, 91, 96, 162–63, 164, 182, 213, 243

Charleston County, S.C., 58, 63, 77, 175, 345

Charleston Messenger, 90, 95

Charleston NAACP branch, 81, 85, 86–88, 214, 223, 225, 233, 238, 240–41; and teacher campaign, 89–92, 93–96, 106, 114, 166, 184

Charleston News and Courier, 64–65, 165, 191, 207, 260–61

Chattin, Chester C., 271, 274

Child Development Group of Mississippi, 337–38

Christianity, 219; and civil rights movement, 231, 260, 304, 328

Citizens' Councils, 34, 236, 239, 242, 267, 277, 281, 321

Citizenship Education Program. *See* Citizenship Schools, SCLC-sponsored

Citizenship Schools, 3; and voter registration, 1, 3, 257–58, 302–3, 324; Highlander-sponsored, 2, 217, 248–57, 274–75; SCLC-sponsored, 2, 5–6, 7, 302–4, 319, 332, 333–34, 343; students, 3, 5, 6, 251, 252–53, 255, 256–57, 258–60, 263, 309, 324–25, 326, 328, 329, 339, 344, 354; pedagogy of, 6, 248, 251–53, 257, 262–63, 302; and black women's activism, 6–7, 260, 282, 304–5, 310, 312–14, 323–44 passim; curriculum of, 283, 326, 328; expansion of, 283–87; problems of, 285, 314–15, 316–18; transfer to SCLC, 293–97; in Mississippi, 322–31

—teachers, 1, 2–3, 249, 279, 302, 324–27, 328, 331, 332, 344; training of, 1, 6, 7, 255, 274, 276, 278, 282–83, 306–8, 309; and War on Poverty, 8, 336–39; and racial violence, 320–21

Civil Rights Act of 1957, 277

Civil Rights Act of 1964, 329

Civil rights movement, 7, 8, 10, 179, 332–33; and white reprisals, 238–39, 277–78. *See also* Gender

Civil War, 15, 23–24, 25, 26, 40, 47

Clark, David (grandson), 11, 312

Clark, George W. and Matilda (in-laws), 109, 113, 117

Clark, Nerie David (husband), 101–2, 103, 107, 108, 109, 110, 112, 115, 232

Clark, Nerie David, Jr. (son), 109, 110, 112, 113, 116–17, 125, 127, 161, 162, 312

Clark, Septima Poinsette: activist approach of, 1, 4, 12, 47–48, 80, 166, 188, 194, 197–98, 202, 214, 216, 225, 228, 231–32, 240–42, 244, 257, 276–77, 282, 299, 314, 319, 341–42, 347, 349, 350–51, 354; activist motivations of, 2, 88, 114, 162, 261, 351–52; and Charleston teacher campaign, 2, 89, 90, 91–92, 95; as member of the PSTA, 2, 131, 132, 133–34; as clubwoman, 2, 134, 135–36, 137, 205; and salary equalization, 2, 156, 157, 158, 166, 169, 170, 176, 177–78; and integration, 2, 5, 6, 201, 212, 218, 239–40, 241, 287–89, 399 (n. 61); firing of, 2, 243–44; and increasing women's participation in civil rights movement, 2, 228, 260, 280, 304, 343; involvement with Highlander, 2, 5, 217, 221–23, 227–29, 230, 235, 240, 244, 246–47, 262, 265; involvement with SCLC, 2, 299, 305, 310, 314, 316, 317; view of teaching citizenship, 3, 5, 79, 132–33, 147, 202, 247, 248, 250, 252, 262, 302, 309, 346–47; leadership philosophy of, 5, 137, 147, 293, 315–16; evaluations of Citizenship Schools, 5, 284–85, 319–20, 322, 332, 335; and women's movement, 7, 9–10, 349–50; as autobiographer, 9–10, 11, 297–99, 383 (nn. 72, 78); marriage of, 10, 83, 103, 104, 107, 109–10, 112, 114, 115; and self-doubt, 10, 108, 110, 246; and motherhood, 11, 107, 109–10, 116–17, 127, 161–62, 242; concern with finances, 11, 229, 296, 352; public persona of, 11, 265, 271, 273; and relationship with family members, 11, 32–33, 48, 101, 102, 109, 113–14, 185–86, 200, 225, 242; radicalism of, 11–12, 150, 181, 242, 262, 342, 350; as mentor, 12, 279, 310, 311,